The Writings of Baal HaSulam

Volume Two

Laitman
Kabbalah
Publishers

Yehuda Leib HaLevi Ashlag

The Writings of Baal HaSulam
Volume One

Copyright © 2019 by Michael Laitman

All rights reserved

Published by Laitman Kabbalah Publishers

Contact Information

E-mail: info@kabbalah.info

Website: www.kabbalah.info

Toll free in USA and Canada: 1-866-LAITMAN

1057 Steeles Avenue West, Suite 532, Toronto,
ON, M2R 3X1, Canada
Tel. 1-416-274-7287

2009 85th Street #51, Brooklyn, New York, 11214, USA
Tel. 1-800-540-3234

Printed in the USA

No part of this book may be used or reproduced
in any manner without written permission of the publisher,
except in the case of brief quotations embodied
in critical articles or reviews.

ISBN: 978-1-77228-146-0

Library of Congress Control Number: 2019939696

Translation: Chaim Ratz

Translation Assistance: Mickey Cohen, Moshe Eisenberg

Content Review: Noga Bar Noye

Editing and Proofreading: Mary Pennock, Mary Miesem,
Joseph Donnelly, Michael Kellogg, Debbie Wood

Internal Design: Chaim Ratz

Cover Design: Baruch Khovov/Inna Smirnova

Executive Editor: Chaim Ratz

Printing and Post Production: Uri Laitman

FIRST EDITION: May 2019

Second printing

Table of Contents

The Articles of Shamati 4
Letters 249
The Gatehouse of Intentions 406
The Writings of the Last Generation 572

The Articles of Shamati

About the Articles

Among all the books and manuscripts in which my teacher, Rav Baruch Shalom HaLevi Ashlag (RABASH)—the firstborn son and successor of Baal HaSulam—used to study, there was one special notebook that he always took with him. On its cover was a single word written in my teacher's handwriting: *Shamati* [I heard]. RABASH would not go anywhere without this notebook. Wherever he went, he took it with him and delved into it at every opportunity.

On his deathbed, late at night, he suddenly handed me the notebook and said, "Take the notebook and study it." Early next morning, with me at his bedside, he passed away.

The notebook contains transcripts of words that RABASH had heard from his father, Rav Yehuda Leib Halevi Ashlag (Baal HaSulam), author of the *Sulam* (Ladder) commentary on *The Book of Zohar*, *The Study of the Ten Sefirot* (a commentary on the texts of the Kabbalist, the ARI), and many other works on Kabbalah.

Because of the uniqueness of the contents, we kept the colloquial style in the articles which RABASH drank with such thirst, and on which he based his teaching.

Michael Laitman

1. There Is None Else Besides Him
I heard on *Parashat Yitro*, 12 *Shevat*, *Tav-Shin-Dalet*, February 6, 1944

It is written, "There is none else besides Him." This means that there is no other force in the world that has the ability to do anything against Him. And what one sees, that there are things in the world that deny the upper household, the reason is that this is His will.

This is deemed a correction called "the left rejects and the right pulls closer," meaning that what the left rejects is considered a correction. This means that there are things in the world that, to begin with, aim to divert a person from the right way, and by which he is rejected from *Kedusha* [holiness].

The benefit from the rejections is that through them a person receives a complete need and desire for the Creator to help him since he sees that otherwise he is lost; not only is he not progressing in the work, he even sees that he regresses. That is, he lacks the strength to observe Torah and *Mitzvot* [commandments] even *Lo Lishma* [not for Her sake], for only by genuinely overcoming all the obstacles, above reason, can he observe the Torah and *Mitzvot*. But he does not always have the strength to overcome above reason; otherwise, he is forced to deviate, God forbid, from the way of the Creator, even from *Lo Lishma*.

And he, who always feels that the shattered is greater than the whole, meaning that there are many more descents than ascents, and he does not see an end to these states, and he will forever remain outside of holiness, for he sees that it is difficult for him to observe even in the slightest bit, unless by overcoming above reason. But he cannot always overcome, so what will be in the end?

Then he comes to the decision that no one can help but the Creator Himself. This causes him to make a heartfelt demand that the Creator will open his eyes and heart and truly bring him closer to eternal *Dvekut* [adhesion] with the Creator. It therefore follows that all the rejections that he had were all from the Creator.

This means that it was not because he was at fault that he did not have the ability to overcome. Rather, for those people who truly want to draw near to the Creator, so they do not settle for little, meaning remain as senseless children, he is therefore given help from above so he will not be able to say, "Thank God, I have Torah and *Mitzvot* and good deeds, and what else do I need?"

Only if that person has a true desire will he receive help from above, and he will always be shown that he is at fault in the present state. Namely, he is sent thoughts and views that are against the work. This is in order for him to see that he is not in wholeness with the Creator. As much as he overcomes, he always sees that he is farther from holiness than others, who feel that they are in wholeness with the Creator.

But he, on the other hand, always has complaints and demands, and he cannot justify the Creator's behavior, the way He behaves with him. This pains him: Why is he not wholly with the Creator? Finally, he comes to feel that he has no part in holiness at all.

Although he occasionally receives an awakening from above, which momentarily revives him, soon after, he falls into the place of baseness. Yet, this is what causes him to come to realize that only the Creator can help and really bring him closer.

One must always try and adhere to the Creator, namely that all his thoughts will be about Him. That is to say, even if he is in the worst state, from which there cannot be a greater decline, he should not leave His domain, namely that there is another authority that prevents him from entering the *Kedusha* [holiness], that can bring benefit or harm.

That is, he must not think that there is a force of the *Sitra Achra* [other side] that does not let a person do good deeds and walk in the ways of the Creator. Rather, all is done by the Creator.

The Baal Shem Tov said that he who says that there is another force in the world, namely *Klipot* [shells], that person is in a state of "serving other gods." It is not necessarily the thought of heresy that is the transgression, but if he thinks that there is another authority and force apart from the Creator, he is committing a transgression.

Furthermore, one who says that man has his own authority, that is, he says that yesterday he himself did not want to follow the Creator's ways, this, too, is considered committing the transgression of heresy, meaning he does not believe that only the Creator is the leader of the world.

But when he has committed a transgression, he must certainly regret it and be sorry for committing the transgression. But here, too, we should place the pain and sorrow in the right order: Where does he place the cause of the transgression, for this is the point that should be regretted.

Then, one should be remorseful and say, "I committed that transgression because the Creator hurled me down from holiness to a place of filth, to the lavatory, the place of filth." That is to say that the Creator gave him a desire and craving to amuse himself and breathe air in a place of stench.

(You might say that it is written in books that sometimes one comes incarnated as a pig. We should interpret this as he says, that a person receives a desire and craving to derive vitality from things he had already determined were litter, and now he wants to receive nourishment from them).

Also, when one feels that now he is in a state of ascent, and feels some good flavor in the work, he must not say, "Now I am in a state that I understand that it is worthwhile to be a servant of the Creator." Rather, he should know that now the Creator favored him; hence, the Creator brought him closer, and this is why now he feels a good taste in the work. He should be careful never to leave the domain of *Kedusha* and say that there is someone else who operates besides the Creator.

(But this means that the matter of being favored by the Creator, or the opposite, does not depend on the person himself, but only on the Creator. And man, with his external mind, cannot comprehend why now the Creator has favored him and afterward did not.)

Likewise, when he regrets that the Creator does not draw him near, he should also be careful that it would not be in relation to himself, meaning that he is removed from the Creator, for by this he becomes a receiver for his own benefit, and a receiver is separated. Rather, he should regret the exile of the *Shechina* [Divinity], meaning that he is causing the sorrow of the *Shechina*.

One should imagine that it is as though a small organ of the person is sore. Nevertheless, the pain is felt primarily in the mind and in the heart. The heart and the mind are the whole of man, and certainly, the sensation of a single organ cannot resemble the sensation of a person's full stature, which is primarily where the pain is felt.

Likewise is the pain that one feels when he is removed from the Creator. Since man is but a single organ of the *Shechina*, for the *Shechina* is the common soul of

Israel, hence, the sensation of a single organ is not like the sensation of the general pain. That is, there is sorrow in the *Shechina* when the organs are removed from her and she cannot nurture her organs.

(We should say that this is as our sages said: "When a man regrets, what does the *Shechina* say? 'It is lighter than my head.'") By not relating the sorrow of remoteness to himself, he is spared falling into the trap of the desire to receive for himself, which is considered separation from the *Kedusha*.

The same applies when one feels some closeness to *Kedusha*, when he feels joy at having been favored by the Creator. Then, too, he must say that his joy is primarily because now there is joy above, in the *Shechina*, at being able to bring her private organ near her, and that she did not have to send her private organ out.

And one derives joy from being rewarded with pleasing the *Shechina*. This is in accord with the above calculation that when there is joy to the part, it is only a part of the joy of the whole. Through these calculations, he loses his individuality and avoids being trapped by the *Sitra Achra*, which is the will to receive for his own benefit.

Although the will to receive is necessary, since this is the whole of man, since anything that exists in a person apart from the will to receive does not belong to the creature, but we attribute it to the Creator, but the will to receive pleasure should be corrected to work in order to bestow.

That is, the pleasure and joy that the will to receive takes should be with the aim that there is contentment above when the creatures feel pleasure, as this was the purpose of creation—to do good to His creations. This is called the joy of the *Shechina* above.

For this reason, one must seek advice how he can bring contentment above. Clearly, if he receives pleasure, there will be contentment above. Therefore, he yearns to always be in the King's palace and to have the ability to play with the King's treasures, and this will certainly bring contentment above. It follows that all his longing should be only for the sake of the Creator.

2. Shechina [Divinity] in Exile

I heard in *Tav-Shin-Bet*, 1941-1942

The Zohar says, "He is the *Shochen* [Dweller], and She is the *Shechina* [Divinity]." We should interpret its words: It is known that regarding the upper light, it is said that there is no change, as it is written, "I the Lord did not change." All the names and appellations relate only to the *Kelim* [vessels], which is the will to receive included in *Malchut*—the root of creation. From there it cascades to this world, to the created beings.

All those discernments, beginning with *Malchut*, the root of the creation of the worlds, through the creatures, are named *Shechina*. The overall correction is for the upper light to shine in them in utter completeness.

The light that shines in the *Kelim* is named *Shochen*, and the *Kelim* are generally named *Shechina*. In other words, the light dwells inside the *Shechina*. This means that the light is called *Shochen* because it dwells within the *Kelim*, that is, the *Kelim* in general are called *Shechina*.

Before the light shines in them in utter completeness, we name that time, "a time of corrections." This means that we make corrections so that the light will shine in them in completeness. Until then, that state is called "*Shechina* in Exile."

This means that there is still no wholeness in the upper worlds. Below, in this world, there should be a state where the upper light is within the will to receive. This correction is deemed receiving in order to bestow.

Meanwhile, the will to receive is filled with ignoble and foolish things that do not make a place where the glory of heaven can be revealed. This means that where the heart should be a tabernacle for the light of the Creator, the heart becomes a place of waste and filth. In other words, ignobility captures the whole of the heart.

This is called "*Shechina* in the dust." It means that she is lowered to the ground, and each and every one loathes matters of *Kedusha* [holiness], and there is no desire whatsoever to raise her from the dust. Instead, they choose ignoble things, and this causes the sorrow of the *Shechina* by not giving her a place in the heart that will become a tabernacle for the light of the Creator.

3. The Matter of Spiritual Attainment

I heard

We discern many degrees and discernments in the worlds. We must know that everything that relates to discernments and degrees speaks of the attainment of the souls with regard to what they receive from the worlds. This follows the rule, "What we do not attain we do not know by name." This is so because the word "name" indicates attainment, like a person who names some object after having attained something about it, and according to one's attainment.

Hence, with respect to spiritual attainment, reality in general is divided into three discernments:

1. *Atzmuto* [His Self]

2. *Ein Sof* [infinity]

3. The Souls

1) We do not speak of His Self at all since the root and the place of the creatures begin in the thought of creation, where they are incorporated in the manner, "The end of an act is in the preliminary thought."

2) *Ein Sof* pertains to the thought of creation, which is "His desire to do good to His creations." This is considered *Ein Sof*, and it is the connection existing between His Self and the souls. We perceive this connection as a "desire to delight the creatures."

Ein Sof is the beginning. It is called "a light without a *Kli* [vessel]," yet there is the root of the creatures, meaning the connection between the Creator and the creatures, called "His desire to do good to His creations." This desire begins in the world of *Ein Sof* and extends through the world of *Assiya*.

3) The souls, which are the receivers of the good that He wishes to do.

He is called *Ein Sof* because this is the connection between His Self and the souls, which we perceive as "His desire to do good to His creations." We have no utterance except for that connection of desire to delight, and this is the beginning of the engagement, and it is called "light without a *Kli*."

Yet, there begins the root of the creatures, meaning the connection between the Creator and the creatures, called "His desire to do good to His creations." This desire begins in the world of *Ein Sof* and extends through the world of *Assiya*.

In and of themselves, all the worlds are considered light without a *Kli*, where there is no utterance. They are discerned as His Self, and there is no attainment in them.

Do not wonder that we discern many discernments there. It is because these discernments are there in potential. Afterward, when the souls come, these discernments will appear in the souls that receive the upper lights according to what they corrected and arranged. Thus, the souls will be able to receive them, each according to his ability and qualification. At that time, these discernments will appear in actual fact. However, while the souls do not attain the upper light, they, in and of themselves, are considered His Self.

With respect to the souls that receive from the worlds, the worlds are considered *Ein Sof*. This is because this connection between the worlds and the souls, meaning what the worlds give to the souls, extends from the thought of creation, which is a correlation between the souls and His Self.

This connection is called *Ein Sof*. When we pray to the Creator and ask Him to help us and give us what we want, we relate to the discernment of *Ein Sof*. There is the root of the creatures, which wants to impart upon them delight and pleasure, called "His desire to do good to His creations."

The prayer is to the Creator who created us, and His Name is "His desire to do good to His creations." He is called *Ein Sof* because this speaks of prior to the restriction. Even after the restriction, no change occurs in Him, as there is no change in the light, and He always remains with this name.

The proliferation of names is only with respect to the receivers. Hence, the first name that appeared, that is, the root for the creatures, is called *Ein Sof*. This name remains unchanged, and all the restrictions and the manifold changes unfold only with regard to the receivers, but He always shines in the first name called "His desire to do good to His creations," endlessly.

This is why we pray to the Creator, called *Ein Sof*, who shines without restriction or end. The end, which appears later, is corrections for the receivers so they may receive His light.

The upper light consists of two discernments: attaining and attained. Everything we say regarding the upper light concerns only how the attaining is impressed by the attained. However, in themselves, meaning only the attaining, or only the attained, they are not called *Ein Sof*. Rather, the attained is called His Self, and the attaining is called "souls," being a new discernment, which is a part of the whole. It is new in the sense that the will to receive is imprinted in it. In that sense, creation is called "existence from absence."

For themselves, all the worlds are regarded as simple unity, and there is no change in Godliness. This is the meaning of "I the Lord did not change." There are no *Sefirot* or *Behinot* [discernments] in Godliness. Even the most subtle appellations do not refer to the light itself, as this is a discernment of His Self where there is no attainment. Rather, all the *Sefirot* and the discernments speak only of what a person attains in them. This is because the Creator wanted us to attain and understand the abundance as "His desire to do good to His creations."

In order for us to attain what He wanted us to attain and understand as "His desire to do good to His creations," He created and imparted us with these senses, and these senses attain their impressions of the upper light.

Accordingly, we have been given many discernments since the general sense called "the will to receive" is divided into many details according to the measure that the receivers are able to receive. Thus, we find many divisions and details called ascents and descents, expansion and departure, etc.

Since the will to receive is called "creature" and a "new discernment," the utterance begins precisely from the place where the will to receive begins to receive impressions. The speech is discernments, parts of impressions. For here there is already a correlation between the light and the will to receive.

This is called "light and *Kli*." However, there is no utterance in the light without a *Kli*, since a light that is not attained by the receiver is considered His Self, where the utterance is forbidden since it is unattainable, and how can we name what we do not attain?

From this we learn that when we pray for the Creator to send us salvation, cure, and so on, there are two things we should distinguish: 1) the Creator, 2) that which extends from Him.

In the first discernment, considered His Self, the utterance is forbidden, as we have said above. In the second discernment, that which extends from Him, which is considered the light that expands into our *Kelim*, into our will to receive, this is what we call *Ein Sof*. This is the connection of the Creator with the creatures, being "His desire to do good to His creations." The will to receive is regarded as the expanding light that finally reaches the will to receive.

When the will to receive receives the expanding light, the expanding light is called *Ein Sof*. It comes to the receivers through many covers so that the lower one will be able to receive them.

It turns out that all the discernments and the changes take place specifically in the receiver, with relation to how the receiver is impressed by them. However, we must discern the matter we are speaking of. When we speak of discernments in the worlds, they are potential discernments. When the receiver attains these discernments, they are called "actual."

Spiritual attainment is when the attaining and the attained come together, as without one who attains, there is no form to the attained, since there is no one to obtain the form of the attained. Hence, this discernment is considered His Self, where there is no room for any utterance. Therefore, how can we say that the attained has its own form?

We can only speak from where our senses are impressed by the expanding light, which is "His desire to do good to His creations," which comes into the hands of the receivers in actual fact.

Similarly, when we examine a table, our sense of touch feels it as something hard, and its length and width, all according to our senses. However, that does not necessitate that the table will appear so to one who has other senses. For example, in the eyes of an angel, when it examines the table, it will see it according to its senses. For this reason, we cannot determine any form with regard to an angel since we do not know its senses.

Thus, since we have no attainment in the Creator, we cannot say which form the worlds have from His perspective. We only attain the worlds according to our senses and sensations, as it was His will for us to attain Him so.

This is the meaning of "There is no change in the light." Rather, all the changes are in the *Kelim*, meaning in our senses. We measure everything according to our imagination. From this it follows that if many people examine one spiritual thing, each will attain according to his imagination and senses, thereby seeing a different form.

In addition, the form itself will change in a person according to his ups and downs, as we have said above that the light is simple light and all the changes are only in the receivers.

May we merit receiving His light and following the ways of the Creator, and to serve Him not in order to receive reward but to give contentment to the Creator and raise the *Shechina* [Divinity] from the dust. May we be rewarded with *Dvekut* [adhesion] with the Creator and the revelation of His Godliness to His creatures.

4. What Is the Reason for the Heaviness One Feels when Annulling before the Creator in the Work?

I heard on Shevat 12, Tav-Shin-Dalet, February 6, 1944

We must know the reason for the heaviness one feels when he wants to work in annulling his self before the Creator and not worry about his own benefit. A person comes to a state as though the entire world stands still, and he alone is now seemingly absent from this world, and leaves his family and friends for the sake of annulling before the Creator.

There is but a simple reason for this, called "lack of faith." It means that one does not see before whom he nullifies, meaning he does not feel the existence of the Creator. This causes him heaviness.

But when he begins to feel the existence of the Creator, his soul immediately yearns to annul and connect with the root, to be contained in it like a candle in a torch, without any mind or reason. However, this comes naturally, as a candle is canceled before a torch.

It therefore follows that the essence of one's work is only to come to feel the existence of the Creator, meaning to feel the existence of the Creator, that "the whole earth is full of His glory," and this will be one's entire work. That is, all the energy one puts into the work will be only to achieve this, and nothing else.

One should not be misled into having to acquire anything. Rather, there is only one thing a person needs: faith in the Creator. He should not think of anything, meaning that the only reward that he wants for his work should be to be rewarded with faith in the Creator.

We must know that there is no difference between a small illumination or a great illumination that a person obtains, since there are no changes in the light. Rather, all the changes are in the *Kelim* [vessels] that receive the abundance, as it is written, "I the Lord did not change." Hence, if one can magnify one's *Kelim*, to that extent he magnifies the illumination.

Yet, the question is, With what can one magnify one's *Kelim*? The answer is that to the extent to which he praises and thanks the Creator for having brought him closer to Him, so he would feel Him a little and think of the importance of the matter, meaning that he was rewarded with having some connection with the Creator.

To the extent of the importance that one pictures for oneself, so the illumination grows in him. One must know that he will never come to know the true measure of the importance of the connection between man and the Creator because one cannot assess its true value. Instead, as much as one appreciates it, so he attains its merit and importance. There is a *Segula* [power/remedy/virtue] in this, since by this he can be rewarded with this illumination staying permanently within him.

5. Lishma Is an Awakening from Above, and Why Do We Need an Awakening from Below?

I heard in *Tav-Shin-Hey*, 1944-1945

In order to attain *Lishma* [for Her sake], it is not within one's hands to understand, as it is not for the human mind to grasp how such a thing can be in the world. This is so because one is only permitted to grasp that if he engages in Torah and *Mitzvot* [commandments] he will attain something. There must be self-benefit there for otherwise, one is unable to do anything. Rather, it is an illumination that comes from above, and only one who tastes it can know and understand. It is written about it, "Taste and see that the Lord is good."

Thus, we must understand why one should seek advice and counsels regarding how to achieve *Lishma*. After all, no counsels will help him, and if the Creator does not give him the second nature, called "the desire to bestow," no labor will help him to attain the matter of *Lishma*.

The answer is, as our sages said (*Avot*, Chapter 2, 21), "It is not for you to complete the work, and you are not free to idle away from it." This means that one must give the awakening from below, since this is regarded as a prayer.

A prayer is considered a deficiency, and without a deficiency there is no filling. Hence, when one has a need for *Lishma*, the filling comes from above, and the answer to the prayer comes from above, meaning he receives fulfillment for his lack. It follows, that the need for man's work in order to receive the *Lishma* from the Creator is only in the form of a lack and a *Kli* [vessel]. Yet, one can never obtain the filling by himself; it is rather a gift from the Creator.

However, the prayer must be a complete prayer, from the bottom of the heart. This means that one knows one hundred percent that there is no one in the world who can help him but the Creator Himself.

Yet, how does one know this, that no one will help him but the Creator Himself? One can acquire that awareness precisely if he has invested all the powers at his disposal and it did not help him. Thus, one must do every possible thing in the world to attain "for the sake of the Creator." Then one can pray from the bottom of the heart, and then the Creator hears his prayer.

However, one must know, when exerting to attain the *Lishma*, to take upon himself to want to work entirely to bestow, completely, meaning only to bestow and not to receive anything. Only then does one begin to see that the organs do not agree to this view.

From this one can come to clear awareness that he has no other choice but to pour out his heart to the Creator to help him so the body will agree to enslave itself to the Creator unconditionally, as he sees that he cannot persuade his body to annul itself completely. It turns out that precisely when one sees that there is no hope that his body will agree to work for the Creator by itself, one's prayer can be from the bottom of the heart, and then his prayer is accepted.

We must know that by attaining *Lishma*, one puts the evil inclination to death. The evil inclination is the will to receive, and acquiring the desire to bestow cancels the will to receive from being able to do anything. This is considered putting it to death. Since it has been removed from its office, and it has nothing more to do since it is no longer in use, when it is revoked from its function, this is considered putting it to death.

When one contemplates "What he has in his work which he works under the sun," one sees that it is not so difficult to enslave oneself to His Name for two reasons:

1. Anyhow, meaning, whether willingly or unwillingly, one must exert in this world, and what has one left from all the efforts he has made?
2. However, if a person works *Lishma*, he receives pleasure during the work, too.

According to the proverb of the Sayer of Dubna, who spoke about the verse, "You did not call Me, Jacob, for you labored about Me, Israel," he said that it is like a rich man who departed the train and had a small bag. He placed it where all the merchants place their baggage, and the porters take the baggage and bring them to the hotel where the merchants stay. The porter thought that clearly the merchant would take a small bag by himself, and there is no need for a porter for this, so he took a big package.

The merchant wanted to pay him a small fee, as he usually pays, but the porter did not want to take it. He said, "I put a big bag into the hotel depository, which exhausted me, and I barely carried your bag, and you want to pay me so little for it?"

The lesson is that when one comes and says that he exerted extensively in observing Torah and *Mitzvot*, the Creator tells him, "You did not call Me, Jacob." In other words, it is not My baggage that you took. Rather, this baggage belongs to someone else. Since you say that you had much effort in Torah and *Mitzvot*, you must have had a different landlord for whom you worked; so go to him to pay you.

This is the meaning of "for you labored about Me, Israel." This means that he who works for the Creator has no labor, but on the contrary, pleasure and elation. But one who works for other goals cannot come to the Creator with complaints that the Creator does not give him vitality in the work, since he did not work for the Creator, for the Creator to pay for his work. Instead, one can complain to those people for whom he worked to give him pleasure and vitality.

And since there are many purposes in *Lo Lishma* [not for Her sake], one should demand of the goal for which he worked to give him the reward, namely pleasure and vitality. It is said about them, "They who make them shall be like them, everyone who trusts them."

However, according to this, it is perplexing. After all, we see that even when one takes upon himself the burden of the kingdom of heaven without any other intention, he still does not feel any vitality, to say that this vitality compels him to take upon himself the burden of the kingdom of heaven. And the reason he does take upon himself the burden is only because of faith above reason.

In other words, he does it by way of coercive overcoming, unwillingly. Thus, we might ask, Why does one feel exertion in this work, with the body constantly seeking a time when it can be rid of this work, as one does not feel any vitality in the work? According to the above, when one works in humbleness, when his only goal is to work in order to bestow, why does the Creator not impart him taste and vitality in the work?

The answer is that we must know that this matter is a great correction. Were it not for this, meaning if light and vitality had illuminated immediately when one began to take upon himself the burden of the kingdom of heaven, he would have vitality in the work. In other words, the will to receive, too, would have consented to this work.

In that state he would certainly agree because he wants to satisfy his desire, meaning he would work for his own benefit. Had that been the case, it would never have been possible to achieve *Lishma* since he would be compelled to work for his own benefit, as he would feel greater pleasure in the work of the Creator than in corporeal desires. Thus, he would have to remain in *Lo Lishma*, since he would have had satisfaction in the work, and where there is satisfaction, one cannot do anything, as without profit, one cannot work. It follows that if one received satisfaction in this work of *Lo Lishma*, he would have to remain in that state.

This would be similar to what people say, that when there are people chasing a thief to catch him, the thief, too, runs and yells, "Catch the thief!" Then, it is impossible to recognize who is the real thief so as to catch him and take the theft out of his hand.

However, when the thief, meaning the will to receive, does not feel any flavor or vitality in the work of accepting the burden of the kingdom of heaven, in that state, if one works with faith above reason, coercively, and the body becomes accustomed to this work against the desire of his will to receive, then he has the means by which to come to work that will be with the purpose of bringing contentment to his Maker, since the primary requirement from a person is to come to *Dvekut* [adhesion] with the Creator through his work, which is discerned as equivalence of form, where all his actions are in order to bestow.

This is as it is written, "Then shall you delight in the Lord." The meaning of "Then" is that first, in the beginning of his work, he did not have pleasure. Instead, his work was coercive.

But afterward, when he has already accustomed himself to work in order to bestow and not examine himself—if he is feeling a good taste in the work—but believes that he is working to bring contentment to his Maker through his work, he should believe that the Creator accepts the work of the lower ones regardless of how and how much is the form of their work. In everything, the Creator examines the intention, and this brings contentment to the Creator. Then one is rewarded with "delight in the Lord."

Even during the work of the Creator he will feel delight and pleasure since now he really does work for the Creator because the effort he made during the coercive work qualifies him to be able to truly work for the Creator. You find that then, too, the pleasure he receives relates to the Creator, meaning specifically for the Creator.

6. What Is Support in the Torah, in the Work?
I heard in Tav-Shin-Dalet, 1943-1944

When one learns Torah and wants all his actions to be in order to bestow, one must try to always have support in the Torah. Support is considered nourishment, which is love, fear, elation, and freshness and so on. One should extract all this from the Torah, meaning the Torah should give him these results.

However, when one learns Torah and does not have these results, it is not considered Torah since Torah refers to the light clothed in the Torah, as our sages said, "I have created the evil inclination; I have created the Torah as a spice." This refers to the light in it, since the light in it reforms him.

We should also know that the Torah is divided into two discernments: 1) Torah, 2) Mitzva [commandment]. In fact, it is impossible to understand these two discernments before one is awarded walking in the path of the Creator by way of "The counsel of the Lord is with those who fear Him." This is so because when one is in a state of preparation to enter the Creator's palace, it is impossible to understand the path of truth.

However, it is possible to give an example that even a person in the preparation period can somewhat understand. It is as our sages said (Sutah 21): "Rabbi Yosef said, 'A Mitzva protects and saves while practiced. The Torah protects and saves both when practiced and when not practiced.'"

The thing is that "when practiced" refers to when one has some light. One can use this light that he obtained only while the light is still with him, as now he is in gladness because of the light that shines for him. This is discerned as a Mitzva, meaning that he has not yet been rewarded with the Torah, but elicits a life of Kedusha [holiness] only from the light.

This is not so with the Torah: When one attains some way in the work, one can use the way he has attained even when he is not practicing it, that is, even while he does not have the light. This is so because only the illumination has departed from him, but he can use the way that he attained in the work even when the illumination leaves him.

Still, we must know that while practiced, a *Mitzva* is greater than the Torah when not practiced. When practiced means that now one receives the light. This is called "practiced," when one receives the light in it.

Hence, while one has the light, a *Mitzva* is more important than the Torah when one has no light, meaning when there is no vitality of the Torah. On one hand, the Torah is important because one can use the way one has acquired in the Torah. On the other hand, it is without vitality, called "light." In a time of *Mitzva* one does receive vitality, called "light." Therefore, in this respect, a *Mitzva* is more important.

Thus, when one is without vitality, he is considered "wicked," since now he cannot say that the Creator leads the world in a manner of "The Good Who Does Good." This is called that he is called "wicked," since he condemns his Maker, as now he feels that he has no vitality, and has nothing to be glad about so he can say that now he thanks the Creator for giving him delight and pleasure.

One cannot say that he believes that the Creator leads His guidance over others in a manner of good and doing good, since we understand the path of Torah as a sensation in the organs. If one does not feel the delight and pleasure, what does it give him that another person has delight and pleasure?

If one had really believed that Providence is revealed as good and doing good to his friend, that faith should have brought him delight and pleasure from believing that the Creator leads the world with a guidance of delight and pleasure. If it does not bring him vitality and joy, what is the benefit in saying that the Creator does watch over his friend with a guidance of good and doing good?

The most important is what one feels in one's own body—whether he feels good or bad. A person enjoys his friend's pleasure only if he enjoys his friend's benefit. In other words, we learn that with the sensation of the body, the reasons are not important. It is only important if he feels good. In that state, he says that the Creator is "good and does good." If one feels bad, he cannot say that the Creator behaves with him in a manner of good and doing good. Thus, precisely if he enjoys his friend's happiness, and receives high spirits from this, and feels gladness because his friend feels good, then he can say that the Creator is a good leader.

If one has no joy, he feels bad. Thus, how can he say that the Creator is good and does good? Therefore, a state where one has no vitality and gladness is already a state where he has no love for the Creator and ability to justify his Maker and be happy, as is appropriate with one who is granted with serving a great and important King.

In general, we must know that the upper light is in a state of complete rest, and the whole expansion of the holy names occurs by the lower ones. In other words, all the names that the upper light has come from the attainment of the lower ones. This means that the upper light is named according to their attainments. Put differently, one names the upper light according to the way in which one attains it, meaning according to one's sensation.

If one does not feel that the Creator is giving him anything, what name can he give to the Creator if he does not receive anything from Him? Rather, when one believes in the Creator, every single state that one feels, he says that it comes from the Creator. In that state, one names the Creator according to one's feeling.

If one feels happy in the state he is in, he says that the Creator is called "The Good Who Does Good," since this is what he feels, that he receives good from Him. In that state, one is called *Tzadik* [righteous], since he *Matzdik* [justifies] his Maker (the Creator).

If one feels bad in the state he is in, he cannot say that the Creator is sending him good. Therefore, in that state one is called *Rasha* [wicked], since he *Marshia* [condemns] his Maker.

However, there is no such thing as in-between, when one says that he feels both good and bad in his state. Instead, one is either happy or unhappy.

This is the meaning of what our sages said (*Berachot* 61), "The world was not created, etc., but either for the complete wicked or for the complete righteous." This is because there is no such reality where one feels good and bad together.

When our sages say that there is in-between, it is that with the creatures, who have a discernment of time, you can say in-between, in two times, one after the other, as we learn that there is a matter of ascents and descents. These are two times: once he is wicked, and once he is righteous. But at the same time, for one to feel good and bad simultaneously, this does not exist.

It follows that when they said that the Torah is more important than a *Mitzva*, it is precisely when he does not engage in it, meaning when he has no vitality. Then the Torah is more important than a *Mitzva*, which has no vitality.

This is so because one cannot receive anything from a *Mitzva*, which has no vitality. But with the Torah, one still has a way in the work from what he had received while he was practicing the Torah. Although the vitality has departed, the way remains in him, and he can use it. There is a time when a *Mitzva* is more important than Torah, meaning when there is vitality in the *Mitzva* and no vitality in the Torah.

Thus, when not practiced, meaning when one has no vitality and gladness in the work, one has no other counsel but prayer. However, during the prayer one must know that he is wicked because he does not feel the delight and pleasure that exist in the world, although he makes calculations that he can believe that the Creator gives only good.

Yet, not all the thoughts that one has are true in the way of the work. In the work, if the thought leads to action, meaning a sensation in the organs, so the organs feel that the Creator is good and does good, the organs should receive from this vitality and gladness. If one has no vitality, what good are all the calculations if now the organs do not love the Creator because He imparts them with abundance?

Therefore, one must know that if he has no vitality and gladness in the work, it is a sign that he is wicked because he is unhappy. All the calculations are untrue if they do not lead to action, meaning to a sensation in the organs that he loves the Creator because He imparts delight and pleasure to the creatures.

7. What Is, "A Habit Becomes a Second Nature," in the Work?

I heard in Tav-Shin-Gimel, 1942-1943

By accustoming oneself to something, that thing becomes a second nature for that person. Hence, there is nothing that one cannot feel its reality. This means that although one has no sensation of the thing, he still comes to feel it by becoming used to that thing.

We must know that there is a difference between the Creator and the creatures regarding sensations. In the creatures, there is the feeler and the felt, the attaining and the attained. This means that we have a feeler who is connected to some reality.

However, a reality without a feeler is only the Creator Himself. In Him, "there is no thought or perception whatsoever." This is not so with a person; his whole existence is only through the sensation of reality. Even the validity of reality is evaluated as valid only with regard to the one who senses the reality.

In other words, what the feeler tastes is what he considers truth. If one tastes a bitter taste in reality, meaning he feels bad in the situation he is in, and suffers because of that state, that person is considered wicked in the work, since he condemns the Creator, as He is called "The Good Who Does Good," for He only bestows goodness to the world. Yet, with respect to that person's feeling, the person feels that he received the opposite from the Creator, meaning the situation he is in is bad.

We should therefore understand what our sages wrote (*Berachot* 61), "The world was created either for the complete wicked or for the complete righteous." This means the following: Either one tastes and feels a good taste in the world and then he justifies the Creator and says that the Creator gives only good to the world. Or, if one feels and tastes a bitter taste in the world then one is wicked because he condemns the Creator.

It turns out that everything is measured according to one's sensation. However, all these sensations have no relation to the Creator, as it is written in the "Poem of

Unification," "As she, so You will always be; shortage and surplus in You will not be." Hence, all the worlds and all the changes are only with respect to the receivers, as one attains them.

8. What Is the Difference between a Shade of Kedusha and a Shade of Sitra Achra?

I heard on Tammuz, Tav-Shin-Dalet, July 1944

It is written (Song of Songs, 2), "Until the day breathes, and the shadows flee away." We must understand what are shadows in the work and what are two shadows. The thing is that when one does not feel His guidance, that He leads the world in a manner of "The Good Who Does Good," it is regarded as a shadow that hides the sun.

In other words, as the corporeal shadow that hides the sun does not change the sun in any way, and the sun shines in all its power, so one who does not feel the existence of His guidance does not induce any change above. Rather, there is no change above, as it is written, "I the Lord did not change."

Instead, all the changes are in the receivers. We must observe two discernments in this shade, meaning in this concealment:

1. When one still has the ability to overcome the darkness and concealments that one feels, justify the Creator, and pray to the Creator that the Creator will open his eyes to see that all the concealments that he feels come from the Creator, meaning that the Creator does all this to him so he may find his prayer and yearn to adhere to Him.

   This is so because only through the suffering that one receives from Him, wishing to break free from the trouble and flee from the torments, then he does everything he can. Hence, when receiving the concealments and afflictions, he is certain to take the known cure—to do much praying for the Creator to help him out of the state he is in. In that state, he still believes in His Providence.

2. When one comes to a state where he can no longer overcome and say that all the suffering and pains he feels are because the Creator sent them to him so as to have a reason to ascend in degree, he comes to a state of heresy, since he cannot believe in His guidance. Naturally, at that time, he cannot pray.

It follows that there are two kinds of shadows, and this is the meaning of "and the shadows flee away," meaning that the shadows will pass away from the world.

The shade of *Klipa* [shell] is called "Another god is sterile and does not bear fruit." In *Kedusha* [holiness], however, it is called "Under its shadow I coveted to sit, and its fruit was sweet to my palate." In other words, he says that all the concealments and afflictions he feels are because the Creator has sent him these states so he would have a place for work above reason.

When one has the strength to say this—that the Creator causes him all this—it is to one's benefit. This means that through this he can come to work in order to bestow and not for his own sake. At that time, one realizes, meaning believes that the Creator enjoys specifically this work, which is built entirely on above reason.

It follows that at that time, one does not pray to the Creator that the shadows will flee from the world. Rather, he says, "I see that the Creator wants me to serve Him in this manner, entirely above reason." Thus, in everything he does he says, "The Creator certainly enjoys this work, so why should I care if I am working in a state of concealment of the face?"

Because one wants to work in order to bestow, meaning that the Creator will enjoy, he feels no lowliness in this work, meaning a sensation that he is in a state of concealment of the face, that the Creator does not enjoy this work. Instead, one agrees to the leadership of the Creator, meaning however the Creator wants him to feel the existence of the Creator during the work, he agrees wholeheartedly. This is so because one does not consider what can please him, but what can please the Creator. Thus, this shade brings him life.

This is called "Under its shadow I coveted," meaning one covets such a state where he can make some overcoming above reason. It follows that if one does not exert in a state of concealment, when there is still room to pray for the Creator to bring him closer, and he is negligent in this, for this reason, he is sent a second concealment in which one cannot even pray. This is because of the sin of not exerting with all one's might to pray to the Creator. For this reason, one comes to a state of such lowliness.

However, after one comes to that state, he is pitied from above and is given another awakening from above. The same order begins anew until finally he strengthens in prayer, the Creator hears his prayer, brings him near, and reforms him.

9. What Are Three Things that Broaden One's Mind in the Work?

I heard on Elul, Tav-Shin-Bet, August 1942

The Zohar interprets what our sages wrote: "Three things broaden one's mind. These are a handsome woman, a handsome abode, and handsome *Kelim* [vessels]." It says, "A sightly woman is the *Shechina* [Divinity]. A sightly abode is his heart, and sightly *Kelim* are his organs."

We must explain that the *Shechina* cannot appear in its true form, which is a state of grace and beauty, except when one has sightly *Kelim*, which are the organs extending from the heart. This means that one must first purify his heart to be a sightly abode by annulling the will to receive for himself and accustoming himself to work so all his actions will be only in order to bestow.

From this extend sightly *Kelim*, meaning his desires, called *Kelim*, will be clean from reception for himself. Rather, they will be pure, called "bestowal."

However, if the abode is not sightly, the Creator says, "he and I cannot dwell in the same abode." This is because there must be equivalence of form between the light and the *Kli* [vessel]. Therefore, when one takes upon himself faith in purity, in mind or in heart, he is imparted with a sightly woman, meaning that the *Shechina* appears to him in a form of grace and beauty, which broadens his mind.

In other words, through the pleasure and gladness he feels at that time, the *Shechina* appears within the organs, filling the outer and inner *Kelim*. This is called "broadening the mind."

This is obtained through envy, lust, and honor, which bring a person out of the world. Envy means through envy in the *Shechina*, regarded as being jealous in "jealously for the Lord of hosts." Honor means that he wants to increase the glory of heaven. Lust is by way of "You have heard the lust of the humble."

10. What Is "Run Away, My Beloved," in the Work?
I heard on *Tammuz*, *Tav-Shin-Dalet*, July 1944

We should know that when one begins to walk on a path of wanting to come to do everything for the sake of the Creator, he comes to states of ascents and descents. Sometimes he comes to such a great decline that he has thoughts of escaping Torah and *Mitzvot* [commandments], meaning thoughts come to a person that he has no desire to be in the domain of *Kedusha* [holiness].

In that state, one should believe that it is to the contrary, meaning that it is the *Kedusha* that runs away from him. The reason is that when one wants to blemish the *Kedusha*, the *Kedusha* moves forward and runs away from him first. If one believes this and overcomes during the escape, then the *Brach* [escape] becomes *Barech* [bless], as it is written, "Bless, Lord, his strength, and accept the work of his hands."

11. Joy with Trembling
I heard in *Tav-Shin-Het*, 1947-1948

Joy is considered love, which is existence. This is similar to one who builds for himself a house without making any holes in the walls. You find that he cannot enter the house, as there is no hollow place in the walls of the house by which to enter the house. Therefore, a hollow space must be made through which he will enter the house.

Therefore, where there is love, there should also be fear, as fear is the hollow. In other words, one must awaken the fear that one might not be able to aim to bestow.

It follows that when there are both, there is wholeness. Otherwise, each wants to revoke the other. For this reason, we must try to have both of them in the same place.

This is the meaning of the need for love and fear. Love is called existence, whereas fear is called a deficiency and a hollow. Only with the two of them together is there wholeness. This is called "two legs," where precisely when one has two legs can one walk.

12. The Essence of Man's Work
I heard during a meal on the 2nd day of Rosh Hashanah, Tav-Shin-Het, October 5, 1948

The essence of man's work should be how to come to feel taste in bestowing contentment to one's Maker, since all that one does for oneself removes him from the Creator due to the disparity of form. Conversely, if one acts in order to benefit the Creator, even if it is the smallest act, it is still considered a *Mitzva* [commandment].

Therefore, one's primary exertion should be to acquire the strength to feel taste in bestowing, which is through lessening the force that feels taste in self-reception. Then one slowly acquires the taste in bestowing.

13. A Pomegranate
I heard during a meal on the 2nd day of Rosh Hashanah, Tav-Shin-Het, October 5, 1948

A pomegranate, he said, implies to what our sages said, "Even the vain ones among you are filled with *Mitzvot* like a pomegranate" (*Iruvin* 19). He said, *Rimon* [pomegranate] comes from the word *Romemut* [exaltedness/sublimity], which is above reason. And the meaning will be that the "The vain among you are filled with *Mitzvot*." The measure of the filling is the extent to which one can go above reason, and this is called *Romemut*.

There is emptiness only in a place where there is no existence, as in "The earth hangs on nothing." You find that what is the measure of the filling of the empty place? The answer is, the extent to which one raises oneself above reason.

This means that the emptiness should be filled with exaltedness, meaning with above reason, and to ask of the Creator to give him that strength. This will mean that all the emptiness was created, meaning it comes to a person to feel this way—that he is empty—only in order to fill it with the *Romemut* of the Creator. In other words, one is to take everything above reason.

This is the meaning of the verse, "God has made it that He will be feared." This means that these thoughts of emptiness come to a person in order for one to have a need to take upon himself faith above reason. And for this we need the help of the

Creator. It follows that at that time, one must ask the Creator to give him the power to believe above reason.

It turns out that it is precisely then that one needs the Creator to help him, since the exterior mind lets him understand the opposite. Hence, at that time, one has no other choice but to ask the Creator to help him.

It is said about this, "One's desire overcomes him every day; and were it not for the Creator, he would not overcome it." It follows that only then is the state when one understands that no one will help him but the Creator. And this is "God has made it that He will be feared." The matter of fear is discerned as faith, and only then is one in need of the salvation of the Creator.

14. What Is the Exaltedness of the Creator?
I heard in Tav-Shin-Het, 1947-1948

The *Romemut* [exaltedness/sublimity] of the Creator means that one should ask the Creator for the strength to go above reason. This means that there are two interpretations to the *Romemut* of the Creator:

1. To not be filled with knowledge, which is intellect with which one can answer one's questions. Rather, he wants the Creator to answer his questions. It is called *Romemut* because all the wisdom comes from above and not from man, meaning that man can answer his own questions.

   Anything that one can answer is regarded as answering everything with the external mind. This means that the will to receive understands that it is worthwhile to observe Torah and *Mitzvot* [commandments]. However, if the above reason compels one to work, it is called "against the opinion of the will to receive."

2. The greatness of the Creator means that one becomes needy of the Creator to grant his wishes. Therefore:

   a. One should go above reason. Then one sees that he is empty and becomes needy of the Creator.

   a. Only the Creator can give him the strength to be able to go above reason. In other words, what the Creator gives is called "The *Romemut* of the Creator."

15. What Is Other Gods in the Work?
I heard on Av 24, Tav-Shin-Hey, August 3, 1945

It is written, "You shall make no other gods over Me." *The Zohar* interprets that there should be stones to weigh with. It asks about it, How is the work weighed with stones, by which one knows one's state in the ways of the Creator? It replies that it is known that when one begins to work more than one is used to, the body begins to kick and object to this work with all its might, since regarding bestowal, it is a load and a burden for the body. It cannot tolerate this work, and the resistance of the body appears in a person in the form of foreign thoughts. It comes and asks the questions of "who" and "what." Through these questions, a person says that all these questions are certainly sent to him by the *Sitra Achra* [other side] to obstruct him in the work.

It says that if, at that time, one says that they come from the *Sitra Achra*, one breaches what is written, "You shall make no other gods over Me." The reason is that one should believe that it comes to him from the *Shechina* [Divinity], since "There is none else besides Him." However, the *Shechina* shows one his true state, how he is walking in the ways of the Creator.

This means that by sending him these questions, called "foreign thoughts," meaning that through these foreign thoughts she sees how he answers the questions regarded as "foreign thoughts." And all this, one should know one's true state in the work so as to know what to do.

It is like an allegory about a friend who wanted to know how much his friend loved him. Certainly, when face to face, his friend hides himself because of shame. Therefore, he sends a person to speak badly about his friend. Then he sees his friend's reaction while he is away from his friend, and then one can know the true measure of his friend's love.

The lesson is that when the *Shechina* shows her face to a person, meaning when the Creator gives one vitality and joy, in that state, one is ashamed to say what he thinks about the work of bestowal without receiving anything for himself. However, when not facing her, meaning when the vitality and gladness cool down, which is considered not facing her, then one can see his true state regarding the aim to bestow.

If one believes that, as it is written, "There is none else besides Him," and that the Creator sends all the foreign thoughts, meaning that He is the operator, he certainly knows what to do and how to answer all the questions. This seems as though she sends him messengers to see how he slanders her, his kingdom of heaven, and this is how we can interpret the above matter.

One can understand this, that everything comes from the Creator, for it is known that the beatings that the body beats a person with its foreign thoughts, since they do not come to a person when he does not engage in the work, but these beatings that come to a person in a complete sensation, to the point that these thoughts smash his mind, they come specifically after preceding Torah and work more than the usual. This is called stones to weigh with.

It means that these stones fall in one's mind when one wants to understand these questions. Afterward, one comes to weigh the purpose of one's work, if it is truly worthwhile to work in order to bestow, to work with all his might and soul, and that all his aspirations will be only to hope that what there is to acquire in this world is only in the purpose of his work to bring contentment to his Maker, and not in any corporeal matter.

At that time begins a bitter argument, since one sees that there are arguments both ways. The writings warn about this, "You shall make no other gods over Me." Do not say that another god gave you the stones with which to weigh your work, but "over Me."

Instead, one should know that this is considered "over Me." This is so that one will see the true form of the basis and the foundation upon which the structure of the work is built.

The heaviness in the work is primarily because they are two texts that deny one another. On one hand, one should try that all his work will be to achieve *Dvekut* [adhesion] with the Creator, that all his desire will be only to bestow contentment upon his Maker, and not at all for himself.

On the other hand, we see that this is not the primary goal, since the purpose of creation was not for the creatures to bestow upon the Creator, since He has no need for the creatures to give Him something. On the contrary, the purpose of creation was due to His desire to do good to His creations, meaning for the creatures to receive delight and pleasure from Him.

These two matters contradict one another from one end to the other, for on one hand, one should bestow, and on the other hand, one should receive. In other words, there is the matter of correction of creation, being to achieve *Dvekut*, discerned as equivalence of form, being that all his actions will be only to bestow. Afterward, it is possible to achieve the purpose of creation—to receive delight and pleasure from the Creator.

Hence, when one has accustomed oneself to walk in ways of bestowal, one has no vessels of reception anyhow. When one walks in ways of reception, he has no vessels of bestowal.

Thus, through the "stones to weigh with" one acquires both, since after the negotiation he had during the work, when he overcomes and takes upon himself the burden of the kingdom of heaven in the form of bestowal in mind and heart, it causes that when he comes to draw the upper abundance, since he already has a solid basis that everything should be in the form of bestowal, hence, even when one receives some illumination, he receives it in order to bestow. This is because the whole basis of his work is built solely on bestowal. This is considered that he "receives in order to bestow."

16. What Is the Day of the Lord and the Night of the Lord, in the Work?

I heard in *Tav-Shin-Aleph*, 1940-1941, Jerusalem

Our sages said about the verse, "Woe unto you who desire the day of the Lord! Why do you need the day of the Lord? It is darkness, and not light" (*Amos* 5): "There is an allegory about a rooster and a bat that were awaiting the light. The rooster said to the bat, 'I am waiting for the light since the light is mine. But you, why do you need its light?'" (*Sanhedrin* 98b). The interpretation is that since the bat has no eyes to see, what does it gain from the sunlight? On the contrary, to one who has no eyes, sunlight only makes it darker.

We must understand that allegory, meaning how the eyes are connected to looking in the light of the Creator, which the text names "the day of the Lord." They gave an allegory in that regard about a bat, that one who has no eyes remains in the dark.

We must also understand what is the day of the Lord, what is the night of the Lord, and what is the difference between them. We discern the day of people by the sunrise, but with the day of the Lord, in what do we discern it?

The answer is, as the appearance of the sun. In other words, when the sun shines on the ground, we call it "day." When the sun does not shine, it is called "darkness." It is the same with the Creator. A day is called "revelation," and darkness is called "concealment of the face."

This means that when there is revelation of the face, when it is as clear as day for a person, this is called "a day." It is as our sages said about the verse, "'The murderer rises at daytime to kill the poor and indigent; and in the night, he is as a thief.' Since he said, 'and in the night, he is as a thief,' it follows that light is day. He says there, that if the matter is as clear to you as light that comes over the souls, he is a murderer, and it is possible to save him in his soul" (*Psachim* 2). Thus, we see that in the matter of "day," the Gemara says that it is a matter as clear as day.

It follows that the day of the Lord will mean that the guidance by which the Creator leads the world will be clearly in the form of good and doing good. For example, when one prays, his prayer is immediately answered and he receives what he has prayed for, and one succeeds wherever one turns. This is called "the day of the Lord."

Conversely, darkness, which is night, will mean concealment of the face. This brings one doubts in the guidance of good and doing good, and foreign thoughts. In other words, the concealment of the guidance brings one all these foreign views and thoughts. This is called "night" and "darkness," meaning that one experiences a state where he feels that the world has turned dark on him.

Now we can interpret what is written, "Woe unto you who desire the day of the Lord! Why do you need the day of the Lord? It is darkness, and not light." The thing is that those who await the day of the Lord, it means that they are waiting to be imparted faith above reason, that faith will be so strong, as if they see with their eyes, with certainty, that it is so, that the Creator watches over the world in a manner of good and doing good.

In other words, they do not want to see how the Creator leads the world as The Good Who Does Good, since seeing is contradictory to faith. In other words, faith is precisely where it is against reason. And when one does what is against one's reason, this is called "faith above reason."

This means that they believe that the guidance of the Creator over the creatures is in a manner of good and doing good. While they do not see it with absolute certainty, they do not say to the Creator, "We want to see the quality of good and doing good as seeing within reason." Rather, they want it to remain in them as faith above reason, but they ask of the Creator to give them such strength that this faith will be so strong, as if they see it within reason, that there will be no difference between faith and knowledge in the mind. This is what they, those who want to adhere to the Creator, refer to as "the day of the Lord."

In other words, if they feel it as knowledge, the light of the Creator, called "the upper abundance," will go to the vessels of reception, called "*Kelim* [vessels] of separation." They do not want this since it will go to the will to receive, which is the opposite of *Kedusha* [holiness], which is against the will to receive for one's own sake. Instead, they want to adhere to the Creator, and this can be only through equivalence of form.

However, to achieve this, meaning in order for one to have desire and craving to adhere to the Creator, since one is born with a nature of a will to receive only for one's own benefit, how is it possible to achieve something that is completely against nature? For this reason, one must make great efforts until he acquires a second nature, which is the desire to bestow.

When one is imparted the desire to bestow, he is qualified to receive the upper abundance and not blemish, since all the flaws come only through the will to receive for oneself. That is, even when doing something in order to bestow, deep inside there is a thought that he will receive something for this act of bestowal that he is now performing.

In a word, man is unable to do anything if he does not receive something in return for the act. In other words, he must enjoy, and any pleasure that one receives for one's own benefit, that pleasure must cause him separation from the Life of Lives, because of the separation.

This stops one from adhering to the Creator, since *Dvekut* [adhesion] is measured by the equivalence of form. It is thus impossible to have pure bestowal without a mixture of reception from one's own powers. Therefore, for one to have the powers of bestowal, we need a second nature, so one will have the strength to achieve equivalence of form.

In other words, the Creator is the giver and does not receive anything, for He lacks nothing, meaning that what He gives is also not because of a lack, that if He has no one to give to, He feels it as a lack.

Rather, we must perceive this as a game. That is, it is not that when He wants to give, it is something that He needs. Instead, this is all like a game. It is as our sages said regarding the queen: She asked, "What does the Creator do after He has created the world?" The answer was, "He sits and plays with a whale," as it is written, "This whale You have created to play with" (*Avoda Zarah*, p 3).

The matter of the whale refers to *Dvekut* and connection (as it is written, "according to the opening of man and the connections"). This means that the purpose, which is the connection of the Creator with the creatures, is only a game; it is not a matter of a desire and a need.

The difference between a game and a desire is that everything that comes in the desire is a necessity. If one does not obtain one's desire, he is deficient. But with games, even if one does not obtain the thing, it is not considered a lack, as they say, "It is not so bad that I did not get what I planned because it is not so important." This is so because the desire he had for it was only a game and not serious.

It follows, that the whole purpose is for one's work to be entirely in bestowal, and he will not have any desire or craving to receive pleasure for his work.

This is a high degree, as it is what happens in the Creator. And this is called "the day of the Lord." The day of the Lord is called "wholeness," as it is written, "Let the stars of morning be dark; let it look for light, but have none," for light is considered wholeness.

When one acquires the second nature, the desire to bestow that the Creator gives him after the first nature, the will to receive, now he receives the desire to bestow, and then one is qualified to serve the Creator in completeness. This is considered "the day of the Lord."

Thus, one who has not been rewarded with the second nature, to be able to serve the Creator in the manner of bestowal, and waits to be rewarded with this, meaning with bestowal, meaning he has already exerted and did what he could to obtain that force, he is considered to be awaiting the day of the Lord—to have equivalence of form with the Creator.

When the day of the Lord comes, he is elated. He is happy that he has emerged from the control of the will to receive for himself which separated him from the Creator. Now he clings to the Creator and considers it as having risen to the top.

It is the opposite for one whose work is only in self-reception: He is happy as long as he thinks that he will receive some reward from his work. When he sees that the will to receive will not receive any reward for his work, he becomes sad and idle. Sometimes he comes to doubt the beginning and says, "I did not swear on this."

Thus, moreover, the day of the Lord is attaining the power to bestow. If one were to be told, "This will be your profit from engaging in Torah and *Mitzvot*," he would say, "I consider it darkness, and not light," since this knowledge brings one to darkness.

17. What Does It Mean that the Sitra Achra Is Called "Malchut without a Crown"?

I heard in *Tav-Shin-Aleph*, 1940-1941, Jerusalem

Crown means *Keter*, and *Keter* is the Emanator and the Root. *Kedusha* [holiness] is connected to the root, meaning that *Kedusha* is considered being in equivalence of form with its root. This means that as our Root, namely the Creator, wants only to bestow, as it is written, "His desire to do good to the creatures," so the *Kedusha* is only to bestow upon the Creator.

The *Sitra Achra* [other side], however, is not so. She aims only to receive for herself. For this reason, she is not adhered to the Root, being *Keter*. This is why the *Sitra Achra* is referred to as having no *Keter* [crown]. In other words, she has no *Keter* because she is separated from the *Keter*.

Now we can understand what our sages said (*Sanhedrin* 29), "All who add, subtract." This means that if you add to the count, it subtracts. It is written (*Zohar*, *Pekudei*, Item 249), "It is the same here, relating to what is inside, it writes, 'Moreover you shall make the tabernacle with ten curtains.' Relating to what is outside, it writes, 'eleven curtains,' adding letters, meaning adding the *Ayin* [the added Hebrew letter] to the twelve, and subtracting from the count. It subtracts one from the number twelve because of the addition of the *Ayin* to the twelve."

It is known that calculation is implemented only in *Malchut*, who calculates the height of the degree (through the *Ohr Hozer* [reflected light] in her). Also, it is known that *Malchut* is called "the will to receive for oneself."

When she annuls her will to receive before the Root, and does not want to receive but only to give to the Root, like the Root, which is a desire to bestow, then *Malchut*, called *Ani* [I], becomes *Ein* [nothing], with an *Aleph*. Only then does she extend the light of *Keter* to build her *Partzuf* and becomes twelve *Partzufim* of *Kedusha*.

However, when she wants to receive for herself, she becomes the evil *Ayin* [eye]. In other words, where there was a combination of *Ein*, meaning annulment before the root, which is *Keter*, it has become *Ayin* (meaning seeing and knowing within reason).

This is called "adding." It means that one wants to add knowing to faith, and work within reason. In other words, she says that it is more worthwhile to work within reason, and then the will to receive will not object to the work.

This causes a flaw, meaning that they were separated from the *Keter*, called "the desire to bestow," which is the Root. There is no longer the matter of equivalence of form with the Root, called *Keter*. For this reason, the *Sitra Achra* is called "*Malchut* without a Crown." It means that *Malchut* of the *Sitra Achra* does not have *Dvekut* [adhesion] with the *Keter*. For this reason, they have only eleven *Partzufim*, without *Partzuf Keter*.

This is the meaning of what our sages said, "ninety nine died of evil eye," meaning because they have no quality of *Keter*. It means that the *Malchut* in them, being the will to receive, does not want to annul before the Root, called *Keter*. This means that they do not want to make of the *Ani* [I], called "the will to receive," a quality of *Ein* [nothing], which is the annulment of the will to receive.

Instead, they want to add. And this is called "the evil *Ayin*" [eye]. That is, where there should be *Ein* with *Aleph* [the first letter in the word *Ein*], they insert the evil *Ayin* [eye, the first letter in the word]. Thus, they fall from their degree due to lack of *Dvekut* with the Root.

This is the meaning of what our sages said, "Anyone who is proud, the Creator says, 'He and I cannot dwell in the same abode,'" as he makes two authorities. However, when one is in a state of *Ein*, and annuls himself before the Root, meaning that one's sole intention is only to bestow, like the Root, you find that there is only one authority here—the authority of the Creator. Then, all that one receives in the world is only in order to bestow upon the Creator.

This is the meaning of what he had said, "The whole world was created only for me, and I, to serve my Maker." For this reason, I must receive all the degrees in the world so that I can give everything to the Creator, which is called "to serve my Maker."

18. My Soul Shall Weep in Secret - 1
I heard in *Tav-Shin*, 1939-1940, Jerusalem

When concealment overpowers a person and he comes to a state where the work becomes tasteless, and he cannot picture or feel any love and fear, and he cannot do anything in *Kedusha* [holiness], his only counsel is to cry to the Creator to have mercy on him and remove the screen from his eyes and heart.

Crying is a very important matter. It is as our sages write: "All the gates were locked except for the gates of tears." The world asks about this: If the gates of tears are not locked, what is the need for the gates at all? He said that it is like a person who asks his friend for some necessary object. This object touches his heart, and he asks and begs him in every manner of prayer and plea. Yet, his friend pays no attention to all this. And when he sees that there is no longer reason for prayers and pleas then he raises his voice in weeping.

It is said about this: "All the gates were locked except for the gates of tears." That is, when were the gates of tears not locked? Precisely when all the gates were locked. It is then that there is room for the gates of tears, and then we see that they were not locked.

However, when the gates of prayer are open, the gates of tears and weeping are irrelevant. This is the meaning of the gates of tears being locked. Thus, when are the gates of tears not locked? Precisely when all the gates are locked, the gates of tears are open since one still has the choice of prayer and plea.

This is the meaning of "My soul shall weep in secret," meaning when one comes to a state of concealment, then "My soul shall weep," because one has no other option. This is the meaning of "All that your hand and strength can do, do."

19. What Is "The Creator Hates the Bodies," in the Work?

I heard in Tav-Shin-Gimel, 1942-1943, Jerusalem

The Zohar says that the Creator hates the bodies. He said that we should interpret it as referring to the will to receive, called *Guf* [body]. The Creator created His world for His glory, as it is written, "Every one who is called by My Name, for My glory, I have created him, formed him, and also I made him."

Therefore, this contradicts the body's argument that everything is for it, meaning only for its own benefit, while the Creator says the opposite, that everything should be for the sake of the Creator. This is why our sages said that the Creator said, "he and I cannot dwell in the same abode."

It follows that the primary separator from being in *Dvekut* [adhesion] with the Creator is the will to receive. This is apparent when the evil comes, meaning the will to receive for oneself comes and asks, "Why do you want to work for the sake of the Creator?" We think that it speaks as people do, that it wants to understand with its intellect. Yet, this is not the truth, since it does not ask for whom one is working. This is certainly a rational argument, as this argument awakens in a reasonable person.

Instead, the argument of the wicked is a bodily question. That is, it asks, "What is this work?" In other words, What will you profit for the exertion you are making? It means that it asks, "If you are not working for your own benefit, what will the body, called 'the will to receive for oneself,' get out of it?"

Since this is a bodily argument, the only reply is a bodily reply, which is "He blunted its teeth, and had he not been there, he would not have been redeemed." Why? Because the will to receive for oneself has no redemption even at the time of redemption, since redemption will be when all the profits enter the vessels of bestowal and not the vessels of reception.

The will to receive for oneself must always remain in deficit, since satisfying the will to receive is actual death. The reason is, as said above, that creation was primarily for His glory (and this is an answer to what is written, that His wish is to do good to His creations and not for Himself).

The interpretation will be that the essence of creation is to reveal to all that the purpose of creation is to do good to His creations. This is specifically when one says that he was born to honor the Creator. At that time, in these vessels, the purpose of creation appears, which is to do good to His creations.

For this reason, one must always examine oneself, the purpose of one's work, meaning if the Creator receives contentment in every act that one performs, because he wants equivalence of form with the Creator. This is called "All your actions will be for the sake of the Creator," meaning that one wants the Creator to enjoy everything he does, as it is written, "to bring contentment to his Maker."

Also, one needs to conduct oneself with the will to receive and say to it, "I have already decided that I do not want to receive any pleasure because you want to enjoy, since with your desire I am forced to be separated from the Creator, for disparity of form causes separation and distance from the Creator."

One's hope should be that since he cannot break free from the power of the will to receive, he is therefore in perpetual ascents and descents. Hence, he awaits the Creator, to be rewarded with the Creator opening his eyes, and to have the strength to overcome and work only for the sake of the Creator. It is as it is written, "One have I asked of the Lord; her will I seek." "Her" means the *Shechina* [Divinity]. And one asks "that I may dwell in the house of the Lord all the days of my life."

The house of the Lord is the *Shechina*. And now we can understand what our sages said about the verse, "And you shall take for you on the first day," the first to count the iniquities. We must understand why is there joy if there is room for a count of iniquities here. He said that we must know that there is a matter of importance in the labor when there is contact between the individual and the Creator.

It means that one feels that he needs the Creator since, in the state of labor, he sees that no one in the world can save him from the state he is in except for the Creator. Then he sees that "There is none else besides Him," who can save him from the state he is in, and from which he cannot escape.

This is called having close contact with the Creator. If one knows how to appreciate that contact, meaning that one should believe that then he is adhered to the Creator, meaning that all his thought is of the Creator, meaning that He will help him, for otherwise he sees that he is lost.

Conversely, one who is rewarded with private Providence and sees that the Creator does everything, as it is written, "He alone does and will do all the deeds," naturally has nothing to add, and in any case, he has no room for prayer for the Creator's help, since he sees that even without his prayer the Creator still does everything.

Hence, at that time one has no place to be able to do good deeds since he sees that without him, too, everything is done by the Creator. Thus, one has no need for the Creator to help him do anything. In that state, he has no contact with the Creator, to need Him to the extent that he is lost if the Creator does not help him.

It follows that he does not have the contact that he had with the Creator during the labor. He said that it is like a person who is hanging between life and death, and asks of his friend to save him from death. How does he ask his friend? He certainly tries to ask his friend to have mercy on him and save him from death with every power at his disposal. He certainly never forgets to pray to his friend, since he sees that otherwise he will lose his life.

However, one who asks of his friend for luxuries, which are not so necessary, the pleading person is not so attached to his friend to give him what he asks for to the point that his mind will not be distracted from asking. You find that with things that are not related to life-saving, the pleading person is not so adhered to the giver.

Thus, when one feels that he should ask the Creator to save him from death, meaning from the state of "The wicked in their lives are called 'dead,'" the contact between the person and the Creator is close contact. For this reason, for the righteous, a place of work is to need the Creator's help. Otherwise, he is lost. This is what the righteous crave: a place to work so they will have close contact with the Creator.

It follows that if the Creator gives room for work, these righteous are very happy. This is why they said, "first to the count of iniquities." For them it is joyous to now have a place to work, meaning that now they have become needy of the Creator and can now come into close contact with the Creator, since one can come to the King's palace only for some purpose.

This is the meaning of the verse, "And you shall take for you." It specifies "for you," since everything is in the hands of heaven but the fear of heaven. In other words, the Creator can give abundance of light because He has it. But the darkness, the place of lack, this is not in His domain.

Since there is a rule that there is fear of heaven only from a place of lack, and a place of lack is called "the will to receive," it means that only then is there a place for labor. In what? In that it resists.

The body comes and asks, "What is the work?" and one has nothing to answer to its question. Then one must assume the burden of the kingdom of heaven above reason as an ox to the burden and as a donkey to the load without any arguments. Rather, He said and His will was done. This is called "for you," meaning this work belongs precisely to you, and not to Me, meaning the work that your will to receive requires.

However, if the Creator gives one some illumination from above, the will to receive surrenders and annuls like a candle before a torch. Then one has no labor anyhow, since he no longer needs to take upon himself the burden of the kingdom of heaven coercively as an ox to the burden and as a donkey to the load, as it is written, "You who love the Lord, hate evil."

This means that the love of the Creator extends only from the place of evil. In other words, to the extent that one has hatred for evil, meaning that he sees how the will to receive obstructs him from achieving the completeness of the goal, to that extent he needs to be imparted the love of the Creator. If one does and feel that he has evil, he cannot be granted the love of the Creator since he has no need for it, as he already has satisfaction in the work.

As we have said, one must not be angry when he has work with the will to receive, that it obstructs him in the work. One would certainly be more satisfied if the will to receive were absent from the body, meaning that it would not bring its questions to a person, obstructing him in the work of observing Torah and *Mitzvot* [commandments].

However, one should believe that the obstructions of the will to receive in the work come to him from above. One is given the force to discover the will to receive from above because there is room for work precisely when the will to receive awakens.

Then one has close contact with the Creator to help him turn the will to receive to work in order to bestow. One must believe that from this extends contentment to the Creator, from his praying to Him to draw him near in the manner of *Dvekut* [adhesion], called "equivalence of form," discerned as the annulment of the will to receive, so it is in order to bestow. The Creator says about this, "My sons defeated Me." That is, I gave you the will to receive, and you ask Me to give you a desire to bestow instead.

Now we can interpret what is brought in the Gemara (*Hulin* p 7): "Rabbi Pinhas Ben Yair was going to redeem the captive. He came across the river Ginai (the name of the river was Ginai). He said to Ginai, 'Split your water and I will pass through you.' It told him: 'You are going to do your Maker's will, and I am going to do my Maker's will. You perhaps do, perhaps not do, while I certainly do.'"

He said that the meaning is that he told the river, meaning the will to receive, to let him through it and reach the degree of doing the will of the Creator, meaning to do everything in order to bestow contentment upon his Maker. The river, the will to receive, replied that since the Creator created it with this nature of wanting to receive delight and pleasure, it therefore does not want to change the nature in which the Creator created it.

Rabbi Pinhas Ben Yair waged war against it, meaning he wanted to invert it to a desire to bestow. This is regarded as waging war against the creation that the Creator created in nature, called "the will to receive," which the Creator created, which is the whole of creation, called "existence from absence."

We must know that during the work, when the will to receive comes to a person with its arguments, no arguments or rationalizations help with it. Though one thinks that they are just arguments, it will not help one defeat his evil.

Instead, as it is written, "Blunt its teeth." This means to advance only by actions, and not by arguments. This is considered that one must add powers coercively. This is the meaning of what our sages said, "He is coerced until he says 'I want.'" In other words, through persistence, habit becomes a second nature.

One must especially try to have a strong desire to obtain the desire to bestow and overcome the will to receive. A strong desire means that a strong desire is measured by the increment of the in-between rests and the arrests, meaning the time gaps between each overcoming.

Sometimes one receives a cessation in the middle, meaning a descent. This descent can be a cessation of a minute, an hour, a day, or a month. Afterward, he resumes the work of overcoming the will to receive and the attempts to achieve the desire to bestow. A strong desire means that the cessation does not take him a long time and he is immediately reawakened to the work.

It is like a person who wants to break a big rock. He takes a big hammer and hammers many times all day long, but they are weak. In other words, he does not hammer the rock with one swing but brings down the big hammer slowly. Afterward, he complains that this work of breaking the rock is not for him, that it must take a very strong man to be able to break this big rock. He says that he was not born with such great powers to be able to break the rock.

However, one who lifts this big hammer and strikes the rock with a big swing, not slowly but with a great effort, the rock immediately surrenders to him and breaks. This is the meaning of "like a strong hammer that shatters the rock."

Similarly, in the holy work, which is to bring the vessels of reception into *Kedusha* [holiness], we have a strong hammer, meaning words of Torah that give us good counsels. However, if it is not consistent, but with long intermissions in between, one escapes the campaign and says that he was not made for this, but this work requires one who was born with special skills for it. Nevertheless, one should believe that anyone can achieve the goal, but he should try to always increase his efforts to overcome, and then one can break the rock in a short time.

We must also know that for the effort to make contact with the Creator, there is a very harsh condition here: The effort must be in the form of adornment. "Adornment" means something that is important to a person. One cannot work gladly if the labor is not of importance, meaning that one is happy that now he has contact with the Creator.

This matter is implied in the citron. It is written about the citron, "a fruit of the citrus tree,"* that it should be clean above its nose. It is known that there are three discernments: A) adornment, B) scent, C) taste.

Taste means that the lights are poured from above downward, meaning below the *Peh* [mouth], where there are the palate and the taste. This means that the lights come in vessels of reception.

Scent means that the lights come from below upward. This means that the lights come in vessels of bestowal, in the form of receiving and not bestowing below the

---

* In Hebrew, citrus is *Hadar*, from the word *Hidur* (adornment).

palate and the throat. This is discerned as "and he shall smell in the fear of the Lord," said about the Messiah. It is known that scent is attributed to the nose.

Adornment is beauty, discerned as above one's nose, meaning scentless. It means that there is neither taste nor smell there. Thus, what is there by which one can endure? There is only the adornment in it, and this is what sustains him.

We see about the citron that the adornment is in it precisely before it is suitable for eating. However, when it is suitable for eating, there is no adornment in it anymore.

This comes to tell us about the work of the first to count the iniquities. This means that precisely when one works in the form of "And you shall take for you," meaning the work during the acceptance of the burden of the kingdom of heaven, when the body resists this work, then there is room for the joy of adornment.

This means that during this work the adornment is apparent. This means that if he has gladness from this work, it is because he considers this work as adornment, and not as disgrace.

In other words, sometimes one despises this work of assuming the burden of the kingdom of heaven, which is a time of a sensation of darkness, when one sees that no one can save him from the state he is in but the Creator. Then he takes upon himself the kingdom of heaven above reason, as an ox to the burden and as a donkey to the load.

One should be glad that now he has something to give to the Creator, and the Creator enjoys him having something to give to the Creator. But one does not always have the strength to say that this is beautiful work, called "adornment," but he despises this work.

This is a harsh condition for one, to be able to say that he chooses this work over the work of whiteness, meaning than a state where he does not feel a taste of darkness during the work. Rather, at that time, he does feel a taste in the work meaning that then he does not have to work with the will to receive, so it will agree to take upon itself the kingdom of heaven above reason.

If he does overcome himself and can say that this work is pleasant to him that now he is observing the Mitzva [commandment] of faith above reason, and he accepts this work as beauty and adornment, this is called "A joy of Mitzva."

This is the meaning of the prayer being more important than the response to the prayer, since in prayer one has a place for labor and he needs the Creator, meaning he awaits heaven's mercy. At that time, one has a true contact with the Creator and he is in the King's palace. However, when the prayer is answered, he has already departed the King's palace since he has already taken what he had asked for and left.

Accordingly, we should understand the verse, "Your oils have a good fragrance; your name is as oil poured forth." Oil is called "the upper light" when it flows. "Poured forth" means during the cessation of the abundance. At that time, the scent from the oil remains. (Scent means that a *Reshimo* [reminiscence] of what he had remains nonetheless. Adornment, however, is called so in a place where there is no grip at all, meaning that even the *Reshimo* does not shine.)

This is the meaning of *Atik* and *AA*. During the expansion, the abundance is called *AA*, which is *Hochma* [wisdom], meaning open Providence. *Atik* comes from the [Hebrew] word *VaYe'atek* [detachment], meaning the departure of the light. In other words, it does not shine, and this is called "concealment."

This is the time of rejection to clothing, which is the time of the reception of the King's crown, which is considered *Malchut* [kingdom] of lights, regarded as the kingdom of heaven.

It is written about it in *The Zohar*, "the *Shechina* [Divinity] said to Rabbi Shimon, 'There is no place to hide from you' (meaning there is no place where I can hide Myself from you)." This means that even in the greatest concealment in reality, he still takes upon himself the burden of the kingdom of heaven with great joy.

The reason is that he follows a line of a desire to bestow, and therefore gives what he has in his hand. If the Creator gives him more, he gives more. And if he has nothing to give, he stands and cries like a crane for the Creator to save him from the evil water. Hence, in this manner, too, he has contact with the Creator.

The reason that this discernment is called *Atik*, since *Atik* is the highest degree, is that the farther the thing is from clothing, the higher it is. One can feel in the most abstract thing, called "the absolute zero," since there man's hand does not reach.

This means that the will to receive can grip only in a place where there is some expansion of light. Before one purifies one's *Kelim* [vessels] so as to not blemish the light, he is unable for the light to come to him in a form of expansion in the *Kelim*. Only when one marches on the path of bestowal, in a place where the will to receive is not present, whether in mind or in heart, there the light can come in utter completeness. Then the light comes to him in a sensation that he can feel the exaltedness of the upper light.

However, when one has not corrected the *Kelim* to work in order to bestow, when the light expands, it must be restricted and shine only according to the purity of the *Kelim*. Hence, at that time, the light appears to be in utter smallness. Therefore, when the light is abstracted from clothing in the *Kelim*, the light can shine in utter completeness and clarity without any restrictions for the sake of the lower one.

It follows that the importance of the work is precisely when one comes to a state of zero, when one sees that he annuls his whole existence and being, for then the will to receive has no power. Only then does one enter the *Kedusha*.

We must know that "God has made the one opposite the other." It means that as much as there is disclosure in *Kedusha*, to that extent the *Sitra Achra* [other side] awakens. In other words, when one claims, "It is all mine," meaning the entire body belongs to *Kedusha*, the *Sitra Achra*, too, argues against him that the whole body should serve the *Sitra Achra*.

Hence, one must know that when he sees that the body claims that it belongs to the *Sitra Achra*, and cries the famous questions of "Who" and "What" with all its might, it is a sign that one is walking on the path of truth, meaning that one's sole intention is to bestow contentment upon one's Maker. Thus, the primary work is precisely in this state.

One must know that it is a sign that this work hits the target. The sign is that he fights and sends his arrows to the head of the serpent, since it yells and argues the argument of "What" and "Who," meaning "What is this work for you?" meaning what will you gain by working only for the Creator and not for yourselves? And the argument of "Who" means that this is Pharaoh's complaint who said, "Who is the Lord that I should obey His voice?"

It seems as if the "Who" argument is a rational argument. Normally, when someone is told to go and work for someone, the person asks, "For whom?" Hence, when the body claims, "Who is the Lord that I should obey His voice," it is a rational argument.

However, according to the rule that the intellect is not an object in itself, but is rather a mirror of what is found in the senses, it appears so in the mind. This is the meaning of "The sons of Dan: Hushim." That is, the mind judges only according to what the senses let it scrutinize and devise some inventions and tactics to suit the demands of the senses.

In other words, what the senses demand, the mind tries to provide their wish. However, the mind itself has no need for itself, for any demand. Hence, if there is a demand for bestowal in the senses, the mind operates according to a line of bestowal, and the mind does not ask questions, since it is merely serving the senses.

The mind is like a person looking in the mirror to see if he is dirty. And all the places where the mirror shows that he is dirty, he goes and washes and cleans, since the mirror showed him that there are ugly things in his face that need to be cleaned.

However, the hardest thing of all is to know what is considered ugly. Is it the will to receive, meaning the body's demand to do everything only for oneself, or is the desire to bestow the ugly thing, which the body cannot tolerate? The mind cannot scrutinize it, like the mirror, which cannot say what is ugly and what is beauty; rather, it all depends on the senses, and only the senses determine this.

Hence, when one accustoms oneself to work coercively, to work in bestowal, the mind, too, operates by lines of bestowal. At that time, it is impossible that the mind will pose the "Who" question, when the senses have already grown accustomed to work in bestowal.

In other words, the senses no longer ask the question, "What is this work?" since they are already working in order to bestow, and, naturally, the mind does not ask the "Who" question.

You find that the primary work is in "What is this work for you?" And what one hears, that the body does ask the "Who" question, it is because the body does not want to degrade itself so much. This is why it asks the "Who" question. It appears to be asking a rational question, but the truth is that, as we have said above, the primary work is in the "What."

20. Lishma [for Her sake]
I heard in Tav-Shin-Hey, 1944-1945

Concerning *Lishma* [for Her sake]. In order for a person to obtain *Lishma*, one needs an awakening from above, as it is an illumination from above and it is not for the human mind to understand. Rather, he who tastes, knows. It is said about this, "Taste and see that the Lord is good."

Because of this, upon assuming the burden of the kingdom of heaven, one needs it to be in utter completeness, meaning entirely to bestow and not at all to receive. If a person sees that the organs do not agree with this view, he has no other choice but prayer—to pour out his heart to the Creator to help him make his body agree to enslave itself to the Creator.

Do not say that if *Lishma* [for Her sake] is a gift from above, what good is one's overcoming and efforts, and all the remedies and corrections that he makes in order to achieve *Lishma*, if it depends on the Creator? Our sages said about it, "You are not free to exempt yourself from it." Rather, one must give the awakening from below, and this is considered "prayer." Yet, there cannot be a real prayer if he does not know first that without prayer it cannot be obtained.

Therefore, the acts and remedies he makes in order to obtain *Lishma* create the corrected *Kelim* [vessels] in him that want to receive the *Lishma*. Then, after all the actions and the remedies he can pray in earnest since he saw that all his actions did not help him whatsoever. Only then can he make an honest prayer from the bottom of his heart, and then the Creator hears his prayer and gives him the gift of *Lishma*.

We should also know that by obtaining *Lishma*, one puts the evil inclination to death. The evil inclination is called "receiving for one's own benefit." By obtaining the aim to bestow, one cancels the self-benefit. "Putting to death" means that one no longer uses one's vessel of reception for oneself. And since it is no longer active, it is considered dead.

If one considers what one receives for his work under the sun, he will find that it is not so difficult to submit himself to the Creator, for two reasons:

1. One must strain oneself in this world in any case, whether one wants to or not.
2. During the work, too, if one works *Lishma*, he receives pleasure from the work itself.

It is as the Sayer from Dubna said about the verse, "You did not call Me, Jacob, for you labored about Me, Israel." It means that he who works for the Creator has no labor. On the contrary, one has pleasure and elation.

But he who does not work for the Creator, but for other goals, cannot complain to the Creator that He is not giving him vitality in the work, since he is working for another goal. One can complain only to the one for whom he works, to give vitality and pleasure during his work. It is said about him: "They who make them shall be like them, everyone who trusts them."

Do not be surprised that when one assumes the burden of the kingdom of heaven, when he wants to work in order to bestow upon the Creator, he still feels no vitality at all, vitality which would compel one to assume the burden of the kingdom of heaven. Rather, one should accept it coercively, against his better judgment. That is, the body does not agree to this enslavement, why does the Creator not shower him with vitality and pleasure.

The reason is that this is a great correction. Were it not for this, if the will to receive had agreed to this work, one would never have been able to achieve *Lishma*. Rather, he would always work for his own benefit, to satisfy his own desires. It is as people say, that the thief himself yells, "Catch the thief!" and then you cannot tell which is the real thief in order to catch him and reclaim the theft from him.

But when the thief, meaning the will to receive, does not find the work of accepting the burden of the kingdom of heaven tasteful, since the body accustoms itself to work against its will, one has the means by which to come to work only in order to bring contentment to his Maker, since his sole intention should be only for the Creator, as it is written, "Then shall you delight yourself in the Lord." Thus, when he served the Creator in the past, he did not sense any pleasure in the work. Rather his work was compulsory.

But now that he has accustomed himself to work in order to bestow, he is rewarded with delighting in the Creator, and the work itself renders him pleasure and vitality. This is considered that the pleasure, too, is specifically for the Creator.

21. When One Feels Oneself in a State of Ascent
I heard on *Heshvan* 23, *Tav-Shin-Hey*, November 9, 1944

When one feels oneself in a state of ascent, that he is high-spirited, when he feels that he has no desire but only for spirituality, it is then good to delve in the secrets of the Torah in order to attain its internality. Even if one sees that although he exerts to understand something, and still does not know anything, it is still worthwhile to delve in the secrets of the Torah even a hundred times in a single thing.

One should not despair, meaning say that it is useless since he does not understand anything. This is so for two reasons:

A) When one delves into something and yearns to understand it, that yearning is called a "prayer." This is because a prayer is a lack, meaning that one is craving what he lacks, that the Creator will satisfy his desire.

The extent of the prayer is measured by the desire, since the thing that one needs most, the desire for it is greater, for according to the measure of the need, so is the measure of the yearning.

There is a rule that in the thing that one makes the most effort, the exertion increases the lack, and he wants to receive filling for his deficiency. Also, a desire is called "a prayer," regarded as "the work in the heart," since "the Merciful One wants the hearts."

It turns out that then one can give a true prayer because when he delves into the words of the Torah, the heart must be freed from other desires and give the mind the strength to be able to think and scrutinize. If there is no desire in the heart, the mind cannot scrutinize, as our sages said, "One always learns where one's heart desires."

In order for one's prayer to be accepted, it must be a complete prayer. Hence, when scrutinizing to the full extent, one elicits from it a complete prayer, and then one's prayer can be accepted because the Creator hears a prayer. But there is a condition: The prayer must be a complete prayer, and not have other things mixed in the middle of the prayer.

The second reason is that at that time, since one is separated from corporeality to some extent, and is closer to the quality of bestowal, the time is better suited to connect with the internality of the Torah, which is revealed to those who have equivalence with the Creator. This is because the Torah, the Creator, and Israel are one. However, when one is in a state of self-reception he belongs to the externality, and not to the internality.

22. Torah Lishma

I heard on *Shevat 9, Tav-Shin-Aleph*, February 6, 1941

Torah is called *Lishma* [for Her sake] primarily when one learns in order to know with utter certainty, within reason, without any doubts of the clarity of the truth, that there is a judge and there is judgment. There is a judgment means that one sees reality as it appears to our eyes. This means that when we work in faith and bestowal, we see that we are growing and climbing daily, since we always see a change for the better.

And it is likewise to the contrary: When we work in a form of reception and knowledge, we see that we are declining every day down to the ultimate lowliness in reality.

When examining these two states, we see that there is judgment and there is a judge, since while we do not follow the laws of the Torah of truth, we are punished instantly. In that state, we see that there is just judgment. In other words, we see that this is precisely the best way, which is fit and can achieve the truth.

This is considered that the judgment is just, that only in this manner can we come to the ultimate goal: to understand within reason, with complete and absolute understanding of which there is no higher, that only by way of faith and bestowal can we achieve the purpose.

Thus, if one studies for this purpose, to understand that there is judgment and there is a judge, this is called Torah *Lishma*. This is also the meaning of what our sages said, "Great is the learning that leads to action."

It seems that it should have said, "that brings to actions," meaning to be able to do many actions, in the plural form, and not in singular form. However, the thing is that, as mentioned above, the learning should bring one only faith, and faith is called one *Mitzva* [commandment], which sentences the whole world to merit.

Faith is called "doing" because normally when one does something, there must first be a reason that makes him do within reason. It is like the correlation between the mind and the action.

However, when something is above reason, when the reason does not let him do that thing, but to the contrary, we must say that there is no reason in this act, but only an act. This is the meaning of "If one performs one *Mitzva*, happy is he for he has sentenced himself, etc., to the side of merit." This is the meaning of "Great is the learning that leads to action," meaning an act without reason, called "above reason."

23. You Who Love the Lord, Hate Evil

I heard on *Sivan 17, Tav-Reish-Tzadi-Aleph*, June 2, 1931

In the verse, "You who love the Lord, hate evil; He guards the souls of His followers; He will save them from the hand of the wicked," he interprets that it is not enough to love the Creator, and to want to be awarded *Dvekut* [adhesion] with the Creator. One should also hate evil.

Hatred is expressed by hating the evil, called "the will to receive." One sees that he has no way to get rid of it, and at the same time, he does not want to accept the situation. He feels the losses that the evil causes him, and also sees the truth, that one cannot annul the evil by himself, since it is a natural force from the Creator, who imprinted the will to receive in man.

In that state, the verse tells us what one can do is hate evil. And by this the Creator will guard him from that evil, as it is written, "He guards the souls of His followers." What is guarding? "He will deliver them from the hand of the wicked." In that state, since he has some contact with the Creator, be it the smallest contact, he is already a successful person.

In truth, the matter of evil remains and serves as an *Achoraim* [posterior] to the *Partzuf*. But this is only through one's correction: Through sincere hatred of evil, it is corrected into a form of *Achoraim*. The hatred comes because if one wants to obtain *Dvekut* [adhesion] with the Creator then there is a conduct among friends: If two people realize that each of them hates what his friend hates, and loves what and whom his friend loves, they come into perpetual bonding like a stake that will never fall.

Hence, since the Creator loves to bestow, the lower ones should also adapt to want only to bestow. The Creator also hates to be a receiver, as He is completely whole and does not need anything. Thus, man, too, must hate the matter of reception for oneself.

It follows from all the above, that one must bitterly hate the will to receive, for all the ruins in the world come only from the will to receive. And through the hatred, one corrects it and surrenders under the *Kedusha* [holiness].

24. He Will Save Them from the Hand of the Wicked

I heard on *Av 5, Tav-Shin-Dalet*, July 25, 1944, at the completion of *The Zohar*

It is written, "You who love the Lord, hate evil ... He will save them from the hand of the wicked." He asks, "What is the connection between 'hate evil' and 'He will save them from the hand of the wicked?'"

In order to understand this, we must first bring the words of our sages, "The world was created either for complete righteous or for complete evil." He asks, "Is it worthwhile to create the world for complete evil, but not worthwhile for incomplete righteous?"

He answers that from the perspective of the Creator, there is nothing in the world that has two meanings. It is only from the perspective of the receivers, according to the sensation of the receivers. This means that either the receivers feel a good taste in the world, or they feel a terribly bitter taste in the world, since with every act they do, they calculate it in advance when they do it, since no act is done purposelessly. Either they want to improve their present state or to harm someone. But purposeless things are not worthy of a purposeful operator.

Hence, those who accept the modes of conduct of the Creator in the world determine it as good or bad depending on how they feel: as either good or bad. Because of this, "you who love the Lord," who understand that the purpose of creation was to do good to His creations, in order for them to come to feel it, they understand that it is received precisely by *Dvekut* [adhesion] and nearing the Creator.

Thus, if they feel any remoteness from the Creator, they call it "bad." In that state, one considers oneself evil, since an intermediary state does not exist in reality. In other words, either one feels the existence of the Creator and His guidance, or one imagines that "The earth is given into the hand of the wicked."

Since one feels about himself that he is a man of truth, meaning that he cannot deceive himself and say that he feels when he does not feel, hence, he immediately begins to cry to the Creator to have mercy on him and deliver him from the authority of the *Sitra Achra* [other side] and from all the foreign thoughts. Because he is crying earnestly, the Creator hears his prayer. (Perhaps this is the meaning of "The Lord is near to all who call upon Him in truth.") At that time, "He delivers them from the hand of the wicked."

As long as one does not feel one's true self, meaning the measure of one's evil to a sufficient level to awaken him to cry to the Creator out of the affliction that he feels with his recognition of evil, he is still unworthy of redemption since he has not yet revealed the *Kli* [vessel] for hearing the prayer, called "from the bottom of the heart."

This is so because one still thinks that there is some good in him, meaning he does not descend to the bottom of the heart. In the bottom of the heart, he thinks that he still has some good, and he does not notice with what love and fear he relates to the Torah and the *Mitzvot* [commandments]. This is why he does not see the truth.

25. Things that Come from the Heart

I heard on Av 5, Tav-Shin-Dalet, July 25, 1944, during a festive meal for the completion of part of The Zohar

Regarding things that come from the heart, enter the heart. Hence, why do we see that even if things have already entered the heart, one still falls from his degree?

The thing is that when one hears the words of Torah from his teacher, he immediately agrees with his teacher and resolves to observe the words of his teacher with his heart and soul. But afterward, when he comes out to the world, he sees, covets, and is infected by the multitude of desires roaming the world. Then, he and his mind, his heart, and his will are annulled before the majority.

As long as he has no power to sentence the world to the side of merit, they subdue him, he mingles with their desires, and he is led like sheep to the slaughter. He has no choice; he is compelled to think, want, crave, and demand everything that the majority demands. Then he chooses their foreign thoughts and their loathsome lusts and desires, which are alien to the spirit of the Torah. In that state, he has no strength to subdue the majority.

Instead, there is only one counsel then: to cling to his teacher and to the books. This is called "From the mouth of books and from the mouth of authors." Only by clinging to them can he change his mind and will for the better. However, witty arguments will not help him change his mind, but only the remedy of *Dvekut* [adhesion], for this is a wondrous cure, as the *Dvekut* reforms him.

Only while one is inside *Kedusha* [holiness] can one argue with oneself and indulge in clever polemics, that the mind necessitates that he should always walk on the path of the Creator. However, one should know that even when he is wise and certain that he can already use this wit to defeat the *Sitra Achra* [other side], he must engrave in his mind that all this is worthless, that this is not a weapon that can win the war against the inclination, for all these concepts are but a consequence he has attained after the aforementioned *Dvekut*.

In other words, all the concepts upon which he builds his building, saying one must always follow in the path of the Creator, is founded in *Dvekut* with his teacher. Thus, if he loses the foundation, all the concepts are powerless since they will now be lacking the foundation.

Hence, one must not rely on one's own mind, but adhere once more to books and to authors, for only this can help him, and no wit or intellect, as there is no vitality in them.

26. One's Future Depends and Is Tied to Gratitude for the Past
I heard in *Tav-Shin-Gimel*, 1942-1943

It is written, "The Lord is high and the low will see," that only the low can see the exaltedness. The letters *Yakar* [precious] are the letters of *Yakir* [will know]. This means that one knows the exaltedness of a thing to the extent that it is precious to one.

One is impressed according to the importance of the thing. The impression brings one to a sensation in the heart, and according to the measure of one's recognition of the importance, to that extent, joy is born in him.

Thus, if one knows his lowliness, that he is not more privileged than his contemporaries, meaning he sees that there are many people in the world who were not given the strength to do the holy work even in the simplest way, even without the intention and in *Lo Lishma* [not for Her sake], even in *Lo Lishma* of *Lo Lishma*, and even in preparation for the preparation of the clothing of *Kedusha* [holiness], while he was imparted the desire and thought to at least occasionally do holy work, even in the simplest possible way, if one can appreciate the importance of this, according to the importance one attributes to the holy work, to that extent he should give praise and thanks for it.

This is so because it is true that we cannot appreciate the importance of being able to sometimes observe the *Mitzvot* [commandments] of the Creator, even without any intention. In that state, one comes to feel elation and joy in the heart.

The praise and the gratitude one gives for it expand the feelings, and one is elated by every single point in the holy work, he knows Whose servant he is, and thus soars ever higher. This is the meaning of what is written, "I thank You for the grace that

You have made with me," meaning for the past, and by this one can confidently say, and he does say, "and that You are destined to do with me."

27. What Is "The Lord Is High and the Low Will See"?
I heard on *Shabbat Terumah*, *Tav-Shin-Tet*, March 5, 1949, Tel-Aviv

"The Lord is high and the low will see." How can there be equivalence with the Creator when man is the receiver and the Creator is the Giver? The verse says about this, "The Lord is high and the low..."

If one annuls oneself, then one has no authority that separates him from the Creator. In that state, one "will see," meaning he is imparted *Mochin de Hochma*, "and the high will know from afar." However, someone with pride, meaning one who has his own authority, is distanced, since he lacks the equivalence.

Lowliness is not considered one's lowering oneself before others. This is humbleness, and one feels wholeness in this work. Rather, lowliness means that the world despises him. Precisely when people despise, it is considered lowliness, for then he does not feel any wholeness, for it is a law that what people think influences a person.

Therefore, if people respect him, he feels whole; and those whom people despise think of themselves as low.

28. I Shall Not Die but Live
I heard in *Tav-Shin-Gimel*, 1942-1943

In the verse, "I shall not die but live," in order for one to achieve the truth, there must be a sensation that if one does not obtain the truth, he feels himself as dead, since he wants to live. This means that the verse, "I shall not die but live" is said about one who wants to obtain the truth.

This is the meaning of "Jonah *Ben* [the son of] Amitai." Jonah comes from the [Hebrew] word *Honaa* [fraud], and *Ben* [son] comes from the word *Mevin* [understands]. One understands because one always examines the situation he is in and sees that he has deceived himself, and he is not walking on the path of truth.

Truth means to bestow, meaning *Lishma* [for Her sake], and the opposite of this is fraud and deceit, meaning only to receive, which is *Lo Lishma* [not for Her sake]. By this, one is later imparted the "Amitai," meaning *Emet* [truth].

This is the meaning of "your eyes are as doves." *Eynaim* [eyes] of *Kedusha* [holiness], called *Eynaim* of the *Shechina* [Divinity], are *Yonim* [doves]. They deceive us and we think that she has no *Eynaim*, as it is written in *The Zohar*, "A fair maiden who has no eyes."

The truth is that one who is rewarded the truth sees that she does have eyes. This is the meaning of "A bride whose eyes are pretty, her whole body needs no scrutiny."

29. When Thoughts Come to a Person
I heard in Tav-Shin-Gimel, 1942-1943

"The Lord is your shade." If one thinks, the Creator also thinks of him. And when the Creator thinks, it is called "the mountain of the Lord." This is the meaning of "Who shall ascend on the mountain of the Lord, who shall stand in His holy place?" "He who has clean hands." This is the meaning of "Moses' hands were heavy," "and a pure heart," which is the heart.

30. The Most Important Is to Want Only to Bestow
I heard after Shabbat Vayikra, Tav-Shin-Gimel, March 20, 1943

The most important is not to want anything except to bestow because of His greatness, since any reception is flawed. It is impossible to exit reception, but only to take the other extreme, meaning bestowal.

The moving force, meaning the extending force and the force that compels to work, is only the greatness of the Creator. One must think that, ultimately, the efforts and the labor must be made, but through these forces one can yield some benefit and pleasure. In other words, one can please a limited body with one's work and effort, which is either a passing guest or an eternal one, meaning that one's energy remains in eternity.

This is similar to a person who has the power to build a whole country, and he builds only a shack that is ruined by a strong wind. You find that all the efforts were wasted. However, if one remains in *Kedusha* [holiness], then all the efforts remain in eternity. It is only from this goal that one should take one's basis for the work, and all other bases are flawed.

The power of faith is sufficient for one to work in the manner of bestowal, meaning that he can believe that the Creator accepts his work, even though his work is not so important in one's eyes. Nevertheless, the Creator accepts everything. If one attributes the work to Him, He welcomes and wants all the works, however they are.

Thus, if one wants to use faith in a manner of reception, then the faith is not enough for him. This means that at that time he has doubts in the faith. The reason is that reception is not the truth, meaning in fact, one has nothing from the work; only the Creator will have from his work.

Therefore, one's doubts are true. In other words, these foreign thoughts that come up in his mind are true arguments. But if one wants to use faith to walk in ways of bestowal, he will certainly have no doubts in the faith. If one has doubts, he must know that he probably does not want to walk in a manner of bestowal, since for bestowal, faith is enough.

31. Anyone Who Pleases the Spirit of the People
I heard

Anyone who pleases the spirit of the people. He asked, "But we have found that the greatest and most renowned were in disagreement. Thus, the spirit of the people is not pleased with him."

He answered that they did not say "all the people," but "the spirit of the people." This means that only the bodies are disputed, meaning that each one is working with the will to receive.

However, "the spirit of the people" is already spirituality, and "pleases"—that the righteous who extends the abundance, extends for the whole generation. Only because they have not yet clothed their spirit, they cannot attain and feel the abundance that the righteous extended.

32. A Lot Is an Awakening from Above
I heard on *Terumah 4, Tav-Shin-Gimel*, February 10, 1943

A lot is an awakening from above, when the lower one does not assist in anything. This is the meaning of "cast a pur," "the lot." Haman was complaining and said, "neither do they keep the king's laws."

This means that enslavement begins for the worker in a state of *Lo Lishma* [not for Her sake], meaning for self-reception. Hence, why were they given the Torah, because afterward they are granted *Lishma* [for Her sake] and they are given the lights and the upper attainments.

Then comes the complainant and asks, "Why are they given these sublime things for which they did not work or hope, but their every thought and goal were only over matters that concern their own needs, called *Lo Lishma*?" This is the meaning of "The wicked will prepare and the righteous will wear."

This means that previously he was working in a state of wicked, meaning *Lo Lishma*, but for the receiver. Afterward, he was rewarded with *Lishma*, meaning that all the servitude enters the domain of *Kedusha* [holiness], meaning everything is to bestow. This is the meaning of "the righteous will wear."

This is the meaning of *Purim* as *Yom Kippurim* [Day of Atonement]. *Purim* is an awakening from above, and *Yom Kippurim* is an awakening from below, meaning through repentance. However, there is awakening from above there, too, corresponding to the lots that were there, "one lot for the Lord, and the other lot for Azazel," and the Creator is the scrutinizer.

33. The Lots on Yom Kippur and with Haman
I heard on *Terumah* 6, *Tav-Shin-Gimel*, February 12, 1943

It is written (Leviticus 16:8), "And Aaron shall cast lots upon the two goats: one lot for the Lord, and the other lot for Azazel." Concerning Haman, it is written (Esther 3:7), "they cast a pur, that is, the lot."

A lot applies where there cannot be a scrutiny in the mind because the mind does not reach there so they can sort out which is good and which is evil. In that state, a pur is cast, when they rely not on the mind but on what the lot tells them. It follows that when using the word "lot," it comes to tell us that now we are going above reason.

Regarding the seventh of *Adar* [sixth month of the Hebrew calendar], on which Moses was born and on which Moses died, we must understand what *Adar* means. It comes from the word *Aderet* [mantle], as it is written about Elijah (Kings 1 19:19), "and cast his mantle upon him." *Aderet* comes from the word *Aderet Se'ar* [hair], which are *Se'arot* [hair] and *Dinim* [judgments], which are foreign thoughts and ideas in the work, removing one from the Creator.

Here there is a matter of overcoming them. Although he sees many contradictions in His guidance, he should still overcome them through faith above reason and say that they are guidance in the manner of "The Good Who Does Good." This is the meaning of what is written about Moses, "And Moses hid his face." This means that he saw all the contradictions and held them through exertion by the power of faith above reason.

It is as our sages said, "In return for 'and Moses hid his face for he was afraid to look,' he was rewarded with 'and the image of the Lord does he behold.'" This is the meaning of the verse, "Who is as blind as My servant, and who is as deaf as My angel?"

It is known that *Eynaim* [eyes] are called "reason," "mind," meaning the mind's eyes. This is because with something that we perceive in the mind, we say, "But we see that the mind and the reason require that we say so."

Hence, one who goes above reason is as one who has no eyes, and he is called "blind," meaning pretends to be blind. Also, one who does not want to hear what the spies tell him and pretends to be deaf is called "deaf." This is the meaning of "Who is as blind as My servant, and who is as deaf as My angel?"

However, when one says, "They have eyes but they see not; they have ears but they hear not," it means that he does not want to obey what the reason asserts and what the ears hear, as it is written about Joshua the son of Nun, that a bad thing never entered his ears. This is the meaning of *Aderet Se'ar*, that he had many contradictions and judgments. Each contradiction is called *Se'ar* [hair], and under each *Se'ar* there is a dent.

This means that one makes a dent in the head, meaning the foreign thought fissures and punctures one's head. When one has many foreign thoughts, it is considered having many *Se'arot*, and this is called *Aderet Se'ar*.

This is the meaning of what is written about Elisha: "And he went from there and found Elisha the son of Shaphat, who was plowing with twelve yoke of oxen before him, and he with the twelfth; and Elijah passed over unto him and cast his mantle upon him" (Kings 1, 19). (Yoke means pairs of *Bakar* [oxen], since they would plow with pairs of oxen together that were tightened. This is called a yoke of oxen.) *Bakar* means *Bikoret* [criticism], and twelve refers to the completeness of the degree (like twelve months or twelve hours).

This means that one already has all the discernments of *Se'arot* that can be in the world, and then an *Aderet Se'ar* is made from the *Se'arot*. However, with Elisha, it was in the form of the morning of Joseph, as it is written, "As soon as the morning was light, the men were sent away, they and their asses."

It means that one has already been rewarded the light that rests over these contradictions, since through the contradictions, called criticism, when wanting to overpower them, it is by drawing light on them. It is as it is written, "He who comes to purify is aided."

Because he already drew the light on all the criticism, and he has nothing more to add, since all the criticism has been completed in him, then the criticism and the contradictions in him end by themselves. This follows the rule that no act is in vain, since there is no operator without a purpose.

Indeed, we must know that what appears to one as things that contradict the guidance of "The Good Who Does Good" is only to compel one to draw the upper light on the contradictions, when wanting to prevail over the contradictions. Otherwise, one cannot prevail. This is called "the exaltedness of the Creator," which one extends when having the contradictions, called *Dinim* [judgments].

This means that the contradictions can be annulled if one wants to overcome them, only if he extends the exaltedness of the Creator. You find that these *Dinim* cause the drawing of the exaltedness of the Creator. This is the meaning of what is written, "and cast his mantle upon him."

It means that afterward he attributed the whole mantle of hair to Him, to the Creator. That is, now he saw that the Creator gave him this mantle deliberately, in order to draw the upper light on them.

However, one can only see this later, after one has been granted the light that rests on these contradictions and *Dinim* that he had had in the beginning. This is so because he sees that without the hair, meaning the descents, there would not be a place for the upper light to be there, as there is no light without a *Kli* [vessel].

For this reason, he sees that all the exaltedness of the Creator he had obtained was because of the *Se'arot* and the contradictions he had had. This is the meaning of "The Lord on high is mighty." It means that the exaltedness of the Creator is awarded through the *Aderet*, and this is the meaning of "let the exaltedness of God be in their mouth."

This means that through the faults in the work of the Creator, it causes him to rise up, as without a push one is idle to make a movement and agrees to remain in the state he is in. But if one descends to a lower degree than he understands, this gives one the strength to overcome, for one cannot stay in such a bad state, since one cannot agree to remain like that, in the state to which he has descended.

For this reason, one must always prevail and emerge from the state of descent. In that state, he must draw upon himself the exaltedness of the Creator. This causes him to extend higher forces from above, or he remains in utter lowliness. It follows that through the *Se'arot*, one gradually discovers the exaltedness of the Creator until one finds the names of the Creator, called "the thirteen attributes of Mercy." This is the meaning of "and the elder shall serve the younger," and "the wicked will prepare and the righteous will wear," and also, "and you shall serve your brother."

This means that all the enslavement, meaning the contradictions that there were, which appeared to be obstructing the holy work, and were working against *Kedusha* [holiness]. Now, when granted the light of the Creator, which is placed over these contradictions, we see the opposite—that they were serving the *Kedusha*. That is, through them, there was a place for the *Kedusha* to clothe in their dresses. This is called "the wicked will prepare and the righteous will wear," meaning that they gave the *Kelim* [vessels] and the place for the *Kedusha*.

Now we can interpret what our sages wrote (*Hagigah* 15a), "Rewarded—a righteous. He takes his share and his friend's share in heaven. Convicted—a wicked. He takes his share and his friend's share in hell." It means that one takes the *Dinim* and the foreign thoughts of one's friend, which we should interpret over the whole world, meaning that this is why the world was created filled with so many people, each with his own thoughts and opinions, and all are present in the same world.

It is so deliberately, so that each and every one will be incorporated in all of one's friend's thoughts. Thus, when one repents, there will be benefit from this *Hitkalelut* [mingling/ incorporation].

It is so because when one wants to repent, he must sentence himself and the entire world to the side of merit, since he himself is incorporated in all the foreign notions and thoughts of the entire world. This is the meaning of "Convicted—a wicked. He takes his share and his friend's share in hell."

It follows that when he was still wicked, called "convicted," one's own share was of *Se'arot*, contradictions, and foreign thoughts. But also, he was mingled with one's friend's share in hell, meaning he was incorporated in all the views of all the people in the world.

Therefore, when later he becomes "Rewarded–a righteous," meaning after he repents, he sentences himself and the entire world "to the side of merit, he takes his share and his friend's share in heaven." This is because he must draw upper light for the foreign thoughts of all the people in the world, too, since he is mingled with them and must sentence them to the side of merit.

This is precisely through extending the upper light over these *Dinim* of the general public. Although they themselves cannot receive this light that he had drawn on their behalf because they do not have *Kelim* that are ready for this, but he drew it for them as well.

Yet, we must understand according to the famous rule that one who causes extension of lights in upper degrees, they say that to the extent that one induces light in the upper one, one receives from these lights, too, since he was the cause. Accordingly, the wicked, too, should have received a part of the lights that they induced in the righteous.

To understand this, we must present the matter of the lots. There were two lots, as it is written, "One lot for the Lord, and the other lot for Azazel." It is known that a lot is a matter of above reason. Hence, when the lot is above reason, it causes the other to be for Azazel.

This is the meaning of "It shall whirl upon the head of the wicked." It is so because through these contradictions, he extended the upper light. You find that in this manner, the exaltedness of the Creator increases, and for the wicked it is a drawback since their whole desire is only within reason. When the light that comes based on above reason increases, they wither away and become annulled.

Hence, all the wicked have is their help to the righteous to extend the exaltedness of the Creator, and then they are annulled. This is called "Rewarded–he takes his share and his friend's share in heaven." (Author's comment: This implies that only one who helped make the correction of creating the reality of appearance of the light through good deeds, hence this act remains in *Kedusha*. One receives what one induces above to make a place for the expansion of the light. In that state, the lower one receives what he causes to the upper one. However, the contradictions and the *Dinim* are canceled, since they are replaced by the exaltedness of the Creator, which appears over the above reason, while they want it to appear specifically on *Kelim* of within reason. This is why they are annulled. This is how we can interpret.)

However, the foreign thoughts, too, which the public caused to draw exaltedness over them, that light remains for them. When they are worthy of receiving, they will receive what each causes the drawing of the upper light on them, too.

This is the meaning of "A path that runs through the split of the hair," brought in *The Zohar* (Part 15, and in *The Sulam* [commentary], Item 33, p 56), which distinguishes between right and left. The two lots that were on *Yom Kippurim*, which is repentance from fear. Also, there was a lot on *Purim*, which is repentance from love.

This is so because it was then prior to the building of the Temple, and at that time they needed repentance from love. But first, there had to be a need for them to repent. This need causes *Dinim* and *Se'arot* [pl. of hair]. This is what it means that Haman was given authority from above, by way of, I place government over you, that he will rule over you.

This is why it was written that Haman "had cast pur, that is, the lot," on the month of *Adar*, which is the twelfth, as it is written "twelve oxen," written about Elisha. It is written, "two rows, six in a row," which is the month of *Adar*, as in *Aderet Se'ar*, which are the biggest *Dinim*.

By this Haman knew that he would defeat Israel, since Moses died on the month of *Adar*. However, he did not know that Moses was born on it, as in, "and they saw that it was good." It is so because when one strengthens in the toughest situation, one is granted the greatest lights, called "the exaltedness of the Creator."

This is the meaning of "fine twined linen." In other words, because they have been granted "the path that runs in the split of the hair," "two rows, six in a row," then "twined," from the words "a stranger removed." It means that the stranger, meaning the *Sitra Achra*, is annulled and gone because he has already completed his task.

You find that all the *Dinim* and contradictions came only to show the exaltedness of the Creator. Hence, with Jacob, who was a smooth man, without *Se'arot*, it was impossible to disclose the exaltedness of the Creator, since he had no cause or need to extend them. For this reason, Jacob could not receive the blessings from Isaac, as he had no *Kelim* [vessels], and there is no light without a *Kli* [vessel]. This is why Rebecca advised him to take Esau's clothes.

And this is the meaning of "and his hand had hold on Esau's heel." This means that although he did not have any hair, he took it from Esau. This is what Isaac saw and said, "The hands are the hands of Esau, but the voice is the voice of Jacob." In other words, Isaac liked the correction that Jacob did and by that his *Kelim* for the blessings were made.

This is the reason that we need such a big world with so many people, so that each will be incorporated in his friend. It follows that each individual is incorporated in thoughts and desires of an entire world.

This is why a person is called "a small world" in and of itself, for the above reason. This is also the meaning of "not rewarded." That is, when one has still not been rewarded, "He takes his share and his friend's share in hell." It means that he is incorporated with his friend's hell.

Moreover, even when one has already corrected one's own part of hell, if he has not corrected his friend's share, meaning he has not corrected his part that is incorporated with the world, he is still not considered whole.

Now we understand that although Jacob himself was smooth, without *Se'arot*, he still held the heel of Esau. It means that he takes the *Se'arot* by being incorporated with Esau.

Hence, when he is rewarded with correcting them, he takes his friend's share in Heaven, referring to the measure of the exaltedness of the upper light that he had extended over the *Se'arot* of the general public. He is rewarded that, although the general public still cannot receive because they lack the qualification for it.

Now we can understand the argument of Jacob and Esau. Esau said, "I have enough," and Jacob said, "I have everything," meaning "two rows, six in a row," meaning within reason and above reason, which is the will to receive and the light of *Dvekut* [adhesion].

Esau said, "I have enough," which is a light that comes in vessels of reception, within reason. Jacob said that he had everything, meaning two discernments. In other words, he was using the vessels of reception, and also had the light of *Dvekut*.

This is the meaning of the mixed multitude that made the calf and said, "this is your god oh Israel," meaning *Eleh* [these] without the *Mi* [who], meaning that they wanted to connect only to the *Eleh*, and not to the *Mi*. It means that they did not want both, which is the *Mi* and the *Eleh*, which together make up the name *Elokim* [God], meaning enough and everything. This they did not want.

This is the meaning of the *Cherubim*, which are *Kravia* and *Patia*. One *Cherub* on the one end, which is the discernment of enough, and one *Cherub* on the other end, which is the discernment of everything. This is also the meaning of "the voice speaking to him from between the two cherubim."

But how can this be? After all they are two ends, opposite from one another. Still, he had to make a *Patia* [fool] and thus receive. And this is called "above reason": One does what one is told although he does not understand anything that he is told.

Regarding the "everything," called "above reason," one should try to work with gladness since through gladness the true measure of the everything appears. If one has no gladness, then one should feel sorry that he has no gladness, since this is the primary place of the work, to discover the gladness that he is working above reason.

Hence, when one has no gladness from this work, he should afflict himself for it. This is the meaning of what is written, "whose heart makes him willing," which means being sick and tormented over not having gladness from this work.

This is the meaning of "because you did not serve the Lord your God with gladness because of the abundance of all things." Instead, you left the everything and took only the enough. Hence, in the end you will be far below and without anything, meaning you will lose the enough, too. However, to the extent that one has the "everything," and he is glad, to that extent he is imparted the "enough."

Accordingly, we should interpret the words, "women weeping for Tammuz" (Ezekiel 8). Rashi interprets that "They had idolatry, that he had lead inside his eyes, and they were heating it to melt the lead out of the eyes."

We should interpret the matter of crying, meaning that they have no gladness because there is dust in the eyes. Dust is *Behina Dalet*, meaning the kingdom of heaven, which is faith above reason.

This discernment bears the form of dust, meaning it is unimportant. And this work has the taste of dust, meaning it is only as important as dust. The allegory about the women weeping for Tammuz is that they burn this idolatry so that by heating, the dust will come out from the lead.

It implies that they are crying over the work that they were given to believe above reason that His guidance is good and does good, while within reason they see only contradictions in His guidance. This work is the work of *Kedusha*, and they want to remove the dust, meaning the work of above reason, called "dust." However, the eyes, called "sight," imply seeing His guidance, being within reason; this is called "idolatry."

This resembles a person whose craft is to make pots and vessels from earth, whose work is to make clay pots. The order is that first he makes round balls of clay, and then cuts and makes holes in the balls. And when the young son sees what his father is doing, he cries, "Father, why are you ruining the balls?" The son does not understand that the father's primary goal is the holes, since only the holes can become receptacles, and the son wants to close the holes that the father made in the balls.

So it is here. This dust inside the eyes, which blocks his vision, so that wherever he looks he finds contradictions in Providence, this is the whole *Kli* by which he can discover the sparks of unconditional love, called "a joy of *Mitzva*." It is said about this, "If the Creator does not help him, he cannot overcome it." This means that if the Creator had not given him these thoughts, he would have been unable to receive any ascension.

34. The Advantage of a Land

I heard on *Tevet, Tav-Shin-Bet*, 1942

It is known that nothing is revealed in its true form, only through its opposite, "As the advantage of the light from within the darkness." This means that each thing points to another, and precisely by the opposite of something, the true existence of its opposite can be perceived.

Hence, it is impossible to attain something in complete clarity if its parallel is absent. For example, it is impossible to evaluate and say that something is good, if its opposite, pointing to the bad, is absent. It is the same with bitterness and sweetness, love and hate, hunger and satiation, thirst and saturation, separation and adhesion. It turns out that it is impossible to come to love adhesion prior to acquiring the hate of separation.

To be rewarded with the degree of hating separation, one must first know what is separation, meaning from what he is separated, and then it is possible to say that he wants to correct that separation. In other words, one should examine from what and from whom he has become separated. After this he can try to mend it and connect himself to the one from whom he has become separated. If, for example, he understands that he will benefit from joining with Him, then he can assume and know what is the loss if he remains separated.

Gain and loss are measured according to the pleasure and the suffering. One hates and stays away from something that causes him suffering. The measure of the distance depends on the measure of the suffering, since it is human nature to escape from suffering. Hence, one depends on the other, meaning that to the extent of the suffering, one exerts and does all kinds of actions so as to move away from it. In other words, the torments cause hatred for the thing that induces torments, and to that extent he moves away.

It follows that one should know what is equivalence of form in order to know what he must do to achieve adhesion, called "equivalence of form." By this he will come to know what are disparity of form and separation.

It is known from books and from authors that the Creator is benevolent. This means that His guidance appears to the lower ones as good and doing good, and this is what we must believe.

Therefore, when one examines the conducts of the world, and begins to examine himself or others, how they suffer under Providence instead of delighting, as is fitting for His Name—The Good Who Does Good—in that state, it is hard for him to say that Providence is behaving in a manner of good and doing good and imparts them with abundance.

However, we must know that in that state, when they cannot say that the Creator imparts only good, they are considered wicked because suffering makes them condemn their Maker. Only when they see that the Creator imparts them with pleasures do they justify the Creator. It is as our sages said, "Who is righteous? He who justifies his Maker," meaning he who says that the Creator leads the world in a manner of righteousness.

Thus, when one suffers, he becomes far from the Creator since he naturally becomes hateful of He who imparts him torments. Consequently, where one should have loved the Creator, he now becomes the opposite, for he has come to hate the Creator.

Accordingly, what should one do in order to come to love the Creator? For this purpose we are given the remedy of engaging in Torah and *Mitzvot* [commandments], for the light in it reforms him. There is light there which lets him feel the severity of the state of separation. Bit by bit, as one aims to acquire the light of Torah, hatred for separation is created in him. He begins to feel the reason that causes him and his soul to be separated and far from the Creator.

Thus, one must believe that His guidance is benevolent, but since he is immersed in self-love, it induces disparity of form in him, since there was a correction called "in order to bestow," and it is called "equivalence of form." Only in this manner can we receive this delight and pleasure. The inability to receive the delight and pleasure that the Creator wants to give evokes in the receiver hatred for separation, and then he can discern the great benefit from equivalence of form, and then he begins to yearn for adhesion.

In turns out that every form points to another form. Thus, all the descents where one feels that he has come to separation are an opportunity to discern between something and its opposite. In other words, from the descents, one should learn the benefits of the ascents. Otherwise, he would be unable to appreciate the importance of being brought near from above, and the ascents that he is given. He would not be able to extract the importance that he could extract, as when one is given food without ever having felt hunger.

It turns out that the descents, which are the times of separation, create the importance of adhesion in the ascents, while the ascents make him hate the descents that the separation causes him. In other words, he cannot assess how bad the descents are, when he slanders Providence and does not even feel whom he slanders, to know that he must repent for such a grave sin. This is called "slandering the Creator."

It follows that precisely when one has both forms he can discern the distance between one and the other, "As the advantage of the light from within the darkness." Only then can he assess and appreciate the matter of adhesion by which the delight and pleasure in the thought of creation can be acquired, being "His desire to do good to His creations." Everything that appears to our eyes is but what the Creator wants us to attain the way we do, since they are ways by which to achieve the complete goal.

Yet, it is not so simple to merit adhesion with the Creator. It requires great effort and exertion to acquire the sensation and feeling of delight and pleasure. Before this, one must justify Providence, believe above reason that the Creator behaves with the creatures in a manner of good and doing good, and say, "They have eyes but they see not."

Our sages say, "Habakkuk came and ascribed them to one," as it is written, "The righteous shall live by his faith." It means that one need not engage in details, but concentrate his entire work on a single point, a rule, which is faith in the Creator. This is what he should pray for, meaning for the Creator to help him to be able to go with faith above reason. There is power in the faith: Through it, one comes to hate the separation. This is considered that faith indirectly makes him hate the separation.

We see that there is a great difference between faith, seeing, and knowing. Something that can be seen and known, if the mind asserts that it is worthwhile to do that thing and he decides on it once, that decision is enough regarding that thing that he decided on. In other words, he executes according to how he had decided. This is so because the mind accompanies him in every single act so as not to break what the mind had told him, and lets him understand by one hundred percent, to the extent that the mind brought him to the decision he has reached.

However, faith is a matter of potential agreement. In other words, he overpowers the mind and says that it is indeed worthwhile to work as faith asserts to work—above reason. Hence, faith above reason is useful only during the act, when he believes. Only then is he willing to exert above reason in the work.

Conversely, when he leaves faith for but a moment, meaning when faith weakens for a brief moment, he immediately ceases the Torah and the work. It does not help him that a short while ago he took upon himself the burden of faith above reason.

However, when he perceives in his mind that this is a bad thing for him, that it is something that risks his life, he needs no repetitive explanations and reasoning why it is a dangerous thing. Rather, since he once fully realized in his mind that he should practice these things, of which the mind tells him specifically which is bad and which is good, now he follows that decision.

We see the difference between what the mind asserts and what only faith asserts, and what is the reason that when something is based on faith, we must constantly remember the form of the faith, otherwise he falls from his degree into a state suitable for one who is wicked. These states might happen even in a single day: One may fall from his degree many times in one day since it is impossible that faith above reason will not stop even for a moment during one day.

We must know that the reason for forgetting the faith stems from the fact that faith above the reason and the mind is against all the desires of the body. Since the desires of the body come by the nature imprinted in us, called "will to receive," whether in the mind or in the heart, hence, the body always draws us to our nature. Only when we cling to faith does it have the power to bring us out of the bodily desires and go above reason, meaning against the body's reason.

Hence, before one acquires vessels of bestowal, called *Dvekut* [adhesion], faith cannot be in him on a permanent basis. When faith does not shine for him, he sees that he is in the lowest possible state, and it all comes to him because of the disparity of form, which is the will to receive for himself. This separation causes him all the torments, ruins all the buildings and all the efforts he had put into the work.

He sees that the minute he loses faith, he is in a worse state than when he started on the path of work in bestowal. In this way, one acquires hatred for the separation since he immediately begins to feel torments in himself and in the entire world. It becomes hard for him to justify His Providence over the creatures, that it is in the form of good and doing good. At that time, he feels that the whole world has grown dark on him and he has nothing from which to derive joy.

Hence, every time he begins to correct the flaw of slandering Providence, he receives hatred for the separation. Through the hatred he feels in the separation, he comes to love *Dvekut*. In other words, to the extent that he suffers during the separation, so he draws nearer to *Dvekut* with the Creator. Similarly, to the extent that he feels the darkness as bad, he comes to feel that *Dvekut* is good. Then he knows how to value it when he receives some *Dvekut*, for the time being, and then knows how to appreciate it.

Now we can see that all the torments that exist in the world are but preparation for the real torments. These are the torments that one must reach, or he will not be able to acquire anything spiritual, as there is no light without a *Kli* [vessel]. These torments, the real torments, are called "condemnation of Providence and slandering." This is what one prays for, to not slander Providence, and these are the torments that the Creator accepts. This is the meaning of the Creator hearing the prayer of every mouth.

The reason the Creator responds to these torments is that then one does not ask for help for his own vessels of reception, since we can say that if the Creator grants him everything he wishes, it might make him farther from the Creator due to the disparity of form that he would thus acquire. Rather, it is to the contrary: One asks for faith, for the Creator to give him the strength to prevail so he can be awarded equivalence of form, for he sees that by not having permanent faith, meaning when faith does not shine for him, he comes to doubt Providence, and he comes to a state called "wicked," that he condemns his Maker.

It turns out that all the suffering he feels is because he slanders Providence. It therefore follows that what hurts him is that where he should have been praising the Creator, saying "Blessed is He who has created us in His Glory," meaning that the creatures respect the Creator, he sees that the world's conduct is unfitting for His glory, since everyone complains and demands that first it should be open Providence that the Creator leads the world in a manner of good and doing good. Since it is not revealed, they are saying that this Providence does not glorify Him, and that pains him.

Thus, by the torment one feels, he is compelled to slander. Hence, when he asks of the Creator to impart him the power of faith and to be rewarded with the quality of good and doing good, it is not because he wants to receive good so as to delight himself. Rather, it is so he will not slander; this is what pains him. For himself, he wants to believe above reason that the Creator leads the world in a manner of good and doing good, and he wants his faith to settle in the sensation as though it is within reason.

Therefore, when he practices Torah and *Mitzvot*, he wants to extend the light of the Creator not for his own benefit, but since he cannot bear not being able to justify

His guidance, that it is in a manner of good and doing good. It pains him that he desecrates the name of the Creator, whose name is The Good Who Does Good, and his body claims otherwise.

This is all that pains him since by being in a state of separation, he cannot justify His guidance. This is considered hating the state of separation. And when he feels this suffering, the Creator hears his prayer, brings him near Him, and he is rewarded with *Dvekut*, for the pains that he feels from the separation make him be rewarded with *Dvekut*; and then it is said, "As the advantage of the light from within the darkness."

This is the meaning of "The advantage of a land in everything." Land is creation; "in everything" means that by the advantage, meaning when we see the difference between the state of separation and the state of *Dvekut*, through it we are granted *Dvekut* with everything, since the Creator is called "the root of everything."

35. Concerning the Vitality of Kedusha

I heard in Tav-Shin-Hey, 1944-1945, Jerusalem

The verse says (Psalms 104): "There is the sea, great and broad, in which are swarms without number, small animals with big ones."

We should interpret:

1. "There is the sea" means the sea of the *Sitra Achra* [other side].
2. "Great and broad" means that it manifests itself and shouts "Give! Give!" referring to big vessels of reception.
3. "In which are swarms" means that there are upper lights there, which one steps and tramples with one's feet.
4. "Without number," that there are small with large animals, meaning whether one has small vitality or big vitality, it is all in that sea.

This is so because there is a rule that "From above they give giving, and take, they do not take" (as all that is given from above is not received in return, but stays below). Hence, if one extends something from above and then blemishes it, it remains below, but not with the person. Instead, it falls to the sea of the *Sitra Achra*.

In other words, if one draws some illumination and cannot sustain it permanently because his Kelim [vessels] are not yet clean so as to be fit for the light, meaning that he will receive it in vessels of bestowal like the light that comes from the Giver, the illumination must depart from him.

At that time, this illumination falls into the hands of the *Sitra Achra*. This continues several times, meaning that one extends, and then it departs from him.

Hence, the illuminations multiply in the sea of the *Sitra Achra* until the quota is full. This means that after one reveals the full measure of the effort that one can reveal, the *Sitra Achra* gives him back everything she took into her own authority. This is the meaning of "He has swallowed down riches, and he shall vomit them up again." It follows that all that the *Sitra Achra* received into her own authority was only as a deposit, meaning that as long as she has control over man, and the matter of the control that she has is so that one will be able to scrutinize one's vessels of reception and admit them into *Kedusha* [holiness].

In other words, had she not controlled a person, he would settle for little. Then all of one's vessels of reception would remain separated, and he would never be able to gather all the *Kelim* that belong to the root of his soul, admit them into *Kedusha*, and extend the light that belongs to him.

Hence, it is a correction that each time one extends something and has a descent, he must start anew, meaning new scrutinies. And what one had from the past has fallen into the *Sitra Achra*, who holds it in her authority as a deposit. Afterward, one receives from her everything that she received from him the whole time.

Yet, we must also know that if one could sustain any illumination, even a small one, but if it were permanent, he would already be regarded as whole. That is, one would have been able to advance with this illumination. Hence, if one loses the illumination, he should regret it.

This is similar to a person who placed a seed in the ground so that a big tree would grow out of it, but took the seed out of the ground right away. Thus, what is the benefit in the work of putting the seed in the ground?

Moreover, we can say that he not only took out the seed from the ground and spoiled it; we can say that he dug out a tree with ripe fruits from the ground and spoiled them.

It is the same here: If he had not lost this tiny illumination, a great light would have grown out of it. It follows that it is not necessarily that he lost the power of a small illumination, but it is as though a great light indeed was lost from him.

We must know that it is a rule that one cannot live without vitality and pleasure, since it stems from the root of creation, which is His desire to do good to His creations. Hence, every creature cannot exist without vitality and pleasure. Therefore, every creature must go and look for a place from which to receive delight and pleasure.

But the pleasure is received in three times: in the past, in the present, and in the future. However, the main reception of pleasure is in the present. Although we see that one receives pleasure from the past and from the future, too, it is because the past and the future shine in the present.

Therefore, if one does not find a sensation of pleasure in the present, he receives vitality from the past, and he can tell others how he was happy in past times. One can receive vitality from this in the present, or picture to himself that he hopes that in the future he will be happy. But measuring the sensation of the pleasure from the past and the future depends on the extent to which they shine for him in the present. We must know that this applies both to corporeal pleasures and to spiritual pleasures.

As we see, when a person works, even in corporeality, the order is that during the work he is unhappy because he is exerting himself. And one can continue the work only because the future shines for him, that he will receive a payment for his work. This shines for him in the present, and this is why he can continue the work.

However, if he is unable to picture the reward he will receive in the future, he must take pleasure from the future, not from the reward he will receive for his work in the future. In other words, he will not enjoy the reward, but he will not feel suffering from the exertion. This is what he enjoys now, in the present, what he will have in the future.

The future shines for him in the present, in that soon the work will be over, meaning the time that he must work, and he will receive rest. Thus, the pleasure of rest that one will ultimately receive still shines for him. In other words, his profit will be that he will not be afflicted by what he now feels from the work, and this gives him the strength to be able to work now.

If one is unable to picture to himself that soon he will be rid of the torments that he suffers now, he will come to despair and sadness to the point that that state can bring one to take his own life.

This is why our sages said, "One who takes one's life has no part in the next world," since he denies Providence, that the Creator leads the world in a form of good and doing good. Instead, one should believe that these states come to him because from above they want it to bring him correction, meaning that he will collect *Reshimot* [recollections] from these states so he will be able to understand the conduct of the world more intensely and more strongly.

These states are called *Achoraim* [posterior]. When one overcomes these states, he will be awarded the quality of *Panim* [anterior], meaning that the light will shine into these *Achoraim*.

There is a rule that one cannot live if one has no place from which to receive delight and pleasure. Thus, when one is unable to receive from the present, he must still receive vitality from the past or from the future. In other words, the body seeks for itself vitality in every means at its disposal.

Then, if one does not agree to receive vitality from corporeal things, the body has no choice but to agree to receive vitality from spiritual things because it has no other choice.

Hence, it must agree to receive delight and pleasure from vessels of bestowal, since it is impossible to live without vitality. It follows that when one is accustomed to observe Torah and *Mitzvot* [commandments] *Lo Lishma* [not for Her sake], meaning to receive reward for his work, he can picture to himself that he will receive some reward later on, and he can already work on the calculation that he will receive delight and pleasure later.

However, if one works not in order to receive reward, but wants to work without any reward, how can he picture to himself having anything from which to receive sustenance? After all, he cannot create any picture because he has nothing on which to do it.

Hence, in *Lo Lishma*, there is no necessity to give one vitality from above, since he has vitality from the depiction of the future, and only necessity is given from above, not luxury. Therefore, if one wants to work only for the Creator and has no wish whatsoever to take vitality for other things, there is no other way, but to be given vitality from above, since he demands only the necessary vitality to go on living. Then he receives vitality from the structure of the *Shechina* [Divinity].

It is as our sages said, "Anyone who is sorry for the public is rewarded with seeing the comfort of the public." The public is called "The *Shechina*," since "public" means a collective, meaning the assembly of Israel, for *Malchut* is the collection of all the souls.

Since the person does not want any reward for himself, but wants to work for the sake of the Creator, which is called "raising the *Shechina* from the dust," so she will not be so degraded, meaning that they do not want to work for the sake of the Creator, but all that one sees that will produce benefit for himself, then there is fuel for the work. And what concerns the benefit of the Creator, and one does not see what reward he will receive in return, the body objects to this work because it feels a taste of dust in this work.

And such a person does want to work for the sake of the Creator, but the body resists it. And he asks the Creator to give him strength to nonetheless be able to work to raise the *Shechina* from the dust. Hence, he is awarded the *Panim* [face] of the Creator, Who appears to him, and the concealment departs from him.

36. What Are the Three Bodies in Man?

I heard on *Adar* 24, *Tav-Shin-Dalet*, March 19, 1944, Jerusalem

Man is made of three bodies:

1. the inner body, which is a clothing for the soul of *Kedusha* [holiness];

2. the *Klipa* [shell] of *Noga*;

3. the serpent's skin.

In order to save one from the two bodies, so they do not interfere with the *Kedusha*, and in order for one to be able to use only the inner body, the advice for this is that there is a remedy—to think only about things that concern the inner body.

This means that one's thought should always remain in the singular authority, meaning that "There is none else besides Him." Rather, He does and will do all the deeds, and there is no creation in the world that can detach him from the *Kedusha*.

And because he does not think of those two bodies, they die, since they have no nourishment and nothing to sustain them, since the thoughts we think of them are their provision. This is the meaning of the verse, "In the sweat of your face shall you eat bread." Prior to the sin of the tree of knowledge, vitality was not dependent on the bread. That is, there was no need to extend light and vitality, but it illuminated.

However, after the sin, when *Adam HaRishon* clung to the serpent's body, life became tied to the bread, meaning to nourishment that must always draw anew. And if they are not given nourishment, they die. This became a big correction in order to be saved from those two bodies.

Thus, one must try with all one's might not to think thoughts that concern them, and perhaps this is what our sages said, "thoughts of transgression are harder than a transgression," since thoughts are their nourishment. In other words, they receive vitality from the thoughts one thinks for them.

Hence, one must think only of the inner body, for it is a clothing for the soul of *Kedusha*. That is, one should think thoughts that are after one's skin. This means that after the body's skin is called "outside one's body," meaning outside one's own benefit, but only thoughts of benefiting others. This is called "outside one's skin."

This is so because after one's skin, there is no grip for the *Klipot* [pl. of *Klipa*], for the *Klipot* grip only that which is within one's skin, meaning that which belongs to one's body, and not outside one's body, called "outside one's skin." This means that they possess anything that is clothed in the body, and they cannot hold anything that is not clothed in the body.

When one persists with thoughts that are after one's skin, he will be rewarded with what is written, "And after my skin they broke this, and from my flesh shall I see God" (Job 19, 26). "This" is the *Shechina* [Divinity], and she stands after one's skin. "Broke" means that it has been corrected to be a pillar "after my skin." At that time, one is awarded "and from my flesh shall I see God."

It means that *Kedusha* comes and clothes the interior of the body specifically when one agrees to work outside one's skin, meaning without any clothing. The wicked, however, who want to work precisely when there is clothing in the body, called within the skin, they will die without wisdom. This is because then they have no clothing and they are not awarded anything. However, it is specifically the righteous who are rewarded with clothing in the body.

37. An Article for Purim

I heard in *Tav-Shin-Het*, 1947-1948

We must understand several precisions in the *Megilla**:

1. It is written, "After these things, King Ahasuerus promoted Haman." We must understand what is "After these things," meaning after Mordecai had saved the king. It seems reasonable that the king should have promoted Mordecai. But what does it say? That he promoted Haman.

2. When Ester told the king, "for we are sold, I and my people," the king asked, "Who is he and where is he?" It means that the king knew nothing of it, although it explicitly says that the king told Haman, "The silver is given to you, the people also, to do with them as it seems good to you." Thus, we see that the king did know about the sale.

3. Our sages said about "according to every man's wish": "Raba said, 'to do according to the will of Mordecai and Haman'" (*Megilla* 12). It is known that where it says only "king" it refers to the King of the world. Thus, how can it be that the Creator would act according to the will of a wicked one?

4. It is written, "Mordecai knew all that was done." This implies that only Mordecai knew, since prior to that, it is written, "and the city of Shushan was perplexed." Thus, the whole city of Shushan knew about it.

5. It is written, "for a writing that was written in the king's name and sealed with the king's ring may not be reversed." Thus, how did he give the second letters afterward, which ultimately cancel the first letters?

6. What does it mean that our sages said, "On *Purim*, one must intoxicate until he cannot tell the cursed Haman from the blessed Mordecai"?

7. What does it mean that our sages said about the verse, "And the drinking was according to the law," what is "according to the law?" Rabbi Hanan said in the name of Rabbi Meir, "according to the law of Torah." What is the law of Torah? More eating than drinking.

To understand the above, we must first understand the matter of Haman and Mordecai. Our sages said about the verse, "according to every man's wish," meaning Haman and Mordecai. We should interpret that Mordecai's wish is called "the view of Torah," which is more eating than drinking, and Haman's wish is the opposite, more drinking than eating.

We asked, "How can it be that he would make a meal according to the will of a wicked one"? The answer to this is written next to it: "none did compel." It means that the drinking was not compulsory, and this is the meaning of "none did compel."

---

* *Megillat Ester* (Scroll of Ester), referring to The Book of Esther

It is as our sages said about the verse, "And Moses hid his face for he was afraid to look." They said that in return for "And Moses hid his face," he was rewarded with, "and the image of the Lord does he behold." This means that precisely because he did not need that (meaning he could make a *Masach* [screen] over it), he was permitted to receive. This is the meaning of the verse, "I have laid help upon one who is mighty." It means that the Creator gives help to one who is mighty and can walk in the ways of the Creator.

It is written, "And the drinking was according to the law." What is "according to the law?" Because "none did compel." It means that he did not need the drinking, but once they began to drink, they were taken after it, meaning they were tied to the drinking, they needed the drinking, or else they would not be able to go forward.

This is called "compel," and this is considered that they canceled the method of Mordecai. This is also the meaning of what our sages said, that that generation was sentenced to perish because they enjoyed the meal of a wicked one.

In other words, had they received the drinking in the form of "none did compel," they would not have canceled Mordecai's wish, and this is the method of Israel. However, afterward, when they took the drinking in a form of "did compel," it follows that they themselves sentenced the law of Torah to perish, which is the quality of Israel.

This is the meaning of more eating than drinking. Drinking refers to disclosing *Hochma* [wisdom], called "knowing." Eating, on the other hand, is called *Ohr de Hassadim* [light of mercy], which is faith.

This is the meaning of Bigtan and Teresh, who sought to lay hands on the king of the world. "And the thing became known to Mordecai... ... inquisition was made of the matter, and it was found to be so." The matter of seeking was not at once, and Mordecai did not obtain it easily, but after much work was the matter of this flaw revealed to him. Once it had become evident to him, "they were both hanged." That is, after the sensation of the blemish in it, they were hanged, meaning they removed these actions and desires from the world.

"After these things," meaning after all the labor and the exertions Mordecai had made by the scrutiny that he had made, the king wanted to reward him for his effort of working only *Lishma* [for Her sake] and not for himself. Since there is a rule that the lower one cannot receive anything without a need, as there is no light without a *Kli* [vessel], and a *Kli* is called a "need," since he does not need anything for himself, how can he be given anything?

Had the king asked Mordecai what he should give him for his labor, since Mordecai is righteous, whose work is only to bestow without any need to ascend in degrees, and he is content with little, while the king wished to give the light of wisdom, which extends from the left line, and Mordecai's work was only from the right line.

What did the king do? He promoted Haman, meaning he made the left line important. This is the meaning of "and set his seat above all the ministers." In addition, he gave him the control, meaning that all the king's slaves kneeled and bowed before Haman, "for the king had so commanded," that he would receive control, and everyone accepted him.

The matter of kneeling is the acceptance of the ruling since they liked Haman's way in the work more than Mordecai's way. All the Jews in Shushan accepted Haman's control until it was hard for them to understand Mordecai's view. After all, everyone understands that the work of walking in the left line, called knowing, is easier than walking in the ways of the Creator.

It is written that they asked, "Why are you transgressing against the king's commandment?" Since they saw that Mordecai persisted with his opinion of walking in the way of faith, they became perplexed and did not know who was right.

They went and asked Haman who was right, as it is written, "They told Haman to see whether Mordecai's words would stand, for he had told them that he was a Jew." It means that the way of the Jew is more eating than drinking, meaning faith is the rudiment, and this is the whole basis of Judaism.

This caused Haman a great disturbance; why would Mordecai not agree with his view? Hence, when everyone saw Mordecai's way, who argued that he alone was taking the path of Judaism, and those who take another path are regarded as doing idol worship, as it is written, "Yet all this is worthless to me each time I see Mordecai the Jew sitting at the king's gate," since Mordecai claims that only through him is the gate to the king, and not that of Haman.

Now we can understand why it is written, "Mordecai knew," meaning that it is specifically Mordecai who knew. But it is written, "but the city of Shushan was perplexed," meaning that everyone knew.

We should interpret that the city of Shushan was perplexed and did not know who was right, but Mordecai knew that if there would be Haman's control, that would mean the annihilation of the people of Israel, meaning that he would obliterate the whole of Israel from the world, meaning the people of Israel's way of Judaism, whose basis of the work is faith above reason, called "covered Mercy," to go with the Creator with eyes shut, and to always say about oneself, "They have eyes but they see not," since Haman's whole grip is on the left line, called knowing, the opposite of faith.

This is the meaning of the lots that Haman cast, as it was on *Yom Kippurim* [Day of Atonement], as it is written, "one lot for the Lord, and one lot for Azazel." The lot for the Lord means a discernment of "right," which is *Hassadim* [mercy], called "eating," which is faith. The lot for Azazel is the left line, which is in fact considered "good for nothing," and all the *Sitra Achra* [other side] stems from here.

Hence, a blockage on the lights extends from the left line, as only the left line freezes the lights. This is the meaning of "cast pur, that is, the lot," meaning he interprets what he cast. He says "*pur*," which means *Pi Ohr* (pronounced *Pi Ohr* [a mouth of light]).

All the lights were blocked through the lot for *Azazel*, and you find that he cast all the lights down. Haman thought that "the righteous shall prepare and the wicked shall wear."

In other words, Haman thought that concerning all the efforts and the exertions that Mordecai had made, along with all who accompanied him, the reward that they deserve, Haman thought that he would take that reward. That is, Haman thought that he would take the lights that appear through the corrections of Mordecai into his own authority. All this was because he saw that the king had given him the power to extend light of wisdom below.

Hence, when he came to the king saying "to destroy the Jews," meaning revoke Israel's dominion, which is faith and mercy, and make knowledge disclosed in the world, the king had replied to him, "The silver is given to you, the people also, to do with them as it seems good to you," meaning as Haman sees fit, according to his dominion, which is left and knowing.

The whole difference between the first and second letters is in the word Jews. In "The written synopsis" (the copy refers to the content that came out from the king. Afterward, the written synopsis is interpreted, explaining the intention of the synopsis) it was said, "to be given out for a decree in every state, revealed to all peoples, that they should be ready for this day." It does not say for whom they should be ready, but Haman interpreted the synopsis, as it is written, "and he wrote all that Haman commanded."

The word Jews is written in the second letters, as it is written, "The written synopsis, to be given out for a decree in every state, revealed to all the peoples, and that the Jews should be ready for this day to avenge themselves on their enemies."

Hence, when Haman came to the king, the king told him, "The silver that had been pre-prepared is given to you," meaning you need not do anything more since "the people also [are given to you], to do with them as it seems good to you."

In other words, the people already want to do as seems good to you, meaning the people want to receive your control. Yet, the king did not tell him to revoke the control of Mordecai and the Jews. Instead, it had been preordained that now, at this time, there would be a disclosure of *Hochma*, which is as "being favored by you."

The written synopsis was "to be given out for a decree in every state, revealed to all peoples." It means that the decree was that it will be published that the matter of the disclosure of *Hochma* (is) for all the nations.

However, it did not say that the quality of Mordecai and the Jews would be revoked, which is faith. Instead, the intention was that there would be disclosure of *Hochma* [wisdom], but they would still choose *Hassadim* [mercy].

Haman said that since now is the time of disclosure of *Hochma*, the disclosure of *Hochma* is certainly given so as to use the *Hochma*, as who does something that is not to be used? If it is not used, it follows that the operation was in vain. Hence, it must be the will of the Creator, and the Creator had made that disclosure so as to use the *Hochma*.

Mordecai's argument was that the disclosure is only to show that what they take for themselves, to walk in the right line, which is covered *Hassadim*, is not because there is no choice, and this is why they take this path. This seems like coercion, meaning that they have no other choice since presently there is no revealed *Hochma*. Instead, now that there is revealed *Hochma*, there is room for choosing of their own free will. In other words, they choose a path of *Hassadim* more than the left, which is the disclosure of *Hochma*.

This means that the disclosure was only so they could reveal the importance of *Hassadim*, that it was more important to them than *Hochma*. It is as our sages said, "thus far coercively, henceforth willingly." And this is the meaning of "the Jews observed and took upon them." It follows that the disclosure of *Hochma* came now only so they would be able to receive the way of the Jew willingly.

And this was the dispute between Mordecai and Haman. Mordecai's argument was that what we now see, that the Creator reveals the authority of *Hochma* is not so they would receive the *Hochma*, but in order to improve the *Hassadim*, meaning that now they will be able to show that their reception of the *Hassadim* is voluntary. That is, they have room to receive *Hochma*, since now is the time of the control of the left, which shines *Hochma*, yet they choose *Hassadim*. It follows that now they show—by receiving the *Hassadim*—that the right rules over the left.

Thus, the Jewish law is the important one, and Haman claimed the opposite, that the Creator's current disclosure of the left line, which is *Hochma*, is in order to use the *Hochma*. Otherwise, it would mean that the Creator did something needlessly, meaning that He did something and there is no one to enjoy it. Hence, we should not regard what Mordecai says, but everyone should listen to him and use the disclosure of *Hochma* that now appeared.

It follows that the second letters did not revoke the first. Rather, they presented an explanation and interpretation to the first written synopsis, that the matter of the publication to all the peoples, the matter of the disclosure of *Hochma* that now shines, is for the Jews. In other words, it is so that the Jews would be able to choose *Hassadim* of their own will, and not because there is no other path to choose.

This is why it is written in the second letters, "and that the Jews should be ready for this day to avenge themselves on their enemies." It means that the control that *Hochma* now has is in order to show that they prefer *Hassadim* to *Hochma*. This is called "to avenge themselves on their enemies." This is because their enemies want specifically *Hochma*, whereas the Jews reject the *Hochma*.

Now we can understand what we asked about the question of the king, "Who is he, and where is he, who dared to do so?" And why did He ask? After all, the king himself had told Haman, "The silver is given to you, the people also, to do with them as it seems good to you."

(It is as we have said that the meaning is that the matter of disclosing *Hochma* is with the intention that the people will do as seems good to you, meaning that there would be room for choice. This is called "the people also, to do with them as it seems good to you." However, if there is no disclosure of *Hochma*, there is no room for choice, but the *Hassadim* that they take, it seems that it is because they have no choice.)

It means that all this came about because the king gave the order that now would be the time of disclosing *Hochma*. The intention was that the left would serve the right. By that it would become apparent that the right is more important than the left, and this is why they choose *Hassadim*.

This is the meaning of *Megillat Ester* [the scroll of Ester]. There seems to be a contradiction in terms here, since *Megillah* [scroll] means that it is *Galui* [revealed] to all, while *Ester* means that there is *Hastara* [concealment]. However, we should interpret that the whole disclosure is in order to give room to choose concealment.

Now we can understand what our sages said, "On *Purim*, one must intoxicate until one cannot tell between the cursed Haman and the blessed Mordecai." The matter of Mordecai and Ester was prior to building of the Second Temple, and the building of the Temple signifies the extension of *Hochma*, and *Malchut* is called "The Temple." This is the meaning of Mordecai sending Ester to go to the king and ask for her people, and she replied, "all the king's servants," etc., "who is not called, there is one law for him, that he be put to death," etc., "and I have not been called to come in unto the king these thirty days."

It means that it is forbidden to extend the quality of GAR *de Hochma* below, and one who does extend GAR (which are three *Sefirot*, each comprising ten, which are thirty) is sentenced to death, because the left line causes separation from the life of lives.

"Except he to whom the king shall hold out the golden scepter, that he may live." Gold means *Hochma* and GAR, meaning that only by the awakening of the upper one can one remain alive, meaning in *Dvekut* [adhesion], called life, but not by the awakening of the lower one.

Although Ester is *Malchut*, who needs *Hochma*, it is only by the awakening of the upper one. However, if she extends *Hochma* she loses her own quality entirely. In that regard, Mordecai replied to her, "(if) then relief and deliverance will arise to the Jews from another place," meaning by completely revoking the left line, and the Jews will have only the right line, which is *Hassadim*, then "you and your father's house will perish."

In the state of "Father founded the daughter," she must have *Hochma* within her. But it must be more eating than drinking. However, if the Jews have no counsel, they will have to revoke the left line, and thus her whole quality would be canceled. It is about that that she said, "if I perish, I perish."

In other words, if I go, I am lost, because I might come to separation, as when the lower one awakens, it induces separation from the Life of Lives. And if I do not go "then relief and deliverance will arise to the Jews from another place," meaning in another way. They would completely revoke the left line, as Mordecai had told her. This is why she took the path of Mordecai by inviting Haman to a feast, meaning that she extended the left line as Mordecai had told her.

Afterward, she included the left in the right and thus there could be disclosure of lights below, and also to remain in a state of *Dvekut*. This is the meaning of *Megillat Esther*, meaning although there is disclosure of the light of *Hochma*, she still takes the concealment that is there (because Ester is *Hester* ["concealment," same as *Hastara*]).

In the matter of him not knowing, it is explained in *The Study of the Ten Sefirot* (Part 15, *Ohr Pnimi*, Item 217) that although lights of *Hochma* illuminated, it is impossible to receive without the light of *Hassadim*, as this induces separation. However, a miracle was made where by fasting and crying they extended the light of *Hassadim*, and then they could receive the light of *Hochma*.

However, there is no such thing before the end of correction. But since this discernment is from the discernment of the end of correction, at which time it will already be corrected, as it is written in *The Zohar*: "SAM is destined to be a holy angel." It follows, that then there will be no difference between Haman and Mordecai, for Haman, too, will be corrected. This is the meaning of "on *Purim*, one must intoxicate until one cannot tell the cursed Haman from the blessed Mordecai."

It should also be added with regard to the words that they were hanged, that it is an indication to the hanging on the tree, meaning they understood that it is the same sin as the sin of the tree of knowledge, as there, too, the blemish was in the GAR.

Regarding "sat in the king's gate," it can be added that this implies that he was sitting and not standing, since sitting is called VAK, and standing is called GAR.

38. The Fear of God Is His Treasure

I heard on *Nissan* 10, *Tav-Shin-Zayin*, March 31, 1947

A treasure is a *Kli* [vessel] in which the possession is placed. Grain, for example, is placed in the granary, and precious things are placed in a more guarded place. Thus, everything that is received is called by its correlation to the light, and the *Kli* must be able to receive the things. It is as we learn that there is no light without a *Kli*, and this applies even in corporeality.

Yet, what is the *Kli* in spirituality, in which we can receive the spiritual abundance that the Creator wants to give, which will match the light? That is, as in corporeality, where the *Kli* needs a correlation with the object that is placed in it.

For example, we cannot say that we have treasures of wine, which we poured in new sacks to keep the wine from turning sour, or that we took a lot of flour in barrels. Instead, there is a conduct that the container of wine is barrels and jars, and the container for the flour is sacks and not barrels, etc.

Thus, there is a question, What is the spiritual vessel, the *Kelim* [vessels] from which we can make a big treasure of the upper abundance?

There is a rule that the cow wants to feed more than the calf wants to eat. This is because His wish is to do good to His creations, and the reason for the *Tzimtzum* [restriction], we must believe, is for our own good. And the reason must be that we do not have the right *Kelim* where the abundance can be, like the corporeal *Kelim*, which must be right for what is placed there. Hence, we must say that if we add the *Kelim*, there will be something to hold the added abundance.

The answer to this is that, in His treasury, the Creator has only the treasure of fear of heaven (*Berachot* 33).

Yet, we should interpret what is fear: It is the *Kli*, and the treasure is made of this *Kli*, and all the important things are placed in it. He said that fear is as it is written about Moses: Our sages said (*Berachot*, p 7), "In return for 'And Moses hid his face for he was afraid to look,' was to be rewarded with 'the image of the Lord does he behold.'"

Fear refers to one's fear of the great pleasure that is there, that he will not be able to receive it in order to bestow. The reward for this, for having had fear, is that thus he had made for himself a *Kli* in which to receive the upper abundance. This is man's work, and besides that, we attribute everything to the Creator.

Yet, it is not so with fear, because the meaning of fear is not to receive. And what the Creator gives, He gives only to receive, and this is the meaning of "Everything is in the hands of heaven except the fear of heaven."

This is the *Kli* that we need. Otherwise, we will be considered fools, as our sages said, "Who is a fool? He who loses what he is given." This means that the *Sitra Achra* [other side] will take the abundance from us if we cannot aim in order to bestow, because then it goes to the vessels of reception, which is the *Sitra Achra* and *Tuma'a* [impurity].

This is the meaning of "And you shall observe the commandments." Observing means fear. Although the nature of the light is that it keeps itself, meaning that the light leaves before one wants to receive the light into the vessels of reception, yet one must do it by himself, as much as he can, as our sages said, "You will keep yourselves a little from below, and I will keep you a lot from above."

The reason we attribute fear to people, as our sages said, "Everything is in the hands of heaven but the fear of heaven," is because He can give everything but fear. This is because what the Creator gives is more love, not fear.

Acquiring fear is through the *Segula* [power/remedy] of Torah and *Mitzvot*. It means that when one engages in Torah and *Mitzvot* with the intention to be rewarded with bringing contentment to one's Maker, that aim that rests on the acts of *Mitzvot* and the study of Torah brings one to attain it. Otherwise, one might remain—although he observes Torah and *Mitzvot* in every item and detail—he will still remain merely in the degree of still of *Kedusha* [holiness].

It follows that one should always remember the reason that obligates him to engage in Torah and *Mitzvot*. This is the meaning of what our sages meant by "that your *Kedusha* will be for My Name." It means that I will be your cause, meaning that all your work is in wanting to delight Me, meaning that all your actions will be in order to bestow.

Our sages said (*Berachot* 20), "Everything there is in keeping, there is in remembering." This means that all those who engage in observing Torah and *Mitzvot* with the aim to achieve "remembering," by way of "When I remember Him, He does not let me sleep." It follows, that the keeping is primarily in order to be awarded remembering.

Thus, one's desire to remember the Creator is the cause for observing Torah and *Mitzvot*. This is so because it follows that the reason and the cause to observe the Torah and *Mitzvot* is the Creator, as without it one cannot adhere to the Creator, since "He and I cannot dwell in the same abode" due to the disparity of form.

The reason that the reward and punishment are not revealed, and we must only believe in reward and punishment, is because the Creator wants everyone to work for Him, and not for themselves. This is discerned as disparity of form from the Creator. If the reward and punishment were revealed, one would work because of self-love, so the Creator would love him, or because of self-hate, for fear that the Creator would hate him. It follows that the reason for the work is only the person, not the Creator, and the Creator wants that He will be the compelling reason.

It turns out that fear is precisely when one recognizes one's lowliness and says that his serving the King, meaning that one's wish to bestow upon Him is considered a great privilege, and it is more valuable to him than he can say. It is according to the rule that with an important person, what is given to him is considered receiving from him.

To the extent that one feels one's lowliness, to that extent he can begin to appreciate the greatness of the Creator, and the desire to serve Him will awaken in him. However, if one is proud, the Creator says, "He and I cannot dwell in the same abode."

This is the meaning of "A fool, a wicked one, and a rude one go together." The reason is that since one has no fear, meaning he cannot lower himself before the

Creator and say that it is a great honor for him to be able to serve Him without any reward, he cannot receive any wisdom from the Creator, and he remains a fool, and he who is a fool is wicked, as our sages said, "One does not sin unless the spirit of folly entered him."

39. And They Sewed Fig Leaves
I heard on *Shavat*, 26, *Tav-Shin-Zayin*, February 16, 1947

The leaf refers to the shade that it puts on the light, meaning on the sun. There are two shades: One comes from the side of *Kedusha* [holiness], and the other comes due to a sin.

Thus, there are two kinds of concealment of the light. As the shade conceals the sun in corporeality, so there is concealment on the upper light, called "sun," which comes from the side of *Kedusha*, namely because of a choice. This is as it is written about Moses, "And Moses hid his face, for he was afraid to look."

The shade comes because of fear, and fear means that one is afraid to receive the abundance, that he may not be able to aim to bestow. It follows that the shade comes because of *Kedusha*, meaning that one wants to adhere to the Creator.

In other words, *Dvekut* [adhesion] is called bestowal, and he is afraid that he might not be able to bestow.

It turns out that he is adhered to *Kedusha*, and this is called "A shade that comes from the side of *Kedusha*."

There is also a shade that comes due to a sin. It means that the concealment comes to him not because he does not want to receive, but on the contrary, it is because one wants to receive in order to receive. This is why the light leaves, since the whole difference between *Kedusha* and *Klipa* [shell] is that the *Kedusha* wants to bestow and the *Klipa* wants only to receive, and not to bestow at all. For this reason, that shade is considered to come from the side of the *Klipa*.

There is no counsel to exit that state, except as it is written, "and they sewed fig leaves and made themselves girdles." Girdles refer to forces of the body that joined in the form of a shade of *Kedusha*. It means that although now they do not have light since the abundance departed due to the sin, they still overcame in serving the Creator by mere force, above reason. This is called "by force." This is the meaning of the verse, "And they heard the voice of the Lord, etc., and the man and his wife hid," meaning they went into the shade. This is the meaning of "and Moses hid his face," meaning *Adam HaRishon* did the same as Moses.

"And He said to him, 'Where are you?' And he said, 'I heard Your voice in the garden, and I was afraid because I was naked; and I hid.'" Naked means stripped from the upper light.

Then the Creator asked, What is the reason that you came to the shade, called "and I hid"? It is because I am naked. Is it because of a shade of *Kedusha* or because of a sin? The Creator asked him, "Have you eaten from the tree from which I commanded you not to eat?" meaning because of a sin.

But when the shade comes because of a sin, it is called "images, image makers, and sorcerers," which is "God has made them one opposite the other." As there are forces in *Kedusha* to make changes and to show signs and omens, so there are forces in the *Sitra Achra*. This is why the righteous do not use these forces, because of "one opposite the other," so as not to give strength to the *Sitra Achra* to do as they do.

Only on exceptional occasions does the Creator not give the *Sitra Achra* the same force that is in *Kedusha*. It is like Elijah on Mt. Carmel saying, "Answer me," so they would not say that it is witchcraft, meaning that there is the strength to conceal the upper light.

Hence, girdles that come from the side of the fig leaves, which is from the sin of the tree of knowledge, these leaves, meaning this shade that comes due to the sin, since the cause is not from the side of *Kedusha*, when they choose to take shade by themselves, but they take the shade because they have no other choice, this can work only to exit the state of descent. But afterward, the work must begin anew.

40. What Is the Measure of Faith in the Rav?
I heard in *Tav-Shin-Gimel*, 1942-1943

It is known that there is a right path and a left path. Right comes from the words "to the right," referring to the verse, "And he believed in the Lord." The Targum says, "To the right, when the rav says to the disciple to take the right path."

Right is normally called "wholeness," and left, "incompleteness," that corrections are missing there. In that state the disciple must believe the words of his rav, who tells him to walk in the right line, called "wholeness."

And what is the "wholeness" by which the disciple should walk? It is that one should depict to oneself as if he has already been rewarded with whole faith in the Creator, and already feels in his organs that the Creator leads the whole world in the form of "The Good Who Does Good," meaning that the whole world receives only good from Him.

Yet, when one looks at oneself, he sees that he is poor and indigent. In addition, when he observes the world, he sees that the entire world is tormented, each according to his degree.

One should say about that, "They have eyes but they see not." "They" means that as long as one is in multiple authorities, called "they," they do not see the truth. What are the multiple authorities? As long as one has two desires, even though he believes that the entire world belongs to the Creator, but something belongs to man, too.

But in truth, one must annul one's authority before the authority of the Creator and say that one does not want to live for oneself, and the only reason that he wants to exist is in order to bring contentment to the Creator. Thus, by this one annuls his own authority completely, and then he is in the singular authority, the authority of the Creator. Only then can he see the truth, how the Creator leads the world by the quality of good and doing good.

As long as he is in multiple authorities, meaning when he still has two desires in both mind and heart, he is unable to see the truth. Instead, he must go above reason and say, "they have eyes," but they do not see the truth.

It follows that when one regards oneself and wants to know if he is now in a time of descent or a time of ascent, he cannot know that, too. That is, he thinks that he is in a state of descent, and that, too, is incorrect, since he might be in a state of ascent now, meaning seeing his true state, how far he is from the holy work. Thus, he has now come closer to the truth.

And it might be to the contrary, that now he feels that one is in a state of elation, when in fact he is now controlled by receiving for himself, called "a descent."

Only one who is already in the singular authority can discern and know the truth. Hence, one must trust the opinion of his rav and believe what his rav tells him. It means that one should go as his rav told him to do.

And although he sees many arguments and many teachings that do not go hand in hand with the opinion of his rav, he should nevertheless trust the opinion of his rav and say that what he understands and what he sees in other books that do not coincide with his rav's opinion, he should say that as long as he is in multiple authorities, he cannot understand the truth, and he cannot see what is written in other books, the truth that they say.

It is known that when one is still not rewarded, his Torah becomes to him a potion of death. And why does it say, "Not rewarded, his Torah becomes to him a potion of death"? This is because all the teachings that one learns or hears will not bring him any benefit to make one able to be imparted with life, which is *Dvekut* [adhesion] with the Life of Lives. On the contrary, one is constantly drawn farther from the Life of Lives, since all that he does is only for the needs of the body, called "receiving for oneself," and this is considered separation.

This means that through his actions he becomes more separated from the Life of Lives, and this is called "the potion of death," since it brings him death and not life. It means that one becomes ever farther from bestowal, called "equivalence of form with the Creator," by way of "As He is merciful, so are you merciful."

We must also know that when one is engaged in the right, the time is right to extend upper abundance, because "the blessed adheres to the Blessed." In other words, since one is in a state of wholeness, called "blessed," in that respect one presently has equivalence of form, since the sign of wholeness is if one is in gladness. Otherwise, there is no wholeness.

It is as our sages said, "The *Shechina* [Divinity] is present only out of gladness of a *Mitzva* [commandment]." The meaning is that the reason that brings him joy is the *Mitzva*, meaning the fact that the rav had commanded him to take the right line.

It follows that he keeps the commandment of the rav, that he was allotted a special time to walk on the right and a special time to walk on the left. Left contradicts the right, since left means when one calculates for oneself and begins to examine what he has already acquired in the work of the Creator, and he sees that he is bare and destitute. Thus, how can he be in wholeness?

Still, one goes above reason because of the commandment of the rav. It follows that all his wholeness was built on above reason, and this is called "faith." This is the meaning of "In every place where I mention My Name, I will come to you and bless you." "In every place" means although he is still not worthy of a blessing, nonetheless, I gave My blessing because you make a place, meaning a place of gladness, in which the upper light can be.

41. What Is Greatness and Smallness in Faith?
I heard on the evening following Passover night, *Tav-Shin-Hey*, March 29, 1945

It is written, "And they believed in the Lord, and in His servant Moses." We must know that the lights of *Pesach* [Passover] have the power to impart the light of faith. Yet, do not think that the light of faith is something small, since greatness and smallness depend only on the receivers.

When one does not work on the path of truth, he thinks that he has too much faith, and with the amount of faith he has, he can dispense to several people, and then they will be fearing and whole.

However, one who wants to serve the Creator in truth, and constantly examines himself, if he is willing to work devotedly "and with all your heart," he sees that he is always deficient in faith, meaning that he is always short of it.

Only when one has faith can one feel that he is always seated before the King. When one feels the greatness of the King, one can discover the love in two ways: in a good way, and in a way of harsh judgments. Hence, the one who seeks the truth is the one who needs the light of faith. If such a person hears or sees some way to obtain the light of faith, he is happy as though he has found a great fortune.

Hence, those people who seek the truth, on the holiday of *Pesach*, which is capable of the light of faith, we read in the *Parasha* [Torah portion], "and they believed in the Lord, and in His servant Moses," because then is a time that can impart that.

42. What Is the Acronym Elul (I am for My Beloved, and My Beloved Is for Me) in the Work?

I heard on *Elul* 15, *Tav-Shin-Bet*, August 28, 1942

In order to understand this, we must understand several other things.

1. The matter of the *Malchuiot* [pl. of *Malchut*], memories, and *Shofarot* [pl. of *Shofar*, a ram's horn], and what is the meaning of what our sages said, "Annul your will before His will, so that He will annul His will before your will."

2. The words of our sages, "Evil—at once to death, and righteous—at once to life."

3. The verse, "The sons of Gershon, Libni and Shimei."

4. The words of *The Zohar*: "*Yod* is a black dot that has no white in it."

5. *Malchut* of the upper becomes a *Keter* to the lower.

6. What is, joy testifies if the work is in wholeness.

All these things apply in the preparation of the month of *Elul*.

To understand all the above, we must understand the purpose of creation, which is said to be because He wishes to do good to His creations. And because of the *Tikkun* [correction], so there will not be a matter of the "bread of shame," a *Tzimtzum* [restriction] was made. And from the *Tzimtzum* extended the *Masach* [screen] by which the vessels of reception are turned into bestowal.

When the vessels are prepared to be in order to bestow, we immediately receive the light that is hidden and treasured for His creatures. It means that one receives the delight and pleasure that was in the thought of creation, to do good to His creations.

With that we can interpret what is written, "Annul your will before His will," meaning annul the will to receive in you before the desire to bestow, which is the will of the Creator. This means that one will revoke self-love before the love of the Creator. This is called "annulling oneself before the Creator," and it is called *Dvekut* [adhesion]. Subsequently, the Creator can shine inside your will to receive because it is now corrected in the form of receiving in order to bestow.

This is the meaning of "so that He will annul His will before your will." It means that the Creator annuls His will, meaning the *Tzimtzum* that was because of the disparity of form. Now, however, when there is already equivalence of form, hence now there is expansion of the light into the desire of the lower one, which has been corrected in order to bestow, for this is the purpose of creation, to do good to His creations, and now it can be carried out.

Now we can interpret the verse, "I am for my beloved." It means that by the "I" annulling my will to receive before the Creator in the form of entirely to bestow, he is rewarded with "and my beloved is for me." It means that My beloved, who is the Creator, "is mine," He imparts to me the delight and pleasure found in the thought of creation. Thus, what was hidden and restricted before has now become disclosure of the face, since now the purpose of creation has been revealed—to do good to His creations.

We must know that the vessels of bestowal are called YH [Yod-Hey] of the name HaVaYaH [Yod-Hey-Vav-Hey], which are pure Kelim [vessels]. This is the meaning of "All who receive, receive in the purer Kli [vessel]." In that state, one is awarded, "and my beloved is for me," and He imparts abundance upon him, meaning he is rewarded with the revelation of the Face.

Yet, there is a condition to this: It is impossible to be rewarded with disclosure before one receives the phase of Achoraim [posterior], which is the state of concealment of the Face, and says that it is as important to him as the disclosure of the Face. It means that one should be as glad as though he has already acquired the disclosure of the Face.

However, one cannot persist and appreciate the concealment like the disclosure, except when one works in bestowal. At that time, one can say, "I do not care what I feel during the work because what is important to me is that I want to bestow upon the Creator. If the Creator understands that He will have more contentment if I work in a form of *Achoraim*, I agree."

However, if one still has sparks of reception, he comes to thoughts, and it is then hard for him to believe that the Creator leads the world in a manner of "good and doing good." This is the meaning of the letter *Yod* in the name *HaVaYaH*, which is the first letter, called "a black dot that has no white in it," meaning it is all darkness and concealment of the Face.

It means that when one comes to a state where one has no support, one's state becomes black, which is the lowest quality in the upper world, and that becomes the *Keter* to the lower one, as the *Kli* of *Keter* is a vessel of bestowal.

The lowest quality in the upper one is *Malchut*, which has nothing of its own, meaning that she does not have anything. Only in this manner is it called *Malchut*. It means that if one takes upon himself the kingdom of heaven—which is in a state of not having anything—gladly, afterward, it becomes *Keter*, which is a vessel of bestowal and the purest *Kli*. In other words, the reception of *Malchut* in a state of darkness subsequently becomes a *Kli* of *Keter*, which is a vessel of bestowal.

It is like the verse, "For the ways of the Lord are right; the righteous will walk in it, and transgressors will stumble in it." This means that transgressors, those who are controlled by the vessels of reception, must fall and crouch under their load when they come to that state.

The righteous, however, those who are in the state of bestowal, are elevated by this, meaning by this they are imparted vessels of bestowal. ("Wicked" should be interpreted as those whose heart is still not set on obtaining vessels of bestowal, and "righteous" means those whose heart is already set on obtaining vessels of bestowal but are as yet unable.)

It is as *The Zohar* writes, that the *Shechina* [Divinity] said to Rabbi Shimon Bar-Yochai, "There is no place to hide from you," and this is why she appears to him. This is the meaning of what Rabbi Shimon Bar-Yochai said, "Because of this, and His desire is upon me." This is, "I am for my beloved and my beloved is for me," and then he bestows upon the *VH* [*Vav-Hey*].

This is the meaning of "The Name is incomplete, and the throne is incomplete until the *Hey* bonds with the *Vav*." The *Hey* is called "the will to receive," which is the last and final *Kli* in which the *Vav* will bestow into the *Hey*, and then it will be the end of correction.

This is the meaning of "Righteous—at once to life." It means that the person himself should say in which book he wants his name to be written—whether in the book of the righteous, meaning that he wants to be given the desire to bestow, or not. Since one has many discernments regarding the desire to bestow, meaning that sometimes one says, "Yes, I want to be given the desire to bestow, but not to completely revoke the will to receive." He rather wants both worlds for himself, meaning he wants the desire to bestow for his own delight, as well.

However, only those who wish to turn their vessels of reception to work only in bestowal and not receive anything for themselves are written in the book of the righteous. It is so that there will not be room for one to say, "Had I known that the will to receive must be revoked, I would not have prayed for it" (so that he will not say afterward, "This is not what I had sworn to").

Hence, one must unreservedly say what he means by being registered in the book of the righteous, so he will not complain later.

We must know that in the work, the book of the righteous and the book of the wicked are in the same person. It means that one must make a choice and clearly know what he wants because wicked and righteous relate to the same person. Hence, one must say if he wants to be written in the book of the righteous, to be immediately for life, meaning adhere to the Life of Lives, that he wants to do everything for the Creator. In addition, when he comes to be written in the book of the wicked, where all those who wish to be receivers for themselves are written, he says that they should be written there to death at once, meaning that the will to receive for himself will be revoked in him, as if it had died.

Yet, sometimes one is doubtful. In other words, one does not want his will to receive to be revoked in him at once. It is hard for him to decide at once that all his sparks of reception will be put to death at once, meaning he does not agree that all his desires for reception will be annulled in him at once.

Instead, he wants the sparks of reception to be annulled in him gradually and slowly, not all at once, meaning that the vessels of reception will operate some, and some the vessels of bestowal. It follows that this person has no firm and clear view.

A firm view is that on one hand, he claims "It is all mine," meaning all for the purpose of the will to receive. On the other hand, he claims that it is all for the Creator. This is called a "firm view." Yet, what can one do if the body disagrees with his view of wanting to be entirely for the Creator?

In that state, you can say that this person does everything he can to be entirely for the Creator, meaning he prays to the Creator to help him be able to execute all his desires only for the sake of the Creator. It is for that that we pray, "Remember us for life and write us in the book of life."

This is the meaning of the word "*Malchut*," meaning that one will take upon himself the quality of the black dot that has no white in it. This is the meaning of "Annul your will" so that the memory of you will come up before Me, and then He will annul His will before your will. With what? With a *Shofar* [ram's horn], meaning with the *Shofar* of the mother, meaning the matter depends on repentance.

In other words, if one accepts the blackness, one should also try that it will be in an honorable manner, and not in a disgraceful manner. This is called "the *Shofar* of the Mother," meaning that one will regard it as beauty and honor.

Accordingly, we should interpret what is written, "The sons of Gershon, Libni and Shimei." If one sees that he has been expelled from the work, one should know that this is due to Libni,* meaning because he wants specifically whiteness. In other words, if he is given the whiteness, meaning that everything one does will shine, which means that he will feel a good taste in the Torah and in prayer, he will be willing to listen and engage in Torah and *Mitzvot* [commandments].

This is the meaning of "Shimei."** It means that it is precisely through a form of "whiteness" that one can hear. However, during the work one sees a shape of black and cannot agree to hear of taking upon himself this work. Hence, he must be expelled from the King's hall, for reception of the kingdom of heaven must be unconditional surrender.

However, when one says that he is willing to take upon himself the work on condition that there will be a shape of white, meaning that the day will shine for him, and he does not agree if the work appears to him in a black form, this person has no place in the King's hall. This is because those who wish to work in order to bestow are admitted into the King's hall, and when one works in order to bestow, he does not mind what he feels during the work.

Rather, even in a state where he sees a shape of black, he is not impressed by it, but he only wants the Creator to give him strength to be able to overcome all the

---

* A word that sounds like the Hebrew *Lavan* (white).
** A word that sounds like the Hebrew *Shmi'a* (hearing).

obstacles. It means that he does not ask the Creator to give him a shape of white, but to give him the strength to overcome all the concealments.

Hence, those people who want to work in order to bestow, if there is always a state of whiteness, the whiteness does not allow one to continue in the work. This is because, while it shines, one is able to work even in the form of reception for oneself.

Hence, one will never be able to know if his work is in purity or not, and this causes him never to be able to be awarded *Dvekut* [adhesion] with the Creator. For this reason, he is given from above a form of blackness, and then he sees if his work is in purity.

This means that if one can be in gladness in a state of blackness, too, it is a sign that his work is in purity, since one must be glad and believe that from above he was given an opportunity to be able to work in order to bestow.

This is as our sages said, "All who are gluttonous are angry." It means that one who is immersed in self-reception is angry, since he is always lacking. He forever needs to satisfy his vessels of reception.

However, those who want to walk in the path of bestowal should always be in gladness. This means that in any shape that comes upon him he should be in gladness since he has no intention to receive for himself. This is why he says that either way, if he is really working in order to bestow, he should certainly be glad that he has been granted bringing contentment to his Maker. And if he feels that his work is still not to bestow, he should also be glad because for himself, he says that he does not want anything for himself. He is happy that the will to receive cannot enjoy this work, and that should give him joy. However, if he thinks that he will also have something for himself from this work, he permits the *Sitra Achra* [other side] to cling to his work, and this causes him sadness, anger, and so forth.

43. Concerning Truth and Faith
I heard

Truth is what one feels and sees in his eyes. This discernment is called "reward and punishment," meaning that nothing can be gained without labor. It is like a person who sits in his home and does not want to do anything to provide for his sustenance. He says that since the Creator is good that does good, and provides for all, He will certainly send him his needs, while he himself does not need to do anything.

Of course, if this person behaves in this manner, he will certainly starve to death. Reason, too, asserts it, so it appears to the eyes, and this is indeed the truth, that he will die of starvation.

But at the same time, one must believe above reason that he could obtain all his needs without any exertion and trouble because of private Providence. In other words, the Creator does and will do every deed, and one does not help Him in anything. Rather, the Creator does everything, and one cannot add or take away.

Yet, how can these two things go hand in hand, since one contradicts the other? One discernment is called what one's mind attains, meaning that without man's help, meaning that without preceding labor and exertion, nothing will be attained. This is called "truth," since the Creator wanted man to feel that way. This is why this path is called "the path of truth."

Let it not perplex you that if these two ways are in contradiction, how is it possible that this state will be true? The answer is that the truth does not refer to the way or to the state. Rather, truth refers to the sensation that the Creator wanted him to feel like that way; this is "truth." It follows that the matter of truth can be said precisely about the Creator, meaning about His will, that He wants man to feel and see this way.

Yet, at the same time, one must believe that even though he does not feel and does not see with his mind's eye that the Creator can help him obtain all the profits that can be gained without any exertion, it is only with respect to private Providence.

The reason that one cannot attain the matter of private Providence before one attains the matter of reward and punishment is that private Providence is an eternal thing, and man's mind is not eternal. Hence, something eternal cannot clothe in something not eternal. Thus, once he has been awarded the reward and punishment, the reward and punishment become a *Kli* [vessel] where private Providence can clothe.

Now we can understand the verse, "O Lord, do save, O Lord, do succeed." "Do save" refers to reward and punishment. One must pray that the Creator will provide him with labor and exertion by which he will have reward. At the same time, he should pray for success, which is private Providence, meaning that he will be rewarded with all the profits in the world without any labor or exertion.

We also see this in corporeal possessions (discerned by their separation in places, meaning in two bodies, whereas in spiritual matters everything is examined on a single body but in two times). There are people who obtain their possessions specifically through great exertion, energy, and great wit, and at the same time we see the opposite, that people who are not so witty, who do not have a lot of energy, and do not make great efforts, succeed and become the greatest owners of property and possessions in the world.

The answer is that these corporeal things extend from their upper roots, meaning from reward and punishment and from private Providence. The only difference is that in spirituality it appears in one place, meaning in one carrier, but one-by-one, meaning in one person but in two states, and in corporeality it is in one time, but in two carriers, meaning at the same time and in two different people.

44. Mind and Heart

I heard on *Tevet* 10, *Tav-Reish-Peh-Het*, February 1, 1928, Givat Shaul, Jerusalem

One must examine if the faith is in order, meaning if he has fear and love, as it is written, "If I am a father, where is my honor, and if I am a lord, where is the fear of me?" And this is called "mind."

We must also see that there will not be any desires to delight oneself, that even a thought to want for himself will not arise in him, but all his desires will be only to bestow upon the Creator. This is called "heart," which is the meaning of "The Merciful One wants the heart."

45. Two Discernments in the Torah and in the Work

I heard on *Elul* 1, *Tav-Shin-Het*, September 5, 1948

There are two discernments in the Torah, and there are two discernments in the work. The first is the discernment of fear, and the second is the discernment of love. Torah is called a state of wholeness, meaning we do not speak of the state one's work is in, but we speak with respect to the Torah itself.

The first is called "love," meaning that one has a desire and craving to know the ways of the Creator and His hidden treasures, and for that he makes every effort and exertion to obtain his wish. He regards everything in the Torah that he extracts from what he has learned as having been granted a priceless thing. According to the appreciation from the importance of the Torah, so one gradually grows until he is slowly shown the secrets of the Torah, according to his labor.

The second discernment is fear, meaning that he wants to be a servant of the Creator. Since "He who does not know the commandment of the upper one, how will he serve Him?" he fears and dreads not knowing how to serve the Creator.

When he learns in this way, every time he finds a flavor in the Torah and can use it, he is elated and excited according to the appreciation of the importance from having been granted something in the Torah. And if one persists in this way, one is gradually shown the secrets of the Torah.

Here there is a difference between external teachings and the wisdom of the Torah: In external teachings, the elation lessens the intellect, since emotion is opposite from the intellect. Thus, the elation diminishes the understanding of the intellect.

Conversely, in the wisdom of the Torah, the elation is an essence, like the intellect. The reason for this is that the Torah is life, as it is written, "Wisdom preserves he who has it," as wisdom and life are the same thing.

Hence, as the wisdom appears in the mind, so the wisdom appears in the emotion, since the light of life fills all the organs. (It seems to me that this is why one should see that one is always elated over the wisdom of the Torah, since in the elation there is a big difference between an exterior teaching and the wisdom of the Torah.)

It is likewise in the work, considered the left line, because it is discerned as reception. The matter of reception means that one wants to receive because he feels a lack, and a lack is regarded as three discernments: 1) the want of the individual, 2) the want of the public, 3) the want of the *Shechina* [Divinity].

Any want is regarded as wanting to satisfy the deficiency; hence, it is considered reception and left line. Torah, however, means that one works not because he feels a lack that must be corrected, but that he wants to bestow contentment upon his Maker (through prayer, praise, and gratitude. When one engages in a way that one feels oneself in wholeness and does not see any shortcoming in the world, this is called "Torah." However, if one engages while feeling some shortcoming, this is called "work").

Also, we should make two discernments during the work: 1) due to love of the Creator, when he wants to adhere to the Creator and feels that this is the place where he can bring out the measure of love he feels and love the Creator, 2) because of fear, when he has fear of the Creator.

46. The Domination of Israel over the Klipot

I heard

Concerning the domination of Israel over the *Klipot* [shells], and vice-versa, the domination of the *Klipot* over Israel. First we must understand what is "Israel" and what is "the nations of the world."

It is explained in several places that Israel means "internality," called "the anterior *Kelim* [vessels]," with which one can work in order to bestow contentment upon one's Maker. "The nations of the world" are called "externality," "the posterior *Kelim*," whose sustenance comes solely from reception and not from bestowal.

The domination of the nations of the world over Israel is in that they cannot work in a form of bestowal and in the anterior *Kelim*, but only in the posterior *Kelim*. They entice the servants of the Creator to extend the lights down to the posterior *Kelim*.

The domination of Israel means that if they give power so that each and every one will be able to work in order to bestow contentment upon his Maker, meaning only in anterior *Kelim*, even if they extend *Hochma* [wisdom], it is only in a form of "a path to travel through," and not more.

47. In the Place Where You Find His Greatness

I heard

"In the place where you find His greatness, there you find His humbleness." It means that one who is always in true *Dvekut* [adhesion] sees that the Creator lowers Himself, meaning the Creator is present in the low places.

One does not know what to do, and this is why it is written, "Who sits on high, who looks down on heaven and on earth." A person sees the greatness of the Creator and then "who looks down," meaning he lowers the heaven to the earth. The advice that is given to this is to think that if this desire is from the Creator, we have nothing greater than that, as it is written, "He raises the poor out of the litter."

First, one must see that he has a lack. If he does not, he should pray for it, why does one not have it? The reason he does not have a lack is due to the diminution of awareness.

Hence, in every *Mitzva* [commandment], one must pray, why does he not have awareness, for he is not keeping the *Mitzva* in wholeness. In other words, the will to receive covers so he will not see the truth.

If he would see that he is in such a lowly state, he would certainly not want to be in that state. Instead, one should exert in one's work every time until he comes to repentance, as it is written, "He brings down to the netherworld, and raises up."

This means that when the Creator wants the wicked one to repent, He makes the netherworld so low for him that the wicked one himself does not want to be so. Hence, one needs to pray pleadingly that the Creator will show him the truth by adding to him the light of the Torah.

48. The Primary Basis

I heard on the evening after Shabbat, *Vayera, Tav-Shin-Yod-Gimel*, November 8, 1952

The primary basis is a path that is known to all. The care and the guard regarding the mind is because it is built on the basis of a question. If one encounters the known question, he must be armed and protected to stand guard and instantaneously reply with the known answer.

In other words, the whole structure is built on questions and answers, and this is walking on the path of the Creator and being rewarded with building the structure of the *Shechina* [Divinity]. And when one has no place for questions and answers, he is called "standing."

The Creator has prepared a place even to those who have already been granted the permanent clothing of the *Shechina* and are already on the path of degrees, who no longer have a place for the above-mentioned work. In this place, they have a free basis where faith can be.

Although it is difficult to understand how such a thing can be in high degrees, the Creator Himself can do such a thing. This is the meaning of the correction of the middle line, and the prohibition on reception from the left line.

At the same time, we see that *Hochma* appears only in *Malchut*. And even though *Malchut* is an opposite attribute from *Hochma*, still, the place for the appearance of *Hochma* is precisely here in *Malchut*.

This is the meaning of "and let this obstacle be under your hand." Our sages said that one does not observe a law unless he has failed in it. A law means a discernment of *Malchut* (and this is the meaning of the bride. When going to the bride it is called "law"*). It is built solely on obstacles, meaning on a time of questions. When one has no questions, one does not have the name "faith" or *Shechina*.

49. The Most Important Are the Mind and the Heart

I heard on Thursday, Vayera, Tav-Shin-Yod-Gimel, November 6, 1952

There should be a preparation on the discernment of "mind," in that same work which refers to the quality of faith. This means that if one is negligent in the work of faith, he falls to a state of wanting only knowledge, which is a *Klipa* [shell], which is against the *Shechina* [Divinity]. Hence, one's work is to strengthen the discernment of "mind" every time.

Similarly, if one feels negligence in the work of the heart, he must strengthen the work that relates to the quality of "heart," and perform opposite operations, meaning affliction of the body, which is the opposite of the will to receive. The difference between negligence in the work of the mind and the work of the heart is that there is an evil *Klipa* [shell] against the mind that can prompt a state of "pondering the beginning."

Hence, one must perform opposite actions, meaning in every renewal of the discernment of "mind" he will take upon himself remorse for the past and acceptance of the future. One can receive the source that causes it from the discernment of "still." And the matter of the clothing of faith is a perpetual and eternal thing. Hence, one will always have it as a measurement if one's work is clean or not, since the clothing of *Shechina* departs only due to a flaw, either in the mind or in the heart.

50. Two States

I heard on Sivan 20

There are two states to the world: 1) In the first state the world is called "pain." 2) In the second state, it is called "*Shechina* [Divinity]." It is so because before one is endowed with correcting his deeds to be in order to bestow, he feels the world only in the form of pains and torments.

However, afterward, he is rewarded with seeing that the *Shechina* is clothed in the whole world, and then the Creator is considered to be filling the world. Then the world is called "*Shechina*," who receives from the Creator. This is called "the

---

* In Hebrew, the words "bride" and "law" are written with the same letters in a different order.

unification of the Creator and His *Shechina*," for as the Creator gives, so the world is now occupied solely in bestowal.

It is like a sad tune. Some players know how to perform the suffering about which the tune was composed, because all melodies are like a spoken language where the tune interprets the words that the person wants to say out loud. If the tune evokes crying in the listeners to the extent that each and every one cries because of the suffering that the melody expresses, then it is called "a tune," and everyone loves to listen to it.

However, how can people enjoy suffering? Since the tune does not point to present suffering, but to the past, meaning torments that have already passed, were sweetened, and received their fill, for this reason, people like to listen to them, for it indicates the sweetening of the judgments, that the sufferings one had were sweetened. This is why these sufferings are sweet to hear, and then the world is called "*Shechina*."

The important thing that one should know and feel is that there is a leader to the capital, as our sages said, "Abraham the Patriarch said, 'There is no capital without a leader.'" One must not think that everything that happens in the world is incidental and that the *Sitra Achra* [other side] causes one to sin and say that everything is incidental.

This is the meaning of *Hammat* [vessel of] *Keri* [semen]. There is a *Hammat* filled with *Keri*. The *Keri* brings one to think that everything is *Bemikreh* [incidental]. (Even when the *Sitra Achra* brings one such thoughts—to say that everything is incidental, without guidance, this is also not incidental, but the Creator wanted it this way.)

However, one must believe in reward and punishment, and that there is a judgment and there is a judge, and everything is conducted by guidance of reward and punishment. This is because sometimes when some desire and awakening for the work of the Creator comes to a person, and he thinks that it comes to him by chance, he should know that here, too, he made an effort that preceded the hearing. He prayed to be helped from above to be able to perform an act with intent, and this is called raising MAN.

Yet, he has already forgotten about it and did not regard it as doing, since he did not receive an immediate answer to the prayer, so as to say, "You hear the prayer of every mouth." Still, one should believe that the order from above is that the response for the prayer may come several days and months after he prayed.

One should not think that it is by chance that he received this awakening now. Sometimes a person says, "Now that I feel that I do not need anything and I have no concerns, my mind is clear and sound, for this reason, now I can focus my mind and desire on the work of the Creator."

It follows that he can say that all his engagement in the work of the Creator is "My power and the might of my hand has gotten me this wealth." Thus, when he can engage and attain spiritual needs, he should believe that this is the answer to the prayer. What he prayed for before, that prayer has now been answered.

Also, sometimes when reading some book, and the Creator opens his eyes and he feels some awakening, then, too, his regular conduct is to attribute it to chance. However, it is all guided.

Although one knows that the whole Torah is the names of the Creator, how can he say that through the book he is reading came some sublime sensation? One must know that he often reads the book and knows that the whole Torah is the names of the Creator, yet receives no illumination or sensation. Instead, everything is dry and the knowledge that he knows does not help him at all.

Hence, when one studies in a certain book and hangs his hope on Him, one's study should be on the basis of faith, that he believes in Providence, that the Creator will open his eyes. At that time, he becomes needy of the Creator and thus has contact with the Creator. By this he can be rewarded with *Dvekut* [adhesion] with Him.

There are two forces that contradict one another, an upper force and a lower force. The upper force is, as it is written, "Every one who is called by My Name, I have created him for My glory." This means that the whole world was created only for the glory of the Creator. The lower force is the will to receive, which claims that everything was created for it—both corporeal things and spiritual things—all is for self-love.

The will to receive claims that it deserves this world and the next world. Of course, the Creator is the winner, but this is called "the path of suffering," and it is called "a long way." But there is a short way called "the path of Torah," and this should be everyone's intention—to shorten time.

This is called "I will hasten it." Otherwise, it will be "in its time," as our sages said, "rewarded—I will hasten it; not rewarded—in its time," "when I place upon them a king such as Haman, and he will force you to reform."

The Torah begins from *Beresheet* [in the beginning], etc. "And the earth was unformed and void, and darkness," etc., and ends, "before the eyes of all of Israel."

In the beginning, we see that the land is "unformed and void, and darkness," but then, when they correct themselves to bestow, they are rewarded with "and God said, let there be light," until the light appears "before the eyes of all of Israel."

51. If You Encounter This Villain

I heard after the holiday of Passover, *Tav-Shin-Gimel*, April 27, 1943

"If you encounter this villain, draw him to the seminary, etc., and if not, remind him of the day of death." This means that he will remind him that the work should be in a place where he is not present, which is after one's skin. This is called "working outside one's body," that he has not a single thought about his own body.

52. A Transgression Does Not Extinguish a Mitzva
I heard on the eve of Shabbat, *Iyar* 9, *Tav-Shin-Gimel*, May 14, 1943

"A transgression does not extinguish a *Mitzva* [commandment], and a *Mitzva* does not extinguish a transgression." It is the conduct of the work that one must take the good path. But the bad in a person does not let him take the good path.

However, one must know that one does not need to uproot the bad, as this is impossible. Rather, one must only hate the evil, as it is written, "You who love the Lord, hate evil." Thus, it is only hatred that is needed, since it is the conduct of hate to separate the adhered.

For this reason, evil has no existence on its own. Rather, the existence of evil depends on love for the evil or the hate for the evil. It means that if one has love for evil then one is caught in the authority of the evil. If one hates the evil, he exits their premises and one's evil has no dominion over that person.

It follows that the primary work is not in the actual evil, but in the measure of love and the measure of hate. For this reason, a transgression induces a transgression. We must ask, "Why does he deserve such a punishment?" When one falls from one's work, he must be aided to rise from the fall. But here we see that more obstacles are added to him so he would fall lower than the first fall.

But in order to feel hatred for the evil, he is given more evil, so as to feel how the transgression removes him from the work of the Creator. Although he regretted the first transgression, he still did not feel regret enough to bring him hatred for the evil.

Hence, a transgression prompts a transgression, and every time he regrets, and each remorse certainly instigates hatred for the evil until the measure of his hatred for the evil is completed, and then he is separated from the evil, since hatred induces separation.

It therefore follows that if one finds a certain measure of hate at a level that prompts separation, he does not need a correction of a transgression induces a transgression, and therefore saves time. When one has been rewarded, he is admitted to the love of the Creator. This is the meaning of "You who love the Lord, hate evil." They only hate the evil, but the evil itself remains in its place, and it is only hatred to the evil that we need.

This extends from, "Yet You have made him but little lower than God," and this is the meaning of the serpent's saying, "and you shall be as God, knowing good and evil." It means that when one exerts and wants to understand all the conducts of Providence, like the Creator, this is the meaning of "A man's passion shall bring him low." It means that one wants to understand everything with the exterior mind, and if he does not understand it, he is in lowliness.

The truth is that if one awakens to know something, it is a sign that he needs to know that thing. When one overcomes one's own mind, what he wishes to understand, and takes everything with faith above reason, this is called the greatest lowliness in the human attribute. You find that to the extent that one has a demand to know more, yet takes it in faith above reason, you find that he is in greater lowliness.

Now we can understand what they interpreted about the verse (Numbers 12:3), "And the man Moses was very meek," humble and patient. It means that he tolerated the lowliness in the highest possible measure.

This is the meaning of *Adam HaRishon* eating from the tree of life prior to the sin, and that he was in wholeness. Yet, he could not walk more than the degree he stood on, since he did not feel any lack in his state. Hence, he naturally could not discover all the holy Names.

For this reason, "He is terrible in His doing toward the sons of man" made him eat from the tree of knowledge of good and evil. Through this sin, all the lights departed from him; hence, he was compelled to start his work anew.

The writing says about it that he was expelled from the Garden of Eden because if he had eaten from the tree of life he would have lived forever. This is the meaning of the internality of the worlds. If one enters there, one remains there forever. It means that once more he would remain without any lack. And to be able to go and reveal the holy names, which appear by the correction of good and evil, he therefore had to eat from the tree of knowledge.

It is similar to a person who wants to give his friend a big barrel filled with wine, but his friend has only a small cup. What does he do? He pours wine into that cup and takes the cup home and he pours it. Then he begins to go with the cup once more and once more fills it with wine. Then, he goes to his house once more until he receives all the wine barrels.

I heard another parable that he said about two friends, one of whom became a king and the other became very poor, and he had heard that his friend had become a king. So the poor man went to his friend the king and told him of his bad state.

Then the king gave him a letter to the treasury minister that for two hours he would receive as much money as he wanted. The poor man came to the treasury with a small box, went in, and filled that little box with money.

When he came out, the minister kicked the box and all the money fell on the floor. This continued time and time again, and the poor man was crying, "Why are you doing this to me?" Finally, he said, all the money that you took this whole time is yours and you will take it all. You did not have the receptacles to take enough money from the treasury; this is why that trick was played on you.

53. The Matter of Limitation

I heard on the eve of Shabbat, *Sivan* 1, *Tav-Shin-Gimel*, June 4, 1943

The matter of limitation is to limit the state one is in and not want *Gadlut* [greatness/adulthood]. Instead, one wants to remain in one's present state forever, and this is called eternal *Dvekut* [adhesion]. Regardless of the measure of *Gadlut* that one has, even if he has the smallest *Katnut* [smallness/infancy], if it shines forever, it is considered having been imparted eternal *Dvekut*.

However, one who wants more *Gadlut*, it is considered luxury. This is the meaning of "Any sorrow will be surplus," meaning that sadness comes to a person because he wants luxuries. This is what it means that when Israel came to receive the Torah, Moses led them to the bottom of the mountain, as it is written, "And they stood at the bottom of the mountain."

(A mountain [Hebrew: *Har*] means thoughts [Hebrew: *Hirhurim*]). Moses led them to the end of the thought and the understanding and the reason, the lowest degree there is. Only then, when they agreed to such a state, to walk in it without any wavering or motion, and remain in that state as if they had the greatest *Gadlut*, and to be happy about it, this is the meaning of "Serve the Lord with gladness," since during the *Gadlut*, it cannot be said that He gives them work to be in gladness because during the *Gadlut*, gladness comes by itself. Instead, the work of gladness is given to them for the time of *Katnut*, so they will have joy although they feel *Katnut*. And this is a lot of work.

This is called "the main part of the degree," which is discerned as *Katnut*. This discernment must be permanent, and the *Gadlut* is only an addition. Also, one should yearn for the main part, not for the additions.

54. The Purpose of the Work - 1

What I heard on *Shevat* 16, *Tav-Shin-Aleph*, February 13, 1941

It is known that the servitude is mainly to bestow contentment upon his Maker. Yet, one must know the meaning of bestowing, as this is used by everyone, and it is known that habit wears off the taste. Therefore, we must thoroughly clarify the meaning of the word to bestow.

The thing is that the will to receive is also incorporated in the desire to bestow of the lower one (but the will to receive can be used with corrections), or else there is no connection between the giver and the receiver. This is because it is impossible that one will give and the other will give nothing in return, yet there will be a state of partnership.

Only when both show love to one another is there a connection and friendship between them. But if one shows love and the other shows no response, such a love is unreal and has no right to exist. Our sages stated about the verse, "and say unto Zion: 'You are My people'" (Isaiah 51), do not say *Ami* [My people], but *Imi* [with Me],* "to be My partner" (*Zohar Beresheet* p 5), meaning that the creatures are in partnership with the Creator.

It follows that when the lower one wants to bestow upon the Creator, the lower one, too, should receive from the Creator. This is called partnership, when the lower one gives, and the upper one gives, too.

However, the will to receive should crave to adhere to Him and receive His abundance, sustenance, and goodness; and that was the purpose of creation, to do good to His creations.

However, because of the breaking that occurred in the world of *Nekudim*, the will to receive fell into the domain of the *Klipot* [shells], by which two discernments were made in the *Kli* [vessel]. 1) It developed a relation to the separated pleasures, and the work of exiting the authority of the *Klipot* is called "the work of purification." 2) The second discernment that occurred due to the breaking is the detachment from spiritual pleasures.

In other words, one becomes distant from spirituality and has no desire for spirituality. The correction for this is called *Kedusha* [holiness], where the order of the work is to crave His exaltedness. In that state, the Creator shines for him in these vessels. However, we must know that to the extent that he has *Kelim* [pl. of *Kli*] of purity, called "hate evil," to that extent he can work in *Kedusha*, as it is written, "you who love the Lord, hate evil."

It follows that there are two discernments: 1) purity, 2) *Kedusha*. *Kedusha* is called the *Kli*, the preparation to receive His goodness, by way of to do good to His creations. However, this *Kli* is attributed to the lower one, meaning that it is for us to repair. In other words, it is for us to crave the good, and this means engaging extensively in His exaltedness and his own lowliness.

Yet, the abundance that should appear in the *Kli* of *Kedusha* is in the hands of the Creator; He is the One who imparts the lower one with abundance. At that time, the lower one cannot help in that in any way, and this is called "The hidden things belong to the Lord our God."

The thought of creation, called "to do good to His creations," begins from *Ein Sof* [no end]. For this reason, we pray to *Ein Sof*, meaning to the connection that exists between the Creator and the creatures. This is the meaning of what is written in the writings of the ARI, that we must pray to *Ein Sof*.

It is so because *Atzmuto* [His Self] has no connection with the creatures, since the beginning of the connection starts in *Ein Sof*, where His name is, which is the root of creation. This is the meaning of what is written in the Jerusalem [Talmud], that

---

* Both words consist of the same letters in Hebrew, and when there are no punctuation marks, as in the Bible, they look the same.

one who prays will pray in the Name, meaning that there is His name, and His name and *Ein Sof* are called in the words of the legend, "A tower filled with abundance." This is why we pray to the name, to receive the benefit that has been prepared for us in advance.

This is why *Keter* is called "His desire to do good to His creations," and the benefit itself is called *Hochma* [wisdom], which is the abundance itself. This is why *Keter* is called *Ein Sof* and "Emanator." However, *Hochma* is not called "emanated" yet, since there is still no *Kli* in *Hochma*, and it is considered a light without a *Kli*.

For this reason, *Hochma*, too, is discerned as the Emanator because there is no attainment in the light without a *Kli*, and the whole difference between *Keter* and *Hochma* is that there, the root of the emanated is more disclosed.

55. Haman from the Torah, from Where?
I heard on *Shevat* 16, *Tav-Shin-Aleph*, February 13, 1941

Haman from the Torah, from where? "Have you eaten from the tree from which I commanded you not to eat?" (Genesis 3:11). We must understand the connection between Haman and *Etz ha Daat* [tree of knowledge]. *Etz ha Daat* is considered the state of greatness of reception, which is not in *Kedusha* [holiness] and must be brought into the *Kedusha* through corrections.

The quality of Haman is also the state of greatness of reception, as it is written that Haman said, "Whom would the king," King of the world, "want to honor more than me?" It means that it is discerned as the state of greatness of reception, and this is discerned as "And his heart was lifted up in the ways of the Lord."

56. Torah Is Called Indication
I heard on *BeShalach* 1, *Tav-Shin-Aleph*, February 2, 1941

Torah is called "indication," from the words "shot through."[*] It means that when one engages in the Torah, he feels his remoteness to the extent of his exertion. In other words, he is shown the truth, meaning he is shown his measure of faith, which is the whole basis of the truth.

The basis of observing Torah and *Mitzvot* [commandments] is on one's measure of faith, since then it appears to him that his whole basis is built only on the upbringing he received. This is because the upbringing is sufficient for him to keep Torah and *Mitzvot* in all its intricacies and details, and everything that comes through upbringing is called "faith within reason."

Even though this is against one's mind, meaning reason necessitates that according to one's addition in the Torah, so one should feel closer to the Creator. However,

---

[*] In Hebrew the same word is used for shooting and for indicating something.

the Torah always shows him more of the truth. When he searches for the truth, the Torah brings him closer to the truth and he sees his measure of faith in the Creator.

This is so that he would be able to ask for mercy and pray for the Creator to bring him genuinely closer to Him, which means that he will be awarded faith in the Creator. Then he will be able to give praise and gratitude to the Creator for having been granted being brought closer to Him.

However, when he does not see the measure of his remoteness and thinks that he is constantly adding, you find that he builds all the buildings on a rickety basis, and he has no place to pray for the Creator to bring him closer to Him. It follows that he has no place for exertion to be imparted whole faith, since one exerts only for that which one needs.

Hence, as long as one is not worthy of seeing the truth, it is the opposite. The more one adds in Torah and *Mitzvot*, one adds in the measure of his wholeness and does not see any deficit in himself. Therefore, he has no place to exert and pray to be granted faith in the Creator in truth, because when he feels corruption, you should say correction.

However, when he engages in Torah and *Mitzvot* in truth, the Torah shows him the truth, because the Torah has that power to show one's true state of faith (and this is the meaning of "make it known").

When one engages in the Torah and sees the truth, meaning his measure of remoteness from spirituality, and sees that he is such a lowly being that there is not a worse person than him on earth, then the *Sitra Achra* [other side] comes to one with a different argument: In fact, his body is really very ugly, and it is true that there is not an uglier person in the world than him.

She tells him this so he will despair, since she is afraid that he will notice and come to correct his state. For this reason, she agrees to what one says, that he is an ugly person, and lets him understand that if he had been born with higher skills and better qualities, he could have overcome his evil and corrected it, and he would have been able to achieve *Dvekut* [adhesion] with the Creator.

The answer to this should be that what she tells him is brought in *Masechet Taanit* (p 20), that Rabbi Elazar, son of Rabbi Shimon, came from a fenced tower from the house of his teacher. He was riding his donkey and strolling along the riverbank feeling great joy. And his mind was crude, as he had been studying much Torah.

A person who was very ugly came by his way. He told him, "Hello rabbi," but he did not reply. He told him, "Vain, how ugly is that man, are all your townspeople as ugly as you?" He replied, "I do not know, but go and tell the craftsman who made me, 'How ugly is this vessel that you have made.'" Because he knew that he had sinned, he descended from the donkey.

According to the above, we can see that since he learned much Torah, through it he was granted seeing the truth about the distance between himself and the Creator, meaning the measure of his nearness and the measure of his remoteness. This is the meaning of his mind being crude, meaning that he saw the complete form of one who is proud, which is his will to receive, and then he could see the truth that it was he himself who was very ugly. How did he see the truth? By learning much Torah.

Thus, how will he be able to adhere to Him, since he is such an ugly person? This is why he asked if all the people were as ugly as him or was he the only ugly one and the rest of the people in the world were not ugly.

What was the answer? "I don't know." It means that they do not feel and therefore do not know. And why do they not feel? It is for the simple reason that they were not rewarded with seeing the truth, since they lack Torah, so the Torah will show them the truth.

To that Elijah replied to him, "Go to the craftsman who made me." Because he saw that he came to a state from which he could not ascend, Elijah appeared and told him, "Go to the craftsman who made me." In other words, since the Creator created you so ugly, He must have known that with these *Kelim* [vessels] it is possible to achieve the goal. So do not worry, go forward and succeed.

57. Will Bring Him Closer to His Will
I heard on *Yitro* 1, *Tav-Shin-Dalet*, February 5, 1944

About the verse, "will bring him closer to His will," our sages said, "How so? He is coerced until he says, 'I want.'" We must also understand what we pray, "Let there be a will," since more than the calf wants to eat, the cow wants to feed, so why do we need to pray, "Let there be a will above"?

It is known that in order to extend abundance from above, one must precede an awakening from below. We must understand why we need an awakening from below. Because of this, we pray that there will be a will above. It means that we must evoke a desire from above to impart below.

It is not enough that we have a desire, but there has to be a good will on the part of the Giver, too. Even though above there is a general desire to do good to His creations, He still waits for our desire to awaken His desire.

In other words, if we are unable to evoke His desire, it is a sign that the desire on the part of the receiver is still incomplete. Hence, precisely by praying that there will be a will above, our desire is made to be a genuine desire, to be a fitting *Kli* [vessel] to receive the abundance.

At the same time, we must say that all that we do, both bad and good, everything extends from above (which is the meaning of private Providence), that the Creator does everything. Yet, at the same time we must regret the bad deeds, though it, too, extends from above.

The mind asserts that we must not regret, but justify the judgment, that the bad deeds come to us. Nevertheless, it is to the contrary; we must regret that He does not let us do good deeds, which is certainly a result of a punishment, meaning that we are unworthy of serving the King.

If everything is guided, how can we say that we are unworthy, since there is no act below? For this purpose we are given bad thoughts and desires that distance us from the work of the Creator, that we are not worthy of serving Him. For this reason, there is a prayer for this, that this is a place of correction to be worthy and capable of receiving the work of the King.

Now we can see why there is a prayer regarding some trouble. This trouble must have come as a punishment, and punishments must be corrections, since there is a rule that the punishment is a correction.

Thus, why do we pray to the Creator to cancel our corrections, as our sages said about the verse, "And your brother is ignoble in your eyes," that your brother is afflicted? We must know that the prayer corrects a person even more than punishment. Thus, when prayer appears instead of punishment, the affliction is lifted and the prayer is placed in its place in order to correct the body.

This is the meaning of what our sages said, "Rewarded—through Torah; was not rewarded—through suffering." We must know that the path of Torah is a more successful way and yields more benefits than the path of suffering. This is because the *Kelim* [vessels] that will be fit to receive the upper light are broader and can yield *Dvekut* [adhesion] with Him.

This is the meaning of "He is coerced until he says, 'I want.'" It means that the Creator says, "I want the deeds of the lower ones."

The meaning of prayer is what our sages said, "The Creator craved the prayer of the righteous," for by the prayer, the *Kelim* are made fit for the Creator to later give the abundance, since there is a fit *Kli* to receive the abundance.

58. Joy Is a "Reflection" of Good Deeds
I heard on *Sukkot*, Inter 4

Joy is a "reflection" of good deeds. If the deeds are of *Kedusha* [holiness], hence joy appears. However, we must know that there is also a discernment of a *Klipa* [shell]. In order to know if it is *Kedusha*, the scrutiny is in the reason. In *Kedusha*, there is reason, and in the *Sitra Achra* [other side] there is no reason, since another god is sterile and does not bear fruit. Hence, when gladness comes to a person, he should delve in words of Torah in order to discover the mind of the Torah.

We must also know that gladness is discerned as upper illumination that appears by MAN, which is good deeds. The Creator judges one where one is. In other words, if one takes upon himself the burden of the kingdom of heaven for eternity, there is an immediate upper illumination on this, which is considered eternity, too.

Even if one evidently sees that he will soon fall from his degree, He still judges one where one is. It means that if a person has now made up his mind to take upon himself the burden of the kingdom of heaven for eternity, it is considered wholeness.

However, if he takes upon himself the burden of the kingdom of heaven and does not want that state to remain in him forever, this thing and this deed is not considered wholeness, and naturally, the upper light cannot come and rest on it. This is because it is whole and eternal, and is not about to change. With a person, however, even if he wants, the state one is in will not be forever.

59. Concerning the Staff and the Serpent
I heard on *Adar* 13, *Tav-Shin-Het*, February 23, 1948

"And Moses answered and said: 'But, they will not believe me,'" etc. "And the Lord said to him, 'What is it in your hand?' And he said, 'A staff.' And He said, 'Cast it on the ground...' and it became a serpent; and Moses fled from it" (Exodus 4).

We should interpret that there are not more than two degrees, either *Kedusha* [holiness] or *Sitra Achra* [other side]. There is no intermediary state, but the same staff itself becomes a serpent if thrown to the ground.

In order to understand this, we will first bring the words of our sages, that He had instill His *Shechina* [Divinity] on trees and rocks. Trees and rocks are called things of inferior importance, and specifically in this manner He placed His *Shechina*. This is the meaning of the question, "What is it in your hand?"

A "hand" means attainment, from the words, "If a hand attains." A "staff" means that all his attainments are built on the discernment of inferior importance, which is faith above reason.

(Faith is regarded as having inferior importance, and as lowliness. One appreciates things that clothe within reason. However, if one's mind does not attain it, but it rather opposes one's mind, and then one should say that faith is of superior importance to one's mind, it follows that at that time he lowers his mind and says that what he understands within reason, that he resists the path of the Creator, faith is more important than his own mind. This is because all the concepts that contradict the path of the Creator are worthless concepts.

Rather, "They have eyes but they will see not, they have ears but they will hear not." It means that he annuls everything he hears and sees. This is called "going above reason." And thus it seems to a person as lowness and *Katnut* [smallness/infancy].

However, with the Creator, faith is not considered lowliness, since man, who has no other choice but to take the path of faith, considers faith as lowliness. However, the Creator could have placed His *Shechina* on something other than trees and rocks.

Yet, He chose this way, called faith, specifically. He must have chosen it because it is better and more successful. You find that for Him faith is not regarded as being of inferior importance. On the contrary, specifically this path has many merits, but it appears lowly in the eyes of the creatures.)

If the staff is thrown to the ground and one wants to work with a higher discernment, meaning within reason, degrading the above reason, and this work seems low, one's Torah and work immediately become a serpent. This is the meaning of the primordial serpent, and this is the meaning of "Anyone who is proud, the Creator tells him, 'He and I cannot dwell in the same abode.'"

The reason is, as we have said, that He has placed His *Shechina* on trees and rocks. Hence, if one throws the discernment of the staff to the ground, and raises oneself to work with a higher attribute, this is already a serpent. There is no middle; it is either a serpent, or *Kedusha*, since all the Torah and the work that one had from the discernment of a staff, all has now entered the discernment of a serpent.

It is known that the *Sitra Achra* has no lights. Hence, in corporeality too, the will to receive has only deficiencies, but not satisfaction of the deficiency. And the vessel of reception remains forever in deficit, without fulfillment, because one who has one hundred wants two hundred, etc., and one does not die with half one's wish in one's hand.

This extends from the upper roots. The root of the *Klipa* [shell] is the vessel of reception, and they have no correction during the six thousand years. The *Tzimtzum* [restriction] is placed on them; hence, they do not have lights and abundance.

This is why they entice one to draw light to their degree. And the lights that one receives by being adhered to *Kedusha*, since abundance shines in *Kedusha*, when they entice one to draw abundance to their state, they receive that light. Thus, they have dominion over a person, meaning they give him satisfaction in the state he is in so he will not move from here.

Hence, one cannot go forward through this dominion since he has no need for a higher degree. Since he has no need, he cannot move from his place, even a slight movement.

In that state, he is unable to discern if he is advancing in *Kedusha* or the other way around. This is because the *Sitra Achra* gives him power to work more strongly, since now he is within reason and can therefore work not in a state of lowliness. It follows that thus one would remain in the authority of the *Sitra Achra*.

In order for a person to not remain in the authority of the *Sitra Achra*, the Creator made a correction that if one leaves the discernment of the staff, he immediately falls into the state of a serpent. He immediately falls into a state of failures and has no power to hang on, unless he accepts the discernment of faith, called lowliness, once more.

It follows that the failures themselves cause one to take upon himself the discernment of a staff once more, which is the discernment of faith above reason. This is the meaning of what Moses said, "But they will not believe me." It means that they will not want to take upon themselves the path of working in faith above reason.

Then the Creator told him, "What is it in your hand?" "A staff." "Cast it on the ground," and then, promptly, "it became a serpent." It means that there is no intermediary state between the staff and the serpent. It is rather to know if one is in *Kedusha* or in the *Sitra Achra*.

It turns out that in any case, they do not have any other choice but to assume the discernment of faith above reason, called "a staff." This staff should be in the hand; the staff should not be thrown. This is the meaning of the verse, "The staff of Aaron budded."

It means that all the budding he had in serving the Creator was based specifically on Aaron's staff. This means that He wanted to give us a sign to know if we are walking on the path of truth, or not. He gave us as a sign to know only the basis of the work, meaning what basis one is working on. If one's basis is the staff, it is *Kedusha*, and if the basis is within reason, this is not the way to achieve *Kedusha*.

However, in the work itself, meaning in the Torah and in the prayer, there is no distinction between one who serves Him and one who does not serve Him. This is because there it is to the contrary: If the basis is within reason, meaning based on knowing and receiving, the body gives fuel for work, and he can pray and study more persistently and more enthusiastically, since it is based on within reason.

However, when one takes the path of *Kedusha*, whose basis is bestowal and faith, he needs much preparation so the *Kedusha* will shine for him. Without preparation, the body does not give one the strength for work, and one must always exert extensively, since man's root is reception and within reason.

Therefore, if his work is based on earthliness, he can always be fine. But if the basis for the work is on the discernment of bestowal and above reason, he needs perpetual efforts so as not to fall into his root of reception and within reason.

One must not be distracted for a minute, or he will fall into his root of earthliness, called "dust," as it is written, "for dust you are, and to dust shall you return." And that was after the sin of the tree of knowledge.

One examines if one is advancing in *Kedusha* or to the contrary, since another god is sterile and does not bear fruit. *The Zohar* gives us that sign, that specifically on the basis of faith, called "a staff," is one imparted fruitfulness and multiplication in the Torah. This is the meaning of "the staff of Aaron budded": The budding and growing come specifically through the staff.

Therefore, as one rises from one's bed daily and washes oneself to purify his body from the filth of the body, so one should wash oneself from the filth of the *Klipa*, to examine himself if his quality of staff is in completeness.

This should be a perpetual examination, and if one is distracted from it, he immediately falls to the authority of the *Sitra Achra* called "self-reception." One immediately becomes enslaved to them, as it is known that the light makes the *Kli*. Hence, as much as one works in order to receive, to that extent he needs only a desire to receive for himself and becomes remote from matters concerning bestowal.

Now we can understand the words of our sages, "Be very, very humble." What is that fuss that it says, "very, very"? It is because one becomes needy of people by having been honored once. At first one receives the honor not because he wanted to enjoy the honor, but for other reasons, such as the glory of the Torah, etc. One is certain of this scrutiny since he knows about himself that he has no desire for honor whatsoever.

It follows that it is reasonable to think that he is permitted to receive the honor. However, it is still forbidden to receive since the light makes the *Kli*. Hence, after he has received the honor he becomes needy of the honor, he is already in its dominion, and it is hard to break free from the honor.

By this one acquires one's own reality, and it is now hard to annul before the Creator since through the honor he has become a separate entity, and in order to obtain *Dvekut* [adhesion] one must annul one's reality completely, hence the "very, very." "Very" is that it is forbidden to receive honor for oneself, and the other "very" is that even when one's intention is not for himself, it is still forbidden to receive.

60. A Mitzva that Comes through Transgression

I heard on *Tetzve* 1, *Tav-Shin-Gimel*, February 14, 1943

A *Mitzva* [commandment] that comes through transgression means that if one takes upon himself the work in order to receive a reward, it is divided into two things:

1. The reception of the work, which is called a *Mitzva*.

2. The intention: to receive a reward. It is called a transgression because reception moves one from *Kedusha* [holiness] to the *Sitra Achra* [other side].

The whole basis and the reason that gave one the strength to work was the reward; hence, a *Mitzva* "that comes" means that he was brought to perform the *Mitzva*, this is the transgression. This is why it is called a "*Mitzva* that comes," that the one who brings the *Mitzva* is the transgression, which is only the reward.

The advice for this is to do one's work in the form of "without seeing more," that his whole aim of the work will be to increase the glory of heaven in the world. This is called working in order to raise the *Shechina* [Divinity] from the dust.

The matter of raising the *Shechina* means that the *Shechina* is called "the entirety of the souls." It receives the abundance from the Creator and imparts to the souls. The bestower, who passes the abundance to the souls, is called "the unification of the Creator and His *Shechina*," for at that time the abundance is extended to the lower ones. However, when there is no unification, there is no extension of abundance to the lower ones.

To make it clearer, because the Creator wanted to delight His creatures, therefore, as He thought of dispensing the abundance, He also thought of the reception of the abundance. That is, that the lower ones would receive the abundance. But both were in potential, meaning that afterward, souls will come and receive the abundance in practice.

Also, the receiver of the abundance in potential is called *Shechina*, since the thought of the Creator is a complete reality and He does not need an actual deed. Hence the lower one... (discontinued)

61. Round About Him It Storms Mightily
I heard on *Nisan* 9, *Tav-Shin-Het*, April 18, 1948

Our sages say about the verse, "And round about Him it storms mightily," that the Creator is meticulous with the righteous as a hairsbreadth. He asked: If they are generally righteous, why do they deserve a harsh punishment?

The thing is that all the borders we speak of in the worlds are from the perspective of the receivers, meaning the lower ones limit and restrict themselves to some degree, and thus remain below, since above, they agree to everything that the lower ones do. Hence, to that extent the abundance extends below. Therefore, by their thoughts, words, and actions, the lower ones cause the abundance to come down from above in this manner.

It turns out that if the lower one regards a minor act or word as if it is an important act, such as considering a momentary pause in *Dvekut* [adhesion] with the Creator as breaking the gravest prohibition in the Torah, then there is consent above to the opinion of the lower one, and it is considered above as though he really broke a serious prohibition. Thus, the righteous says that the Creator is meticulous with him as a hairsbreadth, and as the lower one says, so it is agreed above.

When the lower one does not feel a slight prohibition as a serious one, from above they also do not regard the trifle things he breaks as great prohibitions. Hence, such a person is treated as though he is a small person, meaning his *Mitzvot* [commandments] are considered small, and his transgressions are considered small, too. They are regarded as having the same weight, and he is generally considered a small person.

However, one who regards the trifle things and says that the Creator is meticulous about them as a hairsbreadth is considered a great person, and both his transgressions and his *Mitzvot* are great.

One can suffer when committing a transgression to the extent that he feels pleasure when performing a *Mitzva* [commandment]. There is an allegory about this: A man did a terrible crime against the kingship and was sentenced to twenty years in prison with hard labor. The prison was outside the country in some desolate place in the world. The sentence was carried out right away and he was sent to the desolate place at the end of the world.

There, he found other people who were sentenced by the kingdom to be there like him, but he became sick with amnesia and forgot that he had a wife and children, friends and acquaintances. He thought that the whole world is nothing more than the desolate place with the people who are there, that he was born there, and he did not know of more than that. Thus, his truth is according to his present feeling and he has no regard for the actual reality, only according to his knowledge and sensations.

There he was taught rules and regulations so that he would not break the rules once more, and keep himself from the transgression written there, and know how to correct his actions so as to be brought out from there. In the books of the king, he learned that one who breaks this rule, for example, is sent to a punitive land far from any settlement. He is impressed by this harsh punishment and has grievances at why such harsh punishments are given.

Yet, he would never think that he himself is one of those who broke the rules of the state, that he has been sentenced harshly, and the verdict has been carried out. And since he became sick with amnesia, he will never feel his actual state.

This is the meaning of "and round about him it storms mightily": One must consider his every move, that he himself had already broken the king's commandment, and has already been banished from the world. Now, through many good deeds, his memory begins to work and he begins to feel how far he has become from the settled place of the world.

He begins to engage in repentance until he is taken out from there and brought back to the settled place, and this feeling comes specifically through one's work. He begins to feel that he has grown far from his origin and root until he is rewarded with *Dvekut* with the Creator.

62. Descends and Incites, Ascends and Complains
I heard on *Adar Aleph* 19, *Tav-Shin-Het*, February 29, 1948

"Descends and incites, ascends and complains." One must always examine oneself, if one's Torah and work do not descend to the abyss. This is because one's greatness is measured by one's measure of *Dvekut* [adhesion] with the Creator, meaning on one's measure of annulment before the Creator.

In other words, self-love does not merit reference, and one wishes to annul one's self completely. This is because in one who works in order to receive, the measure of one's work is the measure of the greatness of one's self. At that time, he becomes a being, an object, and a separate authority. In that state it is difficult for him to annul before the Creator.

However, when one works in order to bestow, when he completes his work, meaning that he has corrected all his vessels of reception for himself from what he has from the root of his soul, then he has nothing more to do in the world. It follows that one should think and concentrate only on that point.

The sign by which to see if one is walking on the path of truth is if he is in the form of "descending and inciting," meaning that his entire work is in a state of descent. In that state he is in the authority of the *Sitra Achra* [other side], and then he ascends and complains, meaning feels that he is in a state of ascent and complains about others. Yet, one who works in purity, cannot complain about others and always complains about himself, and sees others in a better degree than he feels himself.

63. I Was Borrowed on, and I Repay
I heard on the eve after Shabbat, *Tav-Reish-Tzadi-Het*, 1938

Understand what our sages said, "I was borrowed on, and I repay." It means that the purpose of making the heaven and the earth is the light of *Shabbat* [Sabbath]. This light should be disclosed to the lower ones, and this purpose appears through Torah and *Mitzvot* [commandments] and good deeds.

Gmar Tikkun [end of correction] means when this light appears in full through an awakening from below, meaning preceded by Torah and *Mitzvot*. Before *Gmar Tikkun* there is also a discernment of *Shabbat*, called "A likeness of the next world," when the light of Shabbat shines in both the individual and the public as a whole.

This light of Shabbat comes by credit, meaning without preceding exertion, though afterward, one will pay off for all the credit. In other words, afterward he will give all the labor that he should have given before he was imparted the light; he will pay later.

This is the meaning of "I was borrowed on," meaning draw the light of *Shabbat* by credit, and I will pay, from the verse, "and let the hair of the woman's head go loose."* It means that the Creator will reveal this light only if Israel borrow, meaning extend. Although they are still not worthy, by credit, one can still draw.

64. From Lo Lishma, We Come to Lishma
I heard on VaYechi, Tevet 14, Tav-Shin-Het, December 27, 1947

"From *Lo Lishma* [not for Her sake] we come to *Lishma* [for Her sake]." If we pay close attention, we can say that the period of *Lo Lishma* is the more important time, since it is easier to unite the act with the Creator.

This is so because in *Lishma* one says that he did this good deed because he is serving the Creator in wholeness, and all his actions are for the sake of the Creator. It follows that he is the owner of the act.

However, when one works *Lo Lishma*, one does not do the good deed for the sake of the Creator. Thus, he cannot come to Him with a complaint that he deserves a reward. Thus, for him the Creator does not become indebted.

Hence, why did he do that good deed? Only because the Creator provided him an opportunity that this SAM would compel him and force him to do it.

For example, if people come to one's house, and he is ashamed to sit idly, he takes a book and learns Torah. Thus, for whom is he learning Torah? It is not because of the commandment of the Creator, to be pleasing in the eyes of the Creator, but for the guests who came into his domain, to be pleasing in the eyes of man. Thus, how then can one seek reward from the Creator for this Torah in which he engaged for the guests?

It follows that for him, the Creator did not become indebted, and instead, he can charge the guests, that they would pay him a reward, meaning respect him for learning Torah. However, one cannot obligate the Creator in any way.

When one performs self-examination and says that in the end I am engaging in the Torah, and he tosses off the cause, meaning the guests, and says that now he is working only for the sake of the Creator, then one should immediately say that everything is conducted from above. It means that the Creator wanted to grant him engagement in the Torah, but he is not worthy of receiving an element of truth. For this reason, the Creator gives him a false cause, and through this cause he engages in the Torah.

It follows that the Creator is the operator, and not the person. Then, moreover, he should praise the Creator that even in a state of lowliness that he is in, the Creator does not leave him and gives him strength, meaning fuel to want to engage in words of Torah.

You find that if he pays attention to this act, he notices that the Creator is the operator, as in "He alone does and will do all the deeds." Yet, one does not put any

---
* In Hebrew, the same word is used for letting loose and for paying off.

action in the good deed. Although the person does that *Mitzva* [commandment], he does not do it for a *Mitzva*, but for another cause (man), and the cause extended from the separation.

The truth is that the Creator is the cause and the reason that compels him. But the Creator is robed in him in another clothing, and not in a clothing of a *Mitzva*, but for another fear or another love. It follows that during the *Lo Lishma*, it is easier to attribute the good deed and say that the Creator is the doer of the good deed, and not man.

This is simple, since one does not want to do the thing for a *Mitzva*, but for another cause. However, in *Lishma*, one knows about oneself that he is working because of the *Mitzva*, meaning that he himself was the cause, meaning because of a *Mitzva*, and not because the Creator placed the idea and the desire to make the *Mitzva* in his heart, but he himself chose it. But the truth is that it was all done by the Creator, but private Providence cannot be attained prior to attaining the matter of reward and punishment.

65. Concerning the Revealed and the Concealed
I heard on *Tevet* 29, *Tav-Shin-Bet*, January 18, 1942, Jerusalem

It is written, "The hidden things belong to the Lord our God, and the things that are revealed belong to us and to our children forever, to do all the words of this law." We should ask, "What does the text come to tell us, that the hidden things belong to the Lord?" We should not say that concealed means unattainable and revealed means attainable. We can see that there are people with knowledge in the concealed part, as there are people who have no knowledge in the revealed part, but it cannot be said that this means that there are more people with knowledge in the revealed part than in the concealed part. (If so, you have given only a part of the whole picture.)

The thing is that in this world, we see that there are actions that are revealed as actions to our eyes. This means that man's hand is involved there, and there are actions where we see that an act is done, but man cannot do anything there. Rather, a hidden force operates there.

It is as our sages said, "There are three partners in man—the Creator, his father, and his mother." The revealed part is the commandment to be fruitful and multiply. This act is done by the parents. If the parents do their thing properly, the Creator puts a soul in the newborn. That is, his parents do the revealed part, as they can only do the revealed part, but the hidden part—placing the soul in the newborn—here the parents cannot do a thing; only the Creator Himself does that thing.

Similarly, with the *Mitzvot* [commandments], we must do only the revealed part, as only here can we act, that is, engage in Torah and *Mitzvot* by way of "doers of His word." However, the hidden part, the soul in observing Torah and *Mitzvot*, one cannot do a thing there. When we observe Torah and *Mitzvot* in action, called "doing," we should pray to the Creator that He will do the concealed part, meaning place a soul in our practice.

The practice is called "a candle of a *Mitzva*," which are only candles, which must be lit by the "and the Torah is light." The light of Torah lights the *Mitzva* and gives the soul vitality in the practice, as with the newborn, where there are three partners.

This is the meaning of "The things that are revealed belong to us," meaning that we must work in the form of "All that your hand and strength can do, do." It is only here that we can act, but obtaining the soul and vitality depends on the Creator.

This is the meaning of "The hidden things belong to the Lord our God." The Creator promises us that if we do the part that is revealed to us, acting on the conditions of the Torah and *Mitzvot* in the practical part, the Creator will put a soul in our actions. However, before we are awarded the concealed, called "a soul," our revealed part is like a body without a soul. Thus, we must be awarded the hidden part, and this is only in the hands of the Creator.

66. Concerning the Giving of the Torah - 1
I heard during a meal on the eve of *Shavuot* [Feast of Weeks], *Tav-Shin-Het*, 1948

The matter of the giving of the Torah that occurred on Mount Sinai does not mean that the Torah was given once and then the giving stopped. Rather, there is no absence in spirituality, since spirituality is an eternal matter, unending. But since, from the perspective of the Giver, we are unfit to receive the Torah, we say that the cessation is by the upper one.

However, then, at the foot of Mount Sinai, the whole of Israel were ready to receive the Torah, as it is written, "And the people camped at the bottom of the mount, as one man in one heart." At that time, the public was prepared; they had but one intention, which is a single thought about the reception of the Torah.

However, there are no changes from the perspective of the Giver—He always gives, as it is written in the name of the Baal Shem Tov that each day one must hear the ten commandments on Mount Sinai.

The Torah is called the "potion of life" and the "potion of death." We must understand how two opposites can be said about a single subject.

We must know that we cannot attain any reality as it is in itself. Rather, we attain everything only according to our sensations. And reality, as it is in itself, is of no interest to us at all. Hence, we do not attain the Torah as it is in itself; we attain only our sensations. Thus, all of our impressions follow only our sensations.

Therefore, when a person learns Torah, and the Torah removes him from the love of the Creator, this Torah is certainly considered the "potion of death." Conversely, if this Torah that he is learning brings him closer to the love of the Creator, it is certainly considered the "potion of life."

But the Torah itself, the existence of the Torah in and of itself, without consideration of the lower one who must attain it, is considered "a light without a *Kli* [vessel]," where there is no attainment whatsoever. Hence, when we speak of the Torah, it refers to the sensations that a person receives from the Torah, and only they determine the reality for the creatures.

When one works for oneself, it is called *Lo Lishma* [not for Her sake]. But from *Lo Lishma* we come to *Lishma* [for Her sake]. Hence, if one has not yet been rewarded with the reception of the Torah, he hopes to be rewarded with the reception of the Torah in the following year. But when one has been awarded the wholeness of *Lishma*, he has nothing more to do in this world, since he has already corrected everything to be in the wholeness of *Lishma*.

For this reason, each and every year there is the time of reception of the Torah, since that time is ready for an awakening from below. This is because it is the awakening of the time when the light of the giving of the Torah was revealed in the lower ones. Hence, there is an awakening from above, which gives strength to the lower ones to be able to perform the qualifying act to receive the Torah, as then, when they were ready to receive the Torah.

Therefore, if one marches on a path where the *Lo Lishma* brings him the *Lishma*, then he is marching on the path of truth. One should hope that he will eventually be rewarded with achieving *Lishma* and with the reception of the Torah.

Yet, caution is required to constantly keep the goal before his eyes or he will march on an opposite line, since the root of the body is reception for itself. Thus, it always draws to its root, which is the aim to receive, the opposite of the Torah, called "the tree of life." This is why the body considers the Torah the "potion of death."

67. Depart from Evil

I heard after the holiday of *Sukkot* [the Tabernacles Feast], *Tav-Shin-Gimel*, October 5, 1942, Jerusalem

We must take caution with "depart from evil" to keep the four covenants.

1. The covenant of the eyes, which is caution from looking at women. And the prohibition on looking is not necessarily because it might lead to a thought. The evidence of this is that the prohibition applies also to a hundred-year old man. Rather, the real reason is that it extends from a very high root: This caution is because if one is not careful, he might come to look at the *Shechina* [Divinity].

2. The covenant of the tongue—to be vigilant with truth and falsehood. The scrutinies that exist now, after the sin of *Adam HaRishon*, are scrutinies

of true and false. However, prior to the sin of the tree of knowledge, the scrutinies were about bitter and sweet. Yet, when the scrutiny is about truth and falsehood, it is completely different. At times, it begins sweet and ends bitter, which means that there is a reality of bitter which is nonetheless true.

For this reason, we must be careful with changing our words. Although one thinks that one is only lying to one's friend, we should know that the body is like a machine: As it is accustomed to walk, so it continues to walk. Therefore, when it is accustomed to falsehood and deceit, it is impossible for it to walk by another way, and this forces man to proceed with falsehood and deceit when one is alone, too.

It turns out that one must deceive himself and cannot tell himself the truth at all, since he does not find any special preference to the truth.

We might say that he who thinks that he is deceiving his friend is really deceiving the Creator, since besides man's body there is only the Creator. This is because it is the essence of creation that man is called "creature" only with respect to himself. The Creator wants man to feel that he is a separate reality from Him; but other than this, it is all "The whole earth is full of His glory."

Hence, when lying to one's friend, one is lying to the Creator; and when saddening one's friend, one is saddening the Creator. For this reason, if one is accustomed to say the truth, it will help him with respect to the Creator. That is, if he promised something to the Creator, he will try to keep his promise, since he is not used to changing his word, and by this he will be rewarded with "The Lord is your shade." If one keeps and does what he says, the Creator, too, will keep "Blessed is he who says and does" in return.

There is a sign in the covenant of the tongue, not to say all that can be said, since by speaking, one reveals what is in one's heart, and this gives a hold to the external ones since as long as one is not perfectly clean, when he reveals something of his interior, the *Sitra Achra* [other side] has power to slander above and mock his work. She says, "What kind of work is he giving upward, since his whole intention in this work is only downward?"

This answers a great question: It is known that "a *Mitzva* induces a *Mitzva*," so why do we often see that one falls from one's work? As we have said above, the *Sitra Achra* defames and slanders his work, and then descends and takes his soul. That is, since she has already defamed above and said that his work was not clean, but that he works in the form of reception for oneself, she descends and takes his spirit of life by asking, "What is this work?" Hence, even when one is awarded some illumination of the spirit of life, he loses it again.

The advice for this is to walk humbly, so she does not know about his work, by way of "He does not reveal from the heart to the mouth." Then the *Sitra Achra*, too, cannot know of one's work, as she only knows what is revealed by word or action; this is what she can grip.

We should know that pain and suffering comes primarily through those who slander. Hence, we should be as careful as we can with speaking. Moreover, we should know that even when speaking mundane words, it still reveals the secrets of one's heart. This is the meaning of "My soul went out when he spoke." This is the covenant of the tongue with which we must take caution.

And the keeping should be especially during the ascent, since during the descent it is hard to walk in great degrees and cautions.

68. Man's Connection to the Sefirot
I heard on *Adar 12, Tav-Shin-Gimel*, February 17, 1943

Prior to the sin of *Adam HaRishon*:

1. His *Guf* [body] was from *Bina de Malchut de Malchut de Assiya*,

2. And he had NRN from *Beria* and NRN from *Atzilut*.

After he sinned, his *Guf* fell into the discernment of the serpent's skin, which is the *Klipa* [shell] of *Behina Dalet*, called "the dust of this world." Clothed within it is the inner *Guf* of *Klipat* [*Klipa* (shell) of] *Noga*, which is half good and half bad. And all the good deeds that he does are only with his *Guf* of *Noga*. Through engaging in Torah and *Mitzvot*, he brings this *Guf* back to being all good, and the *Guf* of the serpent's skin departs from him. At that time, he is awarded NRN of *Kedusha* according to his actions.

Man's NRN connection to the *Sefirot*:

The essence of man's NRN is from *Behinat Malchut* of the three *Sefirot*, *Bina* and ZON in each of the worlds from ABYA. If he is awarded the NRN of *Nefesh*, he receives from the three *Behinot Malchut de Bina* and ZON *de Assiya*. If he is awarded NRN *de Ruach*, he receives from the three *Behinot Malchut de Bina* and ZON *de Yetzira*. And if he is awarded NRN *de Neshama*, he receives from the three *Behinot Malchut de Bina* and ZON *de Beria*. And if he is awarded NRN *de Haya*, he receives from the three *Behinot Malchut de Bina* and ZON *de Atzilut*.

And this is what our sages said, that man thinks only from within the thoughts of his heart, that the whole body is regarded as the "heart." Even though man consists of four *Behinot* of still, vegetative, animate, and speaking, they are all registered in the heart.

Since after the sin, the *Guf* of *Adam HaRishon* fell into the serpent's skin, which is the *Klipa* of *Behina Dalet*, called "the dust of this world"; hence, when he calculates, all his thoughts are of his heart, meaning his *Guf* from the *Behina* of the serpent's skin.

When he grows stronger, through his engagement in Torah and *Mitzvot*, which is the only remedy, if he aims to bestow contentment upon his Maker, the Torah and *Mitzvot* cleanse his body. This means that the serpent's skin departs from him. Then, the previous act of the Torah and *Mitzvot*, called "*Klipat* Noga," considered the "inner *Guf*," which was half good and half bad, has now become all good. This means that now he has achieved equivalence of form.

And then he is awarded the *NRN* of *Kedusha* according to his actions. That is, in the beginning he attains *NRN de Nefesh* from the world *Assiya*. Then, when he sorts all the *Behinot* that belong to the world *Assiya*, he is awarded *NRN de Ruach* of the world *Yetzira*, until he achieves *NRN de Haya de Atzilut*.

Thus, a different structure is made within his heart each time: Where there was previously the inner *Guf* from *Klipat* Noga, which was half good and half bad, this *Guf* is now turned into all good through the cleansing he has received from the Torah and *Mitzvot*.

Accordingly, when he had a *Guf* from the serpent's skin, he had to think and calculate his thoughts only from within the thoughts in his heart. This means that all his thoughts were only about how to satisfy the desires to which the *Klipa* compels him. He had no way to think thoughts and aim intentions, but only what settled in his heart, which was then in the form of the serpent's skin, the worst *Klipa*.

Also, when he is rewarded through his engagement in Torah and *Mitzvot*, even *Lo Lishma* [not for Her sake], when he asks and demands of the Creator to help him by engaging in Torah and *Mitzvot* in the form of "All that your hand and strength can do, do," and he awaits mercy from above, that the Creator will help him achieve *Lishma* [for Her sake] by this, where all the reward he is asking for his work is to be rewarded with working in order to bring contentment to his Maker, as our sages said, "the light in it reforms him."

In that state, the body of the serpent's skin is purified, meaning that that body is separated from him and he is awarded a completely different structure—the structure of *Nefesh de Assiya*. He also adds further until he achieves a structure from *Nefesh* and *Ruach de Bina* and *ZA* and *Malchut de Atzilut*.

But even then he has no option to think other thoughts, but only according to what the structure of *Kedusha* [holiness] dictates. This means that he has no room to think thoughts against his own structure, but he must think and act only with the intention to bring contentment to his Maker, as his structure of *Kedusha* necessitates.

All the above means that one cannot correct one's thought, but should only aim the heart—make one's heart straight to the Creator. Then all of his thoughts and actions will naturally be to bestow contentment upon his Maker. When he corrects his heart to be a heart and desire of *Kedusha*, the heart will then be the *Kli* in which to place the upper light. And when the upper light shines in the heart, the heart will grow stronger and he will add and supplement continuously.

Now we can interpret our sages' words, "Great is the learning that yields action." It means that through the light of the Torah he is led into action, as the light in it reforms him. This is called "an act." This means that the light of the Torah builds a new structure in his heart.

Thus, the previous *Guf*, which came to him from the serpent's skin, has been separated from him and he has been awarded a holy *Guf*. The inner *Guf*, called "*Klipat* Noga," which was half good, half bad, has become all good, and now the *NRN* is in it, which he attains through his actions, as he adds and supplements.

Before he is awarded a new structure, although he tries to cleanse his heart, the heart is still unchanged. In that state, it is considered that he is in the form of "doers of His word." Yet, we must know that the beginning of the work is specifically in the form of "doers of His word."

However, this is not completeness since he cannot cleanse his thoughts in that state, since he cannot be saved from thoughts of transgression, as his heart is of a *Guf* of *Klipa*, and one thinks only from the thoughts in his heart, and only the light in it reforms him. At this time, the separating *Guf* departs from him, and the inner *Guf*, the *Klipat* Noga, which was half bad, becomes all good. In that state, the Torah brings him into action through the making of a new structure. And this is called "an act."

69. First Will Be the Correction of the World
I heard on *Sivan*, *Tav-Shin-Gimel*, June 1943

He said that first will be the correction of the world, then there will be the complete redemption, the coming of the Messiah. This is the meaning of "And your eyes shall see your Teacher," etc., "And the whole earth shall be full of knowledge." This is the meaning of what he wrote, that first the interior of the worlds will be corrected, and subsequently the exterior of the worlds. But we must know that the correction of the externality of the worlds is a higher degree than the correction of the internality.

And the root of Israel is from the internality of the worlds. This is the meaning of "for you are the least of all the peoples." However, by correcting the internality, the externality will be corrected, too, though in small pieces. And the externality will be corrected each time (until many pennies accumulate into a great sum), until all the externality is corrected.

The main difference between the internality and the externality is, for example, when one performs a certain *Mitzva* [commandment], not all the organs agree to it. It is like a person who fasts. We say that only his internality agreed with the fast, but his externality is feeling discomfort by the fast, since the body is always in opposition to the soul. Thus, the difference between Israel and the nations of the world should only be made concerning the soul; but concerning the body, they are the same, for the body Israel, too, cares only for its own benefit.

Hence, when individuals in the whole of Israel are corrected, the whole world will naturally be corrected. It follows that the nations of the world will be corrected to the extent that we correct ourselves. This is the meaning of what our sages said, "Rewarded—he sentences himself and the whole world to the side of merit." They did not say, "he sentences the whole of Israel," but "the entire world to the side of merit," meaning that the internality will correct the externality.

70. With a Mighty Hand and with Fury Poured Out
I heard on Sivan 25, Tav-Shin-Gimel, June 28, 1943

To understand what is written, "with a mighty hand ...and with fury poured out, will I be king over you," we should understand that there is a rule that there is no coercion in spirituality, as it is written, "You did not call Me, Jacob, for you labored about Me, Israel," and there is the known interpretation by the Sayer of Dubna. Hence, what does "with a mighty hand ...and with fury poured out, will I be King over you" mean?

He said that we should know that of those who want to come into the work of the Creator in order to truly adhere to Him and enter the King's palace, not everyone is admitted. Rather, he is tested: If he has no other desires but only a desire for *Dvekut* [adhesion], he is admitted.

And how is one tested if he has only one desire? He is given disturbances. This means that he is sent foreign thoughts and foreign messengers to obstruct him so he would leave this path and follow the path of all the people.

If one overcomes all the difficulties and breaks all the bars that block him, and little things cannot push him away, the Creator sends him great *Klipot* [shells/peels] and chariots to deflect one from entering into *Dvekut* with the Creator alone, and with nothing else. This is considered that the Creator is rejecting him with a mighty hand.

If the Creator does not show a mighty hand, it will be hard to push him away since he has a strong desire to adhere only to the Creator and to nothing else.

But when the Creator wants to reject one whose desire is not so strong, He pushes him away with a small thing. By giving him a great desire for corporeality, he already leaves the holy work entirely, and there is no need to repel him with a mighty hand.

Yet, when one overcomes all the hardships and the disturbances, one is not easily repelled, but with a mighty hand. And if one overcomes even the mighty hand and does not want to move from the place of *Kedusha* [holiness] whatsoever, but wants to adhere specifically to Him in truth, and sees that he is repelled, then one says that fury is poured out on him. Otherwise, he would be allowed inside. But because fury is poured out on him by the Creator, he is not admitted into the King's palace to adhere to Him.

It follows that before one wants to move from one's place, and breaks in and wants to enter, it cannot be said that he feels that fury is poured out on him. Rather, after all the rejections that he is rejected, and he does not move from his place, meaning when the mighty hand and the fury poured out have already been revealed upon him, then "I will be King over you" comes true. This is so because only through bursting and great efforts does the kingdom of heaven become revealed to him, and he is rewarded with entering the King's palace.

71. My Soul Shall Weep in Secret - 2
I heard on Sivan 25, June 28, Tav-Shin-Gimel, 1943

"My soul shall weep in secret because of pride," because of the pride of Israel. He asks, "Is there crying before the Creator? After all, 'strength and gladness are in His place!'" We must understand the matter of crying above. Crying is in a place where one cannot help oneself. Then one cries that the other will help him. The meaning of "in secret" is the concealments and contradictions that appear in the world.

This is the meaning of "My soul shall weep in secret," since "all is in the hands of heaven, but for the fear of heaven."

Our sages said about this that there is crying in the inner homes. This means that when the light shines only in the interior and there is no outward disclosure of light, for lack of *Kelim* [vessels] in the lower ones so they can receive, then there is weeping. However, in the outer homes, when the light can be revealed outward, when the abundance becomes revealed below, to the lower ones, then "strength and gladness are in His place," and everything is seen. Yet, when He cannot bestow upon the lower ones, it is called "weeping," since He needs the *Kelim* of the lower ones.

72. Confidence Is the Clothing for the Light
I heard on Nisan 10, Tav-Shin-Zayin, March 31, 1947

Confidence is the clothing for the light, called "life." There is a rule that there is no light without a *Kli* [vessel]. It follows that the light, called "light of life," cannot clothe but must dress in some *Kli*. The *Kli* where the light of life is clothed is usually called "confidence." It means that he sees that he can do every difficult thing.

Thus, the light is felt and recognized in the *Kli* of confidence. Because of this, one's life is measured by the measure of confidence that appears there. One can measure the magnitude of vitality in oneself according to the confidence in himself.

For this reason, one can see in oneself that as long as his level of vitality is high, the confidence shines on every single thing, and he sees nothing that can obstruct him with what he wants. This is because the light of life, which is a force from above, shines for him and he can work with superhuman powers since the upper light is not limited like corporeal forces.

However, when the light of life departs from him, which is considered that he has descended from his previous level of vitality, then he becomes clever and inquisitive. He begins to calculate the profitability of everything, is it worthwhile to do it or not. He becomes temperate and not lively and sizzling as before he began to decline in his level of vitality.

However, one does not have the wisdom to say that all this cleverness and wit, that now he has been rewarded with thinking about everything, are because he'd lost the spirit of life he had then. Instead, he thinks that now he has become smart, not as before he'd lost the light of life. Rather, then he was reckless and careless.

However, he should know that all the wisdom he has now acquired came to him because he has lost the spirit of life that he had had before. Before, he measured all the acts with the light of life that the Creator gave him. But now that he is in decline, the evil inclination has the power to come to him with all their "just arguments."

The advice for this is that one should say that now he cannot speak to his body and argue with it. Rather, he should say, "Now I am dead and I am awaiting the revival of the dead." Then he must begin to work above reason, meaning say to his body, "Everything you say is true, and I have nothing rational to answer you. However, I hope that I will begin to work anew. Now I am taking upon myself Torah and *Mitzvot* [commandments], and now I am becoming a proselyte, and our sages said, 'a proselyte who has converted is like a newborn baby.' Now I await the salvation of the Creator; He will certainly help me and I will come once more into the path of holiness. When I have power in holiness, I will have what to answer you. But in the meantime, I must go above reason for I am still without the mind of holiness. Hence, you can win with your intellect, and there is nothing I can do but believe in our sages who said that I should keep Torah and *Mitzvot* with faith above reason. I must certainly believe that by the power of faith we will be helped from above, as our sages said, 'He who comes to purify is aided.'"

73. After the *Tzimtzum*

I heard in *Tav-Shin-Gimel*, 1942-1943

After the *Tzimtzum* [restriction], the first nine became the place of *Kedusha* [holiness]. And *Malchut*, over which there was the *Tzimtzum*, became the place of the worlds. There are two discernments to be made: 1) a hollow place, which is a place for the *Klipot* [shells/peels], whose essence is the desire to receive only for themselves, and 2) a vacant place, meaning a place that became vacant for inserting what one chooses—*Kedusha* or the opposite.

Had it not been for the *Tzimtzum*, the whole of reality would have been in the form of simple light. Only after the *Tzimtzum* was there room for choosing to do bad or do good.

The abundance extends into that place through choosing the good. This is the meaning of what is written in the writings of the ARI, that the light of *Ein Sof* [infinity] shines to the lower ones.

Ein Sof is called "the desire to do good to His creations." Although we discern many worlds, ten *Sefirot*, and other names, it all extends from *Ein Sof*, called "the thought of creation."

The names, *Sefira* [sing. of *Sefirot*] and "world," are because the abundance that pours out from *Ein Sof* descends through that *Sefira* and world. This means that since the lower ones cannot receive His bounty without preparation and correction, for the lower one to be able to receive, corrections were made by which there is ability to receive. This is called *Sefirot*.

In other words, each *Sefira* has its unique correction. Because of this there are many discernments. But they are only with respect to the receivers, since when the lower one receives the abundance from *Ein Sof*, he receives through a special correction which adapts it to receive the abundance. This is the meaning of receiving through a special *Sefira* although there are no changes whatsoever in the abundance itself.

Now you will understand the matter of the prayer that we pray to the Creator, which is the light of *Ein Sof*, being the connection that the Creator has with the creatures, called "His desire to do good to His creations." Even though there are many names with the aim of the prayer, the interpretation is that the abundance will pour out through the corrections in the names since precisely through the corrections in the names will the abundance be in the hands of the receivers.

74. World, Year, Soul

I heard in *Tav-Shin-Gimel*, 1942-1943

It is known that there is no reality without someone who senses the reality. Hence, when we say *Nefesh de Atzilut*, it means that we are sensing a certain measure of attainment in the upper abundance, and we call this measure *Nefesh*.

And "world" refers to the collective within that attainment, meaning that all the souls have the same form so anyone who attains that degree attains that name, *Nefesh*. This means that it is not necessarily that a specific individual attains that name and in that form, but that anyone who achieves that degree—which is certainly through the preparation of *Kedusha* [holiness] and purity—the abundance appears to him in that form called *Nefesh*.

We can understand that from a corporeal example applied in this world. For example, when one person says to another "Now I am going to Jerusalem," when he says the name of the city, everyone knows and recognizes that city. They are all certain of the place he is speaking of, since those who have been to that city know what this is about.

75. There Is a Discernment of the Next World, and There Is a Discernment of This World

I heard during a meal celebrating a Brit [circumcision], Jerusalem

There is a discernment of "the next world," and there is a discernment of "this world." The next world is called "faith," and this world is called "attainment."

It is written about the next world, "They shall be satiated and delighted," meaning that there is no end to the satiation. This is so because everything that is received by faith has no limits. Conversely, what is received through attainment already has limits since anything that comes in the *Kelim* [vessels] of the lower one, the lower one limits it. Hence, there is a limit to the discernment of this world.

76. On All Your Offerings You Shall Offer Salt

I heard on Shevat 30, January-February, celebrating the completion of Part Six, Tiberias

"On all your offerings you shall offer salt," meaning the covenant of the salt. A covenant is against reason. Normally, when two people do good to one another, when there is love between them, they certainly do not need to make a covenant. But at the same time, we can see that precisely when there is love, this is the usual time for making covenants. Then he said that the making of the covenant is for later.

This means that the agreement is made now so that later, if there comes a state where each of them thinks that the other's heart is not whole with one's friend, they will have an agreement. This agreement will obligate them to remember the covenant that they had made between them, in order to continue the old love in this state, too.

This is the meaning of "On all your offerings you shall offer salt," meaning that all of the *Krevut** in the work of the Creator should be about the covenant of the King.**

---

* In Hebrew *Krevut* means "nearing" but also "battles."
** In Hebrew, the words *Melach* (salt) and *Melech* are spelt the same and pronounced very similarly.

77. One's Soul Shall Teach Him

I heard on *Elul 8, Tav-Shin-Zayin*, August 24, 1947

"One's soul shall teach him."

It is known that the whole Torah is learned primarily for the needs of the soul, for those who have already been rewarded with a discernment of a soul. Nevertheless, they must crave and search words of Torah of others who attained, to learn new ways from them, which the previous ones invented in their innovations in the Torah. By this it will be easy for them to advance in the high degrees, meaning that through them they will advance from degree to degree.

But there is a Torah that is forbidden to disclose, since each soul should make that scrutiny by itself, and not that someone will make that scrutiny for him. Hence, before they make the scrutiny themselves, it is forbidden to disclose to them the words of Torah.

This is why the great ones hide many things. And except for this part, there is great benefit to the souls by what they receive from innovations of the Torah of others. And "One's soul shall teach him" how and what to receive and to be assisted by the innovations in the Torah of others, and what he himself must innovate.

78. The Torah, the Creator, and Israel Are One

I heard on *Sivan, Tav-Shin-Gimel*, June 1943

"The Torah, the Creator, and Israel are one."

Hence, when one learns Torah, he should learn *Lishma* [for Her sake]. This means that he is learning with the intention that the Torah will teach him, as is the name of the Torah, which means "instruction." Because "The Torah, Israel, and the Creator are one," the Torah teaches one the ways of the Creator, how He is clothed in the Torah.

79. Atzilut and BYA

I heard on *Tammuz 15, Pinhas 1, Tav-Shin-Gimel*, July 18, 1943

Atzilut is considered from the *Chazeh* and above, which is only vessels of bestowal. *BYA* means reception in order to bestow, the ascent of the lower *Hey* to the place of *Bina*.

Because man is immersed in the will to receive in order to receive, he cannot do a thing without having reception for oneself there. This is why our sages said, "From *Lo Lishma* [not for Her sake], we come to *Lishma* [for Her sake]." This means that we begin the engagement in Torah and *Mitzvot* [commandments] in order to "Give us the wealth of this world," and afterward, "Give us the wealth of the next world."

When learning in this way, one should come to learn *Lishma*, for the sake of the Torah, meaning that the Torah will teach him the ways of the Creator. And then he should first make the sweetening of *Malchut* in *Bina*, which means that he elevates *Malchut*, called "will to receive," to *Bina*, which is considered bestowal. That is, that all his work will be only in order to bestow.

And then it becomes dark for him. He feels that the world has grown dark on him since the body gives strength to work only in the form of reception, and not in the form of bestowal. In that state, he has but one choice: to pray to the Creator to open his eyes so he can work in the manner of bestowal.

This is the meaning of "Who stands for the question?" It refers to *Bina*, called *Mi* [water] and the question comes from the verse, "asking about the rains," meaning prayer. Since they arrive to the state of "water of *Bina*," there is room to pray for it.

80. Concerning Achor be Achor

I heard

Panim and *Achor* [face and back].

Panim [face/anterior] means reception of abundance or bestowal of abundance.

Negation is called *Achoraim* [back/posterior], meaning neither receiving nor giving.

Hence, in the beginning of the work, one is in a state of *Achor be Achor* [back to back] because he still has the *Kelim* [vessels] of the will to receive. If he extends abundance into these *Kelim*, he could blemish the light, since he is considered opposite in value, since the lights come from the Root, and the Root only bestows.

For this reason, the lower ones use the *Kelim* of *Ima*, called *Achoraim*, meaning that they do not want to receive, so as not to blemish. And the Emanator, too, does not bestow upon them for the above reason, for the lights guard themselves so the lower ones do not blemish them. This is why it is called *Achor be Achor*.

To explain what is written in several places, that "Wherever there is a deficiency, the *Klipa* suckles," we might say that the reason is that this place is still not free from *Aviut* [thickness]. Otherwise, the light would have illuminated in full since the upper light never stops. If there is a place that is corrected with a *Masach* [screen], the upper light immediately grips there. And since there is a place of deficiency, meaning absence of the upper light, there is certainly a discernment of *Aviut*, whose entire grip is in the will to receive.

81. Concerning Raising MAN

I heard

It is known that because of the breaking, sparks of *Kedusha* [holiness] fell into BYA. But there, in BYA, they cannot be corrected. Therefore, they must be raised to *Atzilut*. By doing *Mitzvot* [commandments] and good deeds with the aim to bring contentment to his Maker and not to himself, these sparks rise to *Atzilut*. Then they are included in the *Masach* [screen] of the upper one, at the *Rosh* [head/top] of the degree, where the *Masach* remains in its eternity. At that time, there is a *Zivug* [coupling] on the *Masach* by the *Hitkalelut* [mixture/integration] of the sparks, and the upper light spreads through all the worlds according to the measure of the sparks that they have raised.

This is similar to the *Hizdakchut* [thinning/waning] of the *Partzufim* of *Akudim*. We learned that during its *Hizdakchut*, when the light departs because of it, the *Masach* of the *Guf* [body] ascends along with the *Reshimot* to *Peh de Rosh*. The reason is that when the lower one stops receiving, it is considered that it has been cleansed of its *Aviut* [thickness]. Hence, the *Masach* can rise back to *Peh de Rosh*, as its decline into the degree of *Guf* was only because the light expanded from above downward into the vessels of reception.

Also, the *Rosh* is always discerned as being from below upward, meaning resisting the expansion. When the *Guf* stops receiving the lights from above downward, because of the absence of the *Masach* that had been purified by the *Bitush* [beating] of the internal and the external, it is considered that the *Masach de Guf* has been cleansed of its *Aviut* and ascended to the *Rosh* with the *Reshimot*.

Additionally, when one engages in Torah and *Mitzvot* in order to bestow and not to receive, through it, the sparks rise to the *Masach* in the *Rosh*, in the world of *Atzilut* (and they rise degree by degree until they arrive at the *Rosh de Atzilut*). When they are included in that *Masach* and the level of light appears according to the size of the *Masach*, more light is added in all the worlds. And man, too, who caused that improvement above, receives illumination by having improved above, in the worlds.

82. The Prayer that One Should Always Pray
What I heard in private on *VaYera*, *Tav-Shin-Yod-Gimel*, November 1952

Faith is discerned as *Malchut*, interpreted in the mind and in the heart, that is, bestowal and faith. Opposite faith there is the discernment of the "foreskin," which is knowing, whose way is to appreciate the discernment of the foreskin. Faith, however, called "the *Shechina* [Divinity]," is in the dust. This means that this work is considered disgraceful, and everyone escapes from walking on this path. But only this is called "the path of the righteous and *Kedusha* [holiness]."

The Creator wants His names to be revealed only in this manner, as in this manner it is certain that they will not blemish the upper lights, since the whole basis is bestowal and *Dvekut* [adhesion]. Also, the *Klipot* [shells/peels] cannot suckle from this quality since they nurse only on knowing and receiving.

Where the foreskin rules, the *Shechina* cannot receive the upper lights into it, so the lights do not fall into the *Klipot*. Because of this there is the sorrow of the

Shechina, meaning that the upper lights are detained from being drawn into it, so she can bestow upon the souls.

And this depends only on the lower ones. The upper one can only impart the upper light, but the force of the *Masach*, so the lower one does not want to receive anything in the vessels of reception, depends on the works of the lower ones; that is, the lower ones must make that scrutiny.

83. Concerning the Right Vav and the Left Vav
I heard on *Adar* 19, *Tav-Shin-Gimel*, February 24, 1943

There is the discernment of *Ze* ["this" in male form], and there is the discernment of *Zot* ["this" in female form]. Moses is regarded as *Ze*, which is the King's best man. The rest of the prophets are regarded as *Zot* or *Koh* [the letters *Chaf* and *Hey*], which is the meaning of *Yadecha* [your hand], a left *Vav*. Then there is the discernment of the right *Vav*.

And this is the meaning of "the gathering *Zayins*," which gather two *Vavs*. This is the meaning of "and one that contains them," which is the thirteen, regarded as a complete degree.

There is a right *Vav*, and there is a left *Vav*. The right *Vav* is called "the tree of life," and the left *Vav* is called "the tree of knowledge," where there is the place of the guarding. The two *Vavs* are called "twelve *Challahs*,"* two rows, six in a row, which is the meaning of the thirteen *Tikkunim* [corrections], which are twelve, and one that contains them, called *Mazal ve Nakeh* [luck and cleansed].

It also contains the thirteenth correction, called "shall not be cleansed," which is the meaning of the gathering *Zayins*. The *Zayin* is *Malchut*; she contains them. Before one is rewarded with "shall not return to folly," she is called "shall not be cleansed." And those who have already been rewarded with not returning to folly are called "cleansed."

This is the meaning of "will reveal its flavors in twelve roars, which are a sign in his sky, twice and weak" (in the song, "I will Prepare for a Meal"). It is also written, "she will be crowned with *Vavs* and gathering *Zayins*" (in the song, "I will Praise with a Song"). We should interpret the crowning with the *Vavs*, that the connection through two *Vavs* is the twelve roars (which are the twelve *Challahs*) that are a sign in the sky.

A sign is called *Yesod*, and it is called "twice and weak." This means that the *Vavs* have been doubled: The left *Vav* is called "the tree of knowledge," the place of the guarding. Then they became weak (called "light"), and then a room was made through which it was easy to pass. Had it not been for the doubling with the tree of knowledge, they would have had to work with the right *Vav*, discerned as "the tree of life." And then, who could elevate himself and receive the *Mochin*?

---
* Braided bread (traditionally served during the Sabbath)

However, with the left *Vav*, discerned as the keeping, one is always in this form. And by merit of the keeping, when he takes upon himself the above reason, his work is then desirable. This is why it is called "weak," light, meaning it is easy to find a place for work.

This means that in any state one is in, he can be a servant of the Creator since he does not need anything, but does everything above reason. It turns out that one does not need any *Mochin* with which to be the servant of the Creator.

Now we can interpret what is written, "Set up a table before me, against my enemies." A table means, as it is written, "and sent her out of his house, and she departed his house, and went" (Deuteronomy 24:1-2). A *Shulchan* [table] is like *VeShlacha* [and sent her], meaning exit from the work.

We should interpret that even during the exits from the work, meaning in a state of decline, one still has a place to work. This means that when one prevails above reason during the declines, and says that the descents, too, were given to him from above, by this the enemies are canceled. This is so because the enemies thought that through the declines the person will reach utter lowliness and escape the campaign, but in the end the opposite occurred—the enemies were canceled.

This is the meaning of what is written, "the table that is before the Lord," that precisely in this manner does he receive the face of the Creator. This is the meaning of subduing all the judgments, even the harshest judgments, since he assumes the burden of the kingdom of heaven at all times. That is, he always finds a place for work, as it is written that Rabbi Shimon Bar-Yochai said, "There is no place to hide from You."

84. What Is "He Drove the Man Out of the Garden of Eden so He Would Not Take from the Tree of Life"?

I heard on *Adar* 24, *Tav-Shin-Dalet*, March 19, 1944

It is written, "And He said to him, 'Where are you?' And he said, 'I heard Your voice,'" etc., "'and I was afraid because I was naked, and I hid.' And the Lord said ... lest he stretched out his hand and take also from the tree of life," etc. "So He drove out the man."

We should understand Adam's fear, which was so much that he had to hide because he saw himself naked. The thing is that before he ate from the tree of knowledge, his nourishment was from *Bina*, which is the world of freedom. Afterward, when he ate from the tree of knowledge, he saw that he was naked. This means that he was afraid that he would take the light of Torah and use it in the form of "the herdsmen of Lot's cattle."

"The herdsmen of Lot's cattle" means that there is faith above reason, called "the herdsmen of Abraham's cattle." In other words, one who has been rewarded with attainment of the light of Torah does not take it as the basis of one's work, saying that now he no longer needs strengthening in faith in the Creator, since he already has the foundation of the light of the Torah. This is called "the herdsmen of Lot's cattle," considered "the cursed world," which is considered a curse. This is the opposite of faith, which is a blessing.

Rather, he said, he says that now he sees that if he goes with faith above reason, he will be given from above the light of the Torah, to show him that he is marching on the path of truth. And it is not that he takes it as support, that his work will be within reason, from which one comes into the vessels of reception, on which there was the *Tzimtzum* [restriction]. This is why it is called "the place of the curse," since Lot means the cursed world.

And in that regard, the Creator told him, "Why are you afraid to take these lights for fear that you will blemish them? Who told you that you were naked? It must be because you have eaten from the tree of knowledge, and this brought you the fear. Previously, when you were eating from every tree in the garden, meaning when you were using the lights by way of 'the herdsmen of Abraham's cattle,' you had no fear at all." Hence, he drove him out, "lest he stretched out his hand and ate from the tree of life."

The fear was that he would repent and enter the tree of life. But what is the fear? Since he had sinned in the tree of knowledge, now he must correct the tree of knowledge.

This is the meaning of "He drove him out of the garden of Eden," to correct the sin of the tree of knowledge. And afterward, he will be able to enter the garden of Eden.

The garden of Eden means the ascent of *Malchut* into *Bina* where she receives *Hochma*, as Eden means *Hochma*. And then *Malchut*, called "garden," receives *Hochma* in the form of "Eden," and this is "the garden of Eden."

85. What Is the Fruit of a Citrus Tree, in the Work?

I heard on *Sukkot* Inter 1, *Tav-Shin-Gimel*, September 27, 1942

It is written, "And you shall take you on the first day the fruit of a citrus tree, branches of palm-trees, and boughs of thick trees, and willows of the brook" (Leviticus 23:40).

And we should interpret "fruit of a citrus tree": A tree is considered righteous, called a "tree of the field." The "fruit" is the progeny of the tree, meaning the progeny of the righteous, which are the good deeds, which should be in the form of adornment in his tree.

"From year to year" means a whole year, which are "six months with oil of myrrh, and six months with sweet odors." The wicked, however, are "like the chaff which the wind drives away."

"Branches of palm-trees" are two pans, which are the two *Heys*, the first *Hey* and the last *Hey*, by which one is rewarded with "one golden pan of ten shekels, full of incense."

Kapot [pans] mean *Kefia* [coercion], when one assumes the kingdom of heaven coercively. This means that even when reason disagrees, he goes above reason. This is called "coercive mating." *Tmarim* [palm trees] comes from the word *Morah* [fear], which is fear (by way of "and God has made it that He will be feared").

Because of this, it is called *Lulav* [palm branch]. This means that before one is rewarded, he has two hearts. And this is called *Lo Lev* [no heart], meaning that the heart is not devoted solely to the Creator. When he is rewarded with the *Lo* ["no" or "to Him"], meaning a heart that is for the Creator, this is the *Lulav*.

Also, one should say, "When will my deeds come to be as the deeds of my fathers?" Through it, one is rewarded with being a branch of the holy fathers, and this is the meaning of "boughs of thick trees," which are the three myrtles.

Yet, at the same time, one should be in the form of "willows of the brook," tasteless and scentless. And one should delight in this work, even though he feels no flavor or fragrance in this work. And then this work is called "the letters of Your unified name," by which we are rewarded with complete unification with the Creator.

86. And They Built Arei Miskenot
I heard from my father, Shevat 3, Tav-Shin-Aleph, January 31, 1941

The writing says (Exodus 1): "And they built for Pharaoh *Arei Miskenot*,* Pithom and Raamses." We should ask, "Pithom and Raamses means that they are beautiful cities, while the words *Arei Miskenot* imply poverty and meagerness [see footnote], and they also imply danger!" And we must also understand what Abraham the Patriarch asked, "And he said ... 'How will I know that I will inherit it?'" (Genesis 15:8). What did the Creator reply? It is written, "And He said unto Abram: Know for certain that your seed shall be a stranger in a land that is not theirs, and shall serve them, and they shall afflict them four hundred years."

The literal meaning is hard to understand, since the question was that he wanted guarantees on the inheritance, and there is no apparent guarantee in the Creator's answer, that your seed will be in exile, but it seems that this was a sufficient answer for him. Moreover, we see that when Abraham had an argument with the Creator regarding the people of Sodom, he had a long argument with the Creator, and he kept saying "perhaps." Here, however, when the Creator said that his seed would be in exile, he immediately accepted it as a sufficient answer and did not argue or say, "perhaps?" Instead, he accepted it as a guarantee for the inheritance of the land.

We must understand this answer, and we must also understand what *The Zohar* interprets about the verse "Pharaoh brought near." It interprets that he drew them

---
* *Arei Miskenot* means store-cities, but also "cities of affliction" and "cities of poverty."

toward repentance. Can it be that wicked Pharaoh would want to draw them toward repentance?

In order to understand all that, we must understand what our sages said (*Sukkah* 52a): "Rabbi Yehuda says, 'At the end of days, the Creator brings the evil inclination and slaughters it before the righteous and before the wicked. To the righteous, it seems like a high mountain. To the wicked, it seems as a thread of a hairsbreadth. These cry and those cry. The righteous cry and say 'How could we conquer such a high mountain?' and the wicked cry and say 'How could we not conquer this hairsbreadth?'"

This verse is perplexing through and through:

1. If the evil inclination has already been slaughtered, how are there still wicked?
2. Why do the righteous cry? Quite the contrary, they should have been happy!
3. How can there be two opinions in reality when they have both arrived at the state of truth? This verse speaks of the end of days, which is certainly a state of truth, so how can there be such a difference in reality between a hairsbreadth and a high mountain?

He explains this with the words of our sages (there): "Rabbi Assi says, 'In the beginning, the evil inclination seems like a spiderweb, and in the end, it seems like cart-ropes,' as was said, 'Woe unto them who draw iniquity with cords of vanity, and sin as though with a cart rope'" (Isaiah 5).

There is a great rule we must know. Our work, which was given to us to be based on faith above reason, is not because we are unworthy of a high degree. Hence, this was given to us so as to take it all in a *Kli* [vessel] of faith. It appears to us as ignominy and worthlessness, and we are anxious for the time we can rid ourselves of this burden called "faith above reason." However, it is a great and very important degree, whose exaltedness is immeasurable.

The reason it appears to us as ignominy is because of the will to receive in us. We must discern a *Rosh* [head] and a *Guf* [body] in the will to receive. The *Rosh* is called "knowing," and the *Guf* is called "receiving." Because of this, we consider anything that is against knowing as low and beastly.

Now we can interpret what Abraham the Patriarch asked of the Creator: "How will I know that I will inherit it?" For how will they be able to accept the burden of faith, since it is against reason, and who can go against reason? Thus, how will they come to be granted the light of faith, since perfection depends on this alone?

The Creator answered him about this: "Know for certain, etc., that they will be in exile." This means that He prepared a *Klipa* [shell], which is the evil inclination, an evil person, Pharaoh king of Egypt. The letters of the word Pharaoh are like the letters of the word *Oref* [back of the neck], as the ARI wrote (*Shaar HaKavanot* for *Pesach*) that Pharaoh is considered the *Oref*, the narrow in the sea. He would suck out the abundance that comes to the lower ones with his question (Exodus 5:2), "Who is the Lord that I should obey His voice?" By this very question, they are in the hands of the *Klipot* [shells], as the Maimonides says (*Hilchot Deot*) regarding not turning to idol gods, that with this approach alone, meaning with the very question, the prohibition on turning to them is broken.

The evil inclination wishes to suck abundance from the *Kedusha* [holiness]. Thus, what does it do to suck abundance from the *Kedusha*? The writing tells us, "and Pharaoh brought near." *The Zohar* interprets that he brought them near to repentance. It asked how can we say that Pharaoh brought them close to repentance if the conduct of the *Klipot* is to turn one away from the Creator.

We must understand this by what is written in *The Zohar* ("Introduction of The Book of Zohar," p 41 [in Hebrew]): "Transgression is concealed within you, like the serpent that strikes and hides its head inside its body." Also, in the *Sulam* ["Ladder" commentary on *The Zohar*]: "Like, etc. Since that transgression is concealed, the force of the serpent that strikes the people of the world and brings death to the world is still in all its power and cannot be revoked. It is like a serpent that bites a person and immediately puts its head in its body, and then it is impossible to kill it."

There is yet another saying in *The Zohar*—that the serpent bows its head and strikes with its tail. This means that sometimes it lets one take upon himself the burden of faith, which is above reason, which is the bowing of the head, but it strikes with its tail. The tail can be interpreted as "the end," that it bowed its head so as to ultimately receive in order to receive. In other words, it first gave one permission to take upon himself faith so that afterward it would take everything into its own authority, for the *Klipa* [shell/peel] knows that there is no way to receive abundance except through *Kedusha* [holiness].

This is the meaning of Pharaoh bringing them near. It is explained that he deliberately brought Israel to repentance, so as to afterward take everything from them into his own authority. This is why the ARI wrote that Pharaoh sucked all the abundance that came down to the lower ones. He sucked from the *Oref* and from the throat, which is considered the beginning of the body, meaning he would take everything in his vessels of reception.

This is the meaning of "And they built *Arei Miskenot*," meaning that this was for Israel. In other words, all their work during the exile was taken into Pharaoh's custody, and Israel remained poor, for *Miskena* means poor.

We should also interpret *Miskenot* from the word *Sakana* [danger], meaning that they were in great danger of remaining in that state for the rest of their lives. However, to Pharaoh, the work of Israel was Pithom and Raamses, meaning very beautiful cities.

Thus, the meaning of "And they built *Arei Miskenot*"—to Israel, and to Pharaoh—Pithom and Raamses. This is because all the work of Israel fell into the *Klipot*, and they saw no blessing in their work.

When they prevailed in their work in faith and bestowal, they did see fertility. And the moment they fell into knowing and receiving, they fell into the hands of the *Klipa* of Pharaoh. Finally, they came to a determined resolution that the work must be in faith above reason and in bestowal.

However, they saw that they were unable to come out of Pharaoh's power by themselves. This is why it is written, "And the children of Israel sighed from the work," since they feared that they might stay in exile forever. Then, "their cry came up unto God," and they were rewarded with emerging from the exile in Egypt.

It turns out that before they saw the situation—that they are in the hands of the *Klipot*, and were hurting and afraid that they would remain there forever—they had no need for the Creator's help from vessels of reception, if they do not feel the shortcoming and detriment caused by them, that this is all that obstructs them from adhering to the Creator. This is because otherwise one has a higher regard for work in the form of knowledge and reception, and faith is considered lowliness. They prefer knowledge and reception since this is what man's exterior mind necessitates.

Hence, they were given the exile, to feel that they do not progress in nearing the Creator, and all their work sinks in the *Klipa* of Egypt. Finally, they saw that they had no other choice but to take upon themselves the work of lowliness, which is faith above reason, and yearn for bestowal. Otherwise, they feel that they are in the domain of the *Sitra Achra* [other side].

It turns out that the faith that they took upon themselves was because they saw that otherwise they would have no counsel, and hence agreed to a work of lowliness. This is called "conditional work," that they accepted this work so they would not fall into the net of the *Klipot*. This is why they had taken upon themselves this work.

However, if the reason is revoked, the love for this work is revoked, too. This means that if the evil inclination is canceled, and there is nothing that brings them thoughts of not turning to idol gods, then the love for the work in lowliness is canceled.

Now we can understand what our sages wrote: "In the beginning, the evil inclination seems like a spiderweb, and in the end, it seems like cart-ropes." We know that there is a discernment of "coercive," "mistaken," and "deliberate." The will to receive that is imprinted in man is considered "coercive," since one cannot revoke it, and it is therefore not considered a sin, but an iniquity, as it is written, "Woe unto them who draw iniquity with cords of vanity." It cannot be rejected or hated, since he does not feel that it will be a sin.

However, afterward, it becomes a "sin, as it was with cart-ropes," and the *Klipot* were then made of this will to receive, which have a complete structure, as in "God has made one opposite the other." This is where the evil inclination comes from, meaning everything comes from this hairsbreadth.

Since it has already been revealed that it is a sin, then everyone knows to guard themselves from this hairsbreadth, and they understand that there is no other choice if they want to enter *Kedusha*, except to resolve to work in lowliness, meaning faith and bestowal. Otherwise, they see that they are under the control of the *Klipa* of Pharaoh, King of Egypt.

It follows that the benefit from the exile was that they would feel that the will to receive is a sin, and this is the reason to decide that there is no other choice but to try and acquire vessels of bestowal. This is the meaning of the Creator's answer to Abraham the Patriarch about his request for guarantees for the inheritance of the land: "Know for certain that your descendants will be strangers, etc., and they shall afflict them, etc." Through the exile they would come to discover the hairsbreadth, which is a sin, and then they would accept the real work in order to detach themselves from the sin.

This is the meaning of what Rabbi Yehuda said, that in the future, death shall be swallowed up forever, meaning the Creator will slaughter the evil inclination, and all that will be left of it is but a hairsbreadth, which is not even felt as a sin (The hairsbreadth is something that cannot be seen with the eye).

Yet, some wicked and righteous do remain, and they all want to adhere to Him. The wicked have not yet corrected their hairsbreadth, when the evil inclination still existed, and they could feel that it is a sin. Now, however, when there is no evil inclination, all that is left is but a hairsbreadth, so they have no reason to make them turn their vessels of reception into vessels of bestowal, since a hairsbreadth is unfelt. But nevertheless, they cannot adhere to Him because there is disparity of form, and He and I cannot dwell in the same abode.

Their correction is to be dust under the feet of the righteous. This means that since the evil inclination has been canceled, the righteous have no reason to have to go with faith above reason. Hence, since they have no reason, who would make them?

They see that the wicked are left with the hairsbreadth and did not correct the hairsbreadth while there was evil inclination, and it was the time to correct it since then the will to receive was evidently a sin, whereas now it does not seem like a sin, but like a hairsbreadth. Hence, if there is no reason, there is no place to correct.

Yet, there is also no place for *Dvekut* [adhesion], since the disparity of form remains, and all their correction is that the righteous walk on them. This means that they now see that there is no fear from the network of the *Klipot* since the evil inclination has been slaughtered.

Thus, why do they now have to work in faith above reason? Now they see that the wicked cannot reach *Dvekut* because now they have no reason, meaning an evil inclination that will be distinguished as a sin, yet they remain outside for there is still disparity of form.

Hence, when the righteous see this, they understand how good it was for them that they had a reason to work in bestowal. They thought they were engaged in bestowal only because of the evil inclination, but they see that the sin they saw was for their own good. In other words, this is the real work, and it is not because of fear of falling into the hands of the *Klipot* that they do this work. The evidence of this is that they see that the wicked, who did not correct the hairsbreadth, now they have no reason to, and they remain outside and cannot come to *Dvekut* with the Creator.

It follows that the righteous receive the strength to go from strength to strength through the wicked, the wicked have become dust under the feet of the righteous, and the righteous walk on the discernments that remain as wicked.

Hence, in retrospect, specifically this work is important. And it is not because of coercion, as it seemed to them before while they had the evil inclination. Now they see that even without the evil inclination, it is worthwhile to work in bestowal and faith.

Regarding "these cry and those cry," it is known that weeping is *Katnut* [smallness/infancy], VAK. There is a difference between GAR and VAK. *Mochin de VAK* illuminate from the past, meaning they take sustenance and light from what they experienced in the past. *Mochin de GAR*, however, shine in the present by uniting the *Zivug* [coupling].

This is the meaning of the righteous crying and saying, "How could we conquer such a high mountain?" Now they see what was prior to the slaughtering of the evil inclination, that its dominion was indeed great, as it is written, "God has made one opposite the other," and they received great mercy from the Creator, Who gave them the power to win the war against the inclination, and now they rejoice in the miracle that they had then, meaning in the past. This is called *Mochin de Katnut*.

The wicked cry because now they have no way to adhere to Him, even though now they see that it is only a hairsbreadth. But since now there is no evil inclination, they have no reason to turn the vessels of reception to bestowal; they can only see that they are outside; this is why they cry.

However, their correction is in becoming dust under the feet of the righteous. In other words, by the righteous seeing that although now there is no evil inclination, the wicked still cannot attain *Dvekut*, they say about their thought that they had to follow the path of bestowal only because of the evil inclination, they see that this is the real vessel. This means that even if there were no evil inclination, this path is still true, that the path of faith is a wonderful path.

Now we understand why wicked remain after the slaughtering of the evil inclination; it is so that they will become dust under the feet of the righteous. If no wicked would remain, there would not be anyone to show this great thing, that the path of faith is not because of conditional love. That is, it is not because of the evil inclination that we should follow the path of faith, but this is unconditional love, since now there is no longer any evil inclination, and still, only through faith can we attain *Dvekut* with the Creator.

I heard on another occasion: The reason we need faith specifically is the pride within us, for then it is difficult for us to accept faith. This means that although faith is an exalted and wonderful degree, which the lower one cannot attain and understand its preciousness and sublimity, it is only because of our pride, meaning the will to receive. We imagine it as low and beastly, and for this reason we were given the evil person.

And I heard on another occasion: We see that when we do not want to accept faith, we fall from our state. We rise and fall each time until we resolve that we have no other choice but to set faith permanently. This was in order to receive faith, and this is "And they built *Arei Miskenot*" (for Israel), for Pharaoh.

87. Shabbat Shekalim

I heard on *Adar* 26, *Tav-Shin-Het*, March 7, 1948

On Shabbat *Shekalim* [name of a weekly portion], when he came in for the *Kiddush** ... he said, "There was a custom among the *Admorim* [rabbis, heads of congregations] in Poland, that all the rich men would come to their rabbis on Shabbat [of the portion of] *Shekalim* to receive *Shekalim* [coins] from their rabbis."

He said that it implies that there cannot be obliteration of Amalek without *Shekalim*. This is so because before one receives *Shekalim*, there is still no *Klipa* [shell] of Amalek. Rather, when taking *Shekalim*, the great *Klipa* called "Amalek" comes, and the work of obliterating Amalek begins. However, prior to that, he has nothing to erase.

And he added an explanation to it, concerning what the Sayer of *Kuznitz* said about what is said in the closing prayer: "You have separated man from the beginning and You will recognize him to stand before You." The sayer asked about it: "How is it possible to stand without a *Rosh* [head/beginning]? It means that he separated the *Rosh* from the man, and how can such a thing be?" The explanation is, "When you count the heads of the children of Israel," by which we extend the discernment of *Rosh*. If we give the half *Shekel*, through it we are awarded the *Rosh*.

And he later asked ... "Why does he prepare for the *Kiddush* more drinking than eating? This is not the right order, since the order should be more eating than drinking, as drinking comes only to complement the eating, by way of 'And you shall eat and be satisfied, and bless.' However, it is not so when drinking is more

---

* *Kiddush*—a blessing recited over wine or grape juice to sanctify the *Shabbat* [Sabbath] and Jewish holidays.

than eating." And he interpreted that eating implies *Hassadim* [mercy] and drinking implies *Hochma* [wisdom].

And he said further, that the Shabbat prior to the month of *Adar* contains the whole of the month of *Adar*. Hence, "when *Adar* enters, there is much joy." And he said that there is a difference between a Shabbat and a good day. Shabbat is called "love," and a good day is called "joy." The difference between joy and love is that love is an essence, and joy is only a result, born from some reason. The reason is the essence, and the result is only a progeny of the essence. Hence, Shabbat is called "love and good will," and a good day is called "joy and merriment."

He also explained concerning what Rabbi Yochanan Ben Zakai replied to his wife, that I was like a minister before the King, and he, Rabbi Hanina Ben Dosa, like a slave before the King; this is why he could pray. It seems as though it should have been the opposite—that the minister would have more strength to induce his opinion on the King, and not the slave.

However, a "minister" is one who has already been awarded private Providence. In that state, he sees no room for prayer since everything is good. But a slave is one who is at the degree of reward and punishment, and then he has room to pray since he sees he has more to correct.

And he added an explanation from an article that is presented (*Baba Metzia* 85a). It is written there, "A calf was being led to the slaughter. It went, put its head in the rabbi's lap, and wept. He told it, 'Go, this is what you were made for.' They said, 'Since he has no pity, suffering shall come upon him.'"

"This is what you were made for" means private Providence, that there is nothing to add or take away, since there the sufferings, too, are considered merits. This is why he extended sufferings upon him.

And the *Gemara* says that he was rid of the suffering through an act, by saying, "and His mercies are over all His works." One day, the rabbi's maid was sweeping the house. There were rat young there, and she was sweeping them away. He told her, "Leave them!" It is written, "and His mercies are over all His works." Since he attained that a prayer, too, remains in eternity, he now had room for prayer. This is why the sufferings departed from him.

At the end of Shabbat, he said an interpretation about what *The Zohar* says about the verse, "For the Lord has chosen Jacob for Himself." Who chose whom? And *The Zohar* replies, "The Lord chose Jacob" (*Beresheet* 161b). And he said that the question of *The Zohar* is if the Creator chose Jacob. It follows that Jacob did not do anything, but all was under private Providence. And if Jacob did choose, it means that Jacob is the doer, meaning a matter of reward and punishment.

And he replied that in the beginning, one should begin on the path of reward and punishment. When he completes that phase of reward and punishment, he is rewarded with seeing that everything is under private Providence, that "He alone does and will do all the deeds." However, before one completes one's work in reward and punishment it is impossible to understand private Providence.

And on Sunday night, after the lesson, he explained the matter of Jacob's cunningness, that it is written about Jacob, "Your brother came with guile." There was certainly no issue of falsehood here. Otherwise, the text would not say about Jacob, the senior among the patriarchs, that he was a liar.

Rather, "guile" means that when one performs an act of wisdom without intending for wisdom, but to elicit some benefit that he needs, and sees that it cannot be obtained directly, hence, he performs an act of wisdom to obtain the thing he needs. This is called "wisdom."

This is the meaning of the verse, "be guile with reason," meaning wisdom through reason. This means that the wisdom he wants to obtain is not for the purpose of wisdom, but through something else which forces him to extend wisdom. In other words, he must extend in order to complement the *Hassadim*.

Because before the *Hassadim* obtain *Hochma*, they are discerned as *Katnut* [smallness/infancy]. However, afterward, when he extends *Hochma* but still prefers *Hassadim* to *Hochma*, it is apparent that the *Hassadim* are more important than *Hochma*. This is called GAR *de Bina*, which means that he uses the *Hassadim* because of a choice.

This is the meaning of *Hochma* through *Daat*, that *Hochma* appears in the form of VAK in YESHSUT. And in AVI, *Hochma* appears by improving the *Hassadim* and remaining in *Hassadim*. However, although *Bina* is considered the correction of "desiring mercy," her choice of *Hassadim* is not apparent because of *Tzimtzum Bet*, where there is no *Hochma*. However, in *Gadlut* [greatness/adulthood], when *Hochma* comes, the *Hassadim* she uses are because of a choice.

88. All the Work Is Only Where There Are Two Ways – 1

I heard after Shabbat BeShalach, Tav-Shin-Het, January 24, 1948

All the work is only where there are two ways, as it is written, "And he shall live by them, and he shall not die by them. And the issue of 'shall die and not breach' applies only to three *Mitzvot* [commandments]: idolatry, bloodshed, and incest." And yet, we find that the first *Hassidim* would give their lives over [commandments] to-do.

And we should know that all the work and the labor are only when one should observe the Torah. At that time, one feels the heavy load that the body does not agree to the conditions of the Torah. But when a person is rewarded, and the Torah guards him, no heaviness is sensed in the work of the Creator since the Torah guards a person, as it is written, "One's soul shall teach him."

89. To Understand the Words of The Zohar
I heard on Adar 5, Tav-Shin-Het, February 15, 1948

To understand the words of *The Zohar*, we should first understand what *The Zohar* wants to say. Understanding what *The Zohar* wants to say depends on one's dedication to Torah and *Mitzvot* [commandments], so the Torah and *Mitzvot* will bring him cleanness, to be cleansed of self-love. This is why he engages in Torah and *Mitzvot*. And to that extent we can understand the truth that *The Zohar* wants to say. Otherwise, there are *Klipot* [shells/peels] that hide and block the truth in the words of *The Zohar*.

90. In The Zohar, Beresheet
I heard on Adar Bet 17, Tav-Shin-Het, March 28, 1948

In *The Zohar*, *Beresheet*, p 165, "In the secrets of the Torah, the ministers' defenders are erected from above. And the blaze of the flaming sword is appointed over all the armies and the camps. And in this discernment, several other discernments are interpreted to several other degrees."

He explained that when the left line extends, it must be sweetened with the right line. It spreads in three places:

1. in *AVI*, which is the root;
2. in Malchut;
3. in God's angels.

In *AVI*, they are called "defenders of the ministers," and in *Malchut* they are called "the blaze of the swirling sword." And in the angels they are called "They are in many sides, several other manners are interpreted to several other degrees."

91. Concerning the Replaceable
I heard on Nisan 9, Tav-Shin-Het, April 18, 1948

In *The Zohar* he explains the reason why Reuben was born to Leah while he was thinking of Rachel during the act. The law is that if he thinks of another, the child is called "replaceable." *The Zohar* explains that since he was thinking of Rachel, and he thought that it really was Rachel, and replaceable means that his thought was of Rachel and of the act, he knew that it was Leah. However, here his thought was of Rachel and of the act, and he thought that it really was Rachel.

He explained that in spirituality, it is known that they are as seal and imprint, where each degree is sealed by its upper degree. And the conduct of seals and imprints is that they are always opposites: The imprint is always opposite from the seal. It follows that what is considered *Klipa* [shell] in *Beria* is *Kedusha* [holiness] in *Yetzira*, and what is *Kedusha* in *Yetzira* is *Klipa* in *Assiya*.

Therefore, if the righteous is united in some degree, he certainly unites with the *Kedusha* in the degree. And if, during the act, he thinks of another degree, and what is considered *Kedusha* in that degree is considered *Klipa* in another degree, it is therefore called "replaceable." That means that the offspring of this unification is replaceable because the degrees are opposite from one another.

Jacob, however, was thinking of Rachel, meaning of the *Kedusha* in the quality of Rachel. And of the act, he also thought that it was Rachel. Hence, both the thought was of the *Kedusha* in Rachel, and the act intended to be the degree of Rachel. Therefore, there is no discernment of Leah here, to be considered replaceable.

92. Explaining the Discernment of Luck
I heard on Sivan 7, Tav-Shin-Het, June 14, 1948

"Luck" is something that is above reason. That is, even though it was reasonable that it would be so and so, luck caused his actions to succeed. Reason refers to cause and consequence, meaning that a cause makes the result come out as it does. But above reason, when the initial cause is not the cause of the consequence, this is called "above reason." We refer to it as luck causing the result.

It is known that all bestowals come from the light of *Hochma* [wisdom]. And when *Hochma* shines, it is called "left line" and "darkness." The abundance is blocked, and it is called "ice." This is called "merit" because he is rewarded. That means that the reason that causes the light of wisdom is called "merit," which is cause and consequence.

But "sons, life, and nourishment do not depend on merit, but on luck." This means that *Hochma* shines specifically through the middle line, where the *Hochma* is diminished, and specifically through the diminution, called *Masach de Hirik*. It follows that she does not shine with cause and consequence, meaning that *Hochma* shines through the left line, but precisely through diminution. This is called "above reason," and this is "luck."

93. Concerning Fins and Scales
I heard in Tav-Shin-Hey, 1944-1945

To understand what our sages said, "whatsoever has scales is known to have fins. And whatsoever has fins, it is not known if it has scales."

In the work, we should interpret the matter of *Kaskeset* [scales] as *Kushiot* [questions] that he has in the work of the Creator. The *Kushiot* are *Kelim* [vessels] in which to receive answers, since the answers are not filled in the external mind, but specifically in the internal mind, which is the upper light, clothed within a person. And then all the questions are settled in him.

Hence, to the extent that questions increase, to that extent does the upper light dress within man. This is why the scales are among the signs of purity, since through it one can come to purify oneself by not wanting to have questions. Hence, one does whatever one can to purify oneself, so he can be awarded the upper light.

And a fin, too, is among the signs of purity. *Snapir* [fin] implies *Soneh-Peh-Ohr Elyon* [hating-mouth-upper light]. And since he has questions, it is certainly because he has hatred for the upper light. But one who has fins does not have to have questions. One may hate the upper light not because he has questions but because he is simply greedy, and says, "I will not go anyway."

This is the sign of purity. That is, when he has a fish. A fish implies meat that is clothed in fins and scales. This means that the upper light shines in these two signs.

But one who works without any questions in the work, this is not a sign of purity, that one has no questions. This is so because one has no place in which to place the upper light, as one has no reason that will compel him to draw the upper light, as even without the upper light he thinks he is just fine.

This is why when Pharaoh, King of Egypt, wanted to keep the people of Israel in his domain, he issued an order to not give *Kash* [straw], as it is written, "So the people were scattered... to gather stubble for straw." Then they would never need the Creator to deliver them from the domain of *Tuma'a* [impurity] into the *Kedusha* [holiness].

94. And You Shall Keep Your Souls
I heard in *Tav-Shin-Hey*, 1944-1945

In the verse, "And you shall keep your souls," the keeping refers mainly to the spiritual soul. However, one keeps the corporeal soul even without commandments from the Torah. This is because the rule is that a *Mitzva* [commandment] is primarily evident, meaning it is evident that he does what he does for the purpose of a *Mitzva* when he would not do it were it not for a *Mitzva*. Rather, the reason he does it is because of a *Mitzva*.

Hence, with a *Mitzva* that he performs, if he would do it even if it were not a *Mitzva*, he needs special care, to find a place where he can say that he does this only because of a *Mitzva*. Then the light of the *Mitzva* can shine on the act of the *Mitzva* that he performs. This is called "making a *Kli* [vessel] with the *Mitzva*," in which the upper light can be. Hence, the keeping refers mainly to the spiritual soul.

95. Concerning Removing the Foreskin

I heard during a meal celebrating a circumcision, Tav-Shin-Gimel, 1942-1943, Jerusalem

Malchut in itself is called "lower *Hochma*," and with respect to its connection to *Yesod*, it is called "faith." There is a foreskin over the *Yesod*, whose role is to separate *Malchut* from *Yesod*, and not let it connect to *Yesod*. The foreskin's power is in picturing faith as dust. This is the meaning of *Shechina* [Divinity] in the dust.

When that depicting force is removed, and instead, saying that the depicting force is dust, this is called "circumcision," when the foreskin is cut off and the foreskin is thrown to the dust.

In that state, the *Shechina* comes out of the dust, and the merit of faith becomes apparent. This is called "redemption," being rewarded with raising the *Shechina* from the dust. Hence, we must focus all the work on removing the depicting force, and only faith is considered whole.

"They are meticulous with themselves as much as an olive and as much as an egg." An "olive" is as the dove said, "I prefer my food as bitter as an olive from heaven." And the "egg" means that it is lifeless, although a living animal will emerge from it. But in the meantime, no life is seen in it. And they are meticulous with themselves and prefer to work although that situation is like an olive.

Also, when they see no vitality in the work, and all their strength to work is because their sole aim is to raise the *Shechina* from the dust, then, through this work, they are awarded redemption. Then they see that this meal, which was previously like an olive and an egg, has now become lively and sweet and sublimely pleasant.

This is the meaning of "a converted proselyte is like a newly born child." At that time, he must keep the state of "covenant," too, and then he will be glad.

It follows that when the infant is circumcised, although the child is suffering, the guests and the parents are nonetheless happy, since they believe that the boy's soul is happy. Similarly, in the work of the covenant, we must be happy even though we feel a state of suffering. Nevertheless, we should believe that our soul is happy.

Our whole work should be in gladness. And the evidence to that is from the first commandment man was given to man. The *Mitzva* is done by the parents, and the parents and the guests are happy. So should be all the *Mitzvot* that one performs—only in gladness.

96. What Is Waste of Granary and Winery, in the Work?

I heard on the eve of *Sukkot*, inside the *Sukkah*, Tav-Shin-Gimel, 1942-1943

A granary is male *Dinim* [judgments], as in "hidden and not defiled," when he feels that he is in a state of *Goren* [granary], meaning *Ger* [stranger/not converted] in the work.

A winery is female *Dinim*, as in "hidden and defiled." *Yekev* [winery] is considered *Nekev* [foramen].

And there are two kinds of *Sukkot*: 1) clouds of glory, and 2) waste of granary and winery.

A cloud is considered concealment, when one feels the concealment over the *Kedusha* [holiness]. If a person overcomes the cloud, meaning the concealment that one feels, he is thus rewarded with clouds of glory. This is called MAN *de Ima*, which applies during the six thousand years. It is considered a secret, for it still has not become a nature, called "literal."

And the waste of granary and winery are called "literal and nature," which is considered MAN *de Malchut*, corrected specifically through faith, called an "awakening from below."

And MAN *de Ima* is considered an awakening from above, which is not discerned as nature. This means that with respect to nature, when one is not ready to receive the abundance, he does not receive any bestowal.

However, from the perspective of the awakening from above, which is above nature, the light is indeed poured to the lower ones, by way of "I am the Lord, Who dwells with them in the midst of their impurity," as it is written in *The Zohar*, "Even though he has sinned, it is as if he did not sin at all."

However, with an awakening from below, the light is not dispensed. Rather, precisely when one is qualified by nature—meaning by himself, this is called MAN *de Nukva*—that he can correct through faith. This is called "by himself," considered the seventh millennium, called "and one is ruined," meaning that "she has nothing of her own," considered *Malchut*. When this is corrected, one is awarded the tenth millennium, which is GAR.

Such a soul is found in one of ten generations. However, there is the discernment of the seventh millennium, from the perspective of the six thousand years, called "particular," as the general and the particular are always equal. But this is considered MAN *de Ima*, called "clouds of glory."

The purpose of the work is in the literal and nature, since in this work he no longer has room to fall lower down, since he is already placed on the ground. This is so because he does not need greatness because to him it is always like something new.

That is, he always works as though he had just begun to work. And he works in the form of accepting the burden of the kingdom of heaven above reason. The basis, upon which he built the order of the work, was in the lowest manner, and all of it was truly above reason. Only one who is truly naïve can be so low as to proceed without any basis on which to establish his faith, literally with no support.

Additionally, he accepts this work with great joy, as though he had had real knowledge and vision on which to establish the certainty of faith. And to that exact measure of above reason, to that very measure as though he had reason. Hence, if he persists in this way, he can never fall. Rather, he can always be in gladness, by believing that he is serving a great King.

This is the meaning of the verse, "The one lamb you shall offer in the morning; and the other lamb you shall offer at dusk. ... according to the meal-offering of the morning, and according to the drink-offering thereof." This means that that gladness that he had while he was sacrificing his sacrifice, when it was a morning for him, as morning is called "light," meaning that the light of the Torah was shining for him in utter clarity. In that same gladness, he was making his sacrifice, meaning his work, even though for him it was like evening.

This means that even though he did not have any clarity in the Torah and the work, he still did everything gladly, since he worked above reason. Hence, he could not measure from which state the Creator derives more contentment.

This is the meaning of Rabbi Shimon Ben Menasia's saying "a kind of matter." Matter means without reason and knowledge. "An ear that heard on Mount Sinai, 'You shall not steal.'" This means not receiving anything for oneself, but rather taking upon oneself the burden of the kingdom of heaven without any *Gadlut* [greatness/adulthood], but entirely above reason. And he went and stole some illumination for himself, meaning he said, "Now I can be a servant of the Creator because I already have reason and knowledge in the work, and I understand that it is worthwhile to be the Creator's servant. And now I no longer need faith above reason."

He tells us about that, "and he was sold to the court." "Court" refers to man's reason and knowledge, which judge a person's actions, whether or not they are worth doing. "Sold" means that he has become a stranger in the work of the Creator, that the mind comes and asks him the known question, "What is this work?" And it only comes from the side of stealing, having received some support to the faith. Hence, he comes and wants to cancel the support with his questions. But this is only for "six," meaning "he was sold for six years," considered male *Dinim*.

"But if the servant shall plainly say, 'I love my master... I will not go out free,'" meaning he does not want to go out free without *Mitzvot* [commandments], then the correction is "his master shall bring him," meaning the Master of the earth, "to the door, or to the door-post," meaning give him blockage over the reception of the kingdom of heaven. And "his master shall bore his ear," meaning his ear is pierced. This means that another hole is made in him, so he will be able to hear once more what he had heard on Mount Sinai: "You shall not steal," "and he shall serve him forever," and then he truly becomes a servant of the Creator.

Sukkot is temporary residence. This means that one who has already been awarded permanent residence and has nothing more to do, as with the matter of the first to count the iniquities, the advice is to leave for temporary residence, as when he was on his way to the house of God, before he arrived at the permanent residence. At that time, he constantly needed to reach the Creator's palace, and he had guests, when his work was in the form of "a passing visitor."

And now he can extend from the past work, when he was always thankful and praising the Creator for the Creator always bringing him closer, and from this he had gladness. Now, on *Sukkot*, he can extend the gladness he had then. This is the meaning of temporary residence. This is why they said, "Leave the permanent residence and dwell in temporary residence."

"The learning is not what is most important, but the act." This means that an act is like a substance. Rabbi Shimon Ben Menasia was saying, "a kind of matter," that the act is the most important, and the mind is but a kind of mirror.

However, the act is considered animate, and the mind is considered speaking. The thing is that if there is wholeness in the act, then the act is so great that it brings with it the mind of the Torah. And the mind of the Torah is called "speaking."

97. Waste of Granary and Winery

I heard

Goren [granary] means diminution of good deeds, when a person feels *Gronot* [throats] (*Ger'onot* [deficiencies]) with the Creator. Hence, he lessens the good deeds. Afterward, he comes to a state of *Yekev* [winery], which is "And he that blasphemes the name of the Lord."

Sukkot is considered gladness, considered "rejoicing *Gevurot*," which is repentance from love, when sins become for him as merits. Then, even the granary and winery are admitted into *Kedusha* [holiness]. This is the meaning of *Sukkot's* primary discernment being Isaac, although everyone is included in him (and Passover is considered love, which is right).

This is the meaning of "Abraham begot Isaac." The issue of father and son is cause and consequence, reason and result. Had there not been a discernment of Abraham first, which is the right, there could not have been the discernment of Isaac, which is the left. Rather, the left is integrated in the right, as in "For You are our Father."

Abraham said, "will be destroyed over the sanctity of Your name." And Jacob also said that it means that the sins will be destroyed over the Sanctity of Your name. And if it remains so, then there is a breach in the middle. In other words, the sins that were in the whole of Israel are like a breach in the *Kedusha* [holiness].

Isaac, however, said, "half over me and half over you," meaning the part of the sins and the part of the *Mitzvot*, meaning that both will enter *Kedusha*. This can be through repentance from love, when sins become for him as merits. In that state, there is no breach, as it is written, "No breach and no... outcry," but all is corrected for *Kedusha*.

This is the meaning of our sages' words, "Greater are the dung and mules of Isaac than Abimelech's money and gold." Dung is something inferior, worthless, meaning that they consider the servitude of him as dung. Afterward, there arrives a state of separation. Because he does not appreciate his work, he falls into separation. This is called "the dung and mules of Isaac." Since Isaac corrected everything in the form of repentance from love, and his sins became as merits, the profits that had come to him through his dung and mules are greater than "Abimelech's money and gold."

His *Kesef* [money] means *Kisufim* [longing] for the Creator. *Zahav* [gold] means *Ze Hav* [give this], meaning craving for the Torah, to attain the Torah. Since Isaac corrected everything, meaning achieved repentance from love, the sins, too, were considered for him as merits. And then he is very rich in any case, since in observing *Mitzvot*, there are not more than 613 *Mitzvot*, but sins and transgressions are endless. This is why Isaac became rich, as it is written, "And he found a hundred gates," meaning that he had one hundred percent in *Kedusha*, without any waste, since the waste, too, was corrected in him.

This is why the thatch of the *Sukkah* is made of waste of granary and winery. (And you can say what our sages said, that Moses became rich from waste). Hence, *Sukkot* is named primarily after Isaac, who is the rejoicing *Gevurot*, and *Sukkot* is named after Moses, too.

98. Spirituality Is Called That Which Will Never Be Lost

I heard in Tav-Shin-Het, 1947-1948

Spirituality is called that which will never be lost. Hence, the will to receive, in the form it is in, meaning in order to receive, is called "corporeality," since it will be canceled from this form and will acquire the form of in order to bestow.

A real place in spirituality is called "the place of reality," since anyone who comes there, to that place, sees the same shape as the other. Conversely, something imaginary is not regarded as a real place since it is imaginary, and then everyone imagines it differently.

When we say "seventy faces to the Torah," it means that they are seventy degrees. In each degree, the Torah is interpreted according to the degree one is in. However, a world is a reality, meaning that anyone who comes to any of the seventy degrees in that world attains the same form as all the other attainers who came there.

From this extends what our sages say, who interpret the verses of the Torah. They say that this is what Abraham said to Isaac, and other similar sayings of our sages. They would say what they would say, what is explained in the verses.

The question is, How did they know what one said to the other? But because those who achieved the degree where Abraham (or anyone) stood, they see and know what Abraham knew and saw.

For this reason, they know what Abraham said. It is likewise in all the sayings of our sages that interpret the verses of the Torah. All that was because they, too, attained the degree, and each degree in spirituality is a reality, and everyone sees the reality, just as all those who come to the city of London in England see what is in the city and what is said in the city.

99. He Did Not Say Wicked or Righteous
I heard on *Iyar* 21, Jerusalem

"Rabbi Hanina Bar Papa said, 'That angel, appointed on conception, its name is *Laila* [night]. It takes a drop and places it before the Creator and says to Him: 'Master of the world, this drop, what shall become of it, a hero or a weakling, a wise or a fool, a wealthy or an indigent?' But he did not say 'a wicked or a righteous'" (*Nida* 16b).

We should interpret according to the rule that a fool cannot be righteous, as our sages said, "One does not sin unless a spirit of folly has entered him." It is even more so with one who is a fool his whole life. Hence, one who is born a fool has no choice since he has been sentenced to be a fool. Therefore, saying, "He did not say 'a wicked or a righteous'" is so that he would have a choice. But what is the benefit if he did not say "a righteous or a fool"? After all, if he is sentenced to be a fool, it is the same as being sentenced to become a wicked!

We should also understand the words of our sages: "Rabbi Yochanan said, 'The Creator saw that the righteous are few, He stood and planted them in each generation, as was said, 'For the pillars of the earth are the Lord's, and He has set the world upon them.'" RASHI interprets "'He has set the world upon them'—He dispersed them in all the generations to be an infrastructure and sustenance and foundation to sustain the world" (*Yoma* 38b).

"They are few" means that they are growing fewer. Hence, what did he do to multiply them? "He stood and planted them in each generation." We should ask, "What is the benefit in planting them in each generation, by which they multiply?" We must understand the difference between all the righteous being in a single generation or being dispersed through all the generations, as RASHI interprets. Does being in many generations multiply the righteous?

To understand the above, we must expand and interpret our sages' words, that the Creator sentences the drop to be a wise or a fool, meaning that one who is born weak, without the strength to overcome his inclination, and is born with a weak desire and without talents, since during the preparation, when beginning in the work of the Creator, he must be fit to receive the Torah and the wisdom, as it is written, "will give wisdom to the wise," he asked, "If they are already smart, why do they still need wisdom? It should have been 'will give wisdom to the fools.'"

He explains that "wise" means one who craves wisdom although he still has no wisdom. But because he has a desire, and a desire is called a *Kli* [vessel], it follows that one who has a desire and craving for wisdom is the *Kli* in which wisdom shines. It therefore follows that a fool means one without yearning for wisdom, whose yearning is only for his own needs. In terms of bestowal, a fool is completely incapable of achieving any bestowal whatsoever.

Therefore, one who is born with such qualities, how can he achieve the degree of a righteous? It follows that he does not have a choice. Therefore, what is the benefit from saying, "he did not say, 'a righteous or a wicked'?" So he would have a choice. After all, since he was born unwise and weak, he is no longer capable of having a choice, since he is completely incapable of any overcoming and craving for His wisdom.

To understand this, that even a fool can have a choice, the Creator made a correction, which our sages call, "the Creator saw that the righteous were few; He stood and planted them in each generation." We asked, "What is the benefit of this?"

Now we will understand this matter. It is known that as it is forbidden to bond with the wicked even when one does not do as they do, as it is written, "nor sat in the seat of the scornful." This means that the sin is primarily because he sits among the scornful, even though he sits and learns Torah and keeps *Mitzvot*. Otherwise, the prohibition would be due to the cancellation of Torah and *Mitzvot*. But rather, the sitting itself is forbidden, since man takes the thoughts and desires of those he likes.

And vice versa: If one does not have any desire or craving for spirituality, if he is among people who have a desire and craving for spirituality, if he likes these people, he, too, will take their strength to prevail, and their desires and aspirations, although by his own quality, he does not have these desires and cravings and the power to overcome. But according to the grace and the importance he ascribes to these people, he will receive new powers.

Now we can understand the above words: "The Creator saw that the righteous were few," meaning that not any person can become a righteous, for lack of qualities for it, as it was written, that he is born a fool or a weakling; he, too, has a choice and his own qualities are no excuse. This is because the Creator planted the righteous in every generation.

Hence, a person has the choice of going to a place where there are righteous. One can accept their authority, and then he will receive all the powers that he lacks by the nature of his own qualities. He will receive it from the righteous. This is the benefit in "planted them in each generation," so that each generation would have someone to turn to, adhere to, and from whom to receive the strength required to rise to the degree of a righteous. Thus, they, too, subsequently become righteous.

It follows that "he did not say 'a wicked or a righteous'" means that he does have a choice: He can go and adhere to the righteous for guidance, and through them receive strength, by which they, too, can later become righteous.

However, if all the righteous were in the same generation, the fools and the weak would have no hope of approaching the Creator. Thus, they would not have a choice. But by dispersing the righteous in each generation, each person has the power of choice to approach and draw near to the righteous that exist in every generation. Otherwise, one's Torah must be a potion of death.

We can understand this from a corporeal example. When two people stand one opposite the other, the right hand of one is opposite the left hand of the other, and the left hand of one is opposite one's friend's right hand. There are two ways: the right—the way of the righteous, which is only to bestow, and the path of the left—who want only to receive for themselves, by which they are separated from the Creator, who is only to bestow. Thus, they are naturally separated from the Life of Lives.

This is why the wicked in their lives are called "dead." It therefore follows that as long as one has not been awarded *Dvekut* [adhesion] with the Creator, they are two. Then, when one learns Torah, which is called right, but is to the left of the Creator, meaning he is learning Torah to receive for himself, it separates him from Him, and his Torah becomes a potion of death to him since he remains separated, as he wants his Torah to clothe his body. This means that he wants the Torah to increase his body, and by this his Torah becomes a potion of death to him.

However, when a person becomes adhered to Him, a single authority is made, and that person unites in His uniqueness. Then, the right side of the person is the right side of the Creator, and then the body becomes a clothing for one's soul.

The way to know if one is marching on the path of truth is that when one engages in bodily needs, one should see that he does not engage in them more than is necessary for the needs of his soul. When one thinks that one has more than he needs to clothe the needs of one's soul, it is like a clothing that a person puts over his body. At that time, he is meticulous about keeping the garment not too long or too wide, but clothing his body accurately. Similarly, when engaging in one's bodily needs, he should be meticulous not to have more than he needs for his soul, meaning to clothe his soul.

To come to *Dvekut* with the Creator, not all who wish to take the Lord may come and take, since it is against man's nature, who was created with a will to receive, which is self-love. This is why we need the righteous of the generation.

When a person adheres to a real rav, whose only wish is to do good deeds, but one feels that he cannot do good deeds, that the aim will be to bestow contentment upon the Creator, by adhering to a real rav and wanting the rav's fondness, he does things that his rav likes, and hates the things his rav hates. Then he can have *Dvekut* with his rav and receive his rav's powers, even that which he does not have from birth. This is the meaning of planting the righteous in each generation.

However, according to this, it is hard to see why plant the righteous in each generation. We said that it was for the fools and the weak. But he could have solved it otherwise: not to create fools! Who made him say that this drop will be a weakling or a fool? He could have created everyone wise.

The answer is that the fools are also needed since they are the carriers of the will to receive. They see that they have no counsel of their own by which to draw near to the Creator, so they are as those about whom it is written, "And they shall go forth and look upon the carcasses of the men... for their worm shall not die, neither shall their fire be quenched; and they shall be an abhorring unto all flesh." They have become ashes under the feet of the righteous, by which the righteous can acknowledge the good that the Creator did for them by creating them wise and strong, by which He has brought them closer to Him.

Hence, now they can give thanks and praise the Creator since they see the lowly state they are in. This is called "ashes under the feet of the righteous," meaning that the righteous walk by it and thus thank the Creator.

But we must know that the lower degrees are also needed. The *Katnut* [smallness/infancy] of a degree is not considered superfluous, saying that it would be better if the degrees of *Katnut* were born immediately with the *Gadlut* [greatness/adulthood].

It is like a physical body. There are certainly important organs, such as the brain and the eyes and so forth, and there are organs that are not as important, such as the stomach, intestines, fingers, and toes. But we cannot say that an organ that performs a not-so-important task is redundant. Rather, everything is important. It is the same in spirituality: We also need the fools and the weak.

Now we can understand what is written, that the Creator said, "Return unto Me, and I will return unto you." It means that the Creator says, "Return," and Israel say the opposite: "Bring us back, Lord, and then we shall return."

The meaning is that during the decline from the work, the Creator says "Return" first. This brings a person an ascent in the work of the Creator, and one begins to cry, "Bring us back." But during the decline, one does not cry, "Bring us back." On the contrary, he escapes the work.

Hence, one should know that when he cries, "Bring us back," it stems from an awakening from above, since the Creator previously said "Return," by which one has an ascent and he can say "Bring us back."

This is the meaning of "And it came to pass when the ark journeyed, that Moses said: 'Rise up, O Lord, and let Your enemies be scattered.'" "Journeying" means when advancing in servitude of the Creator, which is an ascent. Then Moses said "Rise." And when they rested, he said "Return, Lord." And during the rest from the work of the Creator, we need the Creator to say, "Return," meaning "Return unto Me," meaning that the Creator gives the awakening. Hence, one should know when to say "Rise" or "Return."

This is the meaning of what is written in *Parashat Akev*, "And you shall remember all the way... to know what was in your heart, whether you would keep His commandments, or not." "Would keep His commandments" is discerned as "Return." "Or not" is discerned as "rise," and we need both. And the rav knows when to "rise" and when to "return," since the forty-two journeys are ascents and descents that unfold in the work of the Creator.

100. The Written Torah and the Oral Torah - 1
I heard on Mishpatim, Tav-Shin-Gimel, 1943

The written Torah is considered "awakening from above," and the oral Torah is an awakening from below. Together, they are called "Six years he shall serve, and in the seventh he shall go out free."

This is so because the essence of the work is specifically where there is resistance. And it is called *Alma* [Aramaic: world] from the word *He'elem* [concealment]. Then, when there is concealment, there is resistance, and then there is room for work. This is the meaning of the words of our sages, "Six thousand years the world, and one ruined." This means that the concealment will be ruined and there will be no more work. Rather, the Creator makes him wings, which are covers, so he would have work.

101. A Commentary on the Psalm, "For the Winner over Roses"
I heard on Adar Aleph 23, Tav-Shin-Gimel, February 28, 1943

"For the winner," one who has already won.

Over *Shoshanim* [roses], meaning the *Shechina* [Divinity], which concerns the inversion from mourning to a good day and *Sasson* [joy]. Since there are many states of ascents and descents, the descents are called *Shoshanim*, from the words "blunt its *Shinaim* [teeth]," the questions of the wicked should not be answered, but rather, "Blunt its teeth." From the multiple beatings, meaning from many blunting of teeth, we come to roses. Hence, there are many discernments of *Sasson* in it, which is why it is spoken of in plural form, "roses."

Of the sons of Korah, from the word *Karachah* [bald], meaning that the hair has gone bald. *Se'arot* mean *Hastarot* [concealments], from the word *Se'ara* [storm]. It is known that "The reward is according to the sorrow." This means that when there are *Se'arot*, it is a place for work. And when corrected, hair comes over the storm, by way of "This is the gate to the Lord." When one has corrected all the storms, and has no more concealments, he has no room for work, and therefore has no place for reward.

It follows that when a person comes to the state of *Korah*, he can no longer extend faith, called "the gate to the Lord." This is so because if there is no gate, he cannot enter the King's palace, since it is the foundation, since the entire structure is built on faith.

"Sons of Korah" comes from the word *Bina*. They understood that *Korah* is considered left, from which Hell extends. This is why they wanted to continue their friendship from before, from the time they were in the form of "Lord, I heard the report of You, and I am afraid" (*Zohar*, *Beresheet*, 4:7). This means that with the strength they had extended from the past, they could endure the states and go from strength to strength. This is the meaning of "the sons of Korah did not die." That is, they understood that if they remained in a state of *Korah*, they would not be able to extend life, so they did not die.

"*Maskil* [learned] a song of loves," meaning that they have learned that the measure of friendship with the Creator is complete.

"My heart overflows." The overflowing in the heart is by way of "does not reveal from heart to mouth." This means that there is nothing to elicit from the mouth, which is only reception in the heart, as in whispered in the lips.

"A good thing"—faith is called "a good thing."

"I say, 'My work is for the king.'" When he receives the light of faith, he says, "My work is for the king," and not for myself. And then he is rewarded with "My tongue is the pen of a quick writer," when he is awarded the discernment of the written Torah, which is the language of Moses.

"You are more beautiful than the children of man," when he says to the *Shechina* that her beauty is from people, meaning from what people think of her, which is considered insignificant. Precisely from this, beauty is born.

"Grace is poured upon your lips." Grace belongs particularly to matters where praise cannot be said, but we still want that thing. Then we say that it is graceful.

"Upon your *Sefataim* [lips]" means at the *Sof* [end]. This is the meaning of "He saw from the end of the world to its end."

102. And You Shall Take You the Fruit of a Citrus Tree
I heard on *Ushpizin de Yosef* [Sukkot]

In the verse, "And you shall take you... the fruit of a citrus tree," meaning a righteous, called a "fruit bearing tree," this is the whole difference between *Kedusha* [holiness] and the *Sitra Achra* [other side], that "another god is sterile and does not bear fruit." Conversely, a righteous is called *Hadar* [citrus/adornment] because he bears fruit; he *Dar* [lives] in his tree from year to year. This is why it is written about Joseph, "he was the one who *Mashbir* [sold] to all the people of the land," for he *Shover* [breaks/feeds] them with the fruits that he had, while they had no fruits. By this, each one felt his state, whether he was from the good side or to the contrary.

This is the meaning of "Joseph sustained... with bread, according to the infants." The "infants" are considered GAR, as in "and they shall be for frontlets between your eyes," which is the head *Tefillin*. For this reason, Joseph is called "the youngest son, a wise son." This is the meaning of "sent me before you to preserve life," which is the "light of *Haya*," considered GAR.

This is the meaning of the verse, "I gave you one portion more than to your brothers, which I took from the Amorite with my sword and with my bow." (His sons took two parts. And according to RASHI, "portion" means part.) That is, through his sons, as sons are called "fruits," and he gave this to Joseph.

This is the meaning of what is written about Saul, "from his shoulders up he was higher than any of the people." And this is the meaning of "You have a mantle, be you our ruler." This is also the meaning of "Infants, why do they come? To give reward to those who bring them." He asked, "Why do they need wisdom if the important thing is not the learning but the act?" He replied, "to give reward to those who bring them," since wisdom yields action.

Concerning the dispute between Saul and David, there was no flaw in Saul. This is why he was one year old when he reigned, and he did not need to prolong the kingship, since he completed everything in a short time. David, however, needed to rule forty years. David was the son of Judah, the son of Leah, the hidden world, while Saul was from Benjamin, the son of Rachel, the revealed world, and hence opposite from David. This is why David said, "I am peace," meaning I attain everyone and I love everyone, "But when I speak, they are for war."

Likewise, Avishalom was the opposite of David. This is the meaning of the sin of Jeroboam, son of Navat: The Creator held him by his garment and said to him, "You and I and the son of *Yishai* [Jesse] will walk in the garden of Eden." He asked, "Who is leading?" And the Creator told him, "The son of *Yishai* is leading." Then he replied, "Don't want."

The thing is that the order of degrees is that the hidden world comes first, and then the revealed world. This is the meaning of "I have enough," "I have everything." "Enough" is GAR, and "everything" is VAK. This is also the meaning of "how shall Jacob stand, for he is small?" This is the meaning of Jacob taking the seniority from him. Afterward, he was given everything, since he had GAR, too, which came to him through Joseph, by way of "And Joseph sustained."

This is the meaning of "Leah was hated," from whom all hatreds and disputes among wise disciples extend. This is also the meaning of the dispute between Shammai and Hillel. In the future, when the two camps unite—the camp of Joseph and the camp of Judah—this is the meaning of what Judah said to Joseph: "Oh my lord," as then was the unification of Judah and Joseph. But Judah must be in the lead.

This explains the ARI being Messiah Son of Joseph, which is why he could reveal such wisdom, since he had permission from the revealed world. This dispute extends from "And the children struggled within her," that Esau had the good clothes that were with Rebecca.

103. Whose Heart Makes Him Willing
I heard on the eve of Shabbat, Beresheet, Tav-Shin-Gimel, October 1942

In the verse, "from every man whose heart makes him willing, you shall take My donation." This is the meaning of "the substance of a donation from sanctity." In other words, how does one come to a state of offering? Through sanctity.

This means that if one sanctifies oneself with the permitted, he thus comes to a state of donation, which is the *Shechina* [Divinity], called "my donation." This is the meaning of "of every man whose heart makes him willing," all of his heart, meaning if he donates all of his heart, he is rewarded with My donation, to adhere to the *Shechina*.

In the verse, "in the day of his espousals and in the day of the gladness of his heart," espousals mean being of inferior degree, which is lowliness. If a person takes upon himself to serve the Creator in a state of lowliness, and at the same time he is happy with this work, this is an important degree, and then one is called "a bridegroom" of the *Shechina*.

104. And the Saboteur Was Sitting
I heard on the eve of Shabbat, Beresheet, Tav-Shin-Gimel, October 1942

In *The Zohar*, Noah, "There was a flood, and the saboteur was sitting in the midst of it." He asked, "A flood means a flood of water. This, in itself, is deadly and a saboteur. So what does it mean that the saboteur was sitting in the midst of it, in the midst of the flood? Also, what is the difference between the flood and the saboteur?"

He replied that the flood is corporeal torments, meaning torments of the body. Within it, meaning within the torments of the body, there is yet another saboteur, who sabotages spirituality. This means that the afflictions of the body bring him foreign thoughts, until these foreign thoughts sabotage and kill his spirituality.

105. A Bastard Wise Disciple Precedes a Commoner High Priest
I heard on Heshvan 15, Tav-Shin-Hey, November 1, 1944, Tel-Aviv

"A bastard wise disciple precedes a commoner high priest."

A bastard means a foreign god, cruel. This refers to bastardy. When one breaches the prohibition of turning to other gods, they beget him a bastard.

Turning to the other gods means that he mates himself with the *Sitra Achra* [other side], which is pudendum. This is called "who comes over the pudendum and begets from it a bastard."

The view of landlords is opposite from the view of Torah. Hence, there is a dispute between commoners and wise disciples. And here there is a big difference if the person begot the bastard. A wise disciple claims that that, too, comes from the Creator, that the form that appears to him—the bastard—he says that the Creator caused him that reason. The wicked, however, says that it is only a foreign thought that came to him because of a sin, and he needs nothing more than to correct his sins.

A wise disciple, however, has the strength to believe that this, too, meaning his present form, he must see its true essence. At the same time, he must take upon himself the burden of the kingdom of heaven to the point of devotion.

This means that on what is considered of little importance, too, the lowest and most concealed, still, at such a time it should be ascribed to the Creator, that the Creator created such a picture of Providence in him, called "foreign thoughts." And he works above reason on such a small thing as though he had great *Daat* [knowledge] in *Kedusha* [holiness].

And a great priest is one who serves the Creator by way of "and they are many..." meaning that they have much Torah and many *Mitzvot* [commandments] and they are not lacking anything. Hence, if one comes to connect and take upon himself some order in the work, the rule is that a bastard who is a wise disciple comes first. This means that one assumes one's bastardy in the form of a wise disciple. "Wise" is the name of the Creator. His disciple is one who learns from the Creator. Only a wise disciple can say that everything, all the shapes that appear during the work are "for it was from the Lord."

But a commoner priest, although he serves the Creator and is great in the Torah and in the work, he has not been rewarded with learning from the Creator's mouth, and he is still not considered "a wise disciple."

Hence, this above state cannot help him achieve true perfection whatsoever, since he has the view of landlords, and the view of Torah is only one who learns from the Creator. Only a wise disciple knows the truth, that the Creator causes all the reasons.

Now we can understand the words of our sages, "Rabbi Shimon Ben Menasia was studying all the *Etin* ['the' (in plural form)] in the Torah." *Et* means including. This means that every day he added Torah and *Mitzvot* more than in the day before. And since he came to "You shall fear the Lord your God," meaning that he could not increase, but came to a point where he could not add, but God forbid, to the contrary.

And RASHI interprets, Ben Menasia means that he understood the *Menusa* [fleeing], which means fleeing and retreat from the campaign. Also, *Ben** *Haamsuny*,

---
* In Hebrew, *Ben* (son) has the same root as *Mevin* (understanding).

meaning that he understood the truth, and what form truth has, and he remained standing guard and could not move forward until Rabbi Akiva came and explained *Et* [the], to include the wise disciples. This means that through adhering to wise disciples, it is possible to receive some support.

In other words, only a wise disciple can help him, and nothing else. Even if he is great in the Torah, he will still be called "a commoner," if he has not been rewarded with learning from the Creator's mouth.

Hence, one must surrender before a wise disciple and accept what the wise disciple places on him without any arguments, but by way of above reason.

"Its measure is longer than the earth." This means that the Torah begins after the earth. That is, if it is greater than the earth. There is a rule that nothing can begin in the middle. Hence, if one wants to begin, the beginning is after the earth, meaning past earthliness. (And this is the meaning of "a commoner high priest," meaning that even if one's work is in greatness, if he has not been awarded the light of the Torah, he is still in earthliness.)

Achieving *Lishma* [for Her sake] requires plenty of learning in *Lo Lishma* [not for Her sake]. This means that one should strain and exert *Lo Lishma*, and then he can see the truth, that he has still not been awarded the *Lishma*. However, when one does not strain oneself with great efforts, one cannot see the truth.

On another occasion, he said that man should study much Torah *Lishma* to be rewarded with seeing the truth—that he is working *Lo Lishma*. The work *Lishma* is considered reward and punishment, which is considered *Malchut*. And Torah *Lo Lishma* is considered *ZA*, considered private Providence.

This is why the kings of Israel, all of whom who were awarded private Providence, had nothing more to do since they had nothing to add. This is why our sages said, "a king of Israel neither judges nor is he judged." Hence, they have no part in the next world since they do not do anything, as they see that the Creator does everything.

This is the meaning of *Izevel* [Jezebel], Ahab's wife. They interpreted that his wife argued, *Ei Zevel* [where is refuse], meaning "Where is there refuse in the world?" She saw that it was all good. And *Ah Av* [Ahab] means that he was *Ah* [brother] to the *Av* [Father] in heaven. But the kings of David's house are judged because the kings of David's house had the power to unite the Creator and His *Shechina* [Divinity], although they are mutually contradictory, as Providence is opposite to the discernment of reward and punishment.

This is the power of the great righteous, that they can unite the Creator with the *Shechina*, meaning private Providence with reward and punishment. And precisely from the two of them emerges the complete and desirable perfection.

106. What the Twelve Challahs on Shabbat Imply
I heard on *Elul*, *Tav-Shin-Bet*, August 1942

In the songs of Shabbat [Sabbath] it is written, "will reveal to us the flavor of twelve challahs [Sabbath bread], which are a letter in His name, multiplied and faint."

We should interpret the words of the holy ARI. It is known that two *Vavs* were made by the second *Tzimtzum* [restriction], meaning the right side and the left side. This is the meaning of the multiplication, from the word "multiply." And from this, from the power of the correction of the second *Tzimtzum* when there was the association of the quality of mercy with the judgment, the judgment became fainter than it was prior to the sweetening.

Afterward, the two *Vavs* shine in *Malchut*, which means "the gathering *Zayins*." The *Zayins* are *Malchut* called "seventh," who gather the two *Vavs* within her.

The seventh day is considered *Gmar Tikkun* [the end of correction], discerned as the end of days. However, it also shines in the six thousand years. This is the meaning of the six workdays, discerned as "that God has created to do." And Shabbat is called "resting" (as it is written, "and on the seventh day He ceased from work and rested").

This is considered *Shabbat* [Sabbath], which shines in the six thousand years, as then the Shabbat is considered resting, like a person carrying a load, and stands to rest along the way to regain his strength. Afterward, he should carry the weight once more. But on the *Shabbat* of *Gmar Tikkun*, there is nothing more to add; hence, there is no more work at all.

107. Concerning the Two Angels
I heard on *Tetzave*, February, *Tav-Shin-Gimel*, 1943, Jerusalem

Concerning the two angels that accompany one on the eve of *Shabbat* [Sabbath], a good angel and a bad angel, a good angel is called "right," by which one comes closer to serving the Creator. This is called "the right brings closer." And the bad angel is considered "left," pushing away. This means that it brings him foreign thoughts, whether in mind or in heart.

When one prevails over the bad and brings himself closer to the Creator, meaning that each time, he overcomes the evil and attaches himself to the Creator, it follows that through the two of them, he has come closer to *Dvekut* [adhesion] with the Creator. This means that both performed a single task—they have caused him to adhere to the Creator. In that state one says, "Come in peace."

And when one has completed all of one's work and has admitted all the left into *Kedusha* [holiness], as it is written, "There is no place to hide from You," the bad angel has nothing more to do, as the person has already overcome all the difficulties that the evil presented. At that time, the bad angel is idle. At that time, the person tells it, "Go in peace."

108. If You Leave Me One Day, I Will Leave You Two
I heard in 1943, Tav-Shin-Gimel, Jerusalem

Every person is remote from the Creator with the quality of reception in him. But he is remote simply because of the will to receive in him. However, since that person does not crave spirituality, but worldly pleasures, his distance from the Creator is one day, meaning a distance of a day, which means that he is far from Him in only one aspect—in being immersed in the will to receive the desires of this world.

However, when a person brings himself closer to the Creator, and dismisses reception in this world, he is then considered close to the Creator. But if he later fails in the reception of the next world, he is then far from the Creator because he wants to receive the pleasures of the next world, and also falls into reception of pleasures of this world, too. It follows that now he has become remote from the Creator by two days: 1) by receiving pleasures in this world, to which he has fallen again, and 2) since he now has the desire to receive the crown of the next world. This is because by engaging in Torah and Mitzvot [commandments], he forces the Creator to reward him for his work in Torah and Mitzvot.

It turns out that in the beginning he walked one day and drew closer to serving the Creator, and afterward he walked two days backwards. Thus, now that person has become needy of two types of reception: 1) of this world, 2) of the next world. Thus, he has been walking in the opposite state.

The advice for this is to always go by the path of Torah, which means to bestow. The order should be that first one must be careful with the two bases: 1) the making of the Mitzva [commandment], 2) the sensation of pleasure from the Mitzva. One should believe that the Creator derives pleasure when we keep His commandments.

It therefore follows that one should keep the Mitzva in practice, and believe that the Creator derives pleasure from the lower one keeping His Mitzvot. In this there is no difference between a big Mitzva and a small Mitzva. That is, the Creator derives pleasure even from the smallest act that is done for Him.

Afterward, there is a result, which is the main goal that one should see to. In other words, a person should feel delight and pleasure in causing contentment to his Maker. This is the main emphasis of the work, and this is called "serve the Lord with gladness." This should be the reward for one's work, to receive delight and pleasure in having been rewarded with delighting the Creator.

This is the meaning of "The stranger that is in the midst of you shall rise above you higher and higher; ... He shall lend to you, and you shall not lend to him." The "stranger" is the will to receive (when beginning to serve the Creator, the will to receive is called "stranger." And prior to that, it is a complete gentile).

"He shall lend to you." When he gives strength for work, he gives the strength by way of lending. This means that when a day in Torah and *Mitzvot* has passed, although he did not receive the reward instantaneously, he still believed him that afterward he would pay for the powers for the work that he gave him.

Hence, after the day's work he comes to him and asks for the debt that he had promised him, the reward for the powers that the body gave him in order to engage in Torah and *Mitzvot*. But he does not give him so the stranger cries, "What is this work? Working without reward?" Hence, afterward, the stranger does not want to give Israel the strength to work.

"And you shall not lend to him." If you give him food and ask that he will give you strength to work, then he tells you that he has no debt to pay you for the food that you are giving him since "Previously, I gave you the strength for the work on condition that you would buy me possessions. Hence, what you are giving me now is all according to the previous condition. Therefore, now you come to me to give you more strength for the work, so that you will bring me new possessions?"

So the will to receive has grown clever and uses its cleverness to calculate the profitability of the matter. Sometimes he says that he is content with little, that the possessions he has are enough, so he does not want to give him strength. And sometimes he says that the way you are going in now is dangerous, and perhaps your efforts will be in vain. Sometimes, he tells him that the effort is greater than the reward; hence, I will not give you strength to work.

Then, when one asks him for strength to walk in the path of the Creator, in order to bestow, and that everything will be only to increase the glory of Heaven, he says, "What will I get out of it?" Then he comes with the famous arguments, such as "Who" and "What," meaning "Who is the Lord that I should obey His voice?" as Pharaoh's argument, or "What is this work for you?" as the argument of the wicked.

All this is because he has a just argument, that this is what they had agreed between them. And this is called, "if you do not obey the voice of the Lord," then he complains because he does not keep the conditions.

But when you obey to the voice of the Creator, meaning right at the entrance (entrance is a constant thing because every time he has a descent he must begin anew. This is why it is called an "entrance." Naturally, there are many exits and many entrances) he tells his body, "Know that I want to begin to serve the Creator and my intention is only to bestow and not to receive any reward. You should not hope that you will receive anything for your efforts, but it is all in order to bestow."

And if the body asks, "What is your benefit from this work?" meaning, "Who receives this work, that I want to exert and toil?" Or he asks more simply, "For whose sake am I working so hard?" The reply should be, "I have faith in the sages, and they said that I should believe in abstract faith, above reason, that the Creator has so commanded us, to take upon ourselves faith, that He commanded us to keep Torah and Mitzvot. And we should also believe that the Creator derives pleasure when we keep the Torah and Mitzvot with faith above reason. Also, one should be glad at the Creator's pleasure from his work."

Thus, there are four things here:

1. Believing in the sages, that what they said is true.
2. Believing that the Creator commanded to engage in Torah and Mitzvot only through faith above reason.
3. There is joy when the creatures keep the Torah and Mitzvot on the basis of faith.
4. One should receive delight, pleasure, and gladness from having been rewarded with pleasing the King. And the measure of the greatness and the importance of man's work is measured by the measure of joy that one derives during his work. This depends on the measure of faith that one believes in the above.

It follows that when you obey the voice of the Creator, all the powers that he receives from the body are not considered receiving a loan from the body, which one should return, as in "If you do not obey the Lord." And if the body asks, "Why should I give you strength to work when you promise me nothing in return?" he should answer, "Because this is what you were made for, and what can I do if the Creator hates you, as it is written in *The Zohar*, that the Creator hates the bodies."

Moreover, when *The Zohar* says that the Creator hates the bodies, this refers specifically to the bodies of the servants of the Creator, since they want to be eternal receivers, as they want to receive the crown of the next world, too.

And this is considered, "and you shall not lend." This means that you do not have to give anything for the strength that the body gave you for the work. But if you lend it, if you give it any pleasure, it is only as a loan, and it should give you strength to work in return, but not for free.

It must always give you strength, meaning for free. You do not give it any pleasure and you always demand of it to have strength for the work, since "the borrower is servant to the lender." Thus, it will always be the servant and you will be the master.

109. Two Kinds of Meat
I heard on Heshvan 20

We usually distinguish between two kinds of meat: beast meat and fish meat, and in both there are signs of *Tuma'a* [impurity]. The Torah gave us signs by which to know how to avoid them so as to not fall into the domain of *Tuma'a* in them.

In fish, it gives us the signs of fins and scales. When one sees these signs in fish, he knows how to be careful and not fall into the hands of *Tuma'a*. *Snapir* [fin] implies *Soneh-Peh-Ohr* [hating-mouth-light]. This refers to *Malchut*, called "mouth," and all the lights come from her, which is discerned as faith.

When one sees that he is in the state of a taste of dust, at a time when one should believe, he knows for certain that he should correct his actions. This is called "*Shechina* [Divinity] in the dust," and one should pray to raise the *Shechina* from the dust.

Kaskeset [scales] means that at a time of *Snapir* he is unable to work at all. But when he overcomes the *Snapir*, a question concerning Providence appears in his mind. This is called *Kash* [straw], and then he falls from his work. Later, he grows stronger and begins to work above reason, and another doubt concerning Providence appears in his mind.

It follows that he has two times *Kash*, which are *Kas-Keset*. Every time one overcomes above reason, he ascends and then he descends. Then one sees that he cannot overcome due to the proliferation of the doubts. In that state, one has no other choice but to cry out to the Creator, as it is written, "And the Children of Israel sighed from the work, and their cry came up unto God," and He delivered them out of Egypt, meaning from all the troubles.

Our sages said a famous rule, that the Creator says, "He and I cannot dwell in the same abode," since they are opposite from one another. This is so because there are two bodies in man—the inner body and the outer body. The spiritual sustenance dresses in the inner body, discerned as faith and bestowal, called "mind and heart." And the outer body has the corporeal sustenance, which is knowing and receiving.

In the middle, between the inner body and the outer body, there is a middle body, which does not bear its own name. Rather, if one performs good deeds, the middle body clings to the inner body. If one does bad deeds, the middle body clings to the outer body. Thus, either one has corporeal sustenance or spiritual sustenance.

It follows that since there is oppositeness between the internal and the external, if the middle body clings to the inner body, it is considered the death of the outer body. And if it clings to the outer body, it is death to the inner body, since in that state, the choice is in the middle body: to continue adhering to *Kedusha* [holiness], or to the contrary.

110. A Field that the Lord Has Blessed
I heard in Tav-Shin-Gimel, 1942-1943

"A field that the Lord has blessed." The *Shechina* [Divinity] is called "a field." Sometimes, a *Sadeh* [field] becomes a *Sheker* [lie]. The *Vav* within the *Hey* is the soul, and the *Dalet* is the *Shechina* [Divinity]. When the soul is dressed in it, it is called *Hey*, and when one wants to add to the faith, he extends the *Vav* below and it becomes a *Kof*.

At that time, the *Dalet* becomes *Reish*, in the form of poor and meager, who wants to add. Then it becomes *Reish*, by way of "A poor was born in his kingdom," when the meager has become poor. In other words, by inserting the evil eye into himself in both mind and heart, by way of "The boar from the wood will gnaw on it," the eye is hung since it returns to the leftovers, that the *Sitra Achra* [other side] is destined to be a holy angel.

This is the meaning of "May the glory of the Lord be forever." Because he has come to a state of the animal of the *Yaar* [forest], from the word *Iro* [his town], it means that all of his vitality has been poured out, yet he constantly grows stronger, then he is awarded the state of "a field which the Lord has blessed," when the evil eye has become a good eye.

This is the meaning of "a hanging eye," meaning it hangs on a doubt, whether with a good eye or with an evil eye. And this is the meaning of returning to leftovers, and this is the meaning of "one, to receive one," as our sages said, "There was no joy before Him as on the day when heaven and earth were created." This is so because at last, the "Lord will be One and His name One," which is the purpose of creation.

But for the Creator, past and present are the same. Hence, the Creator observes creation in its final shape, as it will be at *Gmar Tikkun* [the end of correction], when all the souls in their complete perfection are included in the world *Ein Sof*, as it will be at *Gmar Tikkun*. Their perfect form is already there, and nothing is missing.

But with the receivers it is apparent that they still need to complete what they must complete. This is, "which God has created to do," meaning the deficiencies and the petulance. This is the meaning of what our sages said, "the petulant yields nothing but petulance," and also, "All who are gluttonous are angry."

This is the true form of the will to receive in its true form, as obscene as it is. And all the corrections are to turn it in order to bestow, which is all the work of the lower ones. Before the world was created, it was in the form of "He is one and His name One." This means that even though His name has already departed from the He, and has become revealed and is already called "His Name," He is still one. This is the meaning of "one, to receive one."

111. Breath, Sound, and Speech

I heard on Sivan 29, Tav-Shin-Gimel, July 2, 1943, Jerusalem

There is a discernment of "breath," "sound," and "speech," there is a discernment of "ice," and there is the discernment of "terrible." Breath means *Ohr Hozer* [reflected light], which comes out of the *Masach* [screen]. This is a limiting force. As long as it is not accumulated to the measure of "let them not return to folly," it is called "breath."

When its measure is completed, this limitation, the *Masach* with the reflected light, is called "sound." Sound is like a warning that tells him not to breach the laws of the Torah. And if he should breach, as soon as he breaches he will stop tasting. Hence, when he knows for certain that if he breaches he will come to a cessation, he retains the limitation.

And then he comes to a state of "speech," which is *Malchut*. At that time, there can be the *Zivug* [coupling] of the Creator and His *Shechina* [Divinity], and illumination of *Hochma* [wisdom] will extend below.

It is known that there are two degrees: 1) bestowal without any reception, 2) reception in order to bestow.

Then, when he sees that he has already come to a degree where he can receive in order to bestow, why does he need the servitude, which is only in the form of bestowing in order to bestow? After all, the Creator has more contentment from reception in order to bestow, since the light of wisdom, which enters the vessels of reception, is the light of the purpose of creation. Hence, why should he engage in the work of bestowal in order to bestow, which is the light of the correction of creation?

At that time, he immediately stops tasting and is left bare and destitute. This is because the light of *Hassadim* [mercy] is the light that robes the light of *Hochma*. And if the robe is missing, even though he has light of *Hochma*, he still has nothing with which to clothe the *Hochma*.

At that time, he comes to the state called "the terrible ice." *Yesod de Abba*, which gives *Hochma*, called "narrow of *Hassadim* and long of *Hochma*," is ice. It is like water that has been crystallized: Although there is water, it does not expand below.

Yesod de Ima is called "terrible," considered short and wide. It is called "short" because there is blocking on the *Hochma*, because of the absence of *Hochma* there due to the second *Tzimtzum* [restriction]. And this is "terrible." Hence, it is precisely by both: *Hochma* extends through *Yesod de Abba*, and *Hassadim* extends through *Yesod de Ima*.

112. The Three Angels
I heard on *VaYera*, *Tav-Shin-Gimel*, October 1942

Understand:

1. The matter of the three angels that came to visit Abraham during the circumcision.

2. The matter of the Creator coming to visit him and what He told him during the visit.

3. That our sages said that the visitor takes one sixtieth of the sickness.

4. The separation from Lot.

5. The destruction of Sodom and Gomorrah.

6. Abraham's request not to destroy Sodom.

7. The matter of Lot's wife looking back and becoming a pillar of salt.

8. The matter of Shimon and Levi's deceit of the people of Shechem concerning the circumcision, when they said, "for it is a disgrace to us."

9. The matter of the two separations that came out from Lot, which were erased in the days of David and Solomon, which are opposite to one another.

To understand the above, we should first say that we know that we discern *Olam* [world], *Shanna* [year], and *Nefesh* [soul] in everything. Hence, concerning the circumcision, too, which is the making of the covenant of the skin, applies the matter of *Olam*, *Shanna*, *Nefesh*. (There are four covenants: eyes, tongue, heart, and skin; and the skin includes them all.)

The skin, considered the foreskin, is the *Behina Dalet* [Phase Four], which should be removed to its place, meaning to the dust. This is considered *Malchut* in her place, that is, lowering *Malchut* to a state of dust. This follows the words, "*Abba* [father] gives the white," meaning lowers *Malchut* from all thirty-two paths to its place. And you find that the *Sefirot* have been whitened from the *Aviut* [thickness] of *Malchut* of the quality of judgment that was in them, since the breaking occurred because of this *Malchut*.

Afterward, *Ima* [mother] gives the red, when she receives the *Malchut* that is sweetened in *Bina*, called "earth," and not "dust." This is so because we make two discernments in *Malchut*: 1) earth, 2) dust.

Earth is *Malchut* that is sweetened in *Bina*, called "*Malchut* that has risen to *Bina*." Dust is called "*Malchut* in the place of *Malchut*," which is *Midat ha Din* [the quality of judgment].

When Abraham had to beget Isaac, who is discerned as the whole of Israel, he had to purify himself with the circumcision so that Israel would emerge pure. The circumcision, with respect to its *Nefesh* [soul], is called "circumcision" and concerns the removal of the foreskin and throwing it to a place of dust.

The *Olam* [world] in the circumcision is called "the destruction of Sodom and Gomorrah."

The *Hitkalelut* [mingling/integration] of the souls in the world (a world means *Hitkalelut* of many souls) is called "Lot," and the circumcision in the world is called "the destruction of Sodom." The healing of the pain of circumcision is called "the saving of Lot." Lot comes from the word "cursed land," called *Behina Dalet*.

We should know that when one has been awarded *Dvekut* [adhesion] with the Creator, when he has equivalence of form and his only wish is to bestow and not receive anything for his own benefit, he comes to a state where he has no room to work. This is because that person does not need anything for himself; and for the Creator, he sees that the Creator has no deficiencies. Hence, he remains standing, without work. This causes him the great pain of the circumcision, since the circumcision gave him room to work, as circumcision is the removal of the desire to receive for oneself.

It turns out that by removing the will to receive, when it no longer controls him, he has nothing more to add to his work. There is a correction to this: Even after one has been rewarded with circumcising himself from the will to receive, there still remain sparks of *Behina Dalet* in him, and they, too, are awaiting correction. They are sweetened only by extending lights of *Gadlut* [greatness/adulthood], and thus one has room for work.

This is the meaning of Abraham the Patriarch's pains after the circumcision, and the Creator coming to visit him. This is also the meaning of the angel Raphael healing his pain (and we cannot say that since with the four angels, the order is that Michael is on the right, Gabriel is on the left, and Uriel is at the front, and behind, which is *Malchut*, implied in the west, it is Raphael. This is because he heals *Malchut* after the removal of the foreskin, so there will be more room for work).

And the second angel came to destroy Sodom. This means that the removal of the foreskin in the quality of *Nefesh* is called "circumcision," and in the quality of *Olam*, it is called "the destruction of Sodom." As they said, after the removal of the foreskin there remains pain, and then we need to heal that pain. Similarly, in the destruction of Sodom, the healing is called "the saving of Lot," due to two good separations that were about to unfold.

It is seemingly difficult to understand the matter of the good separation. If it is separation, how can it be good? Rather, following the removal of the foreskin, there is pain. This is because one has no room for work. And those separations, the sparks that remain of *Behina Dalet*, give one room for work in that he needs to correct them.

They cannot be corrected prior to the removal of the foreskin, since first, the 248 sparks must be elevated and corrected. Subsequently, the thirty-two sparks, called "the stony heart," are corrected. Hence, first the foreskin must be removed completely.

This is the meaning of the necessity of having a secret, that one should not know ahead of time, for they should remain in the form of a *Reshimo* [recollection]. And this is the meaning of *Sod* [secret]: Through the correction of the circumcision, which is the disruption of the *Yesod* [foundation], meaning disrupting the *Yod* [the first letter in *Yesod*]. Then, the *Sod* becomes *Yesod*.

This is the meaning of the angel Raphael subsequently going to save Lot because of the "good separations." This is the meaning of Rut and Naomi, considered mind and heart. Rut comes from the word *Re'uia* [worthy], when the *Aleph* is unpronounced.

And Naomi is from the word *Noam* [pleasantness], something that is pleasant to the heart, which were then sweetened in David and Solomon.

However, previously, the angel said, "look not behind you," since "Lot" is *Behina Dalet*, but she is still connected to Abraham. However, "behind you," past *Behina Dalet*, there is only raw *Behina Dalet*, without sweetening. This is the meaning of the great sea monsters, of which our sages said that it is a Leviathan (whale) and his spouse, which killed the *Nukva* and salted her for the righteous in the future. The future means after all the corrections.

This is the meaning of Lot's wife looking behind her, as it is written, "But his wife looked back from behind him, and she became a pillar of salt." However, she first had to be killed, which is the destruction of Sodom. But Lot, who is considered the Leviathan (the connection between *Behina Dalet* and Abraham) had to be saved.

This explains a common question, How could the angel that healed Abraham save Lot? After all, there is a rule: One angel does not perform two missions. However, this is the same issue, since there has to remain a *Reshimo* from *Behina Dalet*. But it must be a secret.

This means that before he circumcised himself, there was no need to know anything of it. Rather, she had to be put to death. And the Creator salted her for the righteous in the future, when the *Sod* became *Yesod*.

This is the meaning of the strife between the herdsmen of Abraham's cattle and the herdsmen of Lot's cattle (*Mikneh* [cattle] means spiritual *Kinyanim* [possessions]). This is because Abraham's cattle was for the purpose of increasing the quality of Abraham—faith. This means that in this manner he took for himself greater forces to go above reason, since he saw that specifically in this way of faith above reason, one is rewarded with all the possessions.

It follows that the reason he wanted the possessions was that these possessions would testify to the way, called "faith above reason," which is a true path. The evidence of this is that since he is given spiritual possessions from above, through the possessions, he strains to go only by way of faith above reason. But he does not want the spiritual possessions because they are great degrees and attainments.

This means that it is not that he believes in the Creator in order to achieve great attainments through faith. Rather, he needs great attainments so as to know that he is treading a true path. Thus, after all the *Gadlut*, he wants specifically to walk in the path of faith, since through it he sees that he is doing something.

However, the only intention of the herdsmen of Lot's cattle was to achieve great possessions and attainments. This is called "increasing the quality of Lot." Lot is called "the cursed land," which is one's will to receive, called *Behina Dalet*, whether in mind or in heart. This is why Abraham said, "Please part from me," that is, that *Behina Dalet* would be separated from him, from the *Behina* of *Olam-Shanna-Nefesh*.

This is the meaning of the removal of the foreskin. The removal of *Behina Dalet* in *Nefesh* is called "circumcision." In the *Behina* of *Olam*, the removal of the foreskin is called "the destruction of Sodom"; and from the *Behina* of *Shanna*, it is the *Hitkalelut* of many souls, and it is called *Shanna* [year]. This is the quality of Lot, from the word "curse," called "the cursed land."

Hence, when Abraham said to Lot, "Please part from me," still, Lot was the son of Haran, referring to the second restriction, called "a river that flows out of Eden to water the garden." And there is the discernment of "beyond the river," being outside the river, meaning the first *Tzimtzum* [restriction], and there is a difference between the first *Tzimtzum* and the second *Tzimtzum*.

In the first *Tzimtzum*, the *Dinim* [judgments] stand below all the *Sefirot* of *Kedusha* [holiness], as they emerged in the beginning, by the order of the hanging down of the worlds. In the second *Tzimtzum*, however, they rose to the place of *Kedusha* and already have a hold of *Kedusha*. Hence, in this respect, they are worse than the first *Tzimtzum*; they have no further expansion.

The "land of Canaan" is from the second *Tzimtzum*, which are very bad because they have a hold on *Kedusha*. This is why it is written about them, "you shall not sustain any soul." The quality of Lot, however, *Behina Dalet*, must be saved. Hence, the three angels came as one: one for the blessing of the seed, considered the whole of Israel, implying also the multiplication in the Torah. This is the meaning of disclosing the secrets of Torah, which is called *Banim* [sons], from the word *Havanah* [understanding]. It is possible to attain all this only after the correction of the circumcision.

This is the meaning of the Creator's words: "Shall I hide from Abraham that which I am doing?" Abraham was afraid of Sodom's destruction, lest he would lose all the vessels of reception. This is why he said, "Perhaps there are fifty righteous within the city?" because a complete *Partzuf* is fifty degrees. And afterwards he asked, "Perhaps there are forty-five righteous?" meaning *Aviut* of *Behina Gimel*, which is forty, and the *Dalet de Hitlabshut* [clothing], which is VAK, half a degree, being five *Sefirot*, etc. Finally, he asked, "Perhaps there are ten righteous?" meaning the level of *Malchut*, which is only ten. Hence, when Abraham saw that even the level of *Malchut* could not emerge from there, he agreed to the destruction of Sodom.

It turns out that when the Creator came to visit him, he prayed for Sodom, as it is written, "according to its cry," meaning that they were all immersed in the will to receive. "Altogether... and if not, I will know." This means that if there are discernments of bestowal in them, then we will know. This is a matter of bonding, meaning He will connect them to the *Kedusha* [holiness]. Since Abraham saw that no good would come from them, he agreed to the destruction of Sodom.

This is why after Lot's separation from Abraham, it is written, "[he] moved his tent as far as Sodom," the dwelling place of the will to receive, with respect to himself.

This is only in the land of Israel. However, beyond the river, which is the first *Tzimtzum*, the domination of *Behina Dalet*, there is no room for work. This is because it rules and prevails in its own place, and only in the land of Israel, considered the second *Tzimtzum*, there is all the work. This is the meaning of Abraham's name *Be Hey Bera'am* [created them with the *Hey*]. This means that the *Yod* of Sarai divided into two *Heys*—the lower *Hey* and the upper *Hey*—where Abraham took form the *Hitkalelut* of the lower *Hey* with the upper *Hey*.

Now we can understand Shimon and Levi who deceived the men of Shechem. Since Shechem wanted Dinah, since his whole intention was the will to receive, they said that they had to be circumcised, meaning to cancel the vessels of reception. Since their only aim was in the will to receive, they were killed by the circumcision, by losing the will to receive through the circumcision. For them, this was considered death.

It therefore follows that they themselves deceived, since their whole intention was in Dinah, their sister. They thought that they could receive Dinah in the vessels of reception. Hence, once they were circumcised, and then wanted to receive Dinah, they could only use the vessels of bestowal, and they had lost the vessels of reception by the circumcision. But since they lacked the spark of bestowal, since Shechem was the son of Hamor, who knows nothing but the vessels of reception, they could not receive Dinah in the vessels of bestowal, as this is against their root, for their root is only *Hamor*, the will to receive. Hence, they came out empty both ways. This is considered that Shimon and Levi caused their death. But actually, it was their own fault, not Shimon's and Levi's.

This is the meaning of the words of our sages: "If you come across a villain, draw him to the seminary." We must understand what "If you come across" means. It means that the villain, meaning the will to receive, is not always found. Rather, it means that not everyone considers their will to receive "a villain." Rather, if someone feels the will to receive as a villain and wants to get rid of it, as it is written, "One should always vex the good inclination over the evil inclination," if he prevails, good; and if not, he should engage in the Torah, and if not, he should read the *Shema* reading, and if not, he should remind him of the day of his death" (*Berachot*, p 5). In that state, he has three counsels together, and one without the others is incomplete.

Now we can understand the common question with which the *Gemara* ends: If the first advice—"pull him to the seminary"—does not help, then "read the *Shema* reading." And if that does not help, "remind him of the day of his death." Thus, if he is doubtful of their help, why does he need the first two counsels? Why should he not take the last advice right away, meaning reminding him of the day of death? He answers that this does not mean that one counsel will help, but that it requires all three counsels together.

And this means:

1. Pull him to the seminary, meaning the Torah.
2. Read the *Shema* reading, meaning the Creator and *Dvekut* [adhesion] with the Creator.
3. Remind him of the day of death, meaning devotion. This is considered Israel, who are likened to a dove that stretches out its neck. In other words, all three discernments are one unity called "The Torah, Israel, and the Creator are one."

One can receive assistance from a rav [great person/teacher] for the quality of the Torah and the reading of *Shema*. However, for the quality of Israel, which is the circumcision, which is devotion, one has to work by himself. Even though there is help from above for this, too, as our sages said, "and made a covenant with him," meaning that the Creator helped him, still, man must begin. This is the meaning of "remind him of the day of death." We must always remember and not forget, since this is the essence of man's work.

And concerning the *Reshimot* that we must leave, by way of Lot's salvation, it is because of two good separations, which is the meaning of Haman and Mordecai. Mordecai wants only to bestow; he has no need to extend lights of *Gadlut*. But through Haman, who wants to swallow all the lights into his authority, through him, he is the cause that evokes man to draw the lights of *Gadlut*.

Yet, after he has already extended the lights, it is forbidden to receive them in Haman's *Kelim* [vessels], called "vessels of reception," but only in the vessels of bestowal. This is the meaning of what is written, that the King told Haman, "and do so to Mordecai the Jew." This is considered the lights of Haman shining in the vessels of Mordecai.

113. The Eighteen Prayer

I heard on Kislev 15, Shabbat

In the *Shmone Esrei* [eighteen] Prayer, "for You hear the prayer of every mouth in Your people, Israel, with mercy," it seems perplexing since first we say, "for You hear the prayer of every mouth," meaning even an unworthy mouth—the Creator still hears. It is written, "every mouth," meaning even an unworthy one. Afterward, it says, "Your people, Israel, with mercy," meaning specifically a prayer that is in mercy. Otherwise, it is not heard.

The thing is that we must know all the heaviness in the work of the Creator is because of the oppositeness that is in every step. For example, there is a rule that man must be humble. But if we follow this end, although our sages said, "be very, very humble," this end still does not mean that it should be a rule, since it is known that one should go against the whole world and not be canceled by the many views that abound in the world, as it is written, "And his heart was high in the ways of the Lord." Hence, this rule is not a rule that we can call complete.

And if we go by the other end, which is pride, that, too, is wrong, since "Anyone who is proud," says the Creator, "he and I cannot dwell in the same abode." And we can also see oppositeness in the matter of suffering. That is, if the Creator sends suffering to some person, and we should believe that the Creator is good and does good, then the suffering He sent is necessarily to that person's benefit. Thus, why do we pray for the Creator to remove the suffering from us?

And concerning suffering, we should know that suffering only comes to correct us to be qualified to receive the light of the Creator. The role of the suffering is only to cleanse the body, as our sages said, "as salt sweetens meat, suffering cleanses the body." In the matter of prayer, they constituted that it would be instead of suffering. Thus, prayer, too, cleanses the body.

However, a prayer is called "the path of Torah." This is why prayer is more effective in sweetening the body than suffering. Therefore, it is a *Mitzva* [commandment] to pray over the suffering, since additional benefit stems from that to the individual and to the whole.

For this reason, the oppositeness causes one heaviness and cessations in the work of the Creator, and he cannot continue the work and feels bad. It seems to him that he is unworthy of assuming the burden of the kingdom of heaven "as an ox to the burden and as a donkey to the load." Thus, at that time, he is called "unwanted."

However, since one's sole intention is to extend faith, called *Malchut*, meaning to raise the *Shechina* [Divinity] from the dust, meaning that his aim is to glorify His Name in the world, His greatness, so the *Shechina* will not take the form of meagerness and poverty, so the Creator hears "the prayer of every mouth," even of one who is not so worthy, who feels that he is still far from the work of the Creator.

This is the meaning of "for You hear the prayer of every mouth." When does He hear every mouth? When Your people, Israel, pray with mercy, meaning simple mercy, when one prays to raise the *Shechina* from the dust, to receive faith.

It is similar to one who has not eaten in three days. Then, when he asks of another to be given something to eat, he is not asking for any luxuries or extras; he is simply asking to be given something to revive his soul.

Similarly, in the work of the Creator, when one finds himself standing between heaven and earth, he is not asking the Creator for something redundant, but only for the light of faith, for the Creator to open his eyes so he can take upon himself the quality of faith. This is called "raising the *Shechina* from the dust." This prayer is accepted from "every mouth." That is, whatever state a person is in, if he asks to revive his soul with faith, his prayer will be answered.

This is called "with mercy," when one's prayer is only to be pitied from above so he can sustain his vitality. This is the meaning of what is written in *The Zohar*, that a prayer for the poor is immediately accepted. That is, when it is for the *Shechina*, it is immediately accepted.

114. Prayer
I heard in *Tav-Shin-Bet*, 1941-1942

We must understand why a prayer is considered "mercy." After all, there is a rule: "I found and did not labor, do not believe." The advice is that one should promise the Creator that he will give Him the labor afterwards.

115. Still, Vegetative, Animate, and Speaking
I heard in *Tav-Shin*, 1939-1940, Jerusalem

Still is something that does not have an authority of its own. Rather, it is under the authority of its landlord and must satisfy every wish and desire of its landlord. Hence, since the Creator created creation for His glory, as it is written, "Every one who is called by My Name, I have created him for My glory," it means that the Creator created creation for His own needs. The nature of the landlord is imprinted in the creatures, meaning all the creatures cannot work for the sake of others but for themselves.

Vegetative is that which already has its own authority to some extent. It can already do something that is contrary to the opinion of the landlord. This means that it can already do things not for one's own benefit but in order to bestow. This is already the opposite of what exists in the will of the landlord, which He imprinted in the lower ones, that they will work only with the will to receive for themselves.

Yet, as we can see in corporeal plants, even though they are mobile and expand in length and in width, still, all the plants have a single property. In other words, there is not a single plant that can go against the method of all the plants. Rather, they must obey the rules of the plants and are incapable of doing anything against their contemporaries.

Thus, they have no life of their own, but are parts of the life of all the plants. This means that all the plants have a single form of life, that the form of life is the same for all the plants. All the plants are like a single creature, and the individual plants are specific organs of that animal.

Similarly, in spirituality there are people who have already acquired the strength to overcome their will to receive to some degree but are enslaved to the environment. They cannot do the opposite of the environment they live in, yet they do the opposite of what their will to receive wants. This means that they already work with the desire to bestow.

Animate: We see that each animal has its own characteristic; they are not enslaved to the environment and each of them has its own sensation and characteristics. They can certainly work against the will of the landlord, meaning they can work in bestowal and are also not enslaved to the environment. Rather, they have their own lives, and their vitality does not depend on their friends' lives. Yet, they cannot feel more than their own being. In other words, they have no sensation of the other. Naturally, they cannot care for others.

The speaking has virtues: 1 - It acts against the will of the Landlord. 2 - It is not confined to its contemporaries like the vegetative, meaning it is independent of the environment. 3 - It also feels others and can therefore care for them and complement them by feeling and regretting with the public, and being able to rejoice in the comfort of the public. Also, they can receive from the past and from the future, while animals feel only the present and only their own being.

116. He Who Said, "Mitzvot Do Not Require Intention"

I heard

"Mitzvot [commandments] do not require intention," and "The reward for a Mitzva [sing. of Mitzvot] is not in this world." This means that one who says that Mitzvot do not require intention believes that the reward for a Mitzva is not in this world. An intention is the reason and the flavor in the Mitzva. And this is the real reward of the Mitzva.

If a person tastes the flavor of a Mitzva and understands its reasoning, no greater reward is needed. Thus, if Mitzvot do not require intention, the reward for a Mitzva is not in this world anyway, since one does not feel any taste or any reason in the Mitzva.

It follows that if one is in a state where he hasn't any intention, then one is in a state that the reward for a Mitzva is not in this world. Because the reward for a Mitzva is the taste and the reason, if one does not have it, he certainly has no reward for a Mitzva in this world.

117. Labored and Did Not Find? Do Not Believe

I heard

Necessity of the labor is a requirement. Since the Creator gives man a present, He wants man to feel the benefit in the present. Otherwise, that person would be like a fool, as our sages said, "Who is a fool? He who loses what he is given." Because he does not appreciate the importance of the matter, he does not pay attention to keeping the present.

There is a rule that one feels no importance in anything if one has no need for that thing. As the measure of the need and the suffering if one does not attain it, to that very extent one feels gladness, pleasure, and joy at the satisfaction of the need. It is similar to one who is given all sorts of good beverages, but if he is not thirsty, he tastes nothing, as it is written, "As cold water to a faint soul."

Hence, when meals are set in order to please people, there is a custom: When we prepare meat and fish and all sorts of good things, we take note to serve bitter and hot things, such as mustard, hot peppers, sour, and salty foods. All of this is to evoke the suffering of hunger, since when the heart tastes a hot and bitter taste, it evokes hunger and deficiency, which one needs to satisfy with the meal of good things.

No one would ask, "Why do I need things to arouse hunger? After all, the host should only prepare satisfaction for the need, meaning the meal, and not prepare things that evoke the need for the satiation?" The obvious answer is that since the host wants people to enjoy the meal, to the extent that they have a need for the food, to that very extent they will enjoy the meal. It follows that if he gives many good things, it will still not help them enjoy the meal due to the above reason that there is no filling without a lack.

Hence, to be rewarded with the light of the Creator, there must also be a need. And the need for this is the labor: To the extent that one exerts and demands the Creator during the greatest concealment, to that extent he becomes needy of the Creator, for the Creator to open his eyes to walk by the path of the Creator. Then, when one has that *Kli* [vessel] of a deficiency, when the Creator gives him some help from above, he will know how to keep this present. It turns out that the labor is considered *Achoraim* [posterior]. And when he receives the *Achoraim*, he has a place in which to be rewarded with the *Panim* [face].

It is said about that, "A fool has no wish for wisdom." This means that he does not have a strong need to exert to obtain wisdom. Thus, he has no *Achoraim*, and he naturally cannot be awarded the discernment of *Panim*.

This is the meaning of "As is the sorrow, so is the reward." That is, the sorrow, called "labor," makes the *Kli* [vessel], so one can be awarded the reward. This means that to the extent that one regrets, to that extent he can later be rewarded with joy and pleasure.

118. To Understand the Matter of the Knees that Have Bowed to Baal

I heard

There is the discernment of a wife, and there is the discernment of a husband. A wife is considered that "she has nothing but what her husband gives her," and a husband is considered extending abundance into his own aspect. Knees are considered "bowing," as it is written, "unto You every knee shall bow."

There are two discernments in bowing:

1. One who bows before one who is greater, and although he does not know his merit, but believes that he is great, he therefore bows before him;

2. When he knows his greatness and merit in utter clarity.

There are also two discernments considering the faith in the greatness of the upper one:

1. He believes that he is great because he has no other choice, that is, he has no way to know his greatness.

2. He has a way to know his greatness in utter certainty, but he still chooses the path of faith because "It is the glory of God to conceal a thing." This means that although there are sparks in his body that want specifically to know His greatness, and not be as a beast, he still chooses faith for the above reason.

It follows that one who has no other choice, and chooses faith, is considered a woman, female—"he grew as weak as a female"—and she only receives from her husband. But one who has a choice yet struggles to go by the path of faith is called "a man of war." Hence, those who choose faith when they had the option of walking by the way of knowing, called *Baal* [husband/Canaanite god], are called "which have not bowed to *Baal*." This means that they did not surrender to the work of *Baal*, considered "knowing," but chose the path of faith.

119. That Disciple Who Learned in Secret
I heard on *Tishrei* 5, *Tav-Shin-Gimel*, September 16, 1942

That disciple who learned in secret, Bruria struck him and said, "ordered in all things," if ordered in the 248, exists. Secret means *Katnut* [smallness/infancy], from the word *Chash-Mal*. *Chash* means *Kelim de Panim* [anterior vessels], and *Mal* means *Kelim de Achor* [posterior vessels], the *Kelim* below the *Chazeh* [chest], which induce *Gadlut* [greatness/adulthood].

That disciple thought that if he had been awarded the state of *Chash*, a desire to bestow, and all his intentions are only to bestow, then he has been awarded everything. But the purpose of creating the worlds was to do good to His creations, to receive all the sublime pleasures, so man would achieve the full stature, even below the *Chazeh*, meaning the whole 248. This is why Bruria told him the verse, "ordered in all things," in all 248.

This means that he would extend below the *Chazeh*, too, meaning that he should extend *Gadlut*, too. This is *Mal*, speech, considered disclosure, to reveal the whole level. However, to avoid impairing, one must first receive the *Katnut*, called *Chash*, which is in secret, not yet revealed. Afterward, one needs to scrutinize the discernment of *Mal*, too, the *Gadlut*, and then the whole level will be revealed.

This is "ordered... and secure," when the *Katnut* is already secured in him and he can already extend the *Gadlut* without fear.

120. The Reason for Not Eating Nuts on Rosh Hashanah

I heard at the end of Rosh Hashanah, *Tav-Shin-Gimel*, 1942, Jerusalem

The reason for not eating nuts on *Rosh Hashanah* [Jewish New Year] is that *Egoz* [nut], in *Gematria*, is *Het* [sin]. And he asked, "But *Egoz*, in *Gematria*, is *Tov* [good]?" And he said that *Egoz* implies the tree of knowledge of good and evil.

And before one repents from love, the *Egoz* in him is still a sin. And one who has already been awarded repentance from love, his sins become for him as merits. It follows that the sin has been turned to good, and then he is permitted to eat nuts. This is why we should see that we eat only things that do not have any hint of a sin, which are considered the tree of life. However, things that have *Gematria* of *Het* imply the tree of knowledge of good and evil.

121. She Is Like Merchant-Ships

I heard

In the verse, "She is like the merchant-ships; she brings her bread from afar," when one demands and insists, "she is all mine," that all the desires will be dedicated to the Creator, the *Sitra Achra* [other side] awakens against him and claims, "She is all mine," too. Then there is a tradeoff. A tradeoff means that a person wants to buy a certain object, and the buyer and seller debate its value, meaning each of them claims that he is right.

And here the body examines to whom it is worthwhile to listen: to the receiver or to the giving force. Both clearly argue, "She is all mine." And since the person sees his lowliness, that in him, too, there are sparks that do not agree to observe the Torah and *Mitzvot* [commandments] even as a dot on the iota, but that the whole body argues, "She is all mine," then, "she brings her bread from afar." This means that from the removals, when one sees how far he is from the Creator and regrets and asks of the Creator to bring him closer, "she brings her bread."

Bread means faith. In that state one is awarded permanent faith, since "God has so made it that He would be feared." This means that all the removals that one feels were brought to him by the Creator, so he would have the need to take upon himself the fear of heaven.

This is the meaning of "Man shall not live on bread alone, but on what proceeds out of the mouth of the Lord." This means that the life of *Kedusha* [holiness] in a person does not come specifically from drawing closer, from entries, meaning admissions into *Kedusha*, but also from the exits, from the removals. This is so because through the dressing of the *Sitra Achra* in one's body, and its claims, "She is all mine," with a just argument, one is awarded permanent faith by overcoming these states.

This means that one should dedicate everything to the Creator, that is, that even the exits stem from Him. When he is rewarded, he sees that both the exits and the entries were all from Him. This forces him to be humble, since he sees that the Creator does everything, the exits as well as the entries.

This is the meaning of what is said about Moses, that he was humble and patient—that one must tolerate the lowliness, meaning that in each degree one should keep the lowliness. The minute he leaves the lowliness, he immediately loses all the degrees of Moses he had already achieved.

This is the meaning of patience. Lowliness exists in everyone, but not every person feels that lowliness is a good thing. It turns out that we do not want to suffer. However, Moses tolerated the humbleness, which is why he was called "humble," since the lowliness made him glad.

This is the rule: "Where there is no joy, the *Shechina* [Divinity] does not dwell." Hence, during the purification period, there cannot be the *Shechina*, although purification is a necessary thing (like the lavatory: although one must go there, one is still certain that this is not the King's palace).

This is the meaning of *Beracha* [blessing] and *Bechora* [seniority], whose letters are the same [in Hebrew]. Seniority is GAR, and the *Sitra Achra* wants the GAR, but not the blessings, since blessing is the clothing over the *Mochin*. And Esau wanted the seniority without the clothing, but it is forbidden to receive *Mochin* without clothing. This is the meaning of Esau's words: "Have you not reserved one blessing for me?" "One blessing" means the opposite of blessings, meaning a curse. It is said about that: "He loved cursing, and it came to him, and he had no desire for a blessing."

122. Understanding What Is Written in Shulchan Aruch

I heard on the eve of Shabbat, *Nitzavim*, Elul 22, *Tav-Shin-Bet*, September 4, 1942

Understand what is explained in *Shulchan Aruch* [Set Table—the Jewish code of Law]: The rule is that one should repeatedly reflect upon the prayers of the Terrible Days so that when the time of prayer comes, he will be accustomed and used to praying.

The thing is that the prayer should be in the heart. This is the meaning of the work in the heart, that the heart will agree to what one says with one's mouth (otherwise, it is deceit, that is, one's mouth and heart are not the same). Hence, on the month of *Elul*, one should accustom oneself to the great work.

And the most important thing is that one can say "Write us to life." This means that when one says "Write us to life," the heart, too, should agree (so it will not be as flattery) that one's mouth and heart will be the same, "for man looks on the eyes, and the Lord looks on the heart."

Accordingly, when one cries "Write us to life," "life" means *Dvekut* [adhesion] with the Life of Lives, which is specifically by a person wanting to work entirely in the form of bestowal, and that all of one's thoughts of his own pleasure will be revoked. Then, when he feels what he is saying, his heart can fear that his prayer might be accepted, meaning that he will have no desire whatsoever for himself.

And concerning self-pleasure, there appears a state where it seems as though he leaves all the pleasures of this world, together with all the people, friends, his kin, all his possessions, and retires to the desert where there is nothing but wild beasts, without anyone knowing of him or of his existence. It seems to him as though he loses his world at once, and feels that he is losing a world filled with the joy of life, and takes upon himself death from this world. He feels as though he is committing suicide when he experiences this image.

Sometimes, the *Sitra Achra* [other side] helps him picture his state with all the dark colors. Then the body repels this prayer, and in such a state, his prayer cannot be accepted since he himself does not want his prayer to be accepted.

For this reason, there must be preparation for the prayer, to accustom oneself to the prayer, as though his mouth and heart are the same. And the heart can come to agree through accustoming, so it would understand that reception means separation, and that the most important is the *Dvekut* with the Life of Lives, which is bestowal.

One must always delve in the work of *Malchut*, called "writing," considered "ink" and *Shacharit* [blackness]. This means that one should not want one's work to be in the form of "Libni and Shimei,"* that only at the time of whiteness does he adhere to the Torah and *Mitzvot* [commandments], but unconditionally. Whether in white or in black, it will always be the same for him, and that come-what-may, he will adhere to the commandments of the Torah and *Mitzvot*.

123. His Divorce and His Hand Come as One

I heard; memories of Baal HaSulam

In the matter of the lower *Hey* in the *Eynaim* [eyes], it means that a *Masach* [screen] and a cover was placed over the eyes. Eyes mean seeing and Providence, when one sees hidden Providence.

Experimenting means that one cannot decide either way, that he cannot clarify the Creator's will and his rav's intention. Although one can work devotedly, he cannot decide if this work in devotion is in its place or, to the contrary, that this hard work will be against his rav's view and the Creator's view.

---
* Libni also means whiteness.

And to determine, one chooses that which adds labor. This means that one should work according to a line that labor is all that is for one to do, and nothing else. Thus, one has no place to doubt one's actions and thoughts and words, but he must always increase labor.

124. A Shabbat of Beresheet and of the Six Thousand Years

I heard

There are two discernments of *Shabbat* [Sabbath]: 1) of *Beresheet* [Genesis/beginning], 2) of the six thousand years. The difference between them is this: It is known that there is a stop, and there is rest. A stop is where there is nothing more to add. A rest, however, stems from the words "He stood and rested," meaning that one is in the middle of his work, and since he has no strength to continue his work, he stands and rests to revive himself, and afterwards continues with his work.

A Shabbat of *Beresheet* is a state of having nothing more to add. This is called "a stop." A Shabbat of the six thousand years is considered rest, by which one receives strength to continue one's work on the weekdays.

Now we can understand the words of our sages: "Shabbat said, 'You have given everyone a mate, but to me You did not.'" And the Creator replied, "Israel will be your partner." A partner means ZA. If there is a *Nukva*, there can be a *Zivug* [coupling], and from the *Zivug* come the offspring, meaning renewal and additions.

Nukva is a deficiency. If there is a deficiency in some place, there is room to correct the deficiency, and all the corrections are considered having been fulfilled by extending the upper light in the place of the lack. It follows that there was no deficiency here to begin with, but all the lack that they previously considered to be a deficiency came in the form of correction to begin with, meaning that thus the upper abundance would flow from above.

This is similar to one who delves in some matter and exerts to understand it. When he attains the meaning, it is to the contrary: He does not feel that he was previously suffering when he did not understand the matter. Rather, he is glad because now he has joy. The joy is measured by the extent of the effort that he made prior to understanding the matter.

Thus, the time of delving is called *Nukva*, a deficiency. And when one unites with the deficiency, he produces the offspring, the renewal. This is what the Shabbat argued, "Since there is no work on Shabbat, there will be no offspring and renewals."

125. He Who Delights the Shabbat
I heard on *Sivan* 8, *Tav-Shin-Tet*, June 15, 1949, Tel-Aviv

"Anyone who delights the *Shabbat* [Sabbath] is given an unbounded domain, as it is said, 'Then shall you delight yourself in the Lord, and I will make you to ride upon the high places of the earth, and I will feed you with the heritage of Jacob your father,' etc. Unlike Abraham, about whom it is written, 'Arise, walk through the land in the length of it,' etc. And not as Isaac, as it is written, 'for unto you and unto your seed I will give all these lands,' but as Jacob, about whom it is written, 'and you shall spread abroad to the west, and to the east, and to the north, and to the south'" (*Shabbat* 118).

It is difficult to understand this *Gemara* as it is. Should every one of Israel be given the whole world, an unbounded domain?

We should begin with the words of our sages: "In the future, the Creator will take the sun out of its sheath and will darken. The wicked are judged by it, and the righteous are healed by it, as it is written, 'For behold, the day comes, it burns as a furnace, and all the evildoers and all that work wickedness shall be stubble; and the day that comes shall set them ablaze, says the Lord of hosts, that it shall leave them neither root nor branch,' neither a root in this world nor a branch in the next world." The righteous are healed by it, as it is written, "'But unto you who fear My Name shall the sun of righteousness arise with healing in its wings.' And moreover, they are refined by it" (*Avoda Zarah* 3b).

We need to understand the riddle of the sages, what is a sun, what is a sheath, and from where this oppositeness comes. Also, what is "neither a root in this world nor a branch in the next world"? And what is "Moreover, they are refined by it"? He should have said, "healed and refined by it." Also, what is the "moreover" that he said?

Now we can understand the words of our sages: "Israel count by the moon and the nations of the world, by the sun" (*Sukkah* 29). Thus, the sunlight is an epithet to the clearest knowledge, as it is written, "as clear as the sun." And the nations of the world, who did not receive the Torah and *Mitzvot* [commandments], as it is written that the Creator brought it to every nation and tongue, since they did not want to enjoy the light of the Torah, considered "the moon," which receives from His light, being the light of the sun, meaning the common light. Yet, they do have craving and desire to study the Creator and to know Him, Himself.

But Israel count by the moon, which are the Torah and *Mitzvot*, where the sunlight is clothed within them. Hence, the Torah is the sheath of the Creator.

It is written in *The Zohar* that "the Torah and the Creator are one." This means that the light of the Creator is clothed in the Torah and *Mitzvot*, and He and His sheath are one. Hence, Israel count by the moon to complement themselves in Torah and *Mitzvot*. Therefore, they are naturally awarded the Creator, too. Yet, since the nations of the world do not keep the Torah and *Mitzvot*, meaning the sheath, they do not have even the light of the sun.

This is the meaning of "In the future, He brings the sun out of its sheath." And they said, "*Shechina* [Divinity] in the lower ones; a high need," meaning that the Creator craves it and yearns for it.

This is the meaning of the six workdays, meaning the work in Torah and *Mitzvot*, since "The Lord has made everything for His own purpose." And even the work on the weekdays is still the work of the Creator, as it is written, "He created it not a waste; He formed it to be inhabited." This is why it is called "a sheath."

And the Shabbat is the light of the sun, the day of rest in the eternal life. That is, He has prepared the world in two degrees: 1) that His *Shechina* [Divinity] would be revealed through the Torah and *Mitzvot* in the six workdays, 2) that He will be revealed in the world without the Torah and *Mitzvot*.

This is the meaning of "in its time, I will hasten it." Rewarded—I will hasten it, meaning through Torah and *Mitzvot*. Not rewarded—in its time, since the evolution of creation with all the suffering brings the end and redemption to humanity, until the Creator places His *Shechina* in the lower ones. This is called "in its time," through evolution over time.

126. A Sage Comes to Town

I heard during the Shavuot meal, Tav-Shin-Zayin, May 1947, Tel-Aviv

"A sage comes to town." The Creator is called "Sage" [or "wise"]. He comes to town, since on *Shavuot* [Feast of Weeks] He shows Himself to the world.

"The sluggard says: 'There is a lion on the way'; perhaps the sage is not at his home? Perhaps the door is locked?" Our sages said that the thing is, "If you labored and did not find, do not believe." Hence, if he sees that he has not found the nearness of the Creator, then he is told that he must have not labored sufficiently. This is why the verse calls him "sluggard."

And what is the reason that he did not labor? If he is seeking the nearness of the Creator, why does he not want to make an effort? After all, even if you want to obtain a corporeal thing, you still cannot obtain it without labor. In truth, he does want to labor, and it is not that he says, "There is a lion on the way," meaning the *Sitra Achra* [other side], as it is written, "A lion lurks in secret places." This means that one who begins the path of the Creator encounters the lion on the way. And those who fail in it cannot recover.

This is why he is afraid to start, for who can defeat it? Then he is told, "There is no lion on the way," meaning "There is none else besides Him," it is written. This is because there is no other force but Him, by way of "and God has made it that He will be feared."

And then he finds another excuse: "Perhaps the Sage is not at home?" His home is *Nukva*, the *Shechina* [Divinity]. Then he cannot know for certain if he is walking on the path of *Kedusha* [holiness] or not.

This is why he says that perhaps the Sage, meaning the Creator, is not at His home. That is, this is not His, not of the *Kedusha*, so how can he know that he is advancing in *Kedusha*? Then he is told: "The Sage is at His home," meaning "One's soul shall teach him," and at last he will know that he is advancing in *Kedusha*.

Then he says, "Perhaps the door is locked, and it is impossible to enter the palace, as in 'Not all who wish to take the Lord will come and take'?" Then he is told, "The door is not locked." After all, we see that many people have been rewarded with entering the palace.

Then he replies, "Either way, I will not go." This means that if he is lazy and does not want to exert, he becomes argumentative and shrewd, and thinks that they are only making the work heavier on him.

But in truth, one who wishes to exert sees the opposite. He sees that many have succeeded. And those who do not want to exert see that there are people who did not succeed. And even though they did not succeed, it is because they discovered that they did not want to exert. But since he is lazy and only wants to justify his actions, he preaches like a wise man. In truth, the burden of Torah and *Mitzvot* [commandments] should be accepted without any arguments or complaints, and then he will succeed.

127. The Difference between Core, Self, and Added Abundance

Sukkot Inter 4, *Tav-Shin-Gimel*, September 30, 1942, Jerusalem

It is known that the departure of the *Mochin* and the cessation of the *Zivug* occur only to the additions of the *Mochin*, and the core of the degree in ZON is *Vav* and a *Nekuda* [dot]. This means that, at its essence, *Malchut* has no more than a dot, a black dot that has no white in it.

If one accepts that dot as the core, and not as something superfluous that one wishes to be rid of, but moreover, he accepts it as adornment, it is called "a handsome abode in one's heart." This is because he does not condemn this servitude, but makes it essential to him. This is called "raising the *Shechina* [Divinity] from the dust." When one sustains the basis as his core, he can never fall from his degree, since there is no departure in the core.

When one takes upon himself to work as a black dot, where even in the blackest darkness in the world, the *Shechina* says, "There is no place to hide from You." Hence,

"I am tied to Him in one knot," "and it will never be detached." Because of this, he has no cessation of *Dvekut* [adhesion].

If some illumination, called "addition," comes to him from above, he accepts it by way of "unavoidable and unintended," since it comes from the Emanator, without the lower one's awakening. This is the meaning of "I am black, but beautiful," because if you can accept the blackness, you will see that I am beautiful.

This is the meaning of "Who is gullible, let him come here." When he turns from all his engagements and wants only to work in order to benefit the Creator, and works by way of "I was a beast with You," then he is rewarded with seeing the final perfection. This is the meaning of "a heartless one, she said to him." This means that since he was heartless, he had to be thoughtless; otherwise, he would not be able to approach.

But sometimes we encounter a state of *Shechina* in exile, when the dot descends to the separated *BYA*. At that time, he is called "As a lily among thorns," since it has the shape of thorns and thistles. In that state, it cannot be accepted, since it is the domination of the *Klipot* [shells/peels].

This comes through man's actions, as man's actions below affect the root of one's soul above, in the *Shechina*. This means that if a person below is enslaved to the will to receive, he thus makes the *Klipa* [sing. of *Klipot*] reign over the *Kedusha* [holiness] above.

This is the meaning of *Tikkun Hatzot* [midnight correction]. We pray to raise the *Shechina* from the dust, meaning to elevate it, to be important, as above and below are calculations of importance. And then it is considered a black dot.

In the *Tikkun Hatzot* he prevails and says that he wants to keep the verse of "Libni and Shimei." Libni means *Lavan* [white], and not black, and Shimei means *Shmi'a* [hearing], meaning reasonability, which means that assuming the burden of the kingdom of heaven is a reasonable and acceptable matter for him. And the *Tikkun Hatzot* is the *Tikkun* of the *Mehitza* [partition], the correction of separating the *Kedusha* from the *Klipa*, meaning to correct the bad feeling within the will to receive, and connect to the desire to bestow.

Golah [exile] has the letters of *Ge'ulah* [redemption], with the difference being the *Aleph*. This means that we must extend the *Aluf* [champion] of the world into the *Golah*, and then we immediately feel the *Ge'ulah*. This is the meaning of "He who could guard the harmful must compensate the harmed with the best kind that one has." This is the meaning of "when there is judgment below, there is no judgment above."

128. Dew Drips from that Galgalta to Zeir Anpin

I heard on *Mishpatim* 3, *Tav-Shin-Gimel*, February 27, 1943

Dew drips from that *Galgalta* to *Zeir Anpin*. And concerning the pale hair, there is a dent under each hair, and this is the meaning of "He that would break me with a tempest." And this is the meaning of "Then the Lord answered Job out of the storm." And this is the meaning of "This they shall give, every one that passes among them that are numbered, half a shekel after the shekel of the holiness." And this is the meaning of "a *Beka* [dent] a head," "to make atonement for your souls."

To understand the issue of the hair, it is the black and the ink. This means that when one feels remoteness from the Creator, because one has foreign thoughts, this is called "hair." And "pale" means whiteness. This means that when the light of the Creator pours onto him it brings him closer to the Creator, and both of them together are called "light and *Kli* [vessel]."

The order of the work is that when one awakens to the work of the Creator, it is by being given paleness. At that time, one feels vitality and light in the work of the Creator. Afterward, a foreign thought comes to him, by which he falls from his degree and drifts away from the work. The foreign thought is called *Se'ara* [storm/hair]. And there is a dent under the hair, which is a dent and a deficiency in the skull.

Before the foreign thoughts came to him, he had a complete *Rosh* [head] and he was close to the Creator, and through the foreign thoughts he drew far from the Creator. This is considered having a deficiency. And by the sorrow, when he regrets it, he extends a flowing of water. Thus, the hair becomes a pipeline for the transferring of abundance, by which it is considered that he has been awarded whiteness.

And afterwards the foreign thoughts come to him again, and he thus becomes remote from the Creator once more. This creates a dent again, a hole and a deficiency in the skull, and through the sorrow, that he regrets it, he extends a flowing of water once again, and the hair becomes a pipeline to transfer the abundance.

This order continues repeatedly, by way of ups and downs, until the hairs are accumulated into the complete measure. This means that each time he corrects, he extends abundance. This abundance is called "dew," as in "my head is filled with dew." This is because the abundance comes intermittently, and each time it is as though he receives a drop. When one's work is complete and he achieves the full amount, until "they will not return to folly," it is considered that from that dew, the dead will be revived.

This is the meaning of the dent, meaning the foreign thoughts that make holes in the head.

And also, concerning the matter of the half-shekel, meaning that he is half guilty, half innocent. But we must understand that the halves are not at the same time. Rather, at each time there must be a complete thing. This is because if he has broken one *Mitzva* and did not keep it, he is no longer considered half, but a complete wicked.

However, it is in two times. At one time he is righteous, adhered to the Creator, and then he is completely innocent. And when he is in descent, he is wicked. This is the meaning of "the world was created either for the complete righteous or for the complete wicked." And this is why it is called "half," having two times.

And this is "to make atonement for your souls." Through the dent, when one feels that one's head is incomplete, because when a foreign thought comes, his mind is not wholly with the Creator. And when he regrets it, it makes him make atonement for his soul. This is so because if he repents every time, then he extends abundance until the abundance is filled by way of "my head is filled with dew."

129. The Shechina in the Dust
I heard

"You are fond of suffering. Then he said, 'neither they nor their reward,' about this beauty, which wears off in the dust." Suffering is primarily in a place that is above reason. And the measure of the suffering depends on the extent to which it contradicts the reason. This is called "faith above reason," and this work gives contentment to the Creator. It follows that the reward is that by this work there is contentment to one's Maker.

However, in between, before one can prevail and justify His guidance, the *Shechina* [Divinity] is in the dust. This means that the work by way of faith, called the *Shechina*, is in exile, canceled in the dust. And he said about that, "Neither they nor their reward." This means that he cannot stand the period in between. And this is the meaning of his reply to him, "I am crying for this and for that."

130. Tiberias of Our Sages, Good Is Your Sight
I heard on *Adar 1, Tav-Shin-Zayin*, February 21, 1947, on a trip to Tiberias

"Tiberias of our sages, good is your sight." Seeing means wisdom. Good means that he can be awarded wisdom there. And Rabbi Shimon Bar-Yochai was purifying the markets of Tiberias. The *Tuma'a* [impurity] of the dead, that is, of the will to receive, means "the wicked, in their lives, are called 'dead.'" And all impurities belong only to *Hochma* [wisdom]. Hence, in Tiberias, where there is the quality of *Hochma*, the market had to be purified.

131. Who Comes to Purify
I heard in *Tav-Shin-Zayin*, 1946-1947

"He who comes to purify is aided." This means that one should always be in a state of "coming." And then, in any case, if he feels that he has purified, he no longer needs to aid him, since He purified and left. And if he feels that he is in a state of coming and going, then he is certainly assisted, since there is no prevention before the desire, as he is seeking the truth.

"For your love is better than wine." This means that wine can cause drunkenness, and a drunk, the whole world is his since he has no deficiencies, even in the six thousand years.

132. In the Sweat of Your Face Shall You Eat Bread - 1
I heard on Adar 14, Tav-Shin-Zayin, March 6, 1947, Tel-Aviv

"In the sweat of your face shall you eat bread." Bread means Torah, which is "Go, fight with My bread." The study of Torah should be with fear, tremor, and sweat, by which the sin of the tree of knowledge is sweetened.

133. The Lights of Shabbat
I heard in Tav-Shin-Zayin, 1946-1947

The lights of Shabbat [Sabbath] come to the discernment of the *Guf* [body]. Hence, on Shabbat we say, "To David. Bless [the Lord] my soul, and all that is within me," meaning the *Guf*. A new head, however, is considered a *Neshama* [soul], which comes only to the discernment of the *Neshama* and not to the *Guf*. This is why we only say, "Bless [the Lord] my soul," and not "and all that is within me," since they do not reach the *Guf* (see *The Zohar* 1, 97).

134. Wine that Causes Drunkenness
I heard in Tav-Shin-Zayin, 1946-1947

It is impossible to be awarded the Torah in its entirety. Through intoxication in the wine of Torah, when one feels that the whole world is his, even though he still does not have the whole of the wisdom, he will think and feel that he has everything in perfection.

135. Clean and Righteous Do Not Kill
I heard on Nisan 2, Tav-Shin-Zayin, March 23, 1947, Tel Aviv

"The clean and righteous do not kill." A righteous is one who justifies the Creator: Whatever he feels, whether good or bad, he takes above reason. This is considered "right." Clean refers to the cleanness of the matter, the state as he sees it. This is so because "a judge has only what his eyes see." And if one does not understand the matter, or cannot attain the matter, he should not blur the forms as they seem to his eyes. This is considered "left," and he should nurture both.

136. The Difference between the First Letters and the Last Letters
I heard on Purim, Tav-Shin-Zayin, 1946-1947

The difference between the first letters and the last letters is only in the written synopsis, meaning the content of the writing that was given by the King's house. And the King's authors elaborate on the content to make it understandable for all.

The content was simply "that they should be ready for that day," and the authors interpreted it as applying to the nations, that they are destined to avenge the Jews. And that force was so that Haman would think, "Whom would the king want to honor more than I?" Hence, in the last letters he wrote specifically, straight from the King, "that the Jews should be ready." Conversely, in the first letters he did not specifically write "the Jews." This is why they had the strength to complain.

The thing is that this force was given because one should not justify any desire for reception of lights, to extend the upper lights below, as the whole work was to bestow. Hence, he cannot extend something from below. Therefore, by giving strength to Haman, who specifically wants the greater lights, as his name testifies, Haman the Agagite, the *Gag* [roof] of the degree, which is GAR.

137. Zelophehad Was Gathering Wood
I heard in *Tav-Shin-Zayin*, 1946-1947

Zelophehad was gathering wood. *The Zohar* interprets that he was measuring which tree was bigger: the tree of life or the tree of knowledge. A righteous is called "the tree of life," who is entirely to bestow. And in that, there is no hold to the external ones. However, wholeness lies in the tree of knowledge, the extension of *Hochma* [wisdom] below. This is the meaning of doing good to His creations. They must not be measured; rather, they should be, "that they may become one in your hand."

This means that one without the other is incomplete. And Mordechai was from the quality of the tree of life, not wanting to extend anything below since he had no deficiencies. Hence, he had to increase the quality of Haman, so he would draw the lights below. Afterward, when he disclosed his deficiency, Mordechai would receive them in the form of reception in order to bestow.

Now we can see why later, when Mordechai said good things about the King, when he saved Him from death, the King promoted Haman, who was his enemy. It is as our sages said, "according to every man's wish," according to the will of Mordechai and Haman, who were hateful of each other.

138. Concerning Fear that Sometimes Comes Upon a Person
I heard in *Tav-Shin-Bet*, 1941-1942

When fear comes upon a person, he should know that there is none else but Him. And even witchcraft. And if he sees that fear overcomes him, he should say that there is no such thing as chance, but the Creator has given him an opportunity from above, and he must contemplate and study the end to which he has been sent this fear. It appears that it is so that he will overcome and say, "There is none else besides Him."

But if after all this, the fear has not departed from him, he should take it as an example and say that his servitude of the Creator should be in the same measure of the fear, meaning that the fear of heaven, which is a merit, should be in the same manner of fear that he now has. That is, the body is impressed by this superficial fear, and exactly in the same way that the body is impressed, so should be the fear of heaven.

139. The Difference between the Six Workdays and Shabbat

I heard

The six workdays are considered ZA, and Shabbat [Sabbath] is considered *Malchut*. And he asked, "But ZA is a higher degree than *Malchut*, so why is Shabbat more important than the weekdays? And also, why are they called *Yemey Hol** [weekdays/days without holiness]?"

The thing is that the world is nourished only through *Malchut*. This is why *Malchut* is called "the assembly of Israel," since all the good influence to the whole of Israel comes from there. Therefore, although the six days imply ZA, there is no unification between ZA and *Malchut*. This is why it is called *Hol* [not holy], since no abundance extends from ZA to *Malchut*.

And when no *Kedusha* [holiness] extends from *Malchut*, it is therefore called *Yemey Hol*. Conversely, on Shabbat there is a unification of ZA and *Malchut*, and then *Kedusha* extends from *Malchut*. This is why it is called Shabbat.

140. How I Love Your Torah

I heard at the conclusion of Passover 7, *Tav-Shin-Gimel*, 1943

"O how I love Your Torah! I speak of it throughout the day." He said that even though King David had already been awarded perfection, he still craved the Torah, because the Torah is greater and more important than any perfection in the world.

141. The Holiday of Passover

I heard

The holiday of Passover concerns *Mochin de Haya*, and the count concerns *Mochin de Haya*. Hence, during the count there is departure of the *Mochin*, since the count is considered raising MAN. It is known that when raising MAN there is departure of lights. But after the count, the *Mochin* returns to its place. This is so because the *Katnut* [smallness/infancy] during the count is *Katnut* of *Yechida*, but along with it

---

* *Yemey*—days; *Hol* comes from the word *Hulin*—secular, not holy.

there is *Mochin* of weekdays, which is *YESHSUT*, and *Mochin* of Shabbat [Sabbath], which are *Mochin* of *AVI*.

142. The Essence of the War
I heard

The essence of the war should be in a place of permission. However, with *Mitzva* [commandment] and transgression, the loss is near and the reward is far. Hence, there he should observe without any considerations.

However, waging war and keeping the *Mitzva* of choice should be made in a place of permission, since the act is only a matter of permission. Hence, even if one fails, the sin will not be so great. This is why it is considered near to the reward, since if he wins the war, he will bring a new authority under the *Kedusha* [holiness].

143. Only Good to Israel
I heard from Baal HaSulam

"Only good to Israel, God is to the pure in heart." It is known that "only" and "just" are diminutives. This means that in every place the Torah writes "only" and "just," it comes to diminish.

Therefore, in work matters we should interpret it as when one diminishes oneself and lowers himself. Lowering applies when one wants to be proud, meaning wants to be in *Gadlut* [greatness/adulthood]. This means that he wants to understand every single thing, that his soul craves seeing and hearing in everything, but he still lowers himself and agrees to go with his eyes shut and keep Torah and *Mitzvot* in utter simplicity. This is "good to Israel." The word *Yashar El* [Israel] is the letters of *Li Rosh* [the head (mind) is mine].

This means that he believes he has a mind of *Kedusha* [holiness] although he is only discerned as "just," meaning that he is in a state of diminution and lowliness. And he says about this "just" that it is absolute good. Then the verse, "God is to the pure in heart" comes true in him, meaning that he is awarded a pure heart. And this is the meaning of "and I will take away the stony heart from your flesh, and I will give you a heart of flesh." The heart of flesh is *Mochin de VAK*, called *Mochin* of clothing, which comes from the upper one. *Mochin de GAR*, however, should come from the lower one, through the scrutinies of the lower one.

The issue of *VAK de Mochin* and *GAR de Mochin* requires explanation: There are many discernments of *VAK* and *GAR* in each degree. And perhaps he is referring to what he wrote in several places, that the *Katnut*, called "*GE* of the lower one," rise to *MAN* through the *Kli* that raises *MAN*, called "*AHP* of the upper one." It therefore follows that the upper one raises the lower one. And then, to receive the GAR of the lights and the AHP of the *Kelim*, the lower one should rise by itself.

144. There Is a Certain People
I heard on the night of *Purim*, after reading the *Megillah*, Tav-Shin-Yod, 1950

"There is a certain people scattered abroad and dispersed among the peoples." Haman said that in his view, we will succeed in destroying the Jews because they are separated from one another; hence, our power against them will certainly prevail, as it causes separation between man and the Creator. And the Creator will not help them anyway, since they are separated from Him. This is why Mordecai went to correct that flaw, as it is explained in the verse, "the Jews gathered," etc., "to gather and to stand up for their lives." This means that they saved themselves by uniting.

145. What Is He Will Give Wisdom Specifically to the Wise
I heard on *Truma* 5, Tav-Shin-Gimel, February 11, 1943

"He will give wisdom to the wise." He asked, "It should have said, 'He will give wisdom to the fools.'"

And he said, "It is known that there is no coercion in spirituality." Rather, everyone is given according to one's wish. The reason is that spirituality is the source of life and pleasure. So how can there be coercion in a good thing? Hence, if we see that when we engage in Torah and *Mitzvot* coercively, meaning that we must overcome the body since it does not agree because it does not feel pleasure in this work, it must be because it does not feel the spirituality in them, as we have said that spirituality is the source of life and pleasure, as it is written in *The Zohar*, "Where there is labor, there is *Sitra Achra* [other side]."

This is the reason that only the wise can be given wisdom, since fools have no need for wisdom. Rather, only the wise can be given wisdom because of their nature. This means that one who is wise loves wisdom, and this is his only wish. And following the rule, "there are no preventions before a desire," he makes every effort to obtain wisdom. Hence, at last he will be awarded wisdom. Therefore, one who loves wisdom can be called "wise," after his end.

But it is written of fools, "A fool has no desire for understanding." The verse, "He will give wisdom to the wise" comes to tell us that one who loves wisdom will not be impressed by not having obtained wisdom despite the great efforts he has made. Rather, he will continue with his work and will certainly achieve wisdom, since he loves wisdom. This is why they say, "Go by this path and you are certain to succeed."

However, we must understand what one can do if by nature "A man is born a wild ass's colt." From where will he take the desire to crave wisdom?

For this, we are given the advice to work by way of "doers of His word," and then, "to hear the voice of His word." This means that one does things to obtain the thing he wants. Hence, here, when he has no desire for wisdom, it means that the thing he lacks is the desire for wisdom. For this reason, he begins to exert and take actions to obtain the desire for wisdom, as this is the only thing he needs.

The order is that one should exert in Torah and work although he has no desire for it. This is called "labor." This means that he does things although he has no desire for the thing he does. It is as our sages said, "All that your hand and strength can do, do." And by the virtue of exerting, a desire and craving for wisdom will form within him.

And then the verse, "He will give wisdom to the wise" will become true in him, and he will be rewarded with "hearing the voice of His word." Thus, that which was previously by way of doing, an act without a will, he has been awarded a desire for it.

Therefore, if we want to know who loves wisdom, we should look at those who strain for wisdom, even though they have not yet been rewarded with being among those who love wisdom. The reason is, as we have said, that through the effort, they will be awarded being among those who love wisdom.

Afterward, when they have a desire for wisdom, they will be awarded wisdom. Thus, the desire for wisdom is the *Kli* [vessel], and the wisdom is the light. This is the meaning of "there is no coercion in spirituality."

The light of wisdom means the light of life. We do not perceive wisdom as an intellectual concept, but as the actual life, the essence of life, to the extent that without it, one is considered dead. (Hence, we can say that for this reason wisdom is called *Haya* [alive].)

146. A Commentary on *The Zohar*
I heard in the year *Tav-Reish-Tzadi-Het*, 1937-1938

In *The Zohar*: "When one is born, he is given a soul from the side of the pure beast." And he interprets that his animate soul, too, agrees to be a servant of the Creator. "If he is further rewarded, he is given a soul of the side of wheels." This means that he has a soul that always longs, and rolls from place to place. Like an ever-turning wheel, it turns and rolls to cling to the *Kedusha* [holiness].

147. The Work of Reception and Bestowal
I heard on Adar 21, Tav-Shin-Yod-Gimel, March 8, 1953

The matter of work in reception and bestowal depends on the heart. This is considered VAK. However, work in faith and knowledge is considered GAR. Although they are one discernment, meaning that faith is accepted by him according to the value of the work in reception and bestowal, they are still two distinct discernments.

This is so because even if one can work in bestowal, he still wants to see to whom he is bestowing and who accepts his work. Hence, he needs to work in the form of Mocha [mind], meaning believe that there is an Overseer who accepts the work of the lower ones.

148. The Scrutiny of Bitter and Sweet, True and False
I heard

There is a scrutiny of "bitter and sweet," and there is a scrutiny of "true and false." The scrutiny of "true and false" is in the mind, and the scrutiny of "bitter and sweet" is in the heart. This is why we must pay attention to the work in the heart, to be in the form of bestowal and not in the form of reception.

By nature, only reception is sweet to man, and bestowal is bitter. And the work—to turn reception to bestowal is called "the work in the heart."

In the mind, the work is of "true and false." And for this, we need to work in faith, meaning have faith in the sages. This is so because the worker cannot clarify the matter of "true and false" to himself.

149. Why We Need to Extend Hochma
I heard on Adar 22, Tav-Shin-Yod-Gimel, March 9, 1953, Tel-Aviv

He asked, "Why do we need to extend the discernment of Hochma [wisdom], which is knowing, if all our work is by way of faith above reason?"

He answered that "If the righteous of the generation were not in the form of knowing, the whole of Israel would not be able to work in the form of faith above reason. Rather, precisely when the righteous of the generation extends illumination of Hochma, his mind shines in the whole of Israel."

For example, if one's mind knows and understands what one wants, the organs perform their action and do not need any intellect. Rather, the hand, the leg, and the rest of the organs do what they must, and no sane person would think of asking or saying that if the hand or the leg had brains, their work would be better.

Thus, the mind does not change the organs, but the organs are set according to the greatness of the mind. This means that if the brain has a great mind, all the organs are named after it; they are called "great organs."

Similarly, if the collective is adhered to a true righteous, who has already been awarded knowing, the collective can do things with faith. They have complete satisfaction, and have no need for any discernment of knowledge.

150. Sing unto the Lord, for He Has Done Pride

I heard on *Shevat* 14

In the verse, "Sing* unto the Lord; for He has done pride," it seems that "prune" is like "[The Lord is] my strength and song." This means that we should always prune and cut the thorns off of the Creator's vineyard. And even when one feels that one is whole, and thinks that he has already removed the thorns, the verse concludes, "for He has done pride."

This means that He has seemingly created pride in this world, that man likes to be honest and true in one's own eyes. And when one feels about himself that he has already removed the thorns and he is a whole man, it is a kind of pride.

Rather, one should always examine one's actions, and check them with ten kinds of examinations, and not rely on one's temporary feeling, for this is only a kind of pride. It is as the verse says in the name of the righteous: "You are idle, you are idle; therefore, you say, 'Let us go and sacrifice to the Lord our God.'"

This means that He said to the children of Israel, "When you say, 'Let us go and sacrifice,' and you feel that you are already willing to go and sacrifice yourselves on the altar before the Lord, it is like idleness and weakness, that you no longer want to work and constantly examine yourselves, to make you ready for this great work. This is why you think that you are already perfect in this servitude, as they interpret at the end of the verse, 'for He has done pride.'"

151. And Israel Saw the Egyptians

I heard on *BeShalach*

In the verse, "and Israel saw the Egyptians dead upon the seashore," "...and the people feared the Lord, and they believed in the Lord and in His servant Moses," we must understand how "they believed" is relevant here. Clearly, the miracle of the exodus from Egypt and the division of the sea brought Israel to greater faith than they had had before. After all, our sages said about the verse, "This is my God, and I will glorify Him," that a maid by the sea saw more than did Ezekiel the prophet.

---

* *Zamru*, in Hebrew means both sing and prune. In this case it is referring to the latter.

Hence, this means that the exodus from Egypt was a case of open miracles, which brings to knowledge of the Lord, which is the opposite of the meaning of "faith," since it does not mean above reason. And when seeing open miracles, it is very hard to be in faith, since, moreover, it is a time of expansion of the reason. Therefore, what is the meaning of the text, "and they believed in the Lord"?

However, we should interpret according to the interpretation of "All believe that He is a God of faith." The verse narrates Israel's praise, who, even after seeing the open miracles, their servitude of the Creator was not reduced in them, which is by way of faith above reason. And it is great work to hold on to the path of faith and not slight it at all once you are awarded and can serve the Creator within reason.

152. For Bribe Blinds the Eyes of the Wise
I heard on *Tevet* 24, *Tav-Shin-Het*, January 6, 1948

"For bribe blinds the eyes of the wise." When one begins to criticize the work and its conditions, he is faced with the possibility that it will be impossible to receive the work, for two reasons:

1. The reward for the work is not one hundred percent certain. He does not see those who have already been rewarded, and when he visits people who have toiled to suffer the weight of the work, he does not see if they have already been rewarded for their work. And if he asks himself, "Why did they not receive?" if he succeeds in giving the highest answer, it is because they did not follow the conditions of the work to the letter. But those who follow the orders to the letter receive their complete rewards.

And then comes a second question: He knows that he is better capable to the conditions of the work than his friend, to be able to cope with all its terms. Hence, he is one hundred percent sure that no one can criticize him for evading, and he is one hundred percent right.

2. Therefore, the question arises: One who begins the work has certainly experienced all the calculations, and yet, took the work upon himself. Thus, how did he answer all the questions to himself? The thing is that to see the truth, we need to look with open eyes. Otherwise, we only think that we see who was right, the righteous or the world. But in truth, we do not see the justice. And to have open eyes, we must be wary of bribery, "for bribe blinds the eyes of the wise and perverts the words of the righteous."

And the essence of the bribe is in the will to receive. Hence, one has no other choice but to first accept the work with all its terms, without any knowledge, but only in the form of faith above reason. Afterward, when he is cleaned from the will to receive, when he criticizes, he can hope to see the truth of the matter. This is why those who only look for guarantees certainly cannot ask a thing, since in truth, he is right, and he will always win the argument, since he will not be able to see the truth.

153. A Thought Is a Result of the Desire

I heard on Shevat 7, Tav-Shin-Het, January 18, 1948, Tel-Aviv

A thought is a result of the desire. A person thinks of what he wants. He will not think of what he does not want. For example, a person never thinks of his day of death. On the contrary, he will always contemplate his eternity, since this is what he wants. Thus, one always thinks of what is desirable for him.

However, there is a special role to the thought: It intensifies the desire. The desire remains in its place; it does not have the strength to expand and perform its action. Yet, because one thinks and contemplates a matter, and the desire asks the thought to provide some counsel and advice to carry out the desire, the desire grows, expands, and performs work in actual practice.

It turns out that the thought serves the desire, and the desire is the "self" of the person. Now, there is a big self or a small self. A big self controls the small selves.

He who is a small self and has no control at all, the advice to magnify the self is through the persistent thought of the desire, since the thought grows to the extent that one thinks of it.

And so, "His law will he contemplate day and night," for by persisting in it, it grows into a big self until it becomes the actual ruler.

154. There Cannot Be an Empty Space in the World

I heard on Shevat 7, Tav-Shin-Het, January 18, 1948, Tel Aviv

There cannot be an empty space in the world. Because man's essence is the desire, as this is the essence of creation, this is where one's greatness and smallness are measured. It follows that one must have some desire—either for corporeality or for spirituality. One who is devoid of these desires is considered dead, since the whole of creation is only the desire, considered existence from absence. And because he lacks this substance, the substance of the whole of creation, it is naturally considered that he is regarded as aborted and he cannot last.

Thus, one should try to have a desire, as this is the whole substance of creation. But the desire must be clarified, as it is natural that each animal feels what is harmful to it. Similarly, we must take note that the desire will be for something.

155. The Cleanness of the Body

I heard during a Shabbat meal, Shevat 13

The cleanness of the body points to the cleanness of the mind. The cleanness of the mind is called "truth," where no falsehood is involved. And not everyone is equal in that, as some are partially meticulous. But the cleanness of the body is not so important to preserve, since the dirt that we so loathe is because the dirt is considered harmful, and we should keep it from harm.

Hence, with the body, it is not so important to be meticulous, since it will finally be canceled, even if we watch over it with all kinds of cares. But with the soul, which is eternal, it is worthwhile to be meticulous with all kinds of cares, to avoid any kind of dirt, since any dirt is considered harmful.

156. Lest He Took from the Tree of Life
I heard on Shevat 15

"Lest he took from the tree of life, and ate, and lived forever." Baal HaSulam interpreted that perhaps he would take from the covered *Hassadim* [mercy], considered from the *Chazeh* [chest] and above. This is because in that, there is complete sufficiency, and by that the sin of the tree of knowledge, considered from the *Chazeh* down, will not be corrected. It follows that the tree of life is called "from the *Chazeh* upward," where there are covered *Hassadim*. And I think that we should accordingly interpret what we say, "a life that has fear of heaven and a life that has fear of sin."

The difference between them, as Baal HaSulam interprets, is that what he takes from life is for fear of sinning, meaning that he has no other choice. But fear of heaven means that he has other choices. That is, even if he does not take this discernment, he will still not sin; but still he chooses it due to fear of the Creator.

But, accordingly, we cannot say that covered *Hassadim* is considered *Katnut* [smallness/infancy]. This is precisely when he has no other choice. But when he achieves the revealed *Hassadim* from the discernment of Rachel, then the discernment of Leah, which is covered *Hassadim*, is called GAR and *Gadlut* [greatness/adulthood].

And this is called "fear of heaven," that he has revealed *Hassadim*, but he nevertheless chooses covered *Hassadim*. Thus, there are two kinds of covered *Hassadim*: 1) when he does not have the quality of Rachel, when he is called VAK; 2) when he does have the quality of Rachel, called "Leah," GAR.

157. I Am Asleep but My Heart Is Awake
I heard on Nisan 9, Tav-Shin-Het, April 18, 1948

It is written in *The Zohar*, (Portion *Emor* 95a): "The assembly of Israel said, 'I sleep in exile in Egypt, where my children were in harsh enslavement.'" The *Mochin* were in the state of sleep, as it is written about the verse, "there is," their God is sleeping.

"But my heart is awake to guard those who will not be extinguished in exile." This means that when they receive the *Mochin* of the *Achoraim*, they are guarded by them, even though they still do not shine in her, and they are still in exile. However, it is still considered awake, by way of "does not reveal from heart to mouth."

The heart is *VAK*, since there is *VAK de Hochma* there. Thus, even at the time of the *Gadlut*, there is no other *Hochma* there, but only from what she received here.

"My Beloved knocks." This is the beating, the *Masach* [screen] *de Hirik* [of *Hirik*—a punctuation mark] in ZA. "And I have remembered My covenant." This is the circumcision, which is *Dinim* [judgments] of *Nukva*, which cancel the *Dinim* of *Dechura* [male]. *Dinim* are the quality that cancels the GAR, and this is considered "cutting."

There are other corrections, called "exposing." "Open for Me an opening like the tip of a needle, and I will open for you the upper gates." The meaning of this slight opening is the tiny lights, as without *Hassadim*, *Hochma* shines very diminutively.

Only afterward, when *Hassadim* are drawn, the *Hochma* is included in the *Hassadim*, VAK, great convoys. And the meaning of the upper gates concerns the *Hassadim* from the perspective of AVI, called "pure air." This is because only once he has *Hochma*, but he draws *Hassadim*, these *Hassadim* are called "pure air," since he prefers *Hassadim* to *Hochma*.

However, when he has *Hassadim* without *Hochma*, it is considered *Katnut* [smallness/infancy]. "Open for Me," that ZA and his sister *Malchut*, in the form of *Hochma*, she would draw *Hochma*. The door to enter Me is within you." Thus, only when you have *Hochma* will I have an opening to enter in the form of *Hassadim*, which I have from AVI, called "pure air."

"Come and see: When the Creator was slaying the firstborn of Egypt, and lowered the degrees from above downward," Egypt is the left line. However, they are in the form of *Klipa* [shell/peel] without any integration of the right. And when Israel were in Egypt, they were under their control, and they, too, had to receive the left.

And the plague of the firstborn, meaning the revoking of the control of the GAR of the left, this is "and lowered the degrees from above downward. At that time, Israel came into the covenant of the holy sign."

Circumcision concerns the *Dinim de Nukva*, which is a *Masach* of *Hirik*, which cancels the *Dinim de Dechura*. In doing so, she cancels the GAR of the left, and only the VAK shine. It follows that by the Creator striking their firstborn, they had the strength to keep the covenant, "as the blood that was shown on the door."

"And they were two bloods: one of Passover and one of the circumcision." The Passover blood is the correction of the integration of the left line, and the circumcision blood is the correction of the *Dinim de Nukva*, which is the *Hirik*. And the Passover blood…

158. The Reason for Not Eating at Each Other's Home on Passover

I heard during a Shacharit [morning] meal on Passover, Tav-Shin-Het, 1948

He explains why it is a custom not to eat at each other's home for reasons of *Kashrut* [Jewish dietary laws], and why it is not so all year long. Also, even if there is one of whom it is known that there it is completely *Kosher*, even better than in one's own home, still the custom is not to eat. This is so because the prohibition on *Hametz* [leavened bread] is on *anything*, and it is impossible to guard oneself from anything. Rather, the Creator can keep him from transgressing even with anything.

This is why it is written that with leavened bread, you should be careful with anything. One is commanded to caution, and he should seek advice how not to come to "anything" leavened.

However, one cannot guard oneself. Hence, only the Creator guards. And certainly, the guard is in such a way that not everyone is equal. Some are better guarded by the Creator, and some are less guarded, depending on one's need. This is so because there are people who know that they need great care, so they draw greater care, and there are people who feel that they do not need such guarding from above. Also, this cannot be said, as it depends on the feeling: Some feel themselves deficient and need greater care.

159. And It Came to Pass in the Course of Those Many Days

I heard

"And it came to pass in the course of those many days that the king of Egypt died; and the children of Israel sighed from the work, and they cried, and their cry came up unto God from the work. And God heard their groaning" (Exodus 2:23-4). This means that they suffered so much that they could not bear it. And they so pleaded with prayer, that "their cry came up unto God."

But we can see that they were saying, "Would that we had... when we sat by the meat-pots, when we ate bread to the full." And they also said, "We remember the fish which we ate in Egypt for nothing, the zucchini, and the watermelons, and the hay, and the onions, and the garlic."

The thing is that indeed, they were very fond of the work in Egypt. This is the meaning of "And they mingled with the nations and learned from their actions." It means that if Israel are under the dominion of a certain nation, that nation controls them and they cannot retire from their control. Thus, they tasted sufficient flavor in that work and could not be redeemed.

So what did the Creator do? "The king of Egypt died," meaning they had lost this servitude. Thus, they could no longer work; they understood that if there is no completeness of the *Mochin*, the servitude is also incomplete. Hence, "and the children of Israel sighed from the work." The work means they had no satisfaction from the work, since they had no vitality in the servitude.

This is the meaning of "the king of Egypt died," that all the dominations of the king of Egypt, who nourished and provided for them, had died. This is why they had room for prayer. And they were immediately saved. Afterward, when they walked in the desert and came to a state of *Katnut* [smallness], they craved the servitude that they had prior to the death of the king of Egypt.

160. The Reason for Concealing the Matzot
I heard

He explains why it is customary that the *Matzot* [unleavened bread] are always placed in concealment, on a matzo-plate or on some other covered thing. It is written, "And the people took their dough before it was leavened, their kneading-troughs being bound up in their clothes upon their shoulders." The hint is in "bound up in their clothes."

The thing is that on Passover, the *Kelim* [vessels] were not yet properly corrected. This is why there is the matter of the count, to correct the *Kelim*. This is the meaning of her words, "I saw the image of a drop of a rose." It means that on Passover night there was a miracle that although there could have been a grip, there still wasn't since it was covered and nothing was showing on the outside. And this is the intimation, "bound up in their clothes."

161. Concerning the Giving of the Torah - 2
I heard during a Shavuot meal

The matter of the giving of the Torah on Mount Sinai does not mean that the Torah was given then, and that now it is not. Rather, the giving of the Torah is an eternal thing—the Creator always gives. However, we are unfit to receive. But then, on Mount Sinai, we were the receivers of the Torah. And the only merit that we had then was that we were "as one man in one heart." This means that we all had but one thought—the reception of the Torah.

However, from the Creator's perspective, He always gives, as it is written in the name of the RIBASH [Rav Isaac ben Sheshet], "Man must hear the ten commandments on Mount Sinai every day."

The Torah is called "the potion of life" and "the potion of death." We should ask, "How can two opposites be in one subject?" Everything we see with our eyes is nothing more than sensations, but reality itself does not interest us. Hence, when one studies Torah and the Torah removes him from the love of the Creator, this Torah is certainly called "the potion of death." And if the Torah brings him closer to the Creator, it is certainly called "the potion of life."

But the Torah itself, meaning reality in itself, is not taken into account. Rather, the sensations determine the reality here below. And the Torah itself, without the receivers, it seems we should interpret the Torah in and of itself as light without a *Kli* [vessel], where we have no attainment. This is considered "essence without matter." And we have no attainment in the essence, even in a corporeal essence, all the more so with a spiritual one.

When one works for oneself, it is considered *Lo Lishma* [not for Her sake], and from *Lo Lishma* we come to *Lishma* [for Her sake]. Hence, if one has not been awarded the reception of the Torah, he hopes that he will receive it next year. And when he receives the complete *Lishma*, he has nothing more to do in this world.

This is why each year there is a time of reception of the Torah, since the time is ripe for an awakening from below, since then it is the awakening of the time when the light of the giving of the Torah is revealed in the lower ones.

This is why there is always an awakening from above, so the lower ones can act as they did then, at that time. Thus, if one continues on the path that the *Lo Lishma* will bring him *Lishma*, he is progressing correctly and hopes that he will eventually be rewarded with the reception of the Torah *Lishma*. But if the goal is not always before his eyes, he is moving in an opposite line from the Torah, called "the tree of life," which is why it is considered "the potion of death," as he is constantly drifting away from the line of life.

"I labored and did not find, do not believe." We must understand the meaning of "I found." What is there to find? "Finding" concerns the Creator finding us agreeable.

"I did not labor and found, do not believe." We must understand, after all, he is not lying; this is not about the person himself, as an individual. Rather, it is the same rule with the whole. And if one sees that the Creator found him agreeable, why "not believe"? The thing is that sometimes the Creator finds a person agreeable as it is in prayer. It is because this is the power of the prayer—it can act like labor. (We also see in corporeality that there are some who provide by labor, and some who provide for themselves through prayer. And by asking for provision, one is allowed to provide for himself.)

But in spirituality, although he is rewarded with being favored, he must still pay the full price later—the measure of the labor that everyone gives. If not, he will lose the *Kli*. This is why he said, "I did not labor and found, do not believe," since he will lose everything. Thus, one should subsequently pay one's full labor.

162. Concerning the Hazak We Say After Completing the Series

I heard during a Shacharit [morning] meal on Shabbat, Av 2, Tel-Aviv

The Hazak* we say after completing the series means that the completion should give us strength to complete all the degrees. As the body has 248 organs and 365 tendons, the soul, too, has 613, which are the channels of the soul by which the bounty extends. And these channels are opened through the Torah. As long as not all of them have been opened, even if a deficiency appears in a particular degree, the particular degree is included in the whole.

Thus, if an element is missing from the whole, that same discernment is missing from the individuals, too, and they gradually incarnate by the order of degrees. And when they are all completed, this will be the end of correction. Prior to this, they will emerge and become corrected one by one.

Now we can understand what our sages said, "the Torah preceded the world." This means that before the limitation of the world appeared, there was already the Torah.

And how could it then shine within the world, which is a boundary? Rather, the Torah shines by way of one after the other. When all the discernments are completed, one must leave this world since he has harvested all the discernments of the Torah. Therefore, each ending should give us strengthening to continue further. And the five books of Torah correspond to the seven *Sefirot*, which are essentially five, since *Yesod* and *Malchut* are not the essence, but only the general.

163. What the Authors of The Zohar Said

I heard after Shabbat, portion Masa'ei, Tav-Shin-Het, August 7, 1948, Tel Aviv

About the authors of *The Zohar* saying their words as morals, it was not necessary. They could have revealed their secrets by other means, too. However, they wanted to clothe their secrets as morals so that the reader would clearly understand that what is important is not the wisdom in the Torah but the Giver of the Torah, that the essence of Torah and *Mitzvot* [commandments] is only to adhere to the Giver of the Torah.

Hence, since the clothing of morals is the most reminiscent of it, they set it up in this dressing. And the many times they give it a clothing of wisdom is so they would not err and say that there is nothing more than morals, that no wisdom is hidden there, but that it is simple morals. This is why they wrote in two dresses, that one points to the other.

---

* *Hazak* means strong; it's a blessing said after finishing each book from the Five Books of Moses (the Pentateuch).

164. There Is a Difference between Corporeality and Spirituality

I heard on *Av 3, Tav-Shin-Het*, August 8, 1948

There is a difference between corporeality and spirituality: In corporeality, the strength precedes the act, as it is written, "Before they call, I will answer." There, the order is according to the end of correction, where nothing is done before there is the strength to do it. In spirituality, however, where it is still not arranged according to the end, but by the order of scrutinies, the work must begin before the attainment of the strength, as it is written, "doers of His word, to hear the voice of His word."

165. An Explanation to Elisha's Request of Elijah

I heard

Elijah asked him: "What I shall do for you?" And he replied, "a double portion of your spirit." And he replied, "You asked a hard thing."

The thing is that there is the sorting of the 288, and there is the stony heart, which cannot be scrutinized. However, when sorting the 288, the stony heart, too, is thus sorted, though it is forbidden to touch it itself. One who scrutinizes these 248, in doing so he scrutinizes the stony heart, as well.

166. Two Discernments in Attainment

I heard

There are two discernments: 1) the cascading of the worlds from above downward, 2) from below upward.

The first discernment: "which God has created to do." This means that the Creator has prepared for us a place for work.

The second discernment: when we begin to engage and clothe from below upward. However, before we achieve the completion of the degree, we cannot know anything for certain. This is called "learning first, understanding next."

A little one, who begins to eat bread, still has no knowledge, but only of the bread. And when beginning to grow, he begins to understand that there is a reason for the bread, which causes the shape of the bread, that shapes it as it appears to our eyes: white, soft, tasty, etc.

Then he attains the shape of the bread, after it has been taken out of the oven: The bread is too soft and very hot, until it is not fit for eating. There is an act missing—the cooling and drying over time, when the air makes the bread fit, giving it the shape of the bread as it appears when it comes to the table.

But then he begins to research further and sees yet another shape—before it is placed in the oven. Although it has a similar shape, there are big differences. That is, the heat of the oven makes the bread bigger and more solid, and crusts its face. Previously, it was white, and now it has a different color. When he begins to research, he sees that the bread acquired its shape and weight even before it was placed in the oven.

So he continues until he comes to the state when the wheat is taken and sowed in the ground. Until then, he can only receive from the bread, meaning reduce the bread that exists in the world. But afterwards he already knows how to add.

Similarly, in spirituality, first one needs to receive from below upward. At that time, he can only receive and not add. But afterwards, in the second state, one can add, as well.

167. The Reason Why It Is Called Shabbat Teshuva
I heard on Shabbat Teshuva, Tav-Shin-Tet, October 9, 1948, Tel-Aviv

The reason why it is called "Shabbat *Teshuva*" [Sabbath of repentance] is that (at the end of the ten penitential days, on the Day of Atonement) we say "for a sin." And anyone who examines the "for a sin" does not find his place there, at least in sixty percent, and forty percent can be explained and excused, perhaps there is a doubt that he does not feel there. But in sixty percent he certainly does not find himself.

This is why there is the *Segula* [power/virtue/cure] of the Shabbat: The light of the Shabbat can shine and show, so one can find himself in all one hundred percent of the "for a sin," that this was established only for him, and not for others. But without the light, we do not feel.

This is why it is called "Shabbat *Teshuva* [repentance]." The Shabbat is good for *Teshuva*, so we can feel the sin. This is because first we must confess the sin, and then ask for forgiveness. But if we say "for a sin" without feeling the sin, what kind of confession is this? After all, he is saying in his heart that he did not sin. And what he says with his mouth when his heart is not with him, such a confession is certainly worthless.

168. The Customs of Israel
I heard

The customs of Israel are so important that it is safe to say that they give more spirituality to a person than the *Mitzvot* [commandments] themselves. This is so although breaking a custom does not yield punishment, and breaking a judgment does yield punishment. Still, concerning the benefit, meaning producing fear of heaven, the customs yield more spirituality, since the great ones, who established the customs, arranged it so that spirituality would shine through them.

This is why he said that he who avoids the custom of eating meat and fish on Shabbat denies himself of spirituality. However, this concerns a person who has not achieved wholeness, meaning to see what he is doing. This means that he has still not been rewarded with the flavors of the *Mitzvot*, so he must observe the customs.

It is like an apple that is spoiled before it rots, but when it is spoiled, rotting is certain. Similarly, when a person becomes free, he rejects the customs, and following the rejection either he becomes free or his sons become free.

169. Concerning a Complete Righteous
I heard

In the matter of "complete righteous" who did not sin. It is written, "There is not a righteous man on earth who does good and will not sin." He replied that in each degree there is a discernment of "complete righteous," where there is no sin. In that degree, he never sinned. This is the discernment of from the *Chazeh* [chest] and above of in each degree, considered "the tree of life" and "covered *Hassadim* [mercy]."

And in the discernment of the *Chazeh* and below, there is sin and repentance. When this is corrected, we arrive at a higher degree. And there, too, begins this order, meaning "complete righteous," and "There is not a righteous man on earth who does good and will not sin."

170. You Shall Not Have in Your Pocket a Big Stone
I heard

"You shall not have in your pocket a big stone and a small stone." *Even* [stone] is called "faith" (stones to weigh with). This is considered small, which is above reason. But at the same time, you should say that you have a "big stone," meaning that you have reason. This means that what you do is not like the rest of the world, but that you have a solid basis, which is *Gadlut* [greatness] and not *Katnut* [smallness], meaning without basis and a complete *Even*.

There must be a "small stone" but it must be "complete," meaning sufficient to keep the whole of the Torah and *Mitzvot* based on the "small stone," and only then is it called "complete."

But if it is "small," and makes you do only small things, it is not considered "a complete stone." Where is it big and where is it small? If you have a small basis, it is considered small with respect to itself. But when you have a "big stone," a large basis, you consider yourself great, meaning that you are great. And a "complete stone" is when he is awarded private Providence.

171. In *The Zohar*, Emor - 1

I heard on Passover Inter 4, *Tav-Shin-Tet*, April 18, 1949

It is written in *The Zohar*, portion *Emor*: "The assembly of Israel said, 'I sleep in the exile in Egypt'" (*Zohar, Emor*, p 43).

The departure of the *Mochin* is called "sleep." "And my heart is awake." "Heart" is considered the thirty-two paths of wisdom. This means that *Hochma* [wisdom] was shining in them, but without the clothing of *Hassadim* [mercy], and this is called "the exile in Egypt." For this reason, it is called "sleep." But at the same time they were worthy of receiving *Mochin de Hochma*, but in the form of *Achoraim* [posterior].

"Hark! my beloved knocks," meaning the voice of ZA, who is considered *Hassadim*. And this is what the Creator said, "Open for Me an opening like the tip of a needle." This means that during the redemption, He told them to draw the quality of *Hochma* once more. And when it is without *Hassadim*, its opening was called "the tip of a needle," since she does not shine without *Hassadim*.

"And I will open for you the upper gates," meaning bestowing upon her the discernment of *Hassadim*, and then she will have abundance, *Hochma* and *Hassadim*.

"Open for Me... for the opening to enter Me is in you, for My children will not enter in Me, except in you." This means that He cannot give to the children, who need *Mochin de Hochma*, as His quality is only *Hassadim*. However, when she draws *Hochma*, it will be possible for the children to receive *Hochma*, too. This is why it is considered that only she can open this opening, whereas "I am closed so they will not find Me," meaning "that they will not find Me in completeness."

When ZA has only *Hassadim*, he has only VAK, and he is called "simply air." However, when he also has *Hochma*, even though he then receives only *Hassadim*, his *Hassadim* are called "pure air." This is because then his *Hassadim* are better than *Hochma*, but without *Hochma*, he will not be found in completeness.

This is the meaning of the words: "To mate with You and to always be at peace with You. Come and see, when the Creator killed the firstborn of Egypt, all those whom He killed at midnight and lowered the degrees from above downward." This is done through the correction of the *Masach de Hirik*, which causes two discernments: the departure of the GAR, and the extension of *Hassadim*, where by this *Hitkalelut* [integration], there is ability for the expansion of *Mochin* from above downward.

"At the time when Israel came into the covenant of the holy sign, they were circumcised." The "plague of the firstborn," the "Passover blood," and the "circumcision blood" are all one discernment. It is a known secret that the God of Egypt was a lamb. This means that the Passover offering was aimed at their God.

The *Klipa* [shell/peel] of Egypt was that they wanted to extend from the end of correction, like the sin of the tree of knowledge, that they wanted to extend the light of GAR from above downward. And through the Passover slaughter, they slaughtered the GAR de Hochma, by which there was the plague of the firstborn.

The firstborn is considered GAR, and they canceled the GAR. This occurred using the *Masach de Hirik*, which is considered raising the lock, which causes the cancellation of the GAR.

Dam [blood] comes from the word *Dmamah* [silence], which puts the GAR to death. This is the meaning of the circumcision blood. The chisel is the *Dinim de Nukva*, and the *Dinim* revoke the *Dinim de Dechura*, as it is written, "they were two bloods: the Passover blood and the circumcision blood." By throwing the Passover blood, the GAR was canceled and there was the *Hitkalelut* in the *Tikkun* [correction] of the lines. This is the meaning of the lintel and the two *Mezuzahs*.

"And on the fourth ... and Israel departed from the other authority, and they were united with a *Matza* holy knot." The leavened bread is the *Mochin* that expand from the *Chazeh* downward, at which time they shine from above downward. The *Matza* is the *Mochin* that shine from the *Chazeh* upward. In this discernment, there is no grip to the outer ones since the lock that appeared on Passover night, by which there was the Passover slaughtering and the plague of the firstborn, acts only from itself downward. This means that it was revealed at the *Chazeh*.

It follows that everything above it does not work with the judgment in it. However, it is not so from the *Chazeh* down, since the whole expansion is below its own discernment. This is why the judgment in it is felt, which is why Israel were cautious on Passover night to eat *Matza* and not leavened bread.

There is a merit to the *Matza* which is not in the leavened bread, and a merit to the leavened bread which is not in the *Matza*. The merit in the *Matza* is that they are complete *Mochin*, GAR de Hochma, which are still considered "the two great lights." However, they are in the form of *Achoraim*, since they cannot shine because of the lack of *Hassadim*.

And there is a merit to the leavened bread: Although it is only VAK, it is already clothed in *Hassadim*. At the Temple, where there was *Mochin de Hochma*, they were also in the form of from the *Chazeh* and above, considered a *Matza*. This is why it is said, "You shall make no leaven, nor any honey, smoke as an offering."

172. The Matter of Preventions and Delays
I heard on Passover 7, *Tav-Shin-Tet*, April 20, 1949, Tel Aviv

All the preventions and delays that appear before our eyes are but a form of nearing—the Creator wants to bring us closer, and all these preventions bring us only nearing, since without them we would have no possibility of approaching Him. This is so because, by nature, there is no greater distance, as we are made of pure matter while the Creator is higher than high. Only when one begins to approach does he begin to feel the distance between us. And any prevention one overcomes brings the way closer for that person.

(This is so because one grows accustomed to moving on a line of growing farther. Hence, whenever one feels that he is distant, it does not induce any change in the process, since he knew in advance that he is moving on a line of growing farther, since this is the truth, that there are not enough words to describe the distance between us and the Creator. Hence, every time he feels that distance to a greater extent than he thought, it causes him no contention.)

173. Why We Say LeChaim

*I heard during a Shabbat meal, portion Acharei-Kedoshim,
Omer Count 23, Tav-Shin-Tet, May 7, 1949*

He said about saying *L'Chaim* [to life—cheers (when toasting a drink)] when drinking wine, that it is as our sages said, "Wine and life according to the sages and their disciples." This is perplexing: Why specifically according to our sages? Why not according to the uneducated?

The thing is that saying *L'Chaim* implies a higher life. When we drink wine, we should remember that wine implies "the wine of Torah," a reminder that we should extend the light of Torah, called "life." The corporeal life, however, is called by our sages, "The wicked, in their lives, are called 'dead.'"

Hence, it is specifically our sages who can say "wine and life." This means that only they are qualified to extend spiritual life. Uneducated people, however, have no tools for it, with which to extend. (And perhaps, "according to our sages" means according to the view of our sages. This means that life, what they call "life," refers to spiritual life.)

174. Concealment

I heard

Concerning the concealment, which is a correction, had it not been for that, man would have been unable to attain any completeness, since he would not be worthy of attaining the importance of the matter. However, when there is concealment, the thing becomes important to him. Even though one cannot appreciate the importance as it truly is, the concealment grants it merit. To the extent that one senses the concealment, a bedding of importance is formed within him.

It is like rungs. He climbs rung by rung until he comes to his designated place. This means that he achieves a certain measure of importance with which he can at least endure, though His true importance and sublimity are immeasurable, but nonetheless a measure that will suffice him to persist.

However, concealment in itself is not considered concealment. Concealment is measured by the demand. The greater the demand for something, the more the concealment is evident. And now we can understand the meaning of "The whole earth is full of His glory." Although we believe it, the concealment still fills the whole earth.

It is written about the future: "For I, ... will be unto her a wall of fire round about, and I will be the glory in the midst of her." Fire means concealment. But still, glory is in the midst of her, meaning that then the glory will be revealed. This is because then the demand will be so great, even though there will be concealment then, too. And the difference is that at this time there is concealment, but no demand. Hence, this is considered "exile." Then, however, although there will be concealment, there will also be demand, and this is what is important—only the demand.

175. And If the Way Be Too Far for You

I heard during a *Shevat* meal, portion *Behar-BeHukotai*, Iyar 22, Tav-Shin-Tet, May 21, 1949

"And if the way be too far for you, so that you are not able to carry it."

He interpreted, Why is the way so far? Because "you are not able to carry it." This is because he cannot carry the burden of Torah and *Mitzvot* [commandments], and hence he regards the way as far. The advice for it, says the verse, "Bind up the money in your hand." *Kesef* [silver/money] means *Kisufin* [longing], to draw longing in the work. Thus, through the desire, the craving for the Creator, he will be able to carry the burden of Torah and *Mitzvot*. *Kesef* also concerns shame. This is because one is created for the goal of glorifying heaven, as it is written, "Blessed is... who created us for His glory."

In general, Torah and *Mitzvot* are things that one does in order to be favored by Him. This is because it is the slave's nature to want to be liked by his master, since then his master's heart is for him. So it is here: The many actions and meticulousness that one becomes proficient in are but a means by which to be favored in His eyes, and then he will have the desired goal of Him.

And a person observes Torah and *Mitzvot* to be liked by people. And he turns the needs of heaven into a means. Meaning, through them he will be liked by people. And as long as one has not been rewarded with the Torah *Lishma* [for Her sake], he works for people.

Although one has no other choice but to work for people, he should still be ashamed of such servitude. Then, through this *Kesef*, he will be awarded the *Kesef* of *Kedusha* [holiness], meaning to want *Kedusha*.

"And bind up the money in your hand." This means that even though the craving is not up to man, if he has no desire for it, he cannot do a thing. Nevertheless, he should show the desire for the *Kisufin*, the desire to want (and perhaps *VeTzarta*

[bind] comes from the word *Ratzita* [wanted]). One needs to show a desire for it, to show the desire and the craving to want the Creator, meaning to want to increase the glory of heaven, to bestow contentment upon Him, to be favored by Him.

There is a discernment of *Zahav* [gold], and there is a discernment of *Kesef*. *Kesef* means having *Kisufin* [longing] in general, and *Zahav* [gold, made of the words "give this"] means that he wants only one thing, and all the longing and the craving that he had for several things are canceled in this desire. And he says "give this" only, meaning he does not want anything but to raise the *Shechina* [Divinity] from the dust. This is all that he wants.

It follows that even though one sees that he does not have the proper yearning and desire, he should still see and exert in deeds and thoughts to obtain the desire. This is called "And bind up the money in your hand." One should not think that if it is in the hands of man, it is a small thing. Rather, "for oxen (with grace), or for sheep," etc., for only by this will he be rewarded with the most sublime lights.

176. When Drinking Brandy after the Havdala*

I heard after *Yom Kippur*, Tav-Shin-Yod-Aleph, September 21, 1950

"And he would make a good day when he came out of the holiness." Holiness is considered wisdom, and left line, where there is fear of the *Dinim* [judgments]. Hence, there is no place for a good day there. But rather, "when he came out of the holiness," called "wisdom" and "left line," he would make a good day, considered light of *Hassadim*.

177. Atonements

I heard

"Atonement of sins" is done through manifestation of the light of *Hochma* [wisdom]. The confession is the drawing of *Hochma*. The more one confesses, the more the *Hochma* appears on him. It is said about that: "In that day, ... the iniquity of Jacob shall be sought, and there shall be none." This is because for all the sin, when it is forgiven, it is not forgiven until *Hochma* is extended on it. This is why they were looking for iniquities, to draw upon him the light of wisdom.

"The embrace of the left" means the extension of the left line. On each of the ten penitential days, one quality of the ten *Sefirot* of *Mochin de Hochma*, called "left line," is extended. And on *Yom Kippur* [Day of Atonement] is the *Zivug* [coupling].

The embrace of the right is the drawing of *Hochma* below the *Chazeh* [chest], the place of the manifestation, where it is already sweetened in *Hassadim* [mercy]. It is primarily considered extending of *Hassadim*. The building of the *Nukva* itself

---

* A ceremony marking the end of the Sabbath

continues until the "eighth of the assembly" [last day of *Sukkot*], and on the eighth day is the *Zivug*.

178. Three Partners in Man

I heard during a meal celebrating the completion of Part Nine of The Zohar, *Iyar 3, Tav-Shin-Yod-Aleph, May 9, 1951*

Concerning the three partners in man: the Creator, the father, and the mother.

And he said that there is a fourth partner: the earth. If one does not take nourishment from the earth, he cannot persist. Earth is considered *Malchut*. In general, it is considered that there are four discernments, called HB TM. The nourishment one receives from the earth is the scrutinies, where through the nourishment, the food is separated from the *Klipa* [shell].

There are two discernments in *Malchut*: 1) *Kedusha* [holiness], 2) The Evil Lilit. Hence, when a person eats and makes the first and last blessings, by this the food emerges from the dominion of the *Sitra Achra* [other side]. Since the food becomes blood, and blood is considered the soul, his soul becomes secular, and not from the *Sitra Achra*.

However, when one eats from a meal of *Mitzva* [commandment], when the food is considered *Kedusha* [holiness], if he eats it with intention, the food becomes blood, and the blood becomes a soul. And then he comes to a state of "a soul of *Kedusha*." This is why the evil inclination always comes to a person and makes him think that it is not worthwhile to eat at a meal of *Mitzva* for several reasons. But its primary aim is not to eat at a meal of *Mitzva* for the above reason, since it is a part of *Kedusha*.

179. Three Lines

I heard on Passover Inter 2, Omer Count 2, Tav-Shin-Yod-Aleph, April 23, 1951

There is the matter of the three lines, and the matter of Israel holding to the body of the King. There is the matter of the exile in Egypt, when the people of Israel had to descend to Egypt, and the matter of the exodus from Egypt. And there is the matter of "he who is about to marry a woman will bring along an uneducated man." And there is the matter of Abraham's question: "How will I know that I will inherit it?" and the Creator's reply: "Know of a surety that your seed will be a stranger in a land that is not theirs, and they shall afflict them four hundred years, and afterward shall they come out with great possessions." There is the matter of GAR, the matter of VAK, and the matter of VAK de GAR.

The thought of creation was to delight His creatures, and the *Tzimtzum* [restriction] and the *Masach* [screen] were only to avoid the bread of shame. What extended from that is the place of work, and from that extended the three lines. The first line is considered right, regarded as VAK without a *Rosh* [head], considered "faith." The second line is considered left, attainment. And then they are disputed since faith contradicts attainment, and attainment contradicts faith.

Then there is the discernment of the middle line, considered VAK de GAR, or *Hochma* and *Hassadim*, or the right and left lines integrated in one another. This means that he receives attainment to the extent that he has faith. Thus, to the extent that he has faith, he receives the same measure of attainment. And where he has no faith, he does not draw attainment to complement it, but always stands and weighs the lines, so one will not overpower the other.

And GAR (that appears before him) is called "attainment without faith." And this is called "the work of the gentiles." The work of Israel is considered faith, where attainment is included. This is called "the King's body," meaning faith and attainment.

Abraham is called "the patriarch of faith," meaning *Hassadim*. Then he will know that anyone who wants to come near Him must first assume the discernment of "right," meaning faith.

But faith contradicts attainment. Thus, how can they draw attainment when they haven't the *Kelim* [vessels] for it? This is why He told him, "Your seed will be a stranger in a land that is not theirs." This is the meaning of "mingled with the nations and learned from their actions," meaning that they will be under the rule of the nations, that they, too, were under their dominion, drawing GAR *de Hochma*.

This is the meaning of the exile in Egypt, that Israel, too, extended GAR *de Hochma*. And this is their exile, when a discernment of darkness was extended.

The exodus from Egypt was through the plague of the firstborn. The firstborn means GAR *de Hochma*, that the Lord struck the firstborn of Egypt. This is the meaning of the Passover blood, and the circumcision blood, and this is what is written in *The Zohar* (Emor 43): "When the Creator was slaying the firstborn of Egypt, at that time, Israel went into the covenant of the holy sign, they were circumcised and bonded in the assembly of Israel."

The left line is called "foreskin," as it blocks the lights. Hence, when He killed the firstborn, meaning canceled the GAR, Israel below were circumcised, meaning cut off their foreskins. This is called *Dinim de Dechura* [male judgments], which block the lights. Thus, through circumcision with a chisel, which is iron, called *Dinim de Nukva* [female judgments], the *Dinim de Dechura* are canceled. And then VAK *de Hochma* extends to them.

This means that in the beginning, there must be drawing of perfection, meaning GAR *de Hochma*. It is impossible to draw half a degree. And this must be specifically through the Egyptians, and this is called "exile," when the Jews, too, must be under their rule. Afterward, through the exodus from Egypt, meaning the correction of the

Masach de Hirik, they exit their rule, meaning the Egyptians themselves shout, "Rise up, get out!"

And this is, "I and not a messenger." "I" means *Malchut*, the lock, which cancels the *GAR*, by which there is the mingling of the left in the right and the right in the left.

And this is "He who wishes to marry a woman," meaning *Hochma*, called "left." "Will bring an uneducated man with him," because he is in a state of "right," which is faith. But he wants attainment. Thus, specifically through the uneducated man he can draw *Hochma*, since he has repentance, but for attainment, not for faith.

"I rose up to open to my beloved, and my hands dripped with myrrh, and my fingers with flowing myrrh, upon the handles of the bar." Myrrh means "Your Teacher shall no longer hide, and your eyes shall see your Teacher." "My hands" means attainment, and "fingers" mean seeing, as in "Each one pointing with his finger, saying, 'this is our God.'" "On the bar" refers to the lock.

180. In The Zohar, Emor – 2

I heard on Passover Inter 2, *Tav-Shin-Yod-Aleph*, April 23, 1951, Tel-Aviv

In *The Zohar* (*Emor* 43): "Rabbi Hiyah opened, 'I am asleep, but my heart is awake,' etc. The assembly of Israel said, 'I am asleep in the exile in Egypt, where my children were in harsh enslavement, and my heart is awake to guard them from perishing in the exile. The voice of my beloved knocks,' this is the Creator, who said, 'And I shall remember My covenant.'"

We must understand the meaning of sleep. When Israel were in Egypt, they were under their governance, and they, too, extended *GAR de Hochma*. Since *Hochma* [wisdom] does not shine without *Hassadim* [mercy], it is called "sleep." This is called "the harsh enslavement in Egypt," meaning with hard work, called *Dinim de Dechura*.

"And in all manner of service in the field," which is considered *Dinim de Nukva*.

"But my heart is awake" means that even though she is asleep from the perspective of the left line, at which time *Malchut* is considered "the two great lights," at that time *Malchut* is called "the fourth leg." She is regarded as *Tifferet*, above the *Chazeh*. "But my heart is awake" means that the point of *Man'ula* [lock] is already there, which causes the determining of the middle line, the return to the dot that is considered *Panim*, by which they will not perish in exile.

This is the meaning of "Open for Me an opening like the tip of a needle." This means that ZA tells *Malchut* to draw *Hochma*. And even though *Hochma* cannot shine without *Hassadim*, for which it is only called "like the tip of a needle," "and I will open for you the upper gates." That is, afterwards he will give her the *Hassadim*, and thus she will be given abundance. However, if she does not draw *Hochma*, meaning there will be no drawing of *Hochma* but of *Hesed*, this is called "Open to me, my sister." Thus, from the perspective of *Hochma*, *Malchut* is called "sister."

181. Honor
I heard on Nisan 25, Tav-Shin-Yod-Aleph, May 1, 1951

Honor is something that stops the body, and to that extent it harms the soul. Hence, all the righteous who became famous and respected, it was a punishment. But the great righteous, when the Creator does not want them to lose by being famous as righteous, the Creator guards them from being honored, so as not to harm their souls.

Hence, to the extent that they are honored on one hand, on the other hand, they are faced with dissenters who degrade them with all kinds of degradations. To the extent that creates an equal weight to the honor given to a righteous, to that very extent the other side gives disgrace.

182. Moses and Solomon
I heard on Iyar 3, Tav-Shin-Yod-Aleph, May 10, 1951

Moses and Solomon are considered *Panim* [anterior/face] and *Achoraim* [posterior/back]. It is written about Moses: "and you will see My back." Solomon, however, is considered *Panim*. And only Solomon used the *Achoraim* of Moses, which is why the letters of *Shlomo* [Solomon] are the same letters as in *LeMoshe* [to Moses].

183. The Discernment of Messiah
I heard

There is a discernment of Messiah Son of Joseph, and Messiah Son of David. Both must unite, and then there will be true wholeness in them.

184. The Difference between Faith and Intellect
I heard on Shevat 15, Tav-Shin-Tet, February 14, 1949, Tiberias

The difference between faith and intellect. There is an advantage to faith because it affects the body more than the intellect because it is closer to the body. Faith is considered *Malchut*, and the body is related to *Malchut*; hence, it influences it.

The intellect, however, is attributed to the first nine, and hence cannot effectively influence the body. Yet, there is an advantage to the intellect, that it is considered spiritual compared to faith, which is attributed to the body.

There is a rule in spirituality: "There is no absence in spirituality," and "each penny is accumulated to a great amount." But faith is considered corporeality, which is considered separation. There is no adding in corporeality, and what is gone, is gone. What happened in the past does not join the present and the future.

Hence, although faith in something affects him during the act one hundred percent more than the effect of the mind, it only works for a time. The mind, however, although it is effective by only one percent, still, that percent remains constant and existing. Hence, after one hundred times, it is added to the amount that faith could affect in a single time. When he works with faith one hundred times, he will remain in the same state. But with the mind, it will remain perpetually existing in him.

It is as we learn something with the intellect. Although we forget, the recollections remain in the brain. This means that the more one learns knowledge, accordingly is one's evolution of the brain. With corporeal things, however, extended over time and place, a place in the east will never come to the west, or the past hour into the present hour. But in spirituality, everything can be simultaneous.

185. The Uneducated, the Fear of Shabbat Is on Him

I heard

Our sages said, "An uneducated man, the fear of Shabbat is on him." A wise disciple is considered Shabbat [Sabbath], and Shabbat is considered *Gmar Tikkun* [the end of correction]. Thus, as in *Gmar Tikkun*, the *Kelim* [vessels] will be corrected and fit to dress the upper light; likewise, Shabbat is considered "end." This means that the upper light can manifest and clothe in the lower ones, but this is only considered an awakening from above.

186. Make Your Shabbat a Weekday, and Do Not Need People

I heard

On Shabbat [Sabbath], it is forbidden to do work, meaning an awakening from below. And a wise disciple, one who has been rewarded with being the disciple of the Creator, who is called "Wise," is also considered an awakening from above by revealing the secrets of the Torah.

Therefore, when an awakening from above comes, that, too, is called "Shabbat." At that time, the uneducated, meaning the body, has fear, and then there is no room for work in any case.

187. Choosing Labor

I heard

The matter of the lower *Hey* in the *Eynaim* [eyes] means that there was a *Masach* [screen] and a cover over the eyes. The eyes mean Providence, when one sees hidden Providence.

A trial means that a person cannot decide either way, when one cannot determine the Creator's will and the will of his teacher. Although one can work devotedly, he is unable to determine if this devoted work is appropriate or not, that this hard work would be against his teacher's view, and the view of the Creator.

To determine, one chooses that which adds labor. This means that one should act according to one's teacher. Only labor is for man to do, and nothing else. Hence, there is no place for doubt in one's actions and thoughts and words. Instead, he should always increase labor.

188. All the Work Is Only Where There Are Two Ways - 2

I heard after Shabbat Beshalach, Shevat 14, Tav-Shin-Het, January 25, 1948

All the work is only where there are two ways, as we have found, "And he shall live in them, and he shall not die in them." And the meaning of "shall be killed but shall not breach" applies only to three *Mitzvot* [commandments]. And yet, we also find that the first *Hassidim* gave their lives on [*Mitzvot*] to do.

But in truth, this is all the work. When one should keep the Torah, this is the time of the heavy load. And when the Torah keeps the person, it is not at all difficult, by way of "one's soul shall teach him." This is considered that the Torah keeps a person.

189. The Action Affects the Thought

I heard on Tishrei 27

Understand the reason for the sharpness, excitement, and shrewdness when all the organs work in coordination at full speed, when one thinks of corporeal possessions. But with matters concerning the soul, the person, the body, and all the senses work heavily with anything that concerns the needs of the soul.

The thing is that man's mind and thought are but projections of man's actions. They are reflected as if from a mirror. Hence, if most of one's actions are of corporeal needs, it is reflected in the mirror of the mind. This means that they are sufficiently perceived in the mind, and then he can use the mind for whatever he wants since the mind receives its sustenance from corporeal things.

Thus, the mind serves that place from which it receives sustenance. And because there are not enough *Reshimot* [recollections] in the brain from the needs of the soul for reception of sustenance and impression, the mind is unwilling to serve it for the needs of the soul.

For this reason, one must overcome and do many things until they are recorded in the mind. And then the knowledge will certainly increase, and the mind will serve him with shrewdness and speed even more than for corporeal needs, since the mind is a close dressing for the soul.

190. Every Act Leaves an Imprint
I heard during a meal, Passover 1, *Tav-Shin-Tet*, April 15, 1949

He asked if the redemption of our land from the oppressors is affecting us. We have been rewarded with liberation from the burden of the nations, and have become like all the nations, where one is not enslaved to another. And if that freedom has acted upon us so that we would have some sensation of the servitude of the Creator, and he said that we should not think that it does not affect us, that no change appears in this servitude from that freedom.

This is impossible, since the Creator does not act in vain. Rather, everything He does affects us, for better or for worse. This means that additional power is extended to us from every act that He performs, positive or negative, light or dark. From this act we can also come to ascend, since there is not always permission and strength in spirituality, as we must continue under this force.

Hence, one cannot say that the freedom he has achieved induced no change in him. Yet, if we do not feel any change for the better, we must say that this is a change for the worse, even though we do not feel.

And he explained it after the good day, after the *Havdala* [end of holiday blessing]. It is like a meal of Shabbat [Sabbath] or a good day, where the corporeal pleasures awaken spiritual pleasures by way of root and branch. It is a kind of "next world." And certainly, tasting from the next world requires great preparation during the six workdays. To the extent of one's preparation, so is one's sensation.

But without any proper preparation to extend the spiritual taste of Shabbat, it is to the contrary: He grows worse due to the corporeal pleasures. This is so because after corporeal meals one is only drawn to sleep, and nothing more, since after eating comes sleep. Thus, his eating brought him lower.

But it requires great exertion to come to spirituality through corporeal pleasures, since this was the King's will. Although they are in contrast, as spirituality is placed under the line of bestowal, and corporeality under reception, and since this was the King's will, spirituality is attracted to corporeal pleasures, placed under His *Mitzvot*, which are the pleasures of Shabbat and a good day.

We should also see that even with this freedom that we have been granted, we need great preparation and intention in order to extend the spiritual freedom, called "freedom from the angel of death." Then we are rewarded with "The whole earth is full of His glory," called *Mochin de AVI*. This means that we do not see a time or a place where the Creator cannot be dressed, that we cannot say that "He cannot be dressed" at that time or at that place, but rather, "The whole earth is full of His glory."

But before that, there is a difference "between light and darkness, and between Israel and the nations": In the lit place the Creator is present, and it is not so in a place of darkness.

Also, in Israel, there is a place for the Godly light of Israel to be. This is not so in the nations of the world: The Creator does not dress in them. "And between the seventh day and the six workdays." Yet, when we are awarded *Mochin de AVI*, we are rewarded with "The whole earth is full of His glory." At that time, there is no difference between the times, and His light is present in all the places and at all times.

This is the meaning of Passover, when Israel were awarded freedom, meaning *Mochin de AVI*, considered "The whole earth is full of His glory." Naturally, there is no place for the evil inclination since one is not distanced by his actions from the work of the Creator. On the contrary, we see how it has brought man closer to His work, although it was only by way of an awakening from above.

This is why they said that the *Shechina* [Divinity] says, "I saw the image of a drop of a red rose." It means that he saw that there was a place that still needs correction, that He cannot shine in this place. This is why they needed to count the seven weeks of the *Omer* count, to correct those places, so we would see that "The whole earth is full of His glory."

It is similar to a king who has a tower filled abundantly but no guests. Hence, He created the people, so they would come and receive His abundance.

But we do not see the tower filled with goodly matters. On the contrary, the whole world is filled with suffering. And the excuse is that "and royal wine in abundance," that from the perspective of *Malchut*, there is no need for the wine, for pleasures that are comparable to the wine. Rather, the deficiency is only from the perspective of the *Kelim* [vessels], that we do not have the appropriate *Kelim* to receive the abundance, as it is specifically in the vessels of bestowal that we can receive.

The measure of the greatness of the abundance is according to the value of the greatness of the *Kelim*. Hence, all the changes are only in the vessels, not in the lights. This is what the text tells us: "Vessels of gold—the vessels being diverse from one another—and royal wine in abundance," as it was in the thought of creation, to do good to His creations, according to His ability.

191. The Time of Descent

I heard on *Sivan* 14, Tav-Reish-Tzadi-Het, June 1938

It is hard to depict the time of descent, when all the works and the efforts made from the beginning of the work until the time of descent are lost. To one who has never tasted the taste of servitude of the Creator, it seems as though this is outside of him, meaning that this happens to those of high degrees. But regular people have no connection to the work of the Creator, only to crave the corporeal will to receive, present in the flow of the world, washing the whole world with this desire.

However, we must understand why they have come to such a state. After all, with or without one's consent, there is no change in the creation of heaven and earth; He behaves in a manner of good and doing good. Thus, what is the outcome of this state?

We should say that it comes to announce His greatness. One does not need to act as though he does not want Her. Rather, one should behave in a manner of fearing the exaltedness, to know the merit and the distance between him and the Creator. It is difficult to understand this with a superficial mind, or have any possibility of connection between the Creator and creation.

During a descent he feels that it is impossible that he will have connection or belonging to the Creator by way of *Dvekut* [adhesion], since he feels that servitude is a foreign thing to the whole world.

In truth, this is so. But "In the place where you find His greatness, there you find His humbleness." This means that it is a matter that is above nature, that the Creator gave this gift to creation in order to allow them to be connected and adhered to Him.

Hence, when one becomes reconnected, he should always remember his time of descent so as to know, understand, appreciate, and value the time of *Dvekut*, so he will know that now he has salvation above the natural way.

192. The Lots

I heard in the year 1949, *Tav-Shin-Tet*, Tel-Aviv

The lots mean that they are both equal, and that it is impossible to examine with the intellect which is more important. This is why a lot is required. In *The Zohar, Emor*, it asks, "How can a goat for the Lord and a goat for *Azazel* be equal?"

The thing is that a goat for the Lord is considered "right," and a goat for *Azazel* is considered "left," where there is GAR *de Hochma*. It is said about that, "rewarded—good; not rewarded—bad." This means that *Malchut* of the quality of *Din* [judgment] appeared. This is considered a lock and a blocking on the lights. The lock is at the place of the *Chazeh* in each *Partzuf*; hence, *Hochma* can shine up to the place of the lock, but stops at the place of the *Chazeh*, since any *Tzimtzum* [restriction] works only from itself downward and not upward.

And the goat for the Lord is integrated with the left of the goat for *Azazel*, meaning with the *Hochma*. However, it is not like the left of *Azazel*, where it is from above downward. This is why the light stops, since the lock takes effect, though only from below upward, at which time the lock is concealed and the key is revealed.

It follows that concerning *Hochma*, the goat for *Azazel* has *Hochma* from the GAR, whereas the goat for the Lord is considered VAK. However, VAK can shine, while GAR must be stopped, hence the goat for *Azazel*, so the devil will not complain.

He complains because his only wish is to extend *Hochma*, which belongs to *Behina Dalet*, since it is not completed by any other degree, as its source is *Behina Dalet*. Therefore, if it does not receive into its own degree, it is not completed.

This is why it always entices man to extend into *Behina Dalet*, and if man is unwilling, it has all kinds of ploys to force man to extend. Hence, when it is given a portion of the quality of *Hochma* it does not complain about Israel, since it is afraid that the abundance it already has would be stopped.

Yet, when it extends GAR de *Hochma*, at that time Israel extends the VAK de *Hochma*. This light of *Hochma* is called "light of absolution," by which one is awarded repentance from love, when sins become as virtues. This is the meaning of the goat for *Azazel* carrying the iniquities of the children of Israel upon it, meaning that all the iniquities of Israel have now become virtues.

There is the parable that *The Zohar* tells of a King's fool. When he is given wine and told of everything that he had done, even the bad deeds that he did, he says about those deeds that they are good deeds, and that there is none other like him in the whole world. In other words, the devil is called "the fool." When it is given wine, meaning *Hochma* [wisdom], when it draws it, it is the light of absolution, and thus all the iniquities become as virtues.

It follows that it says about all the bad deeds that they are good, since the sins have become as virtues. And since the devil wants to be given its share, it does not complain about Israel.

This is the meaning of the complaints that were in Egypt: He asked, "How are these different from those? Either Israel die like the Egyptians, or Israel will return to Egypt." The thing is that Egypt is the source for extension of *Hochma*, but there it is *Hochma* in the form of GAR, and when Israel were in Egypt they were under their control.

193. One Wall Serves Both

The matter of the *Achoraim* [posterior] concerns primarily the absence of light of wisdom, which is the essence of the vitality, called "direct light." And this light was restricted so as not to come to disparity of form. This is why ZON have no GAR when they are not corrected, so the *Sitra Achra* [other side] would not draw.

Yet, since there is a lack of GAR, there is fear that the external ones will have a grip, since they enjoy wherever there is a deficiency in the *Kedusha* [holiness], since they come and ask the "where" question, and it is unrealistic to answer this question before there is *Hochma* [wisdom]. Hence, there is a correction to ZON:

They rise and become included in *Bina*, considered "for he desires mercy," and rejects *Hochma*, while *Bina* herself has no need for *Hochma* since her own essence is *Hochma*.

This is called following their rav's view in everything, that their whole foundation is their root, meaning their rav's view. And the question, "Where is the place of His honor?" is irrelevant there.

And they are in *Bina* until they are corrected by raising MAN of efforts and labors, until they are purified from reception for themselves. Then they are fit to receive *Hochma*, and only then are they permitted to disclose their own quality, as they are deficient since they do not have *Hochma*, and to accept the answer, to extend the light of *Hochma* to shine in them by way of illumination of *Hochma*. In that state, they are in their own authority and not in the authority of *Bina* since they have light of wisdom, and light clears and expels the external ones. And perhaps this is the meaning of "Know what to answer the heretical."

This is called "one wall," meaning the *Achoraim* of *Bina*, which is enough for both, and which is a shield from the *Sitra Achra*. In other words, by relying oneself on the view of one's rav, by being one with one's rav, it means that the wall that his rav has, being "desiring mercy," is enough for him, too. However, afterwards they are separated, when he extends illumination of *Hochma* and can be on his own by being able to answer all the questions of the *Sitra Achra*.

194. The Complete Seven
Copied from a manuscript of Baal HaSulam

In the matter of the seven full ones of the Sanctification of the New Moon, it is customary to wait for seven full ones, and the end of Shabbat [Sabbath], too. It is not like the custom that if the end of Shabbat occurs in the middle of the seven days, we sanctify the moon, or when the seven days have been completed from the time to the time, they do not wait for the end of Shabbat. This is not so, as we should wait the full seven, specifically on the end of Shabbat.

The thing is that the moon is considered *Malchut*, called "seventh," which is "He is in me." This means that when the Shabbat is filled by the six workdays, called "He," the Shabbat says, "He is in me." "He" is the sun, and "me" is the moon, which receives all of its light from the sun, and has nothing of its own.

However, there are two *Behinot* [discernments] in it, called "Shabbat" and "Month," since *Malchut* herself is regarded as the four known discernments HB and TM. The first three *Behinot* (*Hochma, Bina, Tifferet*) are the Shabbat. These are the three meals, called and implied in the Torah in the three times "this day." Indeed, *Behina Dalet* in her is the end of Shabbat or month, and it is not included in the "this day," as she is night, and not day.

We could ask, "The first meal of Shabbat is night, too, so why does the Torah call it 'this day'?" However, the eve of Shabbat is "And there shall be one day which shall be known as the Lord's, neither day, nor night; but it shall come to pass that there shall be light at evening time."

However, the night of the end of Shabbat is still dark, and not light. Hence, our sages instructed us in the oral Torah to set up a table at the end of Shabbat, too, to correct this darkness and night, which are still uncorrected. This is called *"Melaveh Malkah"* [escorting the Queen], sustaining and complementing that Luz bone, which is *Behina Dalet*, which does not receive anything from the three meals of Shabbat. Yet, this *Behina Dalet* is gradually completed by way of "the month, the day." This is the meaning of the sanctification of the month, that Israel sanctify the times, meaning that residue that is not nourished by the meal of Shabbat.

Hence, even the greatest among the priests, of which there is none higher in *Kedusha* [holiness], is warned to caution not to defile any dead from among his relatives. The writing warns him: "except for his kin, ... for her may he defile himself." From all the above, you can understand that any upper *Kedusha* comes from Shabbat. And since that Luz bone, meaning *Behina Dalet*, called "his kin," does not receive from the Shabbat meal, the great priest is not exempted from being defiled by it.

Indeed, the meaning of the correction in the sanctification of the month extends from the Shabbat and its illuminations. This is the meaning of "Moses was perplexed, until the Creator showed him the similitude of a coin of fire and told him, 'Thus behold and sanctify.'" This means that Moses was very confused because he could not sanctify it, since all the power of Moses is the Shabbat, since the Torah was given on Shabbat.

Hence, he could not find a correction to this residue in all the lights of the Torah, since this residue is not fed by all that. This is why Moses was perplexed.

And what did the Creator do? He took it and molded in it a shape within a shape, like a coin of fire, where the shape imprinted in its one side is not like the shape on the other side, as our sages said about the coin of Abraham that an old man and an old woman were on its one side, representing *Behina Bet*, the quality of mercy, and a young man and a virgin on the other side, which are *Behina Dalet*, the harsh quality of judgment, from the words, "neither had any man known her."

These two forms were joined in such a way that when the Creator wants to extend a correction of the lights of Shabbat there through the work of the righteous, the Creator shows the righteous that shape that extended from the first three qualities of *Malchut*, which we call *Behina Bet*, and which the righteous can sanctify with the lights of Shabbat. This is the meaning of...

195. Rewarded—I Will Hasten It

I heard in the year Tav-Reish-Tzadi-Het, 1937-1938

"Rewarded—I will hasten it," meaning the path of Torah; "not rewarded—through suffering," an evolutionary path that will finally lead everything to utter perfection. The path of Torah means that an ordinary person is given virtues by which he can make for himself *Kelim* [vessels] that are ready for it. And the *Kelim* are made through the expansion of the light and its departure.

A *Kli* [vessel] is specifically called "the will to receive." This means that he lacks something, and "there is no light without a *Kli*," for the light must be caught in some *Kli*, so it would have a hold.

But an ordinary person cannot have desires for sublime things, since it is impossible to have a need before there is fulfillment, as it is written, "the expansion of the light, etc." For example, when a person has a thousand pounds, he is rich and content. However, if he subsequently earns more, up to five thousand pounds, and then loses until he is left with two thousand, he is then deficient. Now he has *Kelim* [vessels] for three thousand pounds, since he had already had it. Thus, he has actually been canceled.

And there is a path of Torah for this. When one is accustomed to the path of Torah, to regret the scantiness of attainment, and every time he has some illuminations, and they are divided, they cause him to have more sorrow and more *Kelim*.

This is the meaning of every *Kli* needing light, that it is not filled, that its light is missing. Thus, every deficient place becomes a place for faith. Yet, were it filled, there would be no existence of a *Kli*, existence of a place for faith.

196. A Grip for the External Ones

I heard in the year Tav-Reish-Tzadi-Het, 1937-1938

We should know that the *Klipot* can only get hold in a place of lack. In a place where there is wholeness, they flee and cannot touch.

Now we can understand the matter of the breaking: It is written in several places that it concerns the separation of the light of wisdom from the light of mercy. That is, since a *Parsa* [partition] was made between *Atzilut* and *BYA*, the light of wisdom cannot descend. Only the light of *Hassadim*, which previously contained light of wisdom, has now been separated from the light of wisdom and descended. Thus, they still have powers from what they had before. This is called "lowering *Kedusha* [holiness] into the *Klipa* [shell]."

197. Book, Author, Story
I heard in the year Tav-Reish-Tzadi-Het, 1937-1938

Book, author, story. A book is considered prior to creation. An author is the owner of the book. An author is the unification of the author and the book, which should assume the form of a story, that is, the Torah along with the Giver of the Torah.

198. Freedom
I heard in the year Tav-Reish-Tzadi-Het, 1937-1938

Harut [engraved], do not pronounce it *Harut* but *Herut* [freedom]. This means that it is written, "Write them upon the tablet of your heart." Writing is with ink, which is considered blackness. Each time a person writes, meaning makes decisions about how to behave, and then reverts to his bad ways, it is because the writing was erased. Thus, one should constantly write so it will be as though *Harut*, so it will be *Harut* in his heart so he cannot erase.

And then he is immediately rewarded with *Herut*. Thus, the *Kli* [vessel] for *Herut* is the extent to which it is written in his heart. To the extent of the engraving, so is the salvation. This is because the essence of the *Kli* is the hollow, as it is written, "My heart is *Halal* [hollow/slain] within me," and then he is awarded freedom from the angel of death, since the lowliness is SAM itself, and he must know it to the fullest and overcome it until the Creator helps him.

199. To Every Man of Israel
I heard Inter 3

Every man of Israel has an internal point in the heart, which is considered simple faith. This is an inheritance from our fathers, who stood on Mount Sinai. However, it is covered by many *Klipot* [shells], which are all kinds of dresses of *Lo Lishma* [not for Her sake], and the *Klipot* must be removed. Then his basis will be called "faith alone," without any support and outside help.

200. The Hizdakchut of the Masach
I heard in Tiberias, Kislev 1 [November-December], Shabbat

The *Hizdakchut* [refinement] of the *Masach* [screen], which occurs in the *Partzuf*, causes the departure of the light, too. And the reason is that after the *Tzimtzum* [restriction], the light is captured only in the *Kli* [vessel] of the *Masach*, which is the rejecting force. And this is the essence of the *Kli*.

When that *Kli* departs, the light departs, too. This means that a *Kli* is considered faith above reason. And then the light appears. When the light appears, its nature is to thin out the *Kli*, to cancel the *Kli* of faith. Because this is so, meaning that it comes into a form of knowing in him, the light immediately departs from him. Thus, he should see to increasing the *Kli* of faith, meaning the *Masach* over the knowing, and then the abundance will not stop from him.

This is the meaning of each *Kli* being deficient of light, that it is not filled by the light that it lacks. It follows that every place of lack becomes a place for faith. If it were filled, there would be no possibility for a *Kli*, a place for faith.

201. Spirituality and Corporeality
I heard on *Hanukkah* 1, December 18, *Tav-Reish-Tzadi-Tet*, 1938

Why do we see that there are many people who work so diligently for corporeality, even in life-threatening places, but in spirituality, each and every one examines one's soul very carefully? Moreover, one can exert in corporeality even when he is not given a great reward for his work. But in spirituality, one cannot agree to work unless he knows for certain that he will receive a good reward for his work.

The thing is that it is known that the body is worthless. After all, everyone sees that it is passing and leaves without a trace, so it is easy to abandon it, as it is worthless anyway.

But in spirituality, there are *Klipot* [shells] which guard the body and sustain it. This is why it is hard to abandon it. This is why we see that it is easier for secular people to abandon their body and they do not find heaviness in their body.

But this is not so in spirituality. This is the *Achoraim* [posterior] of *Kedusha* [holiness], called "devotion." It is specifically through this that one is awarded the light. And before one is completely devoted, he cannot achieve any degree.

202. In the Sweat of Your Face Shall You Eat Bread - 2
I heard

Diminishing the light is its correction. That is, nothing is achieved without an effort. Because it is impossible to obtain the complete light in utter clarity, the advice is to diminish the light. In this way, it is possible to obtain it with the little effort that the lower one can make.

This is similar to one who wishes to move a big building; of course, this is impossible. So what does he do? He takes the building apart into small bricks, and he can move each piece. So it is here: Through diminishing the light, one can make a small effort.

203. Man's Pride Shall Bring Him Low

I heard on *Sukkot* Inter 2, *Tav-Reish-Tzadi-Tet*, October 12, 1938

"Man's pride shall bring him low." It is known that a man is born in utter lowliness. However, if the lowly one knows his place then he does not suffer for being low, as this is his place. For example, the legs are not at all degraded because they are always walking in the litter and must carry the full weight of the body, whereas the head is always above, since because they know their place. Hence, the legs are not at all degraded and do not suffer for being on a low degree.

Yet, if they had wanted to be on top but were forced to be below, they would feel the suffering. This is the meaning of "Man's pride shall bring him low." If one wants to remain in one's lowliness, he does not feel any lowliness, meaning no suffering that "Man is born a wild ass's colt." But when they want to be proud they feel the lowliness, and then they suffer.

Suffering and lowliness go hand in hand. If one feels no suffering, it is considered that he has no lowliness. It is precisely according to the measure of one's pride, or that he wants to be but is not, so he feels the lowliness. This lowliness later becomes a *Kli* [vessel] for pride, as it is written, "The Lord reigns; He wears pride." If they adhere to the Creator, they have a clothing of pride, as it is written, "Pride and glory are to the One who lives forever." Those who adhere to the One who lives forever have much pride. And to the extent that he feels the lowliness, and according to the measure of his suffering, so he is rewarded with the clothing of the Creator.

204. The Purpose of the Work – 2

I heard in the year *Tav-Reish-Tzadi-Het*, 1937-1938

During the preparation period, all the work is in the no's, that is, in the "no," as it is written, "and they shall be afflicted in a land that is not." However, with matters of the tongue, which is considered "me," one must first be awarded the discernment of love.

Yet, during the preparation, there is only work in the form of no's, regarded as "You shall not have," and by the profusion of no's, we come to the point of God* of *Hesed* [mercy]. But prior to that, there are many no's, which is other gods, many no's. This is so because from *Lo Lishma* [not for Her sake] we come to *Lishma* [for Her sake].

Since the *Sitra Achra* [other side] provides support, even afterwards, when we work and extend *Kedusha* [holiness], still, when she takes the support, we fall from the degree, and then she takes all the abundance that they extended. By this, the *Sitra Achra* has the power to control a person so he will be compelled to satisfy her wish. And he has no other choice but to raise himself to a higher degree.

---

* In Hebrew, the word God (*El*) and 'no' are written with the same letters but in the opposite order.

Then the sequence begins anew, as before, with the forty-nine gates of *Tuma'a* [impurity]. This means that one walks in the degrees of *Kedusha* until the forty-nine gates. But there she has control to take all the vitality and abundance until a person falls each time into a higher gate of *Tuma'a*, since "God has made them one opposite the other."

When one comes into the 49th gate, he can no longer raise himself until the Creator comes and redeems him. And then "He has swallowed down riches, and he shall vomit them up again; God shall cast them out of his belly." This means that now one takes all the abundance and vitality that the *Klipa* [shell] was taking from all of the forty-nine gates of *Kedusha*. This is the meaning of "the looting of the sea."

Yet, it is impossible to be redeemed before we feel the exile. And when we walk on the forty-nine, we feel the exile, and the Creator redeems on the 50th gate. The only difference between *Gola* [exile] and *Ge'ula* [redemption] is in the *Aleph*, which is *Alupho Shel Olam* [Champion of the world]. Hence, if one does not properly attain the exile, too, he is deficient in the degree.

205. Wisdom Cries Out in the Streets
I heard in the year *Tav-Reish-Tzadi-Het*, 1937-1938

"Wisdom cries out in the streets, she utters her voice in the broad places. He who is a fool, let him come here; 'Heartless!' she said to him." This means that when one is awarded *Dvekut* [adhesion] with the Creator, the *Shechina* [Divinity] tells him that the fact that he first had to be a fool was not because he really is so. The reason was that he was heartless. This is why we say, "And all believe that He is a God of faith."

This means that later, when we are rewarded with true *Dvekut* [adhesion], it is not considered being a fool, that I should say that it is above reason. Moreover, one must work and believe that one's work is above reason even though one's senses tell him that his work is within reason. It is to the contrary: Previously, he saw that the reason did not obligate the servitude, and then he had to work above reason and say that there is real reason in it. This means that he believes that the servitude is the actual reality.

Afterward, it is the opposite: His whole work compels him, his reason. In other words, the *Dvekut* impels him to work. However, he believes that everything he sees within reason is all above reason. And this was not so before, when everything that is in the form of above reason is within reason.

206. Faith and Pleasure
I heard in the year *Tav-Reish-Tzadi-Het*, 1937-1938

One will never ask about pleasure, "What is the purpose of this pleasure?" If even the smallest thought about its purpose appears in one's mind, it is a sign that this is not true pleasure, since pleasure fills all the empty places, and then of course there is no vacant place in the mind to ask about its purpose. If one does ask about its purpose, it is a sign that the pleasure is incomplete, since it has not filled all the places.

So it is with faith. Faith should fill all the places of knowing. Hence, we should imagine what it would be like if we had knowledge, and to that very extent there should be faith.

207. Receiving in order to Bestow
I heard on Shabbat, Tevet 13

People in the world walk on two legs, called "pleasure" and "pain." They always chase after the place of pleasure, and always flee from the place of suffering. Hence, when one is rewarded with tasting the flavor of Torah and *Mitzvot* [commandments], as it is written, "Taste and see that the Lord is good," then he chases the servitude of the Creator. The result of this is that one is always rewarded with degrees of Torah and *Mitzvot*, as it is written, "And His law does he contemplate day and night."

But how can one restrict one's mind to one thing? Rather, love and pleasure always tie one's thoughts so that one's mind and body are attached to the love and the pleasure, as we see with corporeal love. This is so precisely when one has already been awarded the expansion of the mind, which yields love. This discernment is called "within reason." But one should always work above reason, since this is called "faith and bestowal."

This is not so within reason, for then all the organs agree with one's work because they, too, receive delight and pleasure, which is why it is called "within reason."

At such a time one is in a difficult situation: It is forbidden to spoil the discernment, as it is a Godly illumination within him, as this is abundance from above. Instead, one should correct both, meaning the faith and the reason.

And then he needs to arrange it so that everything he has achieved so far, meaning the Torah that he has now achieved and the abundance that he now has, what has this got to do with that? It is only because he had had prior preparation by taking upon himself the above reason.

This means that through engagement in *Dvekut* [adhesion], he attached himself at the root. By this he was awarded reason, meaning that the reason he has obtained by the discernment of faith was a true revelation. It follows that he appreciates primarily the above reason, and also appreciates the reason, that he has now been rewarded with the revelation of His names to extend abundance.

This is why now he should strengthen further through reason, and take upon himself a greater above reason, as *Dvekut* in the root occurs primarily through faith, and this is his whole purpose. This is called "reception," the reason he extended in order to bestow, and by which he will be able to take upon himself faith above reason to the greatest extent in quantity and quality.

208. Labor
I heard

The efforts that one makes are but preparations for achieving devotion. Hence, one should grow accustomed to devotion, since no degree can be achieved without devotion, as this is the only tool that qualifies one to be rewarded with all the degrees.

209. Three Conditions in Prayer
I heard

There are three conditions in prayer:

1. Believing that He can save him. Although he has the worst conditions of all his contemporaries, still, "Will the Lord's hand be too short to save him?" If it is not so, then "the Landlord cannot save His vessels."

2. He no longer has any choice for he has already done all that he could but saw no cure to his plight.

3. If He does not help him, he will be better off dead than alive. Prayer means "lost in the heart." The more one is lost, so is the measure of his prayer. Clearly, one who lacks luxuries is not like one who has been sentenced to death, and only the execution is missing, and he is already tied with iron chains, and he is standing and pleading for his life. He will certainly not rest or sleep or be distracted for even a moment from praying for his life.

210. A Sightly Flaw in You
I heard

It is written in the Talmud: "He who said to her, to his wife, 'Until you see a sightly flaw in you.' Rabbi Ishmael, son of Rabbi Yosi, said that the Creator says that she cannot adhere to him until you see a sightly flaw in you" (*Nedarim* 66b). The first interpretation of the *Tosfot* means that she is forbidden to enjoy until she can find a sightly thing.

This means that if one can say that he, too, has nice things with which he helped the Creator, so they can adhere to one another, so why has He not helped another? This must be since there are things in him, that he has good faith or good qualities, since he has a good heart, that he can pray.

This is the meaning of his commentary: "He said to them, 'Perhaps like a becoming woman?'" This means that there is an external mind, better than all his contemporaries. Or "Perhaps her hair is pretty?" This means that he is as meticulous with himself as a hairsbreadth. Or "Perhaps her eyes are pretty?" This means that he has more grace of holiness than all of his contemporaries. Or "Perhaps his ears are handsome?" This means that he cannot hear any slander.

211. As Though Standing before a King
I heard on *Elul* 1, August 28, *Tav-Reish-Tzadi-Het*, 1938

One who is sitting at one's home is not as one who is standing before a King. This means that faith should be that he will feel all day as though he is standing before the King. Then his love and fear will certainly be complete. As long as he has not achieved this kind of faith, he should not rest, "for this is our lives and the length of our days," and we will accept no recompense.

And the lack of faith should be woven in his limbs until the habit becomes a second nature, to the extent that "When I remember Him, He does not let me sleep." But all the corporeal matters quench this lack, since he sees that anything that gives him pleasure, the pleasure cancels the deficiency and the pain.

Rather, he must want no consolation, and should be careful with any corporeal thing that he receives, so it does not quench his desire. This is done by regretting that by this pleasure, the sparks and powers of the *Kelim* [vessels] of *Kedusha* [holiness] are missing in him, meaning desires for *Kedusha*. Through the sorrow, he can keep from losing *Kelim* of *Kedusha*.

212. Embrace of the Right, Embrace of the Left
I heard on *Kislev* 8, *Tav-Shin-Bet*, November 28, 1941

There is the embrace of the right and there is the embrace of the left, and both must be eternal. This means that when one is in the state of "right," he should think that there is no such quality as "left" in the world. And also, when one is in the left, he should think that there is no such quality as "right" in the world.

"Right" means private Providence, and "left" means guidance of reward and punishment. Although there is reason which says that there is no such thing as right and left together, he must work above reason, meaning that reason will not stop him.

The most important is the above reason. This means that one's whole work is measured by his work above reason. Although he later comes into within, it is nothing, since his basis is the above reason, so he always suckles from his root.

However, if, when he comes into within reason, he wants specifically to be fed within reason, at that time the light immediately departs. If he wants to extend, he must begin with above reason, as this is his whole root. Afterward, he comes to the reason of *Kedusha* [holiness].

213. Revealing the Deficiency

I heard

The basic, primary principle is to increase the deficiency, for this is the basis upon which the whole structure is built. And the strength of the building is measured by the strength of its foundation.

Many things compel one to labor, but they do not aim at the cause. Therefore, the foundation impairs the whole structure. Although from *Lo Lishma* [not for Her sake] we come to *Lishma* [for Her sake], it still requires a long time before one returns to the goal.

Therefore, one must see that the goal is always before his eyes, as it is written in *Shulchan Aruch* [Set Table (Jewish code of law)]: "I see the Lord before me always." And one who stays home is unlike one who stands before the king. He who believes in the existence of the Creator—that the whole earth is full of His glory—is filled with fear and love, and needs no preparations or observation, only to completely nullify before the king from his very nature.

Just as we see in corporeality, that he who truly loves his friend thinks only of the best of his friend, and avoids anything that is not beneficial to his friend. All this is done without any calculation, and it does not require a great mind, since it is as natural as a mother's love for her child, who only wants to benefit her child. She needs no preparations or intellect to love her child, since a natural thing does not require an intellect that will assert it, but it is done by the senses themselves. The senses themselves are devoted, since this is how it is in nature, as due to the love for something, they give their soul until they achieve the goal. And as long as they do not achieve, their lives are not a life.

Thus, whoever feels, as it is written in *Shulchan Aruch*, that for him it is similar, etc., he is certainly in wholeness, meaning that he has faith. As long as one does not feel he is standing before the king, then one is the opposite.

Hence, one should see that servitude is first and foremost. One must regret not having sufficient faith, as the lack of faith is his foundation, and he should pray for requests and labor, to feel that deficiency, for if he has no deficiency, it means he has no *Kli* [vessel] to receive the filling. One must believe that the Creator hears the prayer of every mouth and that he, too, will be delivered in complete faith.

214. Known in the Gates

I Heard on *Shavuot* [Feast of Weeks], *Tav-Reish-Tzadi-Tet*, 1939, Jerusalem

"I am the Lord your God." Also, in *The Zohar*, "known in the gates." Question: Why did our sages change from the written word of calling the festival of the assembly by the name "the giving of our Torah"? In the Torah, this festival is specified by the name "offering of first-fruits," as it is written, "Also in the day of the first-fruits." Our sages came and named it "the giving of our Torah."

The thing is that our sages did not change anything; they only interpreted the matter of the offering of the first-fruit. It is written, "Let the field exult, and all that is in it; then shall the trees of the forest sing for joy." The difference between a field and a wood is that the field bears fruit and woods are infertile trees, which do not bear fruit.

This means that a field is discerned as *Malchut*, which is discerned as acceptance of the burden of the kingdom of heaven, which is faith above reason.

But what is the measure of the faith? This has a measurement, meaning it should fill to the very same extent as the knowledge. Then, it will be called "A field that the Lord has blessed," meaning bearing fruit. This is the only way by which it is possible to adhere to Him since it places no limits on him because it is above reason.

Knowledge, however, is limited. The measure of the greatness is according to the measure of the knowledge. And this is called "Another God is sterile and does not bear." This is why it is called "a wood." However, in any case, both are called "edges." But there should be a discernment of the middle pillar, meaning that he needs knowledge, too, but on condition that he does not spoil the faith above reason.

Yet, if he works with knowledge a little better than with faith, he immediately loses everything. Instead, it should be to him without any difference. Then, "The field will exult, etc., the trees of the wood will sing for joy," for then there is correction even for "another God," discerned as the "wood," because he will be strengthened by faith.

This is the meaning of what is written about Abraham, "Walk before Me, and be wholehearted." RASHI interprets that he does not need support. About Noah, it is written, "Noah walked with God," that he needed support, though in any case it is support from the Creator. However, the worst that can ever be is needing the support of people.

There are two matters:

1. a gift,

2. a loan.

The gift that one takes from people is the support, and he does not want to return it, but wants to use it for the rest of his life.

And a loan is when he takes for the time being, meaning as long as he has no strength or power of his own, but he hopes that through work and labor in sanctity and purity he will obtain his own strength. At that time, he will give back the support he took. Yet, this, too, is not good, because if he is not rewarded with obtaining, he will fall.

Let us return to the issue that the "giving of the Torah" and not the "receiving of the Torah" was because then they were rewarded with the Giver of the Torah, as it is written, "We wish to see our King." Hence, the main thing with which they were rewarded is the "Giver of the Torah." And then it is called "a field that the Lord has blessed," meaning a field that bears fruit.

This is the meaning of the first-fruit, meaning the first fruit of the field. It is a sign of being rewarded with the "Giver of the Torah" and complete awareness. This is why he says, "A wandering Aramean was my father." Previously, he had descents and cunningness, but now it is a sustainable connection. This is why our sages interpret the matter of the first-fruit as the "giving of the Torah," when they are rewarded with "the Giver of the Torah."

215. Concerning Faith
I heard

Faith, specifically, is pure work since the will to receive does not participate in this work. Moreover, the will to receive resists it. The nature of that desire is only to work in a place that it sees and knows. But above reason is not so. Hence, in this manner the *Dvekut* [adhesion] can be complete, since there is an element of equivalence here, meaning it is actually to bestow.

Therefore, when this basis is fixed and exists in him, even when receiving good influences, he considers it an *Atreia* [Aramaic: warning], which, in *Gematria*, is Torah. And there should be fear with this Torah, meaning he should see that he does not receive any support or assistance from the Torah, but from faith. And even when he already considers it superfluous because he is already receiving from the quality of "a pleasant land," he should believe that this is the truth. This is the meaning of "And all believe that He is a God of faith," since specifically through faith can he maintain the degree.

216. Right and Left
I heard on *Tevet* 6

There is the discernment of "right" and there is "left." On the "right" there are *Hochma*, *Hesed*, *Netzah*, and on the "left" there are *Bina*, *Gevura*, and *Hod*. Right is considered "private Providence," and "left" is considered "reward and punishment."

When engaging in the right, we should say that all is in private Providence, and then one does nothing anyhow. Thus, he has no sins. However, the *Mitzvot* [commandments] that one performs are also not his own, but are a gift from above, so he should be thankful for them, as well as for the corporeal benefits that He has done to him.

This is called *Netzah*, when he *Nitzah* [defeated] the *Sitra Achra* [other side], and from this extends *Hesed* [mercy], which is love. By this he comes to *Hochma*, called *Reisha de Lo Etyada* [The Unknown Head]. Afterward, one should go to the left line, which is regarded as *Hod*.

217. If I Am Not for Me, Who Is for Me?
I heard on *Adar Aleph* 27

"If I am not for me who is for me, and when I am for myself, what am I?" This is an inherent contradiction. The thing is that one should do all of one's work by way of "If I am not for me, who is for me," that no one can save him, but "by your mouth, and by your heart to do it," that is, a discernment of reward and punishment. However, to oneself, in private, one should know that "when I am for myself, what am I?" This means that everything is in private Providence and no one can do anything.

If you say that if everything is in private Providence, why is there the issue of working in the form of "If I am not for me, who is for me?" Yet, through working in the form of "If I am not for me, who is for me," one is awarded private Providence, meaning attains it. Thus, everything follows the path of correction, and the distribution of added fondness, called "children of the Creator," is not revealed unless it is preceded by work in the form of "If I am not for me, who is for me."

218. The Torah and the Creator Are One
I heard

"The Torah and the Creator are one." Certainly, during the work they are two things. However, they contradict one another. The discernment of the Creator is *Dvekut* [adhesion], and *Dvekut* means equivalence, being canceled from reality. (And one should always depict how there was a time when he had a little bit of *Dvekut*, how he was filled with vitality and pleasure, and to always crave to be in *Dvekut*, for a spiritual matter is not divided in half. Moreover, if this is something fulfilling, he should always have the good thing. And one should depict the time he had since the body does not feel the negative, but the existing, that is, states he had already had. And the body can take these states as examples.)

The Torah is called "the light" in it. This means that during the study, when we feel the light, and want to give to the Creator with this light, as it is written, "One who knows the commandment the Master will serve Him." Hence, he feels that he exists, that he wants to bestow upon the Creator, and this is the sensation of oneself.

However, when one is awarded the discernment of "the Torah and the Creator are one," one finds that all is one. At that time, one feels the Creator in the Torah. One should always yearn for the light in it; and the light we can with what we learn, although it is easier to find the light in words of Kabbalah.

During the work, they are two ends. One is drawn to the discernment of the Creator, at which time he cannot study the Torah, and he yearns after the books of *Hassidim*. Then there is one who craves the Torah, to know the ways of the Creator, the worlds, their processes, and matters of guidance. These are the two ends. But in the future, "He shall smite the corners of Moab," that is, they are both included in the tree.

219. Devotion
I heard

The work should be with love and fear. With love, it is irrelevant to say that we must be devoted to it, since it is natural, as love is as fierce as death, as it is written, "for love is as strong as death." Rather, devotion should primarily be concerning fear, that is, when one still does not feel the taste of love in the servitude, and the servitude is coercive for him.

There is a rule that the body does not feel a thing that is coercive, as it is built by way of correction. And the correction is that the servitude, too, should be in the form of love, as this is the purpose of the *Dvekut* [adhesion], as it is written, "In a place where there is labor, there is the *Sitra Achra* [other side]."

The servitude that should primarily be in devotion is on the discernment of fear. At that time, the whole body disagrees with one's work, since it does not feel any taste in the servitude. And with each thing that he does, the body calculates that this servitude is not in completeness. Thus, what will you get out of working?

Then, because there is no validity or taste in this servitude, overcoming is only through devotion. This means that the servitude feels bitter, and each act causes him horrendous suffering, since the body is not accustomed to work in vain: either the work should benefit oneself, or others.

But during the *Katnut* [smallness/infancy], one does not feel any benefit for oneself, since he does not presently feel any pleasure in the servitude. And also, he does not believe that there will be benefit to others since it is not important to him, so what pleasure would others have from it? Then the suffering is harsh. And the more he works, the suffering increases proportionally. Finally, the suffering and the labor accumulate to a certain amount where the Creator has mercy on him and gives him a taste in the servitude of the Creator, as it is written, "Until the spirit be poured upon us from on high."

220. Suffering
I heard

The harsh suffering that one feels is only because of the absence of vitality. However, what can one do? It is not within one's power to take vitality. At such a time, one comes to a state of boredom. And it is specifically at such a time that one needs great strengthening, but you are not taking.

221. Multiple Authorities

I heard

A *Kli* [vessel] does not leave its own authority unless it is filled with something else. But it cannot remain empty. Hence, because it is in the authority of the *Sitra Achra* [other side], of course it must be taken out. Therefore, we must try to fill it with other things. This is why it must be filled with love. It is written, "And then he will be taken after her for love of self."

222. The Part Given to the Sitra Achra to Separate It from the Kedusha

I heard

"In the beginning, He created the world with the quality of *Din* [judgment]. He saw that the world did not exist." Interpretation: The quality of *Din* is *Malchut*, the place of the *Tzimtzum* [restriction]. From there down, the external ones stand.

However, in the first nine, there can be reception of the abundance without any fear, but the world would not exist, meaning *Behina Dalet* cannot be corrected because this is her place, and it is impossible to change, meaning revoke the vessels of reception, since this is nature and it is impossible to change. Nature means a higher force, that this was His will, that the will to receive would be in completeness and impossible to cancel.

Also, in man below, it is impossible to change nature. And the advice for this was to associate it with the quality of mercy, meaning to make the boundary that exists in *Malchut* in the place of *Bina*. This means that He made it as though there is a prohibition to receive, and there it is possible to work, meaning receive in order to bestow. This is because this is not the place of *Behina Dalet*; therefore, it can be revoked.

It follows that *Behina Dalet* is actually corrected, that is, by lowering the *Behina Dalet*. This means that she discovers that this is not her place. And this is done through *Mitzvot* [commandments] and good deeds. When he discovers, he scrutinizes *Behina Dalet* in *Behina Bet*, which shows that her place is below.

At that time, the *Zivug* [coupling] rises and the *Mochin* [light] extends below. Then the lower *Hey* rises to the *Eynaim* [eyes] and the work on turning the vessels of reception begins anew.

And the essence of the correction is because he gives a portion to the *Sitra Achra*. That is, previously the place of her suckling was only from *Behina Dalet*, as only there is the quality of *Din*, which is not so in *Bina*. Now, however, *Bina*, too, takes the discernment of diminution, since the quality of *Din* has been mingled with her, too. It follows that the place of the quality of *Din* has grown. Yet, it is through this part that there is room for work, the ability to reject, since this is not her real place. And then, after being accustomed to rejecting it from where it is possible, it results in the ability to reject her from where it was previously impossible.

And this is "He has swallowed down riches, and he shall vomit them up again." Thus, by stretching her boundary and swallowing up great riches, thus she herself is made completely corrected. This is the meaning of "a goat for *Azazel*": She is given a part, by which she is subsequently separated from *Kedusha* [holiness], when she is corrected in the place He gives her, which is not her place.

223. Clothing, Sack, Lie, Almond
I heard

"None might come to the king's gate wearing sackcloth." This means that when one awakens oneself to how remote he is from the Creator, that he is filled with transgressions, sins, and crimes, he cannot be adhered, and he cannot receive any salvation from the Creator. This is because he is wearing sackcloth and cannot enter the King's palace.

Hence, it is necessary for one to see one's true state, as it is, without covering. On the contrary, the whole purpose of the *Klipot* [shells/peels] is to cover, but if one has been rewarded from above, he can discover and see his true state. However, he must know that this is not wholeness but necessity. And a time of bitterness is called *Dalet* [the Hebrew letter]. When it is added by a *Sack* [the Hebrew and English words are the same here], they form *Shakad* [was diligent], which rushes salvation.

Yet, when one makes the bitterness in the work by himself, that is, when one can make the self-scrutiny, he is glad that at least he sees the truth. This is considered making this the *Rosh* [head], that is, important. This is called *Reish* [the Hebrew letter], and joined with the *Sack* it creates *Sheker* [lie]. However, this work should be as the blink of an eye, and he should immediately strengthen himself with complete faith that everything will be corrected.

224. Yesod de Nukva and Yesod de Dechura
I heard

The matter of the ascent of *Malchut* to the place of the *Eynaim* [eyes] is called *Yesod de Nukva*. This is because *Nukva* means deficiency, where diminution is considered a lack. Because it is in the *Eynaim*, which is *Hochma*, it is nevertheless called *Behina Aleph* of the four *Behinot*. However, when the bottom *Hey* is in *Keter*, and *Keter* is a desire to bestow, no diminution applies there, since there is no limitation on the desire to bestow. This is why it is called *Yesod de Dechura*.

225. Raising Oneself
I heard

One cannot raise oneself above one's circle. Hence, one must nurse from one's environment, and he has no other way except through Torah and much work. Therefore, if one chooses for oneself a good environment, he saves time and efforts since he is drawn according to his environment.

226. The Written Torah and the Oral Torah - 2
I heard on *Mishpatim* 3, *Tav-Shin-Gimel*, February 2, 1943, Tel-Aviv

The written Torah is considered an awakening from above, and the oral Torah is considered an awakening from below. Together, they are considered, "Six years he shall work, and in the seventh he shall go out free." The matter of work pertains precisely where there is resistance, and it is called *Alma* [Aramaic: world] from the word *He'elem* [Hebrew: concealment]. Then, during the concealment, there is resistance, and then there is room for work. This is the meaning of the words of our sages: "6,000 years the world exists, and one destroyed," meaning that the concealment will be destroyed, and then there will be no more work. Instead, the Creator makes wings for him, which are covers so we would have work.

227. The Reward for a Mitzva–a Mitzva
I heard

One should crave being awarded the reward of a *Mitzva* [commandment]. This means that through keeping the *Mitzvot* [pl. of *Mitzva*] he will be rewarded with adhering to the *Metzaveh* [Commander].

228. Fish before Meat
I heard on *Adar* 1, *Tav-Shin-Zayin*, February 21, 1947, Tiberias

The reason that in a meal we eat fish first is that fish are given free, without preparation. This is why they are eaten first, as they do not require preparation, as it is written, "We remember the fish that we ate in Egypt for nothing." And *The Zohar* interprets "for nothing" as without *Mitzvot* [commandments], meaning without preparation.

And why do fish not require preparation? The thing is that we see that a fish is only considered *Rosh* [head]; it has no hands or legs. A fish is discerned as "Joseph halved a fish and found a *Margalit* [gemstone] in its flesh."

Margalit means *Meragel* [spy], and a fish means that there is no negotiation there. This is the meaning of the absence of hands and legs. And "halved" means that through the rise of *Malchut* to *Bina*, each degree has been halved, and by this division, a place was made for the *Meragelim*. Thus, the whole negotiation was only over the *Meragelim*, as the whole Torah extends from here. This is the meaning of the *Margalit* hanging on his neck, and anyone who was sick would look at it and heal immediately.

However, there is no reward in the discernment of the fish alone, except that it is free, as it is written, "which we ate in Egypt for nothing." "An open eye, which never sleeps, needs no guarding," since the matter of the fish is considered *Hochma* [wisdom] and *Shabbat* [Sabbath], which precede the Torah.

The Torah means negotiation. This is the meaning of "I could not find my hands and legs in the seminary," meaning that there was no negotiation. "For nothing" means without negotiation, and "Torah" is called "the next world," discerned as "satiated and delighted," and that the satiation does not quench the pleasure, as it is the pleasure of the soul. However, in the discernment of "The Shabbat that precedes the Torah," considered *Hochma*, it comes to a state of *Guf* [body], and the *Guf* is a boundary, where the satiation quenches the pleasure.

229. Haman Pockets
I heard on Purim Night, after reading the *Megillah*, Tav-Shin-Yod, March 3, 1950

Concerning the eating of the *Haman Tashim*, meaning Haman's Pockets,* he said that since "man must be intoxicated on Purim until he cannot tell between the evil Haman and the blessed Mordecai," we eat Haman Pockets, so we remember that Haman did not give us more than pockets, called *Kelim* [vessels], and not the interior. This means that it is only possible to receive Haman's *Kelim*, and not the lights, called "internality," since the big vessels of reception are in Haman's domain, and this is what we must take away from him.

However, it is impossible to extend lights with the *Kelim* of Haman. This occurs specifically through the *Kelim* of Mordecai, which are vessels of bestowal. But there was a *Tzimtzum* [restriction] on the vessels of reception. This is explained in the verse: "And Haman said in his heart, 'Whom would the king delight to honor more than me?'"

This is called "a real will to receive." This is why he said "Let royal apparel be brought which the king uses to wear, and the horse that the king rides upon," etc. But in truth, Haman's *Kelim*, called "vessels of reception," do not receive anything due to the *Tzimtzum*. All he has is a desire and a deficiency, meaning he knows what to demand. This is why it is written, "And the king said to Haman, 'Hurry, and take the apparel and the horse, as you have said, and do so to Mordecai the Jew.'"

This is called "lights of Haman in *Kelim* of Mordecai," meaning in vessels of bestowal.

---

* Haman's Pockets are also known as "Haman's Ears," a traditional Purim pastry.

230. The Lord Is High and the Low Will See

I heard on Shabbat *Teruma*, *Tav-Shin-Tet*, March 5, 1949, Tel-Aviv

"The Lord is high and the low will see." How can there be equivalence with the Creator when man is the receiver and the Creator is the Giver? The verse says about that, "The Lord is high and the low will see." If one annuls oneself, no authority separates him from the Creator, and then he will "see," meaning he will be awarded *Mochin* [lights] of *Hochma* [wisdom].

"And the high will know from afar." One who is proud—who has his own authority—is far because he lacks the equivalence.

Lowliness does not imply lowering oneself before others; this is humbleness, and one feels wholeness in this work. Lowliness means that the world despises him. It is precisely when people despise him that it is considered lowliness, and then one does not feel any wholeness, since it is a law—what people think affects a person. Hence, if people appreciate him, he feels whole, and those whom people despise consider themselves low.

231. The Purity of the Vessels of Reception

I heard on *Tevet*, *Tav-Reish-Peh-Het*, January 1928, Givat Shaul (Jerusalem)

We should be cautious with anything that the body enjoys. One should regret this, since through reception, he becomes removed from the Creator since the Creator is the Giver, and if he will now be a receiver, he thus comes into oppositeness of form. In spirituality, disparity of form is remoteness, and then he does not have *Dvekut* [adhesion] with the Creator.

This is the meaning of "and to adhere to Him." Through the sorrow that one feels upon reception of pleasure, the sorrow revokes the pleasure. It is like a person who suffers from scabbiness in his head. He must scratch his head and it gives him pleasure. However, at the same time he knows that this will only worsen his scabbiness, and his plight will spread and he will not be able to heal. Thus, during the pleasure he has no real delight although he cannot stop receiving the pleasure of scratching.

He should also see that when he feels pleasure from something, he should extend sorrow over the pleasure, since thus he becomes so remote from the Creator that he will feel that the pleasure is not worthwhile compared to the loss that this pleasure will subsequently bring him. This is the work in the heart.

(*Kedusha* [holiness]: that which brings one closer to the work of the Creator is called *Kedusha*.

Tuma'a [impurity]: that which removes one from the work of the Creator is called *Tuma'a*.)

232. Completing the Labor
I heard

"I labored and did not find, do not believe." We must understand the meaning "I found." What is there to find? Finding concerns the Creator finding us agreeable. "I did not labor and found, do not believe."

We must ask, after all, he is not lying; this is not about a person concerning himself as an individual. Rather, it is the same rule with the whole. And if one sees that he is favored by Him, why "not believe"? The thing is that sometimes a person is rewarded with favor through prayer. This is because so is the power of the prayer—it can act like labor. (As we see in corporeality, some get provision through their labor, and some get their provision through prayer. By asking for provision, he is allowed to provide for himself.)

But in spirituality, although he is rewarded with favor, he must still pay the full price later on—the measure of the labor that everyone gives. If not, he will lose the *Kli* [vessel]. This is why he said, "I did not labor and found, do not believe," since he will lose everything. Thus, one should subsequently pay one's full labor.

233. Pardon, Forgiveness, and Atonement
I heard

Mechila [pardon], as in from ruin to praise. This means that sins have become to him as merits specifically through repentance from love. Thus, he turns the sins into a praise, to merits.

Slicha [forgiveness] comes from *VeShalach Et Be'iro* ["and shall let his beast loose," exchanging the [Hebrew letter] *Samech* with a *Shin*]. This means that he sends the sins away from him and says that from now on he will do only merits. This is considered repentance from fear, when sins become to him as mistakes.

Kapara [atonement] comes from *VeKipper Et HaMizbe'ach* ["and he shall make atonement for the altar"], from "wishes to atone his hands in this man." Hence, when one knows that he is dirty, he has not the audacity and impudence to enter the King's palace. Therefore, when one sees and remembers his bad deeds, which are against the King's will, it is difficult for him to engage in Torah and *Mitzvot* [commandments], much less to ask of the King to adhere to Him and unite with Him.

This is why he needs atonement, so he will not see his poor state, that he is in utter lowliness, and so he will not remember his state, so he will have room to receive joy by being able to engage in the Torah and the work. And then, when he has joy, he will have room to ask for bonding with the King, since "the *Shechina* [Divinity] dwells only in a place of joy." Therefore, first we need atonement, and then, when we repent from fear, we are awarded forgiveness. And then repentance from love, we are awarded pardon.

We should believe that everything that happens in our world is guided, and there are no coincidences. We should also know that everything that is written as admonition, meaning the curses, in "If you do not listen," are terrible torments, and not as everyone thinks. Some say that they are blessings and not curses. They bring the Sayer of Kuznitz as evidence to their words. He would always make *Aliyah la Torah* [ritual reading of the Torah during service] on *Parashat Tochachot* [a specific portion of the Torah called "Admonition"]. He says that these are real curses and troubles.

It is as we see for ourselves that curses exist in reality, that they feel in this world unbearable torments. Yet, we should believe that we should attribute all these torments to Providence, that He does everything. Moses took these curses and attributed them to the Creator. This is the meaning of "and in all the great terror."

When you believe in that, you also believe that "there is judgment and there is a judge." This is why the sayer would make *Aliya* on *Parashat Tochachot*, since only he could attribute the curses and the suffering to the Creator, since he believed that "there is judgment and there is a judge." And through that, real blessings stem from all these curses, since "God has made it that He will be feared."

And this is the meaning of "the bandage is made out of the blow itself." That means that from the very place where the wicked fail, the righteous will walk. This is because when coming to a place where there is no support, the *Sitra Achra* [other side] has a hold in that place. Then the wicked fail in them. This wicked, who cannot go above reason, falls because he has no support. Then he remains between heaven and earth, since they are wicked, and can only do things within reason, by way of "evil eye, of haughty eyes."

But the righteous are considered "my eyes are not haughty, nor my heart lofty," and they will walk in it. It follows that it turns into blessings. Thus, by attributing all the suffering to Providence and taking everything above reason, it creates within him the proper *Kelim* [vessels] to receive blessings.

234. He Who Ceases Words of Torah and Engages in Conversation

Adar Aleph, Tav-Shin, 1940, on the way to Gaza

"He who ceases words of Torah and engages in conversation is fed coals of broom." This means that when one engages in Torah and does not stop, the Torah is considered for him a blazing flame that burns the evil inclination, and he can then continue his work. But if he stops in the midst of his learning, even if he immediately starts again, the Torah for him is already like coals of broom. This means that it can no longer burn the evil inclination, and the taste of Torah is spoiled for him, and he must cease his work. Hence, when he resumes his learning, he must take upon himself never to stop in the middle of his learning. And through the decision for the future, the blazing flame of the Torah will reignite.

235. Looking in the Book Again

After one sees some words of Torah in a book and memorizes them, since what enters the mind is already blemished, hence, when looking in the book again, he can elicit the light so as to receive illumination from what he is seeing now. This is already considered new and unblemished.

236. My Adversaries Curse Me All the Day
Tishrei 6, Tav-Shin-Gimel, September 17, 1942

"Because zeal for Your house has eaten me; my adversaries curse me... all the day" (Psalms 69). The form of cursing and swearing appears in several manners:

1. During the work, when he performs an act of *Mitzva* [commandment], the body tells him, "What will you get out of it, what benefit?" Hence, even when he prevails and does it coercively, this *Mitzva* is still considered a burden and a load. This brings up a question: If he really is keeping the King's commandment and is serving the King, he should have been glad, as it is natural for one who is serving the King to be in gladness. But here it is to the contrary. It follows that here he feels a state of cursing and swearing, and this coercion proves that he does not believe that he is serving the King, and there is no greater cursing than that.

2. Or, he sees that he is not adhered to the Creator the whole day, as he does not feel a real thing, and it is impossible to be adhered to an empty thing. Hence, he shifts his mind from the Creator (whereas a real thing, where there is pleasure, is hard to forget. And if he wishes to shift his mind, he must make great efforts to take the matter off his mind). This is, "my adversaries curse me... all the day."

This applies in every person, but the difference is in the feeling. Yet, even if one does not feel it, it is because he lacks the attention to see the situation as it truly is. It is similar to one who has a hole in his pocket, the money falls out through it, and he loses all the money. It makes no difference whether or not he knows that he has a hole. The only difference is that if he knows he has a hole then he can fix it. But this makes no difference regarding the actual losing of the money. Hence, when he feels how the body, called "my adversaries," curses the Creator, he says, "Because zeal for Your house has eaten me," and he wishes to correct it.

237. For Man Shall Not See Me and Live

"For man shall not see Me and live" (Exodus 33:20). This means that if one sees the revelation of Godliness to a greater extent than he is ready to see, he may come into reception, regarded as oppositeness from the Life of Lives, and then he comes to death. Hence, one must advance on the path of faith.

238. Happy Is the Man Who Does Not Forget You and the Son of Man Who Exerts in You

Elul 10

"Happy is the man who does not forget You, and the son of man who exerts in You" (a supplement for the *Rosh Hashanah* prayer). When one advances by way of whiteness, he should always remember that everything he has been granted is only because he took upon himself the discernment of blackness. And he should exert precisely in the "You," by way of "and all believe that He is a God of faith," although he currently does not see any place where he has to work in faith, since everything is revealed to him. Nevertheless, he should believe above reason that there is more room to believe by way of faith.

This is the meaning of "And Israel saw the great work... and they believed in the Lord." Thus, even though they had been awarded the discernment of "saw," which is seeing, they still had the strength to believe by way of faith.

And this requires great exertion; otherwise, one loses one's degree, like Libni and Shimei. This means that if it is not so, it means that one can listen to Torah and *Mitzvot* precisely at a time of whiteness; it is like a condition. However, one should listen unconditionally. Hence, at a time of whiteness, one should be careful not to blemish the blackness.

239. The Difference between Mochin of Shavuot and that of Shabbat at Minchah

There is a difference between *Shavuot* [Feast of Weeks]—considered the ascent of ZA to *Arich Anpin*, to *Behinat Dikna*—and Shabbat [Sabbath], during *Mincha* [midday prayer]—which is an ascent to *Arich Anpin*, too. *Shavuot* is considered Mochin de Hochma from YESHSUT, meaning from *Bina* that returns to being *Hochma*. Conversely, (Shabbat) is considered GAR de Bina, considered the actual *Hochma*. It is regarded as not having left the *Rosh*, and that *Mocha Stima'a* is dressed in it, which is GAR de Hochma and not VAK.

Because she is GAR, she cannot... unless from below upward, without any expansion downward. This is why she is regarded as female light, since she has no expansion below. This is why Shabbat is considered *Nukva*.

A good day, however, is considered ZAT *de Bina*, regarded as VAK—it has expansion below. Hence, even after all the ascents in reality, the ladder of degrees still does not change.

He said that the reason people respect a good day more than Shabbat, although Shabbat is a higher degree, is that a good day is ZAT *de Bina*, which is revealed below, while Shabbat is considered GAR *de Bina*, where there is no revealing below. But certainly, the degree of Shabbat is far higher than a good day.

240. Seek Your Seekers when They Seek Your Face
Slichot 1, from Baal HaSulam

"Seek your seekers when they seek Your face, answer them from the heavens of Your abode, and do not shut Your ear to their pleading cries" (*Slichot* for the first day). It is... that the purpose of the creation of the world was to do good to His creations. But for the correction to be completed, there must be the sweetening of the quality of judgment in mercy.

Judgment is discerned as *Gadlut* [greatness/adulthood]. But to avoid coming into disparity of form by this, there must be a discernment that is a kind of compromise: The judgment says she would have received more, but she was still in danger of coming into disparity of form. However, when mingled with the quality of mercy, she does not receive the *Gadlut* of the light, and can then come into equivalence of form. And the correction is done by turning the vessels of reception into reception in order to bestow.

Hence, when one comes to seek the Creator, he is still attached to reception, and one who has reception is considered lacking, and cursed, and the cursed does not adhere to the Blessed. But one who receives in order to bestow is called "blessed," since he does not lack anything or need anything for himself. It follows that the only difficulty is for one to be in a state of blessed, as only by the virtue of Torah and *Mitzvot* [commandments] can the vessels of reception be turned into vessels of bestowal. This is why we pray, "Seek your seekers."

There are two kinds of seekers: Some seek only for Your face, seeking only to bestow. Hence, when they seek to receive some salvation, it is only for Your face. He said about that, "When they seek your face." Those who seek for Your face, "answer them from the heavens of Your abode," meaning that the heavens of Your abode will become revealed since they will no longer blemish above, as they are cleansed from reception. "Their pleading cries," that all their prayers and pleas are still for themselves, that they want to be close to the Creator, meaning that they are still not cleansed from reception.

This is so because there are two qualities in the work of the Creator: There are those who want the Creator to be revealed in the world, that everyone will know that there is Godliness in the world. In that state, they are not in the middle, but merely want. In that state, it cannot be said that he has a quality of reception since he is not praying to be close to the Creator, only that the glory of Heaven will be revealed in the world.

And there are those who pray to be close to the Creator, and then he is in the middle. Then you can call it reception for oneself since he wants to receive abundance in order to come closer to the Creator. This is called "pleas," and it is also called "cries." Those who are still in a state of pleas, that is, to be closer, they can do the crying, and to them "do not shut Your ear," for only one who is deficient cries. But for another, it is not a cry, only a demand, as in "give my regards."* Hence, with the face, there is only a demand.

"From the heavens of Your abode" means *Eynaim* [eyes], light of wisdom, that they will receive the essence of the abundance, since their *Kelim* [vessels] are already in the form of reception in order to bestow. But those who are still in a state of pleading, "do not shut Your ear." Ear means *Bina*; they need to extend strength so they will have bestowal... over the light of mercy.

241. Call Upon Him When He Is Near

"Call you upon Him when He is near" (Isaiah 55:6). We must understand what "when He is near" means since "The whole earth is full of His glory"! Thus, He is always near, so what does "when He is near" mean? It would seem that there is a time when He is not near.

The thing is that states are always evaluated with respect to the attaining and feeling individual. If one does not feel His nearness, then nothing will come out of it, as everything is measured according to one's feeling. One person may feel the world as filled with abundance, and the other will not feel the goodness of the world, so he cannot say that there is a good world. Instead, he states as he feels—that the world is filled with suffering.

And the prophet warns about that: "Call you upon Him when He is near." He comes and says, "Know that the fact that you are calling on the Creator is because He is near." It means that now you have an opportunity. If you pay attention, you will feel that the Creator is near you; it is a sign of the Creator's nearness.

The evidence of this is that we must know that man is not naturally qualified for *Dvekut* [adhesion] with the Creator since it is against man's nature. By creation, man has only a desire to receive, while *Dvekut* is only to bestow. However, as the Creator calls upon man, it creates a second nature within him where he wants to revoke his own nature and adhere to Him.

---

* The actual phrasing in Hebrew is "demand my regards to..."

Hence, one should know that his speaking words of Torah and prayer is only from the Creator. He should never think of saying that it is "My power and the might of my hand," since it is the complete opposite of his might. This is similar to one who is lost in a dense forest and sees no way out of it to an inhabited place, so he remains despaired and thinks that he will never return to his home. But when he sees a person from afar or hears a human voice, the desire and the craving to return to his origin will immediately awaken in him, and he will begin to shout and ask of someone to come and save him.

Likewise, one who has lost the good way and entered a bad place, and has already accustomed himself to live among beasts, for the part of the will to receive, it will never occur to him that he should return to a place of reason of *Kedusha* [holiness]. Yet, when he hears the voice calling him, he awakens to repent.

But this is the voice of the Creator, not his own voice. But if he has not completed his actions on the path of correction, he cannot feel or believe that this is the voice of the Creator, and he thinks that it is his power and the might of his hand. This is what the prophet warns about, that one should overcome one's view and thought, and believe with complete faith that it is the voice of the Creator.

Hence, when the Creator wishes to bring him out of the dense forest, He shows him a light from afar, and the person gathers and musters the remains of his strength to walk on the path that the light shows him in order to obtain it.

But if he does not attribute the light to the Creator and does not say that the Creator is calling him, the light disappears from him and he remains standing in the forest. Thus, he could have now shown his whole heart to the Creator, to come and save him from the bad place, from the will to receive, and bring him to a place of reason, called a place of the sons of Adam (people), as in *Adameh la Elyon* [I will be like the Most High], meaning the desire to bestow, in *Dvekut*. Instead, he does not use this opportunity and remains once more as before.

242. What Is the Matter of Delighting the Poor on a Good Day, in the Work?

Sukkot Inter 3

In *The Zohar*: "The Creator's share is to delight the poor," etc. In the *Sulam* [Ladder commentary on *The Zohar*], he interprets that since the Creator saw that the *Lo Lishma* [not for Her sake] does not bring him to *Lishma* [for Her sake], He rose up to destroy the world, meaning his abundance is stopped ("Introduction of The Book of Zohar," Item 175).

We could say that when one receives an illumination from above, even while one has not been purified, if he takes this illumination in order to raise himself from his lowliness and approach bestowal, it is considered that the *Lo Lishma* brings him *Lishma*, meaning that he is walking on the path of Torah.

This is called "One who is happy on holidays." A holiday is a good day. And certainly there is no greater good day than when some illumination shines for a person from above, which brings him closer to the Creator.

243. Examining the Shade on the Night of Hosha'ana Rabbah

Adar Aleph, 24, *Tav-Shin-Gimel*, March 1, 1943, Tel-Aviv

Concerning the shade. On the night of *Hosha'ana Rabbah* [the seventh day of the Feast of Tabernacles], it is a custom that each one examines himself to see if he has a shadow, and then he is certain that he will have abundance (*Shaar HaKavanot* (*Gate of Intentions*), *Sukkot* Commentaries, 6-7). The shade implies clothing, the clothing in which the light dresses.

There is no light without clothing, since there is no light without a *Kli* [vessel]. According to the measure of the clothes, the lights increase and multiply. When one loses the clothing, the light that belongs to that clothing is proportionally absent from him.

This is the meaning of truth and faith. Truth is called "light," and faith is called "*Kli*." This is the meaning of "the Creator and His *Shechina* [Divinity]," and the meaning of "Let us make man in our image," and "Surely man walks by the image." Man's walk depends on the *Tzelem* [image], meaning on faith. And this is why on *Hosha'ana Rabbah*, one should see if his faith is complete.

But why do we call the worlds above *Tzelem*? After all, above, there is no weight to faith. However, what appears to us as dryness is a great light above, except that we call that name "above" because it appears to us as a shade, and we name what is above after the lower one.

Bina is called "faith," which is the light of the *Ozen* [ear], meaning hearing. *Hochma* [wisdom] is called "seeing," which is a light that comes into the vessels of reception, considered eyes.

244. All the Worlds

I heard on the 12th of *Adar*, *Tav-Shin-Gimel*, February 17, 1943, Tel-Aviv

All the worlds in which we discern many degrees and covers are all from the perspective of the souls, who are the receivers from the worlds. According to this, we will understand the rule, "Everything that we do not attain, we do not know by name," for a name indicates attainment. This means that all the names, the *Sefirot*, and the numbers, are all from the perspective of the receivers.

Therefore, we have three discernments:

1) *Atzmuto* [His Self], of which we do not speak at all because the place where we begin to speak is from the thought of creation, where we are included in potential, as in "The end of the act is in the preliminary thought."

2) The thought of creation. We call this *Ein Sof* [infinity], and it is the connection between *Atzmuto* and the souls. We understand this connection as a desire to do good to His creations, and besides this connection of a desire to do good, we have no utterance. Therefore, there is no perception or attainment.

Because all the discernments in the world are only from the perspective of the souls, it follows that we have no attainment of the worlds in and of themselves. Therefore, they, too, are regarded as *Atzmut* and there is no attainment in them whatsoever. With regard to the souls, which receive from the worlds, the worlds are regarded as *Ein Sof*.

The reason is that this connection between the worlds and the souls is what the worlds impart upon the souls. This extends from His desire to do good to His creations, which is the correlation between *Atzmuto* and the created being, and this connection is called *Ein Sof*. That is, when we begin to speak of the upper light, it speaks of two discernments together, the attaining and the attained, meaning how the attaining is impressed by the attained

However, individually, they do not come under the name *Ein Sof*. Rather, the attained is called *Atzmuto* and the attaining is called "souls," which is an initiated discernment that is a part of the whole with regard to the desire to receive called "existence from absence" that was imprinted in the souls. (And the Creator created such a reality that we would feel this way.)

It therefore follows that with regard to themselves, all the worlds are regarded as simple unity, and there is no change in Godliness, as in "I the Lord did not change." In godliness, there are no *Sefirot* or *Behinot* [discernments], and even the finest words are absent in them, themselves, as everything is regarded as *Atzmuto*. Rather, all the *Sefirot* and discernments come with the person who attains the upper light, since the Creator wanted us to attain and understand the abundance as "His desire to do good to His creations," and He has given us these senses.

This means that according to how our senses are impressed by the upper light, to that extent we receive many discernments. Our overall sense is called "will to receive," and to the extent of the reception we discern many parts and details, ascents and descents, expansions and departures since the will to receive is already called a "creature" and an initiated discernment existence from absence.

For this reason, precisely from a place where the will to receive begins to be impressed, the utterance of the parts begins, to the extent of the impression. All this is already called a "correlation between the upper light and the will to receive," and this is called "light and *Kli* [vessel]." Conversely, there is no utterance in the light without a *Kli* since light without someone who attains, called a *Kli*, is still regarded as *Atzmuto*, of which speaking is forbidden because He is unattainable, and where there is no attainment, how can we speak of something that we do not attain?

It follows that what we call "light and *Kli*" in spirituality, while they are only in potential, it is called *Ein Sof* prior to the *Tzimtzum* [restriction] of the world, which is regarded as the root, meaning that the potential will yield the actual. There are many worlds and discernments that begin from the *Tzimtzum* through the world of *Assiya* where everything is included in potential, and one who attains, attains them so in practice, for in the attaining, these many details are determined in actual fact.

From this we will understand why we say that the Creator will help us, or that the Creator will send us healing or salvation, or that the Creator has given us a gift; Lord, send me good business, and so forth. There are two discernments about this: 1) the Creator, 2) something that extends from him.

The first is regarded as *Atzmuto*, in which utterance is forbidden since we do not attain Him.

The second is the discernment that extends from Him. This is regarded as the expanding light which enters our *Kelim*, meaning our will to receive. This is regarded as *Ein Sof*, meaning the connection that the Creator has with the lower man, whom the Creator wants to delight. The desire to enjoy is regarded as the light that expands from Him, which finally comes to the will to receive, meaning that the will to receive receives the expanding light.

It follows that the expanding light is called *Ein Sof*, and that expanding light comes to the lower one through many covers by which the lower ones can receive them. This means that all the discernments and the changes were made specifically in the receiver to the extent that he is impressed by the salvation, and all the many names and discernments in the world are according to the impressions of the lower ones. At that time, many discernments are made in potential, from which the lower one will be impressed in practice.

In other words, the attaining and the attained come together, for without one who attains there is no form to the attained, for with regard to whom will he acquire the form, with regard to the one who attains? After all, He does not exist in the world, and with regard to the attained Himself and what form they acquire, this is unattainable. Therefore, if we have no attainment in His Self and we cannot depict any senses there, then how can we say that the attained will acquire some form in and of himself if we have no attainment whatsoever in *Atzmuto*? Thus, we have nothing to speak of but our own senses to the extent that we are impressed by the expanding light.

This is similar to looking at a table. Then, according to our senses, we feel that it is a hard object, through our sense of touch. Also, we can determine length and width, etc., and it is all according to our senses.

However, this does not necessarily mean that the table will appear in the shapes we see to the eyes of someone who has different senses, meaning in the eyes of an angel. Certainly, when he looks at the table, he does not have these forms in the table. Rather, he sees according to his senses. Therefore, we cannot say or determine any form about the table from the perspective of the angel because we do not know the senses of the angel.

It follows that as we have no attainment in Him, we cannot say which form the worlds have from His perspective. We attain in the world only what is attained through our senses and sensations. And this was the will of the Creator, that we will attain in this way in the upper worlds, and this is what it means that there are no changes in the light, but all the changes are in the *Kelim*, meaning in our senses for everything is measured according to our senses and imagination.

It therefore follows that if many people look at one spiritual thing, each one still attains differently, according to each and every one's imagination and senses. Likewise, in a single person, the spiritual thing will change him according to his states.

Therefore, he himself feels a different form each time, and it is all because the light is simple and formless, and all the shapes are from the perspective of the receivers.

245. Prior to the Creation of the Newborn

I heard in Jerusalem, *Iyar* 21, April-May

"Prior to the creation of the newborn, it is declared whether the drop will be a fool or a wise, etc., but righteous or wicked, he did not say."

Accordingly, we should ask: After all, a fool cannot be righteous since "One does not sin unless the spirit of folly has entered him. It is also written, "One who is a fool all his days, how can he have a choice if he is destined to be a fool?"

And we should also understand what is written, "I saw the virtuous, and they are few, He stood and planted them in each and every generation." We should interpret that the word "few" means that they are growing fewer, and by planting them they multiply. We should understand the allegory of "planting them," and also that the word "few" is in present tense. so how do the plants multiply?

We should interpret that fool or wise refer only to the preparation, as in "will give wisdom to the wise." This means that there are people who are born with a strong will, a broad heart, and a keen mind, and we call this "wise" because he is capable of receiving His wisdom. Conversely, there are people who were born fools, meaning they are narrow people whose thoughts and desires are only about themselves. They do not know what it means to feel others since they do not understand what is bestowal upon others, so how can they achieve the degree of righteous? It is impossible to be righteous until we achieve love of the Creator, and if one has no love of others, he cannot come to love the Creator, as is explained in the words of Rabbi Akiva, "love your friend as yourself is a great rule in the Torah." Accordingly, such people have no choice. And yet, "He did not say 'righteous or wicked,'" which means that they do have a choice.

We should understand this the way our sages said, "I saw the virtuous, and they are few." Virtuous means people who are capable and are ready for *Dvekut* [adhesion] with Him; these are few. This is why He planted them in each and every generation. Thus, the fools already have a choice—to go and unite and adhere to the righteous of the generation. By this they will receive the strength and the ability to take upon themselves the burden of the kingdom of heaven. They will be able to do the holy work since the righteous will bestow upon them their thoughts and desires. Through the assistance they will receive from the righteous of the generation, they, too, will be able to rise to the degree of righteous, even though inherently, they do not have these qualities. Yet, through the *Dvekut* with the virtuous ones, they will receive different qualities.

It follows that by planting them in each and every generation, the virtuous can raise their contemporaries to the height of the degrees. Had the virtuous been in one generation, the fools would have no way to ascend to the trail of holiness.

By this we will understand the correction of planting them, for the planting multiplied the virtuous. Likewise, placing a plant in the ground causes many branches to grow.

We can also understand the matter of choice. If one is born a fool, meaning far from matters of bestowal upon others, through connection with the virtuous, they will receive new qualities from the virtuous, who will influence the fools when they make a choice, meaning submit themselves to go and accept the guidance of the virtuous. Without it, their Torah will become to them a potion of death. Only through *Dvekut* with the virtuous will they be rewarded with *Dvekut* with the Creator.

It is known that when two people stand opposite from one another, one's right is opposite the other one's left, and one's left is opposite the other one's right. Therefore, when speaking of two ways, 1) of the right, meaning the path of the righteous, whose interest is only to bestow, and the path of the left is the way of the wicked, for their interest is only their own benefit, for which they are separated from the Life of Lives and are regarded as dead, as our sages said, "The wicked in their lives are called 'dead.'"

It therefore follows that even when a person learns in the path of the right, he is still opposite the left side of the Creator. It follows that his Torah becomes to him a potion of death, for through the Torah and *Mitzvot* [commandments], if it is in the manner of the left then his intention is to increase his body. This means that previously he wanted only to satisfy his body with pleasures of this world. Now, by observing Torah and *Mitzvot*, he wants the Creator to also satisfy his pleasures of the next world. It follows that through the Torah, his vessels of reception grow. That is to say, previously he wanted only the wealth of this world; afterward, by engaging in Torah and *Mitzvot*, he also wants the wealth of the next world. Thus, the Torah causes death, for by this he is completed with a real will to receive.

It is even more so when he engages in Torah and *Mitzvot* on his left side, meaning that his initial intention is only to receive, which is regarded as left. This is certainly wrong. However, we should try to achieve *Dvekut* by becoming one with the Creator, and then there is no right or left; he achieves equivalence of form with the Creator. At that time, his right is the Creator's right. It follows that his body has become a clothing for the soul. Then, when he comes to engage in bodily matters, he will not engage in the needs of his body more than is suitable for his soul. Similarly, when a person makes a clothing for his body, he will not make the garment longer or wider than his body. Rather, he will try to make the garment exactly fitting for his body. Otherwise, he will not wear the garment.

This is like a tailor who brings a suit to a man. When the man wears the suit on his body, if the garment is too long and too wide, he will return the suit to the tailor. Likewise, man's body should clothe the soul, and the body should be no bigger than the soul, meaning the needs of his body must not be too much, beyond what he needs for his soul.

However, we must know that it is not easy to achieve *Dvekut* with Him, and "Not all who want to take the Lord may come and take. This is why we need the righteous of the generation. By adhering to a real teacher, whose desire is only to bestow, and then one should do things that his teacher likes, meaning hate what his teacher hates and love what his teacher loves, then he can learn Torah that will not be a potion of death.

This is the meaning of "He stood and planted them in each and every generation," so that by this they will be able to connect to the virtuous, and they, too, will be able to achieve real *Dvekut* with Him.

Let it not be perplexing to you that there is a need for fools in the world. After all, they could all be wise. However, everything must have a carrier. This is why there is a need for fools—to be the carriers of the will to receive. By this, those who want to walk in the ways of the Creator can receive assistance from them, as it is written, "Then they will go forth and look on the corpses of the men who have transgressed against Me, for their worm will not die and their fire will not be quenched, and they will be an abhorrence to all flesh." As our sages said, they will be ashes under the feet of the righteous, for by this the righteous will be distinguished, so they can praise and thank the Creator for bringing them closer. This is called "ashes under their feet," etc., meaning that they will be able to go forward by seeing the end of the wicked.

246. An Explanation about Luck
I heard on *Sivan* 7

The word "Luck" means something that is above the intellect. That is, even though it is reasonable that it would be so and so, his luck caused it.

By this we will understand what is written, "Sons, life, and nourishment do not depend on merit, but on luck." It is known that all the influences come mainly from *Hochma*, called "left line." Thus, it should have extended specifically from the left line. This is called "by merit." And yet, all that extends from here is darkness.

Rather, it is precisely from the middle line, where the *Hochma* is diminished from GAR to VAK, and there is already the point of *Hirik* there. *Hochma* extends precisely from here although it would make sense that *Hochma* should have been extended from the left line. Nevertheless, this is not the order. Instead, *Hochma* is extended specifically from the middle line, where there is diminution of *Hochma*.

247. A Thought Is Regarded as Nourishment
I heard on *Adar* 24, *Tav-Shin-Dalet*, March 19, 1944, Jerusalem

Man is discerned as having three bodies:

1. The inner body, which is a clothing for the soul of *Kedusha* [holiness].

2. *Klipat* [shell of] *Noga*.

3. The serpent's skin.

In order to save one from the two bodies and be able to use only the inner body, the *Segula* [remedy/power] is to think only about things that concern the inner body. This means that one's thought should always remain in the singular authority, meaning that "There is none else besides him," that He does and will do all the deeds, and there is no creation in the world that can detach him from the *Kedusha*.

And because he does not think of the two bodies, they die, since they have no nourishment and nothing to sustain them. This is why after the sin of the tree of knowledge, the Creator told him: "By the sweat of your face shall you eat bread," since prior to the sin, vitality was not dependent on the bread.

However, after the sin, when he clung to the body of the serpent's skin, life became tied to the bread, meaning to nourishment, and if he is not given nourishment, he dies. This is a big correction, in order to be saved from those bodies, since one must try and exert not to think thoughts for their sake, since the thoughts are their nourishment.

Hence, one must think only of the inner body, for it is a clothing for the soul of *Kedusha*. That is, one should think thoughts that are after one's skin. This means that they benefit outside his skin, outside the will to receive.

After one's skin, there is no grip for the *Klipot* [pl. of *Klipa*], for the *Klipot* grip only that which is within one's skin, and not outside one's skin. This means that they have a grip on anything that is clothed, and they cannot hold anything that is not clothed.

When one persists with thoughts that are after one's skin, he will be rewarded with what is written, "And after my skin they broke this." "This" is the *Shechina* [Divinity], who stands after one's skin. "Broke" means that it has been established only after his skin. At that time, he is awarded "and from my flesh shall I see my God." At that time, he sees his God from this flesh, meaning that the *Kedusha* comes and clothes the interior of the body. But this is specifically when one agrees to work outside one's skin, meaning without any clothing, and then he is rewarded with clothing. The wicked, however—who want to work precisely when there is clothing, meaning within the skin—will die without wisdom. This is because then they have no clothing and they are not awarded anything.

248. Let His Friend Begin

Love of friends is a nature; it is "As in water, face reflects face, so the heart of man reflects man." However, each one wants his friend to begin. It was said about this, "He who rushes—gains."

Letters

Letter No. 1

4 *Iyar*, *Tav-Reish-Peh-Bet*, May 2, 1922, Jerusalem

To my friend...

It is now noon and I have received his letter from the eighth of the first month, and your beggar's complaints against me are an accepted prayer, as it is written in *The Zohar*.

I have already proven to you in my previous letter that while you reproach me for not writing, it is your own languor you should be reproaching. Note, that since the seventh of *Shevat* [Hebrew month around February] to the eighth of *Nissan*, meaning more than two months, you have not written me a word, while I wrote you four letters in that time: on the 22nd of *Shevat*, the 10th of *Adar*, the 1st of *Nissan*, and the 8th of *Nissan*.

And if this wisp still satiates the lion, it is as it is written, "for one higher than the high watches, and high ones are atop them." As for the answer he firmly demands, I shall reply that everyone believes in private Providence, but do not adhere to it at all.

The reason is that an alien and foul thought ... cannot be attributed to the Creator, who is the epitome of the "good who does good." However, only to the true servants of the Creator does the knowledge of private Providence open, that He caused all the reasons that preceded it, both good and bad. Then they are adhered to private Providence, for all who are connected to the pure are pure.

Since the Guardian is united with His guarded, there is no apparent division between bad and good. They are all loved and are all clear, for they are all carriers of the vessels of the Creator, ready to glorify the revelation of His uniqueness. It is known by the senses, and to that extent, they have knowledge in the end that all the actions and the thoughts, both good and bad, are the carriers of the vessels of the Creator. He prepared them, from His mouth they emerged, and at the end of correction it will be known to all.

However, in between, it is a long and threatening exile. The main problem is that when one sees some wrongful action, he falls from his degree (and clings to the famous lie and forgets that he is like an ax in the hand of the cutter). Instead, one thinks of himself as the owner of this act and forgets the reason for all the consequences from whom everything comes, and that there is no other operator in the world but Him.

This is the lesson. Although he knew it at first, still, at the time of need, he will not control this awareness to attribute everything to the cause, which sentences to the side of merit. This is the whole reply to his letter.

I have already told you face to face a true allegory about these two concepts, where one teaches of the other. Yet, the force of concealment overpowers in between, as our sages said about those two jokers before the rabbi, who were amusing all those who were sad.

There is an allegory about a king who grew fond of his servant until he wanted to raise him above all the ministers, for he had recognized true and unwavering love in his heart.

However, it is not royal manners to raise a person to the highest level at once without an apparent reason. Rather, it is royal manners to reveal the reasons to all with profound wisdom.

What did he do? He appointed the servant a guard at the city gate, and told a minister who was a skilled joker to pretend to rebel against the kingship and wage war to conquer the house while the guards are unprepared.

The minister did as the king had commanded, and with great wisdom and craftiness pretended to fight against the king's house. The servant risked his life and saved the king, fighting devotedly and bravely against the minister until his love for the king was evident to all.

Then the minister took off his clothes and there was great laughter (for he had fought so fiercely and bravely, and now he realized that there was only fiction here, and not reality). They laughed the most when the minister told of the depth of the imaginations of his cruelty and the fear he had envisioned, and every single item in this terrible war became a round of laughter and great joy.

Yet, in spite of everything, he is still a servant and is not scholarly, and how can he be raised above all the ministers and the king's servants?

Then the king reflected and said to that minister that he must disguise himself as a robber and a murderer, and wage a clandestine war against him. The king knew that in the second war he would display wondrous wisdom and merit standing at the head of all the ministers.

Hence, he appointed the servant in charge of the kingdom's treasury. The minister now dressed as a ruthless killer and came to loot the king's treasures.

The poor appointee fought courageously and devotedly until the cup was full. Then the minister took off his clothes and there was great joy and laughter in the king's palace, even more than before.

The details of the minister's tricks aroused great laughter since now the minister had to be more clever than before because now it is evidently known that no one is cruel in the king's domain, and all the cruel ones are but jokers. Therefore, the minister used great craftiness to acquire clothes of evil.

Yet, in the meantime, the servant inherited "wisdom" from after-knowledge, and "love" from foreknowledge, and then he is established for eternity.

In truth, all the wars in that exile are a wondrous sight, and everyone knows in their kind interior that it is all a kind of wit and joy that brings only good. Still, there is no tactic to ease the weight of the war and the threat on oneself.

I have elaborated on this to you face to face, and now you have knowledge of one end of this allegory, and with the Creator's help you will also understand it on its other end.

But the thing you want to hear me speak about the most is one to which I cannot answer anything. I have also given you an allegory about this face to face, for "the kingdom of the earth is as the kingdom of the heaven," and the true guidance is given to the ministers.

Yet, everything is done according to the King's counsel and His signature. The King himself does no more than sign the plan that the ministers devised. If He finds a flaw in the plan, He does not correct it, but places another minister in his place, and the first resigns from office.

So is man: a small world behaving according to the letters imprinted in him, since kings rule the seventy nations in him. This is the meaning of what is written in the *Sefer Yetzira* [*Book of Creation*]: "He crowned a certain letter."

Each letter is a minister for its time, making evaluations, and the King of the world signs them. When the letter errs in some plan, it immediately resigns from office and He crowns another letter in its place.

This is the meaning of "Each generation and its judges." At the end of correction, that letter called Messiah will rule. It will complement and tie all the generations to a crown of glory in the hand of God.

Now you can understand how I can interfere with your business of state, that have already …kings and judges, and each must uncover what he has been assigned to uncover. The ferry of unification … he does not want to correct them; I will correct them nonetheless. And yet, all will become clear through incarnations.

Because of it, I yearn to hear all your decisions in their every detail, since there is profound wisdom in every detail, and if I heard some fixed orders from you, I would be able to fill them and delight your heart.

Know that it is very difficult for me to hear your language, for you have no permanence in the names and their meaning. Hence, I will open for you a door in the meaning of the appellations, and you will measure for me the sentence of your wisdom. In this way, I will be able to follow your intention through.

Therefore, I will set the appellations as I have seen from all your letters, to establish between us permanently, to know all that you will write without any scrutiny, like signs on wine-jars.

We shall begin from the root of all roots, and reach the very end. Five degrees are marked in general: *Yechida, Haya, Neshama, Ruach, Nefesh*. All these are grouped together in the correcting body. *Yechida, Haya,* and *Neshama* are above time, and though they are found in a creature's heart, they are regarded as surrounding from afar. They do not come in a body during its correction, for a root, *Rosh, Toch, Sof* [respectively: head, interior, end], is discerned in the hidden source, too.

The *Rosh* is the root for the *Yechida*; it is *Ein Sof* [Infinity]. There, even in its place, its light is undisclosed and everything is nullified as a candle before a torch.

Afterward, the root of the *Toch*, and it is the root for *Haya*. This is the meaning of the light of *Ein Sof*, meaning the appearance of His complete light. While in time, this light is attained only as its sustenance, and this is why it is called the "root for *Haya*."

Subsequently, the root for the *Sof*, and it is the root for the souls. It is just as in the beginning, *Ein Sof*. Here, an upper veil spreads, and the time begins in the form of "six thousand years the world exists, and one is ruined." This is called *Ruach, Nefesh*, and their root is adhered to the *Neshama*.

However, they also expand below as Torah, which is a spirit of life, and *Mitzva* [commandment], which is the *Nefesh*. This *Nefesh* is the permanence, stillness, the embracing force that strengthens the body in a permanent state by the force of females imprinted in this *Nefesh*.

This *Ruach* blows the spirit of life and the light of Torah in the image of the female. Its root explains the meaning of "and breathed into his nostrils the breath of life; and man became a living soul." This pertains to the spirit that rises to the soul and receives from it life in the light of the King's face, bringing this life to the soul, which at that time is called a "living soul."

This is also the order in all the *Zivugim* [couplings] of the seven females of the *Rosh*, and the two below in the *Nefesh*. This is the meaning of "God places the lone ones in the house," meaning when the force of the females appears, by "All the glory of the king's daughter is inside."

The primary corrections and the work are to reveal the forces of the soul, which *The Zohar* calls "the upper world." This, too, belongs to the hidden source, as the root of the end, and every *Zivug* [coupling] is the manifestation of one light in the reality of the upper world. This is the meaning of "We whose sons are as plants grown up in their youth," meaning the *Ibur* [impregnation] in the upper world. By the *Zivug* ... to the lower ones ... so it came upon His thought, and the end of the *Rosh*, the hidden source, will complement all the lights ... a continuation from the book, *Treasure of Knowledge*.

The mind itself is man's soul and the whole of man, for in this he is defined entirely. What emerges from it is its clothes and those who serve it. Some are its branches, and some are considered alien to it.

This force, though it is in his soul, he will still not see it; it is concealed from any living thing. Do not wonder about this, for the eye controls and is the most important among all senses. Yet, one never sees oneself, but only feels one's existence in a way that sight would not add to them any knowledge. Hence, nothing was created in vain, for they are sensations to them and there is no need to add to the sensation.

There is also the mental power, which is the man's self. It is not given in any discernment in the senses, for the sensation of one's existence is quite sufficient, and no person will not suffice for one's own existence and demand testimony to his senses (and the reason that there is no feeling without movement, meaning that sometimes the sensation stops and there is no movement in his self, so it is more like absolute awareness). It is a grave mistake to resemble the form of the essence of the mind to a form of concept gripped in diminution by the mind's eye. This is utter falsehood, for this concept is like a light that emerges and operates. Its light is felt as long as it is active until it ends its activity and its light vanishes.

From this you learn that the concept sensed while active is but a small and feeble branch of it (the essential sensation is considered knowledge, for the power to sense is also a sense, a consequence, and does not need the essential feeling).

It is not at all like the essence, neither in quantity nor in quality, like the beaten stone that displays sparks of light that are renewed by the general embracing force in the stone, although in the form of the embracing force in it there is no light at all. Also, the core of the mind is the comprehensive force in man, and various branches stem from it, as in heroism and power, heat and light, according to the laws of the operated action.

Although we refer to it as the "mind's soul," or the "core of the mind," it is because the mind is also a branch of it, the most important in the world since "One is praised according to his mind."

Since one does not give that which he does not have, we thus define it as "mind," meaning at least no less than the sensed mind, as it is a branch and a part of it. It reigns over all her branches and swallows them like a candle before a torch. The mind does not connect in any action, but the various actions connect and become fixed in the mind.

One discerns that all of reality is but its servants, both in discipline, and in order to improve it, for they are all lost, while the mind in general develops. Hence, all our engagements are only in the ways of the mind and its ambitions, and more than that is not necessary.

Yehuda Leib

Letter No. 2

Tammuz 17, Tav-Reish-Peh-Bet, July 13, 1922

To my flesh and blood ... the exalted and glorified.

Now I have come to reply to your letter from the 33rd of the *Omer* Count [*Lag BaOmer*], along with your letter from the 15th of *Sivan*, which I received yesterday, and for which I refrained from replying to your letter from *Lag BaOmer*, as I had hoped you would inform me of the order of fixed names between us by which to disclose the thoughts in our hearts. However, I received the argument, "I do not know" ... and for which now, too, I will not be able to elaborate due to my fear that you would misunderstand. Therefore, I will wait for the third letter; perhaps I will be able to discern a clear way by which to let you know that which is in my heart and I will not miss the target.

I regret the long time that I had disappointedly spent in vain in three long letters—the first from the 22nd of *Shevat*, in which I wrote you a good poem for the work, which begins:

Indeed, let my tongue stick to the roof of my mouth; all my bones are dried of oil.

And from the work of the Lord is every potion.

And the life of all, in Him shall it be believed.

Another letter from the 10th of *Adar*, in which I interpreted a bewildering *Midrash* [commentary]: "A hegemon asked one of the members of the house of Selini. He said to him, 'Who will take the kingship after us?' He brought a clean piece of paper, took a pen and wrote on it, 'And after that his brother came out,' etc. They said, 'Look, old words from the mouth of a new old man.'" I had explained the wondrous truth in these words.

A third letter was from the third day of [the Torah portion] *VaYikrah*, in which I explained the dispute between the House of Shammai and the House of Hillel regarding how to dance before the bride. I also said a true and pertinent poem that begins:

Please see, whose is the signature?

It is a question for all the people of the world.

And for the burning fire

As a wrongdoing man or as a rebellious woman.

I find no flaw in them that should have caused their loss, except that you might have misunderstood them due to lack of clarity between us. Therefore, it is a great commandment to break this iron wall that stands between us, where one does not understand the language of the other, as in the generation of Babylon.

And what you have proven lengthily in your letter, to evidently show that the foundations of our love are based on "concealed love," and concluded from it what you consider a clear conclusion that there is no fear at all regarding all the questions I had asked you, these are your words, verbatim: "However, I have no fear at all regarding your question concerning me regarding you, or concerning you regarding me. They are all annulled and canceled, and you, too, should not fear at all or look at the façade, but at the internal revealing of the heart, as a lover who hides the myriad thoughts rushing through his heart and makes them one piece, good and strong, to repel from him all the pickles, piquant foods, garlic, and onion. By this request I do not mean to increase the love or not revoke it, for the love stands in its place, perfect and whole, completely unchanged, and there is nothing to add to it or take away.

"However, to not make you sorry needlessly—and why and what for, and by your sorrow you will add to mine, and you certainly do not want me to be sad—I have therefore hinted those two hints for you, for they are true and simple," thus far your words.

What shall I do if I cannot lie even when the truth is bitter? Therefore, I shall tell you the truth: I am still very uncomfortable with all your lofty words. If that pains you, truth is still my most beloved. It is written, "Love your friend as yourself," and "That which you hate, do not do to your friend," so how can I leave you with a "sweet thing" if it is not real? This is truly loathed by me and I shall vomit it and utterly repel it.

Especially, regarding the most important matter, called "love," which is the spiritual connection between Israel and their Father in heaven, as it is written, "And You shall bring us, our King, to Your great name, Selah, in truth and in love," and as it is written, "Who chooses His people, Israel, with love," this is the beginning of the salvation and the end of correction when the Creator reveals to His creations—which He has created—all the love that was previously hidden in His heart, as you well know.

This is why I must disclose to you the flaws that I had tasted in your two dainties. The first reason from the threefold string that is far more valuable than worldly love of friends, you were very wrong in this allegory, comparing and equating rudimentary, spiritual love with love of friends that is conditional—which will be revoked when the matter is revoked. In the other reason, you added insult to injury to support our love by the natural love of equivalence that is present with us to a great extent.

I wonder, "Abraham's master, you have supported the lesson without a source," that our love is rudimentary and everlasting, dependent on the love of natural equivalence, which can be canceled, and "When the supporter fails, the supported falls."

But I am at one, and who can answer me? And I shall tell you, if you are a storyteller, do not compare the rudimentary, spiritual love to love of friends that is dependent on any reason that is to be ultimately canceled, but rather to the love between father and son, which is also rudimentary, unconditional.

Come and see a wondrous custom in this love. It seems that if the child is an only child to his father and mother, the child must love his father and mother even more, for they display toward him more love than parents who have many children.

However, in reality, it is not so. On the contrary, if the parents become extremely attached to their children by their love, the children's love is then greatly decreased and diminished. Sometimes it even becomes apparent among children of this sort of love that "The feeling of love has been quenched entirely in their hearts." This is a custom that is of the laws of nature that is applied in the world.

The reason for it is simple: The father's love for his son is rudimentary and natural. As the father wishes for his son to love him, the son also wishes for his father to love him. That craving in their hearts causes them constant, incessant fear. That is, the father is very much afraid that his son will hate him in any extent, even the slightest of the slightest, and the son, too, fears that his father might hate him in any extent, the slightest of the slightest.

This "constant fear" causes them to display good deeds toward each other. The father always exerts to show his love in practice to his son, and the son, too, constantly exerts to show his love in practice to his father, as much as he can. In this way, the feelings of love always multiply in both their hearts until one prevails over the other in good deeds to a great and complete extent. In other words, the fatherly love of the father appears to the son in full, such as to which there cannot be addition or subtraction.

Upon reaching that state, the son sees "absolute love" in his father's heart. I wish to say that the son has no fear whatsoever that his love will diminish, nor has he hope that his love will grow. This is called "absolute love."

Then, slowly, the son grows idle in displaying good deeds before his father. To the extent of the diminution of good deeds and displays of love in the son's heart toward his father, to that very extent the sparks of "rudimentary love" that has been engraved in the son's heart by nature quench. A second nature is made in him, close to hatred, for all the good deeds his father does for him are low and little in his eyes compared to the obligation of "absolute love" that has been stamped in his organs. This is the meaning of the words, "I am not worthy of all the mercies and of all the truth," and delve deeply in this for it is profound and long.

And since it is always my way to praise nature's systems, which the Creator has imprinted and set up in our favor all the days, I will tell you the reason for instilling that boundary. It is not that He has ill will. On the contrary, it is all the multiplication in spirituality, for the main thing desired of the servants of the Creator is *Dvekut* [adhesion], and there is no *Dvekut* unless from love and pleasure, as it is written, "And bring us closer, our King, to Your great name, Selah, in truth and love." With what love did they say? With complete love, since the complete cannot be on the deficient, and complete love is "absolute love," as said above.

Therefore, how can there be multiplication in the desired *Dvekut* that rises and is obtained by all the adventures that have come upon them? This is the meaning of the Creator clothing a soul in the body and in the murky matter, which finally found out that it needs to actually display love, and the deficiency of the display of love in his own heart, for the nature of the substance is to promptly quench any feelings of love that it has already acquired.

In this manner, "The complete is over the complete," and there is absolute knowing in complete and absolute love on the part of the intellect. And yet, more love can be added, and if he does not add love, he will certainly subtract and quench all the possessions he has already acquired. This is the meaning of "And the land shall not be sold forever." These are all sincere and true words, and you should treasure them for the end of days.

Now you will understand my thoughts about you, as I see that you do not fear that my love for you will cool and that my love for you is absolute love. You wrote explicitly that our love will always stand, "without adding and without taking away." But in the end, our spirituality is clothed in matter, and the nature of matter is to cool because of absolute love. This is an unbreakable law.

Hence, moreover, if you feel our love as complete, you must now begin to perform actual actions "to display love" due to the fear of cooling that rises out of the feeling of absolute love, negating any fear. In this way, the desire and the love increase twofold. This is called "multiplication."

My words are said by seeing, and "A judge has only what his eyes see," and no scrutiny and doubt will repeal my words. If you do not feel my words in your heart, it is due to being troubled with your own loss. But when you find the loss and the trouble is removed, look into your heart and you will find it vacant from any feeling of love due to the lack of actual actions to display the love, and this is clear. Even now, the shackles of our love are being very slightly shaken due to "lack of fear" because of the knowing that is in absolute love.

I wrote you all this to let you know my honest opinion, for how can I deny you a word of truth? However, it is not at all concealed from me that these words are currently disagreeable to you, and are long and tiresome for you, and seem like chatter.

But hear me out and you will always be happy, for there is none so wise as the experienced. Therefore, I shall advise you to evoke within you fear of the coolness of the love between us. Although the intellect denies such a depiction, think for yourself—if there is a tactic by which to increase love and one does not increase it, that, too, is considered a flaw.

It is like a person who gives a great gift to his friend. The love that appears in his heart during the act is not like the love that remains in the heart after the fact. Rather, it gradually wanes each day until the blessing of the love can be entirely forgotten. Thus, each day, the receiver of the gift must find a tactic to make it new in his eyes.

This is all our work—to display love between us, each and every day, just as upon receiving, meaning to increase and multiply the intellect with many additions to the core, until the additional blessings of now will be touching our senses like the essential gift at first. This requires great tactics, set up for the time of need.

This is the meaning of the words, "In those days they shall say no more, 'The fathers have eaten a sour grape, and the children's teeth are made blunt.' ... Any man who eats the sour grapes, his teeth shall become blunt." That is, as long as they did not come to know it—that a display of love is required—they could not correct their father's sin. This is why they said, "The fathers have eaten a sour grape, and the children's teeth are made blunt."

But once they come to that awareness, they are promptly rewarded with correcting their father's sin, and any flaw that they will find, they will know that they will sin with displaying love, as was said above. Therefore, each day will be as new in their eyes, as in the first time. To the extent of the display of love on that day, they will draw the light until it is sensed. And should they feel only a little, it is due to eating the unripe fruit of that day, for on that day they did not display love sufficiently and ate prematurely. This is why it lessened in their senses, for it is not as on the first time.

The words are primarily a law for the Messiah, but it also applies to this world, since by exerting the heart to display love between him and his Maker, the Creator instills His *Shechina* [Divinity] on him in remembrance, as in, "In every place where I mention My name, I will come to you and bless you."

When the remembrance increases by the very work, the desire and longing increase, as in "And spirit draws spirit and brings spirit," and so forth. Finally, the remembrance increases and grows by the craving and ascends in good deeds, for "All the pennies join into a great amount." This is the meaning of "Behold, this one comes and His reward is with Him, and His work is before Him."

I have been lengthy about it although the intellect is short in studying. However, it takes a long time to acquire this intellect until it is absorbed in the organs.

And yet, this is all the awakening from below—that the speed of the correction during the corrections and the measure of multiplication after the end of correction during the work on the desirable side depend on the extent to which it is possessed.

You should not doubt my words, for otherwise "The proselyte is in the earth and the citizen is the heaven," for the measure of love is voluntary, dependent on the heart; it is not intellectual. Therefore, how can it be displayed at the top of all the intellectual degrees, as I have elaborated on?

But all who taste and see that the Lord is good witness all those things, since we are dealing with *Dvekut* [adhesion] with the Creator here, and His uniqueness includes all the discernments in the world. Still, there is no doubt that there is nothing corporeal about His uniqueness, and therefore no step outside of an intellectual object.

For this reason, all who are rewarded with adhering to Him grow wiser, as they adhere with simple intellect. During the *Dvekut*, the worshipper is adhered to the worshipped by the mere strength of displaying his will and love. But in Him, the will, intellect, and knowing are in simple unity, without any difference of form, as in the laws of corporeality, and this is simple. Therefore, obtainment of the disclosure of His love is the very blessing of the intellect.

Come and learn from the complete worker (complete even in awakening from above). Ask your elders and they will tell you that the Complete One is complete in everything and has complete knowledge in the "blessing in his future." And yet, it does not weaken him at all because of it—from the labor in Torah and the searching.

On the contrary, none exert in the Torah and in searching as much as he. This is for a simple reason: His labor is not so much to bring the good future to himself. Rather, all his labor is about displaying love between him and his Maker. This is why the feelings of love grow and multiply each day until the love is completed in the form of "absolute love." Afterward, it leads him to double his wholeness by way of awakening from below.

And by the way, I will clarify for you the meaning of the charity for the poor, which is so praised in *The Zohar*, the *Tikkunim*, and by our sages: There is an organ in man with which it is forbidden to work. Even if the smallest of the small desires to work with it still exists in man, that organ remains afflicted and stricken by the Creator. It is called "poor," for its entire sustenance and provision are by others working for it and pitying it. This is the meaning of "Anyone who sustains a single soul from Israel, it is as though he sustains an entire world." Since the organ depends on others, it has no more than its own sustenance.

And still, the Creator regards it as though he sustained an entire world, and this itself is the entire blessing of the world and everything in it, multiplied and completed solely by the force of that poor soul, which is sustained by the work of other organs.

This is the meaning of "And He took him outside and said, 'Look toward the heavens ...' and he believed in the Lord and regarded it to him as righteousness." That is, by taking him outside, there was some desire to work with this organ; this is why He forbade him the work.

It was said, "Look toward the heavens." At the same time, he was given the promise of the blessing of the seed. These are tantamount to two opposites in the same carrier, since all his seed, which is to be blessed, necessarily comes from this organ. Thus, when he is not working, how will there be a seed?

This is the meaning of "And he believed in the Lord," meaning he accepted those two receptions as they were—the complete prohibition on the work, and the promise of the blessing of the seed.

And how did he receive them? This is why he concludes, "And [he] regarded it to him as righteousness," meaning as the form of charity [*Tzedakah* means both "charity" and "righteousness"], for a poor [person] is sustained by the work of others.

This is the meaning of the two sayings of our sages: One [person] thought that the Creator would treat him with righteousness and will keep and sustain him without work, and one thought that Abraham would act with righteousness toward the Creator. Both are the words of the living God, for prior to the correction, that organ is in heaven, and the charity is attributed to the lower one. At the end of his correction, it is not in heaven, and then the giving of the charity is attributed to the upper one. Know and sanctify for it is true.

Yehuda

Letter No. 3

Tav-Reish-Peh-Bet, 1922, Jerusalem

To ...

"Four entered a PARDESS,"* etc. Before the world was created, there was He is One and His name is One, since the souls were not considered souls, for the issue of name refers to when one turns one's face away from him, and the friend calls upon him to turn his face back to him.

Since prior to creation, the souls were completely adhered to Him, and He placed upon them crowns and wreaths, glory, majesty, and splendor, even what they did not evoke, since He knows their wish by Himself and grants them. Hence, it is certainly irrelevant to state a name that relates to an awakening from below of some side. Hence, it is considered "simple light," since everything is utter simplicity, and this light was understood to every simple person, even to those who had never seen any wisdom.

This is why the sages and the wise called it *Pshat* (literal), since the *Pshat* is the root of everything. Authors and books do not speak of it, as it is one, simple, and famous concept. Although in the lower worlds, two divisions are detected in the *Reshimo* [recollection] of this simple light, it is because of the division in their own hearts, by way of "And I am a smooth man."**

Yet, the above-mentioned place has no changes in any depiction you might make. It is like a king who took his darling son and put him in his grand and wondrous

---

* Translator's note: In Hebrew, a *Pardess* means grove. But in Kabbalah, it is an acronym for *Pshat* (the literal Torah), *Remez* (intimation), *Drush* (interpretations), and *Sod* (secret).
** Translator's note: In Hebrew, *Halak* means both "smooth" and "part."

grove. And when the king's son opened his eyes, he did not look at the place where he stood, since due to the great light in the grove, his eyes wandered far away, as the distance of the east from the west. And he cast his eyes only on the buildings and palaces far to his west, and he walked for days and months, wandering and wondering at the glory and the grandeur he was seeing to the west.

After some months, his spirit rested and his passion was fulfilled, and he was satiated from looking to the west. He reconsidered and thought, "What can be found along the way I have traversed?" He turned his face eastward, to the side from which he'd come, and he was startled. All the grandeur and all the beauty were right next to him. He could not understand how he had failed to notice it thus far, and clung only to the light that shone toward the west. From then on he was attached solely to the light that shines to the east, and he was wandering eastward until he returned right to the entrance.

Now do consider and tell me the difference between the days of the entry and the days of the exit. All that he had seen in the latter months, he'd seen in the early months, as well. But in the beginning, it was without inspiration since his eyes and heart were taken by the light that shone toward the west. And after he was satiated, he turned his face eastward and noticed the light that shines toward the east. But how had it changed?

But being near the entrance, there is room for disclosing the second manner, which the sages call *Remez* [intimation], as in "What do your eyes imply?" It is like a king who hints to his darling son and frightens him with a wink of his eye. Although the king's son does not understand a thing or sees the fear that is hidden in the hint, still, due to his *Dvekut* [adhesion] to his father, he promptly jumps from there to another side.

This is why the second manner is called *Remez*, since the two manners, *Pshat* and *Remez*, are registered in the lower ones as one root, as the meticulous ones write, that there is not a word that does not have a two-letter root, called the "origin of the word." This is so because no meaning can be deduced from a single letter; hence, the acronym for *Pshat* and *Remez* is PR [pronounced *Par*], which is the root of *Par Ben Bakar* [young bull] in this world. And *Pria* and *Revia* [multiplication] comes from that root, as well.

Afterward, the third manner appears, which the sages call *Drush* [interpretation]. Hence, there was no *Drisha* [demand] for anything, as in "He is One and His name One." But in this manner, there is subtraction, addition, interpretation [studying] and finding, as in "I labored and found," as you evidently know. This is why this place is attributed to the lower ones, since there is an awakening from below there, unlike the illumination of the face of the east upward, which was by way of "Before they call, I will answer," for here there was a powerful call, and even exertion and lust, and this is the meaning of "the graves of lust."

Afterward begins the fourth manner, which the sages call *Sod* [secret]. In truth, it is similar to *Remez*, but in the *Remez*, there was no perception whatsoever; it was rather like a shadow following a person. Moreover, the third manner, the *Drush*, has already clothed it.

Yet, here it is like a whisper, like a pregnant woman ... you whisper in her ear that today is *Yom Kippur* [Day of Atonement], so the fetus would not be shaken and fall. And we might say, "Moreover, it is the concealment of the face, and not the face!" For this is the meaning of the words, "The meaning of the Lord is to those who fear Him; and His covenant, to make them know it." This is why he made several circles until a whispering tongue said this to him: "He has given *Teref* [food] to those who fear Him," and not *Trefa* [non-kosher food], as that soldier sneered.

You understood by yourself and wrote me in your letter, though shyly and timidly, that you are a bachelor, and this is not the proper way.

Since this verse came into our hands, I shall clarify it to you, as this is also the poet's question: "The meaning of the Lord is to them who fear Him." And why did he speak in such a way? It is as our sages' question, where we find that the text twists (eight) twelve letters, to speak with a clean language, as it is written, "and of the beasts that are not clean," etc.

But your reason does not suffice the poet, for He could have given abundance to the souls, and with a clean language, as Lavan said to Jacob, "Why did you flee secretly and stole from me, and did not tell me, that I might have sent you away with joy and with songs, with a drum and with a harp." The poet's answer to that is, "and His covenant, to make them know it."

This is the meaning of the cutting, the removal, and the drop of blood, meaning the individual thirteen covenants. Had the meaning not been in this manner, but in another language, four corrections from the thirteen corrections of *Dikna* would have been missing, and only the nine corrections of *Dikna* in ZA would remain. Thus, ZA would not be clothing AA, as is known to those who know the meaning of God. This is the meaning of "and His covenant, to make them know it." This is also the meaning of "Ancestral merit has ended, but ancestral covenant has not ended."

Let us return to our issue, which is *PR* (pronounced *Par*), *PRD* (pronounced *Pered*), and *PRDS* (pronounced *Pardess*). This is their order and combination from above downward. Now you will understand these four sages that entered the *Pardess*, meaning the fourth manner, called *Sod*, since the lower one contains the upper ones that preceded it. Hence, all four manners are included in the fourth manner, and they are right, left, front, and back.

The first two manners are the right and left, meaning *PR* (this is the meaning of his words on the step at the Temple Mount: "All of Israel's sages are worthless in my eyes"). These are Ben Azai and Ben Zuma, as these souls nurtured from the two *PR* manners. And the last two manners are the *Panim* [front] and *Achor* [back], which is Rabbi Akiva who entered in peace and came out in peace. They correctly stated, "It indicates that for every thistle, mountains of laws can be learned."

Achor is Elisha Ben Avoia who went astray. Our sages said about that, "One shall not raise an evil dog within one's home," for it is going astray. Everything that was said about them—"peeped and died," "peeped and was hurt," "went astray"—is said of that generation when they gathered closely together, but were all thoroughly corrected, one at a time, as is known to those who know the secret of reincarnation.

Yet, another he saw the tongue of Hutzpit, the translator, which is why he said, "Return, O naughty children," except for the other, and Rabbi Meir, the disciple of Rabbi Akiva, took his place. It is true that the Gemara, too, finds it difficult; how did Rabbi Meir learn Torah from another? And they said, "He had found a pomegranate, ate its contents, and threw its shell (another)." And some say that he corrected the *Klipa* [shell/peel], too, as in raising smoke over its grave.

Now you can understand Elisha Ben Avoia's words: "He who teaches a child, what is he like? Like ink written on a new paper," meaning the soul of Rabbi Akiva. "And he who teaches an old man, what is he like? Like ink, written on erased paper," he said of himself. This is the meaning of his warning to Rabbi Meir, "Thus far the Shabbat [Sabbath] bounds," for he understood and estimated his horse's steps, since he had never come down from his horse.

This is the meaning of "The transgressors of Israel, the fire of Hell does not govern them and they are as filled with *Mitzvot* [commandments] as a pomegranate." He says that it is all the more so with the golden altar, which is merely as thick as a golden coin. It stood for some years, and the fire did not govern it, etc., "The vain among you are as filled with *Mitzvot* as a pomegranate, all the more so," as he says, that the *Klipa*, too, is corrected.

Know that the great Rabbi Eliezer and Rabbi Yehosha are also from the souls of *PR*, like Ben Azai and Ben Zuma. But Ben Azai and Ben Zuma were in the generation of Rabbi Akiva, and were his students, among the 24,000. But Rabbi Eliezer and Rabbi Yehosha were his teachers.

This is why it is said that instead of Rabbi Eliezer, they were purifying the purifications (*Pshat*) that they had done over Achnai's oven, since they cut it into slices (eighteen slices) and placed sand between each two slices. In other words, the third manner is as the sand between the first slice, which is the second manner, and the second slice, which is the fourth manner. Naturally, the sister and the awareness are conjoined as one. And Rabbi Tarfon and Rabbi Yehosha as one are disciples of the great Rabbi Eliezer, and Rabbi Akiva is seemingly included in them. This is because a second good day, with respect to the first good day, is like a weekday [*Chol* means both "sand" and "weekday"] in the eyes of our sages, since the *Drush*, compared to the *Remez*, is like a candle at noon.

But the sages of his generation defiled all those purifications and burned them, and the great Rabbi Eliezer proved with the aqueduct whose water rose that Rabbi Yehosha was a great sage, and the walls of the Temple will prove. And they began to fall before the glory of Rabbi Eliezer, and did not fall before the glory of Rabbi Yehosha. This is a complete proof that there is no place for any doubt that he is pure.

But the sages took Rabbi Yehosha for himself and did not wish to rule as with Rabbi Eliezer, his teacher, until a voice came down, that Rabbi Yehosha was really his disciple. But Rabbi Yehosha did not connect to his place and said that you do not heed a voice: "It is not in heaven," etc. Then sages blessed him, for the light of *Ozen* [ear] had been canceled from them, since they did not follow the rules of the great Rabbi Eliezer. And Rabbi Akiva, his favorite disciple, told him that his 24,000 disciples had died during the count, and the world was sickened, a third in olives, etc.

Elisha Ben Avoia and Rabbi Tarfon came from the same root. But Elisha Ben Avoia is the *Achoraim* [posterior] itself, and Rabbi Tarfon is the *Panim* [face] *de Achoraim* [of the posterior]. What is this like? In one house lay bitter olives that are good for nothing, and in another house lies the beam of the oil-press, which is good for nothing. Then a man comes and connects the two. He places the beam over the olives and produces a wealth of oil.

It follows that the good oil that is revealed is the *Panim*, and the beam is the *Achoraim*. And the plain wooden tools are thrown away after they have completed their work.

Understand that this custom is in the expansion of the roots to the branches in worlds below it. But at their root, they both appear at once, like a person who suddenly enters the oil-press and sees the beam, and under it, a large pile of olives with oil flowing abundantly from them. This is so because at the root, all is seen at once. This is why one is called "another," and the other is called "Tarfon"; one is "a beam" and the other is "oil," which immediately flows through it.

This is the meaning of going astray. After the desire has emerged, which is the soul of Rabbi Tarfon, the soul of "another" remained as "bad manners" in one's home. This is the meaning of the letter combination, *Sod*: *Samech* is the head of the word *Sod* itself, the soul of "another," and *Dalet* is the head of the word *Drush*, the soul of Rabbi Akiva, because they are the operators. And the *Vav* in the middle is Rabbi Tarfon.

Yehuda Leib

Letter No. 4

15 Heshvan, Tav-Reish-Peh-Bet, November 16, 1921

To my friend,

Indeed, I see your difficulty with simplicity, that you are embarrassed to speak simply. Yet, in all my dealings with you, face to face or in letters, I did not affect your spirit whatsoever, as it is the way most people behave on such matters: They are ashamed as thieves of every organ they sin with or behave with it as do beasts. They cover it with seven covers, as with the circumcision organ, the hind part, and other such organs that do as beasts do.

Hence, I must be lenient with you regarding this change and speak with you as ... under a cover of allegories, for I have grown tired of waiting for solutions to this question, which we both need, and especially for the glory of Heaven, for this is all I need.

I shall speak to you cunningly, in a language that the ministering angels do not need. And therefore, I shall request of you to thoroughly clarify to me the words of *The Zohar* in three places. And even the things that you clearly see that it is considered an advantage, or even a sin to disclose such secrets, especially before those who know and understand, or even with the most ordinary matters, which are so light that they fly like birds in the sky, I need it all. And although there is no need for them in and of themselves, in general, it is still a need.

See in *The Zohar* from the portion *Shemot* [Exodus] through the words of the break after Passover and onward to thoroughly clarify. Afterward, delve in the pages preceding the holiday of *Shavuot* [Feast of Weeks], from nearly there through *Elul* of that year when they crossed into the land of Israel. Thus you have two places, and afterward, from the pages of the virtues of the land of Israel through its end.

First, clarify for me every kind of change and action from this place to that place, meaning with the sustaining of the degrees and understanding of the issue as much as you can. Then, point out for me every good thing in the steps of its body and its parts, which is necessary and which is redundant, in what it is necessary, and in what way it is redundant, and what the world would lack without it, as well as depicting the lines of hope in each and every place.

And most important, the drawings should bring out the features with its shades and lights, with a terrible face or a beautiful face, a laughing face or a welcoming face. On such a living bulge, even simple and redundant and known things must be registered, so that all the drawings are included in one collection in each picture clearly arranged.

And do not repeat the mistake of interpreting the commentary that you have found in the drawings, and the drawings themselves are hidden in your commentary. Moreover, it is the drawings themselves that I need, and to interpret them myself with aptitude such as yours, and especially, as though they have fallen from above prior to the interpretation that you gave them from below.

And because I still fear your idleness, which is only a *Klipa* [shell/peel], or hunts clean and innocent souls, I myself will write to you some innovations in these forms that I request. After you explain to me all the above-mentioned drawings, as much as you can, with simplicity and without commentaries, as though they fell from the sky, then you will interpret for me in your own words what I interpret here in the language of translation [Aramaic]. In this way, I will know how well you understand my writing and my thoughts.

And after you interpret what is in my heart, review my words and add to them, remove from them, or both. And for God's sake, follow my request and do not skip any of your studies or prayers, even for several weeks, until you have completed my request, and until your words reach me with a clear answer. After all, my fingers are tied by fear and I cannot correspond with you under the canopy of the Torah and higher love.

Come and see: There is a holy language for the upper ones and there is a holy language for the lower ones. It is after them that all those sages of the truth are called "God's mouth." What is the reason? It is because the *Shechina* [Divinity] speaks from their mouths, and all that they say, their palates taste, and no other's. Hence, the way of these sages of the truth is to convey wisdom to their friends mouth to mouth.

And what is the reason it is mouth to mouth and not mouth to ear? It is because what the palate tastes is not given to the ears; they are separate. It is written about that: "With him do I speak mouth to mouth, manifestly, and not in riddles." "Manifestly" means by people's vision, and "in riddles" means by people's hearing with the ears.

But these are not at all the ways of the wisdom of truth, which is (the wisdom of truth) given only in the palate, as it is written, "Who will eat and who will feel but me?" By this rule the sages know the judgment in the judgment, each kind with (what is not) its kind, its flavor, since each kind has its own flavor.

And since these wicked have seven abominations in their hearts, their hearts are divided and their flavors are not the same, for "the Lord confused their language," "that they may not understand one another's speech."

But with the sages, no lie comes to their palates. Hence, all that they eat is true, and all their awakenings are for the truth. Therefore, all the sages are as one man, understanding each other's language, since their palate is one. Thus, they necessarily have the power to disclose secrets to each other mouth to mouth.

It is in that regard that the faithful shepherd prayed for Judah, "Bring him in unto his people." Our sages explained that he could stand among the righteous and discuss rules with them, meaning, as it is said, he understood their language.

This is so because one who is flawed—who did not properly correct the sin of the generation of Babylon—is under the dominion of the gods of Babylon, called *Ball*. "And there confound their language," and he did not know what our sages said. Woe unto him and woe unto his soul. "And what does the *Shechina* say? It is lighter than my head, lighter than my arm."

And should you say, "How can such a great sin be corrected?" After all, it is written, "God is in heaven and you on earth; therefore, let your words be few." And it is also written, "Why should God be angry with your voice?" This is undoubtedly true.

But as it is here, it is the force of Moses, the faithful shepherd, that we need, who testifies about himself: "It is not in heaven … it is in your mouth and in your heart to do it." It is known that by the great power of the faithful shepherd, the Torah has already come down to earth, as though in the combinations of the letters in the names of the Torah.

And in all those deeds that he has set up before us and for the whole world, as in "from the permitted which is in your mouth," now they are actually in the earth, as it is written, "It is in your mouth and in your heart to do it." That is, by the *Dvekut* [adhesion] of spirit and mind to all the intelligence and reason that there are in the sayings of the fathers and the sayings of the fathers' servants, and in the 613 *Mitzvot* [commandments]. In each act, one combination becomes known to the eyes in the manners of the ways of the Master of the world, manners within which all the upper light is deposited. One who cleaves to one discernment in complete knowledge did not work in vain, for here is one part of the 613 parts of the soul. Subsequently, he multiplies all those degrees until he finds all the organs of his soul.

If he is rewarded with the wholeness of his soul, he will be confident that he has won everything, for nothing is absent in the King's palace, and there is no poverty in a place of wealth.

Woe unto those fools, destructors of the world. They know full well that it would be better for them had they not been born. There is only one thing that they say, that they had better days than now, meaning before they were born. The Creator does this to them to display their flaw before people. It is written, "Do not say, 'What was it, that the days before were better than these, for it is not with wisdom that you ask this.'" In other words, the text has mercy on them and notifies them to cover this thing in their hearts, as it is a sign of the flaw of folly that is in them.

The faithful prophet Malachi admonished them about it: "You offer soiled bread upon my altar and say, 'With what have we soiled you?' By your saying, 'The table of the Lord is contemptible.'" So is the manner of all the fools of the world. Since their palates taste the sweet as bitter, they say that it is bitter and despise the bread of the holy King.

This is why he curses them and says, "Cursed be the swindler who has a male in his flock," showing them that this swindling is them swindling against their master. What is the reason? It is because there is a male in their flock and they are idle in their work and do not exert to find him. This is why the holy prophet curses them, since they can bring a pure male to the King's palace, yet they bring a lame and blind one.

Woe unto they who show disgrace in the King's palace. This is why they are shown their flaw with great cleverness, as in "Offer it to your Governor; would He be pleased with you?" "Your Governor" implies a place that has been made lower, where they flawed, meaning in the upper lip, a place that according to us is a flaw, and according to them is not a flaw. But that place is not filled by their twisting of their lips and the

Creator shows their wickedness in their faces, as I had said to you when I was with you, as it is written, "The clean and the righteous do not kill." The mind is called "clean," and the heart is called "righteous." Woe unto one who changes his name, who lies in the name of the Creator and reverses the meaning. The text testifies about them and before them: "I will not justify the wicked."

Therefore, you, the love of my life, will not follow in the footsteps of the destructors of the world, the fools, sons of fools, as they are worthless compared to you, whether in trunk, branch, and all the more so in the fruits. In your trunk, you are unique in this generation. In the cleanness of that trunk, you are better than I, as I had told you when I was with you. You lack nothing but to go out to a field that the Lord has blessed, and collect all those flaccid organs that have drooped from your soul, and join them into a single body.

In that complete body, the Creator will instill His *Shechina* incessantly, and the fountain of intelligence and high streams of light will be as a never ending fountain. Each place on which you cast your eye will be blessed, and all will be blessed because of you, for they will bless you constantly, and all the chariots of *Tuma'a* [impurity] will be on them ... forever since it is their wish to curse you. At that time, the blessing of the grandfather, "Those who bless you are blessed," will come true.

Let us return to the issue that we dealt with first: the Lord's mouth. There is an upper lip and there is a lower lip. Those crowns came down equal to each other, but to add to all those worthy ones good upon good and light upon light, four high and holy corrections of the *Dikna* were made on them. Happy is he who has been rewarded with inheriting them, and happy also is he who has been rewarded with adhering to the worthy one who has already inherited them.

It is written in relation to those four corrections: "My thoughts are not your thoughts, nor are your ways My ways." The high and holy thoughts are not as the thoughts of an uneducated one. The high and holy ways are not as the ways of the uneducated. The thought is the *Rosh* [head/mind], and a way is the path by which the *Rosh* spreads and by which it multiplies.

Come and see. There is an upper *Rosh* and an upper path on the upper lip, and there is a lower *Rosh* and a lower path on the lower lip. This is why the mustache hair was established over the upper lip, which is the similitude of the upper *Rosh* that I have said.

This correction is called "merciful" (see *Idra Rabah, Nasso*). When one is rewarded with seeing that vision with the eye, it is full of mercies on all sides, for there is no place in it ... which is why it is indeed "merciful."

Afterward, they are rewarded with seeing the upper path, the path of those who ascend, who are male goats. This is why it is seen by all those lower worlds, like the precious correction of the *Rosh*, called "merciful," which is the praise of all the praises that appear to them.

In this way, there is a stop on those hairs in the middle, and that cessation of this path is seen to the lower ones by the two holes in the nose. There, that path spreads and is imprinted in the middle of the upper lip. This correction is called "and gracious," and all those who know the secrets certainly see it.

Now that you have been rewarded with those two names ... lower ones, and we will see what it is before us in that place where we find a lip ... under the lower lip. There ... meaning a *Rosh* [head/mind] to the lower ones, and all those worthy ones were awarded kisses ... although the kisses ... lower one as one.

Thus, we should ask, "Why did they cling to the *Rosh* of the bottom lip?" ... good reason ... and a holy mouth ... of that path that was imprinted in the upper lip, and shows them that place like ... a path of no flesh ... as it should be with love. ... And then ... they grew stronger in the bottom lip. At that time, "Love is as strong as death." Their soul comes out with upper and lower love together, and when their soul ... lower one.

This is why that place is called "the bottom *Rosh*." What is the reason? It is because it is completely similar to the upper *Rosh*, and everyone knows that one begot the other. This is called "lengthy," since the *Panim* [face/anterior] of the upper *Rosh* grew longer ... is not in everyone for one another. And as they were integrated as one, they are eyes for everyone.

It is in that regard that the sages asserted, "A voice, a vision, and a scent are not considered fraud." What is the reason? It is because in those three, all the ... are seen. And since we have been rewarded with this bottom *Rosh*, it was doubled at its conclusion and came in three praises. ... As the upper *Rosh* came to us, there is certainly no fraud in them, and there is no flaw in those precious corrections that were extended ... theirs, and everyone knows that one begot the other, except for the court's clowns who would say, "Sarah conceived from Avimelech, King of Gerar."

This is why the verse, "'As for Me, this is My covenant with them,' says the Lord: 'My Spirit which is upon you,'" came true in this holy seedling of the seed of Israel. It follows that this correction is certainly the *Rosh* of the lower ones, as it is for the lower ones to keep them and connect them to the bundle of life, as we have said.

But the sages have established, "There is no admission to the Azarah [a special section in the Temple] except for the kings from the House of David." What is the reason? It is because they are in the *Rosh*. But for the rest of the generation, that place was made only to pass by it. Were it not so, that rest would have been an easygoing stroll, which is why a lower path was established and extended from that *Rosh*, and it is similar to the upper path.

However, it appears and comes like an old man weary from the many days, and "There is no reason in the elderly." It is like Barzillai the Gileadite, for because the shape of that bottom path is completely similar, in everything, to the upper path that expanded from the upper *Rosh*, for this reason, he sees that the *Guf* is below, in the bottom path, similar to the upper one as a monkey to a human. And what he saw, he saw well.

This is why that correction is called "face," to show that not all faces are the same, and all the falls of people should be on the face, as in "And they bowed down with faces to the earth."

This is why that path was registered in the bottom lip, directly opposite the path on the upper lip, like the faces of the cherubim "facing one another." Because their shape resembles one another, they were strengthened by one another and were registered in the lips more deeply. This is also the meaning of "face," meaning that until now it was not known at all that there were faces above and faces below, and that not all faces are the same.

And when I hear of that wise disciple who said that he is laughing at the whole world by merit of "The image of the Lord does he behold," and he rejoiced and boasted his degrees, that he, Anah, "found the springs in the desert while pasturing the donkeys of his father Zibeon," and the first iniquity was erased, I say to myself that it is from our sages, who was found on the bottom path and calls it "the bottom path": Anah is the shepherd of his father, Zibeon. He also calls that lower *Rosh*, Zibeon, which is something I had never heard of in the writings before me.

I exert to find these words sufficiently interpreted, 1) to know what these "springs" do, meaning all the *Reshimot* [imprints/recollections] in their faces, to the length, to the width, in sound, vision, and in scent. Also, what is their question, and what is their answer—whether it is a new question or hidden in their ears from the shepherd of his father, Zibeon, of that Anah? And what was Zibeon thinking about this wise son if he had told him, "If your heart is wise, my heart, too, will rejoice"?

In general, was there joy over the question? And how many days did it last, or was it joy for a few hours? All this is clearly interpreted and explained in that clarification of the bottom *Rosh* and the bottom path that I have said. If it is not so for you, but some other way, tell me how the actual work was done.

And now that we are relieved regarding the bottom *Rosh* and the bottom path, and the holy names for those who have been rewarded with their faces with corrections of the hairs under the bottom lip—"long face" indeed, we will descend further, to below the holy curtain. In it, a good reward for the righteous is bundled, concealed, and revealed, as well as bitter and harsh punishments for the wicked. That curtain is called "very merciful," as it was established, as he leans toward *Hesed* [mercy]. It has all the merits and all the bounty of the Master of the world.

Woe unto one who displays incest. He severs his soul from this world, and it is severed from the next world. He is in the form of "Give truth to Jacob," which is why his hand held Esau's heel. He found all this mercy that we mentioned because in his wholeness, that seventh correction—called "and truth"—was revealed and came, since truth and mercy were included here in one another, as in "Give truth to Jacob, mercy to Abraham."

Come, see, and understand the order I have said to you thus far in all the degrees that you have seen thus far, and look upon their depictions properly. You will find them as a depiction of a garden-bed in which plantings have been sown, two opposite two, and one comes out the tail. That is, above is a *Rosh* and a path, and below, directly opposite them, is a *Rosh*, a path, and the one of now, called "very merciful," is in the middle toward everyone and below everyone.

There is also a garden-bed where these plantings are depicted in a different combination—three plantings above, which are considered *Rosh, Toch, Sof*. The upper *Rosh* is called *Rosh*, the upper path is called *Toch*, and the bottom *Rosh* is called *Sof*.

What is the reason that this is their combination? It is because the taste, appearance, and smell of these three plantings are the same. By that, the three conjoin as one, and all three are regarded as superior, as *Rosh, Toch*, and *Sof*.

That lower path, and that unification of "very merciful" are called "two branches of the willow." What is the reason? It is because they exist simultaneously, and the children of the exile that are among the nations and have mingled with them say about those two branches of the willow that they have neither taste nor smell. Thus, there are three above and two below in the garden-bed that I have mentioned.

In those five letters that we said, there are 120 combinations. But I said those two in order to show one combination in "remember," and one combination in "keep." The rest are included in those two sides that I mentioned, and these orders are called "the five letters of the name *Elokim*."

What is the reason? It is because they were set up along their emanation path one below the other. However, there is measuring to the width, and thus far I have not heard from you an interpretation from the text, and so I cannot speak of it at all until I hear that you yourself are in it.

When I said, "above" and "below," I was not implying places, for the spirits have no place. However, they certainly do have a time in which to become known in the world. What I called "above" was because it was seen first, and I call "below" what appeared subsequently.

And I ask more of you: When you interpret, in your own words, all those five chapters that I showed you, in an order of above and below, interpret for me each time, when is it the first chapter, and when is it the following chapter, and likewise all of them, as meticulously as your memory allows, or an approximate calculation, and the duration of each chapter.

And most of all, I long to hear the duration of those two branches of willow that I mentioned regarding the bottom path, called the "correction of the face," and the holy curtain, called "very merciful," and their beginning is "truth."

Although it is a small thing for you, it is great for me. I believe you already implied in another letter that you have forgotten their times, but remember it, for it is as though I am in prison and cannot labor and discuss the matter with you for an important reason which is in my heart.

Therefore, try hard to remember their times, more or less, their durations, as well as their beginnings. And please, have mercy on the time that was regrettably lost in vain, and send me a clear letter with complete explanations of all the questions I have asked of you, so I will not need to correspond with you thereafter.

Now, my dear, come and see how you can furnish me with your true answers. And because I carry the burden with you, I have nothing more than gloom now. Yet, I have no doubts about you, since the answers precede the questions—if he does not spare his life, etc.

Yet, let bygones be bygones, and henceforth count the moments lest you lose even one of them, for there is a herald upon us from above each and every day. It is not authority that I have given you. Rather, it is servitude that I have given you. And who is he and where is he who leads an evil, foreign *Klipa* [shell/peel] of idleness here among the King's children? It is certainly insolence toward heaven, and "The door turns on its hinges, and the idle is in his bed." The holy *Shechina* [Divinity] is cast to the dust under the feet of her maidservants, who regularly walk and trample over her head and arm with great insolence, as foreign maidservants do, wishing only to spit impure spit in their mistress' face, arising contempt and wrath.

For all those who have the power to remove this insolence, yet stand and see all this insolence without protesting, you call them "idle"? Idle is not their name. Rather, they have no perception of the preciousness and glory of the Master of the heaven who is before them.

Likewise, we should announce that there is no labor in extending time, but in studying, for that filthy substance is appeased and desires to work twenty-four hours a day, but not a single hour in the exertion of the study.

And the main labor is in finding all the secrets of the Torah and its reasoning, for there is no other slavery in this exile. This filthy substance would want anything but not to exert in the reasons for the *Mitzvot* [commandments]. And even if some reasons are found, it is shown that it is tiring, and that one novelty is not so different from the other, and then he grows tired and can no longer exert.

This is the heart of the matter. It should be uprooted and taken out from the court of the Lord's house, and one should take upon oneself labor to find the reasons of Torah and the meanings of the *Mitzvot* in the words of the Torah. And then the Maker will be brought back to His throne.

Yesterday evening I received your letter from the fourteenth of *Heshvan*. Now, early in the morning, my letter is complete and ready to be sent. I wanted to know how you know that this man who comes and goes into your house without a son is a true sage and a holy man, as you had said to me ... for the proper order of your body. Let me know in detail in what way is he opposite, for I need to know it, but clarify it thoroughly, and if he is not that bookbinder or bookseller that I saw in your house, and if he looks in letters ... and what he says about them. But most important, do not be frugal with those words that seem redundant to you, for upon increasing such depictions, the knowing between us will increase, and now I need it very much.

Your friend,

Yehuda

Letter No. 5

Tav-Reish-Peh-Aleph, 1920-1921

To my soul mate, may his candle burn forever:

... What you implied in your last letter, that I hide my face from you and regard you as an enemy, your intention is as one who hears his disgrace but keeps silent, and that I am not sharing the burden with my friends or care at all about my friends' pains. I admit that you are right about that; I do not feel those pains that you feel whatsoever. On the contrary, I rejoice in those revealed corruptions and the ones that are being revealed.

I do, however, regret and complain about the corruptions that have still not appeared, but which are destined to appear, for a hidden corruption is hopeless, and its surfacing is a great salvation from heaven. The rule is that one does not give what he does not have. Hence, if it has appeared now, there is no doubt that it was here to begin with but was hidden. This is why I am happy when they come out of their holes because when you cast your eye on them, they become a pile of bones.

But I do not settle for it even for a moment, as I know that those who are with us are more numerous than those who are with them. But weakness stretches time, and those contemptible ants are hidden and their place is unknown. The sage says about this, "The fool folds his hands and eats his own flesh." Moses let down his hands, but when Moses lifts his hands of faith, all that should appear promptly appears, and then Israel triumphs "in all the mighty hand, and in all the great terror."

This is the meaning of "Whatever you find that your hand can do by your strength, do." When the cup is full, the verse, "The wicked are overthrown," comes true. And when the wicked are lost, light and gladness come to the world, and then they are gone.

I remember discussing similarly with you on the first day of *Rosh Hashanah* [the first day of the Jewish year], *Tav-Reish-Peh-Aleph* [September 13, 1920], upon our return from the house of A.M. You shared with me very sad things that you saw that morning during the service [prayer]. I was filled with joy before you and you asked me, "Why this joy?" I replied to you the same, that when buried wicked appear, although they have not been fully conquered, their very appearance is regarded as a great salvation and causes the *Kedusha* [holiness] of the day.

And what you wrote me, that you cannot prefer the son of the loved one over the firstborn son of the hated one, I spoke to you many times about it face to face, that the place of faith is called *Bor* [pit/hole], and the filling of faith is called *Be'er* [well] of living waters, or succinctly, "life." It is not as the nature of ordinary water, that when some water is missing, the well still stands, meaning that this well has the nature of animals and nothing more. Rather, all its parts are organs on which the soul depends. Puncturing them in any way causes the entire animate level to die and disappear. This is the meaning of "They have forsaken Me, the source of living water, to hew them out cisterns, broken cisterns that can hold no water."

Although there is no deficiency in the water, there is some deficiency in the well, so it is completely broken, certainly, beyond any doubt that it will not hold the water in it. This is what the prophet implies in the name of the Creator, and this is true Kabbalah for anyone who is wise and understands with his own mind. If you do not understand, go forth and examine, and then you, too, will be wise and understanding with your own mind.

What you wrote me at the end of your letter, that you would like me to sound my pleasant voice to you, since for me it is no labor at all to delight a bitter soul from its hardships, for a heart filled with love sweetens them at their root, the root of all pleasantness, I will reply to you in brief, that there is a time for everything. You evidently saw that in my first letter, I wrote you and inscribed a very nice thing for its time, rejoicing the heart of God and men, interpreting the true meaning of "They will be satiated and delighted by Your kindness," examine there for it is true, and its end will be pleasant to every palate longing for true words.

You see how I can exert to delight you with words of truth at this time. God forbid that I should sin in delighting you with falsehood, like the false prophets during the ruin, for there is no falsehood in my domain at all. You already know what I say about those who draw their disciples to the truth with a web of falsehood and lies, or with luxuries. I have never been defiled by their idols, and not in those is Jacob's lot. Therefore, all my words are said in truth, and where I cannot disclose the truth, I keep completely silent.

Do not think that if I were close to you I would be saying more than in writing. If I knew that this was so, I would not leave you in the first place. What I said to you is the complete truth, that judging by our preparation, you do not need me, and so it is. Do not suspect me that I fabricated untrustworthy words for my own pleasure. When the Creator helps to be rewarded with the end of correction, you will need me very much, and may the Creator grant us this within twelve months, for the day is still long and you are not as quick as I am. Still, I hope that within twelve months from this day forth you will finish the work, and then you will see with all your efforts that we will be together for some years, since the depth of the work begins primarily at its end.

I have elaborated on all that for you because of thoughts that I detected between the lines of your letter. You have forgotten the absolute truth that is always in my heart and mouth. But let me promise you that more than you have witnessed the truthfulness of my words thus far, you will evidently see that all my words are forever true and will not change even as a hairsbreadth. Also, all the words I wrote you carry a true meaning that will not undergo change but require attention for the time is a time for brevity.

Believe that I could not write to you until now the words that are revealed in this letter, for reasons that I keep to myself. My gaze is fixed on the goal, to make it succeed the most, and this is what surrounds me with a fence of careful guarding over every single word. I know that in time, all my words and conducts toward you will become clear, as it is written, "Happy are you, vessels, who entered in impurity and came out in purity," for this is the path of Torah.

I have grown tired of asking you to write me more, and to promise you that in return, I will write you often. Each day I sit and wait, perhaps a word about you—from your spiritual life or from your corporeal life—will come my way. But there is not a sound. What can you say to justify it? There are no answers here with strong words or with faint words, only answers with dry words uttered in a florid style, as though for being overburdened, but you probably do not even understand yourself.

... And yet, I know that times will be better, and then, to the extent that they improve, their open love will grow, as well. We have yet to be satiated with eternal love together, as a never-ending fountain, satiated and delighted together, for the pleasantness of the Lord is for the complete receiver who feels no satiation. This is why He is called "Almighty," since for those who do His will appears an old light and a new light in one unification.

This is acquired by keeping Sabbaths and remissions for the world of *Yovel* [fifty-year anniversary, as well as jubilee]. This is the meaning of "They left it until morning ... and it did not rot, nor was there any worm in it." It is written, "They will be satiated and delighted by Your kindness," as corporeal eating fills the belly by the corporeal measure. Moreover, it sends up smoke to the brain due to the cooking in the stomach, and one grows tired and weary, and falls asleep.

This is the meaning of Pinhas stabbing the spear into her belly while they were attached. "Then Pinhas stood and prayed, and the plague stopped." This is why he was rewarded with the anointing oil although he was not from the descendants of Aaron, for Moses himself told him, "Behold, I give to him My covenant of peace." First it was with a cut *Vav*, but through the light of Torah, it grew long, and "My covenant was with him, life and peace" together, and "By the light of the king's face is life."

Yehuda Leib

Letter No. 6

1 *Av, Tav-Reish-Peh-Aleph*, August 5, 1921, Sabbath eve, Warsaw

To my soul mate ... may his candle burn forever:

I have already written you two letters but did not have the time to send them to you. In truth, I would like to see you prior to my leaving on the 22nd of *Av*. Now I would like to offer you a taste of the honey from my honeycomb.

It is written, "You destroy those who speak falsehood; the Lord abhors the man of bloodshed and deceit." There is an allegory about a king who took it on himself to teach his son tactics of kingship. He showed him the land, his enemies, and his friends. The king also gave his son a sword from his hidden treasures. The sword possessed a wonderful power: When he showed the sword to enemies, they would promptly fall before him as dung on the earth.

The king's son went and conquered many countries, took much spoil, and succeeded greatly.

In time, the king said to his son, "Now I will go up to the tower and hide myself there, which you will sit on my throne and lead the whole earth with wisdom and might. And here is also this shield, which until now has been hidden in the kingdom's treasury. No enemy or harm-doer will be able to harm you while this shield is in your possession."

The king took the sword, tied it to the shield, gave them to his son, and the king himself went up to the tower and hid there.

But the king's son did not know that the sword and the shield were tied to one another, and since he had no regard at all for the shield, he did not watch it. Thus, the shield was stolen from him, and with it, the sword.

When the news spread through the land that the sword and the shield had been stolen from the king's son, the ruler of the earth, they immediately became brazen and his enemies waged war against him until they took him captive, he and all his many possessions. With their enemy in their hands, they poured out their vengeance on him, and avenged him for all his abuse of them in the days of his father's leadership. Each day they would beat him ferociously.

The son was embarrassed before his father because his father's plight hurt him more than his own, so he resolved to make a sword and a shield just like the first ones, to appease his father and to show him his wisdom and might.

With tactics, he made a sword that was similar to the first, and made a shield similar to the first shield.

With his arms in hand, he called on his father at the top of the tower: "Be proud of me, for a wise son makes a father glad." And while he was calling his father, his enemies were bruising his brain and liver. And the more they beat him, the more he braced himself and overcame in order to appease his father, yelling, "Now, I am afraid of nothing, and who can fight me when I have my sword and shield in my hand?"

And the more he boasted, the more his enemies beat and hurt him, stones and sticks landing on his head, and blood running down his face. And all the while, he tried to keep upright, proudly, like a hero, to show his father that now he is afraid of nothing, that compared to his might they are as the dust on the balance, since the sword helps him, or the shield helps him.

This is what the poet implied, "You destroy those who speak falsehood," meaning those whose faces are as the face of a monkey before the face of a man, who make by their own strength a sword such as the Creator has made. And moreover, they wish to boast of their work as the Creator boasts. It is said about them, "The Lord abhors the man of bloodshed and deceit," for he makes a manmade shield and boasts that he feels no pain, etc., and this, too, the Creator abhors—one who shows false pretense saying that he is wise and strong and fearless, yet he is full of deceit and seeks cunning tactics. This the Creator abhors.

However, all the wholeness is in the holy name, God of my righteousness, whose every organ and tendon knows that the place of instilling of the *Shechina* [Divinity] is in the place of justice, meaning in the absolute knowledge that all His thoughts are just, and never has a man anywhere in the world taken a bad step, just as one will not make a good step by himself.

And although everyone believes it, it is knowing that they need—so it may settle in the heart. It is like a first concept, where the pouring out of a truly faithful heart to the Creator can disclose this concept in the world, like any simple and acceptable thing settles in the heart sufficiently.

This is the meaning of "And you will seek 'from there' the Lord your God and you shall find." This is also the meaning of the blessing, "Good who does good," who does good to others, for His attainment is truly on the good, as this is why He is called "good." This name is easily attainable by any person, and it is also called "God of my mercy." But because it is so easily acceptable, due to the ease of accepting it, the individual does not remain over all the people.

This is why the work in exile and keeping Torah in poverty is evidently revealed to the eye of all the organs of a servant of the Creator—the holy name, "God of my righteousness." That is, it was not at all bad in reality even for the slightest moment, which is the meaning of "and does good," meaning that it does not appear on the "good," but only on the "good to others," as in "That, too, is for the best." This is a very deep and important matter, and that unification leaves no room even for ... at that time, other than him.

This is also the meaning of "The Lord is one and His name is 'One,'" which is attained as simple to the ones who are whole.

Yehuda Leib

Letter No. 7

27 *Kislev, Tav-Reish-Peh-Bet,* December 28, 1921, Hanukkah, Jerusalem

To my friend, my heart and my point, the glory of his name is my glory, may his candle burn and shine for all eternity, Amen, may it be so:

Since the ninth of *Elul* [last month in the Hebrew calendar] to the second day of Hanukkah, some four months, I have been anticipating the joy of your written word. But in the end, a long letter is lying before me, full of poetic phrases and intimations that no one understands, like the dust that a fox lifts up when it walks in a tilled field. What fault have you found in me to make me unworthy of knowing anything about your states, although you know how much I care about them?

I am also surprised that you did not pay attention to what we said, that you would not write me anything that is covered with poetic phrases, in which I flee endlessly, so much so that I cannot find you in even one of them.

I ask of you, for God's sake, that from now on, when you write me some information, write with care and make certain you interpret it simply, as a person speaks to his friend, who is not a prophet, making certain he will not stray or even contemplate, nor note the eloquence, but rather the ease of explanation. And most important, not to mix in his words poetic phrases or intimations, for there is no fear of any foreign eyes ... and in my house there is no entry to foreigners.

When you write me innovations in the Torah, clarify them to me without any names or *Partzufim* that are common in the books, but in ordinary people's terms. For myself, I also take notice to explain my points in ordinary language, and it falls under my senses in complete simplicity, through and through, for it is a near and true way to clarify something to the fullest.

While I clothe the matters in the names of the books, at that time appears in me the desire to know the thoughts of the books, so my mind strays from the goal of my way, and this I have tried and tested. Moreover, when I obtain some direction in the poetic phrases in the books for my way, the joy even increases to mingle falsehood with truth.

Therefore, when I come to scrutinize something that I must, I keep myself carefully from looking in books both before and after. And it is likewise in writing; I do not use poetic phrases with them, so as to always be ready in purity to find a word of truth with admixtures or assistance from something external to it. Only then does the palate taste...

Yehuda Leib

Letter No. 8

5 Nissan, Tav-Reish-Peh-Bet, April 3, 1922, Jerusalem

To my honorable friend...

I must comment on your slacking in your work of writing, to approach me every once in a while with information of your points. It would have added a few benches at the seminary, and I have already proven to you in my previous letter from the first of *Nissan* [March 30].

See in Midrash Rabbah, *Yitro* [Jethro]: "Rabbi Yirmiah [Jeremiah] said, 'What if when He gives life to the world, the earth will quake? When He comes to avenge the wicked, who breached the words of Torah, it will be even more so, as it is said, 'Who can face His wrath, and who can calculate the day of His arrival?' When He desires, no being can face His might. When He rises in His anger, who will stand before Him? Whoa, who will not fear You, King of the nations?'" Although the words of Rabbi Yirmiah make inherent sense, concerning the Torah, as long as you engage in it, you find flavor [reason] in it.

Let me illuminate them for you.

You find in the poem, "You are more terrible than all terrors, prouder than all who are proud; You surround everything and fill everything." Interpretation: We see dreadful terrors and pains that are worse than death. Who is the one doing all that? ... This is His name, "You are more terrible than all terrors," who is removed from them!

Also, we see how many people—since the beginning of time until today—have tormented themselves with afflictions and self-torment, all in order to find some rhyme or reason in the work of God, or to know who is the owner of the capital.

Yet, they have all wasted their lives away and left the world as they came, without finding any relief. Why did the Creator not answer all their prayers? Why was He so haughty over them, so unforgiving? And what is His name? "Prouder than all who are proud," this is His name (see my poem, attached to this mail, which asks for whom the field was sown, for I have the right answer). But they who suffer the terrors and perceive that removed pride know for certain that the Creator is removed from them, although they do not know why He is removed.

What do poets say about this? They say that there is a sublime purpose for all that happens in this world, and it is called "the drop of unification." When those dwellers of clay houses go through all those terrors, through all that totality, in His pride, which is removed from them, a door opens in the walls of their hearts, which are tightly sealed by the nature of creation itself, and by this they become fit for instilling that drop of unification in their hearts. Then they are inverted like an imprinted substance, and they will evidently see that it is to the contrary—that it was precisely in those dreadful terrors that they perceive the totality, which is removed by foreign pride. There, and only there, is the Creator Himself adhered, and there He can instill them with the drop of unification.

He turned everything around for them in such a way that one who has unification knows that he has found ransom and an open door for instilling Him.

This is what is written in the poem, "You surround everything and fill everything." During the attainment, abundance is felt. It appears and sits precisely on all those contradictions. This is the meaning of "more terrible than all terrors, prouder than all who are proud," and naturally, "He fills everything." The poet knew that He fills them abundantly, and none else perceived the pleasantness of unification with Him until it seemed to him, at the time of his wholeness, that the afflictions they had suffered had some merit, to value the savor and pleasantness of the abundance of unification with Him. His every organ and tendon will say and testify that each and every person in the world would chop off his hands and legs seven times a day for a single moment in their entire life, of tasting such a savor.

> This is the law of the leprous on the day of his purification;
> He was brought unto the priest for all his fault.
>
> It is a judgment for every good deed;
> Thus you will meet its operator in a land of duty.
>
> Every passerby shall have it;
> It is known how ... [unclear in Hebrew] and He will dwell.
>
> What is His conversing at that time
> While strolling among great beasts?
>
> There, an ear is lent to very pleasant words;
> Rivers of persimmon are extended, dents over dents.
>
> They see what is heard—that it is only their fault that it is pleasant.
> Their stench goes as far from them as the east is far from the west.
>
> He laughs at them because He has known their souls forever.
> The ransom will not be limited at all in their eyes,

When He gives Himself to them for ransom,

And every stranger will be ears for fine words.

It is a hand for every vessel of purification.

He will grip it to disclose the light,

To create, and to sustain the light on it,

In the sentence of redemption and in the sentence of transformation.

And although all these do not elude you, I wish to fill with them the words of Rabbi Yirmiah. This is his sublime meaning with his allegorical words, "What, etc., ... When He desires, no being can face His might. When He rises in His anger, who will stand before Him? Whoa, who will not fear You, Oh King of the nations?" That is, "more terrible than all terrors, prouder than all who are proud," and all in order to sound "the words of the living God."

In other words, the sublime terrors were established only to see the voices, which the eye cannot see nor the heart think or contemplate. Until He came to that quality, the Creator was operating without any grievance for the operation, as it is sensed that the operation still did not exist. For this reason, throughout this terrible and long process, He desired and consented to His operation, to disclose it for the destined time.

This is what Rabbi Yirmiah said, "When He desires, etc.," meaning that His intention is only to admonish to worshippers of the Creator that that sublime side will always be before them once the act has been sufficiently revealed.

Therefore, who is to be held accountable that His honor will not be desecrated, for what fool would say that the Creator is lenient? He brings the verse, "Who can stand in the day of His wrath, and who can calculate the day of His arrival," from the long and sublime past? The day of His wrath is the one that calculates the day of His arrival; they are weighed together as though on scales.

By this you will understand the words of Rabbi Tarfon, who maintains that they say, "Enough." He proves from the verse, "And her father indeed spat [Hebrew: spat, spat] in her face, she will be disgraced for seven days," much less for the *Shechina* [Divinity] to have at least two weeks. And still he concludes, "She shall be closed up seven days," meaning just as before the action and the *Shechina* were exposed, and there was only "Her father indeed spat in her face," meaning exposing her face.

It is considered two spits—one is considered the heart, and one is considered the mind, as in "more terrible than all terrors, prouder than all who are proud." Saying "enough" before the *Shechina* to begin with, if you are pure-hearted you will understand through your heart the meaning of the words that after being closed up for seven days they went on their way in the campaigns of the Torah, unlike prior to the completion of the quarantine.

Even if my mouth was filled with singing like a sea, my lips with florid praise as its numerous waves, it would not be enough to detail the righteousness of the Creator, who has done, is doing, and will do before His creations, which He has created, is creating, and will create. I have thoroughly learned that great masses were, and are, yelling in the world at the top of their lungs but remain unanswered. They come alone and they leave alone. As they begin, so they end, myriad subtract, but do not add, and woe to that shame, woe to that disgrace.

It is a precise rule that sanctity increases and does not decrease, but the uniqueness of the Creator—who takes pride over the bodies, which are devoid of any desirables—does not wane at all. Rather, He even prides over "the elect men of the assembly, men of renown," and they, too, unless they carefully watch over themselves not to waste their time, He will be able to rid them of their world like the first, since the Glory of the World is strong and does not change for fear of His creations, of course.

Many great people have erred about it because they said that they were certain their hearts were awake. And the writing says, "And Er [Hebrew: awake], the firstborn of Judah, was bad in the eyes of the Lord, and the Lord put him to death." The sages say, "Even one who is slacking in his work is brother to one who destroys," for the most important is to pay attention and be mindful, and "Whatever you find that your hand can do by your strength, do," to extol and to sanctify His great and blessed name.

And precisely in a mindful manner, not as the cry of the fools, who know how to utter words without a wise heart. The wise one, his eyes are in his head, and he knows no bodily forces. He is not Er or Onan, but rather, "The words of sages are heard with contentment, with fervent scrutiny for the Creator alone.

It is written in *The Zohar*, "Everything is clarified in the thought." There are no outcries here, no self-tormenting or any illness or mishap whatsoever. Rather, "Her ways are ways of pleasantness, and all her paths are peace," "All who are gluttonous are angry," and "Anyone who is angry, it is as though he is idol-worshipping," and his soul departs from him.

But we should do much scrutiny and think with all our aim and strength, and "All day and all night they will never keep silent. You who mention the Lord, take no rest for yourselves, and give Him no rest until He establishes and makes (the fearing and the whole) Jerusalem a praise in the earth."

Let me tell you the truth: When I see the most vain ones wasting their lives away, it does not pain me whatsoever because in the end, no spiritual misfortune happens to them, only a body of flesh and bones that is tortured, and for which it was made, as has been elaborated above. The fate of every beast is the slaughter, and being mindless, they are all as beasts.

All of nature's orders do not sadden the pure-hearted. On the contrary, they rejoice the hearts of the understanding. But when I see the fallen ones, the men of renown, it is as though a blazing, fiery sword pierces my heart, for they torture the *Shechina* with the follies that they lie and fabricate.

Woe unto this beauty that withers in this dust, the holy, faithful drop. All the prolonged guidance is turning so as to reveal the face of the truth, and upon its revealing, it returns and throws pure, faithful water on every corner of the guidance and reality. Then, all who are empty fill up, and all the afflicted are bestowed upon, and there is neither an iron-web nor a cobweb here. Rather, there is great glory here and faithful love returning and coming back from the Creator to His creatures, and every place where He lays his eyes heals.

Happy is the ear that has never heard slander, and happy is the eye that has never seen a false thing. All that He curses is utterly cursed, and all that He blesses is utterly blessed. Everything that comes out of His mouth has neither doubt nor surplus. Rather, this is the thing which the Creator commanded, "Adhere to Him."

Dust, dust, how obstinate you are. All that is beautiful to the eye withers in you; how insolent you are. That eye that blesses wherever you turn, how has it become strangeness, and every place He looks burns and becomes consumed? How will those most desperate people be comforted "with a comfort of vanity and joy of the flesh"? What shall they answer in the day of calling? It evokes contempt and wrath.

Therefore, I have spoken at length against those people with whom you are face to face, and of the words they fabricate, such as the expansion of corporeality. As they are, so are their works, "All who trust them," and "Cursed is the man who trusts man and makes flesh his arm," and "Blessed is the man who trusts in the Lord." "Happy is the man who did not follow the counsel of the wicked, ... but delights in the law of the Lord, and on His law does he reflect day and night," as our sages said, "I have created the evil inclination, I have created for it the Torah as a spice," and "If you encounter that villain, draw him to the seminary." How man does not fear or feel that his master is assisting him.

This is what I told you face to face at a time of joy, that the primary sin of the generation of knowledge [generation of the desert] was according to the verse, "Our fathers in Egypt did not perceive Your wonders ... and were rebellious at sea, in the Red Sea." I interpreted that the value of a gift is as the value of the giver. They were the first to blemish it when they "did not perceive Your wonders," but merely "wonders." Thus, the gist is missing from the book, which caused them to turn back at the time of the reception of the Torah, saying, "You speak with us and we will hear." Although the Torah does not attribute them sin in the matter, for it is said, "I wish this heart of theirs was to fear Me all the days," it is because the sin preceded the giving of the Torah and was not written in the Torah, and it is known that the Torah engages in the path of correction and not in the path of sins.

You asked me, "What should I do with it?" I replied that you should exert and give many thanks for the benefit, for it is natural that when the giver sees that the receiver is not grateful, his future giving wanes.

You replied to me that the thanks for His blessings does not appear in the words of a corporeal mouth, but through exertion and broadening the heart in the benefit of the merit of unification, by which the enemies are stopped on the right and on the left, that this is called "gratitude for His blessings," and not the words of a corporeal mouth.

But come and see how lovely is faithful water from the never-ending fountain, of which it was said, "Let them be satisfied and delighted by Your goodness." The satiation does not cancel the pleasure because he has perceived "Your wonders," and not wonders and tokens, as to whom will he answer? Even he himself does not need it, and he never said to them or to the like of them, "Give Me, offer a bribe for Me from your strength." Their father has come to loathe going with his flock's dog for inferior guarding, "and if the helper stumbles, he that is helped shall fall," and "The Almighty, whom we cannot find, is excellent in power."

It all came upon him since the time he forgot the quality of "sublime and exalted, very, very high," and began to engage by measuring of flesh and blood, and from there to measuring the trees, and also wishing to build himself on calculations. He was calculating calculations of others, but it is already written, "And you have found."

Ravnai said, "Until it comes into his hand. This means that he does not purchase just by seeing; this is the simpleton's phrasing: 'He does not buy until he holds it in his hand.'" Therefore, the Tanna teaches of two gates, one in finding, and one in negotiating, to understand and to instruct until he actually holds it in his hand.

It seems that at the end of days he will discover ... our sages: "When he sees from whom he took the coins?" They explain that he took from two people (which implies another thing that will be revealed at the end of days), from one—voluntarily—and from another—involuntarily, and we did not know with whom it was voluntary, and with whom, involuntary. This is the meaning of the verse, "What shall we do to our sister on the day when she is spoken for?" She will appear and be seen at the end of days, for we will wait for the days of the Messiah.

Let us return to our topic, which is primarily to learn more about the Giver of the gift, His greatness, His value, and then he will be rewarded with true *Dvekut* [adhesion] and will obtain the flavors of Torah, for there is no other remedy in our world but that.

I shall recite a fine and pleasant poem about it, which brings joy to a true heart, and which is tried and tested in ten trials.

My drop, my drop, you are so fine, all the expanses of my life,
All my mornings, all my evenings.

The face of the curtain, you raise the cover, in the expanses of my futures,
All my mourning, all my comfort.

The wasteland, the multitudes shall carry you with branches that I added,
All my ruin, all my filling.

You pierce my heart, and your full reward is in my hand, from all the banners of my love, all my gold, all my merchandise.

A good guest, what does he say? "All the troubles that the landlord has troubled himself, he has troubled himself only for me," according to the verse, "One must say, 'The world was created for me.'" So it is, that as the world was created for him, all the elements in his reality were also created for him.

One element—because of the unification—the general and the particular are equal to it, and everything that all the people in the world will attain at the end of correction, complete individuals attain in every generation. This is why each one finds the elements of his organs in the Torah, for because it is generally set up for the whole collective, it is also generally set up for an individual. Moreover, in the collective, there is not more than there is in an individual, and this is a true and complete measure in great scrutiny.

This is why it is written, "With her love you will ravish always," and "You shall contemplate it day and night," and "The Torah, the Creator, and Israel are one." It is a measure completely adapted, for everything is one, and the spiritual cannot be divided into parts. One must sanctify and purify himself in mind and heart, and when you bless with the blessings of the Torah as before, you will attain the distinguished verse, "See now that I am I, and there is no other God with Me."

I ask that for your benefit and delight, do send me frequent information of your situation in the Torah, for it will save much time. Know that prolonging the time of correction diminishes the value of the correction, and anything spiritual improves and ascends when it takes less time. If you knew, as I know, that prolonging the stay on the paths of light is harmful, you would certainly be quicker in your work.

Although I neither wish nor am permitted to study for you, it is permitted and a great *Mitzva* [commandment] to delight and perfume those loved ones that you find in the field that the Lord has blessed. Our whole engagement in life is only to raise the *Shechina* from the dust, to delight her, sing before her with all our might, always praise the Creator with your mouth with what is permitted, and especially where we know that you will certainly succeed. For this reason, I urgently need information from you, and we shall be satiated with love together, to uproot the thorns, and we shall see the high rose soon in our days, Amen, may it be so.

Yehuda

Letter No. 9

7 *Nissan*, *Tav-Reish-Peh-Gimel*, March 24, 1923, Jerusalem

To my friend, may his candle burn:

I can no longer restrain myself regarding all that stands between us, so I shall attempt open and sincere admonition. I need to know the value of a word of truth in our land, for so is always my way—to study all the workings of creation in utter precision and to know its merit, whether it is good or bad. This is the only place my fathers left for me as a boundary, and I have already found precious things and secrets in these passing, trifle images. It is with good reason that this lot has been set up before me, and they are lovely letters for the sentence of every wisdom and every knowledge, and were created only for combinations of wisdom.

First, we shall judge the quality of laziness in this world. ... On the whole, it is not such a negative and contemptible quality. The evidence is that our sages already said, "Sit and do nothing—better." Although common sense and several writings contradict this rule, still, to make the proper precision I shall show that "Both are words of the living God," and all will be settled peacefully.

It is clarified beyond any doubt that there is no other work in the world but His work, and all the other works besides His—even for the souls, if it concerns only oneself—would be better if they did not come into the world, as they turn matters upside down, for a receiver does not become a giver. This is an unbreakable law, and "If he had been there, he would not have been redeemed."

Thus, we should not discuss a work or a worker whose doer is in the form of reception, since this is utter vanity, and there is no doubt that it would be better to "Sit and do nothing," for he is doing harm by his work, either to himself or to others. Its benefit is utterly absent, as we said above.

I do not care at all if part of you finds this ruling uncomfortable, and even openly protesting my words, for so is the nature of every truth—it does not require the consent of any woman-born, great or small, and anyone who has been rewarded with thorough knowledge of the Torah is very opinionated.

Therefore, following this great and famous truth—that one who curses in his work "is a friend of a destroyer"—I feel no mercy or concern for the idle, to seek advice for them, due to the great rule: "Sit and do nothing—better." In any case, if they cherish the word of the Creator and truly wish to worship their Maker, to glorify His works, there is no doubt that the spirit of idleness will not be with them, since the spirit of the Creator robes with strength and might, from which idleness is blown away as straw by the wind. However, if it turns out that they have unity with this spirit of idleness, there is no doubt that at that time their minds are not dedicated only to the Creator. If this is so then "Sit and do nothing" is certainly better.

I have much to say about this matter, but what can I do that time causes you to misunderstand my words, for you are not accustomed to my innovations in the Torah, which are said in utter simplicity. It requires a very high level to be able to lower one's level so much, and raise them. And yet, I cannot change my ways, as I see in it the will of the Creator.

Although you have heard from me many words of Torah said in simplicity, and I also troubled myself extensively to make you understand all my ways and all my wishes in the work of the Creator, I wish to say—regarding that profession—that with the Creator's help, I added to my teachers in my generation and before me, and the Creator permitted me, and you are my witness.

And yet, our study of this matter had been short, approximately ... from the second day of the portion *BeHaalotcha* [When You Mount], *Tav-Reish-Peh* [June 1920] to the portion *Shemot* [Exodus], *Tav-Reish-Peh* [January 1920] (*Tav-Reish-Peh-Aleph* [December 1920]) since your situation during the week ... did not permit me to speak with you more of my innovations in the Torah. Also, I stopped entirely the way that I teach for reasons I keep to myself, and even prior to that, I let you know about it with some explanation.

But since the time was very short, you have not become accustomed to my ways, and my ways were not immersed in you at all. For this reason, you have inserted many changes of your own mind in my teaching ... for which you have lost much time. ...

You said explicitly that you would help me with all your might and power to scrutinize the ways of my teaching and its expansion in the world, but you are sitting and waiting for the right time when you can partake with me in this matter. You promised it wholeheartedly, resolutely, and ceremoniously, without a shred of a doubt, that who knows if you are rewarded with the above-said.

Now, what can you say of all your promises to me ... and I know your tactic and ploy, which you have devised, to wash your whole body all at once in endless water.

I also know the answer that is readily available for you regarding my question—that you are still unfit to display knowledge and to ruin or build, much less bond with me in work, while you yourself have an insufficient grip on it.

And yet, it is the inclination in you, and you inherently contradict yourself. That is, you answer another question without humility, but to the contrary. Thus, how can you grip both ends of the rope?

... And I am telling you that there is no shame here whatsoever, no smallness, and no greatness, only the work of the devil that has succeeded in interfering with every good thing that appears in its ways. After all, why should you mind if I understand your smallness too much? Is it my praise that you crave? I rather know that your soul is purer than such litter.

Also, why should you mind if I understand the exact measure of your greatness as it is within your heart? Do you not fear my mocking you for your obstinacy?

And why this shame to speak before a friend like me with boasting words? And also, all our sages have traversed this road, disclosing their secrets either to a special teacher or to a special and true friend, whether high or low, just as they came in their hearts.

The ways of the path of truth are not impressed at all by the truth, be it bitter or sweet. And most important, each scrutiny is as though accepted at its time, for the mind must be "clean," and God forbid that it should be biased due to one's bitterness. And the heart, too, must be righteous in its place, justifying the Creator under any circumstances.

And as there is no measure to the Creator's merit and Almightiness, there is no measure to the lowliness of a woman-born (and to his weakness), unless that creation, for all its lowliness, is willing to accept a word of truth without any bias, for its afflicted body. It is always as in the verse, "The clean and the righteous do not slay," and so it marches on the rungs of sanctity and purity until ... "What is this work for you?"

I evidently see that you will fall in this pit, whether less or more. This is the final Satan, which I find in my fruitful work for my generation. With the Creator's blessing, I have been found agreeable in the eyes of my Creator, to reveal to me the full lowliness of the generation and all sorts of easy and faithful corrections to bring each soul back to its root as quickly as possible.

But what can I do in the day of calling, for you will have to answer the wicked man's question, "What is this work for you?" Although the answer is clarified in the *Haggadah* [Passover story], "Had he been there, he would not have been redeemed," as there is no need for fools, worshippers of vanity, still, no one is chosen for His work unless his heart is whole with the Creator, to work the work of the burden devotedly, all day and all night, always, endlessly, only to bring a shred of contentment to one's Maker. Thus, why should this wicked one mingle and deliberate with such lovers of the Creator?

And yet, my brother, this is not an intellectual question. It is clear and it is true, and no reflection or doubt is left in the matter. But precisely because of it, it is a question to which there is no answer, for it is the question of a murky and turbid matter, and it is only a demand on the part of the material body to return to the idols of his father, in whose work he shares, or even truer—he is the worker and all the pleasure is his. And since the asker is but a mindless matter and body, the power of the mind is weak in giving it any answers, for it has no ears and it is "like the deaf asp that stops its ear."

I know the great advantage with which the Creator has granted me over my contemporaries, for I have searched a long, long time why I have been chosen by God's will. And after all the lowliness emitted from that son of a wicked one, which is the *Klipa* [shell] that rules in my time, and after I have witnessed its true measure, I realize the Creator's kindness with me, to distract my heart today and always from hearing the above-mentioned question of the wicked.

I find myself committed and obligated, as today and as always, to be as an ox to the burden and as a donkey to the load, all day and all night. I will not rest from searching some place where I can bring some contentment to my Maker. Even in this day that I am in, I am happy to work under a great burden even seventy years, without any knowledge of its success (even my whole life), except that it is certainly the way that I have been commanded to walk in all His ways and to adhere to Him, which I have heard initially.

At the same time, I cannot excuse myself at all by any notion or contemplation from doing any work for His sake because of my lowliness. I crave and think all day about the sublimity of the work of God, in such sublimity that I cannot even write about it.

It is true that as I discussed these matters with my contemporaries, I saw that they have a sort of code of law in which they delve to find their measure of the work of God for all their needs. But I have never seen that code of law, that it allots conditions and amount to the Creator's wish from His creations, which He has created, concerning the rungs of *Dvekut* [adhesion] with Him.

By and large, I have received face to face that small and great are equal before Him, and all creations are ready for the instilling of His *Shechina* in their hearts, and the measure of instilling depends on the Creator's will, and not on him, at all. I therefore wonder—it is a grave disgrace for a woman-born, whoever he may be, to place a limit, or a seeming limit, on the quality of the Creator's will.

These words of mine are utterly simple, yet I have yet to see in my generation anyone who is—in his own eyes—such a simple man as to understand the value of my words as they are, for they cannot lower their bodies so.

And once I have come to this, I will reveal to you all their secrets in the chambers of their figures. If you understand ... that it all came to them because of the question of a wicked man, "What is this work for you?" for they always need blindness toward that wicked man.

... But they are people, and why did they not nonetheless turn their work to that profession? What does the owner of the vineyard receive from his vineyard? And still, they worshipped their Creator intellectually, whether He would pour upon them spirit from on high to see fruits in their work, or not. But they would not be excluded from among the worshippers of the Creator nonetheless.

When they are compared to beasts, carrying the material emotions, such as worshipping the Creator with their will without wanting to understand that they will lose all the substance along with anything they can acquire, their memory shall be severed from the earth forever.

And yet, my brother, I have spoken to you extensively regarding these matters face to face when we were together, and it is impossible to elaborate on them so in writing. Yet, I am certain that if you properly scrutinize these words that I have written in this letter, you are certain to find many matters with which you will be displeased, and which I wrote you deliberately, as I believe that perhaps you *will* understand henceforth.

Do let me know every detail and every root where you do not completely agree with me, for my heart is whole with yours, and you ... and the Creator is my witness that if I could feed you heaven's milk above, I would spare not labor or exertion.

Yehuda Leib

Letter No. 10

21 *Tevet*, *Tav-Reish-Peh-Hey*, January 17, 1925, Warsaw

To the disciples, may the Lord be upon them:

... I terribly regret the dwindling organs that external circumstances overcame them from joining you. May the Creator give them strength so they can join us, and the Creator will be with them.

I understand that you are not engaged in unifications of mind and heart as I would like you to. Still, do what you can and the salvation of the Lord is as the blink of an eye. The most important thing before you today is the unity of friends. Exert in that more and more, for it can recompense for all the faults.

It is said, "An exiled disciple, his rav [teacher] is exiled with him." This was perplexing to our sages, for how can there be slandering in the Torah and work of the disciple to the point of expelling him from the domain of the Creator, especially once he is clung to a true teacher? They explained that when the disciple descends, it seems to him that the rav has descended, too. And because it is so, it really is so, meaning that he can enjoy his rav only to the extent that he assumes in his heart. Therefore, all he has is a low and inferior rav, as much as he values him. Thus, his rav is exiled with him.

The exile and enslavement in Egypt begin with the words, "And a new king arose over Egypt, who did not know Joseph." That is, a new ruling appeared in the minds of each and every one, a newly made ruling, since they fell from their previous degree. We have said that "an exiled disciple, his rav [teacher] is exiled with him." Thus, clearly, they did not know Joseph. In other words, they attained him only to the extent that they valued him in their hearts.

Therefore, they depicted the image of Joseph as they themselves were. Because of it, they did not know Joseph and the enslavement began. Otherwise, the righteous would certainly protect them and exile or enslavement would not be depicted to them at all.

Their enslavement in *Homer* [mortar/plaster] and *Levenim* ["bricks," as well as "white"] is explained: Mortar is the iniquity of the *Hamor* [donkey] by which one is sentenced for the thought. The bricks [also "white"] are the repentance, when they are granted upper mercies and temporarily obtain upper light from the faith of the holy fathers and are whitened from their iniquities. However, it was not permanent, and because of it, they were incarnating and coming into every work of the field, meaning continuation of hard work that concerns the rest of the *Mitzvot* [commandments].

Our sages said, "The intermediate, both judge them." This is why that *Klipa* [shell/peel] is called Pharaoh, with the letters *Peh-Hey Reish-Ayin* [initials of *Peh Ra* (bad mouth)]. That is, the *Malchut* in *Mochin* is called *Peh* [mouth], meaning it is a resolution and consent not to break His word, and all that comes out of His mouth will be done.

In the exile in Egypt, the ruling was that of the above-mentioned bad mouth, and they returned to evil. Thus, although they were rewarded with some upper illumination from the first nine, it could not be absorbed in the *Guf* [body] because of the bad mouth, the opposite of "*Peh* of *Kedusha* [holiness]." That is, the back of the neck was blocking the abundance that comes down from the *Rosh* [head], and sucked out all the abundance that began to come down for Israel. This is why no slave could escape Egypt, since Pharaoh put a great charm over the openings of Egypt, as our sages said.

By this we understand the verse, "And I know that the king of Egypt would not let you go, except by a mighty hand." Through Moses, His servant, the Creator announced that no mighty hand or powers in the world would help with this evil *Klipa* as it surrenders only to the Creator. This is the meaning of "I and not a messenger," and the meaning of "And I will put forth My hand and strike Egypt ... And I will grant this people favor in the eyes of the Egyptians..."

Now we shall interpret the enunciation of redemption and Moses' mission. It is written, "And Moses answered and said, 'But they will not believe me' ... for they will say, 'The Lord did not appear to you.'" Interpretation: Because the mouth of *Kedusha* was in exile, as in, "for I am slow of speech and slow of tongue," Moses, the faithful shepherd, argued before the Creator, "But they will not believe me." Even if I tie Israel to me and bring down some bestowal for them, the *Klipa* of Pharaoh sucks it out and robs it from them. And although they are attached to me, they will still not listen to me. That is, while the *Klipa* of Pharaoh has dominion, and a mouth and speech in the exile, still, if they believed in the faithful shepherd properly, the children of Israel would be able to listen to Moses, who is above the mouth and speech. If they strengthened themselves in that, they would certainly be saved from the *Klipa* of Pharaoh.

This is what Moses, the faithful shepherd, complained about to the Creator, "They will say, 'The Lord did not appear to you,'" as explained above, "And a new king arose over Egypt, who did not know Joseph." Upon their descent into matter [substance], they will also deny the greatness of Moses, the faithful shepherd, so how was it possible for Moses to redeem them from that evil and strong *Klipa*?

Therefore, the Creator gave Moses three signs to show to the children of Israel, and taught him to arrange these signs before them one at a time. The Creator also promised him that He would help him from above so he can show it to them. After the children of Israel accept these signs from him, they will come to listen to Moses, and then he will be able to redeem them from that bitter exile.

Now I will explain the three signs. The first sign is the turning of the staff into a serpent, and the serpent into a staff. The second sign is that by taking out his hand not from his bosom, it was as leprous as snow. And when he took out his hand from his bosom, it returned to be as his flesh. The third sign is that by spilling the water of the Nile on the land it turned into blood.

Now I will interpret how He showed them to Israel. In the hand of the redeemer was a staff, which is the faithful shepherd. He is holding the staff to steer the heart of Israel to their father in heaven. If he throws it to the ground, it means that the children of Israel are taking His staff to do with it as they wish (*Artza* [to the ground] is like *Ratzon* [desire]). "And it turned into a serpent" means that their sin seemed to them like animals.

Before they approached his staff, their sin was considered still. After they brought themselves to his staff, it became an actual serpent until "And Moses fled from it" (according to what Israel valued themselves, as in "Who did not know Joseph").

Subsequently, when Moses came to save them from the serpent's bite, he gripped the serpent by its tail and not by its head because when a false redeemer comes to save Israel, he grips the serpent by its head, to break the serpent's head, as so is the way of all snake-catchers.

But a true redeemer grabs it specifically by its tail (according to the secret that that serpent bends its head and strikes with its tail, which I already interpreted for you), "And it became a staff in his hand," for then it really works in their hearts to turn them to the side of merit. And once the children of Israel receive that sign, the Creator gives him permission and authority to show them the second sign.

I have already interpreted for you the words of our sages, "'Will sacrifice him to His will.' How so? He is forced until he says, 'I want.'" This is so because when discussing the thought, the filth of the serpent will be corrected through the offering that atones for the thought.

Yet, making the offering should be with love and fear, and one who needs a sacrifice can toil over fear, but not over love, so the offering is disqualified for lack of love. Our sages say about that that He—the Creator—is forced, as in "My sons defeated Me," for the *Zivug* of one who works out of fear is called "forced." Until the Creator says and reveals to him His will, and tells him, "I want" this work. Then it becomes apparent that there was no coercion to begin with, but an actual *Zivug* with love and friendship.

This is the meaning of "She opens her mouth in wisdom, and the teaching of mercy is on her tongue." In the opening of the mouth, upper *Hochma* appears because at that time, when the *Klipa* of "bad mouth" parts from the *Kedusha*, the "mouth of *Kedusha*" comes out. This is the meaning of opening the mouth wide, and there are no more harm doers to break his word since "He who knows the mysteries testifies about him that he will not return to folly." Promptly, he is rewarded with upper *Hochma* because the disclosure of law and judgment always come together. This is the meaning of "She opens her mouth in wisdom."

And once he has reached the disclosure of *Hochma*, with which he was rewarded only through his prior labor in his *Zivugim* [couplings], coercively, it turns out that were it not for the tongue of *Nukva*, in which there is the power of labor, he would not have been rewarded with anything. Thus, it becomes apparent that to begin with, even the forced *Zivugim* were actually *Zivugim* of love and empathy. This is the meaning of "and the teaching of mercy is on her tongue," specifically "on her tongue," and not in another tongue.

Let us return to our topic that the first sign—that by Moses gripping its tail, it turned into a staff in his hand. This is the meaning of "repentance from fear," as in "She opens her mouth in wisdom," that from the time it is established as a staff—and the *Klipa* is sent away and does not return—begins the root of disclosure of upper *Hochma*.

The meaning of the second sign is a root for repentance from love. When he brought his hand into his bosom, with upper faith, the law of *Hesed* appears on her tongue, and not on another's.

Scrutinize the words because indeed he must take his hand out of his bosom, as "bosom" means "I, and you will not have." The taking out of the hand is the expansion of knowledge [*Daat*]. If—when he takes out a hand for expansion of flavors [also reasons] of Torah and secrets of Torah—he remembers his root well, not to change its flavor [also reason], and knows the benefit of taking his hand out of his bosom, it follows that law and judgment are tied to one another as two friends that do not separate. At that time, the abundance flows in its ways properly.

By that you will understand the meaning of "And he put his hand into his bosom," which is the acceptance of the law, "and took it out," that he came to extend the expansion of *Daat* without strengthening to be adhered to the root, as well, which is the bosom. Then, "Behold, his hand was as leprous as snow." It is translated in Yonatan Ben Uziel, "His hands were closed," meaning that the fountains of abundance had closed, and there was no correction except to be strengthened once again. "And he put his hand back into his bosom," accepting the law, and then, "when he took it out of his bosom, it returned to be as his flesh." That is, the law accompanies and connects to the taking out of the hand, and law and judgment are connected. At that time, the flow of life and abundance returns to its place.

This is the meaning of "And if it comes to pass that they do not believe ... to the voice of the first sign," he will take out his hand not from his bosom. "And they will believe the voice of the latter sign," since he will show that by taking his hand out of his bosom it regained its health.

The third sign is a profound matter. The Nile is the god of Egypt, and Pharaoh is the god of the Nile, as he said, "My Nile is to me, and I have made me." We have already said that Pharaoh robbed to himself all the abundance that came down from the *Rosh* for Israel.

However, he gave to Israel the extract of the abundance that he robbed, and the extract given by Pharaoh is called "Nile." This is what waters all who dwell in Egypt. It is called "bread of idleness," for it does not require labor. This is why there was fear that the children of Israel would be blemished after the redemption from Egypt with the bread of the mighty, as it happened in the desert when they said, "We remember the fish that we ate in Egypt for free." This is the correction, "And the water ... became blood upon the dry land," for everyone will see that they were disqualified from the drink of Israel. Afterward, the blood of Passover and the circumcision blood came to them from that.

This is also the meaning of "She looks well to the ways of her household." It means that the water of the Nile became blood on the land, and then, "and does not eat the bread of idleness." This is a very deep subject, to be elaborated on elsewhere.

Yehuda Leib

Letter No. 11

6 *Shevat*, *Tav-Reish-Peh-Hey*, January 31, 1925, Warsaw

To the one who is tied to my heart, may his candle burn:

I received your words, and concerning the traveling of ... I can inform you that, God willing, I will bring him with me to Jerusalem. I think I will issue a visa to Beirut for him, and from there to Jerusalem on my permit, for I have no other way at the moment. I have already informed this to my family in a letter.

... Concerning the words of Torah you ask of me, you should have written what it is you lack without them, for you should accept everything with love. Indeed, so is the path of truth, but you should feel the love, and it is felt only in a place of deficiency. This is the meaning of "He who shares the affliction of the public is rewarded with seeing the comfort of the public," and "To the extent that a person allots, he is allotted."

You have often heard that all the good of the awakening from below concerns only our learning how to feel the deficiency, as it is set before us by the Creator. This is the meaning of "A prayer makes half," since as long as one does not feel the deficiency of the half—the part that was cut off from the whole, and the part does not feel as it should—one is incapable of complete *Dvekut* [adhesion] since this will not be considered advantageous for him, and one does not keep or sustain a needless thing.

Our sages told us that there is a remedy for this feeling by the power of the prayer. When one is persistent in praying and craving to adhere to Him perpetually, the prayer can do half, meaning that he will recognize that it is half. When the sparks multiply and become absorbed in the organs, he will certainly be rewarded with complete salvation and the part will be adhered to the whole forever.

This is the meaning of "There is only a hairsbreadth between the upper and lower water," as our sages said, "A thread [or hair] was tied to him," as in, "mountains that hang on a thread." This thread needs a filling, and this is the reason for the division of the lower water from the upper.

This is the meaning of the words, "The head of its mouth was inside of it." That is, as long as the blocked was not opened, meaning the mouth in the head [*Peh de Rosh*], it is fed through its navel [*Tabur*], and the blocked must be open. It turns out that "The head of its mouth was inside of it; it will be a lip around his mouth" means he will not settle for little because "If we permit our share, who will permit the share of the altar?" This is why he will feel the heaviness in the head.

That feeling will give him a language for the mouth, since he will pour out his heart to the Creator extensively, to purify the lower lip [also lower language]. This is the meaning of the verse, "It will be a lip around his mouth, a weaving," meaning that the sparks of craving gather side by side and unite together "like the opening of a coat."

In other words, the reasons that cause the sensation of pain and pouring out of the heart will not be canceled whatsoever, but will gather together and become a mouth, as our sages said, "His sins became to him as merits." It follows that he has two mouths, for "around" [in Aramaic] means *Sechor, Sechor* [circling, as well as merchandise].

Thus, the *Panim* [anterior/face] is a complete *Partzuf*, and the *Achoraim* [back/posterior] is a complete *Partzuf*. If he is rewarded with it, he acquires "the opening of a coat," and then "That man is guaranteed that he will not be torn because his name is Yinon for all eternity." Observe carefully and find, for this is the meaning of "They shall inherit twofold in their land."

There is great depth in my words, but I haven't the strength to interpret them now. But if you understand my words, you will certainly be rewarded with coming and going without needing permission. As the portion ends, "And its sound is heard when he enters the holy place and when he goes out," may it be so.

On the whole, you do not understand the attainment and the merit of the Torah. If you did, you would certainly devote yourself to it and you would be rewarded with it. You see the verse, "A candle is a commandment; the Torah is light." If you have a house full of candles but no light, the candles will be taking up room in vain. The name "Torah" comes from the word *Horaah* [instruction], and from the words *Mar'eh* and *Re'iah* ["vision" and "sight" respectively], meaning complete recognition that leaves no thread behind it. May the Creator make you understand my words henceforth…

I will also ask that you make great efforts in love of friends, to devise tactics that can increase the love among the friends and revoke the lust for bodily matters from among you, as this is what casts hate, and among those who give contentment to their Maker there shall be no hatred. Rather, there are great compassion and love between them.

I ask that each will show his letter to his friends because the matters are said from one to another, and there is one law for you in enslaving the body and sanctifying the soul. But do not change, God forbid, as do those with bodies. You should henceforth heed my words, for it is your life and the length of your days.

It is not for my own favor that I demand, but what can a fine general do when soldiers change his instructions to them?

Yehuda

Letter No. 12

26 Tevet, Tav-Reish-Peh-Hey, January 12, 1926, Warsaw

To the honorable students, may the Lord be upon them:

… You must grow stronger in what concerns our prime wish. You know what I interpreted about the verse, "And the Lord your God will bless you in all that you will do." The lower man must do everything that he can do, and only then is there room for instilling the blessing. However, it is folly to think that this makes the Creator obliged to instill the blessing precisely in the place of one's work.

On the contrary, for the most part, the work is in one place and the blessing is in another, in such a place where the person did not work at all, since he did not know or could not do anything there for his part. In the real blessing, it is an unbreakable law, and this is the meaning of the finding, as in "I labored and found," and I have already elaborated on that.

As for me, I enjoy my labor; hence, "They who seek the Lord will not lack abundance," and it is written, "My salvation is near to come, and my righteousness to be revealed." But what I ask most of all is that you brace yourselves and be strong, and the Creator will be with you. Do speak to the sagging friends to join us, and foreign fears will depart from them, and if they make the house vacant, there will be room for idols. Do not fear the blaze of the swirling sword on the way of the tree of life.

And if you wish to know, I will inform you that I do not find myself far from you at all, and one who feels remoteness, it is because of himself.

There is no more news.

The words of the one who longs to unite with you in complete union...

Yehuda Leib

Letter No. 13

10 *Shevat, Tav-Reish-Peh-Hey*, January 25, 1926, Warsaw

To my dear ... may his candle burn forever:

I received your words with a heart full of longing, for you hide yourself from me. Still, you could speak to me in writing.

What you wrote, letting me know the exile in Egypt, I wonder; it is common knowledge. "They cried, and their cry went up to God from the work." Then "And God knew." If there is no knowledge of the Creator in the exile, redemption is impossible. And knowing the exile is itself the reason for redemption, so how do you intend to let me know at the time of redemption?

Truth will show its way, that one who regrets makes his regret known. He cannot withhold himself or hide. Indeed, I feel all of you together, that today has been replaced for you with tomorrow, and instead of "now," you say "later." There is no cure for this but to exert to understand that mistake and distortion—that one who is saved by the Creator is saved only if he needs salvation today. One who can wait for tomorrow will obtain his understanding after his years, God forbid.

This happened to you due to negligence in my request to exert in love of friends, as I have explained to you in every possible way that this cure is enough to recompense for all your faults. And if you cannot rise to heaven, then I have given you moves on earth. So why have you not added anything in that work?

Besides the great remedy that lies within it, which I cannot interpret, you should know that there are many sparks of holiness in each one in the group. When you assemble all the sparks of holiness to one place, as brothers, with love and friendship, you will certainly have a very high level of holiness for a while, from the light of life, and I have already elaborated on that in all my letters to the friends.

I also asked that each one will show his letter to his friend, and so should you. Test me from this day forth to understand and to hear me, at least with what you can do, for then "The Lord will open to you His good treasure."

Tell ... that he should think for himself. What would he lose by corresponding with me? Why is he hiding himself from me? I do ask of him to make an effort to see the merits of the friends and not their faults at all, and connect in true love, together, until "Love will cover all crimes." Have him look in all the letters I send to the friends, so as to learn, "And let him eat no more the bread of idleness."

Where are ... and ... ? I have not heard a word from them so far. Do tell them to nevertheless hold on to their friends' gowns and read their letters as much as they need, and not to forget that the first question is, "Did you expect salvation?"

If they expect salvation, can it be that they will say, "Is this the work that the Creator wants from them?" And if I had to save the lives of one of them, of the friends, I would certainly toil and labor more than you, much less the life of the King, so to speak.

Therefore, give much dowry and gifts to the King of the world, and you will be rewarded with the King's daughter, and the salvation of the Lord is as the blink of an eye.

Yehuda

Letter No. 14

10 Shevat, Tav-Reish-Peh-Hey, January 25, 1926, Warsaw

To... may his candle burn:

... And scrutinize well in a thousand weekdays, for they are the paths of the river of knowledge. It is as Samuel said, "The paths of heaven are clear to me," in the state of Shabbat [Sabbath], as the paths of the river of knowledge, the weekdays. That is, "One who did not labor on the eve of Shabbat, from where will he eat on Shabbat?" Thus, all the lights of Shabbat are set up in lights that are gained during the weekdays. This is the meaning of "a thousand weekdays."

By this you can understand the verse, "Come to Pharaoh." It is the *Shechina* [Divinity] in disclosure, from the words, "and let the hair of the woman's head go loose," as it is written in *The Zohar*. The thing is that to the extent that the children of Israel thought that Egypt were enslaving them and impeding them from serving the Creator, they truly were in the exile in Egypt. Hence, the Redeemer's only work was to reveal to them that there is no other force involved here, that "I and not a messenger," for there is no other force but Him. This was indeed the light of redemption, as explained in the Passover *Haggadah* [story].

This is what the Creator gave to Moses in the verse, "Come to Pharaoh," meaning unite the truth, for the whole approaching the king of Egypt is only to Pharaoh, to disclose the *Shechina*. This is why He said, "For I have hardened his heart," etc., "that I may place these signs of Mine within him."

In spirituality, there are no letters, as I have already elaborated on before. All the multiplication in spirituality relies on the letters derived from the materiality of this world, as in, "And creator of darkness." There are no additions or initiations here, but the creation of darkness, the *Merkava* [chariot/structure] that is suited to disclose that the light is good. It follows that the Creator Himself hardened his heart. Why? Because it is letters that I need.

This is the meaning of "that I may place these signs of Mine within him, and that you may tell ... that you may know that I am the Lord." Explanation: Once you receive the letters, meaning when you understand that I gave and toiled for you, as in, do not move from "behind" Me, for you will thoroughly keep the *Achoraim* [posterior/back] for Me, for My name, then the abundance will do her thing and fill the letters. The qualities will become *Sefirot*, since before the filling they are called "qualities," and upon their fulfillment for the best, they are called *Sefirot*, sapphire, illuminating the world from one end to the other.

This is the meaning of "that you may tell." I need all this for the end of the matter, meaning "And you shall know that I am the Lord" "and not a messenger." This is the meaning of the fiftieth gate, which cannot appear unless the forty-nine faces of pure and impure appear in one opposite the other, in which the righteous falls [forty-nine in *Gematria*] before the wicked.

This is the meaning of the words, "Let not a wise man boast of his wisdom, and let not the mighty man boast of his might ... but let him who boasts boast of this, that he understands and knows Me." That is, as it is written, "There shall be no one miscarrying or barren in your land." Miscarrying or barren are the same thing, except "barren" means the deficiency and the letter itself, and "miscarrying" is the filling that the *Sitra Achra* [other side] gives to fill that deficiency, which is unsustainable, short-lived, and full of anger. At the time of correction, it becomes evident that that miscarrying becomes understanding, and the barren becomes "Know Me."

This is what the prophet instructs us: "Let not a wise man boast of his wisdom, or the mighty man of his might," since all the being and presence that a person feels in himself holds no spirit, neither for the upper ones nor for the lower ones. It is so because there are no innovations in any being or lights. This is the meaning of "maker of light," meaning that there is no innovation in the light but the making, when one can affect moves over the letters and disclose the shapes of the upper ones.

However, "and creator of darkness," for created means elicitation existence from absence, as Nachmanides wrote. There is no innovation here but darkness, like the ink for a book of Torah. By the exertion of the servant of the Creator to bring contentment to his Maker and to complement the Creator's will, the miscarrying and the barren appear. By accepting the burden of the kingdom of heaven to the fullest, which is the meaning of "this," he is rewarded with seeing the real forms of "maker of light," through questions and troubles. Then he is rewarded with boasting of the knowledge, and it is known that this is a true gain, praised and desirable in the initial thought.

By this we understand the verse, "And he said to them, 'May it be so, the Lord is with you' ... and He drove them out from Pharaoh's presence." The whole strengthening of Pharaoh, king of Egypt, was only in the "little ones" who did not know Joseph, who fed them with bread according to the "little ones." The "little ones" means abundance that is restricted at the time of *Katnut* [smallness/infancy], as our sages said, "Why do infants come? To give reward to they who bring them."

This is why he demonstrated his strength on the little ones and said, "See that evil is before your faces. Not so, go now, you who are men," since one should be thankful for the sparks of *Gevurot* [pl. of *Gevura*] in the work of the Creator, and which come through the Creator. But for the sparks of evil before your faces, it cannot be said that it comes from the Creator.

This is why he said, "For it is her that you seek," meaning that your whole intention is to enhance the sparks of *Gevura* and enhance the sparks of evil, and how can you unite the evil sparks with the Creator? By this they were driven out from Pharaoh's presence.

By this we will understand the plague of the locust, as was said, "And it covered the eye of the earth, etc., and ate that which remained." That is, because the Creator saw that all the gripping of the king of Egypt (until he expelled them) was in sorting the men and repelling the infants (as in, "for that is what you desire"), the plague robbed them of the quality of men, as well, and they lost all the sparks of *Gevura*, as well.

By this you will understand the verse of redemption: "This month is to you the beginning of the months." In Egypt, the month was called *Sivan*, as they said about Mount Sinai, that *Sinaa* [hatred] came down from there, like the hard labor in Egypt being called, in general, *Sivan*, like *Shanaan*, meaning *Sinaa Shelanu* [our hate], as in, "for it is her that you seek," and all their efforts were only to delete the letters because they hated them.

And by the light of redemption, when they were rewarded with *Alphey* [thousands of] *Shanaan*, that *Hidush* [initiation (sounding similar to *Hodesh*—month)] was made the very first. Then, instead of *Sivan*, the letters joined to form *Nissan*, meaning *Nissim she Imanu* [miracles that are with us]. This is what RASHI interpreted about this verse: "'This month' indicates that the Creator showed Moses the moon in its beginning," and the words are ancient.

Yehuda Leib

Letter No. 15

18 *Shevat, Tav-Reish-Peh-Hey*, February 2, 1926, Warsaw

To my friend ... may his candle burn forever.

A reply to your letter from the sixth day of [the portion] *Bo* [come], which I received along with your letter from the fourth day of [the portion] *BeShalach* [When Pharaoh Sent]: Concerning the argument, your last interpretation seems the most proper. But let me fill up your words a little: "I shall open the doors of my heart to a high guest," such as the promise to raise himself to the high guest, who is devoid of any attainments of the lower ones.

"The hooks of the pillars of glory shall pronounce," for in this manner of ascent, ever upward, the pillars of the heart connect in certain ties called "hooks," (as in, "You will connect in hooks") into a real *Dvekut* [adhesion], and then the upper light pours on him.

"I shall send free all my permitted ones," as though abandoning his entire fortune, meaning all that he has attained, since the permissions of the heart are the attainments of the body.

But he is not interested in sending them out free, so they will have the strength to cling to him in arguments. On the contrary, he will surely drive them out from his home, so they will have no contact or connection with him whatsoever.

To fully execute it comes the closing verse and says, "Let them announce on what were her foundations established." It is like a question that he asks the permitted ones. He argues and says, "Perhaps you have small or great foundations in the earth, or some pillars, foundations upon which some intellectual construction is supported?" By this he is telling them to announce if they know how to reply to him regarding the rhymes that extend onward, on which there is no human answer. By this he expels them, to announce that the earth hangs on nothing.

And regarding your letter from the fourth day of *BeShalach*, and what you wrote, that you do not understand my words, I am surprised. It must be that it is only due to idleness in the work, and what can I do? Especially now, receive this thing nonetheless, to have a steadfast bond of love among you, as I have cautioned you prior to my departure from you.

I have already written several letters about it, and my heart tells me that you will be slacking in this, for I sense negligence among you in general.

May the Creator have mercy on us and we will be rewarded with salvation soon...

Yehuda Leib

Letter No. 16

20 Shevat, Tav-Reish-Peh-Hey, February 4, 1926, Warsaw

To my soul mate, may his candle burn forever:

I received your letter yesterday and I enjoyed it because I saw that you want to do as I wish, after all. Regarding your first question, your words are very confused. It is a profound matter, and I am preoccupied now, but I will nevertheless elaborate a little on the matter; perhaps you will understand and accept it from now on.

I have already said in the name of the Baal Shem Tov that prior to making a *Mitzva* [commandment], one must not consider private Providence at all. On the contrary, one should say, "If I am not for me, who is for me?" But after the fact, one must reconsider and believe that it was not by "My power and the might of my hand" that I did the *Mitzva*, but only by the power of the Creator, who contemplated so about me in advance, and so I had to do.

It is likewise in worldly matters because spirituality and corporeality are equal. Therefore, before one goes out to make one's daily bread, he should remove his thoughts from private Providence and say, "If I am not for me, who is?" He should do all the tactics applied in corporeality to earn his living as do others.

But in the evening, when he returns home with his earnings, he must never think that he has earned this profit by his own innovations. Rather, even if he stayed all day in the basement of his home, he would still have earned his pay, for so the Creator contemplated for him in advance, and so it had to be.

Although the matters look the contrary on the surface, and are unreasonable, one must believe that so the Creator has determined for him in His law, from authors and from books.

This is the meaning of the unification of *HaVaYaH Elokim* [God]. *HaVaYaH* means private Providence, where the Creator is everything, and He does not need dwellers of material houses to help Him. *Elokim* in *Gematria* is *HaTeva* [the nature], where man behaves according to the nature that He instilled in the systems of the corporeal heaven and earth, and he keeps those rules as do the rest of the corporeal beings. And yet, he also believes in *HaVaYaH*, meaning in private Providence.

By this he unites them with one another, and "they became as one in his hand." In this way, he brings great contentment to his Maker and brings illumination in all the worlds.

This is the meaning of the three discernments—commandment, transgression, and permission. The commandment is the place of *Kedusha* [holiness], the transgression is the place of the *Sitra Achra* [other side], and permission, which is neither a *Mitzva* nor a transgression, is the place over which the *Kedusha* and the *Sitra Achra* fight.

When a person does permitted things but does not dedicate them to *Kedusha*, that entire place falls into the domain of the *Sitra Achra*. And when a person grows stronger and engages in permitted things to make unifications as much as he can, he returns the permission into the domain of *Kedusha*.

Thus, I have interpreted what our sages said, "It follows that the physician has been given permission to heal." That is, although the healing is certainly in the hands of the Creator, and human tactics will not move Him from His place, the Torah still informs us, "and shall cause him to be thoroughly healed," to let you know that it is permitted, that this is the place of the campaign between *Mitzva* and transgression.

It follows that we ourselves are obliged to conquer that "permission" under the *Kedusha*. But how is it conquered? When a person goes to an expert physician who prescribes him a medication that has been tried and tested a thousand times, and after he takes the medicine he is cured, he must believe that without the doctor, the Creator would still cure him, for his longevity has been preordained. Thus, instead of singing and praising the human doctor, he thanks and praises the Creator. By so doing, he conquers the permitted under the domain of *Kedusha*.

It is likewise in the rest of the matters of "permission." By this he expands the boundaries of *Kedusha* so that the *Kedusha* expands to its fullest measure, and he suddenly sees himself and his full stature standing and living in the palace of holiness. Indeed, the boundaries of *Kedusha* have so expanded that it reached his own place.

I have already explained all the above-said to you several times because this matter is an obstacle to several people who have no clear perception of private Providence, and "a slave feels comfortable with a life without a master." Instead of work, he prefers to trust, and desires even more to revoke the questions from his faith and acquire supernatural omens.

This is why they are punished and put themselves to death, for since the sin of *Adam HaRishon* onward, the Creator has devised a correction to this sin in the form of unification of *HaVaYaH* and *Elokim*, as I have explained.

This is the meaning of "By the sweat of your face you shall eat bread." It is human nature that what one obtains through one's own efforts, it is very hard for him to say that it is the Creator's gift. Thus, he has room for work, to exert in complete faith in private Providence, and decide that he would obtain all this even without his work. By this, that transgression is sweetened.

Therefore, once you knew and wrote that nature is a condition from the Creator, why do you settle once again for occasionally breaching the condition of "it came to pass" in favor of "it will come to pass"? One who breaches the Creator's terms will certainly fail because he does not unite *HaVaYaH* and *Elokim*, and "One who says, 'I will sin and repent,' is not permitted to repent."

Also, why the experiments when there are practical actions? I also understand how you come to think that there is no need to establish private Providence, and I have already warned you about it many times.

And what you wrote about the sentence, to regret the continuation of the flesh, it is certainly a must. If you are a strong man, throughout the day and always, you will not find stains during the examination. That is, you, too, helped a little to this completion.

It is all the more so at a time of anger, as well as during envy and feelings of pride and so forth. All these are stains that come from the creation of ideas that there are my power and the might of my hand in my possessions and property. However, it takes great craftsmanship to avoid falling into negligence in the work because of it, for he will not be able to vex the good inclination over the evil inclination and say, "If I am not for me, who is for me," etc., as it is written, "And the fool is boasting and confident." However, as I have written above in the name of the Baal Shem Tov, all the above are fixed, irrevocable laws; they are eternal.

We need to understand that His thoughts are not our thoughts. When it comes to the Creator, there is no issue of oppositeness in reality; it is all the evaluation of our five senses.

We should also understand that all the letters and the combinations are desired by us, but in the upper one, everything includes two forms—contentment and anger—which surround every incident in the world. Contentment includes rest and all its pleasures, and anger includes all the power of movement. Every ... and every movement ... renewal of creation, which is the meaning of "maker of light and creator of darkness"...

Yehuda Leib

Letter No. 17

6 Tevet, Tav-Reish-Peh-Vav, December 23, 1925

Dear...

... Yet, let me write to you with regard to the middle pillar in the work of God, so as to always be a target for you between right and left. This is because there is he who walks, who is worse than he who sits idly. It is he who deflects from the road, for the path of truth is a very thin line that one walks until one comes to the King's palace.

One who begins to walk in the beginning of the line needs great care so as not to deviate to the right or to the left of the line even as much as a hairsbreadth, for if at first the deviation is as a hairsbreadth, even if one continues completely straight, it is certain that he will no longer come to the King's palace, as he is not stepping on the true line, like this, for example:

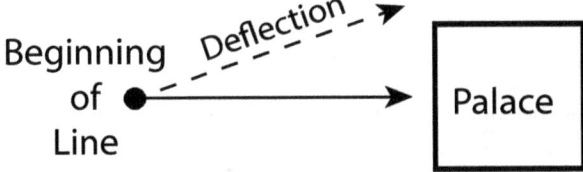

This is a true comparison.

Let me explain to you the meaning of the middle pillar, which is the meaning of "The Torah, the Creator, and Israel are one." The purpose of the soul when it comes in the body is to be rewarded with returning to its root and with *Dvekut* [adhesion] with Him while clothed in the body, as it is written, "To love the Lord your God, to walk in all His ways, to keep His commandments, and to adhere to Him." You see that the matter ends with "to adhere to Him," meaning as it was prior to clothing in the body.

However, great preparation is required, which is to walk in all His ways. Yet, who knows the ways of the Creator? Indeed, this is the meaning of "Torah that has 613 ways." He who walks on them will finally be purified until his body no longer forms an iron partition between him and his Maker, as it is written, "And I will take away the stony heart from your flesh." Then he shall adhere to his Maker just as he was before the clothing of the soul in the body.

It turns out that there are three discernments: 1) Israel is one who exerts to return to his root; 2) The Creator, namely the root he longs for; 3) The 613 ways of the Torah by which one purifies one's soul and body. This is the spice, as it is written, "I have created the evil inclination; I have created for it the Torah as a spice."

However, these three are actually one and the same. In the end, any servant of the Creator attains them as one, unique, and unified discernment, and they only appear to be divided into three because of one's incompleteness in the work of the Creator.

Let me clarify something to you: You shall see its tip, but not its entirety, except when He delivers you. It is known that the soul is a part of God above. Before it comes in a body, it is adhered as a branch to the root. See in the beginning of *Tree of Life*, that He created the worlds because He wanted to manifest His holy names, "Merciful" and "Gracious," etc., and if there are no creatures, there would be no one on which to have mercy. These words are very deep indeed.

However, as much as the pen permits, as "The whole Torah is the names of the Creator," as they said. The meaning of attainment is, "That which we do not attain, we do not define by a name." It is written in the books that all these names are the reward of the souls, which is compelled to come into the body, for it is precisely through the body that it can attain the names of the Creator.

Its stature is according to its attainment. There is a rule: The sustenance of any spiritual thing is according to the merit of knowing it. A corporeal animal feels itself because it consists of mind and matter.

Thus, a spiritual sensation is a known discernment, and the spiritual stature is measured by the value of what is known, as it is written, "One is praised according to one's mind." However, the animal knows; it does not feel at all.

Understand the reward of the souls: Before a soul comes into the body, it is a tiny dot, although it is attached to the root as a branch to a tree. This dot is called "the root of the soul and its world." Had it not entered into this world in a body, it would have had only its own world, meaning its own part in the root.

However, the more it is rewarded with walking in the ways of the Creator, which are the 613 ways of the Torah that return to being the actual names of the Creator, the more its stature grows according to the level of the names it has attained. This is the meaning of the words, "The Creator imparts each and every righteous 310 worlds."

Interpretation: The soul consists of two righteous: upper righteous, and lower righteous, as the body is divided from the *Tabur* [navel] up and from the *Tabur* down. Thus, it is rewarded with the written Torah and the oral Torah, which are two times 310, being 620 in *Gematria*. These are the 613 *Mitzvot* [commandments] of the Torah and the seven *Mitzvot de Rabanan* [of our great teachers].

It is written in *Tree of Life*, "The worlds were created only to disclose the names of the Creator." Thus, you see that since the soul came down to clothe this filthy substance, it could no longer adhere to its root, to its own world, as before it came to this world. Rather, it must increase its stature 620 times, as it previously was in the root. This is the meaning of the entire perfection, the entire *NRNHY* up to *Yechida*, for which *Yechida* is called *Keter*, implying the number 620 [*Keter* is 620 in *Gematria*].

Thus, you see that the meaning of the 620 names, being the 613 *Mitzvot* of the Torah and the seven *Mitzvot de Rabanan*, are, in fact, the five qualities of the soul, meaning NRNHY. This is because the *Kelim* [vessels] of the *NRNHY* are from the above 620 *Mitzvot*, and the lights of *NRNHY* are the very light of the Torah in each and every *Mitzva* [sing. of *Mitzvot*]. It follows, that the Torah and the soul are one.

However, the Creator is the light of *Ein Sof*, clothed in the light of the Torah, which is found in the above 620 *Mitzvot*. Understand that thoroughly, for this is the meaning of their words, "The whole Torah is the names of the Creator." It means that the Creator is the whole, and the 620 names are parts and items. These items are according to degrees and steps of the soul that does not acquire its light at once, but gradually, one at a time.

From all the above, you find that the soul is destined to acquire all 620 holy names, its entire stature, which is 620 more than it had before it came. Its stature appears in the 620 *Mitzvot* where the light of the Torah is clothed, and the Creator in the collective light of the Torah. Thus, you see that "the Torah, the Creator, and Israel" are indeed one.

Examine these words carefully, as they require only a simple explanation. It is about that that they said, "I shall not explain the literal," and you shall be happy if you understand what is before you.

Let us return to the issue that before the completeness in the work of the Creator, the Torah, the Creator, and Israel appear as three discernments. At times, one wishes to complete one's soul and return it to its root, which is considered Israel. At times, one wishes to perceive the ways of the Creator and the secrets of Torah, "for he who does not know the commandments of his Master, how will he serve Him?" This is considered Torah.

Sometimes one wishes to attain the Creator, meaning to adhere to Him with complete perception. One essentially regrets only this and does not agonize over attaining the secrets of the Torah. Also, he does not agonize over returning his soul to its origin, as it was prior to clothing in a body.

Hence, one who walks on the true line of preparing for the work of the Creator must always test himself to see if he wants the three above discernments completely equally, as the end of the act equalizes with its beginning. If one wants one of them more than the second or the third, then one strays from the path of truth.

Thus, you would better hold onto the goal of yearning for the commandment of the Master, for "He who does not know the ways of his Master and the commandments of his Master, which are the secrets of Torah, how will he serve Him?" Among all three, this is what guarantees the middle line most.

This is the meaning of "Open for me one aperture of repentance, such as the tip of a needle, and I will open for you gates where carts and coaches enter." Interpretation: The eye of the needle is not for entry and exit, but to insert the thread for sewing and for work.

Similarly, you are to crave only the commandment of your Master, to work, and then I will open for you a door such as an entry to a hall. This is the meaning of the explicit name in the verse, "But indeed (spelled like Hall in Hebrew) I live, and the glory of the Lord shall fill all the earth."

Yehuda Leib

Letter No. 18

Av, Tav-Reish-Peh-Vav, August 1926

To my soul mate, may his candle burn:

... However, keep away from suffering a man's jolt prematurely, for "Where one thinks is where one is." Therefore, when a person is certain that he will not lack abundance, he can focus his efforts on words of Torah because "the blessed adheres to the Blessed."

But lack of confidence behooves labor, and any labor is from the *Sitra Achra* [other side], and "The cursed does not adhere to the blessed," for he will not be able to focus all his efforts on words of Torah. And yet, if he wishes to travel overseas, he should not contemplate these things at all, but very quickly, as though the blink of an eye, and will return to normalcy, so as not to scatter his sparks in times and places that apart from this are still not sufficiently united.

Know that no flaw comes from the lower ones except in the permitted time and place, as it is now, meaning whether helpful or regretful, or God forbid despairs at the present moment, it is "rushing the end in all the times and in all the places in the world." This is the meaning of "a moment of His fury" and "How much is His fury? A moment."

Therefore, one has no choice but to direct all the present and future moments to be offered and presented to His great name. One who rejects a moment before him for it is difficult, displays his folly openly, for all the worlds and all the times are not worthwhile for him because the light of His face is not clothed in the changing times and occasions although one's work certainly changes because of them. This is why thanks to our holy fathers, faith and confidence above reason have been prepared for us, which one uses in the tougher times effortlessly and tirelessly.

This is the meaning of "By this comes lightly, ready for all His works on those six days." The letter *Hey*, which is the root of creation, is a light letter, and laboring to enhance its level does not help at all, for it is thrown, as in "no reason and no end." Therefore, one who assumes the complete burden of the kingdom of heaven finds no labor in the work of the Creator, and can therefore adhere to the Creator day and night, in light and in darkness. The *Geshem* [Heb: "rain," but also "corporeality"]—which is created in coming and going, changes and exchanges—will not stop him since the *Keter*, which is *Ein Sof*, illuminates to all completely equally. The fool—who walks under a flood of preventions that pour on him from before and from behind—says to all that he does not feel the deficiency of the cessation of *Dvekut* [adhesion] as a corruption or iniquity on his part.

Had he felt it, he would certainly have strained to find some tactic to at least be saved from the cessation of *Dvekut*, whether more or less. This tactic has never been denied of anyone who sought it, either as in "the thought of faith" or as in "confidence," or as in "pleas of his prayer," which are suitable for a person specifically in the narrow and pressured places, for even a thief in hiding calls on the Creator. For this reason, it does not require *Mochin de Gadlut* to keep the branch from being cut off from its root.

"If he does not do these three for her," she shall "go out" into the public domain under the enslavement of people, "free, without money," to this master, because he will not be given anything for his labor in idle things. It is as it is written, "They that make them shall be like them," etc., and what will one who was created by the worshipped—who bows to his own work—ask of them? Therefore, anyone who says he has preventions from above, I say about him that he lies in the name of his Maker. He maliciously pretends to be unable because he does not have the real desire to adhere to the Creator due to his strong ties to the *Ketarim* [pl. of *Keter*] of impurity. That is, he does not wish wholeheartedly to part from them forever.

This is the meaning of the words, "And you who have no money come, buy, and eat. Come, buy wine and milk without money and without cost." In other words, our only prayer to the Creator to give us of His wisdom and splendor is because He desires us to adorn ourselves before Him with these desires, as in, "Spirit draws spirit and brings spirit."

For example, because it is impolite to come before the king without some request ... but in truth, we have no business with the gift itself, but in being granted with *Dvekut* with Him, whether less or more.

Thus, a slave who wants to cling to the king out of the craving in his heart begins to practice royal manners and sets up for him some request. But the king rejects him. If he is clever, he will say to the king the sincerity of the point in his heart—that he desires no gifts, but for the king to assign him any service, the least of the least, in whatever way, as long as he is even slightly attached to the king in a connection that will not be stopped. Instantaneously, the king has revealed it to us in the form of *Dvekut* [adhesion], which is contemptible in the eyes of the lowly and its value is always according to the measure of desire of the point in the heart, meaning the prayer, faith, and confidence that he will never be wanting, even for a moment during the twenty-four hours of the day.

But the lowly—in their point in the heart—do not crave *Dvekut* with the King Himself, with the King's body, but with His numerous gifts, who distributes property and strength with wonderful delights, sparks flow from the bottom of the heart toward His immense gifts. For this reason, they find *Dvekut* with Him laborious, for what will they get out of it and other forms of "so what"?

Rather, "apples of gold..." for which anyone who understands will mock those worshippers whose heart is deficient, who say to all that they are fools because they say they have preventions.

But "The covenant of the fathers did not end," and "He who comes to purify is aided." First thing in the morning, when he rises from his sleep, he should sanctify the first moment with *Dvekut* with Him, pour out his heart to the Creator to keep him throughout the twenty-four hours of the day so that no idle thought will come into his mind, and he will not consider it impossible or above nature.

Indeed, it is the image of nature that makes an iron partition, and one should cancel nature's partitions that he feels. Rather, first he must believe that nature's partitions do not cut off from Him. Afterward, he should pray from the bottom of his heart, even for something that is above his natural desire.

Understand this always, even when forms that are not of *Kedusha* [holiness] traverse you, and they will instantly stop when you remember. See that you pour out your heart that henceforth the Creator will save you from cessations of *Dvekut* with Him. Gradually, your heart will grow accustomed to the Creator and will yearn to adhere to Him in truth, and the Lord's desire will succeed by you.

Yehuda Leib

Letter No. 19

1 *Tishrey, Tav-Reish-Peh-Zayin,* September 9, 1926, *Rosh Hashanah,* London

My dear soul mate and disciple, and all the friends.

I have received all your letters, and may they please the Almighty. However, "Know the God of your father and serve Him." "Know" means recognition, because a soul without knowledge is not good. This means that one who yearns and longs to serve Him, for he has a soul, but he does not know his Master, this is not good.

Even though one has a soul, he is not ready to know Him of his own "Until the spirit be poured upon him from on high." However, one must lend an ear and listen to the words of the sages and believe in them wholeheartedly.

It has already been written, "Only goodness and mercy shall follow me all the days of my life." As The Baal Shem Tov interprets "The Lord is your shade"—like the shade that follows man's movements, and its inclinations lean every way the person does, so is man according to the Creator. This means that when love for the Creator awakens, one must see that the Creator has awakened toward him with intense longing, etc. This is the meaning of the words of Rabbi Akiva: "Happy are you Israel—before whom you purify, and who purifies you."

Hence, in the beginning of one's nearing, he is given a soul in a manner of circles. This means that the Creator awakens toward him every time there is an opportunity on the part of man to cling to the man with longing and yearning. This is what the poet tells us, "Only goodness and mercy shall follow me all the days of my life." King David is the collective soul of the whole of Israel. Hence, he always longed, yearned, and craved true *Dvekut* [adhesion] with Him.

However, one must know in one's heart that the Creator chases him just as much as he chases the Creator. One must never forget that, even during the greatest longing. When remembering that the Creator misses and chases him to cling to him as intensely as one wishes for it himself, he then always goes from strength to strength, with yearning and longing, in a never-ending *Zivug* [coupling], the complete perfection of the soul, until he is rewarded with repentance from love, meaning the return of the *Vav* to the *Hey*, being the unification of the Creator with His *Shechina* [Divinity].

However, a soul without knowledge and recognition of his Master is in great decline when the longing increases to a certain extent, for it seems to him that the Creator dislikes him. Woe to that shame and disgrace; not only does he not complete his yearning and longing to be filled with eternal love, he is even in a state of "A whisperer separates from the champion," since he thinks that only he wishes and longs and yearns for the Creator. He does not believe our sages that to the very same extent the Creator wishes, longs, and yearns for him.

What are we to do to benefit those whose heart has not been fixed with faith in the sages? "From my flesh shall I see God," for I have already proven to you several times that the conducts of this world are *Otiot* [letters] that one must copy to their actual place in spirituality, for spirituality has no *Otiot*.

However, due to the breaking of the vessels, all the *Otiot* were ejected to corporeal conducts and people. When one corrects oneself and reaches one's root, he must collect them by himself, one by one, and bring them back to the root, to holiness. This is the meaning of "to sentence oneself and the entire world to the side of merit."

The matter of the unification of the Creator and His *Shechina* that one induces when he has had his fill of yearning and longing is precisely like the bottom *Zivug* applied in the birth of a corporeal body. It, too, extends necessarily by a prior cause, namely the hardening, which is a certain measure of longing and yearning called "hardness" in the corporeal language. Then, one's seed is also blessed, for it shoots like an arrow in *Nefesh* [soul], *Shanah* [year], *Olam* [world]. This is the meaning of "How is there repentance? In the same place, at the same time, and with the same woman, since the bottom *Hey* consists of *Nefesh*, *Shanah*, *Olam*.

Nefesh is the measure of the longing and the yearning. *Shanah* is the changing stimulations, as complete coitus bears the complete measure to restore past glory, meaning, as they were in *Dvekut* with their root before they separated in the corporeal world. However, one cannot be ready for this sublime *Zivug*, called "complete coitus," all at once. Rather, "Only goodness and mercy shall follow me," etc.

Hence, the stimulus, which is the beginning of the coitus, is the meaning of "a righteous who suffers." The Creator has no wish for his *Dvekut*, so he does not taste love in the longing and yearning that needs "the same thing," and "the same place." Thus, one is found in a state of sorrow, which is a *Nega* [affliction] that is destined to be sweetened into *Oneg* [delight (the words are spelled with the same letters in reverse order)].

However, "time will do what the mind does not do." The Creator counts all the stimuli and collects them into the complete measure, which is the measure of hardness for the intended day. This is what the poet means by "Awaken and sound to sever any shout." *Teki'a* [blowing (of a horn)] is the completion of the coitus, as it is said, "stuck in his brother's wife," which is the *Zivug* of the Creator and His *Shechina* [Divinity] from above downward before the soul clothed in incarnations of this world.

Afterward, when one prepares to return to his root, he does not induce the complete *Zivug* at one time, but creates stimuli, which is the degree of *Nefesh*, by way of cycles, chasing the *Shechina* with all his might, quivering and sweating, until he encircles that extremity all day and all night, incessantly.

It is as the books write concerning the cycles. While one's soul is being completed in the degrees of *Nefesh*, he comes ever closer, and so his yearning and sorrow grow since the unsatisfied desire leaves behind it a great affliction according to the measure of the desire.

This is the meaning of "sound." The poet teaches us and says, "Awaken," meaning that you induce stimuli in the *Shechina*. "Sound," for you cause a great affliction, like no other, which is the meaning of "he groaned and moaned" because "What does the *Shechina* say when one is afflicted?" etc. And why do you do so? It is in order to "sever any shout."

This is the meaning of "The righteousness of the righteous will not save him on the day of his transgression." To Him who knows the mysteries, the desire in one's heart for His nearness is known, and that it might still be interrupted. Hence, He increases His stimuli, meaning the beginnings of the coituses, for if one listens to His voice, as in "The Lord of your shade," one does not fall and descend due to the increasing affliction of the stimuli since he sees and hears that the *Shechina* also suffers as he does by the increased longing. Thus, one's longing grows and intensifies each time until one's point in the heart is completed with complete will in a tight knot that will not crumble.

Rabbi Shimon Bar-Yochai said about this in the Idra: "I am for my beloved and upon me His desire. All the days I was connected to this world, I was connected to the Creator with one knot, and because of it, now, upon me His desire, etc." That is, "Until He who knows the mysteries shall testify that he shall not return to folly." Hence, he is granted the return of the *Hey* to the *Vav* for eternity, meaning the complete coitus and the restoration of past glory, which is the meaning of "the great *Teki'a*."

All this is by the power and the virtue of the blowing, for they have severed any shout, and he shall not return to folly. Then one merits the complete consciousness in a never-ending *Zivug*, called "knowing," and he sees that all the many times of hardships that came to him were but "to know." This is the meaning of "at the same time," meaning "known to Him who knows the mysteries," that times have created that power in him, to remain in his righteousness forever.

"In the same place" is the restoration of past glory, as it was before its diminution, as you have heard from me several times, that the Creator does nothing new at the end of correction, as the fools think. Rather, "And you shall eat old store long kept," meaning until he says, "I want."

"In the same woman ..." "...Grace is deceitful and beauty is vain; but a woman that fears the Lord, she shall be praised." This means that during the preparation, beauty and grace appear as the essence of perfection for which one yearns and longs. However, at the time of correction, when the earth is "full of the knowledge of the Lord," "I shall see an opposite world," as only fear and longing are the desired perfection. Then one feels that during the time of preparation they were lying to themselves. This is the meaning of "a righteous who is happy," meaning the complete coitus for the one who is granted the great *Teki'a*. This is a complete righteous.

Show these words before the eyes of all the friends, and with this I shall bless you with writing and signing in the books of the righteous.

Yehuda Leib

My troubles are many, and I cannot let you know the greatness of my longing for you, but I am certain of the near redemption. Do not deny me your letters, at least one long letter every week. Believe me that while you write me, your answer will come right away.

I have not heard a thing from our friend ... and perhaps there is no need to those who fear Him? That, too, he should let me know. I miss hearing of him and of his household.

All the best, and God willing, we shall speak at length of goodly matters.

Yehuda

Letter No. 20

1 *Tishrey, Tav-Reish-Peh-Zayin*, September 9, 1926, Rosh Hashanah, London

To my soul mate and student ... may his candle burn:

... Why have you not informed me of the *Dvekut* [adhesion] of the friends, if it is going from strength to strength? This is the very basis of our good future and of your success in teaching.

I am not ashamed to admit that my troubles are so numerous that I have no energy to entertain you according to each and every one's wish, but you are engraved within my heart all day and all night. I burn with thirst for your well-being and wholeness, and the Creator knows how much I have labored and exerted on your behalf. We are certain that they will not be in vain, and the word of the Lord will stand forever.

But why have you forgotten the teaching that I said in the holiday of *Shavuot* [Feast of Weeks] about the verse, "My beloved is like a gazelle," concerning "turning the face back," that the face is built during the escape and hiding, but in the form of *Achoraim* [back/posterior], which is the measure of sorrow over the distance and concealment? But in truth, these *Achoraim* are actually *Panim* [face/anterior], as our sages said, "turning the face back," so the face is in the back. This is the meaning of

"I, the Lord, do not change; and you, sons of Jacob, are not consumed," meaning as it is written, "They who seek Me shall find Me."

I wrote you the intention of the blowing [of the *Shofar*], to know why they blow and trumpet standing up ... "For the day is holy to our Lord." Although I know that my words will not reach you while you are hearing the sound of the *Shofar*, but it is written, "Before they hear, I will answer," which is why I wrote in its time.

You, too, show my letter to all the friends and perhaps they will lend an ear to my words.

... From this day forward let us grow strong in Torah and *Mitzvot* [commandments] "as an ox to the burden and as a donkey to the load," to raise the *Shechina* [Divinity] from the dust, "arising contempt and wrath," and the sins will become merits because His glory will fill the whole of the earth.

God willing, I am certain that our salvation is near and we will be rewarded with serving the Creator together abundantly, and the Lord's wish will succeed by us.

Yehuda Leib

Letter No. 21

16 *Heshvan, Tav-Reish-Peh-Zayin*, October 24, 1926, London

To my soul mate ... may his candle burn forever:

I received your letter from the thirteenth of *Tishrey* [the first Hebrew month]. What you write me about, "I recognize how much I need external mortifications to correct my externality," thus far your words, I say that you neither need mortifications nor to correct the externality. Who taught you this new law? It must be that you are not as attached to me as before, and are therefore learning other ways.

Know that you have no other trusted friend in your whole life, and I advise you not to correct your externality at all, but only your internality, for only your internality is destined to be corrected. And the main reason why the internality is corrupted due to the proliferation of sins is the filth, whose sign is pride and self-importance. That filth fears no mortification in the world. On the contrary, it relishes them because the self-importance and pride increase and strengthen by the mortification.

But if you do wish to cleanse the sins off you, you should engage in annulment of self-importance instead of the mortifications, meaning to feel that you are the lowest and the worst of all the people in the world. It requires much learning and education to understand this, and each time you should test yourself to see if you are not fooling and deceiving yourself. It also helps to lower yourself before your friend in practice.

However, you should be mindful that you lower yourself only before the right people. So if you wish to engage in it in practice, you can annul yourself before our group, and not before strangers, God forbid. However, you must know for certain that you are the worst and the lowest of all the people in the world, as this is the truth.

Indeed, my advice is straightforward and easy, and even a weak person can keep it to the fullest, for it does not wear out the strength of the body, and it is the complete purity. Although I have not spoken to you about it, it was because you did not need it so, since while you were with me in the same place, you would gradually recognize your lowliness anyway, without any learning or actions. But now that you are not with me in my place, you must engage in annulment of the self-importance in the manner just mentioned.

And the most important is to pray extensively and strengthen the confidence that the Creator will help you succeed in meriting complete repentance, and to know how to adhere to Him in one connection for eternity. This is the most important, and this is what distinguishes one who serves the Creator from one who does not serve Him. "Do not rest, and give Him no rest" until He forgives all your sins and crimes and brings you close to Him forever and for all eternity.

You should also cling to me in a way that the location does not separate us. Our sages said, "Cling to one who has been anointed and you yourself will be anointed." This is an important principle in the teaching of the Baal Shem Tov, to mate with the righteous, may you be wise enough to understand it.

Believe me that on my part there are no preventions or heaviness. If I knew that there was more that I could do in your favor while being with you in the Land of Israel, I would certainly not leave you. But in truth, my journeying from you was also precisely for your sake.

Yehuda Leib, son of my teacher and Rabbi, Simcha Ashlag

Letter No. 22

16 *Heshvan*, Tav-Reish-Peh-Zayin, October 24, 1926, London

To my soul mate ... may his candle burn:

I received your letter from the fourteenth of *Tishrey* [first month in the Hebrew calendar]. But my friend, why are you not pleased with the first order that I have set up for you, and you are asking for new ones? I have already told you that as long as you are not accustomed to the first order, you are not permitted to make for yourself other orders, neither easy nor strict. But here you are, pretending to forget, and you are knocking on my door seeking new orders. It must be the inciting of the inclination.

I must remind you of the first order I have given you, and may the Creator help you have no breaks with His work going forward, and only ascents ever upward until you are rewarded with *Dvekut* [adhesion] with Him, as it should be:

1. Be prepared for His work, approximately two hours after midnight, and no later (meaning from the eighth hour after *Arvit* [evening service]).

2. On the first two hours, engage in "midnight *Tikkun* [correction]," afflict yourself about the exile of Israel and the affliction of the *Shechina* [Divinity] due to their iniquities, and then prayers and litanies until the tenth hour.

3. From the tenth hour until the prayer is the time of delving in the holy books, *Beresheet Hochma*, and the like, and in the writings of the ARI. See that you thoroughly understand and internalize everything you learn. If you do not fully understand, give the Creator no rest until He opens your heart and you understand Him, for this is the most important—that the Creator gives wisdom.

4. Set times for Torah, without any cessation for idle conversations, God forbid. See that you dedicate no less than five consecutive hours. You can set them for whatever time you wish during the day, as long as you do not stop for any conversation in between, they are consecutive, and specifically in the study of the revealed. Be careful not to forget anything from the study, so repeat the learning as you should. Also, it would be good for you to learn to be a teacher; it will be very helpful for you.

Also, you can study in a group with whomever you want during those five hours, but do not speak of things that do not concern the study, not even of manners of worship. If the partner wishes to study only two or three hours, you can finish afterward by yourself until you complete the five hours. In the rest of the day, succeed in negotiations.

Thus, you have what is yours, now hurry yourself and take the Creator with you, so you will succeed in behaving as I have written for you, and the words of Rashbi in *Idra Zuta* will come true in you: "'I am for my beloved,' etc., all the days when I was tied to this world, I was tied to it in one connection, in the Creator. For this reason, now upon me is 'His passion.'"

After a few months, when you have grown thoroughly accustomed to this order, let me know and I will add to you in the ways of the Creator.

In truth, I am not far from you at all, for it is all up to you, since time or place does not pose any hindrance in spirituality. Why do you not remember what I said on the festival of *Shavuot* [Feast of Weeks] about the verse, "My beloved is like a gazelle"? Our sages said, "As the gazelle turns his face back when he flees, when the Creator leaves Israel, He turns back His face." I interpreted for you that then the face returns to being in the *Achoraim* [back/posterior], meaning craving and longing to cling to Israel once more. This begets in Israel longing and craving to adhere to the Creator, too, and the measure of the longing and craving is actually the face itself, as it is written in "Bless My Soul," by Rabbi Yehuda HaLevi, "My face is to your prayer when you run to meet the Lord God."

Therefore, the most powerful at this time is only to persist and increase the longing and the yearning, for by this appears the face, Amen, may it be so.

Send me many letters, and this will be encouraging to you, as well.

Yehuda Leib, son of my teacher and Rabbi, Simcha Ashlag

Letter No. 23

16 *Heshvan*, *Tav-Reish-Peh-Zayin*, October 24, 1926, London

To my soul mate ... may his candle burn forever:

... Concerning the comparison of your matter to the cascading of the worlds, of which your friends do not approve, it is because they learned from me that first you need to understand the upper worlds, for so is the order—from above downward first, then from below upward. It is so because a corporeal eye can give birth only to corporeality, and wherever he looks, he only materializes. Conversely, from a spiritual eye emerge only spiritual images, and any place he looks at is blessed.

Even the corporeal images, when we sense their origin, return to being truly spiritual, not by comparison or similarity, but rather truly inverted into complete spirituality, as it is written, "It is changed as the material of the seal, and will be fashioned as a garment."

What you are asking of me, to teach you the matter of unifications because you were not rewarded with receiving them from authors, I wonder, how will you receive them from books?

I saw your allegories and poetic phrases that begin, "I shall carry my adages and say, 'Words that are gauged by the *Omer* [count].'" Indeed, you gauge your words with the *Omer*, but exert further to bless the blessing of the *Omer*, for "an *Omer* is the tenth part of an *Ephah* [measuring unit, as well as "where"]." *Ephah* means great bewilderment, as you write, "*Ephah* [written like "where" in Hebrew] is the right [just] side, and *Asirit* [one tenth] comes from the word *Asurot* [forbidden]," for there is a mother to the tradition, and there is a mother to the Pentateuch, as in, "The king is held captive by your tresses."

That measure indicates that through faith and confidence, the heart's bewilderment is forbidden, too, meaning that not even a trace of bewilderment remains. This is the measure of the *Omer*. And yet, we should bless, and this I did not find in your letter.

It is said, "The greedy man curses and spurns the Lord." That is, a prayer does half, and anyone who prays for himself is incomplete, but halved, for the whole one has nothing to pray for. This is why our sages warned us not to work in order to receive reward, but for wholeness. This is a sublime secret, and only those who have no awakening for themselves will understand it.

This is why our sages said, "The host slices and the guest blesses," meaning that one must not lie to himself that the landlord is giving him wholeness. Rather, he must feel the truth as it is, in utter precision. This is why it was said, "The host slices," yet the guest must bless.

"Guest" comes from the words, "and smelled in the fear of the Lord." And because he receives what the host gives him at the cutting, as though it was complete, he is blessing anyway. And the measure of his blessing is as the measure of his joy with the gift, which is possible for him only through "His delight shall be in the fear of the Lord."

This is what our sages said, "If he stole a measure of wheat, ground it, kneaded it, baked it, and separated it, how will he bless? He does not bless, but curses." This is very deep, for one who steals does not thank the robbed one because the robbed one did not give him anything. Rather, he took from him by force, against his will.

The cutting and the reward that a person deserves all stem from the first iniquity, since "a transgression leads to a transgression." "In the beginning it is as a cobweb, and in the end it is as cart-ropes." Everything follows the beginning.

And yet, although he believes that all the deficiencies and cuts were done by the Creator, he still cannot think so about the first iniquity, as it is certain that harm will not come from the upper one. It follows that he truly is a thief, as though he snatched from the Creator against His will.

"The tree of knowledge was wheat," as it is written, "One who robs a measure of wheat." *Se'ah* [measure] is as "In *Se'ahse'ah* [full measure], when You send her away, You will contend with her." Wheat is the first iniquity. Therefore, although "she ground it and baked it"—meaning they became cart-ropes, and then he separated the *Challah* [braided bread for Shabbat] from it, from the word *Hulin* [secular], "It is entirely for the Creator," implying the exaltedness and separation above reason—he is not blessing but curing, as it is a *Mitzva* [commandment] that comes through transgression. For were it not for the first iniquity, this great *Mitzva* would not have happened.

All this is because he is a thief, and does not see that a righteous pardons and gives; hence, he does not bless wholeheartedly and does not make repentance from love, for then sins would become to him as merits. He would recognize that the measure of wheat is the Creator's gift, and not his own power and the might of his hand.

This is why our sages said, "The host slices," and not "the guest," meaning the measure of wheat is also the Creator's gift, to "keep His covenant and to remember His commandments to do them." When the guest grows strong and believes that everything that all the host has troubled Himself with was only for him, he blesses Him wholeheartedly. It turns out that that cutting is itself truly a whole thing, after the blessing of the Creator from above downward.

But first, he must gain strength in his fountain of blessings from below upward. That is, he is called "a guest," for he can gain strength and exert by the scent, as it is written, "and smelled in the fear of the Lord," and as it is written, "One who steals from his father and mother and says, 'it is not a crime,' is a friend to a destroyer." In other words, the first iniquity is rooted in his body because of his father and mother; hence, the person became a thief by saying that he is as above-mentioned, and it is not the gift of the Creator. This is why he is regarded as stealing from his father and mother, and then adding sin to crime because he says, "There is no crime." That is, he grows fond of the Mitzva of destroying, God forbid.

This is the meaning of the blessing of the Omer, that one must feel the Creator's gift even in the measure of wheat, meaning by the scent. At that time, his joy is whole in all his work, and by this the reward becomes whole again, and "The Lord knows the way of the righteous."

Yehuda Leib, son of my teacher and Rabbi Simcha, may his candle burn

Letter No. 24

16 *Heshvan, Tav-Reish-Peh-Zayin*, October 24, 1926, London

To my soul mate ... may his candle burn:

I received your letter from the fourteenth of *Tishrey* [first Hebrew month] and I thoroughly enjoyed it. I commend you on your efforts in adhesion of friends, and may the Creator also give you the complete intention.

Please, my friend, do strengthen in the study of Torah, both revealed and concealed, for all you lack is strengthening in the burden of Torah, for the evil inclination resides only in a heart vacant from wisdom.

Also, be very careful from idleness because "For indolence, the roof leaks," and it is the hardest *Klipa* [shell/peel] in the world. It is all according to the number of actions: The sign of the idle is sadness, and the sign of the nimble is joy.

If it is not too difficult, I would advise you to learn to become a teacher, as it is good for the soul. But most important, pray and trust the Creator with everything you want to do, and it will help you accomplish successfully.

You already know that prayer and confidence go hand in hand. We must believe in complete faith that the Creator hears the prayer of every mouth, especially concerning the *Shechina* [Divinity]. With this faith we acquire confidence, and then his prayer is complete, with confidence that he will be saved, and he is rewarded with confidence and joy all day, as though he has already been saved.

Remember what I told you—during the first hour after rising, break your heart and engage in "midnight *Tikkun* [correction]" by thought. Afflict yourself in the affliction of the *Shechina*, who is suffering because of your actions. However, do not prolong for more than one hour. Afterward, promptly raise your heart in the ways of the Creator, with faith and confidence in wholeness, and engage joyfully in Torah and work all day long. If you wish, you may engage in breaking the heart for half an hour before going to sleep, as well.

However, beware the tricks of the inclination, which wants specifically to sadden us while we engage in the work of the Creator. At such a time, we tell the evil inclination, "Although you are right, wait, for I have a set time for it. Then I will think about it, and not while standing before the King." This is why the priest had special garments for fertilizing the altar, and special garments for doing the work.

If you are mindful of these words of mine, you will be rewarded with bringing yourself close to *Dvekut* [adhesion] with Him, and you will succeed in doing the Creator's will.

Yehuda Leib, son of my teacher and Rabbi, Simcha Ashlag

Letter No. 25

14 *Kislev, Tav-Reish-Peh-Zayin*, November 20, 1926, London

To my soul mate, may his candle burn forever:

... What you wrote, that you do not understand the innovations in the Torah that I wrote to you, they should have been clear to you. When you straighten out the way you work, you will understand them for certain. This is why I wrote them to you.

You explained regarding "sins becoming as merits to him," that when one repents before the Creator, he evidently sees that the Creator forced him into his iniquities, and yet he willingly gives his soul to correct them as though they were his own iniquities. By this, the sins become as merits. But that still does not hit the target, as in the end you turn coercions into merits but not sins.

You also strayed further from the way by interpreting the sin of *Adam HaRishon*, condemning his soul to forced exile, and making the coercion a mistake. And what you explained, that it makes no difference whether the baby makes himself dirty or is made so by his father's deeds, for in the end he is dirty and must wash, I wonder, how did dirt come out of purity?

Your last words are sincere, that because you went into a place that is not yours, and due to your habit to cloak yourself with clothes that are not your own, you did not understand my words, which are aiming precisely and only for you. I wish these words were enough for you to stop wandering in vineyards that are not your own, as it is written in *The Zohar*, "One must not look where he should not."

Regarding what you wrote—that I seem to speak in riddles—it is written, "The needs of Your people, Israel, are many." There is no time that is like another, much less those who go from door to door, to and fro, but the doors won't open. There is no end to the changes in their states. While I write words of Torah, or verbally, I say them so they will furnish for at least a few months, so they will be understood in the good times over time. But what can I do if the good times are few, or the broken is more than the corrected and my words are forgotten?

Of course, the human intellectual mind will not examine my words at all, for they are said and are constructed from the letters of the heart.

And concerning your imagination that you entered and did not know how to come out because you grew tired of examining the matter, I will tell you that in general, one who repents from love is rewarded with complete *Dvekut* [adhesion], meaning the highest degree, and one who is ready for sins is in the netherworld. These are the farthest two points in this entire reality.

It would seem that we should be meticulous with the word "repentance," which should have been called "wholeness," except it is to show that everything is preordained, and each and every soul is already established in all its light, goodness, and eternity. But for the bread of shame, the soul went out in restrictions until it clothed in the murky body, and only through it does it return to its root prior to the *Tzimtzum* [restriction], with its reward in its hand from all the terrible move it had made. The overall reward is the real *Dvekut*, meaning that she [the soul] got rid of the bread of shame because her vessel of reception has become a vessel of bestowal and her form is equal to her Maker, and I have often spoken to you about that.

By this you will see that if the descent is for the purpose of ascending, it is regarded as an ascent and not as a descent. Indeed, the descent itself is the ascent as the letters of the prayer themselves are filled with abundance, and with a short prayer, the abundance is small for lack of letters. Our sages said, "Had Israel not sinned, only the Five Books of Moses and the book of Joshua would have been given to them."

What is this like? It is like a rich man who had a young son. One day, the rich man had to travel far away for many years. The rich man feared that his son would waste his wealth by poor judgment, so he exchanged his properties for gemstones, jewels, and gold, and built a cellar deep in the ground where he hid all the gold, gemstones, and jewels. But he also put his son in there.

He summoned his loyal servants and ordered them to keep his son from leaving the cellar until his twentieth birthday. Each day they were to bring down to him every food and drink, but absolutely no fire or candles. They were also to check the walls and seal every crack so that no sunlight would penetrate. For his health, they were to take him out of the cellar each day for one hour and walk him through the city, but carefully watching that he does not run away. On his twentieth birthday, they were to give him candles, open a window for him, and let him out.

Naturally, the son's affliction was intolerable, especially when he would walk outside and see all the boys eating and drinking merrily on the street, without any guards or time limits, while he was imprisoned with few moments of light. And if he tried to run, he would be beaten mercilessly.

But he was most upset when he heard that his own father had caused him this affliction, for they were his father's servants, carrying out his father's orders. Naturally, he deemed his father the cruelest of all the cruel that ever lived, for who has heard of such a thing?

On his twentieth birthday, the servants lowered down to him a candle, as his father had commanded. The boy took the candle and began to look around. And lo and behold, what did he see? Sacks filled with gold and every royal delight.

Only then did he understand that his father is truly merciful, and that all his trouble was only for his own good. He immediately understood that the servants would certainly let him out of the cellar, and so he did. He came out of the cellar, and there was no guarding, no cruel servants. Instead, he is a noble man, wealthier than the wealthiest people in the land.

But in truth, there is nothing new here, for it becomes revealed that he was so very wealthy to begin with, but in his perception he was poor and destitute, oppressed in the pit all his days. Now, in a single moment, he has gained tremendous riches and rose from the deep pit to the top of the roof.

Who can understand this allegory? One who understands that the "sins" are the deep cellar with the careful watch not to let one out. I wonder if you understand it.

It is simple: The cellar and the careful watch are all "privileges" and the father's mercy over the son. Without it, it would have been impossible for him to be as wealthy as his father. But the "sins" are actual sins and not mistakes. There is no coercion from above. Rather, before he regained his wealth, that feeling dominated in the full sense of the word. But once he has regained his wealth, he saw that all these were a father's mercies and not at all cruelty.

We must understand that the entire connection of love between the father and his only son depends on the recognition of the father's compassion for the son regarding the cellar and the darkness and the careful watch, for the son sees in these mercies of the father a great exertion and profound wisdom.

The Zohar also spoke about it, saying that one who is rewarded with repentance, the *Shechina* [Divinity] appears to him like a soft-hearted mother who has not seen her son for many days, and they made great efforts and experienced ordeals in order to see each other, because of which they both were in great dangers. But in the end, they came to that longed-for freedom and were rewarded with seeing one another. Then the mother fell on him, kissed him, comforted him, and spoke softly to him all day and all night. She told him of the longing and the dangers on the roads she has experienced until today, how she had always been with him, and that the *Shechina* never moved, but suffered with him in all the places, but he could not see it.

These are the words of *The Zohar*: "She says to him, 'Here we slept; here we were attacked by robbers and were saved from them; here we hid in a deep pit,' and so forth. What fool would not understand the great love and pleasantness and delight that burst from these comforting stories?"

In truth, before we met face to face it felt as suffering that is harder than death. But as the word *Nega* [affliction] is because the *Ayin* [the letter] comes at the end of the word, but during the telling of comfort-stories, the *Ayin* is in the beginning of the word, making it *Oneg* [delight/pleasure]. However, they are two points that illuminate only once they are in the same world. Now imagine a father and son who have been anxiously waiting for each other for days and years. When they finally see each other, the son is deaf and mute, and they cannot enjoy one another at all. It follows that the essence of the love is in royal delights.

Yehuda Leib

Letter No. 26

Kislev, Tav-Reish-Peh-Zayin, November-December, 1926, London

To my soul mate ... may his candle burn forever:

I received your last letter, from the fifth of *Kislev* [Hebrew month, roughly December], and regarding your surprise at the scarcity of my letters, I will tell you that I have many troubles, and I pray to the Creator to see me through.

I am surprised that you did not interpret the letters I sent to our friend regarding "The host slices and the guest blesses," as he wrote me that he did not understand it. It seems as though you have grown tired of longing to merit the burden of Torah and *Mitzvot* [commandments] due to the ravages of time.

And what can I tell you from afar, when you cannot hear my voice or my words, but only stare at dry, lifeless letters until a living spirit is blown into them? This requires effort, and in your opinion, effort requires time.

It is written, "A golden bell and a pomegranate, a golden bell and a pomegranate all around the edges of the robe. ... and its sound is heard when he enters the holy place."

The *Ephod* [vest] comes from the words *Ei Po Delet* [where is the door], since the *Delet* [door] is in the place of the opening when it is closed. In corporeality, you can see the door just as you can see the opening. But in spirituality, you see only the opening. But you cannot see the opening unless with complete and pure faith. Then you see the door, and at that moment it turns into an opening because He is one and His name is "One."

That power, to heed the word of the sages in this reality in *Dalet*, is called "faith," as it is not established at once, but through education, adaptation, and through work. It is similar to the tutoring of a child, who would be like an unturned stone were it not for the tutor who rears him. This is why this work is generally called "a robe," as it is an overcoat, "beyond" human conception, and in which there is a combination, as in the edges of the *Kli*, which is the place where the yeast and the filth are collected.

During the training period, he is in a state of "to and fro," as are all those who seek the opening. And in the last moment of the march, when he is close to the opening, then, of all times, he grows weary and turns back. That march is called *Zahav* [gold], from the words *Ze Hav* [give this], as it is written in *The Zohar*, that the walking is done through the craving and the longing for *Dvekut* [adhesion] with Him, and he longs and sings, *Ze Hav, Ze Hav*.

He is also called "a bell" because he does not have the strength to open and he turns back, thus spending his time going to and fro time after time, looking for the opening. Also, he is called *Rimon* [pomegranate] because the *Romemut* [exaltedness] of the above-the-intellect surrounds him from all sides. Hence, *again* he is called *Rimon*, for otherwise he would fall entirely.

In time, great filth and great trembling assemble "all around the edges of the robe," both in the form of the bell and in the form of a *Rimon* (which gathers) around the *Ei Po Delet* [where is the door], which has no edge...

But why did the Creator do so to His creations? It is because He must make the voice for the words, for the "mouth of God" [spelled the same as *Po Delet*] to appear when he comes to the holy place, as it is written, "His voice is heard when he enters the holy place."

Go out and learn from the letters of this world, that there is a sound only in trembling, as is sensed in the strings of a violin. Due to the tension of the strings, there is trembling in the air, which is the sound, and nothing else. Likewise, each human ear contains a kind of twist in the ear that physicians call "a drum." When another person's mouth strikes the air, the beaten sparks of air reach the person's ear, push it, and thereby strike the drum in the ear. The drum trembles differently from each strike, and this is the entire merit of the chosen creature, the speaking species. Because of it, "all things [are] under his feet."

This is the meaning of "rejoice with trembling." Our sages said, "Where there is joy, there shall be trembling." It is abstruse phrasing, for they should have said succinctly, "Joy and trembling will be together."

However, this tells us that the joy has no place without trembling. It is as they said—that where there should be joy and gladness, there is trembling, which is the place of joy.

You can also try it with a clapper [metal striker inside a bell] that is tingling on the iron of a bowl, thus making a sound. If you place your hand on the bowl, the sound will stop at once since the sound emerging from the bowl is the trembling of the bowl, and by striking with the clapper and placing your hand, you strengthen the bowl and reduce the trembling, hence the sound stops.

Thus, you see the sounds—that the sound and the trembling are one and the same. Yet, not all sounds are fit for pleasantness, which is in the quality of the prior form, meaning the trembling. For example, the sound of thunder frightens and is unpleasant to the human ear as the trembling occupies a large amount of the striking force, as well as lasts too long. Even if the striking force were less, it would still be unpleasant to the ear because it is too long.

Conversely, the sound of a violin is pleasant to the listener's ear as it is proportional to the force that strikes, and is precisely proportional to the length of time. One who prolongs the time even a fraction of a minute will spoil the pleasantness.

It is all the more so with understanding the sounds for the word of God. It is precious and clearly requires great precision in the force of the strike, divided into seven degrees. It is even more so with the time, to not spoil even a fraction of a minute, for there is pride there, as it is written, "You put my feet in stocks." Then you will know that all the angels rise in song, and in a place of joy there was trembling first.

Hence, not all trembling is good, but one who is anxious [the same word as trembles in Hebrew] for the word of God collects all the trembling to a place and rushes the joy. This is the meaning of "Let the water gather ... in one place," and not otherwise, God forbid.

Our sages said, "A violin was hanging over David's bed. When the midnight hour came, a northern wind came and blew it, and it would play by itself." One who trembles for the word of God, the trembling comes instead of the northern wind, meaning as the *Rimon* [pomegranate]. By that, "the host slices."

The night divides, as in "A prayer makes half." This is why he is lying in bed, which is the meaning of "He will never allow the righteous to fall." It is as it is written about, "And he lay down in that place." They explained, "There are *Chaf-Bet* [twenty-two] letters, which is a *Chaf* [also a spoon] that holds *Bet* [two] letters—the two farthest points in the reality before us, as I have elaborated in my letter.

Over his bed is the *Rimon*, as said above. And when the point below appears, the Creator goes out to stroll with the righteous in the Garden of Eden because the door is open and the *Shechina* [Divinity] says all her songs and praises. This is why David's violin plays by itself, without any composition except for the trembling of the northern wind.

And if matters are still unclear, go and study the alphabet—that the *Bet*, with which the world was created, lacked nothing but the *Aleph* of *Anochi* [I]. This is its crack in the northern wind of the *Bet*. This is why "Out of the north the evil will break forth," which is a big breach.

Therefore, "Out of the north comes golden splendor." It begins with bells, and when the two letters unite, the mouth of the Creator appears. This is why the anxieties must be collected in one place, to tremble only over the word of the Creator, and then one prepares "a golden bell and a pomegranate, all around the edges of the robe."

In this way, the whole will slowly become more than the broken, and will smell in the fear of God, and will feel that "All that the landlord has troubled Himself with, He has troubled Himself only for me." He will know and see seven parts of the wind trembling, meaning that in addition to the wind of the fear of the Creator there are six more winds hovering over the Creator's Messiah, as it is written, "And the spirit shall rest on him ... the spirit of wisdom and understanding ..."

Our sages said about the likes of it, "The host slices." That is, although the host slices, the guest blesses on the slice as though on a whole one. It is said about one who does not do so, "Robbers shall enter it and profane it," as it is written, "Will he even take the queen with me in the house," to come there with crassness, with more that is broken than is whole, arousing contempt and wrath.

This is the meaning of the chopped *Vav* [*Vav-Yod-Vav*] of Pinhas' *Shalom* [peace, farewell], as it stands with much that is broken before him, and the plague stopped. By his *Kedusha* [holiness], he made the standing more than the broken and the people reunited with Moses. His reward was that the Creator said to Moses, "And ... the covenant of everlasting priesthood," for eternity, as it is written in *The Zohar*.

This clarifies to Abraham the "this memorial" of his, which is there, so that one will not regard the details of the matters in which he is caught up, as this is the counsel of the inclination and the *Sitra Achra* [other side], but only in general, as I have sufficiently explained here. This is the meaning of "All of man's works should be only with the aim to raise the *Shechina* from the dust, from which the primordial serpent feeds."

And what can I do to those who vow and lean toward the view of the masses, and suffice for the halved comfort they receive through them, as people say, "Trouble shared, trouble halved"? This is why they work and settle, to receive reward. But if their ways rose once and for all above ten feet, they would see the door because it is a wide open opening. Then there would no longer be two opposites in the same place and at the same time, as it is above the *Yod* [ten].

... It is written, "Though He scoffs at the scoffers, and He gives grace to the poor" (Proverbs 3:34). I shall start with an allegory, and perhaps you will understand: A great, benevolent king wished only to delight his countryfolk, since he did not need any work to be done for him. Rather, his only wish was to benefit his countryfolk.

However, he knew that there are levels in the recipients of his benefit—to the extent of their love for him and the measure of recognition of the value of his exaltedness. He wished to delight abundantly, especially the worthy ones among his countryfolk, so the rest of the people would see that the king does not deny reward from those who love him dearly. Rather, in his goodness, he showers them with abundant delights that he has prepared for them. And in addition to the pleasures that he showers abundantly upon them, they have a special treat—they feel that they are the chosen ones from among the people. This, too, he wished to give to those who love him.

To keep from the people's complaint, lest they lie or mislead themselves, as well, saying that they, too, are among the king's lovers, and still their reward is denied. And because of the king's wholeness, he kept himself from that, as well, and therefore devised tactics to execute his plans in full.

Finally, he found a wonderful tactic: He sent out a decree to all the people in the country, none excluded, to come to work a full year for the king. He dedicated a place in his palace for that purpose and conditioned explicitly that it is forbidden to work outside the designated area, for it is abomination, and the king will not be pleased with it.

Their reward is in the place where they work. He prepared for them great feasts and every delicacy in the world whenever they wished. At the end of the year's work, he will take all of them to the king's own table, and they will be among those who see his face, the most eminent in the kingdom.

The proclamation went out, and every single one came to the king's city, which is surrounded by guards and a wall. They closed themselves in there for the year, and the work began.

They thought the king had prepared watchmen to oversee their work, to know who served him and who did not. But the king hid, and there was no supervision. Everyone did as he saw fit, or so it seemed to them. However, they did not know about the wonderful tactic—that he placed a kind of bad powder in the delicacies and sweets, and opposite it, he placed a healing powder in the house of work.

That clarified the supervision by itself: His lovers and those truly faithful to him—although they saw that there was no supervision in this place—kept the king's commandments carefully out of their love for him. They did their work as they were told and were careful to work precisely in the designated area. Thus, they inhaled the healing powder into their bodies, and when mealtime came, they tasted the sweets and delicacies and found in them a thousand flavors such as they had never tasted, or ever sensed such sweetness.

Hence, they praised the king extensively, for they were dining at the king's exalted table!

But the lowly did not understand at all the merit of the king, for which he should be loved with devoted and faithful love. When they saw that there was no supervision, they did not keep the king's commandment properly. They slighted the area that was designated for work, and each worked where he saw fit in the king's domain. When mealtime came and they tasted the sweets, they felt a bitter taste because of the above-mentioned dust. They cursed and despised the king and his despicable table, which he had prepared for them as reward for their work. They regarded the king as the greatest liar, who—instead of delicacies and finest delights—gave them these bitter and sour things.

Because of it, they began to devise for themselves foods from what was found in the city, to ease their hunger. Then their suffering was twofold, for their work had doubled, and they did not know the delight in the king's table that was before them.

The lesson is that the Torah is divided into two parts: a part for worshipping the Creator, such as *Tefillin*, *Shofar*, and studying Torah, and a part for working with people, such as robbery, theft, fraud, and slander.

Indeed, the part between man and man is the real work, and the part between man and the Creator is the reward and the delights spread out across the king's table.

However, "All that the Lord has worked, He worked for His sake," so the part of working with people should be in the king's place, too, meaning "to raise the *Shechina* from the dust." In that there is a healing dust to the potion of death that is cast between man and the Creator.

This is the meaning of "He gives grace to the humble," in the Torah and *Mitzvot* between man and man, and between man and the Creator, "...to those who love Me and keep My commandments"—to make them do all the work in the designated place. They are the ones with the grace of holiness, and "they will inherit twofold in their land," for not only are they not working so hard for people, they are delighted all their lives by the grace of the Creator.

However, "He scoffs at the scoffers." They say that the king's table is despicable, God forbid, as they feel the *Kedusha* as a kind of mockery. Therefore, the wicked do not gain by their wickedness, so who would lose anything if he departs from them even when he hopes to be favored?

Yehuda Leib

Letter No. 27

16 *Tevet*, *Tav-Reish-Peh-Zayin*, December 21, 1926, London

To the honorable student ... may his candle burn:

... I do indeed want to unite with you in body and soul, in this and in the next. However, I can only work in the spirit and the soul because I know your souls and can unite with them, but you can only work in the body, since you do not know my spirituality, so as to unite with it. If you understand this, you will also understand that I do not feel any distance from you, but you certainly need the physical closeness. And yet, this is for you and for your own work, not for me or for my work. With this I answer in advance many questions with regard to me.

But I do pray to the Creator to lead you on the path of truth, that you will be saved from all the obstacles along the way, and that the Creator will succeed for you all that you do.

As for you, you should meticulously follow the ways that I have set out for you regarding mind and heart, longing and prayers, and then the Creator will certainly make us succeed and we will soon unite in body and soul, in this and in the next.

To reply to your letter from the 26 of *Kislev*, the second day of Hanukkah [December 2, 1926], you wrote that the world was created for work, and that He has created the darkness for the purpose of work—to have substance on which to work in it—since in the light, there is pleasure and not work. Accordingly, you asked, "What is the *Klipa* [shell/peel] of the right [side] for, for it feels the darkness as light, and the creature feels the darkness as separated from him, as though it is not his, so how can it continue throughout his seventy years? Such a person, why was he born?" You demand a complete answer for it, and it is not the great lights that you need, but only to remove the disgrace of hypocrisy from yourself, which reaches as deep as the soul. And you conclude that you can say about it … "truth will show its way," and "it is already the fifth year," and so forth.

In truth, your words are confused, and therefore I do not know that truth. You said news: The world was created for work. If so, should work remain forever? But it is known that eternity is rest! Also, your question about the creature replacing darkness with light without knowing the darkness in it, we need to know how to discern right from left, and you still have not been rewarded with seeing the darkness, since darkness and light are as the wick and the light. Therefore, we must see the candle and enjoy its light, and then you will know right from left.

However, why are you asking about the Creator, Who gave great powers to the *Klipot* [pl. of *Klipa*]? I have already given you elaborate explanations about it, and primarily that the Creator protects Himself that one who adheres to Him will not doubt Him, and this will never happen because He is Almighty, and I have no wish to elaborate here.

But I consider your words as "a prayer for the poor," which is a prayer in complaint. It is closer to being answered than all other prayers. See in *The Zohar* about the verse, "A prayer for the poor," etc., "And David was poor, but a poor one's prayer is in complaint," etc.

Also, your concern about a good sign, it seems that you need wholeness as merely a sign. This is a good sign because five years ago you were not complaining about this. I have already told you that from "And they journeyed from Rephidim" to the reception of Torah is only one journey. But know that my words must not calm your worry or comfort you, since at the end of the first year you were at a higher level than you are now. And yet, do not give up on mercy.

You bring evidence from the writing to the purpose of creation, that it is for work: "What does the Lord your God ask of you but to fear the Lord your God ... and to serve the Lord your God." Indeed, there are two purposes: One should be before man's eyes, and one is for the Creator Himself. But the writing speaks of what should be before the eyes of the creature.

The matter is as it is written in *Pirkei Avot* [*Chapters of the Fathers*]: "It is not for you to finish the work, nor are you free to idle away from it." That is, since wholeness is the purpose of the work and its conclusion, there is an open side to the *Sitra Achra* [other side] to come near and make one understand that he is incapable of it, and bring one to despair, since we should know that the end of the work is not at all our work, but the Creator's work. Therefore, how can you know the Creator and gauge if He can or, God forbid, cannot finish His work? This is insolence and heresy!

"And you are not free to idle away from it," even in that manner, if the Creator wishes you to work without finishing the work. This is the meaning of what is written, "What does the Lord your God ask of you?" That is, the creature must know only this: The Creator ... work, and will therefore do His will wholeheartedly, as in "Open for Me one opening of repentance, like the tip of a needle." By this he will be saved from the *Sitra Achra* ever approaching him. If a person is completed in this, he can be certain that the Creator will finish His work on His end, "And I open for you gates through which carts and carriages enter."

But if he is not ready to serve Him, even in a manner that he is not rewarded with the completion of the work and the opening of the hall, no fawning or lies will help him. I have already explained what is written in *The Zohar*, "On the evidence of two witnesses ... he who is to die shall be put to death," that it is SAM and he is dead to begin with, and it is not hard to kill the dead, though the dead has the *Klipa* of the right, since the harder *Klipa* is canceled by proliferation of thanksgiving before the Creator, and proliferation of work.

I do not know if my words satisfy you, so do let me know and I will reply in a timely manner since the question, "What is the proof?" is a wise man's question, if he is one who works.

Yehuda

Letter No. 28

10 Adar Bet, Tav-Reish-Peh-Zayin, March 14, 1927, London

To my student ... may his candle burn:

... The above mentioned letter, which was not sent at the time of its writing, I will now reply to you about it. I will also reply to your latest letter from the beginning of the month, *Adar Bet*.

... Regarding your question about NHYM, that I did not explain the right, left, and middle about them, it is also because it belongs to the quality of the *Ohr Hozer* [reflected light], and I have already written you that the qualities of the *Ohr Hozer* need all the clarifications in my books.

How many times have I commented to you that the spiritual qualities can never be better than the corporeal qualities, yet you insist that you do not feel the taste of servitude in cleanness.

In my view, any place where there is a desire for servitude is already lost there ... from the work, since delaying the contentment and the drawn-out abundance is called servitude, as was said, "A servant let loose feels comfortable." Therefore, while being tied under the burden of his master's enslavement, he is called "a servant" and "serving."

See in the "Preface to the Wisdom of Kabbalah," that work and labor extend from the *Masach* [screen] that delays the upper light, which it covets very much, while the reward extends from the *Ohr Hozer*. Thus, *Malchut* returns to being *Keter* and emerges from servitude to complete redemption with simple *Rachamim* [mercies], which is *Keter*.

This is why our sages said, "A servant who is not worth his belly's bread [the bread he eats]," since the *Ohr Hozer* is defined as NHYM, NHY de ZA and *Malchut* that mate in *Hakaa*, as it is known.

If the servant were worth his belly's bread up to *Galgalta* [his head], he would be redeemed. But he is worth only up to his own belly, meaning that his intention to delay does not have the hardness of the *Masach* of *Behina Dalet*, but in order to receive. It follows that his delaying *Masach* will be a vessel of reception, too, and not a *Kli* that delays, for which the *Keter* will become *Malchut*. Thus, only the belly is added from the *Keter*, and NHYM is his belly. Hence, he remains a slave.

All these discernments between the *Masach de Keter* and the *Masach* of the belly come to him by utter and complete loathing the vessels of reception into his own stomach. That is, even the pleasure that extends to his belly by itself seemed to him like the pleasure of one who itches and rubs boils [disease], which is a detestable pleasure to any person because the harm is obvious.

Through the detestable force in nature, a second nature is imprinted in him, to truly loathe the pleasures of his gut. By this, his *Masach* is assisted by the delaying force as *Behina Dalet* that returns to being *Keter*.

But what shall we do to those who are not so meticulous about cleanness and detestable things, even in their first, corporeal nature? We should feel very sorry for them because from their perspective, they are cleansed and have already come to loathe what should be loathed. Yet, they cannot discern very well due to the nature of their corporeality that they are not fleeing as carefully as they should, even with corporeal detestable things.

This answers your question about hypocrisy, for which you came up with the mistake that the world was created for work, and what is to me a reward, you inadvertently mistake for work. You should correct yourself before I come to Jerusalem, and even more so before Passover.

Yehuda Leib

Letter No. 29

10 *Adar Bet, Tav-Reish-Peh-Zayin*, March 14, 1927, London

To my soul mate ... may his candle burn:

I received your letter from the 22nd of *Adar Aleph* [Hebrew month around March]. Although you are displeased with the fact that your innovations are not receiving their due time to ponder and consider them, I regret it, too, and in my opinion, more than you. And yet, hope for the Lord and brace your heart.

Regarding what you wrote, you did well not going, although now is no time for humbleness since the majority of the book has already been printed, and all that is about to be revealed is deemed revealed. Therefore, you can publish the book as you wish.

As for me, I wish to know about those who forbid any innovations in Torah, and take out the new before the old. They treat my book in one of two ways: Either they say that there are no innovations or additions here at all, since everything has already been written in the writings of the ARI, and so it really is. The other option is to say that all my words are my own notions, for why did our sages not mention a word of all that is said in my words? Thus, who knows if you can trust such a person who wishes to create a new method in Kabbalah, which our fathers did not conceive, and then hang on this peg of theirs their entire unclean past?

In truth, I did not add a thing to what is written in the writings of the ARI, with the intention to remove the obstacle from under the feet of the blind and the lame, perhaps they will see the goodness of the Creator in the land of the living. It would be good if you rushed to become proficient in my entire book before it is exposed to the eyes of the external ones, so you may show them every single thing written and interpreted in the writings of the ARI.

The core and the gist of all the explanations in my composition is the revealing of the *Ohr Hozer* [reflected light]. The ARI was succinct about it, as it was sufficiently revealed to all the Kabbalists since the *Rishonim* [Kabbalists in the 11th to the 15th centuries], prior to his arrival in Safed. This is why he did not detail or elaborate on this matter.

However, in Branch Four, he introduces explicitly, and it is presented in *Tree of Life*, p 104b, Gate 47, "The Order of *ABYA*," Chapter 1. In that place, everything that I have innovated regarding the five *Behinot* of *Ohr Yashar* [direct light] is presented there, as well as the matter of the *Ohr Hozer*.

Indeed, know that the five *Behinot* of *Ohr Yashar* presented here are the heart of the innovations of the Kabbalah of the ARI over that of the *Rishonim*. It was his only dispute with his contemporaries, supported by the verse in *The Book of Creation*, "Ten and not nine, ten and not eleven."

And yet, I should tell you that this is what caused great confusion in understanding his words, as in most places, he brings the ten *Sefirot* instead of the five *Behinot*. I also suspect that Rav Chaim Vital did so on purpose, to remove from him obstinacy and slander. In my explanation, I have already noted this complaint, thoroughly proving that both are words of the living God, as explained in "General Preface."

See the essay "The Knowledge," in "Gate to Introductions," where Rav Chaim Vital himself takes great care to show as equal the ten *Sefirot* and the five *Behinot*. However, they are not enough for the diligent students, which is why he only signed his own name on the words.

Regarding the *Zivug de Hakaa*, on which I elaborate and on which the ARI writes very briefly, it is because of the excessive disclosure of the matter among the disciples of the RAMAK [Rav Moshe Kordovero, the prime Kabbalist in Safed before the arrival of the ARI]. The ARI said about it that all the words of RAMAK were said only about the world of *Tohu*, and not about the World of *Tikkun* [correction], since *Zivug de Hakaa* applies only to the worlds preceding *Atzilut*, as well as the externality of ABYA. But inside ABYA there is no *Hakaa* but a *Zivug de Piusa* [coupling of conciliation], called "embrace of kissing," and *Yesodot* [foundations], as I will explain in the beginning of the world of *Tikkun*. But in the *Yesodot* themselves, this matter is applied everywhere, but in the form of reconciliation.

See in the "Gate to the Essays of Rashbi," beginning of the portion *Shemot* [Exodus], in the explanation about *The Zohar*: "And the wise will shine as the brightness of the firmament ... illuminating and sparkling in the upper *Zivug*," concerning the two righteous—the righteous who entered it, called Joseph, and the righteous who exits it, called Benjamin. The first is called "illuminating," which is the expansion of the nine *Sefirot* of *Ohr Yashar* [direct light] to it. The second is called "sparkling," which is "The One Who Lives Forever." Look there and you will see that in my words, I added nothing, only arranged the issues for beginners, and this concerns only Rav Nathan Neta Shapiro and Rav Shmuel Vital, and there is no meticulousness in the matter.

Sometimes I stop an essay midway because it belongs to the world of *Tikkun* and I do not want to confuse the student, only lead him in a safe and faithful way. Once I succinctly interpret the *Partzufim*, worlds, and *Mochin* in general, I will return to the beginning, and then I will be able to explain the complete essays in a wonderful order, as Rav Chaim Vital intended.

... One who is sorry for the public is rewarded with seeing its comfort, as both are the words of the living God. To the extent of the sorrow is the measure of the tranquility, as they are truly one. The only difference is in the *Dvekut* [adhesion] with

Him, as during the *Dvekut*, the judgments turn into simple mercies. The sign of it is that even one who has been sentenced to death but is seen by the king is pardoned and rewarded with life. Therefore, not during the *Dvekut*, the difference between those two *MaT* [fallen] is 98 [*Tzach*-pure] in *Gematria*, for then "a righteous falls before the wicked," and "a righteous falls seven times and rises."

It is very hard for me to be in London during Passover, especially since I am still in the middle of my work. Although I am very hopeful, it is my custom to enjoy only the present, which is the way to draw in the good future. Hence, I have much room for longing.

I am contemplating returning to Jerusalem after Passover, and I want to see you ready and willing in the King's palace, for on the joy of the festival of *Matzot* [unleavened bread (meaning Passover)], you will come out from all those who seek the opening to and fro...

... As it is said, to draw a *Vav* in the *Matza*, and then the *Matza* turns into a *Mitzva* [commandment], and the sliced becomes complete, and how long will you engage in rules of carving? Our sages have already said, "Be not as servants serving the teacher in order to receive reward," for it will not satiate them prior to the actual reception. There is a maxim people use: "One who breaks all his bones, one of them did not break," but is rather strengthened by the crushing in the hand of the giver.

Then each of the two halves becomes wholeness, which is the meaning of "And the righteous inherit twofold in their land," for there is none who is broken here, and both are full and whole. It turns out that one of them did not break, and he has twofold bread because *Malchut* returns to being *Keter*. This is what Elisha asked of Elijah the prophet: "May it be twofold in your spirit to me," meaning the spirit of the giver.

... Our sages said, "A man must be drunk on Purim until he does not know," etc. That is, a man is rewarded with expansion of knowledge through a handsome woman, a handsome house, and handsome tools, as it is said in *The Zohar* about the verse, "And the children of Israel kept the Sabbath..."

But there is one who is rewarded with broadening of the mind through intoxication from wine and rye, as it is written, "Give rye to the lost, and wine to the bitterhearted." Indeed, it is falsehood, for what can broadening of the heart give you and add to you in case of drunkenness, when one is lying merrily as though the whole world is his? This is why it is written, "The wine-joker," as he jokes about people with the gladness of falsehood and groundlessness.

This was Noah's sin, and the ministering angels mocked him for being drunk.

But there is a lowly and despicable *Klipa* [shell/peel] called "the *Klipa* of Amalek." It cuts the words and tosses them up. That is, it is so material that it cannot be reconciled even with thirteen covenants and thirteen rivers of pure persimmon, since it tosses them up, too, and says, "Take what You have given them."

This is the meaning of what is written regarding Elisha, that he was plowing with twelve pairs of oxen, and he with the twelfth. The lowly works are called "plowing," and he was already at the lowest degree, meaning at its end, which is the twelfth.

In the degrees of the year, the month of *Adar* is called "the twelfth month." Then Prophet Elijah threw his mantle and made it an offering to the Creator, since by gripping to the mantle of the giver he was rewarded forever, until the end.

Adar comes from the word *Adir* [huge/great], and extraordinary strengthening is called *Adar*. That strengthening comes to *Adar* only through much Torah. And although there is no wisdom or understanding or counsel in this place, Amalek is still weakened and is ruined and becomes absent, and a righteous comes and inherits his place.

The thing is that idol-worship is canceled only in those who practice it, who have connection with it. It is impossible to strike the wind with an axe. Rather, the wind that strikes repels the wind, and iron to iron, etc. And since the essence of Amalek is a joker, destroying everything in materiality, without knowledge but only with mockery, it is impossible to uproot him from the world with the spirit of knowledge. On the contrary, it is with something that is above reason, meaning through the wine of Torah.

From the whole of the light of Torah, that huge force remains. Through it, you will understand that although the wine is not rife with rye, it is a good remedy for destroying and annihilating the seed of Amalek (as it is written, "to disturb them and destroy them," "an eye for an eye," "it was turned to the contrary"), in the feast of Queen Ester, who stands from the bosom of, etc., and dipping and sitting in the bosom of, etc., meaning that our sages said that it is permitted to change on Purim, in welcoming of guests and with costumes.

It is as they said, "A man must be intoxicated on Purim," meaning that they said, "It did not say, 'learned,' but rather 'poured water,' to teach you that servicing the Torah is greater than learning it." By servicing, he was rewarded twofold, and not at all due to the study, as they are two opposites in the same carrier. This is why they are called "twofold," and the prohibition is the permission, for a key that is fit for closing is fit for opening.

This is the reason for sending [Purim] gifts to one another, see in the commentary on *Tree of Life*, since there is no distinction between one with GAR and one with VAK, because of the two gifts that they send to one another. It is as said in *The Zohar*, Song of Songs: "Your love is better than wine," meaning that the friendship extends from the wine of Torah, as he is attached in utter completeness to the Creator, even in a place devoid of *Hochma*. This is not from the wisdom of Torah itself, but from the wine of Torah, which springs out of the profusion of Torah.

This is the meaning of "And their memory will not perish from their seed," meaning the maleness, as it gazes on the wicked and they are gone, and the matter that there are no *Achoraim* [back/posterior] here at all becomes revealed, and these days of Purim are remembered and done. "And Mordechai went out from before the king in royal apparel." Everything depends on the male, even the displaying of Ester.

I was brief because I have spoken about these matters at length several times. I hope that the Creator will expand your boundaries in all the additions related to the above matters, for the matter is very near to you, and how long will you keep testing the Creator. If you believe in Him, you will certainly not turn back often.

And why did the Creator have faith in Rashbi that he would not turn back? When he said, "I am for my beloved," etc., "All the days when I was connected to this world, I was connected to it in one connection, in the Creator. Therefore, now 'His passion is upon me.'"

However, man sees the eyes, and the Creator sees the heart, for your mouths and hearts are not the same to do them, and the spice for it is the Torah.

Indeed, I have taught you much Torah, but you instilled drops of idle words, but in response to them came forth drops of Torah.

I haven't the strength to fight against your materialism. Instead, the fine light of my teaching has illuminated on you even in previous generations, but you yourselves did not work at all against your materialism, and you are not inspired by the greatness of the Creator and the greatness of His servants, and His holy Torah. I have been standing and warning you about this for a while, and this is the wall that separates you from me for a long time now; woe unto this beauty that has withered in this dust.

Know that this work is highly capable, before I came to you, as it is external work, and one who cleans his clothes in front of the king will not gain honor. Therefore, fix yourselves in time so you may enter the hall, for I see no other fault but that, and "He who said to His world, 'Enough!'" etc. Time is short, and the work is plentiful in the place of Torah, so hurry and journey from Rephidim to the light, by the light of the living, and together we will be blessed with the blessing of redemption that has redeemed us and redeemed our fathers, Amen, may it be so.

Yehuda Leib

Letter No. 30

Nissan, Tav-Reish-Peh-Zayin, April, 1927, London

To my soul mate ... may his candle burn:

I received all of your letters, and regarding your wish to receive an advance for the book, for it is finally to be revealed, happy are you, for the merit of humbleness is to conceal how capable one is. It is as our sages said, "Everyone knows why a bride enters the *Huppah* [wedding canopy]," etc., for all the great and important matters come in humbleness. It is as it is written in *The Zohar* about Rabbi Aba, that he knew how to reveal in intimation, and all according to the ability. Yet, beyond the ability, there is no merit in humbleness, but the initial humbleness is present and instills upon him the blessing forever.

Yehuda Leib

Letter No. 31

Iyar-Sivan Tav-Reish-Peh-Zayin, May-June 1927, London

Leader of the children of Menashe, Gamaliel, son of Pedahzur, *Tav-Reish-Peh-Zayin*, London, May God protect it.

To the students, may the Lord be upon them:

... I shall reply to both of you together, as it all stems from the same desire. The holiday is approaching, and as you know, I tend to keep to myself at such times and not waste time.

Although I do not have many expenses on basic needs for the holiday because I've already obtained the *Matzot* and the wine, I am preoccupied with receiving the newborn child from all that has happened to me during the months of conception since *Tishrey* [approx. September]. The child is very dear to me, a child of entertainment, and so my heart goes out to him and to all his needs.

You must have noted to write in the previous letters to prepare yourselves to long for the Creator and for His goodness in these days, prior to my coming to you, for the time is ripe for this, if you wish, since time and place do not part between us whatsoever concerning the needs of the Creator and the lot of the Creator. As for the box of corporeality? Put it behind you, and we are one.

Our sages have already wondered, "Ester from the Torah, where from?" They said, "I will surely hide." The thing is that from *Lo Lishma* [not for Her sake] one comes to *Lishma* [for Her sake], that the light in it would reform them. Therefore, they were right to ask, "How can there be concealment to any person?" Even if you say that he is wicked, that he engages in Torah and *Mitzvot Lo Lishma*, still, the light in it has to reform him.

They answered that there are two concealments, as in, "I will surely hide" [Heb: *Haster Astir*]. One concealment is due to the diminution of the moon, as it is written, "lights," in deficient writing, since the *Vav* is missing from the *Ohr* [light] in it, *Ohr* without the [letter] *Vav*. The second concealment is due to the sin of *Adam HaRishon*, considered that he cast filth into her, and he was diminished in the first one, too, creating *Mar* [bitter] instead of *Maor* [illumination]. In the work of creation, He brought the medicine before the blow, as it is said in the verse about light, "Let there be light," and "And there was light," to be sufficient for both concealments.

The second light was blemished by the inciting serpent, and *Vav-Reish* remained of it. The *Vav* was already missing in the first light, living a storm over the head of the serpent and his company, "*Arur* [cursed] are you than all the beast," etc. From the first, *Aleph-Reish* remained, and from the second, *Vav-Reish* remained.

This is why its legs were cut off and he walks on his belly, and I have no time to elaborate further. This is the meaning of using the seven days of creation, which were concealed for the righteous in the future.

However, all the corrections are in the receivers of the light. Since they are unfit to receive the upper light, they are rebellious against the light because the light is bestowal, and when it is received, it is called "illumination," which is the internality that reforms him, that which clothes in the vessels of reception. The upper light dresses in the letters of all the prayers, and "He is one and His name, 'One.'" This is the meaning of our fathers being immersed in mire and bricks, from the idols of Egypt on the forty-nine gates of impurity. Then the King of all Kings, the Creator, appeared to them and redeemed them.

The reason is that they had to discover all the letters of the prayer, so the Creator waited for them. However, when the prayers ended, He rushed to them and redeemed them, "And His divorce and His hand come as one."

When righteous Mordechai brought Hadassah, he was rewarded with her because she was the daughter of his uncle, Avichayil. And although "The vision of the glory of the Lord's fire is as consuming fire at the mountain top," she had a good pasture and oil with him, as it is written, "On his right was a fiery law unto them." He understood by the light of his righteousness and extended on her a thread of grace. By that extension, he extended the quality of "line" into holiness for fourteen days (for the quality of "line" is *Hesed* [mercy/grace]), due to the two above-mentioned diminutions, as in, "And her father indeed spat in her face." Finally, he was rewarded with, "And Ester found favor in the eyes of all who saw her," even the actual nations of the world.

First, she corrected in the *Achoraim* [back/posterior], meaning she stands from the bosom of Ahasuerus, dips, and sits in the bosom of righteous Mordechai, which is purity, as in, "interpreted as pure myrrh" (This is why they explained that Mordechai is the translation of the Torah [into Aramaic]), meaning the "bitter" from the serpent. He cast filth in her (which is the meaning of "To most of his brothers," and not "To all his brothers"), and the *Aleph* from "He and I cannot dwell in the world" fled from the illumination in her, for a man cannot dwell in the same place with a serpent. He was rewarded and purified for her because he extended to her his champion, his acquaintance. And yet, the illumination is still written with a deficiency, meaning the *Vav*, due to the diminution of the moon.

However, in return for this, he was later rewarded with "royal apparel" and a great crown of gold, as it is written, "The two great lights." Then, "Mordechai from the

Torah," as it is written, "freedom myrrh," meaning freedom from the angel of death, in the actual holy language.

It is so because the whole purification is in the *Achoraim*—the translation—and complete freedom is in the holy language. The forty-nine pure faces and the forty-nine impure faces are from the diminution of the moon. This is why the first correction is the emergence of the *Kelim* [vessels] in purity, and the second correction is a new name, which the mouth of *HaVaYaH* [the Lord] will determine, "*HaVaYaH* is Her name," and "In every place, offerings are presented unto My name."

I have elaborated thus far to give you a taste of the bitterness of a *Mitzva* [commandment], should you wish, for the meaning of "And made their lives bitter," without the two *Alephs* of *Tohu*. Although the filth of the serpent was only in the first light, he attributed the corruption to the upper one—that the lack of the *Vav* due to the diminution of the moon proved that the *Aleph* was also missing there, God forbid. He dressed them as light [*Ohr*] and *Kli* [vessel], the oil for the illumination and the light, taking the *Aleph* of "illumination" from the "illumination" and from *Ohr* (for the *Vav* was already missing), and the *Aleph* of *Ohr*, assembling them in one another. Thus, he made *Maror* [bitter], meaning the angel of death, where the two *Reish* became *Tav*.

When rewarded with "freedom myrrh," then the Creator came and slaughtered the angel of death, who becomes a holy angel once again. There aren't forty-nine and forty-nine here, the side of merit and the side of fault, which are twenty-two letters. Rather, "He is one and His name, 'One,'" for "The enemy will not deceive him, and the son of wickedness will not afflict him," "The wicked are overthrown and are gone."

Therefore, first, the gods of Egypt must be imprisoned, on the tenth of the month, to be hung in the Torah, "that he cannot prefer, etc., but he shall acknowledge the firstborn, the son of the hated one, by giving him a double portion." This is the meaning of the preparation for the plague of the firstborn, the son of the hated one.

By chaining the gods of Egypt to the legs of the bed, they drew upon them great lights in the cut off place. *Yakir* [recognize] is like *Yakir* [cherish], and there is no "visiting," but there is "preferring," since there is no flaw, as was said, "My darling son, Ephraim, a child of entertainment," for he "folded his hands," and put his right hand on the head of Ephraim.

This is the meaning of ... "a lamb for the fathers' house," from "the hands of the Mighty One of Jacob." And on the four days of the first-fruit, it was slaughtered on the fourteenth and the mouth that forbade (which is the meaning of twice, *Yakir* [recognize] and *Yakir* [cherish]). It is the mouth that permitted, and in the light of "The Lord is to me, and the night will be as light."

Then, "a lamb for a house," and "In that very day, all the hosts of the Lord will come forth," etc., "I and not a messenger," etc., "And you will dip in the blood that is on the doorstep," at the bottom of the legs of the bed. "And you will touch the post, and the two *Mezuzot*," meaning the *Tikkun* [correction] that fills the above-mentioned two diminutions, which is two *Mezuzot*, from the words, "from this" and "this," as in "the faith of the craftsman," and "the faith of a faithful one." The daughter that was trained is really his mother in the faithful one, as I have already interpreted for you. Then, "You will touch the post," etc., for it is literally bloods, and I have no time to elaborate, and the enlightened will understand.

How I long to hear from you the enunciation of redemption and the blessing of redemption, "Who redeemed us," etc., for "On *Nissan* [Hebrew month, spring] they were redeemed, and on *Nissan* they will be redeemed." That is, the past and the present join as one because he sees his back like his face.

This should not surprise you. After all, a box of pests [bad reputation] is hanging behind each one, and how can you equalize with the one before you?

However, this is only in the present, for eternity is present, making the future equal to the present and the past, meaning to the ones rewarded with the light of truth, clothed in only one and unified desire. Anything more than one desire, it was said about it, "Any excess is deemed gone." It is in the unification of the true *Dvekut* [adhesion] from the recognition of his heart that is full of the light of *HaVaYaH* to the brim.

Even when he directs his heart to heaven, one should be very careful with the unity of the desire, to be unified in true unity, internal recognition to the extent of the *Dvekut* on the height of the Lord's palace ... for His hand will not be short, as it is written, "Indeed, I live, and the glory of the Lord shall fill the whole earth."

This is the meaning of Israel's redemption, as in "I am the Lord, I and not a messenger, nor an angel or a seraph."

One who has many desires, the Creator has many messengers and many degrees. The Kabbalists write that there are 125 degrees even in *Nefesh de Assiya*. But one who has only one heart and one desire does not have all the calculations, all the degrees that are made by seraphim [angels] and animals, and holy ofanim [another type of angel]. Rather, "And I was trusted by him," a child of entertainment, for a servant of the Creator who has contentment with his servitude, it is a clear sign that the Creator has contentment with his faithful servant. And conversely, it is, God forbid, to the contrary.

Thus, all we need is to aim the heart to entertain with Him, for the entertainment is for Him alone, and not to cause sadness whatsoever. Also, a wise son always looks at his father's face, whether he is happy with him, as he has one intention—to delight the father, and nothing else.

This is the meaning of "Now it shall be said to Jacob and to Israel, 'What has God wrought?'" Our sages interpreted that angels and seraphim learn the knowledge of the Creator from Israel. This is the meaning of "'And it was very good,' this is SAM," as he blossoms in one, but when that power for holiness is taken from him, then

"And in all your might" comes true in us. This is the meaning of being rewarded with revealing Elijah from the time of the revival of the dead. He flees in four, and then that force to work and to be encouraged is established in us in one, meaning very good, which we hope for soon in our days, Amen.

I have been brief in this letter due to lack of time. But God willing, it will suffice for you to prepare yourselves and be rewarded with all the above-mentioned prior to my coming to you. Then, where there are vegetables on the table, there will be meat and fish, for after all the above-mentioned meriting you will begin to be ready to receive His light through me, as is the Creator's will in advance.

Although it may be a wonder in your eyes, in your minds, you should still believe me that I do not mean to boast, God forbid, for the Creator's benefit is your benefit. If you are small in your own eyes, look at your Maker, the One who made you, for a wonderful craftsman does not do low and lowly things. This false idea is the flaw from the serpent, who casts filth in her, to consider himself low and lowly and not feel that the Creator is by his side, even, and only at the bottom of his lowliness. And what I see, I shall say, perhaps the Creator will be to your liking soon in our days.

Yehuda Leib

I did find one correction on the first page of the preface, second column, where instead of "except," which I wrote, it was written, "but" or "only." It must be from ... may his candle burn, who already argued with me about this word, and then I kept silent about his argument. But now I noticed and found it interpreted in Kings 12, "There was none that followed the house of David, except for the tribe of Judah," as well as in Kings 2:24, "None remained, except for the poorest among the people." And he interpreted the *Metzudat Zion* and replied to me.

And concerning remission of the many debts that some of you ask in letters, I ask, "Why should you not pay me my debt to write me a letter each week as I have asked you?" Indeed, all debts stem from the same *Mitzva*.

The same

Letter No. 32

2 Iyar Tav-Reish-Peh-Zayin, May 4, 1927, London

To the honorable students, may the Lord be upon them:

Yesterday I received the 200 copies of *Pticha* [Preface to the Wisdom of Kabbalah], and today your letter. You are all unanimous about my letters being short, while I myself wrote in detail, for it takes time because the nature of every great thing is that it takes much time to conceive.

What the rav wrote ... that he did not understand my letter because it is all initials, it seems as though he still does not know that he does not know, for in truth, it is the ends of the words and not their beginnings, for each day I wait for the Creator to finish for us, for we are not free to be rid of Him.

Concerning his comment about my writing, that it would be a wonder for them once they are rewarded with all that is written, and then they will need to receive His light through me, he wrote that he is not surprised about it whatsoever. It is because he did not understand my writings, as he himself admits. But how will he understand the wonder? However, I say that it is a wonder in my eyes, too, and may he be experienced and test my words.

And what he wrote concerning settling down in Israel, I agree. I, too, am in favor of enjoying ancestral merit because the covenant of the fathers has not ended and the work is plentiful.

And what ... wrote as an interpretation to my letter, that *Dror* [freedom] in *Gematria* is *Kodesh* [sanctity], he should have said the opposite—that *Kodesh* in *Gematria* is *Dror*. Concerning his writing that he wants to know when I will return to my home, I want to know if he is already ready to receive me and benefit from me, and God willing, I will let him know on my part in due time.

I also received the letter from ... and what he wrote except for *Yakir* [will recognize] and *Yakir* [will cherish], that he cannot properly support, he should know that it is the center of all my letters, and if he does not understand this he will not be able to fully understand the matters.

... It is said in RASHI, *Chayei Sarah* [The Life of Sarah]: "A hundred years old, as twenty years old for punishment (to sin)," (and in *Baba Batra*, 58a), "Everything before Eve is as a monkey before a man." These are only intimations, but simply put, the *Chaf* is replaced with a *Kof* because they are from the same pronunciation, GICHAK. Hence, "Ephraim, my darling son," can be interpreted as the son cherishing the father or the son recognizing [knowing] his father, for in fact, they are one utterance: The one who cherishes recognizes, and the one who recognizes cherishes, without any difference.

There is a clear sign given in the name of the Baal Shem Tov by which to know how much the Creator is playing with a person—to see in one's own heart how much he is playing with the Creator. So are all the matters, as in "The Lord is your shade." This is why one who still feels some difference between cherishing and knowing requires the unification of the heart, as from the perspective of the Creator they are both one.

This is a deep matter, that the Creator is truly in the heart of each one from Israel. But this is on His part, so what does man need? Only to know it—the knowing changes, and the knowing finishes. This is the meaning of "The Lord is your shade."

And what he asked—which one is first, the disclosure of Elijah or the resurrection of the dead, or do both come as one—it is not the same for all and there are several degrees in it. It requires much elaboration to explain this, and there is nothing more to add here.

Rav ... did well ... but it seems that you, too, did not read the pamphlets properly, for you cannot show them that all my words are present in *Tree of Life*, and I did not add a single word, other than writing explicitly that *Malchut* in every place is the will to receive. But this is already accepted from the writings of the ARI in general, without any need to reference it accurately. It is presented explicitly in *The Zohar* and in the *Tikkunim*, and besides this there is no change of wording.

His comparing my book to *The King's Valley*, I saw it here for the first time, and last week I wrote from it. However, all the foundations of this book are renewed and arranged according to the Kabbalah of the *Geonim*, which begins with *Tzimtzum Aleph* [first restriction], followed by the world of *Malchut*, then *Avir Kadmon*, then *Tehiru*, and then *Atzilut*. However, he fills those matters with orders of the ARI ... which are truly not similar because the ARI spoke of nothing more than a line and *Tzimtzum*, and only then AK, *Akudim*, *Nekudim*, and *Atzilut*, as is presented in *Eight Gates* and in all the writings of the ARI.

The studies of the *Atzilut* that are attributed to the ARI are not at all from the ARI but from some abbreviation from the book *The King's Valley*, itself. This is why Kabbalists who follow the ARI did not like this book.

I wrote you that first you should study the pamphlet until you can tell every single one and show their ignorance because you truly will be able to find everything in *Tree of Life* and in *Eight Gates*, especially if you examine closely Branch 3 and Branches 4 and 5 in *Panim Meirot*. Branch 3 explains the *Ohr Hozer* [reflected light], Branch 4—the four *Behinot* of *Ohr Yashar* [direct light], and Branches 5 and 6 explain the *Hizdakchut* [cleansing/purification/weakening] of the *Masach* by which the *Histaklut* [looking] of *Ohr Hozer* is done, and you will be able to prove to anyone who must listen to what he is saying. If you do so, you will certainly prove that you are right.

The book *My Desire Is in Her*, by Rav Chaim Vital was found among my books tied together to the Kabbalah book by Hacham Mas'ud, who gave it to me as a gift. I need it very much, so I ask that to have it sent to me as soon as possible.

Yehuda Leib

Letter No. 33

26 Nissan, Tav-Reish-Peh-Zayin, April 28, 1927, London

To the honorable students, may the Lord be upon them:

Two nights ago, a wonderful thing happened to me: A man asked me to come over to his house to see his books, among which there were also books of Kabbalah...

I saw there a big book, about 180 pages, two printer sheets, titled *The King's Valley* by one of the wondrous ascended ones, Rav Naphtali Ashkenazi, printed in Amsterdam in 1648. The author established a complete order to the wisdom of truth, as in the book *Tree of Life*, beginning with the *Tzimtzum* [restriction] and ending with the lower worlds BYA. It is based on the foundations of the ARI with his own explanations, and he is also assisted by the Kabbalah of the *Geonim* and the *Rishonim*, similar to Rav Yaakov Kafil.

When I opened the book, I saw in it many issues and foundations that were not introduced in any of the books of the ARI or the *Rishonim*, except in the book *Studies of Atzilut*, presented in his book, letter by letter.

This surprised me. I went over the book meticulously until I realized that the book *Studies of Atzilut*, attributed to the ARI, is completely false and fabricated. Instead, a copier abbreviated this book, *The King's Valley*, and turned it into a short composition, which is the book *Studies of Atzilut* that we have.

Moreover, that copier was completely ignorant and did not understand anything about Kabbalah, so he confused the pages of the book in a terrifying manner. Out of every ten pages, he took half or a third of a page and copied them verbatim, then put them together into a single issue.

In consequence, one issue in the book *Studies of Atzilut* consists of ten thirds of pages from ten separate matters in the book *The King's Valley*. This is why it is so perplexing. I cannot put in writing my anger at this wicked fool, since it took me a long time to sort matters out for myself. But because of the sublime holiness of the issues presented there, I was fond of them, and so I spent a great deal of time—above and beyond—on this book.

I understand that the same thing happened to all the great ones; therefore, I wish to make it known that 1) it is not from the writings of the ARI, 2) it is distorted and confused to the point that it is forbidden to look at it. It must be buried so as to remove obstacles from future generations. One who wishes to understand the holiness of the matters will look into the book *The King's Valley*, where the matters are presented in their full and sublime glory. I am contemplating interpreting the matter in the introduction I will write.

That book is priceless. It was probably printed only once, approximately 300 years ago, and this was the first time I saw it. It must have been an act of Providence because I took with me the book *Studies of Atzilut*, but when I wanted to read in it I could not find it. I looked for a place where I could borrow it but could not find it anywhere. In the end I did find it, in my bag, to my surprise.

Regarding the personal questions, I pray that he will succeed wherever he turns, for I cannot settle private affairs these days, as my own troubles surround me. Hence, in His light we will see light.

Yehuda Leib

Letter No. 34

26 Nissan, *Tav-Reish-Peh-Zayin*, April 28, 1927, London

To the honorable students, may the Creator be upon you:

I think that I do not need to write you words of Torah because you have plenty in writing and in print. But who knows if they are still news to you, for "He always renews in His goodness the work of creation each day." Hence, one should be impressed and praise only with news.

Before Passover, I wrote you innovations in the Torah, as it is said, "A good day of labor in the Torah" (the Torah of a festival). With this you will understand the words of our sages concerning fear of heaven, that "the whole world was created only to command this." We should make a precision: It should have said "that" ["this" is used in male form and "that" in female form], since the *Malchut*, which is *Halachah* [code of law] and fear of heaven, is called "that," and the Creator is called "this."

However, it is known to the meticulous that when we speak of male and female together, we pronounce it in male form, and the Creator is called "this." It is as written in the words of our sages, "In the future, the Creator will make a dance for the righteous, and each will point with his finger and say, 'Behold, this is our God ... this is the Lord for whom we hoped.'"

But prior to the correction of making a dance for the righteous, and *Machol* [dance] comes from the word *Mechila* [pardon], it is said, "He shall not enter into the holy place at any time," due to the circle of twenty-eight times, fourteen for better and fourteen to the contrary. Rather, "By that shall Aaron come into the holy place," meaning by the fourteen for the better, which is called "that."

Our sages said, "The whole world was created only to command this," meaning the unification of the Creator and His *Shechina* [Divinity], which are then called "this." That is, up to here we must rise in the fear of exaltedness, in turning his reception into bestowal, while the Giver, who is above the circle, can certainly bestow any time, even to the fourteen that are to the contrary, for in bestowal there is absolutely no evil, as has been thoroughly explained.

This is the meaning of the words, "Keep that forever for the inclination of the heart of Your people." As long as we have not been rewarded with unity with the Creator as one thought, but rather as two thoughts, we therefore ask, "Keep that," give us strength and power to come to the holy place by keeping the word, "By that shall Aaron come into the holy place." "Remember and keep were said in one utterance," and by that it ascended to unite in the true unity, blessed and exalted be His name forever.

It is written, "Take no rest, and give Him no rest until He establishes, and until He makes Jerusalem a praise in the earth." So we rush our pleas above, knock by knock, tirelessly, endlessly, and do not weaken at all when He does not answer us. We believe

He hears our prayer but waits for a time when we have the *Kelim* [vessels] to receive the faithful [guaranteed?] abundance, and then we will receive a reply to each and every prayer at once, since "the hand of the Lord will not be short," God forbid.

This is the meaning of the words, "Children in whom there was no blemish ... and who have the strength to stand in the King's palace." It teaches you that even those who have been rewarded with pardon for iniquities—which became as merits, by which the matter appears after the fact, and in whom there is no blemish—still need more strength to stand in the King's palace, meaning stand and pray, and wait tirelessly, knock by knock, until they elicit the complete desire from the Creator.

This is why we should learn this craft before we enter the King's palace, meaning muster power and might to stand as a pillar of iron until we elicit the desire from the Creator, as it is written, "Take no rest." Although the Creator seems silent and unresponsive, let it not cross your minds to be silent, too, "Take no rest." This is not what the Creator intended by His silence, but rather to give you power to stand afterward in the King's palace when you have no blemish. This is why, "and give Him no rest." Naturally, all the works are taught while one is still outside the palace, for afterward there will be no time to dedicate to crafts.

Give regards to all the students. Due to my troubles, I cannot answer in greater detail, and I hope for the Lord and for His goodness.

Yehuda Leib

Letter No. 35

16 *Iyar, Tav-Reish-Peh-Zayin*, May 18, 1927, London

To the honored disciples, may the Lord be upon them:

The surprise of ... at my zeal and devotion to *The King's Valley*, which I wish to publish, is because he did not understand me. It is not *The King's Valley* that I am zealous about, but its abbreviation, which is *The Studies of Atzilut*, which the copier maliciously attributed to the ARI.

In his abbreviation, he has done two harms: 1) He wasted the time of all who search their hearts for nothing and to cause fear, due to the far ones who are drawing nearer in his lines and cause bewilderment. 2) These are words of the wise rav, author of *The King's Valley*, in the writings of the ARI. By this he caused inconceivable confusion. So I am zealous because of my own time, which was lost.

Concerning the above-mentioned book, the author is undoubtedly a very high and holy man. However, his words are built on the foundations of MAHARI Sruk, who, in my opinion, did not understand the words of his teacher, the ARI, as well.

However, the words of Rav Sruk spread to all the holy ones that were in the land because the Rav Sruk nevertheless arranged the words he had heard from the ARI, so they are understood by anyone with a degree in attainment, for the greatness of mind and attainment of MAHARI Sruk are immeasurable.

For this reason, the author of *The King's Valley* relied entirely on his foundations, along with all the Kabbalists overseas to this day because of the questions in the words of Rav Chaim Vital, which are brief and disordered. This is also one of the reasons why I was moved to put my own words into a book in arranging the Kabbalah of the ARI, which came to us from Rav Chaim Vital, who understood, as the ARI himself testified, and as MAHARI Sruk also admitted.

It is surprising that the HIDA did not resolve to save *The King's Valley* from the quandary of the *Makor Chaim*, who did not lie at all in the Kabbalah of the ARI, God forbid, except that he relied on MAHARI Sruk. This is more or less the case with all the Kabbalists and authors from overseas without exception.

In my view, MAHARI Tzemach, MAHARAM Paprash, MAHARAN Shapira, and MAHARAM Di Lonzano also relied extensively on MAHARI Sruk, so why was he not mad at them?

As for me, I hope, God willing, to purify the words of the ARI without admixtures of names and attainments from others that have mingled into his words to this day, so that in time it will be accepted by all the greats, and they will not need to water the foundations of the ARI with other fountains but his.

It is interesting that ... was surprised that I did not mention the RASHASH? Why did he not reply to him that the RASHASH begins his book from the world of *Nekudim*, while I stand in the middle of *Akudim*? And other than some fragmented words in the sun, which also belong to the five *Partzufim* of *Atzilut*, he did not say a word about these matters.

What he contended regarding the interpretations of *Keter* in the Gate 42 of *Tree of Life*, you can tell him in my name that he does not understand the explanation there. There he speaks of the *Sefira Keter*, which includes the ten *Sefirot* of *Ohr Yashar* [direct light] and ten *Sefirot* of *Ohr Hozer* [reflected light], which is the inner AK, the middle between *Ein Sof* and AB-SAG-MA-BON, but which was revealed outside of it. Similarly, each *Partzuf* contains *Keter*, such as the inner AK, which includes twenty *Sefirot*, for which *The Zohar* calls them "twenty." The *Tree of Life* says about it that it can be called *Ein Sof*, it can be called "emanated," and both are words of the living God.

But I speak only of the *Keter* of the ten *Sefirot* of *Ohr Yashar*, which can only be called *Ein Sof* and Emanator, and cannot be called "middle," and much less by a formless name, and the root of the four *Yesodot* [foundations] of HB TM. It is so because prior to the disclosure of the *Sefira* of *Bina* of *Ohr Yashar*, there is not even a root to the *Kli*, as I have elaborated in Branch 1, for the *Kli*, the potential, and the execution are all from the emanated.

Concerning the inner light of *Igulim*, he confused my words once I divided them into two points—saying that the illumination of the surrounding light is from the surrounding *Ein Sof*, and the inner light is what the *Igulim* can receive by themselves, which are two discernments.

Near there, in the third *Behina*, I interpreted the inner light: The light that comes to them is called *Ohr Pnimi*, meaning that it comes to them by themselves. It is called "the light of the *Reshimo*." That is, the *Reshimo* still has the strength to draw and suckle from *Ein Sof*, except by a limited illumination, which is therefore called "a *Reshimo* that remains after the great light from prior to the *Tzimtzum*," and I have elaborated there.

Conversely, those who imagine that the matter of the *Reshimo* in every place indicates that it is as though a part of the holy light was carved and remained attached to a place after the departure of the light. This is a grave mistake because each light is attached to its root. It extends from its root incessantly, both a great light and a small light, which remains after the departure, called *Reshimo*.

In *Behina Dalet*, I interpreted the surrounding light in the following way: "Now *Ein Sof* illuminates bestowal from its place." What I mean is that that light does not come with the quality of the place of the *Tzimtzum*, which is limited and measured like the *Ohr Pnimi* [inner light]. Rather, it illuminates unboundedly and does not distinguish between great or small that the emanated has made for himself.

These matters are explained in *Mavo She'arim*, in *Gate to Introductions*, and in many places. There is no dispute at all between him and me, except in the meaning, but not in the phrasing whatsoever. I, too, say that the light of *Reshimo* is *Ohr Pnimi*, but I interpreted it so there will not be mistakes about it.

And what he wrote, that he was not set up toward the desired goal, which is the intention, tell him that this is my whole intention with the arrangement of the introductions, since many err in it, and each one builds a podium for himself because the ARI and Rav Chaim Vital did not arrange by themselves. For this reason, I had to clarify my foundations in the explanation of the ten *Sefirot*, in which many grossly err, and in the explanation and order of the *Partzufim* of AK, in which most were grossly mistaken.

Once I explain the order of the *Partzufim* of *Atzilut* and the ascents of the degrees properly, I will explain the book *A River of Peace*, printed with great contradictions because it was printed without the consent of the RASHASH, and things he said in his childhood ... which he regretted as an adult, were published. But if he had composed them himself, he would certainly proofread what was needed.

However, it was known that he did not compile it, but others stole and printed it while he was not at home, and he regretted it, as is known. I saw other commentaries explaining his words, but these commentaries testify that they did not even begin to understand the RASHASH, except for one book, *The Teaching of a Sage*, which attains partially, but not thoroughly. God willing, it will all be explained properly.

However, the method of the RASHASH goes against all the authors until today, for which I could not negotiate with his real words before I demonstrated his real foundations in the studying of *Tree of Life*, which, God willing, I will disclose in the future.

I will also put together an index of all my words in *Meirot Masbirot* and *Panim Meirot*, for I did not add any interpretations to what is written and explained in *Eight Gates*, in *Tree of Life*, or in *Mavo She'arim*. I also accepted some things from the book *My Desire Is in Her*, by Rav Chaim Vital, but I accepted nothing else into my foundations from the rest of the writings of the ARI, fearing for the purity of their compilers.

It is even more so with the Kabbalah of the *Rishonim*, the *Ge'onim*, and all the others, which I hardly saw at all. My reference to Nachmanides in his interpretation to *The Book of Creation* was not to be as a foundation for the wisdom, but as a foundation for purification from corporeality. Rav Chaim Vital also quotes him on this matter, and so I also quoted Maimonides on that matter.

I found it necessary to elaborate on this so you could listen to the ones you should with knowledge and understanding, and the words of the wise are heard in peace. God willing, I will put together an index so you may be able to show each and every word.

Currently, I am preoccupied with setting up the introduction of the book, after which I will set up the index, glossary, and acronyms. My many troubles are delaying me, especially as these are works to which I am not accustomed, which are therefore delayed from day to day.

Concerning the new synagogue, I'm very happy, and I wanted to hear how things are going with the other synagogue, which they were hoping to make in the Old City.

Regards to you,

Yehuda Leib

Letter No. 36

24 *Adar Aleph*, *Tav-Reish-Peh-Zayin*, February 26, 1927, London

To my soul mate ... may his candle burn:

... What you wrote about the cleanness of the clothes, I agree with you. And what is written, "Ten *Sefirot* of *Ohr Hozer* [reflected light]," with what is the light attained, and what is the concept of the *Kli* [vessel]? This is explained in the rest of the book for anyone who seeks—*Behina Dalet* [fourth discernment], which is the one with the *Masach* [screen], is the *Kli*, but she is not a vessel of reception but a vessel of bestowal. By this she returns to being *Keter*.

The concept of the light is all this wisdom, for all that the wisdom discusses is only measures of *Ohr Hozer*, while in the *Ohr Yashar* [direct light] they are all equal, according to the above-mentioned four *Behinot* [discernments], as is explained there. And the division of the nine bottom *Sefirot* of *Ohr Hozer* is already written there—that they connect in the *Kelim* [vessels] of *Ohr Yashar*.

In the fourth pamphlet, which I will send this week, you will see in the introduction of the *AHP* in *Panim Masbirot*, Item 11, the longitude, attributed to the *Ohr Yashar*, and the latitude, to the *Ohr Hozer*. By this you will observe that the *Ohr Hozer* is discerned primarily by the amount of extensions of light of *Atzmut* [essence] in the *Partzuf*, which is not extended to the emanated without the *Ohr Hozer*. This is why it is called "illumination of the line," "thin line," and examine there carefully and implement this rule.

Yehuda Leib

Letter No. 37

20 *Adar Bet, Tav-Reish-Peh-Zayin*, March 24, 1927, London

To my soul mate ... may his candle burn:

I received all your letters. Be strong and we will grow strong; do not fear and do not dread them. Let it be a sign for you that when success approaches, the fear and dread of them grow.

Concerning your question whether to go to America, I do not know how to measure your spirit in the work of the Creator. Perhaps the enemies will find in it a soft spot to weaken you from His work?

Although "emissaries of good deeds are not harmed," meaning when he engages in it—when he does not spend on it more time than necessary for the *Mitzva* [commandment]—if he is slacking and loses more time than keeping the *Mitzva* requires, the *Klipot* [shells/peels] have a place to grip.

Therefore, test yourself: Begin with preparations and supplies, and see and measure your strength. If your thoughts do not trouble you when not in the act, but rather, promptly after the necessary act you take yourself to the work of the Creator and can reject the worldly matters that drip from these matters, you will know that you are a strong man and go, for the Creator has sent you, and the Creator will bless your way and the work of your hands.

But if you cannot take away the excessive thoughts even when they are not necessary and during the engagement, and they trouble you when you do not engage in it, as well, then it is not you whom the Creator has chosen for this great thing. Rather, you still need to cleanse and hurry in everything that helps, as it should be with the emissaries of the Creator.

Yehuda Leib

Letter No. 38

8 *Nissan, Tav-Reish-Peh-Zayin*, April 10, 1927, London

To ... may his candle burn:

I received your letter and I congratulate you for the *Semicha* [rabbinical ordination] you have obtained. This is the first wall that barred you from going forward. I hope that from this day forward you will begin to succeed and go from strength to strength until you come into the King's palace.

I would like you to get another *Semicha*, but from now on hurry yourself and spend the bulk of your time preparing your body to muster strength and courage "as an ox to the burden and as a donkey to the load." Do not lose a minute, "for the way is long and supplies are scarce."

And should you say, "Where is this preparation?" I will tell you as I heard from the ADMOR of Kalshin. In earlier times, prior to the attainment of the Creator, one had to first obtain all seven external teachings, called "the seven maidens that serve the king's daughter," as well as terrible mortification. And yet, not many gained favor in the eyes of the Creator. But since we have been rewarded with the teachings of the ARI and the work-ways of the Baal Shem Tov, it is truly possible for anyone, and the above preparations are no longer necessary.

If you step in those two, which by the Creator's grace I have been favored by Him and have received them firmly, and my view is as close to you as the closeness of the father to his son, I will certainly pass them on to you when you are ready to receive from mouth to mouth.

But the most important is the labor, meaning to crave to labor in His work, for the ordinary work does not count at all, only the bits that are more than usual, which is called "labor." It is like a person who must eat a pound of bread to be full. All his eating does not merit the title, "a satisfying meal," but only the last bit from the pound. That bit, for all its smallness, is what defines the meal as satisfying.

Similarly, out of every service, the Creator draws out only the bits beyond the ordinary, and they will be the letters and the *Kelim* [vessels] in which to receive the light of His face.

Yehuda Leib

Letter No. 39

17 *Sivan, Tav-Reish-Peh-Zayin*, June 17, 1927, London

To the famous *Hassid* ... may his candle burn:

Regards to you.

I must inform you that I just received a very distressing letter about my sacred pamphlet being handed over to external ones to abuse it as they please. Now you will understand my stern warning to keep a secret, and why I have not sent the pamphlets until now. This is what I feared, so I wanted to first send the pamphlets to the MARAN and to the rav.

Indeed, that which I dreaded came to me, and the hands of illiterate have betrayed me, doing what I did not order, after my stern warning not to disclose my secret to any person, whoever he may be. And now they have defamed me in the eyes of the generation and have failed me on the path of my exalted work to bring contentment to my Maker. Who can forgive them this? Heaven will testify to my labor in all my strength to extend His holiness to that generation.

And yet, the *Sitra Achra* [other side] always finds her people, doers of her missions, setting obstacles before me wherever I turn to benefit others. Thus far are my words. "Those who are with us are more than those who are with them," and the Creator does not deny my reward. Bit by bit, I am paving the way, at times less, at times more, but always with profit (reward), until I am rewarded with taking down all the enemies of the Creator with the help of His great and terrible name.

As for you, do not fear the fear of fools. Those who slander, my little finger is bigger than their waist. So the Creator desired, and so He made me, and who will tell Him what to do and what to work? The merit of my law is greater than the merit of their fathers. Similarly, the contemporaries of Prophet Amos defamed him and said that the Creator had no one on whom to instill His *Shechina* [Divinity] but that stutterer, as it is written in the *Psikta* [a Midrash].

However, it is written, "A truthful lip shall be established forever, and a lying tongue is only momentary," for in the end, the truthful people are the winners. Amos remains alive and existing forever, and who has heard or knows what had happened to his adversaries?

So it is here. The sayers can harm only their own kind, so it follows that the storm swirls on the head of the wicked, the truth lives on and does not weaken by all the lies. Instead, it grows even stronger by them, like a sown field that is strengthened by the manure and dung that are thrown in. With the Creator's will, the blessing of the field increases and multiplies by them.

I still do not feel the harm that will come to me through them concerning the dissemination of my teaching, so I do not know how to calculate a way to instill light and save it from their evil. And yet, it is certain that if I feel any harm, I will take my revenge against them, as is the law of Torah, and I will contend forcefully with them. I will do all that is within the power of my hand to do, as it is the Creator I fear, and there is no other force but Him.

As a rule, you should know that it is not for my own need or my own glory that I composed the book. Rather, it is only for His sake, for I noticed great confusions in the writings of the ARI because the ARI did not write or arrange them by himself in the full depth of this sublime wisdom. When Rav Chaim Vital heard and wrote the words, he was still not in the degrees of wholeness necessary for attaining those words at their root. He was young then, thirty years old, when studying with the ARI, as it is written in *Gate to Reincarnations* (Gate 8, p 49). It writes, "Now, in the year *Hey-Shin-Lamed-Aleph* [1571], and I am twenty-nine …" Then, on Passover he was already serving the ARI, and the Rav [ARI] fell ill on Friday, July 21, 1572. The next Tuesday, on the Fifth of *Av* [July 25, 1572], he passed away.

You therefore find that at the time of his demise, he [Chaim Vital] was only thirty, and the ARI lived thirty-eight years, as it is known. And he wrote some more there (Gate 8, p 71), that at the time of his passing, Rav Chaim Vital was not by his side [the ARI's]. These are his words verbatim: "Rav Itzhak HaCohen told me that at the time of my teacher's passing, when I came out of his room, he (Rav Itzhak HaCohen) entered and cried before him saying, 'Is this the hope that we all hoped in your life—to see great good, Torah, and wisdom in the world?' He replied to him, 'If I found even one complete righteous among you, I would not be taken away prematurely.' While saying it, he asked about me (about Rav Chaim Vital). He said, 'Where did Chaim go? Has he left me at such a time?' He was very saddened. He understood from his words that he had some secret to pass on to me, so he (Rav Itzhak HaCohen) said to him, 'What shall we do from now on?' He (the ARI) replied: 'Tell the friends in my name that from this day on they are not to engage at all in this wisdom that I taught, for they did not understand it properly. Only Rav Chaim Vital shall engage in it, alone, in a whisper, and in hiding.' He (Rav Itzhak HaCohen) said, 'But is there no hope at all?' He said, 'If you merit, I will come to you and teach you.' He replied to him, 'How will you come and teach us if you are now departing from this world?' He replied, 'You have no knowledge of the concealed, of how my coming to you will be,' and he promptly passed away."

I have elaborated in copying the words of Rav Chaim Vital's book, *Gate to Reincarnation*, so you would see that the ARI forbade Rav Chaim Vital to teach what he had learned to others because at the time, he did not sufficiently understand what he had heard from the ARI. This is why he would not even arrange the writings he had heard from his teacher, and his successors arranged them, the third generation—Rav Yaakov Tzemach, Rav Meir HaCohen Paprash, and Rav Shmuel Vital.

Each of those compilers did not have the complete writings of the ARI because six hundred pages from the writings were stolen while Rav Chaim Vital was alive. Out of those, Rav Yaakov Tzemach compiled the majority of *Tree of Life*, as well as some other compositions. Rav Chaim Vital ordered another part to be buried along with him in the grave, and so they did. He left a third part as inheritance to his son, Rav Shmuel Vital, from which the famous *Eight Gates* were compiled.

After a long time, Rav Yaakov Tzemach assembled a large group of students, who dug the third portion out of the grave. From them the first and next editions of *Tree of Life* were composed, as well as *Olat Tamid*, and other compositions.

You therefore see that each time, the compiler had only a third of all the writings, which together make up one entity and one structure. I wish it were enough, but since they had only a small portion of the writings, they did not understand the depth of the wisdom at that time, and they terribly confused the matters by not understanding how to arrange them.

Know for certain that since the time of the ARI to this day, there has not been anyone who understood the method of the ARI to the fullest, as it was easier to attain a mind twice as great and twice as holy than the ARI's than to understand his method in which many hands fiddled—from the one who first heard and wrote them through the last compilers, while they still did not attain the matters as they are in their upper root. Thus, each inverted and confused the matters.

And now, by the Creator's will, I have been rewarded with a conception [impregnation] of the soul of the ARI, not because of my good deeds but by a higher will. It is beyond me, too, why I have been chosen for this wonderful soul, with which no one has been granted since his passing until today. I cannot elaborate on this matter as it is not my way to discuss the concealed, but I did find it my duty to ease your mind because ... before a flow of great water from servants that burst out at their master and expel from their water mire and dirt, to fall under the work that their animate soul has worked, since they still did not completely understand how to separate it from the spiritual soul. You should know that one must not fear such forces, which spring forth only to wash away all holiness, and the Creator saves us from them.

I think you will believe me, as it has never been my way to fabricate, exaggerate, or pursue respect and gain a name among the fools, which, until today, I have tolerated and had no desire to even fight with them.

To reinforce your not being confused by their armies of the *Sitra Achra* [other side], I will give you a clear sign that we received from the ARI, by which to know who is a true righteous and who is not a true righteous, but is worthy of being righteous, for which he should be treated respectfully, too. Do you believe that we should cast lots [flip a coin] about it, to know who is serving the Creator and who is not? After all, the signs and the tokens do not determine in this matter, as is known among the *Hassidim*, so it is a lot that we need, God forbid.

Rather, know that Rav Chaim Vital asked the ARI that question, and it is explained in the book *Gate of the Holy Spirit*, the seventh of the *Eight Gates* by the ARI, page 1. Here are his words, word for word: "The sign that my teacher gave me was to see if all his words come true, or if all his words are for the Creator, and he will not be wrong in even one of his words (relating to a letter that he learns from his friend, that he needs, etc., as it is known to those who know the wisdom of the hidden). He should also know the secrets of Torah and how to explain them, and then we can definitely believe in him." Rav Chaim Vital ends with this sign, and these are his words, verbatim: "According to his words we can know and recognize his greatness and merit to the extent of his knowledge."

The explanation is as previously written, that when a person is righteous and *Hassid*, and engages in Torah and prays intently, angels and holy spirits are created out of him. This is the meaning of "One who performs one *Mitzva* [commandment] has acquired for himself one advocate." The follies that come out from his mouth become a chariot to the souls of the first righteous, to go down to teach Torah to that man.

He also says there that if the *Mitzvot* [commandments] are incomplete, incomplete angels and spirits are made of it, which are called "tellers." It is about that that he gave the above-mentioned sign that if the Torah and *Mitzvot* are complete, he is rewarded with complete attainment and knows how to explain all the secrets of Torah. If he is lacking in it, meaning knows how to explain only some of them, his works are certainly incomplete.

Indeed, all those who can be my adversaries, it is because they do not even understand my words, so how can they be deemed complete righteous? Thus, I have given you a clear sign.

I have already written you that my book needs no endorsements because I did not add even a single word to the words of the ARI, and I have also given references to every single concept, showing their place in the writings of the ARI, and the ARI does not need the endorsement of our contemporaries. I did this deliberately, seeing the ways of the *Sitra Achra* against me in advance. My own work and additions in all those two commentaries are hardly recognizable. Thus, how will they hold out the campaign against this notebook? If they do have complaints about my teaching, and I am more proficient in the writings of the ARI than they are, this is not an argument. They should not have spent their time on vanities; they had time to study the words of the ARI, and since they folded their hands idly, now they will eat their own flesh.

My regards to you and to ... and ... Tell him that all his ways are as this deed, whose intention is good but the deeds are not good, and everything follows the act. But what can I do to him? He is my flesh and blood. Therefore, let him inform me in great detail the whole story and how it unfolded from beginning to end, and I will reply to him.

I also ask that you will let me know your thoughts about this letter, and more of what is happening among them in great detail and elaborately, for I need to know all the details in order to maintain the shield, for the work of the Creator is no small matter.

Yehuda

Letter No. 40

29 Sivan, Tav-Reish-Peh-Zayin, June 29, 1927, London

To the honorable students:

This week I received a double portion of letters from the portions *Shlach* [Send] and *Korah*. Last week I did not receive any letters and I thought that you did not write because on the third day of the portion *Korah*, it has been a full year since I have left you.

Regarding the impression of ... with the question ... regarding, "You did not see any image," to the point that he wrote me that even Solomon's wisdom would not be enough to answer such a question, I call on him the words of our sages: "Do not judge your friend until you are in his shoes." If he had even Moses' wisdom, of whom it was said, "And he beholds the image of the Lord," he would be able to blunt his teeth, for there is a form in spirituality.

What I wrote is according to the view of fools who interpreted the word "form" and the word "image" as one. But I am surprised at you—in a place where I ground wheat into flour for human consumption, you turned the flour into wheat again to chew on like a wild beast.

I elaborated extensively on the matter of form and disparity of form, which is only the difference between the Emanator and the emanated. It is necessary that we find some discernment for which it will be called "emanated" and not "Emanator," and I placed "the name" on that discernment, to be able to engage in it and speak of it.

This is why I called it "disparity of form" and "equivalence of form." Sometimes I call it "great *Dvekut* [adhesion]" and "little *Dvekut*." It can also be named by any name we want in order to explain this matter.

After grinding [analyzing] the matters from several pages in the book, he made them wheat once more, and materialized the word "form," clothed it in a corporeal image until his hands and legs were hopelessly tied up in this image. It is written explicitly in the Torah, "For you did not see any image," while here it writes that there is form, disparity of form, and equivalence of form ... I elaborated in your words to evaluate your inclination toward externality, that one needs to look into one's actions.

Concerning the precision that Rav ... makes regarding the name *Ein Sof* [infinity] and "the light of *Ein Sof*," here are the words in the book, *My Desire Is in Her*: "And all those worlds and *Malchut* were included in the upper world, each of them. Also, they are included in *Keter*, and the whole of *Ein Sof*, inside of which all the worlds were hidden, etc., and everything was one unity, and all was *Ein Sof*," thus far his words, word for word.

And what he wrote in the name of the book *The Holy Tongue*, p 20, I did not know the initials of that name, nor the suffixes.

And what he imagines to be my words in the *Pticha* [preface], that "The light and all the abundance are already included in His essence Himself," has no connection to my words regarding the *Hitkalelut* [mingling/inclusion] of the bottom worlds in *Ein Sof*. There, I explain specifically the matter of *Ohr Pashut* [simple light], which does not change wherever it is, and the difference between the Emanator and the emanated is precisely in the darkness. This is why I wrote very precisely, "In His essence," which has neither a name nor a word. I do not even refer there to the light of *Ein Sof*, God forbid.

I do not understand you whatsoever, how you scrutinize but do not taste what you are saying, and compare one issue to another like food to a barrel. It must be due to multiple engagements or a desire for multiple engagements.

And what roams as a "thought"—to know where it belongs, he caught my language in *Bina* and in the order, ABYA—it is said in *Atzilut*, as well as in *Tikkuney Zohar* [*Corrections of The Zohar*], "Upper *Hochma* is called 'a thought.'"

Indeed, it is from the wondrous and concealed secrets. But see in *Gate to the Essays of Rashbi*, these are his words in "The Hidden Midrash of Ruth": Moses means *Daat*, as in *Tifferet*, and Rabbi Akiva is *Bina*, called "being." Had the Torah been given from the part of *Bina*, the *Klipot* would have had no clothing in the Torah. But the Creator wished to give them a part and a grip, similar to how the first sparks in *Hochma* raised 320 sparks. This is the meaning of "So it came about in the Thought."

You find here that Rabbi Akiva as *Bina* is called "being," but this is perplexing because it is known that "being" is the name of *Hochma*. And yet, see in Branch 2 in *Panim Masbirot* (as well as in the introduction on the AHP) in the "Preface" regarding the ascent of *Malchut* to *Bina*. It explains that *Behina Dalet* rose to *Hochma* and became *Nukva* to *Hochma* of *Behina Dalet* that was established as upper *Ima*. This is why *Bina*, which is *Behina Bet*, went out, meaning below *Behina Dalet*, whose *Sium* is called *Parsa*, since out of that *Bina* that went out, the two *Partzufim* YESHSUT were established below the *Parsa*.

By this you will understand that that *Malchut* that went up, really did go up to *Hochma* and acquired upper *Ima* there, and she is called "being." She is also called "a thought," and there is the mitigation of the *Dinim* with *Rachamim*. This is why it is where the 320 sparks rose, as they are from *Behina Dalet*.

However, they did not rise to the actual *Hochma*, but rather to upper *Ima*, who is *Hochma*. This is the meaning of "All is clarified in the thought," since there is their root.

Sometimes *Bina* is called *Nukva* of *Hochma*, which is why I said that *Malchut* rose to *Bina*, meaning received the form of upper *Bina*, which is called "a thought" and "existence from absence." This is the deepest of the deep, which is why the authors were succinct here.

And what I wrote in *Panim Masbirot*, p 6, it writes, "nine *Sefirot*, *Toch* and *Rosh*," it is no longer in the pamphlets, but was written "*Toch* and *Sof*."

And what Rav ... says that I should ask on his behalf, it is similar to a working steam engine. Any machine that you attach to the steam engine with a strap will be just as strong. Thus, it is only *Dvekut* [adhesion] that we need.

Yehuda Leib

Letter No. 41

13 *Tammuz*, *Tav-Reish-Peh-Zayin*, July 13, 1927, London

To the honorable students, may the Lord be upon them:

I received your letter, and I am now sending the introduction. Although I have not proofread it, not even in writing, I trust you to understand how to proofread it perfectly. I cannot send you paper from here, simply for lack of funds.

The introduction will probably take up a printer-sheet and a half, six pages, and with the index and references, it will be two complete pamphlets, eight pages.

But the introduction is one complete thing, and there is no division in it whatsoever, for they are matters that are most sublime, as you will see once you understand. You should hurry with it as much as possible so I can be on the good day.

... And we hope that everything will be for the sake of the Creator and for our sake. We only need to exert in His law and in His work, to fill the lack and to correct what is broken...

I do not understand your lack of longing for my replies. As for me, I find myself truly near you, not in any way less than when I was with you. I share your sorrows and your joys, just as though I were with you in the same house and we were speaking to each other. But you know two, and I know one, hence my words are few.

Please follow everything I wrote above concerning the wholeness of the introduction.

Yehuda

Letter No. 42

14 *Tammuz*, *Tav-Reish-Peh-Zayin*, July 14, 1927, London

To the honorable ... may his candle burn:

With the words below, I will open my heart to you: I am very surprised that the friends are not missing my approaching return home as they should be. But I think of you that you are nonetheless the best among them because you cannot write me and explain your words, so you are more in need of a face to face encounter than the rest. Because of it, I think that you are longing more than they, so I will speak and feel better.

... But on the other hand, let us count the gains you have acquired in all your days with me. Although it is not yet clear who is to blame, but be that as it may, the hope is dwindling and strengthening is required.

On my part, I cannot help you in that, except to guarantee that the fault is not at all mine, but yours alone due to your lack of knowledge or weakness of faith and so forth. This is why all my prayers for you did not help you because you still did not understand how to execute it.

Therefore, let me give you a complete introduction, which you will keep and feel better: When the Creator is fond of a person and He calls him to cling to Him, of course he is ready and willing for it with all his heart and might. Otherwise, He would not invite him to His meal. If the faith in his heart is as a stake that will not fall, he understands this faithful calling and recognizes his place forever. Then, he does so and eats, and welcomes the King's face. And it does not cause him diminution because his mind and faith are complete.

Our sages said, "Fear the Lord your God, to multiply wise disciples." It is to multiply those who unite in true unity, and happy are those who live up to it.

You can see the validity of the words in you, yourself. When the time was ripe and you were fit for bonding, I did not waste time to wait until you came to my house. Rather, I was promptly at your place. And although you did not see me physically, you felt my love and the sublimity of *Kedusha* [holiness] at the bottom of your heart.

Then, all that was left for you to do was hurry and greet me with love. One who craves, does and completes his part. So you did, sending feelings of love, sublimity, and joy to my ears all the way from your home to the hill, with faithful passion.

But once you climbed up the hill and greeted me, the joy and love began to wane. It happened for your lack of faith in me and in my sincere love for you, as you to me, as the water-face to the face. This was the first flaw between me and you, for with that thought you immediately departed and drew far from me to that extent.

Indeed, so is the nature of anything spiritual—the matters are woven in lightning speed, and conception and birth are near. Therefore, once your belly conceived this fear, "You promptly gave birth to straw." That is, you doubted yourself, and your pleasant, sublime, and exalted thoughts about me, that they were exaggerated, that maybe it is not so, and then, "of course it is not so." Thus, I was necessarily separated from you and kept all my work and labor in deposit for a better time.

At the right moment, I returned with you as before, and you, too, repeated your previous acts, more or less. At times you wished to hear from me explicit words about it, as one speaks to one's friend, and not in any way less. But I am not good at that, as it is written, "For I am slow of speech and slow of tongue." You, too, should not hope for it in the future unless you merit sanctifying your corporeal body, with the tongue and ears, to such an extent that it will equal the merit of the spiritual.

But you cannot understand it because you have no perception of the hidden. But I, all that I am permitted, I do not withhold at all, and "more than the calf," etc.

Let me picture for you your above-mentioned issues with me in an allegory: A man walks along the way and sees a lovely garden. He hears a voice calling him, coming from the king, who is walking in the garden. Excited, he jumps the fence in one leap and is inside the garden. For all his excitement and rush, he does not feel that he is walking in front of the king, and the king is near him, strolling behind him.

So he walks and thanks and praises the king with all his might, aiming to prepare himself to meet the king. He does not notice whatsoever that the king is next to him.

But all of a sudden, he turns his face and sees the king right next to him. Naturally, he is overjoyed. He begins to follow the king, praising and glorifying as much as he can, the king in front of him, and he, behind the king.

So they walk and stroll up to the gate. The man walks out the gate and returns to his initial place, while the king remains in the garden and locks the gate. When the man sees that he has been separated and the king is not with him, he begins to look for the gate through which he came out when the king was in front of him. But there is no such gate at all, but only as he came in the first time, when he was walking in front of the king and the king was behind him without his noticing.

So it should be now, but it requires great craftsmanship. Understand it and study this allegory, for it is the same between us. While you were with me and I felt the chill that was born in you compared to the past, you should have nonetheless concealed your face from looking at me, as if I know nothing of all that had happened to you and went through your heart along the way to me.

This is the meaning of "And they believed in the Lord and in His servant, Moses," because in return for, "And Moses hid his face," he was rewarded with, "and the image of the Lord does he behold." That is, if you had believed in my prayer for you, and while I was with you, hearing all the praises and glorifications that you thought of me, there is no doubt you would be ashamed of the coldness instead of the warmth. And if you were properly ashamed and regretful, you would be rewarded with the Creator's mercy over you, and then, more or less, the excitement would return to you, and you would be rewarded with uniting with me properly, as a stake that will not fall forever.

Yehuda Leib

Letter No. 43

14 *Tammuz, Tav-Reish-Peh-Zayin*, July 14, 1927, London

To the honorable ... may his candle burn:

... Our sages have already said, "The fear of your teacher is as the fear of heaven." This, therefore, will be the measure of exaltedness that such a man obtains by his sanctity, for his exaltedness will by no means exceed the exaltedness of his teacher.

What the Rijnaar boasted about—that he was awarded a higher degree than all the sages in his generation because he acquired more faith in the sages than all of his contemporaries—we need to understand that faith does not come by lending. Such faith can be acquired by six-year-old children, too, but as a feeling of the exaltedness and the inspiration to his soul from the wisdom of the sages who have shared from His wisdom to those who fear Him.

I have already said and elaborated that the biggest *Masach* [screen] is in the work in the children of the land of Israel, since the domination of the Canaan *Klipa* [shell/peel] is in this place, and each one is as low as the ground, his friend is even lower than the ground, and his rav [teacher] is like him.

Allegorically, you can say the words of our sages about the verse, "Leave Me and keep My law"—"I wish they would leave Me" means that they were proud of the exaltedness. And although "he and I cannot dwell in the same place," still, "Keep My law," be attached to a genuine righteous with proper faith in the sages. Then there is hope that the righteous will reform them and will sentence them to the side of merit as is appropriate for the presence of the Creator. What could come out of their humbleness and lowliness so the Creator does not move His abode from them, if they have no genuine righteous [person] to guide them in His law and prayer, and lead them to a place of Torah and wisdom?

It is already known that it is forbidden to marry one's daughter to an uneducated man. By this they gradually dry out like dry bones, God forbid. And what can you do for them if not repeat such words from time to time until the living one will pay attention?

... It is written, "And Moses will take the tent," etc. Why did he pitch his tent outside the camp? The fools believe that he did it to stop the flow of *Hochma* due to the sin. This is unthinkable, since after the sin they need the fountains of Torah and *Hochma* thousands of times more than before, as our sages said, "Had Israel not sinned, they would have been given only the *Five Books of Moses* and the book of Joshua."

However, it is to the contrary. It is a true remedy for opening the fountains of wisdom to a faithful source, since once Moses had pitched his tent outside the camp, the craving for him inside the camp increased, as "One who has bread in his basket is not like one who," etc., and along with it the adhesion with Him. Thus, they were rewarded with expansion of Moses' soul among them, for which they were called "the generation of knowledge."

I have already said and reminded you the words of teaching that I said on the festival of *Shavuot* [Feast of Weeks] prior to my departure from you about the verse, "Run My beloved, and be like a gazelle": "As the gazelle turns its face back when it runs," etc., for having no other way to make a *Panim* [face/anterior], they devise this tactic—bringing the *Panim* to the *Achoraim* [back/posterior]. It is as it is written, "So is the Creator when," etc., "He turns His face back," since the sensation of separation and *Achoraim*, and the inability to receive the *Panim* of *Kedusha* [holiness] increase the sparks of craving tremendously, until the *Achoraim* become *Panim*, since the tablets were written on both sides. You should be noticing these things by now.

Yehuda

Letter No. 44

Tammuz, Tav-Reish-Peh-Zayin, July, 1927, London

To the honorable students, may the Lord be upon them:

... and I must praise Rav ... whom I feel closer to me than the rest of the students, and I am deliberately praising him in his presence, so he will give praise and thanksgiving to the Creator for it, that after my leaning away from him for a short while, he was rewarded with connecting to me to a great extent. It must be a present from the Creator.

And concerning my not answering his questions in private, it is because so is my way in important matters—to change addressees from one to the other so as to not give a grip to the *Sitra Achra* [other side]. Hence, each one must exert himself to understand all the letters, without minding the addressee whatsoever.

Do not suspect me that his words are not properly engraved in my heart. Rather, I carry the load with him in all his labors, troubles, and pains.

It is true that for some months now he has been mentioning before me the great pain he has had in the side of his head. I wanted to quickly write him a proven remedy, which is to exert in Torah, but my way has always been that before I make my remedy known, I ask of the Creator that he would obtain by himself. After he obtains by himself, I, too, will come and fill up the words, "For Judah and more to call," and I will tell him the remedy.

This is why I so rejoiced when I received from him after some weeks, words of Torah about the verse, "And the man Moses was very humble," that he discovered it with a genuine mind—that the whole matter of salvation is in obtainment of *Hochma* and the secrets of Torah. I praised and thanked the Creator for it.

But afterward, I received from him a letter from which I understood that he had broken, "Let he not break his word," and once again he perceives ways and salvations prior to attaining the secrets of Torah, since he wrote me that the pain has once again gripped his entire head.

Therefore, I hereby remind him that he had already resolved that there will not be complete, eternal salvation before he attains the flavors of Torah, and the flavors of *Mitzva* [commandment]. Therefore, he must not regret, except over the attainments of the Torah.

It is known that the Creator does not marry His daughter to an uneducated man, as our sages said, "Anyone who marries his daughter to an uneducated man, it is as though he ties her and places her in front of a lion."

... It is known that the woman is always called after the man: He is a *Melech* [king], she is a *Malkah* [queen]; he is *Hacham* [wise], she is *Hochma* [wisdom]; he is *Navon* [intelligent/understanding], she is *Bina* [intelligence/understanding], as it is as is written in *Tikkuney Zohar*. It therefore follows that the wife of an uneducated person is named "folly," since he is a fool, who does not know how to be watchful with kings' honor.

The permanent residence of the evil inclination is a heart that is empty of Torah. But the Torah and *Hochma* reject the evil inclination from the heart, bit by bit. And because he is a fool, a woman of folly is prepared for him—*Klipat* Noga [Noga shell], who seduced Eve.

This is what the writing says, "Anger rests in the hearts of fools." You find a perfect reason why the king should not give his daughter to an uneducated man. Unless your soul truly desires the daughter of Jacob, you need not give many gifts, as is believed by the external ones, of Hamor–father of Shechem the Hivite. Rather, exert for attainment of flavors of Torah and flavors of *Mitzva*, not one of them missing, for then his desire and her desire will meet and unite with one another, and the love will complete its thing by itself, without any assistance from aside, meaning by humans.

Yehuda

Letter No. 45

25 Tammuz, Tav-Reish-Peh-Zayin, July 25, 1927, London

To the honorable students, may the Creator be upon them.

As I prepare myself to return to my home, I so long to find you ready and willing to hear the word of the Creator properly.

Currently, I feel shame for ... and for ... who were among the best and the highest of the friends, and now, who knows? Perhaps ... may his candle burn is drawing nearer to me more than they, and if he is rewarded with complete confidence, he will rise and live, as it is written, "You desire truth in the inward parts, and in blocked wisdom, You let me know." That is, by obtaining confidence, all the wisdom of the worlds, upper and lower, is bundled and revealed, and all that is required for this attainment is a pure heart, which has already loathed self-love and is entirely dedicated to His name.

Therefore, he did well not being impressed at all by ... and ... slighting him for his lack of shrewdness. Rather, let his heart be haughty in the ways of the Creator, and small and great are there.

What else can I do for ... who wishes to learn everything from me, except for the matter of lowliness, for he is thoroughly displeased with this engagement, and he is confident that he is better and more comely than the blind and dry people, and all the more so than his brother, who has an ugly face. He is even certain that I, too, thank him because he was not ashamed to write me. It seemed to me that for his sake, he should dedicate considerable time to this engagement.

And yet, my intention is not as the lowest of the low, meaning as the lowly, who seek lowliness, for that one is even worse than pride itself because who will swear on a stone that it is a stone? Certainly, there is he who thinks that it is gold. However, he should know and believe that all creations are as "clay in the hands of a potter—when He wishes, He makes longer, and when He wishes, He makes shorter."

Also, he should not be angry at the wicked, but rather have mercy on them no less than he has mercy on himself. As long as he has not been rewarded with the higher mercy, how will he know what to detect and be angry over? On the contrary, the mercy on them increases even more because they are robbed without consolation.

Like a father whose two sons are sick, where one has the funds to purchase medicines, and one does not have the funds. Naturally, the father's heart has more mercy on the son without the funds for medicines, for the one with the funds for medicines will be cured if he seeks out cures, and if he does not, it is as though he has committed suicide. But on the other son, the mercy of the father and of all who see him cuts through the heart.

Thus, why do you so slight your brother, who has an ugly face, and you are angry with the world for respecting him more than you? In my view, he is more worthy of respect than you are, and this is simple. So is the nature of the world, and although he did not see, his fortune saw, and this is easy to understand.

Last week, I learned from ... that he has resolved to resign from my engagement, that I had burdened him with too much, and to come to me, to London, without asking my permission, for how will he ask me? Does this relate to me? Also, even a small child running from school knows that to sit next to his teacher's table, with great contentment, and to entertain himself with the secrets of Torah and high secrets, is far more agreeable than to engage in the ways of his teacher, in lowly and contemptible matters. From those, one can only come to great troubles, for lack of ability to pray even as a simpleton.

I reply without question, for one who deals with me in this way at this time, when he is thirsty and longing, I greatly benefit him. Moreover, let his deeds be with me when I am rewarded with bringing him under the wings of the *Shechina* [Divinity], for then he might think, has the Creator spoke only with Moses? The Creator will speak with me, as well. I, too, have a table to set, to furnish all the upper worlds, and how can I annul myself now before the bodily engagements of my teacher and the questions he had taken?

The honor and fear of equalizing with the Creator relate primarily to that time, when he has already been rewarded with the *Shechina* being clothed in his heart forever, for you should believe that your teacher's bodily matters are truly engagements of the soul. This is why our sages said, "It did not say, 'learned,' but 'poured,' implying that serving is greater than learning."

A student should be in true annulment before the teacher, in the full sense of the word, for then he unites with him and he can perform salvations in his favor. A student cannot adhere to his teacher's soul, as it is above his attainment.

As ... may his candle burn, wrote me, he believes that the body of a righteous is as great as the soul of another. While he did not hear what he himself said, for he finished with ... he still agreed with my trip to America. Had he heard what he had said, he would not have agreed so easily. However, it is true that the body of a true righteous is as great as the soul with which the righteous, the saints of the upper one, are rewarded. So may you be rewarded with adhering to my body, and then you will certainly see your world in your life. This is why our sages praised the service, as it is closer to *Dvekut* [adhesion] of the student with the rav.

It is hard for me to understand ... for how can it be that after all the troubles I went through in his favor—composing the handsome and comely composition, namely my book *Ohr HaPanim* [The Light of the Face], with various adornments for him, on fine paper and with a clear type font, a complete introduction, and a general preface, index, and a list of acronyms? These have become the two great lights, properly illuminating and explaining.

Also, almost every single week I write him a long and elaborate letter, sometimes even two in the same week, as best as my fingers can produce. I cannot suspect that he is not a good guest, that he will not say, "All that the landlord has troubled himself with, he has troubled himself only for me." And yet, I find him sitting surrounded by the holy wall, for had he not sat outside the wall, he would certainly not equalize himself with his inclination, conducting this sapless custom.

I also fear that alongside that custom of his, he says to himself that he is adhered and connected to me more than all the friends, for the heart's aim follows the words, and the Creator seeks the heart. And since the point in his heart is adhered to me, he needs nothing more than to repeat the actions. These are needed and appropriate only for those of little knowledge, who have no other way. For a decorated (handsome)

Jew like him, a good heart bests them all, so he no longer needs to display any actions with qualification or advantage.

It is true that I have not yet heard from all the friends any impressions from my book *Ohr HaPanim*, except for ... who wrote me praises and accolades galore from the bottom of his heart for every section I sent. I am therefore certain that it will help him ... and he can more or less feel the value of the man and his work. This is why his heart is a human heart, which is at least behooved to be impressed, as I have already written in the interpretation of the verse, "My darling son, Ephraim." *Yakir* [dear] is like *Yakir* [know/recognize], and *Yakir* [know/recognize] is like *Yakir* [dear], meaning they are interdependent and are as one.

Remember what ... wrote me, admitting without shame that he understood that whole letter well, except for the issue of *Yakir* and *Yakir*, that he must insert an elephant through the eye of the needle [study hard]. He attributed it to the possibility that he needs more forewords and knowledge of the righteous. This is why he was able to write to me in the last letter that there is a hidden lock on my book, which he does not know or understand.

What could I reply to him? Therefore, I said to myself that what the mind does not do, time will do, and it will become clear to him that recognition is according to the appreciation. That is, the inspiration by and annulment before the real good. This is what raises and sustains the exaltedness and preciousness, and then the recognition is accumulated in him, followed by the raising of the preciousness. Thus they rise on the rungs of *Kedusha* [holiness] until they are rewarded with satisfying the deficiency and correcting the wrong, up to the real and complete unification.

In that letter, I wrote that *Yakir* is like *Yakir* on the Creator, but they are one and the same, as it is written, "And they believed in the Lord and in His servant Moses," and as our sages said, "One who doubts his teacher, it is as though he doubts the *Shechina*," since the upper will [desire] is equal in matters that are measured and come in truly the same amount.

And what can I say to you, natives of the land, who believe that I am abroad and you are in the land of Israel!

The holy Torah will testify on my behalf in what Moses commands us in the portion, *Masa'ey* [Journeys]: "Command the children of Israel ... for you are coming unto the land." In these verses, he points out and clearly marks the borders of the land, in a way that anyone who comes to the land of Israel will no longer have any doubt.

He decrees and says, "It shall be to you the side of the Negev ..." "Negev" comes from the word *Negiva* [wiping], for "The salvation of the Lord is as a wet garden." Therefore, the departure from His light is called "Negev." "It shall be" implies joy, indicating the salvation of the Creator, which includes the letter, "It shall be to you the side of the Negev," meaning that they knew that the side of the Negev was considered a recognized side and boundary.

It is written, "And you will soon perish," meaning from Zin Desert, by Edom. "Zin" comes from the words *Tzinim* and *Pachim*, which our sages said are not in the hands of heaven, but rather by Edom, for as soon as Edom is involved, the Creator says, "I and he cannot dwell in the world."

This is why he says, "And it shall be to you the boundary of Negev." "Boundary" is the end, where the above-mentioned wiping ends, "From the end of the Dead Sea eastward" means as soon as you begin to touch the edge of the kingdom of heaven. "Eastward" is like "as before" [the two words contain the same letters in Hebrew], the wiping will promptly end, and the abundance of the goals of His might will begin to appear before you.

It adds further, "And your border shall turn from Negev." That is, because the beginning of sunrise was after the "wiping," and "in its boundary," the narrow turns outward and twists to the north of the world diagonally, as RASHI interpreted, to The Ascent of Akrabim [scorpions]. In other words, this is why scorpions are coming up before you.

"And pass along to Tzina [Tzin]." Terrible *Tzina* [chill] spreads through the bones, bursting forth from Zin Desert on the east, for he is *Tzin*, and she is *Tzina*. It is translated [into Aramaic], "from the south to the ascent" of Akrabim.

"And pass along to Tzin," as our sages said, "Even if a serpent is wrapped around his heel, he will not stop." But according to everyone, a scorpion does stop. Therefore, "And his outcomes shall be from the south to Rekam Ge'ah [Kadesh-Barne'a]," because envy consumes like fire in front of the scorpions until he must come to Kadesh-Barne'a, which is Rekam Ge'ah.

In other words, his thoughts take on a clothing of pride, extraordinarily, until "And it shall go forth to Hatzar-Addar," for although he boasted with a mantle of hair and will not cause to sin, like those who are first to the kingship, he still feels he is standing in the court, standing outside. This is why that place is called *Hatzar* [court] *Addar*, meaning that they contradict one another.

"And pass along to Atzmona," Atzm-on-ah. He is *Etzem*, and he is *Atzmon*, and she is *Atzmona*, for the place causes, and it becomes like a hard, unbreakable *Etzem* [bone/object]. Likewise, the elephant does not have joints in its bones and cannot turn its head back. When it wants to look back, it must turn itself entirely, from head to tail, as is known to those who know the nature of animals.

He concludes and says, "And the border shall turn for you from Atzmon to the brook of Egypt," meaning that Atzmona returned to being Atzmon. This is why he returned to the brook of Egypt, of which the Creator said, "You shall not return that way henceforth." However, it is still not the actual exile in Egypt, but rather the edge of that exile.

"And its exit shall be at the sea." That is, once it was taken and sickened in the brook of Egypt, it is rewarded from there with the offspring of wisdom, to roam in the sea of wisdom. RASHI interpreted it: "That strip that protruded to the north was from Kadesh-Barne'a to Atzmon, and from there on the narrow grew shorter ... to the brook of Egypt."

Interpreting his words: It is written in the name of the ARI in *The Brightness of the Firmament*, and I believe in *Gate to Introductions*, as well, that the world was initially created with a *Bet* ב. It is known that there is a dot in the middle of the *Bet*, which is *Hochma* [wisdom], and the north side is open (see RASHI, *Beresheet*). Afterward, that dot of *Hochma* in the *Bet* expanded like the *Vav* ו and returned to the north of the *Bet*, like this, ם, and became a blocked [final] *Mem*.

This is the meaning of the words of our sages, "But it could be created in one utterance," that *Mem* is one utterance.

However, *Hochma* could not expand because that ם is a blocked letter in all four directions; hence, the *Hochma* was restricted once again as a dot in the middle of the *Bet* ב, like the *Vav*.

At that time, the *Hochma* expanded to be given as a reward for the righteous, which is why "the world was created in ten utterances, to avenge the wicked who are destroying the world, which was created in ten utterances."

Because the border turned from Atzmon to the brook of Egypt, as it is written, "I saw the wicked buried, and they came," and as it is also written, "I was at ease and He shattered me, and He has grasped me by the neck and broken me to pieces. And He set me up as His target." It is all because of the above-mentioned strip, where the *Yod* expanded into a *Vav* to the north of the *Bet*, and the border was necessarily made shorter for the brook of Egypt. This is why all the enemies of Israel are lost there, and the children of Israel come to the sea to draw the fountains of wisdom [*Hochma*] to renew the world as before, meaning to "give good reward to the righteous, who establish the world, which was created in ten utterances."

The writing ends, "As for the western border, you shall have the Great Sea." This is the primary source for being granted with the great *Hochma*, called "the Great Sea." From there begins the drawing of the air of the land of Israel, which the Creator has sworn to give to us.

To rush us toward that thing, the text repeats and says, "This border shall be your western border." That is, all the exits from the sea of wisdom are only that border, meaning the great sea, the sea of the land of Israel, *Mochin de Gadlut*! It is impossible to be rewarded with them unless they have traversed all ten borders. This is the meaning of "and changed my wages ten times," after which one is rewarded with settling in the land of Israel, a land flowing with milk and honey, and a good, broad, and pleasant land.

Behold, I have given you horses. If you can place riders on them, you will come to settle in a good, broad, and pleasant land for all eternity. Until then, do not say that

I have journeyed from the land of Israel. Rather, you are negligent in this and do not properly long to sit in it together with me.

Because I read the portion to you, I will conclude with the prophet: "Hear the word of the Lord, O house of Jacob and all the families of the house of Israel. ... Who say to a tree, 'You are my father,' and to a stone, 'You gave birth to me.' For they have turned their back to Me, ... and where are your gods, which you have made for yourself? Let them arise if they can save you in the time of your trouble ..."

Is it even conceivable that our holy fathers at the time of the Temple and the prophecy were fools, calling the tree and the stone, "Mother and Father"? Only fools who make others fools could think so about our fathers.

Rather, the tree is the tree of life, and the stone is the tree of knowledge. That is, what is revealed to a person, it is tested and tried that it is the counsel of the Creator, since through those tree and counsel he extends the light of the upper life, called "the tree of life." What is hidden from human concepts and tactics—while he is still doubtful whether it is a good tree or a bad one in the eyes of his Master, to be favored by Him—is called "the tree of knowledge of good and evil," or *Even* [stone], from the word *Avin* [I will understand], meaning I will observe and see if it is a good counsel or a bad one.

One who sits and regrets a long time is also called *Meducha* [mortar/issue], as our sages implied, "Prophet Hagai sat on this *Meducha*." It is called *Meducha* because it is ready for the fools to grind and crush their bones there, as it is written, "If you pound a fool in a mortar with a pestle ... his foolishness will not depart from him."

We should ask, "How is the fool placed under the pestle in the mortar in fervent *Dvekut* [adhesion], yet does not depart from his folly whatsoever?" Also, although he sees for himself that the fool is killed like a moth, he will not depart from his filth? But the fool finds for himself a reason even while sitting inside the mortar and seems to find contentment in it.

We need not be surprised at it, for it was said about such matters, "Do not judge your friend until you are in his shoes." This is why this god is called "gods of stone," or a "figured stone," for it does not reward its worshippers whatsoever, who worship it devotedly, and they have no one to save them in their time of trouble.

Opposite the gods of stone are those who worship the tree, who settle for the slight illumination they can salvage for themselves. As the hand of the Creator is too short to save them in their time of trouble, they do not move from the tree that they see because it seems to them that the landlord, too, cannot save his vessels from there because that tree is already tried and tested by them as the father of life. Thus, they forget, or pretend to forget, that holiness is increasing, not decreasing.

This is a sign of sanctification and sanctity, as it is written, "Do not say, 'The first days were better than these,' for it is not out of wisdom that you ask this," as those who serve another god are sterile and do not bear fruit, and wane and diminish like the fruit of the festival. They will die without wisdom and always feel that "the first days were better than these."

This is what the prophet complained about them, for after all their days in the above-mentioned foreign works, as the disgrace of a thief who has been found, "they say to a tree, 'You are my father.'" That is, as though saved from a fire, they delight in their lot, for that tree is to them like the father of life. "... and to a stone, 'You gave birth to me.'"

And once they have received their lot, the prophet compares them to people placed between the mortar and the pestle. The prophet asks further, "And where are your gods which you made for yourself? Let them rise, if they can save you at the time of your trouble." That is, "Think how much those gods have given you and how much they have saved you from your troubles."

He continues and asks about them saying, "According to the number of your cities are your gods, O Judah." That is, in each awakening, these invocators were stubborn and confident compared to the above-mentioned sides—the tree or the stone. Finally, all the kings of the east and the west could not disrupt the works from you, and each city becomes Godly to you, like the word of God.

Do write me and clarify how much of this long letter you understand, and how much you do not. Specifically, detail at length all ten boundaries that I have depicted for you, and interpret for me more than I wrote in it, for I wrote succinctly.

And most of all, do not be ashamed to let me know all that you do not understand, and all your interpretations, for then I "will respond to the grain, to the wine and to the oil," and not one of your words shall be returned empty handed.

Yehuda

Letter No. 46

6 Elul, Tav-Reish-Peh-Zayin, September 3, 1927, London

To the honorable, great *Hassid*, a treasure of wisdom:

I received your letter and I was happy to see his handwriting, which was to me a sign of his good health. Concerning what he says, that he does not consider the rav a Kabbalist, as I think, I do not know who said and who suspected that the rav is a Kabbalist, so I think that the honorable sir thinks that I long for his approval to support my words of Torah. I have already written that I want it only in order to obtain the funds to print the books because I do not have the endorsement of a renowned person who is important in this place, as I have written there.

For this reason, I think that the honorable sir wishes to know more about me and to deliberate with me on that matter. In that, too, I am willing to comply, and I will reply to the best of my ability, especially since he retired from the trying that is mentioned there. For this reason, I am impartial on this matter and I am like a wise disciple who comes prior to the act, who is obeyed, and I will answer first thing first.

1) What he wrote, that he does not see at this time anyone who is a Kabbalist, I wonder how one can sit in a certain place and see throughout the world, and especially, to see who is a Kabbalist. And yet it is true that I, too, have not seen a genuine Kabbalist in my time, but I understand that Israel is not widowed and there is no generation without the likes of Abraham, Isaac, and Jacob. And besides, "We did not see" is not evidence.

2) What he informed me concerning a Kabbalist, as in "Let a double portion of your spirit be upon me," who asked what he asked and what he replied. He explained that he asked to be a receiver and the received together, "And this is why he replied to him, 'If you see that I am receiving from you now that you are receiving from me.'" I admit that I do not understand the brevity of his words. It is similar to one who asks his friend for a gift, and he replies to him, "If you see that I am giving you a gift, then you will have the gift." This is not an answer whatsoever, much less that it does not require a twofold requisite, as written there.

3) "I saw in my teachers from ... and from ... that they had that degree," thus far his words. In my view, there is no doubt that one cannot see any degree in one's teachers, much less if he still has not been rewarded with it himself. Our sages said about the likes of this, "One does not understand his rav before he is forty," and even in one's friend it is impossible to see that which is not in his own possession. I wanted to hear the honorable sir's opinion about that.

Now I will toy a little with his words concerning the receiver and the received as one. These words can be understood only literally, meaning that anyone who receives the abundance from the Creator boasts with the crowns of the Creator, and one who is rewarded with feeling during the act how the Creator, too, boasts about having found him ready to receive His giving is called "a Kabbalist." And this is certainly a high degree, as it is written, "I have found My servant, David; I have anointed him with My holy oil."

By the meaning of the words, "a double portion," I will explain, as in "Let the wise," etc. It means as it is written, "He cannot prefer the son of the loved one," etc., "He shall acknowledge him to give him a double portion." Concerning the birthright, it is known from Rabbi Ber of Mezeritch that "a double portion" is the mouth in which that spirit that the fathers trusted was concealed, see in the *Idra*. I will interpret it below, and from that he will understand the above.

It is known that there are two righteous—a righteous who came into her, and a righteous who came out of her, as in "As her soul went out," for which their *Zivug* [coupling] stopped. It is known in the *Zivugim* [pl. of *Zivug*] of ZON that in the future, their *Zivug* will be complete, and then she will be called "a double portion." This is why

Elijah told him, "You ask a hard question," implying to him how far it reaches. That is, "If you see me being taken from you," taken is with a *Kubutz* [a punctuation mark], which means taken from you, meaning the opposite of what you thought thus far, that I was your master and you were taken from me. Rather, I am taken from you, and then "It shall be so unto you" because then you will be rewarded with "a double portion." This is why Elisha did not have the strength to ask him about it anymore. (It is somewhat similar to what is written about the pious man [*Hassid*] who considered him his rav [teacher].)

But in the end he was rewarded with it, as it is written, "And Elisha sees and he cries out, 'My father, my father, the vehicle of Israel and his horsemen.'" That is, he saw how all the lights of Israel that were included in his master, Elijah, are all drawn and ignited from him, himself. This is why he found it very difficult, as it is written, "a hard question." In other words, he could not tolerate it until he cried out, "My father, my father," which is the double portion, where the bottom ZON are as the upper AVI.

This is why "he saw him no more," since he saw only himself. He was very stressed by that; hence, "he held his clothes and tore them into two tears." Explanation: The lights in general, "the vehicle of Israel and his horsemen," are implied in the words "his clothes," ... until he was rewarded, as it is written, "And he picked up Elijah's mantle that fell from him." This is the mantle ... which until now he regarded as lowly and externality, but now he understood, picked it up to its place, and then he was indeed rewarded with a double portion.

Henceforth, he had the fall of Elijah's mantle as an example for raising MAN. This is the meaning of the words, "And he took ... which fell from him ... and said, 'Where is the Lord, God of Elijah, too?'" "Too" is the *Kli* [vessel] of *Nefesh* [soul, spirit], as it is written, "And He breathed into his nostrils the breath [also "soul"] of life, and the man became a living soul." This is the fall of in between, as mentioned regarding the tearing of the clothes that became for him, as in "Too ... and Elisha went over." "And they said, 'The spirit of Elijah rests on Elisha,'" meaning all the degrees of Elijah, his master, were connected in Elisha.

By this we understand what is written in the ARI's *Assortments from the Torah*, that Elisha is an incarnation of Cain, of whom it is written, "and his offering He did not accept." Indeed, Elisha consists of the letters *Eli Sha'ah* [my God accepted], meaning as we said, "a double portion."

(the rest is missing)

Yehuda Leib

Letter No. 47

Tav-Reish-Peh-Zayin, 1927

To my dearest ... forever and ever:

I received your words today and there is one thing that I see in them: your great fear of my moving away from you even as a hairsbreadth.

It is inherent in people, and also gives permission ... to draw true abundance to the other side. And where the abundance of fear should work on you, to look into your own heart, always and forever—so as not to distance your heart from me as a hairsbreadth—you turn this fear on me, that my heart will not draw far from you. Thus, you are laboring to correct what is fixed, what was never broken, while the broken place remains broken and without attention. I know that these words, too, will be unclear to you and you will not understand where they are coming from, and at a time of joy you might think more, God forbid.

I do feel for you, my dear, to toss into your mouth a drop of truth, which is not obligated by any of the 613 organs of the human body. How many times have you learned it from me? And still, whenever I offer you a word of truth, you fight me fiercely.

Indeed, so is the nature of spirituality: One who is adhered to the Creator feels himself as not adhered. He worries and is insecure about it and does all that he can do by his strength to be rewarded with *Dvekut* [adhesion]. A wise one feels opposite from one who is not adhered to the Creator, who feels content and satisfied, and does not worry properly, except to keep the *Mitzvot* [commandments] of worry and longing, for "a fool does not feel." Just as one cannot teach one who is blind from birth the essence of absence of vision, except when he is given eyesight, so is this matter.

I have already written that you are wrong to say that I have journeyed from you. You should instead understand that you have journeyed from me. Believe me that my eyes and heart are always with you, without feeling a distance of place or time at all. Were it not required for the listener to know, you would be witnessing it.

On the contrary, physical remoteness from you can act within you faster. In truth, this is what I hoped, and do hope for, if you understand more.

It is also true that I judge you favorably, assuming the air of Jerusalem while I am still before you, and especially during concealment from you. This is why I have established for you conducts by which you can still hang on and not turn back.

And the single most special one among them is the *Dvekut* of friends. I sincerely promise that this love is able. And I shall remind you of every good thing that you need. And if you nonetheless braced yourselves in that, you would certainly go from strength to strength on the rungs of holiness, as I have promised earlier.

How can I forgive this to you while the ladder that is placed on the ground is empty? No one climbs it, and instead of today you say "tomorrow." You tell me, what would you gain from my forgiveness? Let me know and I will answer you.

I am not an issuer of decrees or a maker of laws, and this, too, you should know. Unless I feared sliding back, I would not go out of my way, for it was very, very difficult for me. But I am as one who regrets the loss of time ... but my soul suffers from it more than was anticipated, even in a standstill, much less when you, God forbid, fall back. This I saw ahead of time and wished to correct in advance.

Therefore, let me remind you of the validity of love of friends in spite of everything at this time, for it is upon this that our right to exist depends, and upon this our near-to-come success is measured.

Hence, turn away from all the imaginary engagements and set your hearts on thinking thoughts and devising proper tactics to truly connect your hearts as one, so the words "Love your friend as yourself" will literally come true in you, for a verse does not reach beyond the literal, and you will be cleaned by the thought of love that will cover all crimes. Test me in that, and begin to truly connect in love, and then you will see, "the palate will taste," and all the people will not separate between me and you.

Concerning your negligence in coming to the prayer, I know and feel your fate and sorrow. Unless I saw that the measure of loss does not decrease by the justness of the cause, I would not say a word.

Yehuda Leib

Letter No. 48

9 *Elul*, *Tav-Reish-Peh-Zayin*, September 6, 1927, London

To the students, may the Lord be upon you:

I received all your letters, and what ... wrote me about the humiliations and the papers about him, he should believe me that I share and fully sympathize with his pain and misery. He should know that I feel his pain more than he himself.

But the Creator will grant him doubly, and if he could brace himself and act by the conduct of a servant of the Creator to say with honesty, "The Creator permitted all who afflict me," I would advise him to greatly strengthen himself in this, and it will help him in all his ways.

Concerning his questions whether he can show the letter and the words of Torah of the sage's fruit, "And you will be only joyful," he can certainly show it to all the friends.

In the letter of ... may his candle burn, I am glad to see that he has already begun to do what I want him to in this matter.

And what ... wrote, that he sees no other way but come to my house himself, I agree with him on that, and my thoughts are already occupied with preparing supplies for the way and to rush my arrival at my home as much as possible. I have much work to do regarding that, to stand up to all the preventions that rise against me to detain me here for longer.

He should ask my son ... why he has not informed me of the complete reconciliation that I learned about.

And thank ... for the information concerning the friends' party on the fifth of *Sukkot*, and concerning the whole issue between the friends, I have already written that we need not do much about it because with the Creator's help, He will finish for us, who have already begun for the glory of His name.

Yehuda Leib

Letter No. 49

9 Elul, Tav-Reish-Peh-Zayin, September 6, 1927, London

To the students, may the Lord be upon them:

While I trust you to keep your commitment to devotedly observe every utterance I utter right away, I order you to begin to love one another as yourselves with all your might, to ache with your friends' pains, and rejoice in your friends' joys as much as possible. I hope that you will keep these words of mine and execute this matter to the fullest.

I received the letters and everything in them, but at the moment, I cannot answer in person. Besides what I have already replied to each and every one in the previous letters, I promise to speak more elaborately.

Concerning the above-mentioned order, I mean specifically among the friends, because it is written, "your friend." About people from the outside, it requires much scrutiny because there is more to lose than to gain due to their clinging to corporeality and self-importance, while among the friends this must never be accepted; be very careful.

Awaiting salvation for it is near...

Yehuda

Letter No. 50

11 Elul, Tav-Reish-Peh-Zayin, September 8, 1927, London

To the honorable students, may the Creator be upon you:

I received your letter from the portion *Shoftim* [Judges], along with the innovations in the Torah of all except for ... and I do hope to receive his letter today.

It would be very good if you wrote your innovations in the work of the Creator, as well as your questions on the matter. And it makes no difference whether I answer you and comment, or I do not write and do not comment, because your very question is half the answer, while I bring before the Creator to answer you in due time. I am surprised that you still do not sufficiently understand it.

I do have one comment for you: When you write me innovations in the Torah, you do not understand at all if the ways of which you speak are already in your possession, or at least on your degree, meaning whether you can do them or they are above your degree. Rather, wait for the Creator to grant you the understanding how to do them. Likewise, you should be mindful to always interpret as a prayer to the Creator, so you are rewarded with the innovation you have attained or an intimation, as an apology for not being rewarded with it yet, and so on.

The beginning of our longed for, pleasant future is approaching us, and so I crave and long for you to be next to me in body and in soul (meaning that you would draw near me, and not me to you, which is impossible, as well as pointless).

I must also apologize that last *Tishrey* [first Hebrew month] was a very favorable time but you were not near me then. I looked for ... all through that month but he was nowhere in my area, and I only saw one or two of you. Naturally, I was sorry about that all through last year.

The reason for it is the pride and self-importance that have snuck into you, and to that extent the unfounded hatred among you (due to it) in clinging to materialistic friends who are not from our society. ... Clearly, if you hate one of the members of the group, it is a clear sign that you are not in complete love with me, as well.

And although the evil inclination shows you that friend's death, meaning that his actions are bad and sinful toward the Creator, you should have prayed and trusted the Creator for his sake, that He will certainly help him because he is my student.

And if you already understand about that friend that the Creator cannot help him, and that my prayers also cannot help him at a time of need, then the judgment reflects back on the hater. From now on, come and see, and pay attention that you do not fall into that trap again.

... You also need not notice at all if I actually, verbally expel a friend ... judge him favorably, in truth.

Let me tell you the truth: There is greater unity in my departure than in my nearing. Like any craftsman who toils in his craft to complete his work in the best way, a stranger must not look at him in the middle of his work because he will not understand his conduct in his work, except for a craftsman as great as he.

I have elaborated on that so you may know that your soul depends on it.

Although I do not tend to offer private guidance, I must still comment on what I have already warned you several times: No one should share the "innovations in the Torah" that he attained, nor should he "admonish" whatsoever. Even the desire for it is a terrible flaw.

The exception is what I have permitted while I am away—to share innovations in the Torah with one another from what I have already said, as accurately as can be explained, but very precisely, without any additions of one's own.

Also, you must not speak of the words of Torah that I said, and which that friend has not heard from my mouth. It must be concealed attentively and wisely.

I find it necessary to warn about the above because I feel that you have already stretched the line that you have given yourselves. Know for certain that by this keeping you will be granted with saying innovations in the Torah before the Creator, and to admonish yourselves. But one who scatters his qualities in those will not be established in the eyes of the Creator. In that matter, an ounce is as much as a pound, and the Creator will help you and guide you to the doors of truth.

Yehuda Leib

Letter No. 51

3 Tishrey, Tav-Reish-Peh-Het, September 29, 1927, London

To the faithful soul mates:

Because the time of our celebration is approaching, I hereby point to it.

It is written, "And you will be only glad." The grammar feels as though it should have said, "And you will be glad." But this is what I have explained several times, that the whole difficulty in serving Him is that in the worker, there are always two opposites in the same carrier, that His uniqueness is simple, but must clothe in man's body, which consists of a body and a soul, which are two opposites.

Therefore, in any spiritual concept that one attains, two opposite forms are immediately created in him—one form on the part of the body, and one form on the part of the soul. By nature, a person cannot scrutinize the body and the soul as two carriers. Rather, he is composed by the Creator as one, meaning as one carrier. For this reason, spiritual attainment is as difficult for him as two opposites that cannot properly clothe in one carrier.

It is similar to the binding of Isaac, when the Creator said to Abraham, "For in Isaac shall a seed be called to you," and the Creator said to him, "And offer him there for a burnt-offering." From the perspective of the Creator, it is as was written, "I the Lord do not change." But in the perception of the receiver, they are opposites.

This is why it is written, "And you will be only glad," for "'but' and 'only' are diminutions," and the joy of the festival certainly requires wholeness. However, both must be perceived by the receiver as they are for the joy of the festival.

It is also written, "Who is as blind as My servant, or as deaf as My messenger whom I send?" And it is also written, "The deaf heard and the blind looked, so as to see." There are many others likewise, meaning as our sages said, "You, too, listen carefully," as though he was never in the court of hearing, the sentence of choice, to find out who is guilty and who is innocent, for both are the words of the living God. That is, it is written, "I the Lord do not change," as from His perspective there is but one form here.

This is the meaning of the *Mitzva* [commandment], "Sit," as in "dwell," meaning as King David asked, "that I may dwell in the house of the Lord all the days of my life, to behold the pleasantness of the Lord." The "House of the Lord" is the *Shechina* [Divinity], as in "The righteous sit with their crowns on their heads." When they are granted the most, then You are to him like a home, constant and eternal.

The Creator wished to say to His servants, "Go out of the permanent housing and sit in temporary housing," meaning only under His shade. This is the meaning of a "light *Mitzva* [commandment]," the *Mitzva* of the *Sukkah* [hut], where a person sits under the shade of the waste of granary and winery, which is the actual shade of the Creator. Although they contradict one another—for in corporeal eyes and in corporeal hands we see and feel that the shade comes from the waste, in truth it is the Creator Himself. However, from the perspective of the receiver, it is necessary that those two opposite forms will be depicted in him.

The thing is that before the complex man was created, there was no waste here. But once man was created and the waste and the judgment were felt, the quarrel began in his organs. It is as our sages said, "The hay, the straw, and the chaff deliberate with one another. One says, 'The field was sown for me,' and one says, 'The field was sown for me,' etc. When it is time for the harvest, everyone knows for whom the field was sown." All these quarrels and deliberations continued through the terrible days because three books were opened because of them: righteous, wicked, and intermediate.

Once those who were acquitted in the judgment were sorted out and whitened as wheat through the Day of Atonement, and the wicked went promptly to death, as "chaff that is blown by the wind," everyone knows for whom the field was sown. Then we arrive at the commandment, "Go out of the permanent housing and sit in temporary housing." That is, know that it is only temporary housing, and "the outcast one will not be cast out from Him." It is as was said, "Even if the whole world tells you that you are righteous, be wicked in your own eyes." This is also the meaning of the words, "And you will be only glad."

This is why the festival of harvest [*Sukkot*] is called "the time of our joy," to tell you that one should sit in the shade of a *Sukkah* in great joy, just as in the king's house, the kingdom's most eminent. "Sit" is as "dwell," without any difference whatsoever.

And yet, he should know that he is sitting in the shade of a *Sukkah*, meaning the waste of granary and winery. However, "Under His shade I delighted to sit," since he hears His word, "Go out of the permanent housing and sit in temporary housing," and both are words of the living God. Then his exit delights him as much as his entry, as it is precisely the above-mentioned precision, "The deaf heard, and the blind looked, so as to see."

Otherwise, there would not even be a shadow of a *Sukkah*, for it is not toward us, those who scrape the walls as blind, sitting under the shade of a shade, meaning twofold darkness. It was said about them, "shall inherit locust," two words [locust is a translation of *Tzaltzal=Tzel Tzel* (shade, shade)], since their thatch is still fit for reception of *Tuma'a* [impurity] like one who puts thatch in pegs, which have no *Rosh* [head], or in broken *Kelim* [vessels], where there is still dross, since they are still in a state of *Tohu* and the breaking of the vessels.

By this you will see that one cannot observe the *Mitzva* of *Sukkah* before he has been rewarded the degree of uniting *HaVaYaH ADNI*, which is the meaning of "The sun in its sheath."

It was also said explicitly regarding the nations of the world: "In the future, when the Creator brings out the sun from its sheath, and each one kicks his *Sukkah* and leaves, and he asks, Israel too?" They explained, "Kick, they do not kick." It explains that if a person is not rewarded with a sun in its sheath, he cannot keep the *Mitzva* of *Sukkah* altogether. This is the meaning of *HaVaYaH ADNI* being 91 in *Gematria*, implying "Go [91 in *Gematria*] out of the permanent housing."

This is the meaning of "Stay with me one more day," as in the small meal of the *Atzeret* [assembly on the eighth day], meaning that thanks to the complete joy of the festival, as in "only glad"—accepting the two opposites in the same carrier and not revoking one before the other—one is rewarded with the eighth day. This is the meaning of "Stay with me one more day," the day of which it is written, "a day which shall be known as the Lord's, neither day nor night, and it shall come to pass that in the evening there will be light."

Explanation: A "day" is the works of the righteous, and a night is the works of the wicked, as it is written in *Midrash Rabbah* regarding "And God said, 'Let there be light.'" I still do not know which has the Lord chosen—the works of the righteous or the works of the wicked, when he says, "And God called the light 'day,'" to teach you that He chose the works of the righteous.

Therefore, at the end of correction, as in, "The outcast will not be cast out from him," it is written, "a day which shall be known as the Lord's, neither day nor night," meaning the above-mentioned choice. But in the evening, which pertains to the waste of granary and winery, "there will be light," and all thanks to the delay on the eighth day.

This is why it is called "the festival of the *Atzeret*," as though *Otzrin* [gathering] the oil from the olive, meaning "oil squashing," which is the extract ... of all the servitude of "only" a day, and it is crushed in a crusher for the glory of His name, and "Truth shall spring forth from the earth," "And the Lord shall be king over all the earth," for it will be entirely for the Creator, for "only" is part—half permitted and half forbidden, "half of it for you, and half of it for the Lord." But in the eighth day, the *Atzeret*, it becomes entirely for the Creator.

Yehuda Leib

Letter No. 52

14 *Tishrey, Tav-Reish-Peh-Het*, October 10, 1927, *Sukkot* Eve, London

To ... may his candle burn:

I received your letter and the notes. ...interpreted for me the verse, "Seek the Lord while He is found; call upon Him while He is near." This is perplexing. If the Creator is already with him, and He is already close, why is there still a need to seek and call upon Him? He explained that the writing speaks to those who have already been rewarded with constant closeness to the Creator. The prophet warns them that although it seems to them that there is nothing more to seek or to obtain, we should never think like that, for it is like cutting down the plantings. Rather, one should seek further and call upon the Creator for greater attainments.

Let me interpret this according to our way. Clearly, anyone who has been rewarded with his Maker's fondness, the Creator grants all his wishes, as do lovers and friends who complement each other's wants, each according to his ability. Because that person has been rewarded with befriending the Creator, he necessarily consists of body and soul. Therefore, he is not ... for them room to display them before the Creator.

Still, "Love will cover all crimes." Especially before Him there are no obscenities or crimes, as it is written, "No filth will defile You; a fire that consumes fire will not burn You" (see "Poem of Unification"). Therefore, through the genuine love between him and the Creator, it is inevitable that man will also reveal bodily desires before Him.

Clearly, the Creator will not fail in fulfilling His loved one's every wish, both proper and improper, since the Creator's capability is tied to His will. But once the Creator has satisfied his desire, that person himself seemingly regrets the excessive wishes he presented before the Creator, and we learned that from above there is giving and not taking, since the Creator has already sanctified him.

It therefore follows that the person must mend the above-mentioned wrong, in two: 1) that he insulted the Creator's honor by presenting bodily wishes before the King, 2) that he was not careful in appreciating the gift of the King of all kings, the Creator, whether great or small.

This is so because there are two values to each gift. The first value is the gift—whether it is great or small. The second value is the giver—whether he is important or unimportant.

Naturally, when an important person gives even a small thing, the gift has great value, according to the importance of the giver. It is as our sages said ... to be in the king's palace and must come out to be corrected. And once he goes outside, he loses all the attainments he has already been rewarded with attaining because the Creator's gifts are united in "world, year, soul." That is, there must be a chosen "soul," a chosen "time," and a chosen "place." And since he has changed his place, his year and soul change, too, and then a person is in great bewilderment.

The prophet warns about that: "Seek the Lord while He is found," meaning return and continue to attain all the matters of spirituality that he attained, for in matters that concern the soul, the Creator is found for all. It is written about that: When He is found, "Call upon Him when He is near," being the bodily matters, which he has already attained because He is near.

The prophet warns that here it is forbidden to ask because it is an insult to the King to come to Him with bodily wishes. Rather, one must "call" Him only "by that name." That is, when he presents his prayer before the Creator, one must mention all His benefits, which He has done for him before with benevolence, satisfying bodily wishes for him, so it is a given that He will satisfy the matters of the soul for him now.

This is the meaning of the words of our sages: "The heaven between me and you will make a way for a plea." The words are profound. In these words, the rest of the *Haftarah* [final part of each Torah portion] is explained—that the foreigner concerns bodily matters, and the eunuch concerns matters of the soul, and the enlightened will understand.

The above interpretation is immensely profound; who will understand it? Therefore, I will explain by way of "seventy faces to the Torah": When a person introspects and feels his poor state, he awakens to return to the Creator and pours out his prayer in great longing to adhere to the Creator. He thinks that all those prayers and all that awakening are by his own power. He sits and awaits the Creator's salvation, small or great. When time passes and he sees no sign of welcome from the Creator, he falls into despair because the Creator does not want him, since after all this longing, He did not turn to him at all.

It is written about this: "Seek the Lord while He is found." That is, when the Creator presents Himself to you for asking, then you will necessarily seek Him, too, for it is man's way to move first. In other words, the Creator first gives you the heart to seek Him. When you know this, you are certain to strengthen yourself as much as you can, to demand more forcefully and more vigorously, for the King is calling you.

So it says, "Call upon Him when He is near." That is, when you call on the Creator to bring you closer to Him, know that He is already near you, for otherwise there is no doubt you would not be calling Him. This is also the meaning of the verse, "Before they call, I will answer," meaning that if you are calling Him, then He has already turned to you to give you the awakening to call upon Him.

"While they speak, I listen," meaning the measure of the Creator's listening depends precisely on the measure of the longing that appears during the saying of the prayer. When one feels excessive longing, he should know at that time that the Creator is listening to him attentively.

Clearly, when he knows this, he pours his heart out even stronger, for there is no greater privilege than the King of the world being attentive to him. This is quite similar to what our sages said, "The Creator longs for the prayer of righteous," for the Creator's desire for a person to draw near Him awakens great power and longing in the person to crave for the Creator, for "As in water of the face to the face, so the heart of man to man."

It follows that the saying of the prayer and the hearing of the prayer go hand in hand until they accumulate to the full measure and he acquires everything. This is the meaning of "spirit draws spirit and brings spirit." Note these words, for they are the first foundations in the ways of the Creator.

You wrote and asked that I would accept you as a student. You also suspected that I am displeased with you because I already have enough students. But to tell you the truth, it is harder for me with you than with others, as you are of a more eminent lineage. You must have heard that Rabbi Elimelech refused any students with eminent lineages, and the rav of Rufshitz pleaded with him and cried bitterly, but to no avail, until all scent of eminence had faded from him. This is what he said to him: "Why is it my fault that my father is so eminent?" Once he recognized the sincerity of his words, he accepted him.

Do not be surprised that in the eyes of landlords, it seems that the eminent is closer to the Creator than an ordinary person, as he sees and observes the good deeds of his father from his youth, and the childhood upbringing is set more firmly in the heart.

But the thing is that in each and every movement in His work there are two opposites in the same carrier, as I have elaborated in previous letters, as the receiver consists of body and soul, which are opposites. Hence, in each attainment, great or small, He makes two opposite forms.

There are two concepts in the work of the Creator: 1) "prayer and plea," 2) "praise and gratitude." Naturally, both must be at their highest. To complete the prayer, a person must feel the Creator's closeness to him as mandatory, like an organ that is hanging loosely, for then he can complain and pour out his heart before Him.

But opposite that, regarding the complete praise and gratitude, a person must feel the Creator's closeness to him as an addition, a supplement, as something that does not belong to him at all, for "What is man that You should know him, the son of man that You should think of him?" Then he can certainly give complete praise and gratitude to His great name for choosing him from among all those who are standing ready to serve the Creator.

It is great work for the complex man to be completed in both those opposites, so they are set in his heart forever at the same time. The second discernment, to feel himself lowly and far, and the kindness of the Creator as a supplement, is a far harder concept than the first. For the most part, all those who are rejected fail only in the second concept.

By this you know that the one of eminent lineage is farther from the second concept than an ordinary person because he feels the Creator's kindness toward him as mandatory.

Nonetheless, I have no such suspicion because I have already enslaved myself to the Creator, to serve Him in any way I can. No work is too heavy for me to do for His great name. On the contrary, I always love and relish at great exertions that bring Him contentment, and the evidence is that I chose the land of Israel as my workplace, where the ruling of SAM is the most. And not only that, but in *Jerusalem*, where even the ARI was afraid to open his seminary. ... I also collected into my seminary all the eminent ones from Jerusalem ... by which you can know that I am not avoiding work. Thus, everything depends only on you; always remember that.

Time is short, and the good day is approaching, so I cannot elaborate for you on that. But if you believe me, you will also be rewarded with understanding me...

Yehuda Leib

Letter No. 53

27 *Tishrey*, *Tav-Reish-Peh-Het*, October 23, 1927

To my soul mate ... may his candle burn:

... Indeed, you have caused me much work concerning the separation and hatred that has been sown and grown among you to an extent that I did not foresee. Each of the students, may they live forever, is like an organ in my own body, and behold, there is no peace among my bones because of my sin. Therefore, I must begin to cleanse myself like a newborn baby until I merit making peace among the students, may they live forever.

In truth, prior to my departure from my home, I hoped that I would be rewarded with seeing all the kids [young goats] as grownup goats upon my return, for which I have taken upon myself these man's jolts and huge troubles, which I had never experienced previously, nor even something near it. Because of it, I have truly been rewarded with great and wonderful salvation for all of you, and the gates of heaven have been opened for us.

Yet, the separation and hatred, whose only root is in the *Klipot* [shells/peels] and the yeast of the *Klipot*, have been against us, obstructing our ways because through there, the *Klipot* have found a way to sneak into the bodies and twist the holy channels.

I need not interpret for you the measure of longing and sorrow that you have caused me by this. I openly admit that until now I did not understand the ARI, who so regretted the dispute that occurred within his group until the manuscript came through. Now I see that there is none so wise as the experienced. Still, with the Creator's help, I hope to mend everything upon my return home.

The prophet asks and answers, "What does the Lord require of you? Only to do justice, to love mercy, and to walk humbly with your God." These words are very profound, and who will find them?

It is brought in *The Zohar*: "The Creator has three worlds, and this is the meaning of 'Holy! Holy! Holy!' concerning the above-mentioned three worlds. And in each one, the whole earth is full of His glory." Interpretation: It is as it is written, "Justice and law are the foundation of Your throne." It is also written, "Open for me the gates of justice," and it is known that justice becomes Godliness to you, such as a word of Godliness, etc.

Yehuda Leib

Letter No. 54

15 *Tevet*, Tav-Reish-Peh-Het, January 8, 1928

To my soul mate ... may his candle burn:

Today I received your letter with all the adventures that had happened to you, and what you wrote from the night of fourth of [the Torah portion] *VaYechi* [Jacob Lived]: "If the light had surrounded your entire body, you would have been saved from all your troubles."

It seems that you have not fully grasped what I said to you before your journey: "There is no other salvation but the attainment of the Torah." The whole *Merkava* [chariot/structure] of the *Sitra Achra* [other side] is only to fool people in other matters in order to deny them this truth. This is the meaning of the exile in Egypt in mortar and bricks, and the boasting of their king, "My Nile is mine and I have made it."

See what is written in that portion: "This shall be the sign to you that I have sent you: When you have brought the people out of Egypt, you shall serve God on this mountain." That is, when the Creator wished to verify for him the sacred situation with which he has been rewarded then (as explained in the writings), He verified it with that sign, that he will undoubtedly be once again rewarded with the reception of the Torah in that place.

Understand that thoroughly: Even though the face of the Creator appeared to Moses in complete clarity, so much so that he was afraid to look at the Creator, he still needed the guarantee of the Torah, for otherwise the Creator would certainly not make him look.

It is written, "Seek the Lord while He is found, call upon Him while He is near." "Seek the Lord while He is found" means where He is present, and you will not fail with the *Sitra Achra*, who always deflects a person to seek Him where He is not present. Thus, one scatters one's labor in vain. Hence the prophet warns, "Seek the

Lord where He is found," meaning in a place of Torah, and not in a place where there is no Torah, for He is not present there at all.

He also says, "Call upon Him while He is near." When the Creator shows you a bright face, it is the time to call Him—to contemplate and reflect on the secrets and the reasons [also flavors] of Torah, which is the reading—perhaps the Creator will open man's heart to be rewarded with the blessing of the Torah.

This is the meaning of "The Creator, the Torah, and Israel are one." By this you can also observe the need that the Creator had at the event of the first prophecy to Moses to pledge to him with this sign of acceptance of the Torah.

This is the meaning of the words, "Who will ascend into the mountain of the Lord, and who will stand in His holy place? He who has clean hands and a pure heart, who has not lifted up his soul to falsehood and has not sworn deceitfully."

It is said that prior to a person's exit from the mother's womb, he is sworn: "Even if the whole world tells you that you are righteous, be as a wicked one in your eyes." This matter requires explanation: Our sages have already said, "Do not be wicked in your own eyes," much less when the whole world testifies that he is righteous, should he regard himself as wicked? I wonder. We should also understand the words, "Be as a wicked one in your eyes," which implies that in his own heart he can know the truth—that he is righteous.

The thing is that there are two works: one is in the heart, and one is in the mind. That is, to turn the vessels of reception in both of them to work in order to bestow. At the time and moment when a person purifies the vessels of reception of the heart, he immediately becomes worthy of His light, which pours out incessantly. That light is called *Nefesh* [soul], after the disclosure of the *Nefisha* [rest] in all the organs.

This is the meaning of the words, "Who will ascend into the mountain of the Lord, and who will stand ...?" meaning gain an eternal level and will not fall again. It is precisely "He ... who has not lifted up his soul in vain." In other words, once the Creator has turned to him and brought him a little closer, he needs to strengthen himself immensely and take that light for scrutiny of the Torah, to find its secrets and increase his knowledge of the Creator. This is the meaning of raising the eyes of the *Shechina* [Divinity], as it is written, "A bride whose eyes are beautiful, the rest of her body does not require examination."

If a person does not pay attention to raising the eyes, then he carries the light of *Nefesh* futilely. Even worse, he swears deceitfully, for at the time of birth he was sworn, "Even if the whole world tells you that you are righteous." That is, even if he is rewarded with the light of *Nefesh*, where all the organs and tendons of his small world feel that he is a complete righteous, placed in the Garden of Eden, he must still not believe it whatsoever until he raises up the eyes of *Kedusha* [holiness].

This is the meaning of "Who will ascend" and "Who will stand"—precisely "He who has clean hands," who has been rewarded with cleaning both his forms of reception—of mind and of heart. "And a pure heart" means that he has already been rewarded with attaining the flavors [also "reasons"] of Torah and all its secrets, as it is written, "And you will know this day and reply to your heart that the Lord, He is the God ... there is none else."

"Who has not lifted up his soul to falsehood" means that he understood how to work and use the light of *Nefesh* that the Creator illuminated for him, "And has not sworn deceitfully," but raised the eyes, as said above. Delve deeply into all that is said here for it is a true and sincere counsel to avoid being trapped by the counsel of the *Sitra Achra*, who always fools into seeking the Creator where He is not found. Hence, each day one should remind oneself of this.

But what can I do for you if you do not appreciate my words properly, and therefore scatter your energy futilely? I wish you would hear me from now on because my words are always in "neither add nor take away," and are therefore still standing and waiting for a listening heart.

My words are being said in due time because the above-mentioned precise work is very capable in these days, which are called in the books, "*Tikkun Shovavim TaT* [correction of the naughty, *Tav-Tav* (acronym)]."

Let me disclose to you that the books offer only intimations that are completely abstruse to the masses. Indeed, its mark is *Shovavim TaT* as an acronym for *Talmud Torah* [Torah study], and there is no other correction but *TaT*, and "One who does not know the commandment of the upper one," etc.

The thing is that the upper light that approaches a person to direct him toward revival is called *Nefesh*, due to the reception of *Nefisha* [rest] in the organs, each according to its measure in its time. However, it cannot exist without *Ruach* [spirit], meaning attainment of the Torah.

This is why that person is called "naughty," like a little boy who places both hands in a bag full of money, jumping and dancing about, not knowing what to do with the money because he does not know the shape of the money or how to trade. It turns out that one who gives a gift of a bag of money to a little boy does not do him any good by this. On the contrary, he makes him naughty and drives him crazy.

This is the meaning of the words, "He will make my soul naughty." In other words, if the Creator does not give the *Ruach*, but only the *Nefesh*, He makes a person naughty and crazy. However, from *Lo Lishma* [not for Her sake] one comes to *Lishma* [for Her sake], meaning as he ends, "for His name," meaning that through this he will be rewarded with *Lishma*.

This is why he said, "Return, oh naughty boys," meaning those who have not yet been granted with *Ruach*. This is the meaning of attainment of the Torah. Also, as I spoke to you prior to your journey, this is the meaning of the *Klipa* [shell] of Pharaoh, king of Egypt, which was such a hard *Klipa* that no slave could escape from Egypt because of the lights that they had to give to all those who fell into their hands, until they could not retire from them.

It is as is written, "My Nile is mine and I have made it," as I interpreted for you while you were still here … This is why the enslavement in the [Torah] portion *Shemot* [Exodus] begins with the exile in Egypt, and does not end before the portion *Yitro* [Jethro], at the time of the reception of the Torah, as in "This shall be the sign to you that I have sent you: When you brought the people out of Egypt, you shall worship God on this mountain," as I have explained above.

Therefore, it is very possible for any person who wishes to complete what is desired of him, for in these sequences—*Shovavim*, *Teruma* [donation/contribution], *Tetzaveh* [command (verb, imperative form)]—he will examine his works and correct his ways for the reception of Torah. … He will gather all the sparks of light of his soul that were captured by the *Klipa* of Egypt into a place of Torah with great longing and yearning. Through studying with the external mind, as in "Whatever you find that your hand can do by your strength, that do," we will be rewarded with our hearts' opening in His law and the depths of His secrets, and we will be granted the reception of Torah as explained in the portion, *Yitro*. The rest of the sequences, *Mishpatim* [ordinances], *Teruma* [donation/contribution], *Tetzaveh* [command] are the teaching from the making of the calf and the breaking of the tablets.

The *Tikkun Shovavim* is implied in the books in relation to ejaculation in vain, called "nocturnal ejaculation." However, they are the same issue, as I have explained that one who did not purify the vessels of reception of the heart, the vessels of reception of the mind are necessarily filthy, too, and his faith is flawed because he cannot believe what his eyes do not see.

Just so, one whose vessels of reception of the heart are flawed necessarily contemplates once a day or so and will come to nocturnal ejaculation.

At the same time, it is necessary that he will come by a thought of heresy, called "a bag of ejaculation," since the vessels of reception of the heart and the vessels of reception of the mind go hand in hand, and then "The righteousness of the righteous will not save him on the day of his transgression."

It follows that all the lights he had received fall into the hands of the *Sitra Achra*, and delve in it, for I have been brief. All this continues until one is rewarded with extending *Ruach* along with the *Nefesh*, meaning reception of the Torah.

I cannot continue with this any longer, and it is time you took my words to heart, perhaps the Creator will resolve to pour upon us spirit from on high until the will of the Creator succeeds by you…

Yehuda Leib

Letter No. 55

1 *Kislev, Tav-Reish-Tzadi-Bet*, November 11, 1931, Jerusalem

To my dearest ...

Today I received your letter with the news about the sons, may the Creator give the blessing.

By and large, I had some contentment with that letter. Although you did not altogether refrain from giving bodily matters the lead here, too, there is still much of the point in the writing, as you yourself wrote.

As for your saying that I am angry or concerned about you for not writing me anything for two years now, it is how you feel. My reply is that although this feeling is not disappointing in general, it is disappointing in its form, as the Creator knows that nothing bad can come to me from those who perceive the body. As then, so now, I am the same: "Woe to this beauty that withers in this dust," and from here are all my joys and sorrows.

Following this introduction, I will grant your wish. You wrote, "I ask very much that you will write me some innovations in the Torah."

We should carefully consider the words of our sages, whose every word is like embers. They said, "An hour of repentance and good deeds in this world is better than all the life of the next world, and an hour of contentment in the next world is better than all the life of this world." It seems as though the beginning and the end contradict one another, for once they determined that an hour of the next world is better than all the life of this world, they must be referring to the spiritual life in this world, meaning repentance and good deeds. After all, we cannot suspect that the Mishnah speaks of a life of imaginary pleasure, as it is for the wicked, the fools, and the insensitive.

Our sages have already instructed us: "The wicked, in their lives, are called 'dead.'" That is, the form of life that the wicked can resemble, that form is death itself, the opposite of life and happiness. Thus, the death that the wicked perceives, being the absence of the perceived pleasure, is a false perception, since absence of bodily pleasure is not the opposite of life, to merit being defined as death.

Rather, the presence of bodily pleasures, which the wicked received and with which they rejoice, are woven for them into an iron partition that separates them from the life of lives, and they sink in the world of death, as it is written, "He is Satan; he is the evil inclination; he is the angel of death."

Accordingly, it is evident that the words of the Mishnah, "the life of this world," indicate the spiritual life in this world, for the words of the sages heal and they will not speak falsehood.

It was of this that they said, "An hour of contentment in this world is better." Thus, why did they add, "An hour of repentance and good deeds in this world is better than all the life of the next world"? We must not press toward the part that repentance and good deeds require labor and patience, for which they are separated from the life of this world. This is why they first said, "An hour of contentment of this world" is better.

However, labor and exertion that are devoid of pleasure are better than the spiritual pleasure in this world, for it is even higher than all the life of the next world. However, such words are acceptable only among those with little knowledge. They will never be accepted by the wise. Our sages have already determined for us in *The Zohar* that "Where there is labor, there is the *Sitra Achra* [other side], for the *Sitra Achra* is in deficiency," as are all who follow her. But regarding the *Kedusha* [holiness], there is wholeness there, and all who work in *Kedusha* are in wholeness, without any effort, and only in delights and happiness.

Before we delve into the heart of their words, I will thoroughly define for you the meaning of these words—"this world," "the next [world]"—in the words of our sages. It is as presented in *The Zohar* in the title, *Sefer HaBahir* [*The Book of the Bright One*]: "Rabbi Rechimai was asked, 'What is 'the next world,' and what is 'in the future'?' He replied to them, 'In the next world and came.'" In other words, the abundance is still to come.

You can evidently see the difference between this world and the next world. This one is what we attain in the present or attained in the past. The next world, however, is what we have not attained, but which should come to us in the future, after some time. However, both speak of what one attains and receives in this world, since the meaning of the anticipated reward of the soul is presented in the above-mentioned *Zohar*, defined only in the words, "in the future."

In other words, prior to the correction, people in this world are utterly unfit to receive it, but only the souls, which are devoid of bodies, or after the end of correction, when this world rises in the great merit of the world of *Atzilut*. Yet, we should not elaborate on it for now.

It is said, "Initially, our fathers were idol-worshippers. Now the Creator has brought us closer to His work, Terah, Abraham's father," etc. We must understand the intention of the sayer with this reference to Terah, Abraham's father. Is it to remind us of the best of times, the time of our freedom?

But we find such as this in the Torah, as well, as it is written, "And Terah died in Haran. And the Lord said unto Abram, 'Go forth from your country,'" etc. This proximity is perplexing and bewildering, for the first appearance of the Creator to the first father, who is the root and the kernel of all of Israel, and the entire correction containing all the hoped for abundance and happiness to be revealed to us, and the abundance in the worlds to all the righteous and the prophets from beginning to end.

It is so because the law in *Kedusha* [holiness] and spirituality is that the root contains within it all the offspring that come and appear because of it, as it was said about *Adam*

HaRishon that he included all the souls that would appear in the world. Likewise, the firstborn includes all the children born after him, as is known in the books.

Thus, there should have been secession in several writings between Terah's name and the first appearance of Abraham, for he is the root of everything, as said above.

Here I must explain the basis of idolatry. It is as the books write about the verse, "There shall be no foreign god within you." It means that the Creator should not be to you like a stranger, since working for a stranger is a burden. This is why it is idol-worship [the literal translation of idol-worship is "foreign (strange) work"]. Rather, worshipping the Creator should be with love and joy, and then its place is in *Kedusha*, and not otherwise.

It is also said in the name of the Baal Shem Tov, "You shall have no other gods over Me," for one who believes that there are other forces (over Me) besides the force of the Creator, who is called *Elokim* [God], is idol-worshipping, and this is profound.

It is so because a servant of the Creator does not need any change in the corporeal set up. It is beautifully and wondrously arranged, as written in the "Poem of Unification," "You forgot none of Your wishes, nor missed a thing. You did not subtract, and You did not add, and You did not work in them in vain."

The corporeal setup is arranged in such a way that all the people of the world will unite and be qualified for His work, as it is written, "All of the Lord's works are for His sake." This is the meaning of "There has never been joy before Him as the day when heaven and earth were created." It is also written, "And God saw all that He had done, and behold, it was very good."

However, it is arranged in a manner suitable for such work, suitable for the wonderful reward, which "Neither has the eye seen a God besides You." This is the meaning of the work and the reward that are set up before us in this world, in corporeality.

We see here that any reward is according to the pain that the worker feels during the work. But the concept of labor and suffering that appear during the work is valued and measured according to the postponement of the payment from the time of the labor, for it is natural that the payment puts out and uproots the suffering from the labor. That is, it is not perceived as sorrow, not even a bit.

Think for yourself: If you swap a cow for a donkey, then you've received the contentment you feel with the donkey, completely equal to the cow. At the very least, it is not less than that, or you would not swap it for the donkey.

Likewise, if the owner paid the worshipper such payments and rewards that were not satisfactory for him, at least as much as before he worked, it is certain that he would not swap his work with the reward. After all, the worker's intention is to gain and receive contentment through the swap, and not increase his sadness even more; this is clear to all and simple.

Indeed, there are exceptions, but this refers to the majority of people, for the real price of labor is true only in the majority of people, not in specific individuals.

But for all the above-said, common sense denies that at the end of the day, it seems that the body will not make rational calculations, and that it feels the work more or less as debt, and the payment does not put out the present fiery pain of labor.

But in truth, the calculation is correct, for the body does not enjoy or suffer from the future, but from the present. Therefore, if the owner paid the worker his payments in the present, meaning moment by moment, where for every feeling he would pay him a penny, there is no doubt that he would not feel his effort whatsoever, as the payments would put out the pain and uproot it.

But the owner will not do so. Rather, he pays his payments and the reward at the end of the work, after a day, a week, or a month. This is why the animal body, which does not enjoy or suffer from the future, will pain and worry, as it truly loses all its labor for the animal sensation.

It follows that the body that receives the payments did not work at all, and the body that worked did not receive a thing for it. This is why it is separated, for it enjoys only the present moment, and the sensation of the future feels for it like a foreign body.

Come and see: The merchant, owner of the shop, who really does receive his pay in the present, meaning for each minute that he troubles himself and suffers while serving the customers, really does not feel his effort whatsoever. On the contrary, he is delighted during the pay. The labor, which is tied to the pay, is uprooted for him. He is not like the worker who receives his salary in the evening and feels unhappiness and sorrow during this work.

This is what I said, that any sense of pain and suffering in reality is only for the removal of the payment from the time of the work. Also, if you scrutinize further you will find that according to the time gap between them, so the pain increases during the work, as accurately equal as two identical drops of water.

With the above said, we understand the two names, "righteous" and "wicked," for one does not go idle in this world; we necessarily have some sense of the reason for our being in the world—for blessing or, God forbid, for cursing. That is, the blessing we are commanded to bless the Creator is done by itself.

Likewise, a rich person who gives a gift to a poor one knows for certain that the poor person blesses him for it. He does not need to lend his ear to what he utters from his mouth. But if a person strikes and curses another, he knows for certain that the other one is cursing him; he does not need to think about it.

Just so, one who enjoys being in the Creator's world, at that time he is blessing his Maker, who has created him in order to delight him. He hardly needs to utter anything.

Conversely, when a person feels some pain while in the Creator's world, at that time he does the opposite. And although he does not utter any condemnable words from his mouth, still, the feeling rules. This is the title "wicked," for when he feels some pain, he necessarily condemns, as the grievance is expressed in the feeling itself, and need not be shown publicly.

Even if he utters a blessing, it is akin to blarney, like a landlord who is beating his servant while the servant is saying, "I so enjoy the beating; I am simply overjoyed." It was said about the such, "He who speaks falsehood shall not be established."

By these words you will also understand the definition of the title, "righteous." It refers to a person who is in the world of the Creator, yet always receives good and pleasant sensations, and is in constant pleasure. For this reason, he always blesses the Creator, Who created him in order to furnish him with such a good and delightful world. He, too, certainly does not need to explicitly utter the words, for the feelings themselves are the blessings that he blesses the Creator, as explained in the above allegory. This is why he is called "righteous" [also "just"], for he justifies creation and feels it as it truly is, as it is written, "And God saw all that He had done, and behold, it was very good."

This is the meaning of "A righteous lives by his faith." It comes to teach us the power of the righteous, for it seems to be incomprehensible for an ordinary person since how can a person be in this world yet be spared pain and suffering? Even more perplexing, he is in constant pleasure. It seems to contradict reason.

And yet, with the above said, you will understand that the very concept of labor and pain that exist in life is present only in the form of removal of payment from the work. Therefore, although the payments can put out the suffering and uproot it, they do not affect him during the work, and he has time to experience them, as detailed above.

It is as the store owner, whose pain from the labor is completely uprooted. When he searches for it, it is gone during the payment and the servicing of the customers because the reward and the labor come together, without any time gap for the pain of labor to appear.

Now you will clearly understand the words of *The Zohar*, "Where there is labor, there is the *Sitra Achra* [other side], since she is deficient and all her works are in deficiency." It is so because one who has been rewarded with complete faith, the future is to him exactly as the present; otherwise, it would not be considered complete.

For example, if a trusted person promises me something, it is as though I have actually received it. If my sensation is somewhat deficient, meaning that I feel it would be more pleasant if I actually received that thing, then that very extent is missing in my faith in him.

It is therefore obvious that a righteous person, who has been rewarded with complete faith—to the extent that our sages said, "Your employer is trusted to pay you the reward for your work"—necessarily feels every ounce of the pain of his labor in the payments he receives from the Creator, although he has not received them in the present. But for this, his faith illuminates for him completely, in a manner that the giving itself has no room for adding even the smallest bit of contentment.

Had the giving been slightly less valuable than the promise, even in the slightest bit, then he has yet to reach complete faith, and he would therefore not be considered righteous. However, he has necessarily reached the completion of faith, where the promise serves for him as giving, and he feels no division between future and present. Thus, he is like the store owner, for whom the pain from the labor cannot appear while he is serving the customers because the labor and the payment come together. This is the meaning of "A righteous lives by his faith."

By this we can understand the words of *The Zohar*: "Where there is labor, there is the *Sitra Achra*, etc., and there is *Kedusha* only in wholeness." It is a clear sign; if he has been rewarded with clinging to *Kedusha*, he has necessarily been rewarded with complete faith.

Therefore, from where did he get the sensation of labor? It must be that the *Sitra Achra* is on him because his faith is incomplete. Thus, he necessarily feels pain, and then he is called "wicked," as detailed above at length.

This is the meaning of "The wicked, in their lives, are called 'dead,'" The wicked is "short lived and full of anger," and "A righteous lives by his faith."

Now you will understand the philosophers' question about our Torah in the commandment to love the Creator. By nature's law, there cannot be commandments or coercion in love. Rather, it is something that comes by itself, etc., as they elaborated in their foolishness.

According to the above, you will understand the question here, about the Torah being given only to the children of Israel, who were rewarded first with complete faith, as it is written, "And they believed in the Lord and in His servant, Moses," and also first to place "We shall do" before "We shall hear."

In this manner we have attained all 613 *Mitzvot* [commandments] to do them with complete faith first, as it is known that this is the house's door. Therefore, the extent of the words, "And you shall love the Lord your God," depends completely on the individual, on trying as hard as one can to come to that perpetual level of always receiving abundance of sanctity, strength, and every delight in endless pleasure.

Then the love is guaranteed for him by itself, as it is arranged in the laws of nature, in a way that the measure of the love and its commandment are tantamount to our qualification to receive from Him endless pleasure, pleasantness upon pleasantness, as is the way with *Kedusha*—it increases.

This is certainly in our hands, meaning the correction of the faith. With this, the light of His love will certainly come by itself because the sensation of receiving the pleasure is itself the expression of love and blessing for the Giver, like a candle and its light, and this is simple.

Yehuda Leib

Letter No. 56

23 *Kislev, Tav-Reish-Tzadi-Bet*, December 3, 1931

To ... may his candle burn:

I received your letter today and I understood it. And yet, I believe that you should also know my view regarding your words, although in my estimate, you still do not perceive them. For this reason, the words will not delight you, nor will they be pleasant in your eyes, and for that, the truth will show its way.

Many say, "Who will show me good?" And yet, very few find it. We should therefore understand where is that great and relentless obstacle that mercilessly fails so many.

I have already pointed out to you several times the famous law in the holy books, that nothing is given unless by merit, meaning through labor, which everyone calls "awakening from below." Without it, no bestowal from above, called "awakening from above," will ever happen.

These words and laws are known to all, but their extent is not known, or they do not want to know it. For this reason, there is a big edifice of the *Sitra Achra* [other side], which stands and makes allowances in the matter—that it is not necessary to exert beyond human capability. In dire times, one has an entire lore from authors and books showing the kindness and mercy of His guidance with a person who is not so meticulous. He has a thousand pre-prepared proofs for it, instantaneously, as it is written, "The Creator does not criticize His creations."

Our sages said about the such, that the Torah is called SAM, for if he is not rewarded, the Torah itself becomes to him a potion [SAM] of death, for they are learning Torah from wicked SAM, and from him they understand. His words of Torah are immediately accepted by the heart, and are always kept in the memory, for they contemplated them day and night, God save us from him and from his followers.

What shall we do for those, and how can we reach out to them, or slightly move them from their places when they are not at all ready for an awakening from below? I wish to say that even if we succeed, with the Creator's help, to draw upon them the greatest awakening of the body, to crave and covet Him, they will still not want, or will not be able to—with that power of theirs—to give the measure of awakening from below that is needed for an awakening from above. This is something about which the Creator has never made allowances, since days of old until this day and always, for "He has given an unbreakable law."

It is said about it, "In full measure, when You send her away, You contend with her." The Creator measures a person one portion at a time. It is also written, "For the iniquity of the Amorite is not yet full," referring also to our topic. The iniquity of the Amorite is the *Klipa* [shell/peel] that keeps and surrounds the fruit, called "awakening from above," or "the land of Israel." That *Klipa* will not move from its place even as a hairsbreadth before Israel complement entirely the necessary measure of awakening from below, called "merit," meaning the labor and exertion beyond human capability.

Anything that one can do is merely called "work"; it is still not considered "labor." When Israel reach that point, they complement their amount, and then it is called "The iniquity of the Amorite is full." In other words, it is evident that the land of Israel and the glory of the Creator, being the *Shechina* [Divinity], do not belong to them.

Then they break that *Klipa* called "Amorite," and raise the *Shechina* from the dust, and not a moment sooner, as in the verse. This is the meaning of the explicit number, four hundred years, which shows the great precision in that matter, that there are no concessions here at all. As our sages said, the matter of skipping over the end, which was mandatory and obligatory for Israel, that skipping caused all the exiles to this day.

It is also known that the general and particular are equal. That is, in each one from Israel, concerning his soul, there is the matter of coming to the land, and all that is said concerning the whole of Israel, and that in his awakening from below there is that same number, 400 years, which is 400 of death, and 400 of life. Our sages said that the meaning of 400 years of enslavement refers to the place in which he is permitted to pay back the measure of his labor precisely, for in that there are no concessions even as a hairsbreadth.

This is why our sages said, "I did not labor and found, do not believe," and also, "The Torah exists only in one who puts himself to death over it," as well as "He who wishes to live shall put himself to death," and many others likewise.

In contrast, they said, "I labored and did not find? Do not believe," for they knew that that wicked SAM, whose lore is in his hand to show that it is possible to find the Creator's salvation without labor beyond human capability, by which one is made to release one's grip on the awakening from below and is repelled each day into a great abyss.

Afterward, when he returns and recognizes his falsehood and finds his faith in the words of our sages—that the lack of labor and awakening from below had lowered him to the netherworld, he therefore wishes to strengthen himself and dedicate himself to serving the Creator—he promptly returns to him with new heresy, that labor, too, does not help at all because He, God forbid, does not hear the prayer of every mouth. That is, he has pre-prepared proofs to show that there are those who exert but do not find at all. This is why they warned, "I labored and did not find, do not believe."

Thus, I have shown you the web in which the robbed souls that have no comfort are judged, meaning that mistake in interpreting the word, "labor." However, truthful is the verse, "They who seek Me shall find Me."

I still see much evil in the world, where those caught in the web of the *Sitra Achra* labor needlessly, which is only a depiction of punishment. That is, it does not join the count of 400 years whatsoever, and for this my heart aches more than anything.

About the such, a person should brace himself with prayer, "May He grant, etc., that we will not labor in vain," for it requires great success in that matter.

You should also know that the labor and exertion that appear in one's heart during the prayer is the most reliable and most guaranteed to reach its goal than any other matter in reality.

Yehuda Leib

Letter No. 57

Iyar Tav-Reish-Tzadi-Aleph, May 1931, Jerusalem

To the famous and pious student ... may his candle burn:

I received your letter, and while you are sorry for what is not missing, you should be sorry for what is missing. This is the rule: Anything that depends on the Creator exists in abundance, but the vessels of reception can be activated only by the lower ones, since it is their labor in *Kedusha* [holiness] and purity for which He stands and waits. This is what we are concerned with—how to be rewarded with adding labor. One who adds to that and worries needlessly is only subtracting. Not only is it needless, it is also harmful.

Regarding the friend's question that you ask, at the moment, I have no objection, and "Anyone who is shrewd acts with knowledge." Regarding the rest of the questions to which you seek my answers, I will give you my one answer to all of them.

There is no happier state in man's world than when he finds himself despaired with his own strength. That is, he has already labored and done all that he could possibly imagine he could do, but found no remedy. It is then that he is fit for a wholehearted prayer for His help because he knows for certain that his own work will not help him.

As long as he feels some strength of his own, his prayer will not be whole because the evil inclination rushes first and tells him, "First you must do what you can, and then you will be worthy of the Creator."

It was said about this, "The Lord is high and the low will see." For once a person has labored in all kinds of work, and has become disillusioned, he comes into real lowliness, knowing that he is the lowest of all the people, as there is nothing good in the structure of his body. At that time, his prayer is complete and he is granted by His generous hand.

The writing says about this, "And the children of Israel sighed from the work, etc., and their cry went up." It is so because at that time they came into a state of despair from the work. It is as one who pumps into a punctured bucket. He pumps all day but does not have a drop of water to quench his thirst.

So were the children of Israel in Egypt: Everything they built was promptly swallowed in its place in the ground, as our sages said.

Similarly, one who has not been rewarded with His love, all that he has done in his work on purifying the soul the day before is as though completely burned the next day. And each day and each moment he must start anew as though he has not done a thing in his entire life.

Then, "The children of Israel sighed from the work," for they evidently saw that they were unfit to ever produce something by their own work. This is why their sigh and prayer were complete, as it should be, and this is why "Their cry went up," since the Creator hears the prayer, and He only awaits a wholehearted prayer.

It follows from the above that everything, small or great, is obtained only by the power of prayer. All the labor and work to which we are obligated are only to discover our lack of strength and our lowliness—that we are unfit for anything by our own strength—for then we can pour out a wholehearted prayer before Him.

We could argue about this, "So I can decide in advance that I am unfit for anything, and why all the labor and exertion?" However, there is a natural law that there is none so wise as the experienced, and before one tries to actually do all he can do, he is utterly incapable of arriving at true lowliness, to the real extent, as said above.

This is why we must toil in *Kedusha* [holiness] and purity, as it is written, "Whatever you find that your hand can do by your strength, that do," and understand this for it is true and deep.

I revealed this truth to you only so you would not weaken or give up on mercy. Although you do not see anything, for even when the measure of labor is complete, it is the time of prayer, but until then, believe in our sages: "I did not labor and found, do not believe."

When the measure is full, your prayer will be complete and the Creator will grant generously, as our sages instructed us, "I labored and found, believe," for one is unfit for a prayer prior to this, and the Creator hears a prayer.

Yehuda Leib

Letter No. 58

8 *Adar, Tav-Shin-Aleph*, March 7, 1941, Jerusalem

To the holy rav whose light will shine forever...:

... The question was, "What does 'Haman from the Torah, where from?' imply," from the verse, "Have you eaten from the tree of which I commanded you not to eat?" He said that the question was, "Where do we find in the Torah that the Creator summons a messenger to reform a person against his will, as was with Haman, and as it is written, 'I will place over you a king such as Haman, and you will repent against your will'?"

This is what our sages showed about the verse, "Have you eaten from the tree of which I commanded you," etc., for then the evil inclination—the angel of death—was created, forcing the man to engage in Torah, as it is written, "I have created the evil inclination, I have created the Torah as a spice." If one is not to engage in Torah, the evil inclination will put him to death.

It follows that the disclosure of the sin of the tree of knowledge that puts to death—explained in the words, "from the tree," etc., is the messenger that compels a person to reform against his will. This is similar to "I will place over you a king such as Haman, and you will repent against your will."

Had he not been trapped in the serpent's net and had waited for Shabbat [Sabbath], and ate from the tree of life prior to eating from the tree of knowledge, he would have been granted the *Tikkun* [correction] of the evil inclination being a spice for the Torah. He would not need a forcing messenger such as Haman, as in "I have created the evil inclination, I have created the Torah as a spice." On the contrary, the evil inclination would have become a spice for the Torah, and now that he sinned, he needs a forcing messenger.

I added to it according to a higher source that there is in the sanctity of the Sabbath, that the evil inclination becoming a spice for the Torah is the meal on the Sabbath evening. This is what is implied in the songs of the ARI, "To enter the openings in the field of apples," as in "This is the gate to the Lord," and as is explained through the rest of those songs.

On Shabbat, at the meal of holy *Atik*, it is possible to receive from the highest place, where the Torah needs no spice, as in "The Torah and the Creator are one," by ascending to the world of *Atzilut*, where it was said, "No harm shall come to you." It therefore follows that if *Adam HaRishon* had waited with his *Zivug* for Shabbat, he would have been rewarded with the wonderful degree, "The Torah and the Creator are one," for at the time of *Adam HaRishon* the worlds were very high, as stated in Rashbi's essay, *Kedoshim*.

Indeed, even after the sin he could have risen to *Atzilut*, through the ascent of Shabbat, and not come down from there. This is the meaning of what is written, "lest he stretch out his hand and take also from the tree of life, and eat, and live forever." There it was in the form of "The Torah and the Creator are one." But the Creator drove him out from there, as it is written, "And He drove out the man." We should ask, "Why should the Creator mind if he ate from the tree of life and lived forever?"

The answer is that all the wonderful *Kedusha* [holiness] of "the Torah and the Creator are one" that was revealed on Shabbat was only as a loan. Shabbat is an awakening from above, without any awakening from below. But the Torah is completed only through an awakening from below, by observing Torah and *Mitzvot* [commandments]. We should therefore wonder why he was rewarded wholeness on the part of the Creator if his Torah was still incomplete.

This is what our sages answered regarding what the Creator said, "They borrowed on My guarantee, and I collect." That is, "I can lend you the complete Torah to the fullest, until it is enough for "The Torah and the Creator are one" because "I collect." That is, I have no fear at all of "Lend to the wicked and he will not pay," for I can place over you a king such as Haman, and you will repent against your will and observe the Torah from love.

"'All that is destined to be collected is deemed collected.' Therefore, I am lending you on Shabbat, as it is written, 'and a righteous pardons and gives.'" This is why the Creator did not want him to "stretch out his hand and take from the tree of life," since then *Adam HaRishon* would not pay and reveal the Torah as an awakening from below, and it would have remained as a loan.

This would make it groundless from the start because a Torah that is not completed does not merit being "The Torah and the Creator are one." However, the Creator considers the loan as though it was already paid back, since He can force it, and "All that is destined to be collected is deemed collected." Hence, He really did force him: "And He drove out the man," to pay back the loan.

In truth, the suspension also extends from the eating of the tree of knowledge, and this is the meaning of what our sages said about the verse, "Libel is terrible to people," the sin of the tree of knowledge, "You came unto him with libel." With the above-said we understand that it is to force him to pay back his loan.

With these words we also understand his words when he said the intimation that it is Haman from the Torah, since the tree of knowledge is the discernment of "I place over you a king such as Haman," etc. Just as Haman wished to destroy, kill, and annihilate all the Jews—women and children—in a single day, so is the tree of knowledge, "for in the day you eat from it you will surely die."

And just as He forced them to repent from love through the fear of death through Haman's decree, so the above-mentioned disclosure of the sin, explained in the verse, "Have you eaten from the tree of which I commanded you?", etc., will compel man to repent from love, as in "I have created the evil inclination, I have created the Torah as a spice." It is so because if he does not engage in Torah, he will promptly die because of the serpent.

May the Creator help us pay for what we borrowed, and may we be granted complete redemption.

Yehuda Leib

Letter No. 59

A letter that Baal HaSulam wrote to his disciple regarding the dissemination of the wisdom of Kabbalah in English in the United States

To the famous kabbalist, my great teacher and rav, Rav Levi Yitzhak, may he live long and well,

I received your latest letter, and for the first time since you went to America, you have given me a sliver of hope that you will succeed in your mission. I am certain that you understand that I am referring to the English replication that you did, from which you wish to give lectures in English, as this is the only way you will be able to make money in America, and perhaps even substantially, which was my intention.

I do ask that you will send me a complete copy of the book you wrote, to see if you have not veered from the path. In the first book that you copied, I did find a big mistake concerning the conveyance of Kabbalah, where you did not give Moses his rightful place, but I did not send my comments because you had already printed it.

Indeed, there is one drawback that you must remove from within you, which is like an iron partition between you and obtaining funds from anyone: Since you know that the distance between you and the donors of the money is as the distance between heaven and earth, you try to elevate the donors to your place, to heaven, so you can receive the money from them, since you must be with them in the same place, of course. However, they are heavier and stronger than you are, and I guarantee that you will never be able to raise them to heaven, and therefore, you will not be able to stretch out your hand to them and receive money. This way will never succeed, and no grievances or anger will help you.

If you want your mission to succeed, do the opposite, the complete opposite. Let those who listen to your words, the donors, stay in their place on earth. Do not move then one bit from their earthliness or from their views and wishes. I mean, deliberately prepare such words that will not soften their earthly heart or bring them any faith in anything at all, so that you will come down from heaven to earth and be with the listeners in the same world and in the same view.

What you want from them, prove to them with clear evidence that they themselves should have known before they heard your words. That is, not because of faith in the next world and so forth, but out of national pride and recognition of self-value, that the wisdom of Kabbalah is an important asset to the Israeli nation, which has been forgotten in recent generations and must be expanded and revealed, and this will be our glory before the nations so countries will see us as we truly are—a nation of an ancient culture.

At the same time, you should add that the nations are vying to rob this wisdom from us and equate it with Christianity, and it is a commandment of paramount importance to save it from their thick and crass hands no less than what we do to save the souls of Israel from assimilation. The only way toward salvation is to slightly lift the veil from the wisdom of Kabbalah, and reveal some of its luster and beauty to all before the eyes of the nations so they will see that there is none like it in depth or wisdom, and will be embarrassed and ashamed of their notion to compare this wisdom with the arid Christianity.

At that time, it will be clear that "It is a wise and intelligent people," a nation of an ancient and persisting culture, and not as they boast among themselves, that they are the true heirs of the Bible and the people of Israel—by which they involuntarily admit to the antiquity of our culture while degrading the teaching of our sages for two thousand years and mock us. Naturally, this great cessation and vacuum revokes all the merit of our ancient sages, similar to cursing a man who had many millions for a few days in his youth, but since then and until now he has been frayed, barefoot, penniless and indigent, and devoid of the sanctity of the Creator and the name of the whole of Israel to show them a portion of this wisdom, which can present the beauty of our ancient culture through the days of our exile since our Temple was ruined to this day. Thus, they will see the difference between the wisdom of the hidden that is present among the nations of the world and our own wisdom of the hidden, and do add of your own understanding similar to these words.

Speak to them with love and humility, with confidence that they will accept your words, and then I hope that they will open their pockets before you willingly, and you will connect with them in true friendship, you will benefit from them and they from you, and you will be rid of any strife or quarrel, and you will see before you a new world. But the strict condition is that you do not cut off their corporeal, earthly threads. Be very careful not to make them faithful in any way at all. Leave them completely as they are, and lower yourself to them, to their very place, and then they will listen to you.

All these words and points that I have given you, expand them as much as you can and replicate them in the best English, spiced up with commentaries on a verse or two, but under a strict condition not to fill your words with moralism, but with contemporary phrases and praises. Compile sermons of half an hour, which is more than enough. Do not jump too high, and there is no need to make a name for yourself as a first-rate speaker, but only as a first-rate fundraiser. Remember will this point.

Also, to the above points, you can add what the nations of the world do in order to preserve their ancient culture, how they invest on it, and how every nation respects the benefit and necessity to cherish all the great ones they had had throughout the generations, and the words of our sages will come true in us, "Worthless is the dough whose owner testifies that it is bad." If we do not respect ourselves, we cannot hope that others will respect [us].

Hence, a heavy duty lies on us to reveal the truth also among ourselves, that our culture is ancient and persisting, and yet, that even today, as far as religion goes, we are in the first place, and not necessarily only as the cradle of religions.

You should also promise the listeners that after you publish your book and advertise it in the masses, you are completely certain that the intellectuals of the generation will set their hearts and minds on replicating all the necessary books and establishing seminaries to make the wisdom known to all.

It would be good if you suggested these ideas before the best speaker, so he will embellish them with appealing and attractive expressions. It might be good to spend some money on this.

I should not elaborate any further; remember not to let a day go by without learning in my books.

Hoping for your success,

Yehuda HaLevi Ashlag

But most importantly, see that you have a regular yearly order of study for the seminary, and collect for half a year or more, and know what is before you.

Letter No. 60

Introduction

Baal HaSulam wrote this letter in response to a question that was sent to him following the publication of the essay *Matan Torah* ["The Giving of the Torah"], where he elaborates on the commandment, "Love your neighbor as yourself," being the whole of the Torah, and that it means that one should be care for one's friend's benefit no less than one cares for one's own benefit. The sender of the question did not know Baal HaSulam at all, but came across his essay. Baal HaSulam copied the question and underneath it wrote his reply. According to the manner of the writing, it seems as though he intended to publish it in future publications.

The Question

...I am not against, on the contrary, I wish the two hundred thousand people in the country would see only to their benefit... the needs, indeed... if... the essence of the Torah is only to be concerned with people and nothing more, why do all of the Torah, the authors of the Talmud, the rabbinical authorities hardly speak of it at all? Did they all abandon the main issue and dealt only with the marginal? In my view, all your words in this regard completely contradict conventional religion in Israel, and as has been the norm among us. In my opinion, this required force is a new construction, a new method that you have invented from your own mind. Of course, I am only expressing my opinion.

Signed, M.L. Petah Tikva

The Reply

It seems as though you did not delve in my words sufficiently. All I wrote was that there was a precondition from the beginning of the reception of the Torah, but afterward, since the time of the making of the calf, the package has been taken apart, since wars occurred and the children of Levi killed three thousand men by the word of the Creator, and then the grievances against Moses and Aaron, and the spies. Naturally, all those did not add love or unity.

Afterward, after the coming to the land [of Israel], it was still not quiet. Hence, it was irrelevant to ask anyone to uphold this prime commandment. However, in order for the Torah not to be forgotten from Israel, they began to engage in the rest of the commandments although they had abandoned its main point, since they had no other choice. Perhaps this is what our sages meant when they asked about the ruin of the Second Temple, that there was no idolatry there and they were proficient in Torah, so why was it ruined? They said it was for unfounded hatred. Perhaps this means that it was because they could not engage in the heart of the construction of the Torah, which is "love your neighbor as yourself" (Leviticus 19:18).

Letter No. 61

A letter that Baal HaSulam wrote to his brother-in-law in 1928 about the secret teacher

Tuesday, 10 Tevet, Tav-Reish-Peh-Het (January 3, 1928)

Here, in the city of Givat Shaul, a suburb of Jerusalem, may it be built soon in our days, Amen.

To the famous, honorable Hassid, Basket Full of Books [an honorary epithet], Our Teacher Abraham Handil, blessings and peace, Braunstein, may his light shine.

I indeed received your letter from December 16, where you asked me many questions. Particularly, you wanted to know on what I have built foundations in the wisdom of Kabbalah, requiring dwelling over a drop of ink seven clean [days]. Thus far are your words.

As for me, I do not find myself obligated to sympathize with this grief of yours. Nevertheless, for reasons I keep to myself, I will reply to the best of my ability. I will tell you about the main things that happened to me from the beginning of the learning to the end, and for which I have been rewarded with the wisdom, thanks to the Creator's mercy.

On Friday morning, the 12th of the month of Heshvan, a certain man came to me. It was known to me that he was a great and wondrous sage in the wisdom of Kabbalah, as well as in other teachings. Indeed, as soon as he began to speak, I sensed and tasted in him that God's wisdom was in him, and all his words were in great exaggeration and self-aggrandizement.

Nevertheless, I truly believed, with all my being and senses, and he promised to reveal to me the wisdom of truth to the fullest. I studied with him some three months each night after midnight at his house. The majority of the study was in the ways of holiness and purity. However, each time, I implored him to reveal to me some secret from the wisdom of Kabbalah. He would begin to say the headlines, but never completed it for me. Naturally, this made my longing very strong. Finally, once, after great pleading, he completed one secret to me, and my joy was immeasurable.

From then on, I began to acquire some being by myself. But the more my being grew, the further my holy teacher grew from me. Yet, I did not feel it. This continued for some three months until in the last days, I did not find him at his home at all. I searched for him but did not find him. Then I felt that he had truly grown far from me, and I regretted it very much and began to improve my ways.

Then, on the morning of the 9th of the month of Nissan, I found him and I appeased him extensively for the matter, and then he was just as appeased as before, and revealed to me a great and all-inclusive secret in about a Mikveh (a place for ritual bathing) that was measured and found deficient. I, of course, was overjoyed.

However, I saw him appearing to be weakening, and I would not leave his house. The following day, on the 10th of Nissan, Tav-Reish-Ayin-Tet (April 10, 1919), he passed away.

My grief cannot be expressed in writing, for my heart was filled with hope to be rewarded with wisdom and knowledge as one of the first ones, and behold, I had been left bare and destitute. Even what I did receive from him, I had forgotten at the time because of the great grief.

From then on, I have been gazing upward with endless longing and yearning, not resting for even one moment in the day, until I was found favorable in the eyes of the Creator and my teacher's merit and his teaching came to my aid, and my heart was opened with the sublime wisdom flowing on and on like a wellspring.

By the mercy of the Creator, I also remembered all the secrets I had received from my teacher, thank God for sustaining me and keeping me. How can one as poor as I thank Him? He knew my indigence from the beginning, that I had neither the knowledge nor the understanding even to thank and praise for His great favors.

However, who will tell Him, "What You will do and how You will work?" My above-mentioned holy teacher made a living from big business; he was famous all over the city as a good merchant, but to this day, no one knows about him and the wisdom of Kabbalah, and he did not permit me to reveal his name.

Now I will answer the rest of your questions: I make a living being a Rabbi here. Although the salary is very low, the Creator provides for my needs in various ways. As a whole, I currently enjoy dwelling in the land of Israel, and I always hang my hope on the Creator, for His mercies do not end.

I engage in Kabbalah openly, in public. However, in private, to a select few, I sometimes show ways and outlines according to the hour and the time.

I engage in the revealed a few hours a day besides teaching a lesson in rules of permitted and forbidden to the students at the seminary that I watch over, called "a seminary for rabbis."

Your niece, Leah Tehiya, is to be married in the coming days. The groom is a great wise disciple and teacher, with more fear of the Creator [in the Orthodox sense] than most, of a great lineage, the grandson of the holy Rabbi of Stratin, and the holy Sayer of Maazritch, and his lineage encompasses almost all the disciples of The Baal Shem Tov.

Concerning my health and the health of my household, all is well, thank God. May God let us hear good news and to be rewarded with the comfort of Zion.

Your sister's groom [brother-in-law],

Yehuda Leib

The Gatehouse of Intentions

Chapter 1

1*) There is an Emanator and there is an emanated being. The emanated being contains four elements: fire, wind, water, and dust. These are the four letters HaVaYaH [Yod-Hey-Vav-Hey], and they are HB TM, and they are TANTA, and they are ABYA, which are the four phases in man: One is the inner man, which is the spirituality. It is called NRNHY. Two is the body, three is the garments on the body, and four is the house in which man and his body and garment dwell.

Simple Light

1) There is an Emanator and there is an emanated being. The emanated being contains four elements, etc.

This teaches us a great rule that contains the entire wisdom, to learn to know how the entire whole, with even its tiniest details, are all similar, since all of reality, upper and lower together, are but five phases: Keter, Hochma, Bina, Tifferet, and Malchut. These are called by the names of five worlds: Adam Kadmon, Atzilut, Beria, Yetzira, and Assiya. AK [Adam Kadmon] is Keter, meaning the root of everything and the Emanator. The world of Atzilut is Hochma, the world of Beria is Bina, the world of Yetzira is Tifferet, and the world of Assiya is Malchut. These are the four letters in the name HaVaYaH: Yod is Hochma, the first Hey is Bina, Vav is Tifferet, and the bottom Hey is Malchut. They are also called tastes, dots, tags, and letters. It follows that all the worlds are included in one HaVaYaH, meaning Hochma and Bina, Tifferet and Malchut, and the tip of the Yod is regarded as the Emanator, meaning the world of AK. Correspondingly, there is not a tiny element in all of reality that does not contain these five phases KHB TM.

The reason for this is that everything is emanated and created only by the Sefira of Malchut, and Malchut necessarily contains the four phases above it, which precede it, since she is the lowest of the five phases. Hence, the first ten Sefirot that emerged after the first restriction, which are called "the world of AK" or "the line of Ein Sof," which begins near Ein Sof and ends at the point of this world, emerged by a coupling in the Sefira of Malchut, and therefore necessarily contains the above-mentioned five phases, as well as the four worlds ABYA and all the details in them, which also emerge through a coupling in the Sefira of Malchut. Thus, there are the same five phases in them, as well.

We should know that the ten Sefirot KHB HGT NHYM are but five phases, which are KHB TM. We count ten Sefirot because Tifferet contains six Sefirot HGT NHY

---

* Tree of Life, Part 2, Gate 42, Chapter 1

within it. The reason Tifferet contains six Sefirot is because of the incorporation of the Sefirot in one another, where each one is incorporated in all of them.

Thus, there are five phases in Keter, five phases in Hochma, five phases in Bina, five phases in ZA, and five phases in Malchut. However, the incorporation of GAR in Tifferet is not complete incorporation because the Sefira Tifferet is light of Hassadim and is regarded as Guf [body], so how can it contain within it the three phases KHB, which are essentially light of Hochma? For this reason, incorporation of KHB is discerned in it, which descended from their degree and became three Hassadim. This is why their name was changed to HGT, and this is why the five phases in it are called HGT NH, indicating that KHB that were included in Tifferet became Hassadim in it, there is no Hochma in them, Netzah is its own phase, and Hod is the inclusion of Malchut in it. For this reason, they are also called "five Hassadim."

There is also no complete incorporation of KHB in Malchut, and in her, too, they are called HGT, as in ZA, and the five phases HGT NH in her are called "five Gevurot," since they are all regarded as Gevurot. Also, the Sefira of Yesod is an incorporation of the five Hassadim in Tifferet and is not a new phase in and of herself.

Thus, these ten Sefirot are no more and no less than five phases, where each of them includes all of them. Also, there is a difference in this matter of incorporation, since only GAR incorporate all five phases in full, which is why they are considered to have complete KHB TM in each of them. But in Tifferet, where KHB became Hassadim, although it includes KHB, it still lacks them because they became HGT in it. This is why Tifferet is regarded as having six Sefirot HGT NHY, to emphasize the absence of KHB in it. It follows that each KHB contains ten actual Sefirot, which are the three phases KHB, the six Sefirot of ZA, and Malchut, since this innovation that was done in ZA, whose five phases became five Hassadim, is also included in each of the KHB. However, ZA has only six Sefirot HGT NHY because it does not contain the three phases KHB, but only the three Hassadim called HGT. It follows that these HGT NHY, which are incorporated only in Tifferet, are not because of its merit over GAR, but on the contrary, it indicates the lack of GAR in it.

The reason why the ARI counts only four phases HB TM and not five phases KHB TM is that Keter is regarded as the root of all four phases and is not counted along with them.

2) **All of these phases incorporate four phases, and these are they: Phase one of spirituality is Neshama to Neshama and NRN. Phase two, which is the body, is the bones, in which there is the marrow, and the tendons, flesh, and skin, as it is written, "Clothe me with skin and flesh, and knit me with bones and tendons."**

3) **The third phase is the garments. It is known that they are mandatory garments for a regular priest [as opposed to the high priest]: a shirt, trousers, a bonnet, and a belt. The same four of the high priest are higher garments than these, as is mentioned in** *The Zohar.* **These are the garments of the name ADNI, and these**

are the garments of the name *HaVaYaH*. However, essentially, they are only four phases. The fourth phase is the house, and there are house, yard, field, and desert. However, in all those four particular phases there is one phase that incorporates all of them; it is the medium between each two phases and incorporates both.

4*) Once we have clarified that all the emanated beings are one phase that incorporates all four elements, which are the four letters Yod-Hey-Vav-Hey, and which are the four worlds ABYA and have an upper, fifth phase between them and Ein Sof, now we will elaborate on each world in general, and then we will return to explain them all together as one whole.

5) Everything that was created in all the worlds is only four phases, which are HaVaYaH. These are the spiritual, which is called soul, the organs of the body, the garments, and the house.

6) Let us speak of the world of Atzilut, and from there we will understand the rest. The internality of the whole of Atzilut is the spirituality called soul. It is clothed inside the organs of the body, which are called vessels. These are the ten Sefirot called Rosh [head], Zero'ot [arms], and Guf [body].

7) Let us return to the matter of the body, for this phase is ten Sefirot, ten qualities, for there is a boundary and a measure to them. It is written in Pirkey Heichalot, in the measure of the level, that it is 2 billion, 236 million parsas. This body is clothed inside the garments of Atzilut, and as our sages said, the Creator clothed in ten garments, a garment of pride, as was said, "The Lord is King, He wears pride." This is the meaning of what is mentioned in Pirkey Heichalot, that there the robe of the Creator is called Zahariel, but the soul within has no measure at all. However, compared to Ein Sof, we can call them "measures and Sefirot" to the soul, as well.

8) These garments are inside the houses, which are the seven halls of Atzilut, which are the world itself. These are the heaven and the earth, and the air between them, for all this is regarded as "houses." They are called "the world of Atzilut," within which dwells the upper Adam, who is a soul and a body, and royal garments placed in the hall of the upper King, who is the whole of the world of Atzilut.

9) These four phases are regarded as the ten Sefirot that begin from Hochma and contain four phases. There is also the phase of Keter, which is the fifth phase, the root of all of them, and which also contains the root of the four above-mentioned phases. It follows that the light and the soul in Keter are the root of the ten Sefirot of the souls of Atzilut that begin from Hochma, and the body in Keter is the root of the ten Sefirot of bodies in the ten Sefirot of Atzilut that begin from Hochma. Also, the garments in Keter is the root of the ten Sefirot of garments in the ten Sefirot of Atzilut that begin from Hochma, and the hall in Keter is the root of the ten Sefirot of halls in the ten Sefirot of Atzilut that begin from Hochma.

---

* *Tree of Life*, Part 2, Gate 42, Chapter 2

10) Afterward, the world of Beria was created in the exact same manner, where through the screen that is the bottom of the hall of Atzilut, it illuminated downward and imprinted there an imprint of all that was in the world of Atzilut. It is called "the world of Beria" since it is a light of consequence and not the upper light itself. However, since it is the seal of Atzilut, it must contain all the phases that exist in Atzilut.

11') Indeed, the medium rule that is shorter than all is this: In all ten Sefirot of Atzilut, including Keter, there are root, soul, body, garment, hall. It is likewise in BYA, and likewise in AK, which is the root of all of ABYA.

12) It follows that all that was emanated is one HaVaYaH, which comprises five phases, which are the tip of the Yod in AK, Yod in Atzilut, Hey in Beria, Vav in Yetzira, and Hey in Assiya, and each of these phases comprises all five.

Simple Light

12) All that is emanated is one HaVaYaH that comprises five phases, which are the tip of the Yod in AK, Yod in Atzilut, etc., and each of these phases comprises all five. These five phases are in the upper light itself. From their perspective, there is no change from world to world or from degree to degree. All the changes in the worlds and the degrees are only in the screens in the vessels of Malchut, on which a coupling by striking was made, raising reflected light that clothes the upper light.

There are four phases of coarseness in this screen. The coarsest screen reveals the highest level through its coupling with the upper light, since the coarseness in phase four elicits a complete level of reflected light through Keter; the level of coarseness of phase three is only up to Hochma; the coarseness of phase two is only up to Bina; and that of phase one is only up to ZA. If there is only root of coarseness in the screen, it elicits only the level of Malchut.

These are all the changes between those five worlds AK and ABYA, since the screen of phase four operates in AK; hence, the reflected light there extends the level of Keter. For this reason, it is regarded as the Keter of all the worlds. The screen of phase three operates in the world of Atzilut, and the reflected light there extends the level of Hochma. This is why the world of Atzilut is regarded as the Hochma of the worlds. The screen on phase two operates in the world of Beria, which extends only the level of Bina. For this reason, it is regarded as Bina of the worlds. The screen of phase one operates in the world of Yetzira, which extends only the level of ZA, and is therefore regarded as ZA of the worlds, meaning Tifferet. The faintest screen of all is in the world of Assiya; hence, there is only the level of Malchut there.

Although the four phases of direct light are all equal, even in Assiya, they only have the level of Malchut in Assiya, and in Yetzira there is only the level of ZA in all four phases, and so forth likewise.

---

* *Tree of Life*, Part 2, Gate 42, end of Chapter 2

We could ask: There are five Partzufim in AK, which are five levels one below the other, and likewise in Atzilut, where they are called AA [Arich Anpin], AVI [Abba veIma], and ZON [Zeir Anpin and Nukva]. Thus, how do ZON of AK differ from ZON of Atzilut and from ZON of the rest of the worlds, which are Yetzira and Assiya? The thing is that each world is discerned primarily according to its uppermost phase. Since Partzuf Galgalta of AK, which is its highest, has the level of Keter, the rest of the Partzufim are regarded as degrees in Keter. It is likewise in the world of Atzilut whose highest Partzuf, called AA, has the level of Hochma. Thus, all the Partzufim are regarded as degrees of Hochma. It is likewise in Beria: Since the highest Partzuf in it has the level of Bina, they are all degrees of Bina. Likewise, in Yetzira, its highest Partzuf has only the level of ZA, so all the degrees in it are only degrees of ZA. And in Assiya they are regarded as degrees of Malchut. The rule is that all the degrees in any world are related to and regarded as branches of the highest Partzuf in it, whose level shines in all its branches.

13) The tip of the Yod in AK contains the first HaVaYaH of five other phases, which are the above-mentioned five phases in AK itself. These are the AK and ABYA in it, which are five phases: root, soul, body, garment, and hall. Also, the Yod of Atzilut contains one HaVaYaH that incorporates all above-mentioned five phases, and likewise in the rest of the letters in BYA. Thus, they are five letters where each one incorporates all of them, making them twenty-five phases.

14) Afterward, in the same manner, there is another incorporation, where each of them incorporates all twenty-five phases. This is so because the Yod of Atzilut contains one HaVaYaH that incorporates all five phases, and each of the five phases incorporates five. These are the ten Sefirot of the root, ten Sefirot of the soul, ten Sefirot of the body, ten Sefirot of the garment, and ten Sefirot of the hall. It is likewise in the tip of the Yod in AK, Yod in Atzilut, in the letter Hey in Beria, in the letter Vav in Yetzira, etc.

15) It follows that in short, AK is the tip of the Yod and contains one HaVaYaH that incorporates five phases: root, soul, body, garment, and hall. Each of these phases incorporates five, which are ten Sefirot of the root, ten Sefirot of the soul, ten Sefirot of the body, ten Sefirot of the garment, and ten Sefirot of the hall. Also, each Sefira of these ten Sefirot is incorporated in the five Partzufim [pl. of Partzuf], which are the root and ABYA.

Chapter 2

16) Now we will discuss the meaning of each of these worlds. Know that the root and the souls and the bodies are one phase and there is no separation between them. However, the garments and halls are two phases that are separate from the three above phases.

Simple Light

16) *the root and the souls and the bodies are one phase and there is no separation between them. However, the garments and halls are two phases that are separate, etc.* To understand these matters, we must know the meaning of the association of the quality of mercy with judgment that was done during the second restriction of AK, as it is written, "On the day when the Lord God made earth and heaven," when He associated the quality of mercy with judgment. This is also as our sages said, "In the beginning, He contemplated creating the world with the quality of judgment. He saw that the world did not exist; He put the quality of mercy first and associated it with the quality of judgment." That is, Malchut is called "the quality of judgment," and Bina is called "the quality of mercy." In order to sweeten the quality of judgment in Malchut, He associated and connected Malchut with Bina, as it is written, "And they both went," connecting the bottom Hey, which is Malchut, with the first Hey, which is Bina, so the bottom Hey was sweetened by the first Hey.

The beginning of this correction took place when Nekudim emerged from the light of Eynaim [eyes], for by the expansion of SAG through the Sium Raglin of the inner Partzuf of AK, called Galgalta, SAG, which is the level of Bina, merged and connected with the Malchut in TNHY of the inner AK, and the two Heys connected to each other on all the degrees until the bottom Hey rose to the place of Nikvey Eynaim. Eynaim is Hochma and Nikvey Eynaim means the Nukva of Hochma. It follows that the Eynaim have the last Hey and the first Hey, as in "I am asleep, and I am second." It follows that by this, the quality of mercy, which is Bina, was associated with the quality of judgment, which is Malchut.

However, although this association is a very valuable merit for Malchut, it caused a new restriction in the worlds, since the first restriction impacted only the Sefira of Malchut, while all of the first nine Sefirot were clean of any restriction. But now that Malchut rose and connected to Bina, along with it, she elevated the restriction to Bina, which is called Nikvey Eynaim. Thus, now each degree ended at the Sefira of Bina, as it previously ended in the place of Malchut. And since the Sium [ending] of each degree was made in the place of Bina, the two Sefirot ZA and Malchut parted and went outside of each and every degree, leaving only the three Sefirot KHB in the degree.

This is why he said, **"Know that the root and the souls and the bodies are one phase and there is no separation between them. However, the garments and halls** are two phases that are separate from the three above phases." The root, soul, and body, which are the three Sefirot Keter, Hochma, Bina remained in each degree after the second restriction, too, which is why they are united in the degree. However, the garments and halls, which are ZA and Malchut, separated from each degree in the second restriction because it ended at the Sefira of Bina. For this reason, they parted and became surrounding of the degree, since anything that the degree cannot receive now, but only some time later, is regarded as having become surrounding. Therefore, ZA and Malchut that parted from each degree are destined to reunite with it in the future, at the end of correction. This is why it is considered that they have become surrounding.

This is the meaning of what the ARI wrote, "However, from the world of Nekudim downward, which is the world of Atzilut, there was one lack that did not appear in them in all their details more than five internal lights and two surrounding lights, which are surrounding for Haya and surrounding for Yechida." This is so because there were five internal phases KHB ZON in the Partzufim of AK before the world of Nekudim, and opposite them five phases KHB ZON of surrounding lights, since there is no light that does not have inner and surrounding within it, for every inner light has its own surrounding. However, in the world of Nekudim, when the place of the restriction ascended to the Sefira of Bina, a lack was created in the inner ones themselves, as well, since the two internal Sefirot ZON separated from the degree and became surrounding, and only the three vessels KHB remained in the degree, in which three inner lights NRN clothe, while Haya and Yechida do not have corresponding vessels in the Partzuf and they remain outside as surrounding.

We might ask: The three great lights—Neshama, Haya, Yechida—should have remained in the Partzuf, and only Ruach and Nefesh should have become surrounding, since the lights of Neshama, Haya, Yechida always clothe the vessels of Keter, Hochma, Bina, and Nefesh Ruach in the vessels of ZA and Malchut. Thus, why does he say that NRN remained in the Partzuf and Yechida Haya have no vessels? We must remember here what the ARI wrote, that the rule is that in the vessels, the higher ones grow first, and it is the opposite in the lights. Upon the entry of the lights into the vessels, the lower lights enter first, since when there is only light of Nefesh there, it dresses in the vessel of Keter. When the light of Ruach comes, the light of Nefesh descends to the vessel of Hochma and the Ruach dresses in the vessel of Keter. When the light of Neshama comes, the light of Nefesh descends to the vessel of Bina, the light of Ruach to the vessel of Hochma, and the light of Neshama dresses in the vessel of Keter. When the light of Haya comes, the Nefesh descends to the vessel of ZA, Ruach to the vessel of Bina, Neshama to the vessel of Hochma, and the light of Haya dresses in the vessel of Keter. When the light of Yechida comes, the Nefesh descends to its place in the vessel of Malchut, and likewise Ruach to the vessel of ZA, Neshama to the vessel of Bina, Haya to the vessel of Hochma, and Yechida to the vessel of Keter.

Thus, as long as not all five lights NRNHY enter the Partzuf, not only are the lights not clothed in their respective vessels, but there is also an inverse relation between them: When Yechida is absent, the four lights NRNH do not clothe HB TM and the vessel of Keter is empty of its light. Rather, it is the complete opposite: the vessel of Malchut is empty of any light because the four lights clothe the vessels KHB and ZA. And when there are only three lights NRN there, they do not clothe in vessels Bina, ZA, and Malchut, and the two vessels Keter and Hochma remain empty of light. Rather, they clothe KHB, and the two bottom vessels remain empty. Thus, there is always an inverse relation between the vessels and the lights. You should always remember this for without this rule there cannot be any understanding of the writings of the ARI.

By this we thoroughly understand that from the world of Nekudim onward, after a new place of restriction was made in the vessel of Bina, and the two vessels ZA and Malchut separated from each degree and became surrounding, only three lights NRN can clothe in each degree: Neshama in the vessel of Keter, Ruach in vessel of Hochma, and Nefesh in vessel of Bina, while the two lights Yechida and Haya have no vessels in which to clothe.

However, in the end of correction, when the two vessels ZA and Malchut reconnect to the degree as they were in the first restriction, Nefesh will descend to vessel of Malchut and Ruach to vessel of ZA, and Neshama will be able to descend to vessel of Bina. At that time there will be room for the two lights Haya Yechida to clothe in the vessels of Keter Hochma. Thus, the absence of the vessels of ZA and Malchut eliminates the lights of Haya Yechida, for they have no place in which to clothe. For this reason, the vessels of ZA and Malchut are considered to have become surrounding for Haya and Yechida. That is, it is impossible for Haya and Yechida to return to the degree if not through them, since by the return of the vessel of ZA, room is made for the light of Haya to clothe in the degree, and by the return of vessel of Malchut, room is made for the light of Yechida, as well.

This is why the ARI says, **"From Nekudim onward, the five surrounding disappeared from each Partzuf, and there are only two surrounding now, Haya and Yechida, and they themselves are also not surrounding."** This is so because prior to the second restriction of AK that was in Nekudim, when five inner lights NRNHY dressed in their respective vessels, they also had five respective surrounding lights. Each surrounding was in itself: The inner one of Yechida had a surrounding light of Yechida, and the inner one of Haya had a surrounding light of Haya, etc. However, after the second restriction of Nekudim, when the two lights Haya Yechida disappeared from each degree, now there are no five surrounding opposite the five complete internal, since the internal themselves lack the Haya and Yechida in them. Hence, those Haya and Yechida will now be regarded as surrounding the NRN that remained in the degree. Once they fully enter the inner ones, meaning after the two vessels of ZA and Malchut reconnect to the degree and all five inner ones are properly completed, the five surrounding from before will return, as well.

It follows that now there are two deficiencies: The first deficiency is that the previous five surrounding have disappeared due to the lack that made in the internal ones themselves. The second deficiency is that even the two surrounding Haya and Yechida that remained are not surrounding in and of themselves, since there are no internal Haya and Yechida in the Partzuf, which relate to these surrounding. Rather, the surrounding Haya and Yechida illuminate to NRN that are not of their own phase, since they are actually internal and the only reason they became surrounding is due to the separation of the two vessels ZA and Malchut.

This is why it is written, **"The other three inner ones do not have surrounding from the phase of NRN, but only from the phase of Yechida and Haya, which surround everyone, and not from their own phase,"** as has been explained.

We could ask why in the Tree of Life, Gate 40, the ARI says that there are three internal and two surrounding, while in the Tree of Life, Gate 6, Chapter 2, he says that there are five internal and two surrounding. The thing is that in truth, there are two vessels of ZA and Malchut in each degree even after the second restriction, as well. However, they are not from their own phase but from the expansion of Bina, since the vessel of Bina itself expanded to ZA and Malchut, too. Since these ZA and Malchut are not original but are from Bina, now, too, we should not count more than three vessels KHB in each degree. However, this expansion of the vessel of Bina to ZA and Malchut made it possible for the two lights Haya and Yechida to clothe in the Partzuf, as well. However, they do not have a designated vessel, and they clothe inside the light of Neshama. For this reason, these lights of Haya and Yechida are not in in this completeness, as when they had five designated vessels for clothing.

Hence, considering the degrees of AK when there were five vessels in the Partzuf, the lights of Haya and Yechida are completely absent after they separated and became surrounding of garment and hall. This is why he says that **only three inner lights NRN remained in the Partzuf**. However, when considering the degrees of the second restriction themselves, it is possible that they, too, will have five inner [lights] NRNHY through the two new vessels of ZON that expand from Bina, but Haya and Yechida clothe inside the light of Neshama, as is known.

17) **Between those two, between the bodies and the garments, is the section of the shells. They truly attach themselves to the posterior of the light of the body. This is so because the three internal phases contain inner light and the worst of the inner light comes out inside the skin, and there it ends. The surrounding light is the opposite, since the more external light is also greater. It follows that surrounding light in the most internal garment that is attached to the body is the smallest surrounding light in all of them.**

Simple Light

17) The surrounding light in the garment, etc., is the smallest surrounding light, etc. It has already been explained that the vessel of ZA that was separated because of the second restriction became surrounding of Haya and is called garment. Also, the vessel of Malchut that was separated from the degree became a surrounding of light of Yechida because of the inverse relation between the vessels and the clothing of the lights. Hence, the surrounding of the garment is smaller than the surrounding of the hall, since the surrounding of garment is Haya and the surrounding of hall is Yechida.

18) For this reason, the section of the shells is there in the middle, where there are neither inner light nor surrounding light. It is in the middle between the inner and the surrounding, and it is called "the place of darkness." That matter applies to each and every world with regard to the shells in that world.

19) However, after we explained the matter in particular, we shall speak in general. It is known that inside AK is the Ein Sof that dresses in the root of the souls of the ten Sefirot in it, and these clothe the souls of all ten Sefirot in him, which clothe the ten Sefirot of the body of AK.

20) The ten Sefirot of the bodies should have clothed the ten Sefirot of garments, but this is not so for the above-said reason. Rather, the three phases Atik of Atzilut surround these three phases of AK. How? The ten Sefirot of the bodies of AK clothe inside the ten Sefirot of roots of the souls of the ten Sefirot of Atik of Atzilut, which clothe the ten Sefirot of the souls of Atik of Atzilut, which clothe the ten Sefirot of the bodies of Atik of Atzilut.

21) Likewise, the roots and bodies and souls of AA clothe the bodies of Atik, and likewise the three phases of Abba clothe AA. Similarly, the three phases of Ima toward Abba, the three phases of ZA toward Ima, and the three phases of Nukva toward ZA. Thus, now all the bodies have been completed through the Nukva of ZA. And here, in the posterior of the bodies of the Nukva, all the shells of Atzilut of ten Sefirot in them are attached.

22*) This requires that we notify you the meaning of garments and halls. Know that the garments are the vessels for the surrounding light, and between each two garments there is one surrounding light. These are phases of surrounding lights of straightness over all of Atzilut, as mentioned elsewhere that there are three phases of surrounding vessels and over them surrounding (lights) of NRN.

Simple Light

22) There are three phases of surrounding vessels and over them surrounding (lights) of NRN. There are books where it is written that the lights of NRN surround them. However, the word "lights" is a writer's mistake, since the surrounding vessels of straightness, which are the garments, are the vessels of ZA, and the surrounding light

---

* *Tree of Life*, Gate 42, Chapter 3

over these surrounding vessels are the surrounding of Haya and not lights of NRN, as the ARI wrote, that **"The other three inner ones do not have surrounding from the phase of NRN, but only from the phase of Yechida and Haya, which surround everyone, and not from their own phase."** Thus, there are no surrounding lights at all from the **phase** of NRN. However, it is written in other books, **"and over them surrounding of NRN,"** and the word "lights" is not written there. This is the true version.

This means that as there are three inner vessels—outer, middle, and inner—in which three inner lights of NRN clothe, so there are three phases of surrounding vessels—inner, middle, and outer—in the garments, encircled by the surrounding lights that illuminate to the inner NRN. Although this surrounding light is discerned as surrounding light of Haya, it still illuminates to the inner NRN although this surrounding light is not from their own phase, which is why it is considered surrounding of NRN.

23) Those surrounding vessels are the garments. Also, the halls are the circles, as mentioned everywhere that they encircle the surrounding lights, which are the garments. These are discerned as the encircling firmaments, which are discerned as the halls of that world.

24) For this reason, these circles encircle all the phases because they are as houses in which man lives, and over them is an illumination of very big surrounding, which cannot be placed in a boundary or measure, for they cannot be restricted even inside the houses and halls, which are very, very big vessels, and all the more so in small vessels such as bodies. Therefore, do not be surprised if the surrounding lights are in the circles and garments, for due to their great measure, they do not clothe in a body but rather in a very wide place, and the wider the place, the greater the surrounding light.

Simple Light

24) **...as houses in which man lives, and over them is an illumination of very big surrounding.** It has already been explained that the halls and the houses are surrounding light of Yechida, as it is written that there is a very big illumination of surrounding over them, since the light of Yechida is the greatest of all the lights.

The wider the place, the greater the surrounding light. This means that the wide expanse in the place indicates the distancing of the surrounding light from the person who sits within it, meaning from his inner vessels. Thus, the surrounding light of garments, which is surrounding light only in the phase of Haya, which is smaller than the light of Yechida, does not have such remoteness and space between the garments and man's body, since it is close to illuminate to the inner vessels. But the houses and halls, which are surrounding to the light of Yechida, which is very big, the inner vessels are very far from receiving that surrounding light since it is big. Hence, there is a great distance between man and his inner vessels, and the walls of the houses and halls, which are the surrounding vessels.

Chapter 3

25') Let us explain what was the state of the worlds of BYA themselves. Know that there is nothing that does not have internality and externality, even in the vessels. Indeed, from half of Tifferet and NHY of Adam Kadmon through his Sium Raglin, their externality is divided into two phases. Their externality from the side of the anterior is called Beria, and from the posterior, it is called Yetzira.

Simple Light

25) **There is nothing that does not have internality and externality, even in the vessels.** The vessels that are fit to receive the lights of GAR are called "internality," and the vessels that are unfit to receive lights of GAR are called "externality." Therefore, each Partzuf is divided at its Tabur [navel]: From its Tabur up it is fit to receive GAR and is called "internality," and from its Tabur down, where it is unfit to receive GAR, it is called "externality."

Also, the vessels from its Tabur down are divided into internality and externality in and of themselves. That is, when Mochin dresses and is made in the lower one, the NHY of the upper one are divided into three thirds—Rosh, Toch, Sof, meaning HBD HGT, NHY—since they expand and become a complete Partzuf of Rosh-Toch-Sof in the lower one. For this reason, the NHY from Tabur down are also divided into internality and externality where HBD-HGT in it through Tabur are called "internality," and the three bottom thirds of NHY, namely NHY of NHY, are called "externality" in it.

From half of Tifferet and NHY of Adam Kadmon through his Sium Raglin, their externality is divided into two phases, etc. From the side of the anterior is called Beria. Here we must know the state of the Partzufim of AK and Nekudim. This was explained in the book The Study of Ten Sefirot, Part 6, and here we will present it in brief. The first ten Sefirot that emerged after the first restriction are called "inner HaVaYaH of AK," or "inner AK." This is the line of Ein Sof that begins near the surrounding of Ein Sof and ends at the point of this world. Partzuf AB of AK clothes it from its Peh of Rosh through the Tabur, and from Peh of Rosh of this AB through the Sium Raglin [Aramaic: legs] of the inner AK clothes Partzuf SAG of AK, which is until the point of this world.

However, this Partzuf SAG of AK is divided in itself into two special Partzufim called tastes and Nekudot [dots]. Its Partzuf of tastes begins at the Peh of the Rosh of AB of AK and ends evenly with the Raglaim [feet/legs] of AB, meaning through Tabur of the inner AK, where it stops. Partzuf Nekudot of SAG of AK begins at the place of Tabur of the inner AK after the Sium of the tastes of SAG and ends evenly with the Raglaim of the inner AK, which is the place of the point of this world.

---

* *Shaar HaHakdamot [Gate to Introductions]*

These TNHY of AK that the ARI brings here is TNHY of the inner AK, which is the inner HaVaYaH that clothes from its Tabur down inside the whole of Partzuf Nekudot of SAG of AK. Hence, it is regarded as a complete Partzuf, Rosh-Toch-Sof, and is therefore divided into four divisions: internality and externality, anterior and posterior. First, it divides into internality and externality, where HBD HGT in it through the Chazeh are called "internality," and from the Chazeh through its Sium Raglaim in this world, it is called "externality." Afterward, from the Chazeh down in it, it also divides into two phases—anterior and the posterior—where from the Chazeh through the Sium of Tifferet, it is called anterior, and its NHY is called posterior. The anterior is regarded as Beria, and the posterior is regarded as Yetzira and Assiya.

26) **When the Emanator wished to emanate the world of Nekudim, it has already been explained above that Adam Kadmon restricted himself once more and raised the internality of the light from half of Tifferet in him and below. He raised it up, and then that light emerged through the Eynaim [eyes] and expanded outside from half of Tifferet in him and below, and the world of Nekudim was made.**

Simple Light

26) **Restricted himself once more and raised the internality of the light from half of Tifferet in him and below. He raised it up and then that light emerged through the Eynaim.** This matter of the second restriction of AK has already been explained in Item 16, that the first restriction was only on the Sefira of Malchut so she would not receive the upper light into her. It therefore follows that Malchut stopped and ended the upper light. However, the second restriction was done in the place of Bina, since Malchut rose and connected to Bina herself, for which the upper light ended in the place of the Sefira of Bina.

This does not mean that Bina herself was restricted so as not to receive the upper light, but rather that since the restricted Malchut was already incorporated in and connected to Bina, the upper light stopped there because of the Malchut in Bina. For this reason, the upper light stopped at the place of Bina.

There are two phases in this restricted Malchut: The first is Malchut that makes a coupling by striking with the upper light. By this she raises reflected light from-below-upward and dresses the upper light. This clothing makes the ten Sefirot of the Rosh of the Partzuf. Also, through this reflected light that she raised to the ten Sefirot from her and within her, she expands and elicits the ten Sefirot of the Guf of the Partzuf through the Sium Raglin.

The second phase of Malchut is the Malchut that ends the upper light. Once Malchut expanded from-above-downward through the reflected light in her, from her and within her, into ten Sefirot of the Guf, only the upper nine Sefirot in her reflected light are fit to receive the upper light within them, but her Malchut is unfit to receive due to the restriction that was made on her. Because she is unfit to receive, she stops the upper light, and the Guf ends. Thus, any Sium Raglin of a Partzuf is done because of the ending Malchut. These two phases are also called Malchut of the Rosh and Malchut of the Guf, since Malchut of the Rosh is the mating Malchut, and Malchut of the Guf is the ending Malchut.

It has also been explained above (item 1) that only the ten Sefirot of Rosh and GAR are called KHB TM, but the ten Sefirot of VAK and Guf are not called KHB TM, but rather HGT NH. It is known that each Guf is regarded as VAK compared to its Rosh, and you find that HGT is just like KHB, except that in the Guf, KHB is called HGT.

It follows that now, in the second restriction, when the restricted Malchut rose to the Sefira of Bina, we should also discern the two above phases of Malchut, where Malchut of the Guf, regarded as the ending Malchut, rose to the place of Bina of the Guf, meaning the Sefira of Tifferet, since Tifferet is the Sefira of Bina of the Guf. The second phase of Malchut, which is Malchut of the Rosh, which makes a coupling, rose to the Sefira of Bina of the Rosh called Nikvey Eynaim, since the ten Sefirot of Rosh are called Galgalta-Eynaim-Ozen [ear]-Hotem [nose]-Peh [mouth]. Eynaim is Hochma of the Rosh, Nikvey Eynaim is Bina, Nukva of Hochma, and you find that now the place of the coupling of Malchut of the Rosh, which makes a coupling by striking with the upper light, is in the place of Nikvey Eynaim since the mating Malchut rose from the place of the Peh to the Nikvey Eynaim, as has been explained.

It was written, **"Adam Kadmon restricted himself once more and raised the internality of the light from half of Tifferet in him and below. He raised it up and then that light emerged through the Eynaim."** That is, Malchut of the Guf, which ends the Guf, ascended into Bina of the Guf called Tifferet, so now the Guf ends inside Tifferet. It follows that all the light that expanded from half of Tifferet and below was now forced to depart from there and rise above the half of Tifferet, meaning above the ending Malchut.

Likewise, the Malchut of the Rosh, which makes a coupling, now rose from the place of the Peh to the Nikvey Eynaim where a coupling by striking was done, as he writes, "then that light emerged through the Eynaim," since through this new restriction, the coupling was done in the Nikvey Eynaim and the level of the coupling expands and emerges downward through the Eynaim. This is the level of the ten Sefirot of Nekudim that expand from Tabur of AK downward, meaning into the vessels of Partzuf Nekudot of SAG that stand from the Tabur of AK downward.

It will be explained below that Partzuf Nekudot of SAG itself, which stands from Tabur and below, also divides because of the second restriction, as the ARI explained with regard to the general SAG of AK in which the coupling was done for the Nekudot. This is so because as soon as the new restriction took place, the ending Malchut rose from the place of Raglaim of Partzuf Nekudot of SAG to the place of Chazeh in it. It follows that all the vessels from the Chazeh and below separated from this Partzuf and fell below the Raglaim of the inner AK, since they were already below the ending Malchut, which now stands at the place of the Chazeh.

27) Indeed, immediately upon the restriction, which is the ascent of the light upward, before it exits the Eynaim, and before the Nekudim were made, the two external phases were promptly darkened, since the inner light departed upward and they could not stand there. Hence, they descended below the Raglaim of straightness of Adam Kadmon, in the place of the surrounding light under the Raglaim of straightness of only Adam Kadmon.

Simple Light

27) **Immediately upon the restriction ... before it exits the Eynaim ...the two external phases were darkened.** Interpretation: The ascent of the ending Malchut to half of Tifferet of AK that the ARI explained above did not really leave any impression in AK itself. These ascents of Malchut were in order to make a new coupling for the lower one, which are the Nekudim. However, there was no change at all in AK itself, since any restriction that is emerges anew acts only from the place of its emergence onward, but does not operate on the ones above it whatsoever. For this reason, no new Sium was made inside Partzuf AK itself. Rather, the whole of the new Sium that was initiated by this restriction operated only on the vessels of the Partzuf below AK, called Nekudot of SAG, which begins from Tabur of AK and below, and ends at the point of this world.

A new Sium was made in that Partzuf of Nekudot of SAG of AK, too, through the ascent of Malchut to the place of Bina. Here the restriction caused the separation of the vessels below its Chazeh because of the ending Malchut that arose there. It follows that this entire part from the Chazeh down to the point of this world was separated from the Partzuf and is unfit to receive any light, just like the point of this world below the Raglaim of the inner AK. (The ARI calls this Partzuf "half of Tifferet of AK and below," and elsewhere, he calls it Nekudot of SAG. This is a complete Partzuf, Rosh and Guf, where by the new restriction, all the light departed from it and rose above Tabur of AK.)

It was said, **"Immediately upon the restriction ...before it exits the Eynaim..., the two external phases were darkened since the inner light departed upward."** As it is written above, there are four divisions in this Partzuf of Nekudot of SAG. From the Chazeh and above, it is called "internality"; from the Chazeh and below, it is called "externality." Also, from the Chazeh and below it divides into two phases: anterior and posterior. Those two phases of externality, meaning the anterior and posterior from the Chazeh and below, fell and separated from it due to the ascent of the ending Malchut to the place of the Chazeh. This is why it is written, **"the two external phases were darkened since the inner light departed upward."** That is, due to the ascent of the ending Malchut above them, they were emptied of all their inner light.

The words **"immediately upon the restriction, before it exits the Eynaim"** mean before the coupling was made on Malchut of the Rosh that ascended to the place of the Eynaim, for then this entire Partzuf was really emptied, even the inner vessels in it from the Chazeh and above, since all the lights from Tabur of AK and below departed. However, although the lights departed from the vessels from the Chazeh and above, they nonetheless did not separate from Atzilut because the ending Malchut stands below them now, as well. Hence, after the coupling, they are fit to receive the upper light. Conversely, those two external phases, which are below the ending Malchut, completely separated from Atzilut, and as they are similar to being below the point of this world. Even afterward, when the coupling is made in the Eynaim, they will still not be fit to receive the upper light because they are below the point of Sium.

They descended below the Raglaim of straightness of AK in the place of the surrounding light under the Raglaim of straightness of AK. This means that the two external, above-mentioned phases from the Chazeh and below of Nekudot of SAG have now descended below the Raglaim of AK in the place where the surrounding light of straightness is destined to stand. The Sium Raglaim of AK is at the point of this world, and now they have descended and fell below the point of this world, since with regard to Partzuf Nekudot of SAG, in whom the ending Malchut rose to the place of Bina of Guf, which is the point of Chazeh in Tifferet. Hence, there, at the point of Chazeh, it is already the Sium on the upper light, and the vessels from the Chazeh and below became completely dark, just like this world, which is below the Raglaim of AK. For this reason, it is considered that the two external phases descended below the Raglaim of AK into the place of darkness. Afterward, when the coupling is done in the Nikvey Eynaim, the surrounding light of straightness and the circles of Nekudim is destined to emerge there and they will illuminate there. But now, before the coupling was done in the Nikvey Eynaim, and the surrounding light of straightness has not emerged there below the Raglaim of AK, this place is completely dark.

We should remember what is written above, that the new Sium at the place of Bina of the Guf that was made in the second restriction is completely unknown to Partzuf AK itself, and it always ends at the point of this world, as before the second restriction took place. The whole matter of the new Sium operated only on Partzuf Nekudot of SAG of AK, called Partzuf TNHY of AK. For this reason, the ARI values the fall of the vessels from Chazeh of SAG and below the same as the inner AK that fell below the Raglaim, since the same point that ends the Raglaim of the inner AK rose to the Chazeh of Partzuf Nekudot of SAG and ended the upper light there. Thus, the vessels from Chazeh and below are considered to be below the Raglaim of the inner AK.

28) It did not take the rest of the place of the surrounding light or below it, and the surrounding light of straightness that is below its Raglaim rose to their place above, around the internality of NHY of Adam Kadmon.

Simple Light

28) It did not take the rest of the place of the surrounding light or below it. This indicates that it does not mean that the vessels took all the place of the surrounding of straightness, since this surrounding is destined to emerge and become circular very far from the Raglaim of AK, meaning in the full measure that it encircles above the center of Tabur of AK. This is so because this is the manner of the circle: It encircles its center at an even distance, since in a circle, the center is regarded as its end. It follows that the middle point of this surrounding of straightness is at the point of Chazeh of Partzuf Nekudot of SAG, since the ending Malchut ascended there and the surrounding of straightness encircles around it at an even distance from above as from below.

Also, the uppermost circle, which is the most external, is the Sefira of Keter of surrounding light. Following it is Hochma of the surrounding, until Malchut of the surrounding light is at the very center. Accordingly, there is no division of above and below in the surrounding light because its Keter is far from the center from above just as it is far from the center from below.

It follows that the farther it is from the center, the more important it is, since the circle of Malchut is close to the center from below, as well, and below it is the circle of ZA, below which is the circle of Bina, below it is the circle of Hochma, and the lowest of all is the circle of Keter. Accordingly, even before the emergence of the surrounding light of straightness from the Eynaim, you find that the lower its place, the better it is. Therefore, the fallen vessels from Chazeh of Nekudot of SAG and below did not take all of the place of the surrounding light of straightness, but remained standing nearby, below the Raglaim of AK, which is still regarded as the place of Malchut of the surrounding of straightness and not below there, which is more important since there is the place of the first nine of the surrounding of straightness. This is the meaning of the words **"It did not take the rest of the place of the surrounding light or below it,"** but only some of the place, meaning that which is close to the Raglaim of AK, and not below it.

The surrounding light of straightness that is below its Raglaim rose to their place above, around the internality of NHY of AK. This does not refer to the actual surrounding light of straightness, since this surrounding light has not emerged yet, for it emerges from the coupling in Nikvey Eynaim, while here it is before the coupling there took place. Rather, this refers to the light that departs from those fallen vessels of the two external phases from the Chazeh and below. This light that departs from them is destined to be included in the two surrounding of garments and halls, as written above in the words of the ARI. With regard to ZON that separated from the degree because of the second restriction, two surrounding were made—garment and hall. The surrounding light of straightness was made from the garments that are the vessels of ZA that were separated, and the surrounding light of circles was made from the halls, which are the vessels of Malchut that were separated.

The ARI tells us that this light that was separated from the vessels of ZA, which is destined to be a surrounding of straightness, departed from the fallen vessels that stand below the Raglaim of AK, and rose to its preliminary place, namely the place of NHY of AK where it clothed prior to the second restriction. The rule is that there is no falling in the lights; therefore, they remained in the place of their vessels as before, without any change, and only the vessels fell below the Raglaim of AK. This is the meaning of the words, **"and the surrounding light of straightness that is below its Raglaim rose to their place above,"** to the place where they clothed their vessels.

We should know that those two phases of externality of TNHY of AK from the Chazeh of Nekudot of SAG and below, which fell below the Raglaim of AK, are actually only the vessels of ZA and Malchut of that Partzuf, since through the ascent of Malchut to the place of Bina, Bina was divided in two: GAR and ZON. Her GAR remained in the degree, and only her ZON fell below. It follows that there are ZON of Bina here and general ZON. Thus, only the vessels of ZON fell, since ZON of Bina are also regarded as ZA and Malchut. It follows that not all of Bina of the Guf, called Tifferet, fell down, but only its half, meaning this ZON of Tifferet, which is regarded as from the Chazeh down to the Sium of Tifferet.

By this you will thoroughly understand the two external phases that the ARI regards as anterior and posterior. It is so because there are two phases of ZON here: 1) the actual ZON, and 2) ZON of Bina, which is the bottom half of Tifferet. Hence, ZON of Bina are regarded as the anterior, and the real vessels of ZON are regarded as posterior. For this reason, the world of Beria was made from the vessels of the anterior since they are discerned as Bina, and Beria is Bina, and Yetzira and Assiya were made from the vessels of the posterior, since they are real ZON.

29) When Beria and Yetzira descend below his Raglaim, they did not stand in their proper place. Through their descent, the externality of the posterior side was darkened in them more and more because it drew farther from the upper light. At that time, the externality of the externality of the posterior descended to the place called Assiya.

Simple Light

29) When Beria and Yetzira descend below his Raglaim, they did not stand in their proper place. ... At that time, the externality of the externality of the posterior descended to the place called Assiya. It has been explained above that there are anterior and posterior in these vessels that fell. The anterior is Beria, and the posterior consists of Yetzira and Assiya. They are also called "internality and externality of the posterior," where the internality of the posterior is Yetzira, and the externality of the posterior is Assiya. This is the meaning of what the ARI wrote, that the vessels fell below the Raglaim of AK and did not stand in their proper place, for had they stood in their proper place, they would have clothed the inner NHY of AK like today's corrected BYA, and would end equally with the inner NHY of AK, meaning the Raglaim of AK. This is so because today's world of Assiya is in the place of Sium Raglaim of AK, but then, before the coupling was made in Nikvey Eynaim, they all fell below the Raglaim of AK, and they all stand below their place, to the point that the world of Assiya, the externality of the posterior, descended below the place called Assiya, and likewise, Beria is below the place which is called Beria today, and so is the world of Yetzira below the place called Yetzira today, since they are all below the point of Sium Raglaim of AK, which is the point of this world. When it says "descended to the place called Assiya," it should say below the place called Assiya since the Raglaim of AK end at the point of this world, which is below the place called Assiya.

30) **Afterward, an illumination of upper light emerged through the Eynaim and clothed from half of Tifferet of Adam Kadmon downward, and the world of Nekudim was made, while the main light, which is the root, remained inside. It has already been explained that the circles of Nekudim emerge first, and when they encircle the NHY of Adam Kadmon, they also encircle under his Raglaim of straightness and stop between under his feet and the externality, which are Beria and Yetzira that had descended there, and were expelled from there and did not find a place, and they raised those two phases of externality to their place above, in the posterior of these Nekudim.**

Simple Light

30) **The circles of Nekudim emerge first ... they also encircle under his Raglaim of straightness.** So it is in all the Partzufim—the circles precede the straightness. It is so because the circles emerge from the coupling of Malchut of the Rosh from the discernment of from-below-upward, and all their illumination is only an illumination of Rosh. But with regard to the expansion of Malchut from above downward to the ten Sefirot of Guf, called straightness, the circles have no part in them at all, as it is written in *Tree of Life*. For this reason, the circles always come before the straightness as the Rosh comes before the Guf. This matter is thoroughly explained in *The Study of the Ten Sefirot*, Part 2.

There are two types of circles: circles from the first restriction, and circles from the second restriction. Circles are discerned as surrounding, since after Malchut was restricted from receiving light into her, a deficiency of one vessel was made in the ten Sefirot. This vessel of reception that became deficient in the first restriction was separated from the internal ones and became surrounding in the Partzufim of AK. With respect to the coupling from-below-upward that was done in the Malchut of the Roshim [pl. of Rosh] of AK, the surrounding light went out to these circles, since all of this part that Malchut of the Rosh had to receive, were it not for the restriction on her, emerged from the Rosh and became surrounding on the vessels of circles. Thus, the vessels of circles are from the receiving Malchut that was eliminated from the inner ten Sefirot of the Roshim of AK, and the surrounding light of the circles is the full measure of light that was received in the ten Sefirot of the Rosh had there not been a restriction on Malchut.

However, with regard to the expansion of Malchut into ten Sefirot of Guf, there are still no circles since this expansion from-above-downward is by the reflected light of the restricted Malchut from before, in the coupling by striking of the Rosh, and that same receiving Malchut that will make of her vessels of circles is no longer in her, and no light that belongs to that receiving Malchut expanded whatsoever, which would become surrounding light, since they are already below the screen in Malchut of the Rosh. It follows that after the straightness of AK expanded, meaning the ten Sefirot of Guf from-above-downward, there are no more circles that are fit to emerge from it.

However, during the second restriction of AK, when the restriction was made in the place of Bina and the two vessels of ZON departed and were separated from receiving lights within them, and are unfit for internal vessels, at that time, completely new circles were made with regard to these two vessels. These are also called garments and halls. Circles that are made of vessels of ZA are called garments, and the surrounding light in them is called surrounding of straightness. Circles that are made of vessels of Malchut are called halls or houses, and the surrounding light in them is called surrounding light of circles. Thus, there are two phases of circles from the two phases of restriction.

This is the meaning of "God has made man straight, and they sought many calculations." After AK came out in its phase of straightness, which are the ten Sefirot of the Guf, it no longer needs circles to emerge from it at all, since all that was separated from the ten Sefirot of AK, which is the receiving Malchut from before the restriction, has already departed in the coupling of the Rosh, and from the screen and below she expanded only in the phase of the first nine expanded in the inner vessels. Thus, there are no more vessels there to be separated and become circles. This is the meaning of "God has made man straight," meaning that the Guf of Adam was already established and emerged in the form of straightness, "but they sought many calculations." "They" pertains to the ten Sefirot of Nekudim that were made in the second restriction, where the two Heys conjoined, when the bottom Hey rose and connected to the first Hey. By this, new circles emerged after the straightness of AK, meaning also from vessels of ZA that were also parted from the inner ones and became vessels of circles.

By this you will understand why the garments that are made of vessels of ZA are called surrounding of straightness although they are regarded as circles like the halls, since they encircle inside the circles of halls (as it is written in *Tree of Life*). Hence, why are they called surrounding of straightness? It cannot be said that they were called so because they illuminate to the straightness, since the surrounding of circsles also illuminate to the straightness, like they do. Rather, with the above said, you will thoroughly understand that surrounding of circles that are made of the vessel of Malchut, because they were still in the first restriction in the Partzufim of AK and did not have any straightness before them, they are regarded as surrounding light of circles. However, the surrounding of garments that are made of vessels of ZA that were now renewed in the second restriction, where in the Partzufim of AK from the first restriction there were straightness and internal vessels of the Guf there, are therefore called surrounding of straightness, meaning that in their root, in AK, they are actual straightness there and are regarded as internal vessels.

... and were expelled from there and did not find a place, and they raised these two phases of externality to their place above, in the posterior of these Nekudim. This is so because before the coupling was made in Nikvey Eynaim, the surrounding of straightness did not come out at all since it emerges only when the coupling is made in Malchut of the Rosh through an expansion of the upper light into her. When she rejects all the parts of the upper light that want to spread and be received within her through the coupling by striking (as it is written in *The Study of the Ten Sefirot*, Part 2, Inner Observation), those rejected parts emerge outside and become surrounding light. Thus, the surrounding light emerges only after the coupling that is done in Malchut of the Rosh.

For this reason, immediately upon the restriction, before the light emerged through the Eynaim to become surrounding light, meaning at the moment when the ending Malchut rose to Bina of the Guf, which is the place of the Chazeh in Tifferet, those vessels from the Chazeh and below were separated in their anterior and posterior and fell below the point of Sium of the inner AK, meaning below its Raglaim, since the point of Sium of Partzuf Nekudot of SAG is already in the place of the Chazeh above them. This is because they could no longer clothe the inner NHY of AK as before for now their value is completely below those NHY of AK, as they are below the point of Sium, which to AK is regarded as being below its Raglaim, at the point of this world.

However, now that the coupling was done in Nikvey Eynaim and the surrounding light of garments and halls came out and encircled around NHY of AK and below its Raglaim like onionskins, and separated between below its Raglaim and the two external phases that fell there, meaning that that space of those garments and halls that emerged from Nikvey Eynaim was filled with their ten Sefirot of surrounding, and it is known that in the circles, their end is discerned at their center, but the above and below are even in them. Thus, the last Sefira in them, meaning Malchut of these surrounding, surrounds that Malchut that has now risen to the place of Chazeh.

Also, below Malchut of the circles is ZA of the circles, and below ZA there is Bina of the circles, etc. It follows that compared to their current value, this fall of the externality that they fell below the Raglaim of AK is now regarded as an ascent, since there is no above or below in the surrounding light. It follows that the lower place is more important.

This is why the ARI says that the surrounding light of circles that has now emerged reversed the importance of the places, for which they expelled the empty vessels from this space below the Raglaim of AK, for now the first nine of surrounding shine there, as these vessels are not worthy of being received. Hence, this surrounding light rejected them back to their place above, which has now become a worse place as it is closer to the center of the new second restriction. This is why he says that they were expelled from there.

31) Now that Nekudim separated the internality of the vessels of NHY of Adam Kadmon from the externality, they can stand there although they were darkened, and they already have the power to receive the light intended for them, as will be explained regarding the correction of Nekudim below.

Simple Light

31) Now that Nekudim separated the internality of the vessels of NHY of Adam Kadmon from the externality, they can stand there although they were darkened, and they already have the power to receive the light intended for them. Interpretation: the surrounding light of circles, which are the garments that were renewed now in the second restriction, expelled the vessels of externality to their Sof [end], meaning close to their center. By this they returned to the actual place where they stood prior to the fall, meaning in all the place from the point of the second restriction that was done at the point of Chazeh of Nekudot of SAG, to the point of the first restriction below the Raglaim of the inner AK. And the vessels of the anterior of the externality, which are the two thirds of Tifferet, reconnected to the point of Chazeh as in the beginning, and the internality of the posterior, which is the vessels of NHY from the phase of ZA, reconnected to the two thirds of Tifferet. Also, the bottom thirds of those NHY, which are discerned as the vessels of Malchut, reconnected with the vessels of ZA, meaning precisely as they stood prior to the second restriction. By this they were established as three worlds: Beria, Yetzira, and Assiya. The two thirds of Tifferet from the Chazeh down to his Sium became the world of Beria, although they are discerned as ZON. However, they are discerned as ZON of Bina, and therefore became the world of Beria, which is discerned as Bina. The two external phases of the posterior, which are NHY, became Yetzira and Assiya because they are discerned as ZON completely, since NH [Netzah-Hod] of the Guf are ZON of the Guf.

We should not be mistaken that they returned to being Atzilut just like the vessels from the Chazeh of Nekudot of SAG and above, since the Parsa has already been established there, meaning a new screen of the second restriction in the place of that Chazeh. Thus, the upper light cannot expand from there and below. Rather, they receive a lessened light that can pass through the Parsa downward. This is the meaning of the words, **"they already have the power to receive the light intended for them,"** meaning the light that can pass through the Parsa, which is called a light of consequence, and not a light of Atzilut.

We could say that since the surrounding light of circles expelled the vessels below the Raglaim of AK because in them, the lower place is more important, therefore, these vessels of BYA should have all been inverted: Assiya should have been close to the point of the Chazeh, where it is the end of the circles and the worst place, and below it Yetzira, and below it Beria, according to the order of the circles. The thing is that the illumination of the circles does not work at all in the place of straightness of AK. The rule is that illumination of circles works only in the Rosh. Hence, after they returned to the place of NHY of the inner AK, they received the order of straightness, where each higher one is more important, and the whole matter of the expulsion was only in the space below the Raglaim of AK.

32) Beria returned opposite the anterior, and Yetzira opposite the posterior, as it was in the beginning, and with it, a fourth reason was clarified concerning the Nekudim emerging in a manner of circles, as mentioned above. Now, the place of BYA has returned to being a vacant space as in the beginning.

33*) Know that when I heard this fourth reason, I wrote it very succinctly, and I will copy it for you here because in my humble opinion, I seem to have heard that the place of BYA is the posterior of the Nekudim of the circles, which is truly this externality that ascended. However, here it seems the opposite—that the place of BYA is below, in the above-mentioned space, and this requires scrutiny.

Simple Light

33) **The place of BYA is the posterior of the Nekudim of the circles, etc. However, here it seems the opposite—that the place of BYA is below, in the space.** Rav Chaim Vital was perplexed because it is known from all the teachings of the ARI that the place of BYA is below the whole of the world of Nekudim, while here he heard that the circles of Nekudim encircle the Raglaim of AK. It follows that all three worlds BYA stand in the space below the Raglaim of AK, meaning below the circles of Nekudim that surround the Raglaim of AK.

However, this baffled him before he saw the great tractate of AK, when he thought that the straightness did not emerge in Nekudim at all, but only circles, while straightness emerged only in the new MA. Thus, if we say that BYA stand below the circles of Nekudim, it necessarily means that they are in the space below the Raglaim of AK, and this cannot be for several reasons. This is why he wondered about it here.

However, after he saw the great tractate of AK, he saw that circles and straightness emerged in Nekudim, as well, so it was not perplexing at all because what he had

---

* *Mavo She'arim*, Gate 2, Part 1, Chapter 3.

heard, that the worlds BYA stand below the Nekudim, meaning below the straightness of Nekudim, since the straightness of Nekudim begins at the Tabur of AK, like Partzuf Nekudot of SAG, and ends at the point of Chazeh of Partzuf Nekudot of SAG where the Parsa was set up, which is the new point of Sium of the second restriction that was done in the world of Nekudim. Below this Parsa through the Sium Raglaim of AK of straightness to the point of this world, it is the place where the three worlds Beria, Yetzira, and Assiya stand. But the circles of Nekudim, which are the surrounding of Nekudim, truly encircle the space below the Raglaim of AK.

34) These are the words of the copy that I wrote. In the above-mentioned restriction, the externality of the anterior and the posterior descended from Tabur of AK and below, Beria and Yetzira, and descended in a surrounding of straightness below the Raglaim, but not in all of it, and the surrounding ascended instead of it. When the posterior descended, the externality was darkened even more and descended lower, to Assiya. This is the fourth reason that the Nekudim are circles and surrounding, in order to raise them.

35) How? This surrounding descended and entered between the Raglaim, to Beria, and they were expelled and did not find a place, and they ascended behind this surrounding of Nekudim, opposite from their first place. Below, a space remained called "the place of Beria." The place is bigger than the whole world. Therefore, the vessels of Nekudim are spoiled although they were corrected into vessels of Atzilut.

Chapter 4

36*) After we briefly explained the teachings about the circles and straightness in the order of the clothing of all the worlds, now we must explain how far the expansion of the Raglaim of AK of straightness reaches in each world. The straight line must be completely attached to the encircling Ein Sof, and from it, it expands and descends, and dresses in the internality of AK, and extends and expands through the Sium Raglaim of the straight AK, which is truly until half of the circles of Atik Yomin that encircle under his Raglaim. There the Raglaim of straightness of AK end.

37) If it were said that the Raglaim of AK reach and expand down into its own circles until their Sium and end, it follows that it becomes reattached to the circle of Ein Sof in the bottom half under the Raglaim of AK. If this is so, it follows that Ein Sof will shine in it from there and below through the straight line, and there will not be a discernment of above and below, giving and receiving. This is why the Rosh of the line was not extended below.

38) Succinctly, the resulting rule is this: The Raglaim of AK of straightness expand and extend to the bottom half of the circles of Atik Yomin from below, in a manner that the circles of Atik Yomin surround the Raglaim of straightness of AK. However, all the other Raglaim of straightness, such as the Raglaim of Atik and Raglaim of AA, Raglaim of ZA and Raglaim of Nukva, all end evenly, through the bottom half of the circles of AA from below. Thus, the circles of AA surround and encircle below all the Raglaim of all of them.

Simple Light

38) The resulting rule is that the Raglaim of AK of straightness expand and extend to the bottom half of the circles ... from below ... However, all the other Raglaim ... through the bottom half of the circles of AA: The big difference that was made in the world of Nekudim by the new restriction has already been explained above. It elevated the bottom Hey to the Nikvey Eynaim, and the point of Sium of the upper light was made in the place of Bina of the Guf, and only three vessels KHB remained in each degree, in which there are lights of NRN. You find that now there are two points of Sium: The first is the point of Sium of the second restriction, which is at the place of the Chazeh of Nekudot of SAG above the world of Beria, where the Parsa between Atzilut and Beria was set up. The second point of Sium is below the Raglaim of AK. This is the point of this world, as in the verse, "And His feet shall stand on the Mount of Olives." Thus, the three worlds BYA stand right between these two points of Sium. Accordingly, you find that the distance between the Raglaim of AK and the Raglaim of the Partzufim of the world of Atzilut that emerged through the second restriction is as the distance between these two points of Sium, meaning according to the measure of the three worlds BYA.

* *Tree of Life*, Gate 1, Branch 4.

It is known that Partzuf Atik Yomin of Atzilut, which is discerned as the first Rosh of Atzilut, is not counted among the five Partzufim of Atzilut, and is still regarded as the first restriction, like AK. It also expands evenly with the Raglaim of AK down to the point of this world, and nurses the fallen Partzufim after they are born into BYA, as in suckling from Dadei Behema [udders of a beast].

Accordingly, there is a big difference between the circles of Atik Yomin and the circles of AA. The center of the circles of Atik Yomin is the point of this world, and their Sium is at their center. But the circles of all five Partzufim of Atzilut, which come from the second restriction, their center is at the point of Sium of Atzilut, where the Parsa is.

It was said, "The Raglaim of AK of straightness expand and extend through the bottom half of the circles of Atik Yomin from below," meaning until the point of Sium of this world, in a manner that they touch the bottom halves of the circles, since the center point stands in the middle between the bottom halves and the upper halves. Hence, the Raglaim of AK that end at the point of Sium touch the bottom halves of the circles of Atik Yomin, as he says, "However, all the other Raglaim of straightness, such as the Raglaim of Atik and Raglaim of AA, etc., all end evenly, through the bottom half of the circles of AA." That is, they end at the point of Sium of the second restriction, the center of the circles of AA, which is truly at the place of the Parsa of Atzilut. Since it necessarily touches the point of Sium of this center, it follows that it also touches the bottom halves of the circles of AA.

The reason he regards the Raglaim of *Atik*, too, as ending at the point of Sium of the second restriction, meaning at the bottom halves of AA, although in truth, it extends through the point of this world and ends evenly with the Raglaim of AK, is that with regard to its own Partzuf, it extends through the point of this world. However, the Parsa controls it so it does not pass the illumination of Atzilut to the worlds of BYA. For this reason, in this regard, meaning with regard to Atzilut of Atik Yomin, it ends evenly with all the Raglaim of the five Partzufim of Atzilut. And with regard to the illumination of BYA, it extends through the point of this world, evenly with the Raglaim of AK. This is the meaning of the two surplus bottom thirds of Atik that emerge from under the Parsa of Atzilut and are extended to BYA as Dadei Behema.

39) However, there are Partzufim whose level is not high, such as AVI, whose level is only from the Garon [throat] of AA through the Tabur of AA. Likewise, the Partzuf of Leah, which begins from Daat of ZA through its Chazeh. The Raglaim of these Partzufim do not reach down to the Raglaim of AA since they are short, and each will be explained in its place in detail.

40) Another time, I heard from my teacher concerning the correction of AA, how it was born and emerged and suckled from the two bottom joints of the Raglaim of Atik Yomin. There, we explained how the two bottom joints, called Akevim [heels] of Atik Yomin, expand lower than the Raglaim of AA and enter the boundary of the

world of Beria. It can be said that this was so only prior to the correction of Atzilut, and after the correction, there was no need for it since Atik lifted up its Raglaim once more, evenly with the Raglaim of AA, and this requires scrutiny.

Simple Light

40) After the correction, there was no need for it since Atik lifted up its Raglaim once more. We already explained this issue above, that from the perspective of Atzilut, it ends in Atzilut, but it always shines in BYA, in its two bottom thirds. However, this is not regarded as illumination of Atzilut because the Parsa covers them. With regard to the circles, we should remember that this does not mean flat circles, but rather spherical circles, like onionskins enveloping one another.

41*) However, know that every phase of the five Partzufim in each of the above-mentioned worlds consists of 248 organs and 365 tendons. The reader should delve into analyzing the organs in each and every Partzuf, how one organ of a Partzuf meets an organ of a Partzuf that clothes it, since not all the Partzufim stand evenly and on the same level. It follows that the Rosh of Malchut of Assiya met the bottom of the Akev [heel] of AK, and likewise in all the other phases, the eye cannot encompass them for they have been rolled up like the book of heaven. To the extent that this organ in this Partzuf is attached to the organ of the Partzuf opposite from it, sometimes they will meet eye against nose or ear against heel, and so forth indefinitely.

42) This is the meaning of the wisdom of the combinations of the twenty-two letters of the alphabet: One with all and all with one, and likewise the rest of the letters. They cause the change so that no day is like another, no righteous is like another, no created being is like another, and all created beings are for a high purpose, since the suckling is not the same for all of them, nor is the correction of all of them the same, and the Helbona [Galbanum] in the incense will correct what the Levona [frankincense (a.k.a. olibanum)] does not correct. Hence, there was a need for these worlds, the good, bad, and medium, and numerous kinds within each one.

43) This is the meaning of BeHibara'am [when they were created], Be Hey Bera'am [He created them with a Hey], since all the created beings were as five Partzufim, both in Atzilut and in BYA. This is also the meaning of the small Hey, since they all emerged from the small Hey of Malchut of AK after it was diminished at the end of her ZAT, and then she became their Rosh. This is why they were implied in a small Hey.

Simple Light

43) BeHibara'am [when they were created], Be Hey Bera'am [He created them with a Hey], since all the created beings were as five Partzufim, etc. This is also the

---

* *Tree of Life*, Gate 3, Chapter 2.

meaning of the small Hey, since they all emerged from the small Hey of Malchut of AK. Initially, Partzuf Keter emerges in Rosh-Toch-Sof and is called "inner HaVaYaH," consisting of five phases KHB TM, which are the tip of the Yod and the four letters of this inner HaVaYaH. Afterward, four garments expand from it: AB, SAG, MA, and BON, which clothe the inner HaVaYaH. These four garments, AB, SAG, MA, and BON expand from the four letters of the inner HaVaYaH: HaVaYaH filled with AB from its Yod, filled with SAG from its Hey, filled with MA from its Vav, and filled with BON from its bottom Hey. These five Partzufim pertain to AK, as well as to Atzilut, Beria, Yetzira, and Assiya. This is what he implies by "He created them with a Hey [5 in Gematria]," meaning in five Partzufim.

However, it is written BeHibara'am with a small Hey, implying that there is a diminution here in these five Partzufim. This is so because the text speaks of worlds that emerged after the second restriction of AK, when a diminution and Katnut [smallness/infancy] took place in these five Partzufim, where the two Sefirot ZA and Malchut were separated from each Partzuf and only three vessels KHB remained in each Partzuf, with three lights NRN within them, while Haya and Yechida became only surrounding. Thus, the five Partzufim were greatly diminished by the second restriction, and this is what the word BeHibara'am, with a small Hey, implies.

He said, "since they all emerged from the small Hey of Malchut of AK after it was diminished at the end of her ZAT," meaning that all four worlds ABYA emerged from the second restriction when the bottom Hey rose to the first Hey and the vessels were diminished from the two Sefirot ZA and Malchut, and the lights were diminished from Haya and Yechida. It is known that Malchut of AK from the Tabur down connected with the first Hey of Nekudot of SAG, and through the two of them the second restriction emerged. This is why it is written that they all emerged from Malchut of AK, and through her force, the heaven and earth of Atzilut were created.

44) Since the ten Sefirot of Atzilut clothe Malchut of AK, the dross started in them and they were implied in those kings mentioned in the beginning of the *Idra Rabah*, for they are all children of kings. "In the beginning God created," which is Malchut of AK, who is called Elokim [God], and by her force were the heaven and earth of Atzilut created.

45) In the beginning, they were not established until Haddar, the eighth king, the name HaVaYaH, came out. He is the consequence of Yesod of AK, the circumcision that was given on the eighth, and it is "Hadarta [honor] the face of an old man." He begot the drop of whiteness called Hassadim, and cast it in the MAN in Malchut in him, which is a drop of Odem [redness], the land of Edom [red], and then the worlds were established. These are the seven kings that include the ten Sefirot of Atzilut, since the first includes GAR. At that time, the worlds were perfumed by the coupling of Yesod and Malchut of AK, and this is "On the day the Lord God made heaven and earth," associating mercy with judgment, and then Atzilut was established. Malchut of AK herself, which is the beginning of Atzilut and is Atik Yomin, her drop of redness was established, and it was said about her in the *Idra Rabah*, p 135a [in Hebrew], "Any leader of a nation who is not corrected first, the nation is not corrected."

Simple Light

45) Haddar, the eighth king, the name HaVaYaH, came out. He is the consequence of Yesod of AK, etc., He begot the drop of whiteness, etc., and cast it in the MAN in Malchut in him. All the worlds emerged from TNHY of AK, from the association of the quality of mercy with judgment that was done there, as the ARI said above, that they emerged from the small Hey of AK. However, in the first ten Sefirot of Atzilut that emerged in the world of Nekudim, this association of the quality of mercy sufficed only for the GAR of TNHY of AK, meaning for the GAR of Nekudim that clothe the GAR of TNHY of AK. Hence, only the GAR emerged in the correction of lines, but this association was not enough for the ZAT of Nekudim, and they emerged one below the other without a correction of lines. As a result, the ZAT of Nekudim were broken and only the GAR persisted.

However, afterward, through raising MAN once more from TNHY of AK to SAG of AK, this association of the quality of mercy took place in ZAT of TNHY of AK, as well, and a new, deciding line emerged in the middle thirds of NHY of AK, called Yesod, the eighth king. Thus, in Nekudim, only the two upper thirds of NHY of AK were established with a correction of lines, which corrected the Yesod of Nukva [female], the small Hey, since the Yesod of Nukva is in the upper thirds of TNHY. But there was still no correction in Yesod of the male, since he is regarded as the middle thirds of TNHY. Therefore, the ZAT of Nekudim that emerged through Yesod of AK, which gave Vav and Nekuda [dot] to GAR of Nekudim, regarded as Yesod of Nukva, could not persist because there was still no correction of lines in Yesod of AK, which comes through the association of the quality of mercy with judgment. This is why these ZAT were broken.

This is what the ARI implies (item 44), "In the beginning God created," namely Malchut of AK, who is called "God." In other words, before Yesod of AK in Nekudim was corrected through the association, only the name Elokim [God] governed there, which is judgment. But afterward, when there was raising of MAN and a new coupling for the purpose of Atzilut took place, and the ZAT of Atzilut were also corrected with a correction of lines, namely in the middle thirds of TNHY of AK, Haddar emerged, which is Yesod of AK, and which is the name HaVaYaH, which is the quality of mercy.

Elokim indicates the quality of judgment, and HaVaYaH indicates the quality of mercy. It was explained that only Yesod of Nukva was established in Nekudim, but in the world of Atzilut, the Yesod of the male was corrected, too. This is a profound matter, which is elaborated in the book *The Study of the Ten Sefirot*, Part 10, from answer 88 to answer 93.

And this is "On the day the Lord God made heaven and earth," associating mercy with judgment. In the first association, which was done in the world of Nekudim, the heaven and earth, which are ZAT, did not persist there because they only emerged from the name Elokim, lacking a correction of lines in the middle thirds of NHY. Also, ZAT emerged without an association of the quality of mercy with judgment because in them Malchut was not associated with Bina, but only in the GAR of Nekudim. This is why the ZAT broke. This is the meaning of "In the beginning, He contemplated creating the world with the quality of judgment," meaning Malchut in her place, without associating her with Bina. "He saw that the world could not exist" because ZAT were broken and the heaven and earth did not persist. Hence, a new coupling was made, which established the association of the quality of mercy in the ZAT, as well, and this is Yesod of AK. At that time, the name HaVaYaH Elokim was revealed over creation, as it is written, "On the day when the Lord God made earth and heaven," and then they persisted. This is the meaning of "Then the worlds were perfumed."

Malchut of AK herself, which is the beginning of Atzilut and is Atik Yomin, her drop of redness was established. By this he implies the real Malchut of AK before she was diminished, which is in the form of big Hey and not the small Hey of BeHibara'am [when they were created]. She herself was clothed and established in the GAR of Atik Yomin, called RADLA, and she was established there in concealment so as not to be revealed in Atzilut unless in the form of the small Hey called "a drop of redness." This is the meaning of her drop of redness being established, since Malchut that is incorporated in Bina is called "the land of Edom [red]." From the correction of RADLA onward, no coupling was done on Malchut of phase four that is not associated with the quality of mercy. In the future , too, [at the end of correction], she will be revealed only from the place of RADLA herself, as in "The stone that the builders loathed shall become the corner stone." This is the meaning of the correction of the leaders of the nation that the ARI speaks of here, and there is nothing to add. This has already been explained in *The Study of the Ten Sefirot*, Part 13.

46) **This does not refer to herself, but only to the illumination of ZAT in her, which clothe in the ten Sefirot of Atzilut. But the actual ZAT themselves in her remained above in its place, and only the sparks of their light descend to clothe in Atzilut, and they are called "the leaders of the nation." This is why it is called Ani [I] and Ain [none/nothing], and this is Malchut of AK and Keter of Atzilut.**

47) **This is the meaning of what is written in *Idra Zuta* (Tractate 88), "Because of it, Atika Kadisha [Aramaic: holy Atik] is called Ain,"** for Ain depends on him because that concealed Hochma is called Ain. They depend on it, for in it, three

times are explained, etc., which is Hochma of AK that clothes in Atik, which is Keter of Atzilut, and then it is called Ain.

48) Should the reader delve deeper in our words, he should look, since Ein Sof is inside all the worlds and surrounds all the worlds, and the Raglaim of the level of AK that clothes Ein Sof extend through the Sium of all the worlds ABYA. Atzilut is a clothing for ZAT of Malchut in it, all of Beria is a clothing for ZAT of Malchut of Atzilut, all of Yetzira is a clothing for ZAT of Malchut of Beria, and all of Assiya is a clothing for ZAT of Malchut of Yetzira.

Simple Light

48) **The Raglaim of the level of AK that clothes Ein Sof extend through the Sium of all the worlds ABYA,** meaning only the inner AK, called "inner HaVaYaH." However, Partzuf AB of AK does not extend down to this world because it ends at the Tabur of the inner AK. Also, although Partzuf SAG of AK initially expanded evenly with the Raglaim of the inner AK, in the second restriction of AK, it ascended above the Tabur of AK once more. Thus, only the inner AK expands through the Sium of all the worlds ABYA. This is why the ARI makes the precision of saying "AK that clothes Ein Sof," as it is only the inner AK within which is the line of Ein Sof.

49) The Akevim [heels] of AK clothe the ten Sefirot of Assiya, and each one consists of 100. Thus, there are 1,000 weekdays, since there, there are all the shells. When the light from the world of Assiya—which is Yesod of Jacob [Ya'akov], Yod Akev—is completely refined and sorted, since they are ten sparks of light that are placed in the Akev, which is the world of Assiya, then, at the time of the Messiah, which is AK, insolence will soar.

Simple Light

49) **The Akevim of AK clothe the ten Sefirot of Assiya.** It has already been explained above that although in the second restriction, a new Sium was made in TNHY of AK, on the Chazeh of this Partzuf, this restriction still concerns only the ten Sefirot of Nekudim and the world of Atzilut, for only they became limited by the second restriction. All the Raglaim of the five Partzufim of Atzilut had to end on the Parsa, while AK himself did not change at all and ends at the point of this world as prior to the second restriction. This is why he said, "The Akevim [heels] of AK clothe in the ten Sefirot of Assiya." However, we must not be mistaken that they shine there with their own phase, since AK shines only to Atzilut, and this Parsa that had been spread between Atzilut and Beria, and covers the lights of Atzilut from passing onto Beria, also covers the Akevim of AK in BYA, and BYA can receive of their lights, only a light of consequence, which the Parsa does not detain.

Ten sparks of light that are placed in the Akev, which is the world of Assiya. This is so because of Malchut that was concealed in RADLA and Arich Anpin emerged with only nine Sefirot lacking Malchut, meaning Malchut of the first restriction that was concealed in RADLA, as in "The stone that the builders loathed became the corner stone." This is the meaning of the three Roshim that *The Zohar* speaks of, where RADLA was established as one above the other, and AA was established as one within the other. Because the true Malchut of AK does not operate at all in Atzilut and was concealed in RADLA, he therefore drew far from illuminating in Atzilut because he was separated from them as in one above the other, since he departed into himself above, and does not shine at all in Atzilut. This is why AA emerged without Malchut.

Also, it is known that there is an inverse relation between vessels and lights, since the absence of Malchut means that the light of Keter, which is Yechida, is missing, for then Hochma ascends in vessel of Keter and Bina in vessel of Hochma, etc., until the light of Malchut is in the vessel of Yesod, as the ARI explained concerning AB of AK. This is the meaning of AA being established one within the other, meaning light of Hochma in a vessel of Keter, which is the two Roshim—Kitra [Aramaic: Keter] and Mocha Stimaa [concealed Mocha/brain]—which are one within the other.

It is also known that the seven kings of Nekudim expanded down to this world, meaning to the Sium of all of BYA, since through the illumination of AB SAG, the bottom Hey descended from the Nikvey Eynaim once again to the place of the Peh of GAR of Nekudim. Then they broke and revoked the Parsa that was made from the new Sium since they worked with Malchut of AK from the first restriction. Hence, they were broken and fell to the shells.

In the world of correction, when the vessels were sorted out from the shells of BYA once again, they were sorted only from the first nine, meaning from the nine Sefirot of AA. They could not be sorted from Malchut of the seven kings because there is no coupling at all on this Malchut since she was concealed in RADLA, as one above the other. It therefore follows that throughout the six thousand years before the coupling on Malchut of RADLA is revealed, as in "The stone that the builders loathed became the corner stone," the vessels of the phase of Malchut of the seven kings remain inside the shells of the world of Assiya. This is the meaning of the words, "ten sparks of light that are placed in the Akev, which is the world of Assiya," meaning ten sparks of Malchuts of the seven kings that are stuck inside the shells and cannot be sorted prior to the end of correction.

This is the meaning of "When the light from the world of Assiya is completely refined and sorted, etc., his legs will stand on Mount Olives, etc., and his level will be completed." That is, at the end of correction, when all the phases of the 248 sparks are completely sorted, those sparks of light that are placed in the Akev will also be sorted, for then Malchut of AK, which is the big Hey, will be revealed, meaning Malchut of the first restriction, and the coupling of RADLA will be done on her. This level of coupling will sort out and raise the ten sparks of light placed in the Akev, since the second restriction will be revoked along with the Parsa between Atzilut and Beria. At that time, the Raglaim will extend through all the Partzufim of Atzilut down to the point of this world evenly with the Raglaim of AK. This is the meaning of touching legs with legs, since the Raglaim of the Partzufim of Atzilut will touch the Raglaim of AK and then the Messiah will come and will strike the statue on his legs.

50) **Afterward, his legs will stand on Mount Olives, as it is written, "And his legs shall stand," etc., and his level will be completed. It was said about him, "Behold, My servant will succeed, he will be high and lifted up and greatly exalted."** He will succeed more than Assiya, as in "And the tree was good," to succeed [over] the tree of knowledge. "Will be high" above Yetzira "and lifted up" above Beria, and greatly exalted above Atzilut. Meod [very] has the letters of Adam [in Hebrew], which is AK. At that time, the Messiah will come and will strike the statue on his legs. These are the shells opposite the three worlds BYA.

Simple Light

50) **His legs will stand on Mount Olives etc., and his level will be completed.** "His legs will stand" means that his Raglaim [legs] will be revealed on Mount Olives. Now, although he is standing there, he is not revealed because the Parsa that covers BYA above, below Atzilut, also covers the Raglaim of AK. But at the end of correction, when the second restriction is revoked and the worlds are fit to receive from Malchut of the first restriction, the Parsa between Atzilut and BYA will be revoked and the Raglaim of the five Partzufim of Atzilut will extend through the point of this world on Mount Olives, evenly with the Raglaim of AK. Then BYA will return to being Atzilut, BON, which was made by the second restriction, will return to being SAG of AK, and the new MA that was made by the second restriction, will return to being AB of AK. Then the Raglaim of AK will be revealed and shine, as in the verse, "And his legs shall stand on Mount Olives."

It is written, "His level will be completed." The thing is that all the worlds came only to complete TNHY of AK, since when the Rosh and Guf of the inner AK emerged, called the "inner HaVaYaH," there was a departure of lights in his Guf–from the Peh of Rosh through the Sium of the Raglaim. At that time, a second expansion emerged, called Partzuf AB of AK, and refilled the Guf of the inner AK through the Tabur. However, in this second expansion, the lights departed also from his Guf, and Partzuf SAG of AK emerged and refilled the vessels of the Guf of AB of AK that were emptied of their previous lights.

Initially, the Raglaim of this SAG expanded evenly with the Raglaim of AK. But during the second restriction, he, too, rose to the Tabur of AK. Thus, those two fillings–AB and SAG–filled the Guf of the inner AK only through the Tabur. From the Tabur down, the Guf of the inner AK remained as in the beginning, in the first departure. For this reason, the four worlds ABYA emerged in this place from the Tabur down, to fill the absence of light in that place. Thus, before the ten sparks of light in the Akev of Assiya are completed, the level of the inner AK is not complete, since the filling from the Tabur down depends on the completeness of ABYA. This is the meaning of "Afterward, his legs will stand on Mount Olives and his level will be completed," for his level is completed only after BYA return to being Atzilut and fill the Tabur and below of the inner AK with lights of Atzilut. This is the meaning of "It was said about him, 'Behold, My servant will succeed,' etc., He will succeed more than Assiya," "above Yetzira," etc., "at that time, the Messiah will come," after BYA ascend to being Atzilut. At that time, Atzilut will return to being as AK, meaning the first restriction. Then the inner AK will be completed with the lights of ABYA, and this is the meaning of "Meod [very] has the letters of Adam [man], which is AK." He will succeed and [be] high and lifted up and higher than ABYA, as explained, that they will fill his Tabur and below. At that time, the light of Yechida will be revealed in the worlds, which is the Messiah.

51) It was said about Atzilut, "I am the Lord, this is My name, and I will not give My glory to another. Beria is the Rosh of gold, for it is regarded as gold, "From the north, gold shall come." This is Bina, the covered world that dresses and nests in Beria. The shell of Yetzira is silver and copper, and the shell of Assiya is iron and clay. This is the last stone of Malchut in all the world, the Akev [heel] of AK, "And you shall bruise him on the heel." With that stone, he will smash the serpent's brain and will strike the statue on his legs in Assiya.

52) At that time, it was said about the heaven of Assiya and earth of Assiya, "For the heaven will be tattered like smoke, and the earth will be worn out like a garment." When the Raglaim of AK appear on Mount Olives, within which Ein Sof clothes, the light of the moon will be as the light of the sun, and the light of the sun will be sevenfold, like the light of the first seven days, ZAT of Malchut of AK, called Atik Yomin of Atzilut.

Simple Light

52) The light of the moon will be as the light of the sun, and the light of the sun will be sevenfold, like the light of the first seven days, ZAT of Malchut of AK, called Atik Yomin of Atzilut. This means that the sun and the moon will return to being the two great lights on an equal level through Keter, face to face. This is the seventh degree that the ARI wrote about, when Nukva of ZA ascends with ZA to the level of GAR of AA and to incorporation with the coupling in GAR of Atik. At that time, ZA will dress the full level of ZAT of Atik which extend equally with the Raglaim of AK through the point of this world, since the Parsa of the second restriction will be completely revoked.

Chapter 5

53*) It has been clarified how all the worlds in general are one Partzuf of Adam in the self, vessels, and garments. Indeed, each particular world in and of itself has all these phases, which are the self, vessels, and garments. Likewise, each and every one of their elements is divided in the above-mentioned manner. Remember this and you will not need to mention it each and every time. This is implied in the portion *Toldot*, 134.

Simple Light

53) **One Partzuf of Adam in the self, vessels, and garments. Indeed, each particular world in and of itself has all these phases.** This is so because AK is regarded as root, Atzilut is the self, Beria is Guf and vessels, Yetzira is garments, and Assiya is hall. In this manner, AK and ABYA are one Adam in whom there are these five phases: root, soul, body, garment, hall. It is also called marrow, bones, tendons, flesh, and skin. They are also KHB TM, and they are the four letters HaVaYaH and the tip of the Yod. Also, they are called five lights: Nefesh, Ruach, Neshama, Haya, Yechida.

54) Now we will explain from the world of Atzilut downward, that in Atzilut there are NRNHY and organs of the Guf which are called vessels. Because the Yechida and Haya are surrounding, the vessels were also only three phases, corresponding to the inner NRN.

55) You already know that the Moach [brain] is a vessel for the Neshama, the Lev [heart] for the Ruach, and the Kavved [liver] for the Nefesh. The Neshama spreads throughout the Guf [body] from the Moach to the Raglaim [feet], and this is called Gadlut of ZA, which are Mochin. Afterward, the Ruach spreads through the Lev and from there down throughout the Guf. This is the middle vessel called Yenika, since the Lev stands in the VAK, which is Yenika, clothes the Neshama and the Moach, and covers it. For this reason, the Neshama is apparent only in the Moach, since it was concealed in the Guf. Afterward, the Nefesh spreads inside the Kavved, and from there downward it clothes over the Ruach and the heart. Hence, the Ruach is apparent only in the heart.

Simple Light

55) **The Neshama spreads throughout the Guf from the Moach to the Raglaim, etc. Afterward, the Ruach spreads through the Lev and from there down throughout the Guf.** This means that these three vessels, Moach, Lev, and Kavved, the garments of NRN, are three complete Partzufim called Ibur, Yenika, Mochin. The Kavved is Partzuf Ibur in ten complete Sefirot in which the light of Nefesh clothes. The Lev is Partzuf Yenika in the ten Sefirot in which the light of Ruach clothes, and the Moach is Partzuf Mochin in ten Sefirot in which the light of Neshama clothes. These

---

* *Tree of Life*, Part 2, Gate 49, Chapter 1.

three Partzufim clothe one another from the Chazeh [chest] and below, where from his Chazeh and below, Partzuf Mochin is clothed with Partzuf Yenika, and Partzuf Yenika is clothed from his Chazeh and below with Partzuf *Ibur*. Thus, the Raglaim of all three Partzufim end evenly. This is as was said, "The Neshama spreads throughout the Guf from the Moach to the Raglaim." Also, the Ruach begins at the Garon and spreads throughout the Guf through the Raglaim, and the Nefesh begins at the Kavved and spreads through the Raglaim.

The Lev stands in the VAK ... and clothes the Neshama and the Moach, and covers it. The Lev is Partzuf Yenika that clothes the light of Ruach. It clothes from the Chazeh and below of Partzuf Mochin. Likewise, the Kavved, which is Partzuf Ibur, clothes from the Chazeh and below of Partzuf of Yenika so that HBD HGT of each Partzuf are revealed, and from the Chazeh down they are covered and concealed, each one in its lower one. When they are clothed one inside the other, they are regarded as one body where HBD HGT of the revealed Partzuf Mochin is discerned as the Rosh through the Garon [throat]. From there down, it is covered and clothed in Partzuf Yenika that begins at the Garon. This is regarded as VAK. HBD HGT of the revealed Partzuf Yenika are from the Garon to the Chazeh with the Yadayim [hands], and from there down it is covered and concealed in the Partzuf Ibur that begins at the place of the Chazeh.

This is the meaning of "The Lev stands in the VAK, which is Yenika, and clothes the Neshama and the Moach and covers it. For this reason, the Neshama is apparent only in the Moach," since VAK, which is Partzuf Yenika, clothes Partzuf Mochin from its Chazeh down, meaning from the place of the Garon of the whole Partzuf, and only the Rosh of the whole Partzuf is revealed. For this reason, the Neshama is no longer apparent below the Rosh, as it is covered and concealed from the Garon down inside the Partzuf Yenika. Also, the Ruach is apparent only from the Garon to the Chazeh, which is where the Lev is, as it is covered and concealed from the Chazeh down inside the Partzuf of Ibur.

You find how three complete Partzufim clothed in one another from the Chazeh down are discerned in one Partzuf, so that HBD HGT of each one are revealed, and NHY of each one are covered and clothed in its lower one. The Rosh is the GAR of Neshama, the Guf is HBD HGT of Ruach, and from the Chazeh to the Sof it includes HBD HGT NHY of Nefesh. However, in a general overview, they are all only one Partzuf whose Rosh is regarded as merely its HBD, and from the Garon to the Chazeh it is only its HGT, and from the Chazeh to the Sof it is only its NHY.

56) This is by the order of their roots, that you know what all of Atzilut is like, that Bina, who is Neshama, is half revealed and half concealed in ZA, who is Ruach. ZA, too, is half revealed and half covered by the Nukva, who is Nefesh.

57) It follows that the expansion of the vessels of the marrow throughout the Guf are the tendons that are not hollow inside, and the marrow. On top of them

are the veins, which are called arteries that beat without blood, but only the Ruach of the Lev is inside of them. These clothe the above-mentioned tendons that are extended from the Moach, as well as the marrow. Afterward are the arteries that are full of blood and are extended from the Kavved. They clothe the arteries without blood, as is known from surgeons, since the beating arteries are under the arteries of the blood.

58) Thus we have explained how they are three vessels one inside the other, and are regarded as Ibur, Yenika, Mochin. They are also vessels for NRN, since there are no vessels opposite Yechida and Haya because they are not internal. The flesh surrounds them and covers them, and it is called Bisra Sumka [Aramaic: red flesh]. This is also the HASHMAL [also means electricity] that surrounds all the vessels, and it is like the HASHMAL out of the fire, a red fire, and it is the red flesh. Afterward is the skin, which is the tree of knowledge of good in Atzilut.

Simple Light

58) **Three vessels one inside the other, and they are regarded as Ibur, Yenika, Mochin. ...The flesh surrounds them and covers them, and it is called Bisra Sumka.** It has already been explained above that from Nekudim onward, the two vessels of ZA and Malchut of each degree have been separated and become surrounding vessels of Haya and Yechida, leaving only three vessels in the degree—Keter, Hochma, Bina—in which three lights Nefesh-Ruach-Neshama clothe. It has also been explained above that these five vessels KHB ZON are sometimes called marrow, bones, tendons, flesh, and skin, where marrow, bones, tendons are KHB, and flesh and skin are ZON. According to these appellations, it follows that the three vessels found in each degree are marrow, bones, and tendons, and the two bottom vessels of flesh and skin were separated from the degree and became surrounding of Haya and Yechida, which are called garments and halls.

It follows that had the two bottom vessels not been separated from the degree, there would have been five complete Partzufim in each general Partzuf: marrow, bones, tendons, flesh, and skin. Now that the two Partzufim, flesh and skin, have become absent in each general Partzuf, there is a grip for the outer ones opposite them, since wherever there is a deficiency in Kedusha [holiness], the outer ones grip there. Hence, there is a grip for the outer ones at the Sium [end] of each Partzuf. This requires a special correction called "circumcision," since they have a strong grip on the skin, which is Malchut. For this reason, at the Sium of the Partzuf, a shell is made, whose only correction is to cut it and throw it away, hence the foreskin that is thrown to the dust. But they do not have that much of a grip on the flesh at the Sium, and it is corrected by [the act of] exposing.

There are no vessels opposite Yechida and Haya because they are not internal. The flesh surrounds them, etc., and afterward is the skin. Yechida and Haya are not internal, since ZA and Malchut were separated from each degree due to the second restriction. Hence, the flesh and skin were not regarded as vessels of the Guf. Rather, there are only three vessels of KHB in the Guf, which are called marrow-bones-tendons, in which the Neshama is clothed. The Neshama does not clothe in the two vessels of flesh and skin at all, and they are interchangeable in man, meaning they are replaced and renewed each day in the human body. It is so because the real vessels of ZA and Malchut are not at all in the Partzuf, since they were separated and became garments and halls, while the two vessels of ZON that are in the Partzuf are only an expansion from Bina. This is the meaning of what the ARI wrote, that at their end, the tendons of the blood dissolve and become flesh, implying that the vessel of flesh, which is the vessel of ZA, is actually from the expansion of the vessel of Bina called tendons.

The HASHMAL that surrounds all the vessels, and it is like the HASHMAL out of the fire, etc., and afterward is the skin, which is the tree of knowledge of good that is in Atzilut. The flesh in the Partzuf is regarded as HASHMAL, and the skin is regarded as the Noga shell. This is only after it obtains the phase of Haya, since as long as there is only the phase of Neshama in the Partzuf, the vessel of flesh is still not apparent and it is regarded as merely skin, though it incorporates both skins together. That is, the two vessels ZA and Malchut are not regarded as flesh and skin but as two skins attached to one another back-to-back. This is so because as long as there are only three lights NRN in ZA, they are clothed in the three vessels of marrow-bones-tendons, and no light reaches from the tendons down, meaning in the flesh and skin. Because it is known that the lights sort out the vessels, they are regarded as unsorted whatsoever. Therefore, both are regarded as skins, since everything that is not sorted is called skin.

However, when ZA obtains the phase of the light of Haya, the Haya dresses in the marrow, the Neshama that was in marrow descends to the vessel of bones, the Ruach that was in the vessel of bones descends to the vessel of tendons, and the Nefesh that was in the vessel of tendons descends to the vessel of flesh. It follows that now the vessel of ZA is also sorted by obtaining of the light of Haya. Hence, now it has four vessels: marrow, bones, tendons, and flesh. The skin surrounds them, and only the skin remains unsorted.

Nevertheless, the flesh is not regarded as a completed vessel because it is from the expansion of Bina. This is why it is called HASHMAL, meaning a garment, clothing the three vessels. It is called garment because the light of Haya that sorts for it the vessel of flesh is extended from the surrounding of garments. Hence, the vessel of flesh is also regarded as garment.

There is another reason: The light of Haya it receives through sorting the vessel of flesh is only VAK of Haya, since it cannot receive GAR of Haya prior to the end of correction, when the second restriction is revoked and the surrounding of garments, namely the vessel of ZA that was separated by the second restriction, reconnects to the Partzuf like the three vessels KHB. It has been explained above that prior to the end of correction, the vessel of ZA is only from the expansion of Bina, and it receives only the VAK of the light of Haya. Hence, it is considered a vessel of flesh that is still not connected to the Guf, since Neshama of Haya does not illuminate in the Guf. Since it is still separated from the Guf, it is called garment or HASHMAL, indicating that it is not connected to the Guf like the three vessels marrow-bones-tendons.

It has been explained that when ZA has only NRN, it does not have a vessel for flesh at all, and it is still regarded as skin. When it obtains the light of Haya, the vessel of flesh is sorted out for it, yet it is not an actual vessel, connected to the Guf, due to the absence of GAR of Haya throughout the six thousand years. For this reason, the vessel of flesh does not have a complete light that belongs to it, but only VAK from the light that belongs to it. It is known that in all the phases, the VAK are always regarded as merely a vessel, and only the GAR are regarded as complete lights. It follows that there is only an illumination of vessels in flesh, meaning VAK and not GAR.

The skin, which is the tree of knowledge of good that is in Atzilut.

59) **The flesh is the surrounding name Elokim and is called Kursaya of Shvivin [Aramaic: a throne (or chair) of sparks].** It is so because Elokim filled with Yods is 300 in Gematria, and in square Gematria it is 200, and the two incorporators are Bassar [flesh] in Gematria. We have explained that the Or [skin] is Ra [bad] and the letter Vav is the good within it, as mentioned in the Tikkunim 69, p. 150 [in Hebrew], that it is the tree of knowledge of good and bad. However, in Atzilut, the bad was separated outward, as it is written in Tree of Life.

Simple Light

59) **The flesh is the surrounding name Elokim, etc. Elokim filled with Yods is 300 in Gematria, and in square Gematria it is 200, and the two incorporators are Bassar in Gematria.** Mochin of GAR are called HaVaYaH, and Mochin of VAK are called Elokim. Since there is only Mochin of VAK in the vessel of flesh, it is called Elokim. It is known that there are three phases of Ibur-Yenika-Mochin in VAK, and all are the names of Elokim. However, the Mochin of Ibur are Aleph-Lamed-Mem of Elokim, indicating that it lacks the Yod-Hey of Elokim. The Mochin of Yenika are called "simple Elokim" without a filling, since any filling implies a coupling of Mochin. Because there is only VAK of VAK in Yenika, meaning Nefesh-Ruach of Ruach, and there is not even GAR of Ruach there, called Mochin of VAK, they are regarded as simple Elokim without a filling. The Mochin of VAK, meaning the GAR of Ruach, are regarded as Elokim with a filling, and it is known that there are three Mochin HBD, which have three fillings: Moach Hochma is Elokim filled with Yods, Moach Bina is Elokim filled with Heys, and Moach Daat is Elokim filled with Alephs.

It was said, **"Elokim filled with Yods is 300 in Gematria."** This indicates that there is Moach of Hochma of VAK in the vessel of flesh there, since Elokim filled with Yods is Hochma. However, with regard to the Moach Bina of VAK, it only has the posterior because it does not have Elokim filled with Heys, but the posterior of Elokim, which is 200 in Gematria, like this: Aleph, Aleph-Lamed, Aleph-Lamed-Hey, Aleph-Lamed-Hey-Yod, Aleph-Lamed-Hey-Yod-Mem. This indicates that it does not have the Hassadim that are imparted from the Moach of Bina, which is Elokim filled with Heys, and this Moach is regarded as posterior to it. Hence, with regard to Daat, it has only two inclusions—an inclusion of Hassadim and an inclusion of Gevurot. These are the letters Bet-Shin-Reish [the letters of Bassar (flesh)]: Shin is Hochma, Reish is Bina, and Bet is Daat, and this is why it is called "a throne of sparks," implying judgments, due to the lack of Hassadim [mercies] there, for as long as it is devoid of Hassadim, the Hochma will also not be able to clothe in it in full.

60) Afterward there are the worlds BYA, and they are the garments of Atzilut. It is in this manner because when Malchut descends to be the Rosh to the foxes, the upper bodies clothe below.

Simple Light

60) When Malchut descends to be the Rosh to the foxes, the upper bodies clothe below. This was done during the diminution of the moon on the fourth day of the days of creation. First, the ZON were in the form of the two great lights, on an equal level back-to-back. At that time, the Nukva was a complete Partzuf in ten Sefirot of the posterior. That is, she was complete in Ibur-Yenika-Mochin of the posterior, which is all the completeness of Partzuf VAK. When the moon complained and said, "Two kings cannot use the same Keter [crown]," she was told, "Go and diminish yourself." At that time, she returned to being a dot under the Yesod as before, and all ten Sefirot of her Partzuf of posterior descended to Beria as Rosh to the foxes, since she became the phase of Atik and a revealed Rosh in Beria.

It is known that everything that was as a Guf for ZA in the state of Ibur and Yenika became skin in the state of Gadlut. This means that the state of Ibur-Yenika is lights of VAK, which are Ruach-Nefesh. It is also known that when he has only two lights, Ruach-Nefesh, he has two vessels of Keter-Hochma, which are called marrow and bones. The light of Ruach dresses in the vessel of Keter, which is marrow, and the light of Nefesh in vessel of Hochma, which is bones. Obtaining Neshama sorts out for him the vessel of Bina, which is tendons, and then the Neshama dresses in the vessel of marrow, the light of Ruach that was there descends to the vessel of bones, and the light of Nefesh that was in the vessel of bones descends to the vessel of tendons. Obtaining Haya sorts for it the vessel of flesh, and then the light of Haya dresses in the vessel of marrow, the light of Neshama that was there descends to the vessel of bones, the Ruach that was in the vessel of bones descends to the vessel of tendons, while the Nefesh that was in the vessel of tendons now descends to the vessel of flesh that has been sorted anew. Obtaining the light of Yechida sorts out for him the vessel of skin, the Yechida dresses in the marrow, and so forth likewise, and the light of Nefesh that was in vessel of flesh now descends to the vessel of skin that is sorted through the light of Yechida.

You find that when ZA had only Ibur-Yenika, which are Nefesh-Ruach, they clothe in the complete vessels of the Guf of ZA, meaning in the vessels of marrow and bones. However, at the time of Gadlut [greatness/adulthood], when he obtains Haya and Yechida, the Haya and Yechida take those vessels of marrow and bones, and the Neshama takes the vessel of tendons. Thus, now Ruach-Nefesh clothe in vessels that are outside the Guf, called flesh and skin. This is the meaning of what the ARI says, that everything that was regarded as Guf for ZA in Ibur and Yenika has become skin in the state of Gadlut. It is explained that lights of VAK were clothed in the Guf in the days of Ibur and Yenika, meaning in the marrow and bones, and now they are clothed in the flesh and skin, which together are called skin. This indicates that they are incomplete vessels because as long as the second restriction rules, it is impossible to fully sort these vessels of ZA and Malchut called flesh and skin. Hence, they are called skin, where the vessel of skin is called parchment and the vessel of flesh is called Duchsustus.

It was said **"When Malchut descends to be the Rosh to the foxes, the upper bodies clothe below,"** since any clothing of Malchut in BYA is only in her Partzuf of posterior that fell to BYA during the diminution of the moon since she is the Rosh [head] of the foxes. This is only VAK, which is Ruach-Nefesh, so even the lights in her are regarded as body and vessels, as it is known that the light of VAK is called "illumination of vessels" and lights are only GAR, which are Neshama-Haya-Yechida.

This is why he says that only the bodies of Atzilut were clothed through Malchut in BYA, since there are three phases in this posterior Partzuf that fell to BYA. These are Ibur, Yenika, Mochin, and they are only three phases of body, meaning lights of VAK. A phase of body of Mochin clothed in Beria and became Neshama, and a phase of the body of Yenika clothed in Yetzira and became a Neshama there. The phase of the body of Ibur clothed in Assiya and became Neshama there, and he said precisely "Behina of bodies," indicating that these VAK that clothe in Beria are not flesh and skin as in Atzilut during Gadlut. Rather, they are actual vessels of body, which are marrow and bones, since the Partzuf of the posterior of Nukva is Katnut.

61) **The inner vessel of the marrow for Neshama descends in Beria where it becomes Neshama. Although she is discerned as a vessel, a Neshama for the world below it is still made there. However, in the world itself, it is never made from a vessel of Neshama since the Haya and Yechida never clothe.**

Simple Light

61) **However, in the world itself, it is never made from a vessel of Neshama since the Haya and Yechida never clothe.** In BYA there are these lights of VAK that are

Ruach-Nefesh of Malchut of Atzilut that became Neshama there. But this will never happen in the world of Atzilut itself, since it has been explained above that even in Mochin of Gadlut, the lights of VAK descend to flesh and skin, which are incomplete vessels and can never receive the phase of Neshama that belongs to them. Rather, throughout the six thousand years, they remain as light of VAK from the light that belongs to their share. It is so because sorting these vessels depends on the Mochin of Haya and Yechida, and as long as the second restriction rules, the vessels of ZA and Malchut are separated into garments and halls by the ascent of the ending Malchut to the vessel of Bina. Hence, the vessels of flesh and skin are lacking the GAR of Haya of their share since they are merely an expansion of Bina.

This is why he says that these lights of Ruach-Nefesh that are regarded as a vessel become Neshama in BYA, since BYA receive from the Ibur-Yenika of the Katnut of Malchut, which is Ibur-Yenika-Mochin of the posterior, and in Katnut the Nefesh-Ruach are clothed in complete vessels of body, meaning the bones and marrow. For this reason, they can become a phase of Neshama there in BYA. But in Atzilut, the Nukva cannot stand in these Mochin of the posterior. Instead, she returns to being a dot under Yesod. That is, she comes in Ibur for Mochin of face to face and receives Mochin of Gadlut from NHY of ZA. At that time, the lights of VAK descend to the vessels of skin, meaning to flesh and skin, which never become Neshama and are always lacking the GAR that belongs to their share, which is called a vessel. Thus, the illumination of vessels will never rise to become Neshama in Atzilut.

62) **The middle vessel is the Lev [heart], a vessel for Ruach. It descends in Yetzira where it becomes Neshama. At that time, Yetzira covers and clothes some of Beria like the Lev that covers the Moach in Atzilut, and like ZA toward Bina, while the outer vessel of the Kavved of Nefesh of Atzilut, it itself becomes a Neshama to Assiya.**

63) **Indeed, the Neshama in Yetzira is Neshama in relation to Yetzira itself, but in fact, it is only Ruach in relation to the three general worlds BYA. Likewise, the Neshama of Assiya is only Nefesh in relation to the general state because in Atzilut NRN had only three vessels.**

64) **You should know that the internality and externality of the vessels, although each one has three phases of Ibur-Yenika-Mochin, all three phases of externality are nevertheless called body, and all the internality is called Mochin in relation to it, as mentioned in the Tikkunim 121. Hence, for the most part, we call the internal ones Mochin, and it is known that Mochin is not Neshama, but only the inner body.**

Simple Light

64) **All three phases of externality are called body, and all the internality is called Mochin in relation to it.** This concerns what is written above, that the Partzuf of the posterior of the Nukva that descended to BYA is regarded as clothing of the bodies of Atzilut. He says that all three phases of externality, meaning Ibur-Yenika-Mochin

of the posterior, where Ibur-Yenika are VAK of VAK, and Mochin are GAR of VAK, all of these lights are called body and not lights, since even the Mochin of VAK are regarded as body. Hence, this Partzuf of Ibur-Yenika-Mochin of the posterior that fell and clothed in BYA is called "the bodies of Atzilut," since only the three phases Ibur-Yenika-Mochin of the anterior, which are NRNHY of the three lights of Neshama Haya Yechida, only they are called "lights" and Mochin.

65) It follows that the Mochin of externality has become a receptacle for the Mochin of internality and is called "its air," like the Mochin of Katnut, which became "crusts" of the Mochin of Gadlut. This is why it is written in the *Tikkunim*, p. 121, that the name SAG is the marrow inside, the three Yods are as three Mochin, and that the name MA is outside, three Alephs, three airs that clothe in those three Mochin.

Chapter 6

66*) Now we will explain the chariot of Ezekiel, which is in Yetzira, and from it you will deduce about the rest. Know that it has been explained that in all the worlds there are inner lights and surrounding lights, and the vessels of all the worlds stop in the middle between the surrounding lights and the inner lights.

67) The inner lights and their vessels are the higher ones inside and the lower ones outside, since the inner Atik and its vessel are inside everything and on top of it are the inner light and vessel of AA, and likewise through Assiya, whose inner light and vessel clothe all the worlds. The surrounding lights are the opposite because the lower ones are more internal since the surrounding of Assiya is on top of the vessels of Assiya, and on top of it the surrounding of Yetzira, etc.

68) It therefore follows that the vessels of Assiya are the middle point of the whole of Assiya, and all the worlds are in the middle of the inner and surrounding lights, and this earth of ours is the middle point of Assiya and all the worlds.

Simple Light

68) **The vessels of Assiya are the middle point of the whole of Assiya, and all the worlds are in the middle of the inner and surrounding lights.** This means that the Sium of the world of Assiya of straightness is at the ending point of the Raglaim of AK, which is the point of this world. Likewise, the Sium of the vessels of circles of AK is also at the ending point of straightness, which is the point of this world, since in the circles, their end is at their center, for there is no above or below in the circles.

Thus, that same point of Sium that ends the straightness is the central point of the circles of AK, which are from the first restriction. However, remember that the point of Sium of the second restriction of the straightness is in the Parsa below Atzilut, where all the Raglaim of Atzilut end, and it is also the central point of the circles of the second restriction. However, here it refers to the worlds BYA, which clothe NHY of AK of the first restriction through the point of this world. This is why here he points to the central point of the circles of the first restriction.

69) Once we know this, let us return to our matter, that the shells of Assiya are more at the center than all of Assiya and all the worlds except for this earth. However, with respect to the inner light alone, the shells clothe them and surround them and are outside of all of them.

70) Let us begin with Atzilut. First, there are the shells, which are stormy wind, etc. They are called skin, since skin is the shell, which is why it is called shell. They are also the three shells, cloud, stormy wind, and fire, corresponding to the three foreskins, circumcision, exposing, and sucking of blood, and within them is the flesh, the crown of the tendon, which is the HASHMAL.

---

* *Tree of Life*, Part 2, Gate 49, Chapter 2.

Simple Light

70) There are the shells, which are stormy wind, etc. They are called skin, since skin is the shell, which is why it is called shell. They are also the three shells, etc. We should know that although the root of all the judgments in the worlds are still in the first restriction, in the screen that was made there in the vessel of Malchut, nevertheless, the shells were made only by the breaking of the vessels that took place in ZAT of the world of Nekudim. Until there, although there was already a lack of Kedusha [holiness] due to the first restriction, since the receiving Malchut, which was diminished from receiving due to the first restriction, was separated from the internal ones and became vessels of the circles of AK. Nevertheless, by this, no corruption occurred in the worlds.

However, after the second restriction was done in the world of Nekudim, the ending Malchut ascended to the place of the vessel of Bina of the Guf of Partzuf TNHY of AK, which is in the place of the Chazeh of this Partzuf, and the Parsa was placed there as the point of Sium, and the vessels of half of Tifferet and NHY that became the three worlds BYA can no longer receive any of the light of Atzilut due to the point of Sium above them. Hence, after ZAT of Nekudim drew the light of Atzilut to BYA once again, since they revoked the new boundary of the Parsa and expanded to BYA, the breaking occurred in them anterior and posterior, and they fell to the shells in BYA. This was because now a big corruption occurred, where even the anterior vessels of ZAT that stand above the Parsa, and are fit to receive the light of Atzilut, also broke, died, and fell to the shells.

We should thoroughly understand the meaning of the anterior and posterior of ZAT of Nekudim. The thing is that first, the vessels of Nekudim emerged, which are the vessels of Nekudot of SAG of AK that were diminished by the second restriction, where a Parsa and Sium were made at the place of their Chazeh, and TNHY in them fell to BYA together with the Chazeh and below of Partzuf TNHY of AK. It follows that now, after the restriction that took place, there are only six vessels HBD HGT through the Chazeh, and the point of Chazeh is the point of Malchut in them, which ends those vessels. From there down they are unfit to receive lights of Atzilut. Hence, those seven vessels HBD HGT and the point of Chazeh are regarded as vessels of Atzilut and are called anterior vessels, while those vessels of TNHYM below the Parsa that are unfit to receive the light of Atzilut are called posterior vessels.

First, the light of Katnut emerged in the world of Nekudim and clothed in those seven vessels HBD HGT through the Chazeh. The lights of Ruach-Nefesh clothed in them: Ruach in vessels of HBD, and Nefesh in vessels of HGT. This is why they are called HGT NHYM, since lights of Ruach are called HGT, and lights of Nefesh are called NHYM. These lights ended at the point of Chazeh at the Sium of the Parsa, and this clothing is in utter completeness since nothing descended from them to the posterior vessels. Rather, it caused the separation of the two vessels of ZA and Malchut that became the surrounding of garment and hall.

However, afterward, through the coupling of Yesod of AK in the GAR of Nekudim, when the lights were extended from the coupling of AB SAG of AK, since the light of AB precedes the second restriction, this light caused the revoking of the Parsa of the second restriction. After these Mochin reached the ZAT of Nekudim, they, too, were extended through the Sium Raglaim of AK into their posterior vessels in BYA, and reconnected those two vessels that became garments and halls, into inner vessels. However, the force of the boundary of the Parsa overpowered them and the lights of Atzilut that they drew promptly departed from all the ZAT, even from the anterior vessels above the Parsa, and they all broke and died. This happened because the anterior vessels had already connected with the posterior vessels into one Partzuf. Therefore, the anterior vessels were blemished, too, because of the reception of the lights of the posterior vessels. Thus, all the vessels were spoiled since the anterior vessels were merged in a single form with the posterior vessels.

We should discern four phases in those ZAT of Nekudim that fell to the shells: The first is the anterior vessels, meaning the vessels from the Chazeh and above. These are vessels of Atzilut that did not break because of themselves but due to their mixing with the posterior vessels. There are three additional phases in the posterior vessels: In general, they are ZA and Malchut, but there are also ZON of Bina in them. Thus, they are three phases: 1) ZON of Bina, 2) ZA, 3) Malchut. These four phases completely mingled with one another in a way that you have not a spark or a tiny item in those ZAT that fell to BYA where these four phases are not mixed together.

When the ZAT were sorted out from the breaking in the world of Atzilut and were established there as Partzuf ZON of Atzilut, initially, only the anterior vessels were sorted from among them, meaning from the Chazeh and above. These are the vessels of HBD HGT through the point of Chazeh in which the lights of Ruach-Nefesh clothe, Ruach in the vessels of HBD and Nefesh in the vessels of HGT. For this reason, they are called HGT NHYM. They are present in ZA permanently, and no further diminution will occur in them since their breaking was only due to the mixing with the posterior vessels. Once they were sorted out from the mixture, they will never again be blemished.

However, in the three posterior phases that remained in the shells, the anterior vessels still remained mixed with them, for there is no item in the broken vessels that does not have within them all four phases together. They are sorted out by raising MAN since the vessels of the new NHY for the level of Neshama are sorted out from ZON of Bina in the posterior vessels, and the new NHY for the level of Haya are sorted out from ZA of posterior vessels, and the new NHY for the level of Yechida are sorted out from Malchut of the posterior vessels. However, these three levels—Neshama-Haya-Yechida—are not permanent in ZA because the vessels were sorted out from the posterior vessels, whose breaking was because of themselves. Hence, there is power in the work of the lower ones to raise them through MAN or to corrupt them again by committing iniquities.

There is another distinction in this sorting of the posterior vessels for Neshama-Haya-Yechida. Only the vessels for the level of Neshama that come from phase one of the posterior vessels are sorted in full and connect to the body of ZON, since they are regarded as ZON of Bina. But the vessels that are sorted for the level of Haya, which come from phase two of posterior vessels, which are vessels of ZA, cannot be fully sorted because the vessels of ZA have already been separated into garments, which are surrounding vessels. Hence, phase two of the posterior vessels that operated in Nekudim broke, and actual shells were made of them, since they drew surrounding vessels and used them as inner vessels. This is why those vessels were spoiled and became shells, and Partzuf ZA of the shell was made of them.

However, there is also a mixture of anterior vessels in these shells, as well as phase one of the posterior vessels, which are fit for sorting into Kedusha, as was said, that there is not an item that does not contain all four phases mixed together. For this reason, those two above-mentioned phases are fit to be sorted out of the shells. But phase two of the posterior, which is the actual vessel of ZA, is unfit for sorting and is called shell.

In the same manner, the vessels that are sorted out from phase three of the posterior, which is the vessel of Malchut, are not from the vessel of Malchut herself, since she was corrupted by using the inner vessels in Nekudim, and thereby became a shell from which the Nukva of the shells was made. However, because she, too, necessarily incorporates all four phases, only the first two phases that are mixed within her can be sorted, from which they are sorted for the level of Yechida.

This explains how all the shells came only due to the breaking of the vessels, and they are from those two vessels of ZA and Malchut that were used in ZAT of Nekudim as internal after they were separated into surrounding vessels and were therefore corrupted and became ZA and Malchut of the shell. They are called shells to indicate that they are unfit for sorting throughout the six thousand years, for as long as the first two phases have not been fully sorted from within them, which are the anterior vessels and phase one of the posterior, which are ZON of Bina, the Parsa of the second restriction is fixed and sustained, and the vessels of ZA and Malchut remain as surrounding, and what has been put together from them during the reign of ZAT of Nekudim has become ZON of the shells.

Indeed, there are three degrees in these ZON of the shells. They are called "stormy wind," "big cloud," and "flaming fire." They correspond to Bina, ZA, and Malchut, as in "God has made one opposite the other." For this reason, there is ZON in the stormy wind, ZON in the big cloud, and ZON in the flaming fire.

Skin is the shell ... corresponding to the three foreskins, circumcision, exposing, and sucking of blood. This means that while ZA has only NRN, they sort for it only three vessels of marrow-bones-tendons, which are vessels of KHB. The two vessels of flesh and skin are still unsorted. At that time, the vessel of flesh is also called skin since any unsorted phase is called skin, which means good and bad mixed with one another. At that time, the three shells are mixed in these two vessels of flesh and skin which are complete evil. This is why the ARI wrote, "Skin is the shell," etc., meaning that as long as it does not have Mochin of Haya, the flesh and skin of ZA are called only skin since the three shells are still included in his flesh and skin. This is why they are all together, meaning that the flesh, the skin, and the three shells are regarded as one, and they are all shells.

However, when he obtains the Mochin of Haya, the correction of the circumcision is done in him. This is the sorting of the vessel of flesh and the separation of the three shells, since the skin that is cut off and thrown away is the separation of the shell of stormy wind, which is the root and the essence of all three shells. The exposing is done in him corresponding to the separation of the shell of big cloud, and the sucking of blood is done in him corresponding to the shell of flaming fire. At that time, the sorting of the vessel of flesh appears in him in the Ateret [crown] of Yesod, called HASHMAL, for the above-mentioned reason. The vessel of skin on the flesh is now called "the Noga shell" since it is still unsorted, since the Mochin of Haya sort only the vessel of flesh, and any unsorted phase is called skin, or "the Noga shell." This is the meaning of "Noga surrounds this HASHMAL," as is explained that the HASHMAL is the flesh and the skin is Noga.

We should know that the matter of the above-said sorting of the vessels occurs in each and every Sefira of the ten Sefirot of ZA since they are incorporated in one another. In each Sefira five vessels must be sorted: marrow, bones, tendons, flesh, skin. It follows that the correction of the circumcision actually occurs in all the Sefirot, but the shells grip mainly only to the Sium of the Partzuf, meaning the Sefira of Yesod. For this reason, the corrections were done only in Yesod, and it helps and corrects all the phases of flesh and skin in each Sefira.

71) **Noga, the fourth shell, a sound of faint silence in secret, surrounds that HASHMAL. This is the meaning of the HASH of HASHMAL, and in it is the MAL, which is the self of the HASHMAL and is the flesh. This HASHMAL is speaking animals of fire, a filling of Elokim of Yods, the Gematria of [the letter] Shin of Bassar [flesh].**

Simple Light

71) **Noga, the fourth shell, a sound of faint silence in secret. This is the meaning of the HASH of HASHMAL, and in it is the MAL, which is the self of the HASHMAL, etc., a filling of Elokim of Yods, the Gematria of [the letter] Shin of Bassar.** Interpretation: It has already been explained that prior to the end of correction there is no complete sorting of the vessel of flesh since the Mochin of Haya are also only VAK of Haya. Hence, they do not connect to the actual body of the Partzuf, but rather as a garment, clothing over the three vessels marrow-bones-

tendons. Know that these remnants from the vessel of flesh that cannot be sorted before the end of correction since they require GAR of Haya in order to be sorted out are called "The Noga shell," since she is unsorted.

It has been explained that the sorting of the vessels occurs in all the Sefirot of the level of ZA. It follows that there is a complete Partzuf of flesh, as well as a complete Partzuf of the Noga shell, since the vessel of flesh in each Sefira of ZA from its Rosh-Toch-Sof connects into a complete Partzuf. Also, the unsorted remnants that remain in the vessel of flesh, called Noga, connect from all the Sefirot of its Rosh-Toch-Sof and become Partzuf Noga.

You therefore find that HASHMAL and Noga are two Partzufim one atop the other although their root is one: the vessel of flesh in each of the ten Sefirot of Rosh-Toch-Sof of ZA. The sorted part is called HASHMAL, and the unsorted part is called Noga. In that sense, they are only one Partzuf where VAK of the Mochin of Haya, of which only the vessels from the Chazeh and above, which are called HBD HGT, can be sorted, and Nefesh-Ruach of Haya clothe in them, Ruach in the vessels of HBD, for which it is called HGT, Nefesh is in the vessels of HGT, for which it is called NHYM, as is known in the inverse relation between vessels and lights, and those six sorted vessels of HBD HGT are called HASHMAL. The remnants from this Partzuf, meaning the TNHY from the Chazeh down, whose sorting is only in the GAR of Mochin of Haya, which does not occur prior to the end of correction, are called Partzuf Noga. Thus, at their root, they are one Partzuf which is called HASHMAL from the Chazeh and above, and it is called Noga from the Chazeh and below. However, since this sorting occurs in each and every Sefira of the ten Sefirot of the Rosh-Toch-Sof of ZA, they necessarily become two complete Partzufim with Rosh-Toch-Sof for each of them, and they clothe over one another.

For this reason, in relation to HASHMAL and Noga being one Partzuf, the name HASHMAL is divided between them, where the six vessels from the Chazeh and above are called MAL of HASHMAL, which means speaking animals of fire, indicating that the Mochin of Haya [animal] clothe there. In them is the speech, for there is speech only in Mochin of Haya. This is why they are implied by MAL, from the words "speaking animals." However, the vessels of TNHY from the Chazeh and below of this Partzuf, which cannot be sorted prior to the end of correction, and which are called Noga, are HASH of HASHMAL, indicating that they are Hashot [silent] and there is no speech in them. This is why the ARI writes that HASHMAL is MAL and Noga is HASH.

However, with regard to their being two Partzufim with Rosh-Toch-Sof that clothe over one another, you find that in Partzuf HASHMAL, for itself, there are all ten Sefirot in Rosh-Toch-Sof, and in Partzuf Noga, for itself, there are also ten Sefirot in Rosh-Toch-Sof. It follows there are vessels from the Chazeh and above in Partzuf HASHMAL, as well as vessels from the Chazeh and below. This is why the full name

HASHMAL exists only in Partzuf HASHMAL, since from its Chazeh and above, it is MAL from HASHMAL, speaking animals of fire where the light of Haya is clothed, in whom there is speech, and from its Chazeh and below, it is also in HASH from HASHMAL, for the light of Haya does not fully shine in it before it obtains GAR of Haya. Hence, there is no speech there and they are silent. Thus, the matter of HASH and MAL occurs only in Partzuf HASHMAL.

Likewise, in Partzuf Noga, for itself, there are ten Sefirot Rosh-Toch-Sof, where from the Chazeh and above it can receive illumination from Partzuf HASHMAL since usually, VAK of Haya correct the vessels from the Chazeh and above, so it is regarded as being all good there without any bad at all. However, in the vessels from the Chazeh and below of Partzuf Noga, the light of Haya does not shine at all even in Partzuf HASHMAL. Hence, in Noga, they are regarded as good and bad mixed together, and remember these words for the rest of the explanations of the ARI.

We could ask about this from what has been explained by the ARI in several places, that any revealing of Hochma in the Partzuf is only from the Chazeh and below, but from the Chazeh and above, the Hassadim are covered inside the Yesod of Ima and no revealing of Hochma can be seen in them. This seems opposite to what is explained here. Indeed, the thing is that all that is spoken of here is the two vessels of flesh and skin, which are the vessels of ZA and Malchut that were separated from the Partzuf by the second restriction, since Malchut rose to Bina of the body, called Tifferet, and ended the Partzuf there, and from the Chazeh and below they were separated from the Partzuf and became surrounding, which are this ZON of Tifferet, meaning from the Chazeh down to the Sium of Tifferet and the true ZON of the Guf, which are Netzah and Hod.

Thus, those vessels of flesh and skin are regarded as from the Chazeh and below of each Partzuf in general, as well as from the Chazeh and below of each particular Sefira of the ten Sefirot of Rosh-Toch-Sof, since all that applies to the whole applies also to all the parts of that whole. Thus, the whole of the Partzuf HASHMAL that is spoken of here is only from the Chazeh and below, where the ARI says in several places that it is the place of revealing of Hochma, but only in particular, when each of the ten Sefirot of ZA is divided into Rosh-Toch-Sof, Rosh and Toch from the Chazeh and above, and Sof from the Chazeh and below. Hence, they join and become a complete Partzuf in the HASHMAL, with Rosh-Toch-Sof, since the vessels of flesh in the Sefirot from the Chazeh and above of Partzuf ZA are from the Chazeh and above of Partzuf HASHMAL, and the vessels of flesh that comes from the Sefirot from the Chazeh and below of ZA are from the Chazeh and below of HASHMAL.

There is another reason: All the revealing of Hochma in TNHY of ZA itself, from the Chazeh and below of the general ZA, is from below upward. This is the nature of the lights of VAK of Haya: They are not revealed from above downward. For this reason, it is considered that they themselves are divided into from-the-Chazeh-and-above of this Partzuf TNHY, and from-the-Chazeh-and-below of this Partzuf TNHY. From below upward, the Mochin of Haya shine, and from above downward, they do not shine, and understand all this well.

Speaking animals of fire, a filling of Elokim of Yods, the Gematria of [the letter] Shin of Bassar. It has already been explained above that the marrow of Hochma of GAR of VAK is Elokim filled with Yods. Hence, they are called "speaking animals of fire" because the light of Hochma is called Haya [animal], which is the meaning of "animals." Also, the speech is in them because any speech is from an illumination of Mochin of Haya, which explains the "speaking." They are regarded as "animals of fire" because they are VAK of Haya and not GAR of Haya, and in every VAK there is a grip to the judgments, which require extra care. This is why they are called by the names of Elokim, and this is why they are "animals of fire."

72) This is the tree of knowledge of good in Atzilut, as mentioned in the *Tikkunim* [corrections of The Zohar]. This is why it is the name YAHDONHY, for it is the name of HASHMAL, as mentioned in many places. But in BYA, it is the tree of knowledge of good and bad and not HASHMAL itself, but rather the Noga shell that surrounds it and separates the HASHMAL from the shells. This shell of good and bad is in BYA, but in Atzilut itself it is good without bad.

Simple Light

72) **The tree of knowledge of good in Atzilut, etc. The tree of knowledge of good and bad, etc., and this shell of good and bad is in BYA, but in Atzilut itself, good without bad.** In the beginning, before the Mochin of Haya was extended into ZA of Atzilut, the HASHMAL, which is the flesh with the Noga and the three shells, were included in Atzilut under the name skin, since they are good and bad. Thus, before they extend Mochin of Haya, Atzilut is also regarded as good and bad. However, after the Mochin of Haya are extended, the HASHMAL and Noga are sorted to Kedusha and are good without bad, since the bad in them, which is the three shells of the stormy wind, etc., have been rejected from there by the circumcision, exposing, and sucking of blood. However, in BYA, where the Mochin of Haya cannot spread from Parsa of Atzilut and below, the three foreskins are no longer separated from the Noga shell, and it is still mixed with them there. For this reason, she is regarded as the tree of knowledge of good and bad.

There is another reason: In Atzilut, the HASHMAL of Ima separates the skin, which is the inner Noga, from the Noga that is a shell. For this reason, the inner Noga is all good.

73) **For this reason, you find that HASHMAL has the Gematria of MALBUSH [garment], and it is the flesh that covers the three vessels called body, since the flesh is not included in them. This Noga shell is skin that separates the three shells from the HASHMAL since it is a very fine and thin skin that it is not apparent.** It

is over the flesh, where the crude skins are the three other shells. In Atzilut, this is called "the tree of knowledge of good," and in BYA, "the tree of knowledge of good and bad."

Simple Light

73) This Noga shell is skin that separates the three shells from the HASHMAL, etc. In Atzilut, this is called "the tree of knowledge of good," and in BYA, "the tree of knowledge of good and bad." Before the Mochin of Haya shine, they are all incorporated in the skin. At that time, even the HASHMAL is called skin. However, they are two skins attached to one another. Then the outer skin, which is Noga, is one with the three shells. Therefore, in BYA, where the light of Haya does not reach, because of the Parsa, Noga is mixed with the three shells, which is why it is good and bad.

74) You should know that there is no phase in the world that does not consist of self and vessels. It follows that since this Noga is the shell of the skin, it is not because of this that it does not consist of a body and Neshama.

75) This Noga is Batia, daughter of Pharaoh. Pharaoh sent the mixed multitude that came from the Noga shells who is called Lilit, obstinate, dressed as Eve, Adam's wife. But there is a more external Lilit, and she is the wife of Sam'el. Also, in this Noga, there are other Sam'el and Lilit, internal, of which our sages said that he was an angel who was expelled from heaven. It is called "the blaze of the swirling sword," at times an angel and at times a demon, and it is called Lilit. Because the Nukva governs at night (and the demons govern at night), it is called Lilit, as mentioned in the *Tikkunim*, p. 124 [in Hebrew].

76) It is said in the *Tikkunim*, p. 44, that Sam'el emerged from his Kedusha because the three other shells have Sam'el and Lilit there—true, bad, and sinful in every shell in them. This is implied in The Zohar, portion Beresheet, 29: There is SAM and there is SAM, and they are not all the same. This explains several writings about SAM and Lilit.

77) It turns out that SAM and Lilit, who seduced Adam and Eve, are three external shells where there are also other SAM and Lilit. However, the seduction was done by the Noga shell, which includes other SAM and Lilit. This Noga mingled with Adam and Eve and then man became good and bad, see portions VaYechi 221 and VaYakhel 203. This is the meaning of "With this Noga, the Sitra Achra [other side] seduces the woman to take the light," etc.

Simple Light

77) SAM and Lilit, who seduced Adam and Eve, are three external shells, etc. However, the seduction was done by the Noga shell. It has already been explained that these remnants of the seven kings who died, who are unfit to be sorted during

the six thousand years, meaning the vessels of ZA and Malchut that were separated due to the restriction into garment and hall, and the seven kings returned and extended them into the inner vessels, these are the three shells, in each of which there are ZA and Malchut as the ARI wrote here. Since the seven kings used the lights of Atzilut, they court the souls to seduce them so they will draw to them the lights of Atzilut once more. Hence, they seduced Adam and Eve to reconnect them to the inner vessels of Atzilut as they were at the time of the breaking of the vessels. However, Noga is not a shell because she has been corrected not to receive the illumination of Haya into her, as she is discerned as from-the-Chazeh and below of Partzuf HASHMAL, and the HASHMAL has been established as at times speaking, from the Chazeh and above, and at times silent, from the Chazeh and below. Hence, she has no interest in seducing the man to draw the light of Haya. This is why the ARI writes that the seduction was done by the three shells that have a great craving to draw the light of Haya. However, they did this through the Noga shell because they themselves have no contact with the Kedusha of Atzilut, but only with the Noga shell.

Chapter 7

78*) Before Adam HaRishon came, and prior to the creation of the world, ZON were back-to-back. For this reason, all the worlds were back-to-back, like Assiya, which is back-to-back. This is why the thirty-nine works are in Assiya, for there is the action, and they were all in back-to-back.

Simple Light

78) **Before Adam HaRishon came, and prior to the creation of the world, etc., all the worlds were back-to-back, like Assiya.** From the Chazeh and below of each Partzuf, it is called Assiya. It pertains to the Partzuf having only NRN from Nekudim onward. It therefore follows that the Rosh is regarded as Beria and Neshama, HGT as Yetzira and Ruach, and TNHY from the Chazeh down to Assiya and Nefesh. The meaning of back-to-back is that there are judgments there, which are corrected by concealment, as it is written, "Their posteriors turned inward." This is why it is written that before Adam HaRishon was created, Assiya could not be purified of judgments, for although the illumination of Neshama is regarded as GAR and there is no control or grip to the outer ones in an illumination of GAR, nevertheless, these GAR, which are called Neshama, do not correct the Partzuf but only the HBD HGT in it through the Chazeh, which are Beria and Yetzira. But from the Chazeh and below in it, called Assiya, it cannot receive GAR from the light of Neshama and still remains in a state of back-to-back, as in "Their posteriors turned inward," for they are corrected only in Mochin of Haya, for a reason that will explained below.

We should know what is written, that in each degree there are two conceptions [pl. of Ibur (conception)], and the first Ibur of the degree is done without raising MAN from the lower one but merely by him wanting. This means that the upper one raises the MAN of the lower one to him by himself and corrects it in a manner of Ibur, without any assistance from the lower one, as in "There is no man to till the land." It is so because in the first Ibur, the lower one still does not exist, so as to be able to assist in raising its MAN from BYA. But the second Ibur is done only by raising MAN through the power of the lower one itself, since once the lower one exists in Katnut [smallness/infancy], it can sort for itself MAN from BYA and rise to the upper one in a second Ibur.

Adam HaRishon is regarded as a lower one and a son of ZON. When ZON obtained Neshama of Haya, called phase three of the seven phases, they raised the MAN of Adam HaRishon to them as in him wanting, meaning without any assistance from Adam HaRishon himself, for he still did not have any existence in and of himself so that he could assist in this. Instead, ZON raised him and corrected him in a first Ibur for Katnut. After he was born, he raised MAN from BYA by himself, and rose to MAN to ZON and returned then to face-to-face. Thus, through

---

* *Tree of Life*, Part 2, Gate 47, "Order of ABYA," middle of Chapter 5.

his MAN, ZON drew Mochin of Haya because there is no face-to-face unless through Mochin of Haya.

Thus, Adam HaRishon was born from ZON while they still had only Mochin of Neshama of Haya. These Mochin are not enough to be GAR for the Chazeh and below of the Partzuf called Assiya, so at that time, the Chazeh and below were in a state of back-to-back. However, after he was born and obtained his complete Katnut through Yenika [suckling], he hoed and removed the stones and fenced the vineyard, etc., meaning that he raised MAN for his Ibur of Mochin. At that time, ZON draw the Mochin of Haya which returns them to face-to-face. This is the meaning of "Before Adam HaRishon came, etc., all the worlds were back-to-back, like Assiya." That is, although they already had GAR in the phase of Neshama of Haya, still, with regard to Assiya, meaning from the Chazeh of ZON and below, which is called Assiya, the illumination of GAR of Neshama does not help at all since it is specifically the illumination of Haya of Haya that is required. It follows that this is why Assiya of ZON are in back-to-back, and so it is in all the degrees.

79) **After Adam HaRishon came and corrected the worlds through his prayer in the manner of "to till it and to keep it,"** until Adam HaRishon came, the six workdays were in the manner of thirty-nine works since they are back-to-back. At that time, he caused the upper sowing off, and ZON returned to face-to-face, and it was the day of Shabbat. This is why all thirty-nine works were prohibited on Shabbat, since it causes the return of the worlds to back-to-back as in the beginning.

80) **The reason why they were initially back-to-back is that when the GAR were still not established and the light descended in the ZAT, they could not tolerate it and died.** This is the meaning of "These kings," etc. When the GAR were established as a Partzuf, the light was diminished and ZA could tolerate it, as it is explained by us that the diminution is a reason for correction among the receivers. Indeed, the shells were made of the remnants of those kings.

Simple Light

80) **The reason why they were initially back-to-back is that when the GAR were still not established, etc., they could not tolerate it and died etc. Indeed, the shells, etc.** This means that through the second restriction of AK, when the ending Malchut rose to Bina of the Guf and the coupling Malchut to Bina of the Rosh, which is called Nikvey Eynaim, and the light of the level of ten Sefirot of Nekudim emerged through the Eynaim, only the level of VAK came out there, without GAR. This is why AVI of Nekudim emerged back-to-back, for only two Sefirot remained in the degree: Galgalta and Eynaim, which are Keter and Hochma. The light of Ruach dresses in the Keter and the light of Nefesh in the Eynaim, as said about the inverse relation between vessels and lights.

However, afterward, through the ascent of MAN from TNHY of AK to AB SAG of AK, a new light emerged and GAR of Nekudim were extended on the level of Keter. This is called a looking of the Eynaim [eyes] of AVI at each other. The ARI says here about these GAR of the looking of the Eynaim of AVI that they were not corrected. Therefore, when the light descended from them to ZAT of Nekudim, they broke and died. In the world of Tikkun, these GAR were corrected, which is why ZAT exist.

This matter is the very basis and requires thorough understanding of what was missing in the GAR at the time of the Nekudim, and what was corrected at the time of the correction.

First, we must understand how these GAR emerge once more after the ascent of the bottom Hey to the Eynaim, which separates Bina and ZON from the degree and leaves only Keter-Hochma in them, so they could receive only Nefesh-Ruach. From where did they regain five vessels that are fit for the all the NRNHY to clothe in them? The thing is that the second restriction was done only in Partzuf SAG of AK. It is known that any screen has power and operates only from the place of its emergence downward, but not at all above the place of its emergence. It follows that in AB of AK the screen of the second restriction has no power whatsoever to be apparent in it or even to restrict its illumination.

Therefore, when the MAN rose from TNHY of AK to AB SAG of AK and a new light emerged from AB of AK, when that light was extended to the GAR of Nekudim, it lowered the bottom Hey that rose to the Eynaim to its initial place once more, meaning to the Peh, which is Malchut of the first restriction, meaning as the Malchut stands in AB of AK. Thus, now those AHP that were separated from the GAR of Nekudim reunite with the degree as prior to the second restriction. Since now there are five vessels in the GAR of Nekudim, AVI returned to being face-to-face and coupled and elicited the level of Keter in a manner of looking of the Eynaim.

It therefore follows that later, when this light of the level of Keter of GAR of Nekudim expanded and descended to ZAT of Nekudim, the ending Malchut that stands in the place of their Chazeh descended in them once more to the place of Sium Raglaim of AK, where she stood before the second restriction. For this reason, ZAT expanded to BYA, and they, too, reconnected the same three phases of the posterior vessels that have already been separated from them by the second restriction. And since they breached the boundary of the second restriction, they broke and died, since the ending bottom Hey in the Parsa removed the upper light from them.

But not only the three posterior vessels below the Parsa broke. Rather, even the anterior vessels, meaning the HBD HGT through the Chazeh that stand above the *Parsa*, they, too, broke and died because they had already connected to the posterior vessels into one Partzuf and one degree.

This is why it was said, "When the GAR were still not established and the light descended in the ZAT, they could not tolerate it and died," since it is the nature of those GAR that emerge from the coupling of AB SAG to revoke the boundary of the second restriction, and they reconnect to Bina and ZON that were separated by the second restriction. Hence, they expanded down to BYA because of this great light of AB of AK, but they could not tolerate it because the record of the ending bottom Hey remained in Parsa and detains the upper light from expanding from it onward. Therefore, the light departed from them and they died.

For this reason, a correction was made in the Rosh of Atik of Atzilut, that this bottom Hey of the first restriction was concealed there, and he emanated to AA in the first nine without the Malchut. AA ends at the Yesod since its Malchut is in RADLA, meaning in the Rosh of Atik. By this you find that when the illumination of AB of AK is extended, to lower the bottom Hey from the Eynaim to Malchut and elicit the GAR in the Partzufim of Atzilut, the bottom Hey does not descend to Malchut of the first restriction as it happened in GAR of Nekudim. Rather, it descends only to Yesod since the bottom Hey of the first restriction has already been concealed in RADLA. By this, the boundary of the second restriction is kept and ZAT can receive this light of GAR since they are already corrected not to expand to BYA as it happened in ZAT of Nekudim.

The shells were made of the remnants of those kings. That correction, which was made in GAR of Atzilut with the concealment of Malchut of the first restriction in RADLA, caused that level of AVI that emerged in Nekudim not to be able to emerge any longer in Atzilut, and ZAT could no longer expand in BYA. Hence, those three posterior phases of the kings that died remained, for they could not receive any illumination through the Mochin of Atzilut, and they will not be able to be sorted until the end of correction when the Malchut in RADLA is revealed as the cornerstone. This is why they became shells, which make the souls sin and tempt them to extend to them once more the illumination of Atzilut as they had during the kings of Nekudim.

81) When AVI were established, the judgments descended below to ZON. When ZON were established, the Emanator saw that if they are established in a state of face-to-face, the shells and the judgments would grip their posterior because they are judgments, especially since they are below. Hence, He established them back-to-back and by this they could not grip there. There is no need to keep them from gripping to the face; they certainly have no grip there. Afterward, when Adam HaRishon came and corrected his actions, and through the correction of his actions, he fenced the vineyard and cut the thorns that were gripping there, and cut all the shells from there, he returned them to being face-to-face. However, Adam HaRishon could correct only the upper worlds, but he did not correct the world of Assiya, which is all shells, and that world remained in the state of back-to-back.

Simple Light

81) When AVI were established, the judgments descended below to ZON. Initially, the judgments of the screen of the second restriction, the small Hey of Hibara'am [when they were created], were in the Peh and Garon of AA, which is the first Partzuf that was established by the small Hey that was established in RADLA. For this reason, only Keter and Hochma remained in the Rosh of AA, and Bina and ZON exited its Rosh since the screen of the second restriction was established in its Malchut of Hochma as Nikvey Eynaim. It follows that the Garon of AA was its Bina, which is discerned as VAK without a Rosh. However, afterward, AVI of Atzilut emerged and clothed the Garon and HGT of AA through the Chazeh on the level of SAG, which is discerned as GAR and Neshama. At that time, the Garon and HGT of AA also became discerned as Rosh, though as light of Neshama. Then the judgments, which are the screen of the second restriction, descended from the place of the Peh of AA to below the level of AVI, which is the place of Chazeh of AA, from which down is the place of ZON, meaning ZON of AVI and the general ZON of Atzilut. This is the meaning of "When AVI were established, the judgments descended below to ZON," since now this screen rides on ZON and restricts it to VAK without a Rosh.

When ZON were established, etc. Hence, He established them back-to-back. After ZON were established with those Mochin of SAG of AVI, and they, too, obtained Mochin of GAR of the light of Neshama, and these Mochin shine in ZON only through the Chazeh, as in AA. However, from the Chazeh of ZON and below they cannot receive GAR from those Mochin of Neshama, and therefore, the shells can grip from the Chazeh of ZON and below. This is why they were established there back-to-back, as in "Their posterior turned inward," and their anterior revealed outward.

We should know that this screen of the second restriction that rejects Bina and ZON of the Rosh outside into the phase of VAK, and rejects Bina and ZON of the Guf below the Parsa, does not pertain to GAR of Bina, but only to ZON of Bina, since no screen or force of restriction governs GAR of Bina for by their nature, the GAR of Bina are covered Hassadim, which never receive Hochma, as in the verse, "Because he desires mercy." It is known that the restriction applies only to the illumination of Hochma and not at all to the light of Hassadim. However, the whole correction of ZON is in illumination of Hochma, as is the nature of the ZON of direct light. For this reason, the power of the screen of the second restriction governs only the ZON, both to repel them from the ten Sefirot of the Rosh and to repel them from the ten Sefirot of the Guf.

However, when Bina must emanate the illumination of Hochma to ZON, she must receive Hochma, as well, so as to have what to give to ZON. In this manner, the screen of the second restriction also controls Bina, since when Malchut of the Rosh is above her, she cannot receive anything from Hochma. Yet, this does not concern

Bina herself at all, but only her ZON, meaning the root of the ZON, since the roots of ZON in Bina are called ZON of Bina.

Thus, even when Bina receives Hochma for ZON, it is not her GAR that do it but only her ZON. This is the meaning of the division of Partzuf Bina into two Partzufim, where her GAR, which never receive Hochma, are called "upper AVI," and the ZON in her, which receive Hochma again for the ZON, are called YESHSUT.

By this you will understand the meaning of the descent of the judgments from the Peh and Garon of AA to his Chazeh when AVI were established there. After they were established there from the Garon down to the Chazeh on the level of AVI which are the phase of GAR of Bina on which no restriction or screen can govern, it is considered that the screen in the Peh of AA descended from AVI to the place of the Chazeh. However, from the Chazeh to the Tabur, where YESHSUT stand, the screen governs them because they are the roots of ZON, and they must receive Hochma for ZON, and all the more so for ZON themselves.

Thus, it has been explained that there is no correction for AA and AVI through Mochin of Neshama, but only up to the Chazeh. However, from Chazeh of AA and AVI downward, their correction is only with Mochin of Haya, which lowers the screen of the second restriction from Nikvey Eynaim to Yesod of Malchut of the first restriction. At that time, the illumination of GAR of Haya also reaches the Chazeh and below of AA and AVI.

This is so in ZON themselves, as well. When they obtained Mochin of Neshama, these are not enough for from the Chazeh and below, since from the Chazeh and below, the illumination of Hochma is required, since ZON, too, consist of ten Sefirot. Up to the Chazeh, it is from the inclusion of GAR in them. This is why they can be established there with Mochin of Neshama like AVI. However, from the Chazeh down, it is discerned as ZON themselves, which require illumination of Hochma, which is Mochin of Haya. This is why it is written, "If they are established in a state of face-to-face, the shells and the judgments would grip their posterior," since in their posterior, which is from the Chazeh and below where there is the phase of ZON of ZON, they do not receive any correction through Mochin of Neshama, which is why He established them back-to-back. That is, He established them with illumination of covered Hassadim like the illumination of HGT, which conceals the NHY in them so they cannot awaken and draw illumination of Hochma according to their nature. This is the meaning of "Their posterior turned inward," that the quality of NHY in them was concealed within them and they have no strength to draw Hochma. "And their anterior revealed outward," since only illumination of HGT, which is covered Hassadim, illuminates and governs them and this illumination belongs to the anterior vessels, meaning to HGT. This is why the shells have no grip from the Chazeh and below, as well, since in covered Hassadim, there is no grip to the shells.

He returned them to being face-to-face. However, Adam HaRishon could correct only the upper worlds, etc., but [he did not correct] the world of Assiya, etc., in the state of back-to-back. During the first Ibur of Adam HaRishon, ZON were from the Chazeh and below in a state of back-to-back, for at that time there was only Neshama of Haya in them, and the light of Neshama remains from the Chazeh down in a state of back-to-back. But after Adam HaRishon was born, he corrected his actions and fenced the vineyard, etc., meaning raised MAN for his second Ibur of Mochin. Through those MAN that he had raised, he returned ZON to face-to-face and they made a coupling and delivered the Mochin of Gadlut for Adam HaRishon.

However, there are two degrees in these Mochin of Gadlut, as well. Initially, he receives Mochin of Neshama from ZON, then he raises additional MAN to ZON, and then receives Mochin of Haya. However, at that time, Adam HaRishon had the strength to raise MAN only for his Mochin of Neshama, and he drew Mochin of Neshama to him. It follows that Adam HaRishon himself was still in the form of from his Chazeh and below, in a state of back-to-back, since from the Chazeh down he is corrected only in Mochin of Haya.

It therefore follows that the Rosh of Adam HaRishon, discerned as the ten Sefirot of the world of Beria, rose to the place of Ima, called YESHSUT. This is discerned as Mochin of Neshama that he obtained now. His Garon and HGT up to the Chazeh, discerned as the ten Sefirot of the world of Yetzira, rose to the place of ZA of Atzilut, and GAR of Assiya, which are discerned as the two bottom thirds of Tifferet of Adam HaRishon, rose to the place of Nukva of Atzilut.

However, ZAT of Assiya, which are NHY of Adam HaRishon, still could not be sorted by these Mochin of Neshama that he obtained from ZON, and remained below the Parsa in Beria. It follows that although the GAR of Assiya rose to Nukva of Atzilut, she stands back-to-back with Yetzira because there is no correction to her ZAT, which are NHY of Adam HaRishon, as they are with their posterior turned inward.

It was said, "[Adam HaRishon] could correct only the upper worlds, but he did not correct the world of Assiya, which is all shells, and this world remained in the state of back-to-back," since the upper worlds, which are ZON, he could correct them face-to-face in the place where they rose in AVI. There, in the place of AVI, they are face-to-face. But in the place of ZON themselves, which Yetzira and Assiya took, where Yetzira took the place of ZA and Assiya took the place of Nukva, Adam HaRishon corrected only in a state of back-to-back since there are Mochin of Neshama there, which do not sort the NHY. For this reason, these NHY, which are the bottom six of Assiya, remained below the Parsa in BYA and they are still all shells.

For this reason, he was forbidden to eat from the tree of knowledge, which is regarded as from the Chazeh and below, called Assiya, since Assiya had still not been sorted by his Mochin and was still full of shells, and other gods were clung to those posteriors. Had he waited until Shabbat, then promptly, even on the eve of Shabbat, at dusk, which is the "addition of Shabbat," the last six of Assiya also rose to the place of Nukva of Atzilut, at which time the Yetzira and Assiya also returned to being face-to-face and all the shells were cleansed from the world of Assiya, and then he would not fail at all by eating from the tree of knowledge.

82) There, in those posteriors, since there are many shells there, the waste is more than the food, there is a grip to the outer ones there among those posteriors among those that cling, and they are the other gods, meaning gods that cling to the posteriors. They are in Assiya because Ima nests in Beria, and she is HaVaYaH with punctuation of Elokim. But here in Assiya they are other gods.

83*) Know that all the sorting of all the worlds and all the souls was done in Adam HaRishon in a state of back-to-back, and the state of face-to-face were missing. Also, all the beasts were sorted except for the beasts in the mountains of Elef [1,000], but the still and vegetative were not fully sorted. Therefore, they ate in order to sort them.

Simple Light

83) **All the sorting of all the worlds and all the souls was done in Adam HaRishon in a state of back-to-back, and the state of face-to-face were missing.** In other words, from the Chazeh and below, called Assiya, it was back-to-back.

Also, all the beasts were sorted, etc., but the still and vegetative were not fully sorted. The four phases of still, vegetative, animate, and speaking are HB TM, and they are the phases of soul, body, garment, hall. Hochma is the phase of souls and speaking, Bina is body and the phase of animate, meaning beasts, ZA is a garment and the phase of vegetative, and Malchut is a hall and the phase of still.

It was explained above that Adam HaRishon obtained NRN of Atzilut that sort and dress in the three vessels KHB, which are root, soul, and body, and he lacks the two vessels of ZA and Malchut, which are garment and hall and the phases of vegetative and still. But the phases of souls and beasts, which are the phases of soul, body, and the vessels of Hochma and Bina, were already fully sorted. This is why it is written, "Also, all the beasts were sorted, etc., but the still and vegetative were not fully sorted," since only root, soul, and body were sorted, which are the phases of root, speaking, and animate. But the garment and hall, which are vegetative and animate, are not sorted at all with Mochin of Neshama because they are regarded as from the Chazeh and below, which remain back-to-back. This is the meaning of "Therefore, they ate in order to sort them," since eating is raising MAN and MAD and sorting, and the still and vegetative had to be sorted. For this reason, they were given to him to eat, but the quality of animate, which was already fully sorted, was not given to him to eat, since there was no need to sort it.

---

* *Tree of Life*, Part 2, Gate 49, Chapter 3.

84) When they sinned, the souls and beasts returned to the depth of the shells, and now the souls ascend as MAN, and only the pure beasts are sorted through our eating, and so do the still and vegetative. In the future, the beasts in the mountains of Elef will be sorted, as well as the impure ones, see in Portion Pinhas, p 240 [in Hebrew].

Simple Light

84) When they sinned, the souls and beasts returned to the depth of the shells, since through the sin, all his sorting of Ruach and Neshama, which are the phases of souls and animate, as well as the vessels of Bina and Hochma, were spoiled once more, and only the vessel of Keter remained in him, in which the light of Nefesh dresses, meaning only the root, while all four phases of self-body-garment-hall fell together to the depth of the shells. This is the meaning of "the souls and beasts returned to the depth of the shells," for the correction and sorting of the souls out of the shells is through MAN, and the sorting of the beasts is by our eating.

85) By this you will know what is the beastly soul in man, and it is the good inclination and the evil inclination in man. The souls of the gentiles are from the three shells—wind, cloud, and fire—which are all bad. The same goes for the impure beasts, animals, and fowls. But the beastly soul in Israel and the beastly soul of the pure beasts, animals, and fowls are all from Noga.

Simple Light

85) By this you will know what is the beastly soul in man. We should remember what the ARI wrote, that there are no more than five general phases, which are root, soul, body, garment, and hall, in each of which there are five such phases. Prior to the sin of the tree of knowledge, there were sorting only in the last two phases, garment and hall, which are still and animate, and the phases of ZA and Malchut. These are the vessels that fell to BYA due to the second restriction, and from the Chazeh and below of each degree. It is so because in each body there are also five phases of KHB ZON, which are called HGT NH. It follows that Tifferet is the vessel of Bina, and this vessel is also divided according to the five discernments HGT NH, which are KHB ZON. Until the Chazeh, it is KHB, and from the Chazeh down to the Sium of Tifferet it is ZON of Bina of the Guf, and NH are the general ZON of the Guf. Thus, from the Chazeh and below of each degree there are only ZON, which are called garment and hall, and are also the phases of still and vegetative.

Even before the sin of Adam HaRishon, not all the phase of from-the-Chazeh-and-below in BYA was sorted, since only the back-to-back were established, which raise only the GAR of Assiya, being the two bottom thirds of Tifferet from the Chazeh, but VAK of Assiya—which are the phases of NHY and the general ZON of the Guf—were not sorted by Adam HaRishon with his Mochin of Neshama. Hence, those two phases of still and vegetative, which are the bottom six phases of Assiya, were given to him to eat in order to sort them.

The matter of the sorting has been explained above in item 70, that there is no item in BYA and in the shells that does not incorporate all five phases of the Guf of ZAT of Nekudim, since due to the breaking of the vessels, they were all mixed and incorporated in one another. Hence, you find the three phases of KHB that are fit for inner vessels also in those two vessels of ZA and Malchut that were separated from all the inner degrees and became surrounding. This is all the sorting that was given to Adam HaRishon in eating the still and vegetative, meaning to sort the KHB that are mixed in them.

However, through the sin of the tree of knowledge, two more phases fell from him to the shells, which are the soul and body. The soul, which is the self and lights in him, did not fall to the shells but only departed to their root, since there is no descent or fall in the lights. But the body, which are the vessels that clothe the self that is called a soul, fell into the shells and mixed with them like the garment and hall, meaning the still and vegetative from before.

It follows that now only the body was added to the mixture of the shells. Prior to the sin, it was all good and completely sorted, but now it has mixed with the shells and the body, too, which is the vessels of all the degrees, has become good and bad.

Now this body is called the Noga shell, meaning unsorted. This is the beastly soul in man, meaning the phase of animal in man, which are the four foundations in the body itself. Within man there are the spiritual soul, which is extended to him from the wheels, and it is discerned as light, since there is no falling to the shells in the lights and no issue of good or bad. Only in the quality of beastliness in man, meaning the animate part in him, which exists in every animal in the world, as well, this is called "the beastly soul" in man, and it is called the Noga shell, which mixed with the shells and contains good and bad. In it, there is all the distinction, for prior to the sin of Adam HaRishon she was all good without any bad. Only after the sin did the Noga shell become good and bad.

By this you will also understand that the beastly soul in man, with all the qualities of animals in the world, are regarded as one quality. As with man's body, all the animals, meaning pure beasts, come from the Noga shell of good and bad, since the two of them are one quality.

However, what is added in man compared to animals is that he has the quality of Neshama, called "speaking." These are the NRN that are fit to draw. Therefore, it is upon him to sort his own beastly soul, and that of all the animals, since when he raises MAN from his Neshama to ZON of Atzilut, and a coupling and bringing down of MAD over the MAN that he had raised was done there. Thus, according to the level of the coupling that emerged on the MAN he had raised, called NRN, he sorts out his beastly soul, which has become vessels that clothe that level of

NRN that emerged for him in ZON. The matter of impure beasts and the souls of the gentiles will be explained shortly.

86) This is why there is milk from the Chazeh and below of all the beasts: impure milk and pure milk, good and bad, opposite the above-mentioned Nukva of Noga. It is written in *Tree of Life* and in Tikkun 43 [correction no. 43 in the *Tikkuney Zohar*] that these are the remnants of the kings who died and were not sorted yet. This is called "the eleven signs of incense." This is the meaning of the altar of earth, as in "the kings of the land of Edom," as mentioned in the portion Teruma. This is the meaning of "All was from the dust," and it is the meaning of "earth of dust," as mentioned in the portion Mishpatim.

87) Know that the complete bad that was sorted, in which there is no good at all, are the three external shells. However, the fourth shell was not fully sorted. Therefore, it remained in the form of garment and skin, and is sorted gradually and becomes a complete body, since they are broken vessels that return to life, and the good was sorted and the worlds ABYA were made. However, there is a discernment of "this is better than that and that is better than this" from Atik of Atzilut through the end of Assiya.

Simple Light

87) **The complete bad that was sorted, in which there is no good at all, are the three external shells. However, the fourth shell, etc., is sorted gradually and becomes a complete body,** since those remnants of the kings that cannot be sorted prior to the end of correction are regarded as three shells. It has already been explained that essentially, they are two vessels of ZA and Malchut that were separated from the inner ones during the emergence of the world of Nekudim, after which the ZAT of Nekudim returned to using them. Through this usage, they became shells that cause the souls to sin, to draw for them the lights of Atzilut that the ZAT of Nekudim drew for them at the time of the breaking of the vessels.

However, there is a big difference between the vessel of ZA and the vessel of Malchut, which are the male and female of the shells. The ZA of shell has only the corruption of the second restriction, since in the first restriction ZA was among the inner vessels, as in "And God created man straight," etc. But the Nukva of the shell was never an inner vessel since the first restriction was also on her. For this reason, she is very harsh judgments. These ZON of shells exist in each of the three impure shells, and from them come the souls of the gentiles, as well as the impure beasts.

The fourth shell was not fully sorted. Therefore, it remained in the form of garment and skin. That is, as long as it was not sorted, it is called the Noga shell good and bad. It is called skin or garment, since when there is only the root phase in it, meaning the vessel of Keter with the light of Nefesh, called the Ibur of each degree, it is considered that he still did not sort his body and it is Noga, good and bad, unsorted, since then he is corrected only by the root and not by his own body. This is why at that time, the whole body is called skin, meaning it is still mixed good and bad and is all Noga. When he obtains the phase of Yenika, he acquires a vessel of Hochma in which the light of Ruach is clothed, and then it is considered that he has a vessel of body since the light of Ruach sorts for him the vessel of Hochma. Afterward, when he obtains Neshama, the vessel of Bina is sorted for him and the three phases of vessels of the body—Keter-Hochma-Bina—are completed. At that time, the Neshama dresses in the vessel of Keter, Ruach in the vessel of Hochma, and Nefesh in the vessel of Bina.

It was said, "Therefore, it remained in the form of garment and skin, and is sorted gradually and becomes a complete body." In Ibur, his whole body is still regarded as skin. But when he obtains Ruach and Neshama, the skin, which is the Noga shell, is sorted for him and he becomes a complete body with three vessels KHB where NRN are clothed. Now they are all good without any bad at all, and are therefore regarded as a complete body. This applies to all the Partzufim and all the degrees, as the ARI wrote, "the good was sorted and the worlds ABYA were made."

88) **Noga in all the worlds is what has not been sorted yet. This is the scales that rob the souls,** as mentioned in the portion *Mishpatim* 95b, **since when Noga clings to the sapphire brick, Yesod, and it is the foreskin on the circumcision, she then robs the souls. When she departs, she does not rob. This is why the coupling is on the night of Shabbat, for there is no attachment of Noga there, and what was attached returned to being an addition of Shabbat, complete good. This is not so on weekdays,** as mentioned in the portion *VaYakhel*.

Simple Light

88) **The scales that rob the souls, etc. When Noga clings to the sapphire brick, Yesod, etc., Shabbat, for there is no attachment of Noga there.** As long as there is no Mochin of Haya in the Partzuf, his from Chazeh and below are established only back-to-back, as in "Their posterior turned inward." They remain unsorted, and then the foreskin is attached to the circumcision, which is Yesod. This means that those unsorted NHY occur in each of the ten Sefirot of Rosh-Toch-Sof of the Partzuf. You find that even from the Chazeh and below there are vessels of KHB that are sorted, and the phase of flesh and skin of each Sefira in those NHY are unsorted.

However, all the forces of judgment appear at the Sium of the Partzuf, in its Yesod. For this reason, there are three sorted vessels in Yesod, too, but the phases of flesh and skin of Yesod are unsorted and are called the Noga shell, good and bad. The three shells are included in her, as well, and all together are called "foreskin." The rule is that in each unsorted phase there is Noga and three shells mixed together. At that time, Noga is called "The scales that rob the souls," since the Noga shell receives the abundance emerging from Yesod, which is called Neshama, and from her to the three shells because they are included in her. This is during the weekdays, for illumination of Haya does not shine during the weekdays.

However, on Shabbat, when the illumination of Haya shines in the worlds, a fourth vessel is added to the Partzuf, called HASHMAL. It is so because when there are four lights, they sort four vessels, but the fourth vessel is called HASHMAL. The light of Haya is in Keter, the light of Neshama in Hochma, the light of Ruach in Bina, and the light of Nefesh in ZA, which is the fourth vessel called HASHMAL. At that time, the flesh of Yesod is sorted for him, which is the Atara [crown], and the three foreskins are separated from there. Although there is still a fifth vessel there, which is unsorted—the vessel of the skin which must be sorted by the light of Yechida—it is corrected with the HASHMAL as an "addition of Shabbat." At that time, it is considered that there is no attachment of Noga there at all, since even the skin is regarded as sorted, so there is no Noga there, meaning an unsorted phase. This is why it was said, "This is why the coupling is on the night of Shabbat, for there is no attachment of Noga there, and what was attached returned to being an addition of Shabbat, complete good." This means that even the skin that is attached to the Yesod is not regarded as unsorted because it was established as an addition of Shabbat, although it still does not have the light of Yechida that sorts it.

89) This is the meaning of the portion *Mishpatim* 96b, that Elokim is the above-mentioned Noga, since as we explained, there are 120 combinations of Elokim from ZA of Beria to the Sium of Malchut, which are the external vessels there, and outside of them is the HASHMAL. Outside of them is Elokim of Noga, and there the other gods begin.

Simple Light

89) Elokim is the above-mentioned Noga, since only GAR is called HaVaYaH, but VAK, which are Nefesh-Ruach, are called Elokim. For this reason, the 120 combinations of Elokim begin from ZA of Beria, which is Ruach, and expand through Malchut of Assiya, and they are regarded as holy Elokim. Their remnants, which were not fully sorted, are called Elokim of Noga, indicating the mixture of the forces of good and bad in them, and there begin other gods, the forces of idol-worship.

90) This is the meaning of the 288 sparks that remained to be sorted in the Noga shells. From there is the bastard, for he is 288 in Gematria, and there it is called a throne (or chair) of sparks in the Idra, and see there in our explanation. The Noga shell opposite Atzilut is holy Elokim, the throne of sparks, and from ZA of Beria downward they are good and bad.

Simple Light

90) The Noga shell opposite the Atzilut is holy Elokim. In Atzilut, Noga is attached to the HASHMAL. Hence, she is all good without any bad. Hence, she is regarded as holy Elokim.

91) This is the meaning of the red cow, and understand this thoroughly, for in this, Moses and Solomon could not grasp its scrutinies, how the good and bad are together. See in Tikkun 20: She purifies the impure and defiles the pure in the manner of good and bad. She is a cow because she is in the Nukva of Noga, as MANTZEPACH, five pure bloods and five impure bloods, which is the Gematria of Parah [cow], and see in the portion *Pekudey*, p 37.

Chapter 8

92*) Now we will explain the meaning of the man [Adam], since he has self and vessels. The self are NRN, and the vessels are the garments that NRN have, as mentioned in the portion *VaYechi*, p 224. Initially, these vessels called the body and garments of Adam HaRishon were gowns of light. They were from the HASHMAL, which is one thin gown over the garment of the upper body, which are the three vessels. From the HASHMAL of Beria is the garment of Neshama, from the HASHMAL of Yetzira is the garment Ruach, and from the HASHMAL of Assiya is the garment of Nefesh.

Simple Light

92) The garments of Adam HaRishon were gowns of light. They were from the HASHMAL, which is one thin gown on the garment of the upper body, which are the three vessels. ZON is the upper one of Adam HaRishon, from whom his soul was emanated. It has been explained above that he has only three vessels KHB, and the fourth vessel that was sorted for ZON during the obtainment of Mochin of Haya is the garment of HASHMAL. Here the ARI tells us that the vessels of Adam HaRishon are not as the three vessels of ZA, which are the unseparated KHB. Rather, they are extended only from the fourth vessel of ZA, which is the garment of the HASHMAL that dresses over the body of ZON, which is originally a separate phase from ZA, discerned as surrounding. However, it was sorted from the vessels of ZAT of Nekudim that fell to the shells.

The reason for it is that the soul of Adam HaRishon extends only from the Chazeh and below of ZA, and he has no part in Chazeh of ZA and above. Even the Nukva of ZA has no part from the Chazeh and above but only from his Chazeh down, and all the more so Adam HaRishon, who is a consequence of the Nukva of ZA. For this reason, the first Ibur [conception] of Adam HaRishon began only after ZON obtained NRN of the phase of Mochin of Haya, since Mochin of Haya begin to sort the phases from Chazeh of ZON and below, when ZON clothe upper AVI.

It is known that Mochin of Haya sort the fourth vessel of ZA, called HASHMAL. For this reason, all the vessels of Adam HaRishon were extended only from that fourth vessel called HASHMAL, and not from the first three vessels KHB of ZA, which are discerned as the body of ZON. However, it has been explained above that although this fourth vessel is regarded as being from the Chazeh of ZA and below, there is still a complete Partzuf in it, Rosh-Toch-Sof, since the matter of from the Chazeh and below of the general Partzuf of ZA applies also to each and every Sefira of the Rosh-Toch-Sof of ZA, meaning the two bottom thirds of each Sefira, and all those bottom thirds join into one Partzuf called HASHMAL. Thus, in this Partzuf HASHMAL there are all five phases KHB ZON, since the bottom thirds of KHB

---

* *Tree of Life*, Part 2, Gate 49, Chapter 4.

of ZA are KHB of Partzuf HASHMAL, and the bottom thirds of NHY of ZA are regarded as ZA and Malchut of Partzuf HASHMAL.

It was said, "Initially, these vessels called body and garments of Adam HaRishon were gowns of light. They were from the HASHMAL, which is one thin gown over the garment of the upper body," since the three vessels KHB that clothed NRN of Adam HaRishon prior to the sin were not extended from the three vessels of his upper one, which is ZA, but only from the HASHMAL which clothes the three vessels of its upper one, and KHB of that HASHMAL became the three vessels of the body of Adam HaRishon.

It was said, "From the HASHMAL of Beria is the garment of Neshama, and from the HASHMAL of Yetzira is garment of Ruach, and from the HASHMAL of Assiya is the garment of Nefesh," since from the Chazeh and below of each Partzuf it is regarded as its BYA, where the two bottom thirds of Tifferet are Beria, and NHY are Yetzira and Assiya. Hence, the Chazeh of ZA and below of each Partzuf is regarded as its BYA. For this reason, at that time he ascended and clothed BYA of Atzilut, meaning BYA that ascended to the place of YESHSUT and ZON of Atzilut, regarded as BYA of Atzilut. From there, the three general vessels of the body were extended to him: from HASHMAL of Beria, the vessel of Keter to the light of Neshama; from HASHMAL of Yetzira, the vessel of Hochma to the light of Ruach; and from HASHMAL of Assiya, the vessel of Bina to the light of Nefesh. However, the two vessels of ZA and Malchut were not sorted then, which is why NHY of Adam HaRishon, which are the six vessels of the world of Assiya could not rise to Atzilut but remained below the Parsa in BYA.

93) **This HASHMAL is the upper Tzipornayim [nails], and only the fingertips remained of it, from which the Noga shell suckles, as mentioned in** *The Zohar, VaYakhel*, **p 208. It is called "gowns of light," and it is called "illuminations of fire that separate the holy [day], marrow, from the regular [day], the Noga shell, which rules during the weekdays, as mentioned in the Tikkunim [corrections of** *The Zohar*]**, 36. This is like the HASHMAL out of the fire, since the HASHMAL shines out of the upper fire, and it is called "illuminations of fire." This is why at the end of Shabbat we do the Havdalah [lit. separation, the rite that ends the Shabbat] with the Tzipornayim.**

Simple Light

93) **The upper Tzipornayim [nails], and only the fingertips remained of it, etc.** After the sin, all those three vessels of HASHMAL fell to the shells, but a new vessel was created for him from HASHMAL of Bina of Malchut of Malchut called Garden of Eden of the earth, which clothes the light of Nefesh of Nefesh that remained for him after the sin. This is regarded as his inner body, but an illumination from the outside was also extended from it, called "the Tzipornayim on the fingertips," which

guard him from the Noga shell, and the Noga shell also suckles a small illumination from there, enough to sustain herself.

94) When Adam sinned, the Neshama and Ruach departed because they lost their garments, since the Noga shell, called "foreskin," takes those garments of HASHMAL, which are 378 lights, like the number of HASHMAL, as it is written in the portion VaYakhel, 203b, "With this Noga, he seduces the woman to take the light."

95) It is the light of that HASHMAL, since it does not suckle from the marrow but only from the HASHMAL, and remember this rule. It follows that he took his garments, and it is possible that from the garments of HASHMAL is Adam HaRishon who was seduced inside the tent, as mentioned in the portion Teruma 144b, and in The Zohar, Song of Songs, in the verse, "I am black," etc., and in the portion *VaYakhel*, 208.

96) At that time, the Neshama and Ruach of Adam HaRishon, called "the upper radiance," which are Neshama and Ruach of Atzilut, vanished and Nefesh remained in him. Although the outer ones took the garment of Nefesh of Atzilut, as well, the Creator made for them a clothing from HASHMAL of Assiya, once more, but not from all of it, only from Galgalta Eynaim of Assiya from the HASHMAL surrounding it.

Simple Light

96) **The Neshama and Ruach of Adam HaRishon, etc., vanished and Nefesh remained in him,** meaning Nefesh of Nefesh. Had all of Nefesh remained in him, the entire vessel of Keter would have had to remain in him because the light of Nefesh dresses in the vessel of Keter. However, only the tenth part of Keter remained in him, namely the Keter of Keter in the light of Nefesh of Nefesh.

Although the outer ones took the garment of Nefesh of Atzilut, as well, the Creator made for them a clothing from HASHMAL of Assiya, once more, but not from all of it, only from HASHMAL of Assiya, once more, but not from all of it, only from Galgalta Eynaim of Assiya. The first nine of Nefesh vanished from him because the outer ones took also the HASHMAL of Assiya that the Nefesh clothed. For this reason, the Creator has now made for him a clothing only from HASHMAL of Assiya, once more, but not from all of it, only from Galgalta Eynaim of Assiya, which is Bina of Malchut of Malchut, which clothes the light of Nefesh of Nefesh that remained in him. This garment guards the light of Nefesh of Nefesh from the Noga shell, which is the body of the serpent's skin that was made for him after the sin.

97) Afterward, He made for him another garment from the Noga shells, and they are leather gowns. Opposite the garment of gowns of light, the Garden of Eden of the earth, it was written in the book of Rabbi Meir, "gowns of light."

This Noga shell is the serpent's skin, since with regard to the serpent, she is the outermost shell that is attached to Kedusha [holiness].

98) The shell of stormy wind is the inner vitality of the serpent, and this world is placed inside the serpent. This is why he begins from below upward, stormy wind, etc. Understand how from above downward, Noga is the highest and most internal of all of them and is close to Kedusha, and it is called "the serpent's skin" in *Tikkunim*, 36.

Simple Light

98) **The shell of stormy wind is the inner vitality of the serpent, and this world is placed inside the serpent. This is why he begins from below upward, etc.** In the shells, the coarsest is most important. Hence, the lowest shell, which is stormy wind, is regarded as Malchut of the first restriction, like the point of this world that ends the Raglaim of the inner AK, they are all the strength of the serpent and are regarded as its internality. It was said, "The shell of stormy wind, etc., and this world is placed inside the serpent," for they are all of his internality and insides.

Also, in the shells, the more refined is worse. Hence, the great cloud is more external than stormy wind, etc., until Noga, which is the most refined. is the most external of the serpent, and is called its skin, meaning the serpent's skin, from which comes the body of Adam HaRishon after the sin.

99) **This is the true sin of Adam HaRishon in the tree of knowledge of good and bad, since the Noga shell took his garments which are from the HASHMAL, through the Noga shell. At that time, he clothed in the Noga shell, which is good and bad, the serpent's skin.**

100) **It therefore follows that after the sin of Adam HaRishon all his garments were lost, which include all the garments of all the people of Israel and in the world, and they entered the Noga shell. After they were sorted, good and bad were mixed once more.**

101) **At that time, you find that the Noga shell is the man who ruled the man to harm him, as mentioned in Saba of *Mishpatim*, and all the garments entered her and mixed with the bad of this shell. You find that the garment of all the people, which is called "their body," is good and bad, and they must be sorted once again through the Mitzvot [commandments], as it is written in *Tree of Life*.**

102*) However, the actual body of the substance of man is a different quality, Moses' "Take off your shoes" is from the Noga shell, and was said about the bad in her, since Lilit who is there is called "evil handmaid," "black spleen" from the side of the bad in her. Nevertheless, it is kosher [suitable/permissible] and pure to eat because the blood and the milk, which is the bad in her, are removed, and the rest is eaten. This is the Lilit that wanted to make a coupling with Adam HaRishon as a garment for his soul.

---

* *Tree of Life*, Part 2, Gate 49, Chapter 5.

Simple Light

102) The actual body of the substance of man is a different quality. The serpent's skin, which is the Noga shell, is a clothing on the HASHMAL of the Garden of Eden of the earth. The serpent's skin is actually from the three vessels of HASHMAL that he had before the sin, but which, through the sin, fell and mixed with the shells and have become the Noga shell, good and bad. All the sorting done by the commandments apply to this body of Noga, and it is a spiritual body called "the beastly soul." It contains four elements, and the good inclination and evil inclination, which are the good and bad in this Noga, are discerned in it.

However, Adam's material body was never sorted in Adam HaRishon even prior to the sin of the tree of knowledge, since it is from the point of this world which is placed inside the serpent. Conversely, the body of the serpent's skin was already fully sorted prior to the sin of the tree of knowledge, but became mixed with bad again due to the sin.

103) Yet, the murky body is this world, which incorporates all the worlds and is the waste of everything and the material of everything. Therefore, you will see that the Nefesh of the firmaments are the angels of good and bad in the Noga shell, as it is written in the *Tikkunim*, 66, and they themselves are substances, and the body of Adam has this substance.

104) Inside of it, he has two other bodies: The first is the refined and pure body from the above-mentioned HASHMAL, with which Moses was rewarded by the bush. The second is from the Noga shell, and consists of the good inclination and the evil inclination, an angel and a demon, and is called "the beastly soul, good and bad."

Simple Light

103-104) The murky body is this world, etc. Inside of it he has two other bodies. It follows that he has three bodies clothed in one another: The first is the body of the HASHMAL of GAR of Assiya, which is the most internal and separates the light of Nefesh within it from the second body, called "leather gowns," the "serpent's skin," which is the Noga shell good and bad, and this is the middle body. The third is the murky body which is this world, and is the waste of everything.

The inner body is all good and needs no sorting. The outer, murky body is mostly bad and in it, too, there is no sorting. All the sorting is only in the middle, intermediate body, which is the Noga shell, which is half good and half bad. From his waist and up he is good, and from his waist down he is bad and is called "death," the "tree of death."

105) This real body, from the Noga shell, is a clothing for the NRN, and it is called "leather gowns" because it consists of good and bad after it became mixed through the sin of Adam HaRishon. It must be sorted, which is done by the Torah and the Mitzva [sing. for Mitzvot], and this is all the action that Israel do until the coming of the Messiah.

106) There is the falling of the face, the place where her Raglaim [legs] go down to death. From his waist and up he is good, as written in the *Tikkunim*, p 100, and from his waist down he is bad, and the bad in him is called "death," the "tree of death," as mentioned in the *Tikkunim* 101, and there is the place of the falling of the face, to sort the scrutinies from there.

107) The Creator gave the Torah and Mitzvot to Israel only in order to sort and cleanse and remove the dross from the silver, which is the garment of the Neshama. Through man's intention in Torah and Mitzvot [commandments], the garment of the Neshama is completed, as mentioned in the portion *VaYechi*, 227. Noga of Yetzira, the garment of Ruach, is refined through the Torah, and through practical Mitzvot, Noga of Assiya becomes refined and becomes the garment of the Nefesh.

108) You find that those garments mentioned in the portion *VaYechi* do not mean that it was done once more through the Torah and Mitzvot. Rather, they are sorted from the bad that was mixed by the sin of Adam HaRishon and become truly new. Thus, according to what one needs in order to complete it, so his days are allotted, as it is written in the portion *VaYechi*, p 224, that his garments were made from the actual days of BON.

Chapter 9

109*) Let us explain the matter of HASHMAL and the Noga shell mentioned in the portion *VaYakhel*. As the three bodies of Bina entered into ZA, so the outermost Guf, which is the skin, remained outside around the skin of ZA.

110) The thing is that the vessel of flesh of NHY of Ima entered the vessel of flesh of ZA, and within it is the inner Nefesh of ZA. Afterward, a second vessel, the tendons of Ima, entered a second vessel, which is the tendons of ZA, and within them the inner Ruach of ZA. Afterward, there is a third vessel, the bones of ZA, within them the third vessel of the bones of Ima, and within them the inner Neshama of ZA. Now remains the skin of Bina, which should have entered the vessel of skin of ZA as with the others, too. Yet, this is not what happened. Rather, it remained outside, over the skin of ZA himself, remaining as skin over skin.

Simple Light

110) The skin of Bina, which should have entered the vessel of skin of ZA as with the others, too. Yet, this is not what happened. Rather, it remained outside. The reason for it is that all the Mochin of ZA emerge only on the MAN of Mazla which couples with AVI through their incorporation with the MAN of Dikna of AA. Since there is no phase of Malchut in the Dikna since Mazal and Nakkeh are the phase of Yesod and Malchut is missing there, therefore only NHY of Ima can be included in the MAN of Dikna and not her Malchut. It follows that Malchut of Ima is not included in those Mochin of ZA.

Therefore, when NHY of Ima clothe with the Mochin of ZA in his inner vessels, Malchut of Ima remains outside of ZA over his skin, since she has no part in the inner Mochin of ZA. However, for the Mochin of face-to-face for Nukva of ZA, she is incorporated inside the Mochin of ZA, too.

111) Outside of everyone are the images, which are the surrounding lights of straightness of ZA, which are his garments. It has already been explained that the shell is between the garments and the surrounding light of straightness and skin of ZA. For this reason, the skin of Bina was placed outside the skin of ZA so the shells there would not be able to suckle from ZA, since the skin of Bina separates.

112) It is the phases of HASHMAL and garment, as we mentioned that it became ZON from Bina, as in, "Like a vulture awakens its nest, hovers over its nestlings." But this is not regarded among the actual garments, but as actual skin.

113) The thinnest shell of all, called the Noga shell, grips this skin, since inside of it there is Noga, and the light of the 288 sparks of the kings that remain to be sorted. This shell wants to cling to ZA or to the Nukva, and that HASHMAL guards them.

---

* *Tree of Life*, Part 2, Gate 42, Chapter 4.

Simple Light

113) The thinnest shell of all, called the Noga shell, grips this skin, since inside of it there is Noga, and the light of the 288 sparks. The skin of ZA also consists of the Noga shell, which explains why although it is implied from the ARI's words that the skin of ZA is itself the Noga shell and the three shells are attached to it, it is merely a incorporation. The actual Noga shell is completely outside of ZA, since he says here explicitly that the HASHMAL of Ima dresses over the skin of ZA and separates the skin of ZA from the Noga shell, and the Noga shell does not grip the skin of ZA but rather the skin of Ima that clothes it from outside as HASHMAL, and remember this.

114) When the iniquities cause it, the HASHMAL departs and the skin of ZA remains alone. And there is a spark of Kedusha inside of it, which is the Vav inside the skin [Or (skin) is written with a Vav in the middle], and the skin itself remains bad as it is the Noga shell and she suckles from there. When ZA bestows in the Nukva, that shell suckles from there and grips the skin, Yesod of the Nukva, and draws to her the drop of Yesod of the male, and takes it out, as in emitting a layer of semen.

115) This is why it is written in the portion *Truma*, 144, "With this Noga, the Sitra Achra seduces Eve," since it clings to her as the foreskin that is the bad in the skin of the Hey, which is the Nukva, called Hey, and she suckles from the holy drop.

116) By this you will understand what is written about the screen between Atzilut and Beria, etc., which is that same skin of Bina that covers all of ZON. Understand that as there is an image inside the five inner lights NRNHY that are clothed in NHY of Ima, and opposite them there are five surrounding as NHY of the garments of Bina that dress in the three surrounding vessels of garments of ZA himself, so there is another illumination, external to all of them. This is the illumination of the skin of ZA, called the vapor of the bones, and this illumination also clothes inside the skin of Bina and surrounds the skin of ZA, and there is an image of vapor of the bones in it. It seems to me that these are the 288 sparks.

Simple Light

115-116) "With this Noga, the Sitra Achra seduces Eve," since it clings to her as the foreskin, etc., By this you will understand what is written about the screen between Atzilut and Beria, etc., which is that same skin of Bina. Malchut of Ima that is not included in Mochin of ZA that becomes HASHMAL, which guards it from the Noga shell, is regarded as Malchut of the second restriction, the small Hey that was established as female in Atik toward all the Partzufim of Atzilut and ended them at the place of Chazeh of TNHY of AK, where the Parsa between Atzilut and Beria was placed during the emergence of Katnut of Nekudim. For this reason, during the illumination of the coupling of AB SAG of AK, which lowers the bottom Hey from the place of Nikvey Einayim to the Peh and returns the GAR to the degree, the Parsa between Atzilut and Beria does not weaken whatsoever because of it, as it happened during the Gadlut of ZAT of Nekudim, since there is lowering of the bottom Hey there only to Yesod and not to Malchut. Even in the Dikna of AA there is no discernment of Malchut, for by this, Malchut of Ima is not included in these Mochin of GAR. Therefore, the Parsa maintains its strength since she is the very same Malchut of Ima that is not included in the Mochin of ZA and does not suffer any change bt all the Mochin of Gadlut that emerge by the lowering of the bottom Hey back to the place of the Peh. This is the meaning of guarding her so that no illumination of Atzilut will spread to BYA, as it happened in the breaking of the vessels.

This is the meaning of the HASHMAL of Ima that cloths the entire Partzuf of ZA from his Rosh to his Raglayim, since the matter of HASHMAL and skin of ZA that applies from his Chazeh and below applies in each and every Sefira of his Rosh-Toch-Sof. You find that the Noga shell has a grip in all the bottom thirds in each Sefira in it, meaning in the skin that is there. Hence, there is the matter of Parsa there, which is the HASHMAL of Ima that keeps the illumination of Atzilut from reaching Noga and the three shells. It follows that the same Parsa that operates between Atzilut and Beria also operates throughout the level of ZA in each Sefira on her skin. However, there she is called HASHMAL and clothing over the skin, while under his Raglayim she is called Parsa.

This is why it was said, "When the iniquities cause it, the HASHMAL departs and the skin of ZA remains alone, and there is a spark of Kedusha inside of it, and it is the Vav inside the skin, and the skin itself remains bad as it is the Noga shell and she suckles from there." That is, it has been explained that all the vessels of Adam HaRishon were from HASHMAL of ZA himself. Therefore, he could sort only the phase of Neshama of Haya which shines in it only through the Chazeh, while from the Chazeh down it remained back-to-back since Partzuf HASHMAL of ZA itself shines only through its Chazeh and from the Chazeh down it is discerned as Noga: unsorted. The skin of ZA is called Noga, and she is truly the phase of from the Chazeh of his HASHMAL and below, which is the Partzuf of flesh, as it is written there. However, both from the Chazeh and below of the Partzuf of flesh, and the Partzuf of skin are regarded as ZA, that it is all good without any bad at all, since the HASHMAL of Ima, which is the Parsa, guards the HASHMAL of ZA and his skin from drawing any illumination of GAR of Neshama to from-the-the-Chazeh-downward. Since they draw only a small illumination, meaning illumination of VAK, they are regarded as good without any bad at all. Moreover, even the essence of the Noga shell that is outside the Parsa of Atzilut and outside of HASHMAL of Ima is regarded as all good without any bad at all, since she, too, is attached and suckles from the HASHMAL of Ima, and this adhesion allots to her a small illumination that suffices to sustain her, and then she is good without bad.

However, when Adam and Eve were seduced to follow the serpent's advice and ate from the tree of knowledge, meaning sorted and drew illumination of GAR from their Chazeh and below, which is discerned as the bottom six of Assiya, below the Parsa of Atzilut, and breached the boundary of the Parsa, which is the HASHMAL of Ima, by this they caused the departure of the HASHMAL of Ima from the skin of ZA, as the ARI says here. They also caused the flaming fire, the third shell of the three shells, to connect and become one with the Noga shell and with the other two shells. At that time, Noga becomes completely bad like the three shells, and she, too, clung to the skin of ZA and to the HASHMAL of ZA itself. But now the HASHMAL of Ima does not guard it, and then this HASHMAL, too, became skin, meaning good and bad, and they fell to the shells, ZA returned to the state of VAK of Yenika, and the Nukva of ZA to being a dot under the Yesod. Because after his vessels of HASHMAL and skin were blemished and fell to the shells, only the anterior vessels remained in it, which are HBD HGT through the Chazeh, and the point of Chazeh is the Keter of Nukva in which only the lights of Ruach-Nefesh clothe, while the vessels of HBD descended to HGT, and the vessels of HGT to NHY, and the point of Chazeh to the dot under the Yesod, which is the level of VAK of Yenika, in which there can never be any diminution.

However, with regard to the vessels of Adam HaRishon, all of his three vessels fell because they were all from the HASHMAL of ZA that were blemished by the three shells. For this reason, only the phase of HASHMAL of the GE of Assiya remained in it with only the light of Nefesh of Nefesh. By this we find that the sin of the tree of knowledge is the same matter as the breaking of the vessels in Nekudim, since Adam HaRishon, too, drew from the illumination of Atzilut to BYA and breached the boundary of the Parsa like the ZAT of Nekudim. Hence, the NRN departed from him to their root, and his vessels fell to the shells as it happened to the lower seven of Nekudim in the breaking of the vessels. Understand well all that is explained and then you will fully understand the sin of the tree of knowledge.

117) This phase is called HASHMAL, which is the image of vapor of the bones in the skin. These are the actual other garments between the garments of ZA and the garments of NHY of Ima, which are vessels for surrounding lights, and they are all called HASHMAL.

118) There is a male HASHMAL and there is a female HASHMAL. These are the true garments, but the skin is not considered a complete HASHMAL because it is not a separate garment. Rather, it is similar to HASHMAL and not actual HASHMAL.

119) Within this skin is the vessel of Nefesh, which is the flesh, and there are wheels, animals, and Seraphim there, and opposite them the four directions of the body—east and west, etc. Within them all are the bones, like the similitude of

man, discerned as Neshama to Neshama, which never dresses in a vessel. It is called Adam because of Hochma: Koah [power of] MA, which is Adam [man].

120) It is written above that the garments are surrounding light, and atop them are the circles which are the firmaments and the halls called heavens. Understand the verse, "He wears light like a garment." For the Creator cloaked in His Talit, which is surrounding light that is cloaked in a Talit, which are the true, more internal garments. At that time, "He stretches the heavens like a curtain," since the circles emerged from the remnants of the illumination of the garments, which are the heavens, outside the garments.

Simple Light

120) **The Creator cloaked in His Talit, etc., "He stretches the heavens like a curtain," since the circles emerged from the remnants of the illumination of garments, which are the heavens.** It has already been explained that through the ascent of the bottom Hey to the Einayim during the second restriction, the garment and hall, which are the two vessels of ZA and Malchut, were separated from the inner vessels of each degree and became surrounding vessels called garment and hall. It follows that the garments, which are the surrounding of straightness called Talit, are from the remnants of the inner vessels, meaning the vessel of ZA that was separated from them. The halls, which are called "heavens," emerged from the remnants of the garments since the vessel of Malchut is from the remnants of ZA.

However, both are discerned as circles since the surrounding of garments encircle inside the circles of halls, and the reason they are called surrounding of straightness is that before the second restriction they were operating in AK in a phase of straightness, meaning in his inner vessels. But the phase of circles of halls, which are regarded as Malchut, did not operate in a phase of straightness even in the inner AK. This is why they are called surrounding of circles.

We should also interpret the words of the ARI here that it is known that the circles receive their lights only from the GAR of straightness. Hence, the surrounding of straightness receive their illuminations before the surrounding of circles because they are closer to the inner vessels, as written above, that in the first restriction, they operated in the inner vessels. However, we should remember that although from the perspective of the vessels, the surrounding of straightness are more important than the surrounding of circles, from the perspective of the lights it is the opposite, since the surrounding of straightness are discerned as surrounding of Haya and the surrounding of circles are discerned as surrounding of Yechida.

121) **Now we will explain the matter of this world. The firmaments we see with our eyes are ten circles in the Rosh of Malchut of Assiya. In the middle of their space expands the Guf of the line of straightness of Malchut of Assiya through the middle of the space, and it is in the Garden of Eden of the earth.**

Atop this Guf is the skin, and atop the skin is the shell. Around them are the garments of Malchut of Assiya with their surrounding lights, and around them are the above-mentioned firmaments.

Simple Light

121) **The ten circles in the Rosh of Malchut of Assiya. In the middle of their space expands the Guf of the line of straightness of Malchut of Assiya.** There are circles only in the ten Sefirot of the Rosh. Hence, all ten circles of Assiya surround only the Rosh of Assiya, and from the Peh of Rosh Assiya and below through the Garden of Eden of the earth there is already only the discernment of straightness. You should also remember what was written above, that the circles are as onionskins surrounding one another. In that regard, they necessarily surround the Guf, as well. However, it means that the thickness of the circles that touch the straightness and traverse it touch only the ten Sefirot of Rosh.

The line of straightness of Malchut of Assiya through the middle of the space, and it is in the Garden of Eden of the earth. The line of Assiya extends from the second restriction since all the lights of ABYA are from the second restriction. It is known that the point of Sium of the second restriction is in the place of Bina because the ending Malchut rose to the place of Bina. This is the meaning of the line ending in the Garden of Eden of the earth, which is regarded as Bina of Malchut of Assiya, and does not end at the point of this material world, like the Sium Raglayim of the inner AK, which ends on the Malchut who is the actual material earth in this world, since she is discerned as the first restriction.

It follows that there is a difference between the point of Sium of AK and the point of Sium of the line of straightness of Assiya as the measure of ZAT of Malchut of Assiya. However, the Akevim [heels] of AK do not illuminate during the sixth thousand years since the Parsa of the second restriction guards their illumination and covers them from BYA. But in the future, his Akevim will be revealed in the manner of "His legs shall stand on Mount Olives." Therefore, before the end of correction, this earth is in complete coarseness of all the shells since no illumination of straightness reaches here, for even the line of straightness of Assiya ends in Bina of Assiya and the Akevim of AK are covered.

122) This is the meaning of "This is Jerusalem; I placed her among the gentiles and around her are lands," since Malchut of Assiya is called "Jerusalem," and its surroundings are the shell that are the seventy ministers, as mentioned in the portion *VaYakhel*, 209.

123) This line extends through the ground. It follows that the middle of the ground is the Garden of Eden of the earth, and it is a refined substance, very holy, and around it, this earth is very material, where the shell govern, and in it are the yeast of the crude shells, and there is no greater crudeness than theirs. This is the

complete sorting and coarseness, since as the Garden of Eden of the earth is the complete crudeness and coarseness of all the upper worlds and halls of Kedusha, so this earth is the complete coarseness of the shells. Hence, all the actions of this world are hard and bad, and the wicked prevail in it, as in "there is vapor that is done on the earth."

124) By this you will understand the meaning of the appellations found in each and every Sefira in the book. We have found appellations in the still, such as silver and gold, gemstones and rocks, land and rivers and Niles, and mountains and hills, and all the other elements of the halls called houses, fields, and soils, and in which all the kinds of still are included in the ten Sefirot of halls in every detail, and all are completely true. In the same manner, there are many appellations in the garments, and likewise many appellations in organs, and all are true and valid to those who find them.

125*) An explanation about the Garden of Eden of the earth. It has already been explained that it is the middle point of today's equator of the whole world. It is south of the land of Israel and stands opposite Bina of Malchut of Assiya, which is the next world that is hidden for the righteous in the next world. It is known that the Sitra Achra has no grip on Bina; therefore, there is no Sitra Achra in the Garden of Eden.

126) This is not so in the Temple. Although it is the point of Yesod, it is Yesod of Malchut, and the Garden of Eden is Bina of Malchut. It is known that the outer ones have no grip on Bina or on Hesed, which is the right arm, but rather on Yesod of Nukva. Sometimes there is menstruation blood in them, which is the days of the ruin when the Sitra Achra ruled her. When the blood runs out, she promptly leaves. It is also when there is keeping of the dead overnight in Jerusalem, but not in his essence. But in the Garden of Eden, she has no grip at all.

127) Indeed, the ground of the garden, which is his earth, which is Bina of Malchut, touches and does not touch this earth of ours. It is far, far more refined, like Yesod compared to Bina, and her firmaments are her first nine Sefirot, as we explained about this world of ours. The river is the Yesod in it, and the tree of life is Tifferet in it.

Simple Light

127) Her firmaments are her first nine Sefirot. This means that the firmaments, which are the surrounding of circles and straightness, surround her nine Sefirot of the Rosh, and from the Peh of Rosh downward, her ZAT of straightness are extended, where the tree of life is Tifferet in her, the river is her Yesod, and the tree of knowledge is the Ateret [crown of] Yesod in her.

---

* *Tree of Life*, Part 2, Gate 43, Chapter 3.

128) The tree of knowledge is the Ateret Yesod in her; the river emerges from underneath it, and the tree of knowledge is adjacent to it. Since the Garden of Eden is earthly, there is some grip in it from there to the outer ones. It is good and bad, but they do not enter it.

129) The sin of Adam HaRishon caused the serpent to enter up to the tree of knowledge and touch it. The tree yelled, "Wicked! Do not touch me!" And the citron, which, as is explained, corresponds to the Atara [crown], was as the Lulav [palm branch], which is the tree of life, seventy dates, seventy branches, twelve springs, twelve tribes.

Simple Light

129) **The sin of Adam HaRishon caused the serpent to enter up to the tree of knowledge and touch it. The tree yelled, "Wicked! Do not touch me!", etc., as the Lulav, which is the tree of life, seventy dates, etc.** This seems perplexing since the Lulav is regarded as Yesod, and he said above that below the Chazeh it is the tree of knowledge. Indeed, there is great depth here and we must understand it thoroughly. There is always an inverse relation between vessels and lights. Yesod of Katnut of lights stands at the place of the Chazeh of the Partzuf. When the coupling is done in this Yesod of Katnut to draw Mochin of Haya, this Yesod ascends to the place of Daat of Mochin. Hence, it is called the "tree of knowledge," indicating that the coupling is done in the place of Daat. By this it blemishes the Parsa of the second restriction, which is Malchut of Ima that is not included in the Mochin of ZA.

The reason for this ascent of Yesod of Katnut is that ZA is essentially from the phase of anterior vessels of ZAT of Nekudim that emerged above the Parsa, meaning above the Chazeh of Partzuf TNHY of AK, in which there is no flaw at all because they are vessels of Atzilut above the Parsa of the second restriction. These are seven vessels HBD HGT through the Chazeh, in which lights of Nefesh-Ruach are clothed—Ruach in HBD, and Nefesh in HGT. Hence, from the perspective of the clothing of these lights in them, they are called HGT NHY because the light of Ruach is called HGT, and the light of Nefesh is called NHY. It follows that the place of Chazeh of vessels is from the phase of the lights of Yesod.

Know that the ARI always refers to this Yesod, when it is in the place of Chazeh, as Yesod of Katnut, since when it acquires a Neshama, the vessels of HGT ascend and become HBD, in which the GAR of Neshama clothes, and HGT, which were NHY, ascend and become HGT, since now the light of Ruach dresses in them, and obtains new NHY in which the Nefesh clothes. Now it is considered that he has two Yesodot [pl. of Yesod], since there is no absence in the spiritual. It follows that the Yesod of Katnut that was in the place of Chazeh during the Katnut stands there now, as well, during the Gadlut of Neshama. Now, Yesod from the new NHY is added to it, and it is called Yesod of the first Gadlut. When he draws lights of Haya, which is the second Gadlut, it is considered in relation to it that HBD and HGT of Neshama are discerned as only HGT with respect to it, and now through the light of Haya, HBD HGT of Neshama ascend and become the vessels of HBD of Haya, while NHY of Neshama ascend and become the vessels for HGT of Haya, and new NHY emerge for him from the phase of Haya.

Since HBD HGT of Neshama both ascended and became HBD of Haya, it follows that now the place of Chazeh where Yesod of Katnut stands has become Daat of Haya. Thus, through the light of Haya, Yesod of Katnut ascends to the place of Daat. This is why the coupling of Yesod of Katnut is called the "tree of knowledge." Remember this, for it is very deep.

However, the coupling of Yesod of Gadlut of Haya, meaning the new Yesod of NHY that he obtained while drawing Mochin of Haya, where the light of Nefesh of Haya dresses, is called the "tree of life," since he draws only VAK of Haya from the Daat of RADLA that is revealed in the Moach of the Avir [air] of AA. According to the phase of light of Haya in RADLA, it is VAK, since the GAR of AVI of Nekudim were concealed in RADLA, and are revealed only at the end of correction. This is the concealment of Malchut of AK, the big Hey that operated in Nekudim, and the RADLA imparts to Atzilut only in the manner of the small Hey of BeHibara'am [when they were created]. Hence, it is called the "Tree of Life," since all the Mochin of Atzilut and lights of Haya are through the new coupling of the Yesod of Gadlut of NHY of Mochin of Haya. However, what emerges through the coupling of Yesod of Katnut, which is a coupling of the Mochin of the GAR of Haya, for the place of Chazeh where the Yesod of Katnut stands in Daat, in the Mochin between Hochma and Bina, which are GAR of Haya, blemishes the small Hey of BeHibara'am that was set up in RADLA, which is the HASHMAL of Ima and the Parsa below Atzilut. At that time, the abundance is extended to the three impure shells, which is the impure serpent, and one who draws them falls with them to the place of the shells and death. This is the meaning of the verse, "On the day when you eat of it you will surely die." Thus, the coupling of Yesod of Gadlut draws all the life, and the coupling of Yesod of Katnut puts all that is alive to death, and understand this.

This is why the ARI writes that the Lulav is the tree of life since the Lulav is discerned as Yesod of Gadlut from which all of life is extended. He says that this is the meaning of the seventy dates, etc., implying that it is the meaning of the good Ayin ["eye" or "seventy"], because the coupling is called the looking of the Einayim, as the ARI wrote in Shaar HaNekudim. Through this coupling the twelve Partzufim of Atzilut emerge, and it is known that there are four Partzufim in Keter: Atik and Nukva, Arich and Nukva, and also in HB: AVI and YESHSUT, and in ZON: the big ZON, Jacob, and Leah.

This is the intimation of twelve springs, since they emerge on twelve couplings. But the Sitra Achra has only eleven, as in "Anyone who adds—detracts" as it is written in *The Zohar* that one who adds [the letter] Ayin to twelve makes it eleven. It is so because the Sitra Achra is a king without a crown, which is the male of Atik, who is Ein Sof that promptly departed from them and they remained with a grip only on eleven. This is why the tree yelled, "Wicked! Do not touch me!" implying the above.

130) The rest of the Sefirot there are the rest of the trees of the garden, as it is written, "From all the trees of the garden, you will surely eat." The hall is a bird's nest in which there is the Messiah, the son of the upper Leah. She is Bina in Bina from the discernment of Malchut in her, as in "the mother lays." The firmaments are her upper nine Sefirot, and in the middle of those firmaments is one dot called Eden, which is Hochma, and the Keter is incorporated in it. This completes all ten Sefirot of Malchut of Assiya.

131) The above-mentioned firmament of the garden is the phase of Daat, and the middle point is Hochma, Eden, and it is the right arm in which there is no shell. Hence, this firmament is better than the firmament of this world, as mentioned in *VaYakhel* p 209, that it was made of upper fire and water. This firmament is inside the firmament of this world of Assiya, and it is a firmament that overlaps the garden and not more, and it is under the firmament of Assiya, attached to it within it.

132*) *Tree of Life*, Part 2, Gate 41, Chapter 1.) When Adam HaRishon sinned, the Mochin departed from him and [ZA] returned to being only Yenika. Then the HASHMAL, the skin of Tevuna, departed, and he and his wife remained naked. Then the outer ones suckle from him and that skin becomes good and bad.

Simple Light

132) When Adam HaRishon sinned, the Mochin departed from him and [ZA] returned to being only Yenika. Then the HASHMAL, the skin of Tevuna, departed from ZA. We should also say that after the sin, only the phase of Nefesh remained in Adam HaRishon. In *Shaar HaPsukim*, Mark 2, it is explained that only Nefesh of Nefesh remained in him. However, only ZA remained in the form of Yenika, as explained below, that as long as ZA returns to being in Yenika, the HASHMAL departs from him. Thus, this pertains to ZA.

He tells us that due to the departure of the HASHMAL from ZA, the man and his wife remained bare of all their vessels that clothed the NRN of Atzilut that he had, since they fell to the shells and have become good and bad. It is so because all the vessels of Adam HaRishon were only from the HASHMAL of ZA.

133) The thing is that at that time, their garment is from the phase of holy Elokim, Katnut of Yenika, called a "serpent that bites her pudendum," as in the tearing of the Red Sea. This is regarded as holy Elokim of Katnut, as mentioned elsewhere. For this reason, this garment of Katnut in its entirety is called "the serpent's skin." This is the meaning of what our sages said, "leather gowns, the serpent's skin," and

---

* *Tree of Life*, Part 2, Gate 41, Chapter 1.

then the outer, impure serpent suckles from there and becomes skin, good and bad. This is the meaning of HASHMAL. When he seduced Eve, it was by the force of the coupling of Yesod of Yenika with the light of Elokim, from which they grip and suckle. You should understand the meaning of the filth of the serpent.

Simple Light

133) **At that time, their garment is from the phase of holy Elokim, Katnut of Yenika called a "serpent that bites her pudendum," etc.** The matter of the sin of the tree of knowledge is from Yesod of Katnut, and Katnut is always called by the names Elokim. This is why it is called "The coupling of Yesod of Yenika with the light of Elokim." Yesod is called a "serpent that bites her pudendum," since it removes the HASHMAL of Ima, and then the impure serpent that consists of the ten shells clings and suckles from the skin and HASHMAL of ZA and make it good and bad.

134) The resulting rule is that as long as ZA returns to being in Yenika, it dresses in leather gowns, HASHMAL, and this is at night. At that time, the outer ones suckle at night as two birds. In the morning, the Mochin return and we bless in the morning "He dresses the naked," as mentioned elsewhere. However, although the HASHMAL departs, the phase of Tzipornayim [nails] remain to protect, for if they were to suckle from there, their suckling would be very big.

Simple Light

134) **In Yenika, it dresses in leather gowns, HASHMAL, and this is at night.** This means that the HASHMAL of Ima departs and the HASHMAL of ZA becomes leather gowns, meaning the good and bad of Noga. For this reason, there is Yenika to HB of the shell called "two birds."

Chapter 10

135*) By this we will understand the matter of Adam HaRishon, who had two women: One is called Lilit, and the other is Eve. The thing is that Adam HaRishon is a similitude of ZA, and ZA has two females, Leah and Rachel. We have already explained that Leah is very harsh judgments because she is the posterior of Ima, especially since she is above, in the concealed place. But Rachel is sweetened because she is in the revealed place of Hassadim.

Simple Light

135) **Leah is very harsh judgments because she is the posterior of Ima.** She is discerned as the posterior of the upper AVI of Nekudim that were revoked and fell to the place of ZON during the breaking of the vessels. Since these GAR of AVI were concealed in RADLA, there is no correction to their posterior to return and rise to AVI as they were during the Nekudim, prior to the end of correction, meaning after Malchut of the first restriction that was concealed in RADLA is revealed, since then the level of the look of Einayim of Nekudim will be revealed in Atzilut once more, and the posterior that fell to the place of ZON will reconnect to AVI as previously, during the Gadlut of Nekudim. These posteriors are called Leah, which is why her correction is only in ZA, in the place of the falling, for she was established here to be the Nukva of ZA since her entire correction is only from him, as long as she cannot return to her place in upper AVI.

It was said, "Leah is very harsh judgments because she is the posterior of Ima." It is so because there is no correction to her judgments in all six thousand years since she is corrected only in a coupling of the upper Mochin of Haya as the Daat that draws GAR of Haya, which is the phase of GAR of Nekudim. Hence, she is regarded as very harsh judgments.

Especially since she is above, in the concealed place. But Rachel is sweetened because she is in the revealed place of Hassadim. This second reason depends on the first reason, since the Mochin of Haya drawn by the coupling of Yesod of Gadlut of NHY of Haya cannot be revealed from the Chazeh and above of ZA but only from the Chazeh of ZA and below in a manner that even when ZA has Mochin of Haya, he remains in covered Hassadim from his Chazeh and above, and the illumination of Hochma in Hassadim, called "revealing of Hassadim," is only from the Chazeh and below. This is why it is written that since Leah was established as a Nukva only from the Chazeh of ZA and above, where the illumination of Haya is not revealed, her judgments from the time of the revoking of the GAR of AVI are still in her without correction, while Partzuf Rachel, which is his Nukva of NHY from the Chazeh and below, has from the place of the revelation of the Mochin of Haya, and the illumination of Haya completely cancels the grip of the outer ones.

---

* *Tree of Life*, Part 2, Gate 38, Chapter 2.

For this reason, she is completely sweetened. Conversely, Leah is sweetened only in the Mochin of Neshama that illuminate from the Chazeh and above, since there is no revelation of illumination of Haya in her. For this reason, she is regarded as completely unsweetened.

136) ZA is called Adam because he is MA, which is HaVaYaH filled with Alephs, which is forty-five in Gematria [Mem-Hey, the letters of MA], and Aleph-Dalet-Mem [the letters of Adam]. It is known that the simple HaVaYaH is the primary one since the filling is regarded as a female since she is all judgments. A filling with Gematria Elokim is also regarded as a filling because all the power of the Nukva and the self of her lights and powers are concealed inside ZA, since the Keter of Gevura is inside ZA and afterward emerges from him.

Simple Light

136) The filling is regarded as a female since she is all judgments. The four letters of the simple HaVaYaH imply the self of the Sefirot in the degree with regard to the ten Sefirot of direct light in them. The filling of the four letters implies the phase of Malchut and the screen in each Sefira on which the coupling by striking is performed, which raises reflected light and clothes the ten Sefirot of direct light. On one hand, the simple letters are more important as they are the self of the Sefirot and the core of the Partzuf. On the other hand, the filling is more important as it determines the level of the Partzuf, since the direct light shines in the Partzuf only according to the measure of the reflected light that rises. In a filling of AB, reflected light rises up to Hochma. Hence, there is light of Hochma in the Partzuf. With a filling of SAG, reflected light rises and clothes only up to Bina. Hence, that degree is only on the level of Bina and lacks the light of Hochma, and so forth likewise. This is so because there is no attainment in the light without a vessel, so although there are ten Sefirot of direct light in each degree, she still receives only according to the level of the garment, which is the reflected light. For this reason, the filling is regarded as female and judgments, since Malchut and the screen in her is discerned as female and judgments.

All the power of the Nukva and the self of her lights and powers are concealed inside ZA, etc., and afterward emerges from him. Interpretation: When ZA imparts to Nukva, a coupling by striking is done in ZA himself, in the phase of his crown of Gevura, which is the Nukva in his own Guf, and a level emerges according to the measure of reflected light that the Nukva in his Guf raises in him. Afterward, he imparts this level as it is clothed in the reflected light to his separated Nukva, Rachel. It follows that all the Mochin of the Nukva are regarded as mere filling, since the coupling is done inside ZA and she takes the level that is already made. This is the second reason why the filling is Nukva. This pertains especially to what is written below, that the females Leah and Rachel are implied in the letters of the filling of HaVaYaH of MA of ZA. However, the first reason is over all the degrees, they are all males and females.

137) The Nukva is a filling of ZA since a filling is the Ibur [impregnation] that fills the insides of its mother's abdomen. Hence, the filling is the phase of Nukva. The filling of the name MA has the Gematria of nineteen as once you remove the simple letters, which are twenty-six in Gematria, a filling of nineteen in Gematria remains, the Gematria of Het-Vav-Hey [the letters of Eve].

Simple Light

137) A filling is the Ibur that fills the insides of its mother's abdomen. This implies that every lower one is discerned as the filling of the Partzuf above it since it emerges from the Ibur of the upper one. This is a long matter, and we must remember everything that he explained about the departure and second expansion concerning the Partzufim of AK. Here we will explain very briefly, and it will help only those proficient in the above-mentioned parts. The cascading of the Partzufim from one another comes by a clash of inner light with surrounding light, causing the refinement of the screen of Guf into a screen of Rosh. By this, all the lights of the Guf depart. However, a coupling is done in the screen at the Rosh of the Partzuf by which a new expansion of the level of ten Sefirot emerges. This expansion is regarded as a son of the Partzuf and its lower one, and the Guf of the upper one is filled once more by this expansion of its lower one. For this reason, the lower one clothes the upper one with the full measure that it fills the empty vessels of the upper one, meaning only the phase of Guf. Hence, the matter of the refinement of the screen of the Guf into Malchut of the Rosh is regarded as Ibur, since through this ascent of the screen of Guf to Malchut of Rosh, the whole of lower one is born.

We will explain about the cascading of the five Partzufim of AK. First, the inner HaVaYaH of AK emerged, which is its Partzuf Keter. These are the first ten Sefirot that came with the line of Ein Sof after the first restriction. His screen of Guf was refined into a root of the screen, which is the Malchut of Rosh, and all his lights of Guf departed. Afterward, a coupling was done on the screen that rose and was incorporated in Malchut of the Rosh, and a new expansion of ten Sefirot emerged in the coarseness of phase three called "the filling of AB," where the reflected light ascends and clothes up to Hochma, and the Guf of the inner Partzuf was also filled with this expansion of AB. Afterward, a refinement of the screen took place and the lights of the Guf of AB departed, as well, and it ascended and was incorporated in its Malchut of Rosh, and a new coupling was done in the coarseness of phase two. Then a new expansion emerged called Partzuf SAG of AK, which also fills the Guf of its upper one, which is AB. Likewise, a new expansion emerged at the Rosh of Partzuf SAG in the coarseness of phase one, which elicits the level of MA, and fills the Guf of SAG, as well. These are the ten Sefirot of Nekudim called BON. You find how each Partzuf is from the screen of the Guf of the upper one that ascended and was incorporated in the Peh of the Rosh of the upper one, where the ten Sefirot of its level emerge. For this reason, this ascent is called "The Ibur of the lower one," which fills the inside of the upper one.

As it was in the cascading of the Partzufim of AK, so it was in Atzilut in the first three Partzufim called Atik and Nukva, Arich and Nukva, and AVI. The Ibur of each lower one is done at the Peh of the Rosh of the upper one, which fills the upper one from the Peh of the Rosh downward. However, after the Partzuf of upper AVI emerged, which fill AA from his Peh of the Rosh through the Chazeh, there is no more departure in the Gufim [pl. of Guf] of AVI because they are already corrected by this in a never-ending coupling. However, from the Chazeh of AVI and below, which stand from the Chazeh of AA downward, there is still departure. Therefore, regarding the ascent of the screen for an Ibur for ZON, it does not rise to the Peh of the Rosh of AVI, but rather from their Tabur down, called the Peh of the Rosh in relation to YESHSUT. However, in relation to AVI, it is regarded as being from the Tabur down and is called "abdomen." For this reason, the Ibur of ZA is in the abdomen of AVI and Yisrael Saba and Tevuna, which then become one Partzuf. This is the meaning of "A filling is the Ibur that fills the insides of its mother's abdomen," for as ZA emerges only from the Tabur of AVI and below, it therefore fills only their abdomen.

138) By this you will understand how Eve is Adam's wife and truly a flesh of his flesh. We have already explained that ZA has two phases in it: One is from the Rosh to the Chazeh, where he has the first Yesod and in which he makes a coupling with Leah, and his latter half is from the Chazeh down, which is the place of revealed Hassadim. It follows that he has two names of MA of Alephs, as mentioned in the verse, "Lord, let me know my end." From the two of them, two fillings emerge, in each of which there is Gematria of Hava [Eve]. However, the first, upper Eve is regarded as Leah, and the bottom Eve is Rachel.

Simple Light

138) **The Chazeh, where he has the first Yesod and in which he makes a coupling with Leah.** Initially, there were only six vessels, HBD HGT, in him through the Chazeh, in which Nefesh-Ruach clothe—Ruach in HBD, for which it became HGT, and Nefesh in HGT, for which it became NHY. Thus, the Sefira Yesod is in the place of the Chazeh. It was said, "The first phase is from the Rosh to the Chazeh, where he has the first Yesod," since in his phase of Katnut he has only six vessels from the Rosh to the Chazeh, which are HBD HGT, which with regard to the lights in them they became HGT NHY, and you find that Yesod of Katnut is in the place of the Chazeh.

From the Chazeh down, which is the place of revealed Hassadim. This is regarded as phase two of ZA, which is his state of Gadlut. At the time of Gadlut, when he obtains the GAR, HGT return to being HBD since the lights are GAR like the vessels, NHY return to being HGT, and the lights of GAR sort for him new NHY from BYA. You find that now he obtained a new Yesod of Gadlut.

However, there is no absence in the spiritual and the first Yesod of Katnut, which was at the place of the Chazeh, remains there now, as well, during the Gadlut. For this reason, there are two Yesodot [pl. of Yesod] in him.

We already said that revealed Hassadim means that the illumination of Hochma is revealed in Hassadim in the manner that Bina that returns to the Rosh of AA and couples there with Hochma in order to impart illumination of Hochma to ZON, as Bina of direct light emanates to ZA of direct light. However, for herself, Bina is always in a state of desiring mercy and does not receive Hochma. This is the meaning of the upper AVI at the level of Bina being in a never-ending coupling. It follows that even after Bina returned to Hochma, the Hochma is not revealed in her own place but in the place of ZON. This applies both in ZON of the ten Sefirot of Rosh called Daat, and in ZON of the ten Sefirot of Guf called NHY. For this reason, the illumination of Hochma is not revealed from the Chazeh and above, where there is the phase of KHB of Guf, but only from the Chazeh and below, where there is the phase of ZON of Guf.

We could say that this is acceptable in Hochma in the phase of Bina of GAR, but in Hochma of GAR itself, in which this distinction does not exist, why then does she not illuminate in the GAR of the Rosh and GAR of the Guf? Indeed, we should know what the ARI wrote for us here, that after Hochma-Stimaa [concealed Hochma] of AA was concealed, Hochma does not shine in Atzilut, except for the Hochma of the thirty-two paths, which is received from Bina that returns to the Rosh of AA where she receives Hochma for ZA. Thus, all the Hochma that there is after AA is only Hochma of the phase of Bina.

This is why this phase of Hochma is called "thirty-two paths of Hochma [wisdom]," as it implies twenty-two letters, which is Bina, with the ten Sefirot of ZON impregnated inside her, which are thirty-two in Gematria as the ARI wrote there. This means that Bina does not draw Hochma except through ZON that ascend to her in Ibur as MAN. Hence, Bina and ZON are implied in her together.

Since she herself is always in the state of Hassadim, therefore even when she receives Hochma, it is not revealed in her HB, but only in ZON, both in the Rosh and in the Guf, and remember these words always. He says here "His latter half is from the Chazeh down, which is the place of revealed Hassadim," since there, it is the phase of ZON of Guf. Thus, illumination of Hochma is revealed in Hassadim. However, from the Chazeh and above, where it is the phase of GAR of Guf, the Hassadim are always covered from Hochma. Therefore, he divides them into two phases and two names of MA of Alephs, since they are regarded as two separate levels, where the filling of Alephs from the Chazeh and above is Leah, and the filling of Alephs from the Chazeh and below is Rachel.

139) Since the phase of Leah is regarded as very harsh judgments for the above-mentioned reason, although there, in the upper world of Atzilut, it is complete Kedusha [holiness], yet, in this bottom world, which is material, the phase of Leah could not emerge sweetened in Kedusha at the time of the creation of Adam

HaRishon, and she emerged as very harsh judgments, as the shell of the evil serpent. This is discerned as Lilit, the first Eve, who made a coupling with Adam before the second Eve was created.

Simple Light

139) In this bottom world, which is material, the phase of Leah could not emerge sweetened, etc. This is discerned as Lilit, the first Eve, since even in Atzilut, her correction is only in a filling of Alephs from the Chazeh of ZA and above, which is covered Hassadim.

It follows that Leah, too, was corrected only from the Chazeh and above in her, which are KHB, but from the Chazeh and below in her, which are the ZON in her, which need the revelation of illumination of Haya, they still remained in her in the phase of skin. Hence, in the bottom world, in the phase of Leah of Adam HaRishon, where all the self of his vessels is only from the phase of HASHMAL of ZA, it is discerned as flesh and skin of ZA. Thus, his phase of Leah is also discerned as flesh and skin of the upper Leah, which is the phase of her Akevim [heels], whose correction begins only in the Mochin of GAR of Haya, which are AVI of Nekudim that were concealed in Atzilut. For this reason, she is regarded as an actual shell, called Lilit. The rule is that any discernment from the breaking of the vessels that is not sorted during the six thousand years is called a shell, and it is also called "the first Eve."

140) Afterward, a second Eve emerged sweetened, and remained as Adam's wife, while the other one departed since she was still completely mixed with the shells, which is why the first Eve was called Lilit. But afterward, when Jacob came, whose beauty is like the beauty of Adam, and corrected Adam HaRishon's flaw of incest, as mentioned in *The Zohar, Kedoshim,* and in the portion *Toldot,* concerning the blessings he took by deceit from his brother Esau. He took both because then Leah was sweetened and was in Kedusha and departed from the shell.

Simple Light

140) Leah was sweetened and was in Kedusha and departed from the shell. This does not mean that this Leah of Adam HaRishon is Leah Jacob's wife since he already said that she became a shell. Rather, she is an illumination of Leah from the upper Leah of ZA and was so sweetened that she received a correction of completely departing from the phase of flesh and skin, which becomes a shell. The precision he makes, "and departed from the shell," means from her own shell. Thus, Leah, Jacob's wife, can receive illumination of GAR from covered Hassadim, too, like Leah, the wife of ZA. This is what it means that she was in Kedusha.

141) This is why our sages said that Leah's eyes were soft, from tears she cried for being destined to be in the part of Esau. But through her prayers and her tears she was sweetened and given to the part of Jacob. Understand this well.

142) Concerning Adam HaRishon, it is written in this verse, "The man said, 'This is now a bone of my bones and flesh of my flesh.'" It is said in the *Tikkunim*, p. 99, that they are two women, one of the bones and one of the flesh. The thing is that Leah is called a "bone," which is judgments that are as hard as a bone. Also, she is regarded as the rib since the place of Leah is behind the ribs, which are bones. But Rachel is a flesh of his flesh, a soft judgment in the place of the revealing of Hassadim.

Simple Light

142) Two women, one of the bones and one of the flesh, etc. It has already been explained that KHB ZON are called marrow-bones-tendons-flesh-skin. It follows that bones are Hochma and flesh is ZA. It has also been explained that all the phases of the soul of Adam HaRishon are from Mochin of Haya of ZON, and even his vessels came from the HASHMAL of ZA, which are the fourth vessels that are sorted through Mochin of Haya. It has also been clarified that Leah is the posterior of the inner AVI, which are GAR of Haya. Since the inner AVI were concealed in Atzilut, she cannot return to her degree, to AVI, before the end of correction, when GAR of Haya are revealed. All their correction prior to this is through ZA from the Chazeh and above. Hence, Leah, too, is sweetened only from her Chazeh and above, while her Raglayim, which are flesh and skin, have no correction whatsoever. For this reason, Adam HaRishon, whose entire phase is only from the phase of HASHMAL of ZA, which is flesh and skin, his two females are also only the phase of flesh and skin of the two females Leah and Rachel of ZA. This is why his Leah emerged as a shell, called Lilit, since she is the flesh and skin of the upper Leah, who is not corrected during the six thousand years.

For this reason, the two females of Adam HaRishon are called "bone" and "flesh," since bones means Haya of Haya, and it is Leah, since she is the posterior of the inner AVI, who is corrected only in the GAR of Haya, called Haya of Haya. Flesh is Rachel, which means Ruach of Haya. She receives her complete correction in ZA since Mochin of VAK of Haya, called "flesh," are extended to ZA in full. Hence, the Nukva of the flesh is the second Eve of Adam HaRishon, who was completely sweetened, but the Nukva of the bones, which is the first Eve of Adam HaRishon and is regarded as the Raglayim of Leah, the wife of ZA, which cannot be sweetened prior to the end of correction, becomes a shell. We must not be confused in that flesh and skin are sometimes named after their vessels, and sometimes after their lights, since the ARI is not so meticulous about the definition of the words because matters become clarified according to the context. But the reader himself should always remember the inverse relation between vessels and lights, and then he will be able to understand them according to the context.

143) The rest of the chronicles of Adam HaRishon are as follows: He had two women, one was a bone of his bones, and one, flesh of his flesh. But the second one, called "flesh," he will call a "woman," and not the first one, who is a bone and is still not sweetened. Afterward, in the time of Jacob, she is sweetened as Leah.

144) However, there are two reasons why he says that Jacob loved Rachel and not Leah: The first is that the lower Jacob in that world did not yet attain the full existence of Partzuf ZA, but only from opposite the Chazeh and below, the place of Rachel. This is why at that time, Jacob loved Rachel, and it does not say, "Israel loved," which is ZA, who had both Leah and Rachel.

Simple Light

144) **The lower Jacob in that world did not yet attain the full existence of Partzuf ZA, but only from opposite the Chazeh and below.** ZA is divided into two phases, and his Partzuf GAR from the Chazeh and above is called "Israel." His Partzuf VAK from the Chazeh and below is called Jacob. Hence, as long as he attained only the VAK of ZA, he is called Jacob. Once he attained the GAR, the Creator named him Israel.

145) However, Jacob loved the lower Rachel, like himself, who is the revealed world. Leah, on the other hand, is the covered world, as we explain that it is the form of the [letter] Dalet in the knot of the head Tefillin. This is why Jacob did not want to make a coupling with her, since he did not attain that far.

Simple Light

145) **Leah is the covered world etc., in the form of the Dalet in the knot of the head Tefillin.** Since Leah is Partzuf Nukva of GAR of ZA, and her sweetening is only through the GAR of Haya, the Mochin of Haya she receives from ZA are merely as posterior to her, since they are discerned as VAK of Haya that do not sort the vessels that need the lights of GAR of Haya. Hence, those vessels which the Mochin of VAK of Haya sort in Leah and clothe in them are called skin and posterior because any phase that is not sufficiently sorted is called skin, (see item 59). This is why Leah is called "the covered world," since the illumination of Mochin of Haya is covered in her because it is clothed in skin, which "is the form of the Dalet," the knot of the Tefillin.

Likewise, her illumination is called "covered Hassadim" since the illumination of Hochma is covered in her. For this reason, Jacob did not want to make a coupling with her, since Jacob is discerned as VAK of ZA, the place of revealed Hassadim, and covered Hassadim can receive only VAK without a Rosh.

146) This is the meaning of what is written in *The Zohar*, portion *VaYetze*, 123b, "Leah and Rachel are two worlds, from the world and to the world, seven years of the covered world," etc. It is so because Leah emerged from the posterior of Malchut of Ima in Daat of ZA, as the Dalet in the knot of the head Tefillin. Since Leah is from the phase of Ima, her seven years are covered.

147) The seven are KHBD HG and a third of Tifferet through the Chazeh of ZA, since these seven phases were covered, undisclosed to Jacob before he was called Israel, for then he attained the entire Partzuf ZA, which is called Israel. This is why it is written in *The Zohar VaYetze*, page 154, about the verse, "And the Lord saw that Leah was hated": "This means that a person hates his mother's nakedness," since Leah is extended from Malchut of Ima, who is Jacob's mother.

148) Know that half of Ima is called MI, and when they expand here in the phase of Leah, which are the letters ELEH, she becomes Elokim, since the upper phases of Ima are called MI, but from half her Tifferet and below, which clothe ZA, it is called ELEH, and the connection of everything together is called Elokim.

149) The phase of Leah is made of these above-mentioned ELEH. This is the meaning of what is written in *Saba of Mishpatim* about the verse, "Who are these who fly like a cloud," and you will understand his words by what we have explained here. Know that this Leah always has a complete Partzuf like ZA, and her level is from Keter of ZA to his Chazeh (and see below where it is explained that her beginning is from Daat of ZA. This requires scrutiny and perhaps it will be understood by what we said above).

150) It has already been explained above that Yesod Ima expands up to the Chazeh of ZA where there is the phase of Daddim [udders] of ZA that were made there as the axes and doors that there are in Yesod Ima that is there. This is the meaning of the Daddim of ZA.

151) Yesod of Leah is also there outside, opposite the Daddim of ZA. You should also know that the upper half of Tifferet of ZA was initially discerned as Yesod, as we explained concerning the Gadlut of ZA, which was from VAK. His HGT ascended and became HBD, NHY became HGT, and thus Yesod has become Tifferet.

152) Now it follows that there are three phases of Yesod there in one place. These are Yesod of Ima, Yesod of Leah when she returns to being face-to-face with ZA himself in order to make a coupling with him, and Yesod of ZA himself, which is now called Tifferet. It follows that Yesod of Ima and Yesod of Leah join together and both become one womb, to make a coupling in it with Yesod of ZA himself, which is called Tifferet. This is the meaning of "A person hates his mother's nakedness, nakedness in its literal meaning."

153) (Know that another time, I heard from my teacher that when the phase of Leah makes a coupling with ZA himself, he makes a coupling with her through the actual Daat itself. This is the meaning of "Adam knew Eve, his wife," since this coupling is done by Daat [knowledge], and it is a coupling in concealment. This is why it was initially concealed from Jacob and it was not known that it was Leah until morning. We must reconcile how these ideas coincide. Perhaps this upper Yesod, which is the Rosh of Tifferet, the phase of Daat of ZA is also there sometimes, when he descends there. This requires scrutiny.)

Simple Light

153) When the phase of Leah she makes a coupling with ZA himself, he makes a coupling with her through the actual Daat itself. Just as Partzuf ZA is divided into Partzuf GAR from the Chazeh and above, and Partzuf VAK from the Chazeh and below, so the coupling in Mochin is divided into a coupling of GAR of Mochin and a coupling of VAK of Mochin. It therefore follows that the coupling of the Nukva of GAR, who is Leah, is from the coupling of GAR of Mochin, and she receives from the actual Daat of the Rosh, since the Yesod of GAR is called Daat, but Rachel, who is the phase of VAK, her coupling is not from the GAR of Mochin but from the VAK of Mochin. Also, it is not from the actual Daat of the Rosh, but from Daat that spreads to the Guf, which is the phase of VAK of Daat of the Rosh and not actual Daat.

The thing is that there are three Mochin in the Moach of Daat, which are HBD of Daat. HB of Daat are GAR of Daat, and Daat of Daat is VAK of Daat. They determine with regard to the upper Mochin called HB of the general Rosh, and when the coupling is in the GAR of these HB, it is done by HB of Daat, and that drop of coupling is called "the drop of coupling of the actual GAR of that level." This is discerned as the coupling of ZA with Leah, and this is why they are called "the big ZON." But the coupling with Rachel is through the third Moach of Daat, called Daat of Daat. It makes a coupling only of VAK of HB of the Rosh. Hence, that drop of the coupling is a drop of VAK of that level. Remember this, as this is the key to understand the discernment of the coupling of ZA with Leah in all the places in the ARI's words.

With it you will also understand why Leah is called "the covered world," for because her coupling with ZA is from HB of Daat, which makes a coupling of GAR of HB of the Rosh, it follows that if the coupling were on the level of Hochma, they would draw GAR of Hochma, which are the inner AVI that were concealed in RADLA and are still not revealed in Atzilut. Thus, it is impossible for ZA to make a coupling with Leah on the level of Haya, and all the couplings of ZA with Leah are only in the phase of covered Hassadim, where the illumination of Haya is covered and concealed. This is why she is called "the covered world."

154) Know that even Moses, of whom it was said in *The Zohar* that he attained up to Bina, is from this Leah, who is extended from Malchut of Bina and becomes the Dalet of the knot of the Tefillin, and this is the meaning of "You will see My back," as our sages said in the Gemara, teaching that He showed him the knot of Tefillin.

155) It also means that Leah, who stands in the knot of the Tefillin, sees the back of ZA because she stands with her face opposite the back of ZA. Since Moses is in Leah, this is "And you will see My back," and the matters are clear.

Simple Light

155) Her face opposite the back of ZA. She can receive only the posterior from the phase of Mochin of Haya, which is discerned as the vessel of skin, called "the knot of Tefillin." For this reason, this is called "her face opposite the back of ZA," for her face are Mochin of Haya, since she is the posterior of AVI of Nekudim and receives only the posterior of these Mochin. However, in the phase of Neshama, and even Neshama of Haya, she can stand with ZA face-to-face.

156) Yet, the second reason it was said that Jacob loved Rachel is clear through what is written in the verse, "Skin for skin, and all that a man has will he give for his soul." Interpretation: That man is ZA, and he has two women, Leah and Rachel. Leah is discerned as the skin, but Rachel is his actual soul. This is why ZA would give his skin for the skin of Leah out of his love for her. However, Rachel has an advantage over Leah, since all that the above-mentioned man has will he give for his soul, which is Rachel, and he will not settle for giving his skin for her.

157) This explains the reason why Leah is called skin and Rachel Nefesh [soul]. The thing is that Rachel is the real Nukva of ZA; she is his actual spouse, since he is from the ten general points of the world of Atzilut, and she is the last Malchut in them. But the essence of Leah is the posterior of Ima, which fell down here in this place. She is the wife of ZA only as a lending for since she fell down here, she is attached to the skin of ZA. But Rachel is his soul [Nefesh] since Malchut is Nefesh and ZA is Ruach.

Simple Light

157) Rachel is the real Nukva of ZA, etc. There are three main points to know about this Rachel: 1) her root with regard to the vessels, 2) her root with regard to the lights, 3) her source with regard to the construction of the Partzuf. All three main points are from the world of Nekudim, since it is known that in Katnut of Nekudim only seven vessels HBD HGT through the Chazeh emerged, and the point of Chazeh ends them at the Parsa that was established by the second restriction, and the vessels from the Chazeh down departed and became BYA. It follows that the root of the Nukva in this regard is only the point of Chazeh. With regard to the lights that clothed them, they became HGT NHY, since the lights of VAK are called HGT NHYM.

You therefore find that the point of Chazeh is called "the point of Malchut of the ZAT of Nekudim." However, of these two phases there is only one point in her, which is the phase that ends ZA, but there is no construction of a Partzuf in her.

This began in the Gadlut of Nekudim, for through the new light that emerged from AB SAG of AK, the Parsa was fissured and the ZAT of Nekudim expanded through the point of this world like the Raglayim of AK, while those NHYM that were separated from ZAT of Nekudim to below the Parsa, which became BYA, reconnected with ZAT of ZA. Also, they are regarded as the part of the point of Chazeh of ZA, which is Malchut, and they connected to her. At that time, she is temporarily built in a complete Partzuf called "the seventh king of Nekudim," since during the Katnut they already belonged to her part, since all of BYA, which are restricted through the Parsa, are in the domain of the Nukva and below her. Hence, even when they connected, they became a part of her and of her structure. Thus, the whole root of the construction of the Nukva is from the posterior vessels of Nekudim, which are the NHY below the Parsa.

For this reason, the point of Chazeh is considered the Keter of Nukva since after she is built by the NHY that ascended from BYA, the point of Chazeh becomes the Keter above them. Sometimes, the point of Chazeh is called only her Malchut since with regard to the clothing of the lights, you find that during the Katnut of Nekudim, there was only the force of Sium of Malchut in her. These three main points are called 1) the point of Keter of Nukva, 2) the point of Malchut of Nukva, 3) the bottom nine Sefirot of Nukva. Remember this in all the places that discuss them.

The essence of Leah is the posterior of Ima, which fell down here in this place, meaning during the breaking of the vessels of Nekudim. We should know that this Ima does not mean the level of Neshama but rather Ima at the level of Haya, since AVI of Nekudim were on an even level at the level of Haya. You find that Leah is the posterior that fell from the level of Haya of Ima. Hence, she is not at all from the degree of ZA. Rather, her place of descent is in the place of ZA. Therefore, he corrects her and she is regarded as his Nukva only in a manner of lending, meaning that finally, at the end of correction, she will depart from him and return to the upper Ima, to her degree. Since the phase of Haya of Nekudim was concealed in the six thousand years, the correction of Leah is incomplete, for which she is regarded as judgments.

158) Another reason is that the place of Leah is above, in the place of the concealed lights, since Yesod Ima reaches up to the Chazeh. For this reason, her illumination is only the phase of skin, as we say about the form of Dalet of the knot of the head Tefillin, which is Leah. The knot is only the phase of skin, but Rachel, which is a hand Tefillin, has skin in it, the boxes of the hand Tefillin, as well as actual Mochin as portions.

159) In short, Leah corresponds to the place of the covering of the lights. A small illumination passes through the skin of ZA out to her from his Mochin, and not from the Mochin themselves but only from their garments and vessels, which are NHY of Ima. This is why she is implied in the Dalet of the knot of the head Tefillin, for she is Dalah [poor] and meager. The form of Dalet that she takes, corresponding to the four Mochin, is only an illumination through the skin, and skin means as in the verse, "After my skin they struck this," and see there how the inner illuminations strike one another, and the number of their strikes is as the number of skins, which is why it is called skin.

160) We shall explain further and say that NHY of Abba stand and clothe inside NHY of Ima at the Rosh of ZA. AVI and ZA are the first two letters of HaVaYaH, which are Yod-Hey, and they strike each other—the inner Abba on Ima, who is outside, in order to elicit her lights outside. At that time, it becomes ten times

Hey [Hey-Aleph], which is 120 in Gematria. Subsequently, the illumination of Hey, which is Ima, strikes the Vav [Vav-Aleph-Vav], which is ZA, to come outside, and they are 78 in Gematria. Then the illumination of Vav strikes the Hey, which is ZA, on the outer Leah, which is 78 in Gematria. The sum of the strikes is 276. This is how the sum of the lights of Leah is 276 and they emerge through the skin [Or, 276 in Gematria] of ZA.

161) This is the meaning of "skin for skin," since the skin, called Leah, her illuminations pass through the skin of ZA. But Rachel, who corresponds to the revealed lights, is simple, for the lights that come to her part, which is the Keter of Daat in Gevura, as well as the rest of the Mochin, are given to her only as actual Mochin. It follows that all that there is in ZA has, there is in Rachel, too.

Simple Light

161) **It follows that all that there is in ZA has, there is in Rachel, too.** This concerns only the level of Mochin, for Rachel takes the full level of the Mochin. However, Leah has only the skin from them. Yet, in the essence of the Mochin, there are many divisions between ZA and Rachel. The main one is that in ZA, there is the root of the Keter of Gevura from the phase of NHY of Ima that is included in Mazal and Nakeh. But the Nukva has only the phase of the Keter of Gevura from Malchut of Ima, which is not included in Mazal and Nakeh, and is not included in the Mochin of ZA. This is why her Daat [mind] is light.

162) This is the meaning of what is written, "All that a man has will he give for his Nefesh [soul]." You already know that Rachel is called Nefesh [soul] and ZA is called Ruach [spirit]. We can also say that the two times skin mentioned here are Rachel and Leah, since the illuminations of Rachel also emerge and pass through the skin of ZA outward. The intention of the verse is to say that although both are regarded as skin and are equal in that sense, since the illumination of both of them emerges through the skin of ZA, nevertheless, there is an advantage to Rachel over Leah, since "all that a man," ZA, "has," meaning the actual Mochin, "will he give for his soul," which is the above-mentioned Rachel.

163) Let us return to the matter that it is written that Jacob loved Rachel, since ZA loved Rachel more than Leah because to this one, he gave actual Mochin, and to that one, a mere illumination. Even though in truth, if the verse speaks of ZA, we should have said, "And Israel loved Rachel," since ZA is Israel and is not Jacob. Still, it is for the reason that was explained concerning what our sages said, that Jacob is the senior among the patriarchs.

164) The reason is that initially, Jacob was the Jacob that is made of the posterior of Abba, and the posterior of Abba is very high. Moreover, afterward, through his actions, he ascended more and a Neshama was extended to him from the actual ZA, called Israel. Sometimes he uses the name Jacob and sometimes Israel. This is why

anyone who calls him Jacob does not transgress on the "to do" [commandment] because of the above reason.

165) However, Abraham and Isaac are discerned as HG in ZA, they are particular phases in ZA and are not a complete Partzuf on its own. This is why Jacob is the senior patriarch. Also, one who calls Abraham Abram transgresses on the "to do" [commandment], since the letter Hey that was added to the name Abraham is the five Hassadim that never change and are never absent.

166) However, the Partzuf of Israel, or Jacob, changes according to the times. You find that even when it is written "And Jacob loved Rachel," it is possible that it speaks of ZA himself, since when he is in the state of VAK he is like Jacob, and in his Gadlut, he is called Israel.

167) This is the meaning of the words, "Your name shall no longer be Jacob, but Israel, for you have wrestled with God." Interpretation: In Katnut, ZA has Mochin of Katnut discerned as the name Elokim, since during the Katnut he has only two Mochin, for one who is small has no Daat in him, which is the third Moach, only HB. They are two names of Elokim, which are Gematria Jacob. During his Gadlut, he is called Israel since Mochin of Gadlut enter and push down the Mochin of Katnut. This is the meaning of "for you have wrestled with God," since he wrestles with them and can push them down.

168*) Now we will explain the meaning of the connection between Leah and Rachel together, and in it we will explain several verses and several sayings of our sages. Our sages interpret the verse, "Because of humbleness is the fear of God," that as she made fear a crown on her head so she made humbleness a heel on her sole.

169) Explanation of these words: The root of these wives of ZA, Leah and Rachel, is called humbleness and fear of God. Rachel is called "Fear of God is the beginning of wisdom," since she is the beginning of all the Sefirot from below upward, and she is the door to all of them. She is called "A virtuous woman fears the Lord," which are "I placed Your Chaf-Dalet Chaf-Dalet suns," which are Gematria Hayil [power/heroism/valor]. But Leah is called "humbleness" since she is above, in the posterior of the Rosh of ZA.

170) It is known that the humbleness is apparent in man when he lowers his head and bows it down before a person's face due to his humbleness, and he yields before one who is greater than him. This is the meaning of "And the man Moses was very humble," for we learn elsewhere that Moses took Zipporah and she is one of the four phases that Leah has, which are all called Leah after her. Zipporah is one of them for she, too, stands above, opposite Daat ZA.

171) Thus, it has been explained how Moses took the upper quality of humbleness, but Rachel, who is the small bottom Hey called "the fear of God," is small in relation to Moses, as in "The name of the elder was Leah and the name

---

* *Tree of Life*, Part 2, Gate 38, Chapter 3.

of the younger was Rachel." This is the meaning of what our sages said, "And now Israel, what does the Lord your God ask of you but fear," is fear is a small matter? And they replied, "Yes, for Moses, it is a small matter."

172) It has been explained above that Leah emerges from the illumination of Malchut of Ima that dresses in ZA as Mochin. Indeed, her NHY become garments of the three Mochin of HBD of ZA, although Malchut of Ima does not operate in ZA at all. This is the meaning of what our sages said about the seven firmaments, that the lower one among them is called "a curtain" and does not operate at all but rather exits in the evening and enters in the morning.

Simple Light

172) Leah emerges from the illumination of Malchut of Ima that dresses in ZA as Mochin. He says below that Malchut of Ima does not operate in the Mochin of ZA whatsoever but only NHY of Ima, and here he says that she dresses as Mochin. Indeed, this matter is explained thoroughly, that although she does not operate at all for the purpose of the Mochin of ZA himself, for the Mochin of Rachel, she dresses in the Mochin of ZA and is incorporated in his Mochin. By this incorporation of Malchut of Ima with the Mochin of ZA, the Mochin of Rachel exit there in the Rosh of ZA and return from there to the posterior of the Mochin of ZA on the back of the neck, where they make the knot of the Tefillin as a Dalet, which is the phase of Leah.

With regard to the Mochin of the Nukva Rachel, she is regarded as a second phase of her Mochin and from there they are extended to the internality of NHY of ZA, and this is regarded as the third phase of the Mochin of Rachel. Afterward, the Mochin come out as surrounding on NHY of ZA, which is regarded as phase four of the Mochin of Rachel, and from here they are drawn to the Rosh of Rachel herself, which is the fifth phase. Thus, Malchut of Ima dresses as the Mochin of ZA for the purpose of the Mochin of Rachel, where the second phase of those Mochin—which are the Dalet in the knot of the Tefillin—come for Mochin for Leah, too.

Her NHY become garments of the three Mochin of HBD of ZA, although Malchut of Ima does not operate in ZA at all, since the Mochin of ZA emerge from NHY of AVI that are included in Mazla, and there is no quality of Malchut in Mazla because the Mazal veNakeh is the phase of Yesod. Hence, Malchut of Ima is not included in the overall Mochin of ZA of Gadlut, and this Malchut remains in the state of the second restriction. For this reason, she does not operate at all in the Mochin of Gadlut of ZA. But for the purpose of the Mochin of Nukva, Rachel, she is included in Yesod of Ima, and then a new level emerges on this incorporation for the Mochin of Rachel. Explaining this requires extensive elaboration.

It has already been explained above that these Mochin of Leah from the Dalet of the knot of Tefillin are the second phase of Mochin of Rachel. Also, we should know that these Mochin are Mochin of Haya. Therefore, Leah receives from them only the phase of skin and not portions, since she needs Mochin of GAR of Haya from the inner AVI, and these Mochin are not revealed before the end of correction. Hence, throughout the six thousand years, she does not have Mochin of Haya from her own phase and she uses the Mochin of VAK of Haya of Rachel.

173) The thing is that the firmament that is simply called firmament, in which the sun and the moon, the stars, and the signs are set, is the phase of Yesod of Tevuna, which is called "firmament" in several places. It is the small Vav, as in "Stretching out heaven like a curtain," and the sun and moon, etc., are set in it, since all the lights emerge from there, as it is known, for the sun and the moon, which are ZON, are set in it and suckle from there, one from Hassadim and one from Gevurot, which stand in the Daat that is clothed in this Yesod of Tevuna.

174) The stars are the lights of Hassadim that emerge from there and fall into Yesod of ZA and strike there with force and disperse and become thin sparks. These are the stars that shine, and this is the meaning of "Those who lead the many to righteousness are as stars" since the root of those who lead the many to righteousness is from Yesod, which is called righteous, and they receive the illumination of the stars of Hassadim that shine like them inside the Yesod. (It seems to me that I heard from my teacher that the signs are Nekudot and are from the sparks that are made in Yesod from the falling of the Gevurot. Also, they are from above through Yesod of ZA, where they strike, fall, disperse, and become sparks.)

175) Malchut of Tevuna is called a "curtain," which does not operate at all in ZA. Rather, it shines its illumination and elicits for Leah who stands outside ZA. Hence, since Leah emerges from this quality of Malchut of Tevuna, which is discerned as the crown of the Yesod in her. It therefore follows that her place is in Daat of ZA since there is her main place. Also, it is necessary that the level of Keter down to the Chazeh begins in Leah who exits her illumination.

176) However, the Keter of Rachel begins from the Chazeh down to the actual Sium Raglayim of ZA, in a manner that at the Sium of the Raglayim and Akevim of Leah, from there begins the Keter of Rachel below the Raglayim of Leah. This is why our sages said, "As she made fear a crown on her head so she made humbleness a heel on her sole." That is, the Raglayim of Leah, who is called "humbleness," made fear, which is Rachel, a crown on her head.

177) Yet, these words still require clarification. From the words of our sages, it seems that the heel of humbleness itself becomes the crown of fear, and they did not say that the Keter [crown] of fear is under the heel of humbleness. Therefore, the matter requires a more detailed clarification.

178) According to the above, it turns out that from the Rosh of Keter of Leah to the Sium Raglayim of Rachel, they are seven Sefirot Daat, HGT, NHY, since Malchut in ZA is herself the root of Rachel, and it would be appropriate that of these two women, one would be loved, Rachel, and one would be hated, Leah. He would

not be able to remove the part of the hated one for the part of the loved one, since they will both eat equal parts and inherit the place of their husband, ZA, equally. Leah will take three Sefirot and a half, which are Daat, HG, and the upper half of Tifferet, and Rachel will take from half of Tifferet down to the Sium Raglayim of ZA, which are the other three Sefirot and the bottom half of Tifferet.

Simple Light

178) Leah will take three Sefirot and a half, etc., and Rachel will take from half of Tifferet down. Explanation: The main carrier of the revelation of the Mochin of Haya is ZA, called Tifferet. It is so because Bina herself is always in covered Hassadim and does not make a coupling with Hochma in order to draw Mochin of Haya, unless for ZA. Therefore, the phase of ZA exists also in the Mochin of AVI, where he is called Daat, since his existence there causes the coupling of Bina with Hochma as MAN to them. In other words, Bina maintains the coupling with Hochma for him. But when he descends from there, the coupling of Bina with Hochma is immediately canceled, since Bina returns to being covered Hassadim and the Mochin of Haya are canceled.

This is why Tifferet of Ima became Keter to ZA, for because the main thing that sustains the Mochin of Haya in AVI is ZA, which is Tifferet, this Tifferet of Ima is regarded as giving those Mochin to ZA in his own place. The rule is that all the benefit that the lower one causes to the upper one, the lower one, too, inherits all of that benefit since he causes him to become the phase of Keter and it bestows upon him. That is, just as Tifferet of Ima sustains the Mochin of Haya in upper Ima, so he gives these Mochin to ZA himself. Understand this well.

When ZA himself receives these Mochin, it follows that Tifferet of ZA, which is the essence of ZA, has the main carriers of the Mochin of Haya as in Ima. These are the phase of Tifferet of Mochin, called Daat, and the phase of Tifferet of the Guf. Know that the essence of Tifferet is the middle third in it, since the upper third is an incorporation of the ten Sefirot of Tifferet with the ones above it, meaning KHB of Tifferet. The bottom third of Tifferet is regarded as its incorporation with the Malchut below it, which is discerned as NHYM of Tifferet, but the middle third is its own phase, which is HGT of Tifferet. Therefore, it is considered that the main carrier of the illumination of Mochin of Haya is the middle third of Tifferet.

With this you will understand what the ARI wrote, that when ZA has only Mochin of Neshama, it clothes only the bottom third of Tifferet of Ima. Only when he obtains Mochin of Haya does he rise and clothe the middle third of Tifferet, since there is Haya only from the middle third that carries the illumination of Hochma, as it is regarded as Tifferet of Tifferet and the core of Tifferet. Conversely, the bottom third of Tifferet is the phase of Malchut that is incorporated in it, and the upper third is the phase of GAR incorporated in it.

It was said, "It would be appropriate for these two women," etc., to "inherit the place of their husband, ZA, equally. Leah would take three Sefirot and a half, which are Daat, HG, and the upper half of Tifferet, and Rachel would take from half of Tifferet down," meaning that both will take the middle third of Tifferet that imparts Mochin of Haya. That is, Leah would take a part of the Mochin of Haya of ZA like Rachel, and they would share the middle third of Tifferet equally. This is why it says, "However, this is not so. Rather, Leah takes the upper third and Rachel takes all of the two bottom thirds of Tifferet of ZA to her Keter." That is, only Rachel takes the middle third that imparts Mochin of Haya, and not Leah, since Leah takes only the upper third where there is no revelation of Mochin of Haya.

179) However, this is not so. Rather, Leah takes the upper third from the three thirds of Tifferet, and Rachel takes all of the two bottom thirds of Tifferet of ZA to her Keter, as explained elsewhere. Many reasons are explained there, one of which is that Yesod of Ima is completed in the Chazeh. For this reason, from there down, when the lights of Hassadim are revealed, Rachel is built in the posterior of ZA, and all this was explained above. By this they will be each other's enemies and there will be envy between them over this matter.

180) Therefore, what did the upper Emanator do? He made it so the upper third of Tifferet would be entirely for Leah, the bottom third entirely for Rachel, but the two sisters would use the middle third equally and would share authority over it. That is, it is impossible to divide the middle third into two parts since it is all a single, indivisible phase. However, the Keter of Rachel will rise to there and the Raglayim of Leah will descend to there, and the Raglayim of Leah clothe in the Keter of Rachel only as the measure of the middle third. Thus, both use equally. This is why our sages said "She made humbleness a heel on her sole," which are the Raglayim of Leah. From them, themselves, the Rosh and Keter of Rachel, which is called "fear," were made.

Simple Light

180) The two sisters would use the middle third equally, etc., and the Raglayim of Leah clothe in the Keter of Rachel. In other words, this was done only during the Katnut of Rachel, when the Raglayim of Leah clothe in the Keter of Rachel. At that time, Rachel, too, has no Mochin of Haya and then she is back-to-back with ZA. Because the Raglayim of Leah clothe the middle third of Tifferet of ZA and Leah is unfit to receive the Mochin of Haya, the Raglayim of Leah darken the Keter of Rachel, meaning that Rachel, too, cannot receive Mochin of Haya and she is as she was initially, from the Tabur of ZA and below, since in her own part there is only the bottom third of Tifferet where there is no revelation of Mochin of Haya.

However, when Rachel obtains the Mochin of Haya, she necessarily takes the entire middle third of ZA to her own part, and the Raglayim of Leah disappear there, as it was written before, "However, know that sometimes Rachel takes that entire place of the middle third, and the Raglayim of Leah do not expand inside the Keter of Rachel," since only when Rachel is back-to-back with ZA, the Raglayim of Leah expand in the Keter of Rachel. However, when Rachel obtains face-to-face with ZA, meaning when receiving Mochin of Haya, the Raglayim of Leah depart from the Keter of Rachel and the entire middle third of Tifferet of ZA becomes her Keter, which imparts these Mochin to her. The rule is that imparting Mochin of Haya is only from the middle third, both in ZA from upper Ima and in Nukva from ZA, and the bestowing root is called Keter.

181) However, know that sometimes Rachel takes the entire place of that middle third and the Raglayim of Leah do not expand into the Keter of Rachel as far as that third. This is what we wrote about the intention of the Shema reading in the verse veAhavta [You shall love], that we must aim to give two lights to Rachel according to the count [in Gematria] of veAhavta, which are two times Ohr [light], and Rachel is called Aleph-Tav [pronounced Et (the)], as will be written below. It is as our sages said, "the" and "also" are plural. This is the meaning of "and you shall love the," meaning that you will love Rachel, who is called "the," and he elicits by the word "love," as in "And Jacob loved Rachel," since the love is an addition, for he gave her one portion more than to Leah, and they are those two lights, as in the count of veAhavta.

182) These lights are regarded as the two bottom thirds of Tifferet. The upper third is in the concealed place, but those two thirds are in the revealed place where the Hassadim shine. This is why it is called Ohr, Ohr [light, light]. This matter was explained above concerning Rachel's Keter, which is two thirds of Tifferet of ZA, called "two times light, light," as in "I placed Your Chaf-Dalet Chaf-Dalet suns." But the Keter of Leah has only one light, as elaborated there and it will be explained below.

Simple Light

182) **In the revealed place where the Hassadim shine, this is why it is called Ohr, Ohr [light, light], etc., but the Keter of Leah has only one light.** There are two lights in the revealing of the light of Haya: light of Hochma and light of Hassadim. The meaning of the revealing of Hassadim is that illumination of Hochma is revealed in them, which is why it is called light, light. But Leah is regarded as the covered world because she is only the upper third where there is no revealing of Hochma in Hassadim; hence, there is only one light there, meaning only light of Hassadim, since there the Hassadim are covered from Hochma.

183) It follows that there is a time when Rachel takes two thirds by herself, and there is a time of a middle third. Although it is always hers, there is still a time when Leah's Raglayim dress in her Keter, truly inside of it, as the

measure of the middle third alone (also, sometimes Rachel takes a third by stealing, precisely as the measure of this middle third). However, the measure of Rachel's Keter is always two thirds. This is the meaning of "And Rachel stole her father's Teraphim [household idols]," since the place of the middle third, which Rachel sometimes takes for herself alone through snatching and stealing, is called Teraphim.

Simple Light

183) **Snatching and stealing is called Teraphim.** That is, Leah's Raglayim, which Rachel takes into her own part through her ascent and clothing of the upper third of ZA, are regarded in her as snatching and stealing. It is so because since they are from the phase of Leah, they are unfit to receive any illumination of Haya because a coupling of Mochin of Haya is done only on the VAK of AVI, which ZA can shine only to the phase of Rachel, who is his Nukva of VAK, but not to Leah, who is his Nukva of GAR. It follows that the Raglayim of Leah are unfit for illumination of Haya in and of themselves, but since Rachel takes them into her share, they, too, receive illumination of Haya like Rachel, and this is stealing, meaning that those vessels do not belong to the structure of her Partzuf at all and are unfit to receive her illumination, but Rachel stole them. As a result, they also receive her illumination. However, her taking the middle third of Tifferet of ZA is not stealing whatsoever since this is truly her part which imparts her Mochin of Haya.

184) It follows that Laban is the upper Loven [whiteness], who is the upper Abba, who has two daughters, Rachel and Leah, as mentioned in *The Zohar*, portion *VaYetze* p 162, concerning "And Laban had two daughters." Sometimes Rachel steals from Leah the middle third of Tifferet, called Teraphim, and takes it only to herself, since it is her father's fortune and she does not give of it to her sister Leah.

185) Teraphim comes from the word Toref, which is a place of pudendum, like the house of Torpa that is mentioned in the Gemara. These are the two Raglayim of Leah that enter and clothe inside the Keter of Rachel. This is why he said Teraphim, in plural form, which are the two Raglayim.

Simple Light

185) **Teraphim, in plural form, which are the two Raglayim.** Below, he says that "Since the two Akevim [heels] are concealed inside the Keter of Rachel, they unite and become one Akev [heel]." The thing is that below he speaks of when they clothe inside Rachel's Keter and darken her. At that time, Rachel is back-to-back with ZA, hence NH of Leah are regarded as one phase. It is as the ARI wrote, that when NH are in the posterior, they are one phase. This is why he calls them Akev, in singular

form. But here, where it speaks of stealing the Teraphim, which is by obtaining Rachel's Mochin of Haya, by these Teraphim receiving the illumination of Rachel, they are in a state of anterior. In a state of anterior, the NH are regarded as two distinct phases. This is why it is called Teraphim, in plural form.

186) **Explanation:** The place of the opening of Yesod of Ima inside ZA is in his Chazeh. It follows that its revealing and opening are in the middle third, and this is the opening and revealing of the house of the Toref of the Tevuna that is there. However, the matter of Rachel's stealing of the Teraphim and how by this they did not tell Laban that Jacob had fled is as it is written in the explanation about Balak and Balaam, and Aza and Azael.

187) It is explained there that that place is the phase of the tree of knowledge of good and bad, in which Adam HaRishon and Eve sinned, for that is the place of revealing the Hassadim of Daat of ZA in his Chazeh. Hence, there is Yenika there and a grip to the outer ones, which is actually called "bad."

Simple Light

187) **That place is the phase of the tree of knowledge of good and bad, in which Adam HaRishon and Eve sinned, for that is the place of revealing the Hassadim of Daat of ZA.** The middle third of Tifferet is the root that imparts Hochma, as Tifferet that rises and makes a coupling with HB, since Bina makes a coupling with Hochma only through MAN of Tifferet. For this reason, ZA rose and acquired a place inside the Mochin of AVI in order to sustain the coupling of Hochma in AVI. And that Tifferet that sustains the Mochin of Haya in AVI is called Daat.

For this reason, the middle third of Tifferet of ZA is called "the tree of knowledge," since it left its root in AVI as their Moach of Daat. However, according to this, we could be mistaken that the Keter of Rachel is also called so, since she, too, takes Mochin of Haya from the middle third of Tifferet of ZA. Indeed, this refers to the coupling of the GAR of Mochin of Haya, which are the inner AVI that were concealed as "the great ring [or seal]," regarded as the Mochin that operated in AVI of Nekudim as the looking of Einayim of AVI on each other. It is after this that the middle third of Tifferet of ZA is called the "tree of knowledge," since there is the prohibition in it not to raise Tifferet as MAN to the inner AVI and make a coupling between them in order to draw GAR of Haya as in Nekudim. Conversely, the ascent of this Tifferet as MAN to AVI of Mazla, as is done in all the Mochin of Haya of Atzilut is not forbidden whatsoever. On the contrary, all the corrections are dependent on this because there is no coupling whatsoever without Mochin of Haya.

However, it has been explained that this Daat is discerned as VAK of Daat, through which the VAK of inner AVI make a coupling. It has already been explained that this is why Leah is called "the covered world," since she needs GAR of Haya, and there is no coupling on them at that time. For this reason, Rachel is called "the revealed world" because she needs only VAK of Haya, and they are revealed in her also in this time, before the end of correction.

188) Conversely, above, when the lights are covered, the illumination of these five Hassadim that are revealed and emerge to the outer ones is by those Raglayim of Leah that enter the Keter of Rachel, which correspond to the opening of the mouth of Yesod of Tevuna.

189) When those lights emerge from Yesod of Tevuna through outside of ZA to make a Keter for Rachel, the light wanes and darkens through the clothing of Leah's Raglayim inside Rachel's Keter. That light cannot exit and pass through the anterior of Rachel because she stands back-to-back with ZA. In the beginning, the lights strike the posterior and subsequently pass from there through her anterior. Since the Akevim of Leah are there in the middle of Rachel's Keter, the light does not travel through to the anterior of Rachel's Keter since those two Akevim of Leah completely stop and take the lights that emerge from within.

Simple Light

189) **Those two Akevim of Leah completely stop and take the lights that emerge from within.** This concerns the lights of the anterior of the Neshama in which the Akevim of Leah are established completely for themselves, since the lights of GAR of Neshama are actual illumination of GAR, completely in the phase of from the Chazeh and above. However, from the Chazeh and below they do not suffice for illumination of the anterior because there is no phase of anterior from the Chazeh and below, but only through Mochin of Haya. This is the meaning of "Those two Akevim of Leah completely stop and take the lights of the anterior." Yet, Rachel has only lights of posterior from them, which are VAK without a Rosh, since she cannot enjoy them as they are covered Hassadim while she needs revealed Hassadim. Hence, Leah's Raglayim in the place of Rachel's Keter are regarded as harsh judgments, because in her, the judgments in them are apparent, which position Rachel in the state of posterior. Understand this well because although Leah's Raglayim are sweetened in the phase of anterior to the phase of Leah herself, they are nonetheless complete judgments for the phase of Rachel, which make her a posterior with ZA for the above-mentioned reason.

190) It is known that the Akevim of Leah are complete and harsh judgments since they are NH, and all the phases of NH are judgments because they are the edges near the shell, especially that it is called "outside the Guf," as it is known that NH are outside the Guf.

191) Additionally, they are Leah's Raglayim, whose every phase is harsh judgments because she is discerned as Malchut of Tevuna, and Tevuna herself is NHY of Bina, which are the last ones in her, and it was said about Bina herself in *The Zohar* that judgments are awakened from her.

192) Moreover, Leah herself is from the posterior of Malchut of Tevuna and is not the phase of anterior, especially since she is not her Raglayim but rather the bottom phase of her Raglayim, which are the Akevim, as written in Tree of Life.

193) According to all the above arguments, you find that those Akevim of Leah are complete judgments. Therefore, there is a place for gripping and suckling to the shells, as it is written in the explanation about Balak and Balaam, and Aza and Azael, whose root is phase four of the above lights in those two Raglayim and Akevim of Leah, from which the outer ones suckle. This is why Balaam went to the mountains of the east, to Aza and Azael, as it is written in *The Zohar*, that before Balaam came to Balak he went and closed himself in the mountains of the east with Aza and Azael.

Simple Light

193) And Aza and Azael, whose root is phase four of the above lights in those two Raglayim and Akevim of Leah. It has already been explained that those Akevim of Leah are complete judgments with their illumination below the Chazeh after the end of Yesod of Ima, since the light of Ima, which is illumination of GAR, ends already at the place of the Chazeh, and from the Chazeh and below it is sweetened only by illumination of Haya. Since the illumination of Haya from the phase of Mochin of Leah do not appear throughout the six thousand years, all those judgments are therefore without any sweetening at all. For this reason, they have become the roots of the two angels, Aza and Azael, where Aza was made of the right Akev [heel] and Azael from the left Akev.

194) This is the meaning of "From Aram Balak will lead me, the king of Moab from the mountains of the east." We have already explained in the teaching about Balak and Balaam that the phase of Balaam was from the lights that emerge from those Akevim of Leah that are swallowed inside the Keter of Rachel to the outer ones. This is the meaning of Balaam [Hebrew: he swallowed them], and this is why he went to the mountains of the east, to Aza and Azael, whose suckling is from there.

195) We have already explained that Laban the Aramaic is Balaam's father's father, and he himself was incarnated in Balaam, and from him Balaam, his son's son, learned witchcraft. This wisdom is the wisdom of Laban the Aramaic who praised himself and said, "I can do you harm," and as was said about Balaam, "For I know that he whom you bless is blessed, and he whom you curse is cursed."

196) This is the meaning of the wisdom of the Teraphim that Laban had. Through those Teraphim, he obtained all his illuminations. When Rachel stole them, those lights did not come out to the Akevim of Leah, outside, to the outer ones to shine for them, and he did not know that he had fled. Thus, Teraphim are lights that come out to the outer ones from the Toreph of Tevuna, which is her Yesod that is clothed in the place of the Chazeh of ZA.

Simple Light

196) When Rachel stole them, those lights did not come out to the Akevim of Leah, outside. The matter of this stealing was done by Rachel's obtaining of Mochin of Haya, for then those Akevim shine as though they are of her organs. For this reason, all the forces of judgment that were mixed with them are separated and the illumination of the outer ones, which are the gods of Laban, was completely revoked. This is the meaning of "Why did you steal my gods?" and all his wisdom departed, too, and he did not know that he had fled.

197*) This matter, too, is the sin of Adam HaRishon with the tree of knowledge of good and bad as we explained above that this is his place. He himself is as our sages said, that Eve's sin was that she pressed grapes and gave him. The meaning of the matter is that Leah's Akevim that enter Rachel's Keter are regarded as grapes, which are Akev in Gematria, as in Akev [heel, but also spelled as Ekev (because)] of humbleness, and the wine in the grapes are the judgments in those Akevim.

198) It is known that the outer ones are nourished only by the waste of wine, from the yeast in it, which are residue of the holy judgment. This abundance that the outer ones suckle is harsh judgment, and it is murky wine full of yeast, swallowed inside Leah's Akevim like the wine that is swallowed in the grapes.

Simple Light

198) Murky wine full of yeast, swallowed inside Leah's Akevim like the wine that is swallowed in the grapes. Interpretation: All the Partzufim of ABYA emerged from the second restriction, as in "He created them with a small Hey." Also, it is known that the shells were made from those vessels of ZA and Malchut of the posterior of Nekudim that they used at the time of the Melachim [kings], after they were separated into external and surrounding vessels called garment and hall. It has also been explained above that there was another flaw in the vessels of the kings that were used in Nekudim since the judgments of the first restriction also rides on it. Know that this quality in the shells is the cup of poison and is called "the yeast of the shells," and remember this. All the shells were made from using the separated vessels of ZA and Malchut that were separated by the second restriction, and the yeast of the shells were made from the Malchut of the first restriction that was mixed with them, and from her is all their power, as with yeast, which are all the power of the strength in the wine.

It was said, "Murky wine full of yeast, swallowed inside Leah's Akevim," since it has been explained above that any phase that was not fully sorted, all the shells are mixed there. You find that there are two qualities of judgments in the Akevim of Leah, and they are the roots of the shells and the yeast of the shells. The Akevim of Leah themselves are from the sorting of the second restriction as in all the Partzufim, and only the shells suckle from them. However, the yeast of

---

* Tree of Life, Part 2, Gate 38, Chapter 4.

wine is also mixed with them, as in "swallowed inside Leah's Akevim," meaning that they are not apparent on the outside because the whole structure of Leah is from the second restriction. Rather, they are concealed there and are swallowed within them.

It was said, "Eve squeezed those grapes" since her eating from the tree of knowledge means that she wanted to draw GAR of Haya that sort those Akevim of Leah. It follows that she squeezed those grapes and then the yeast were revealed outside. This is the meaning of the filth that the serpent cast in Eve, since by drawing illumination to the yeast of the shells, they clung to her and caused her death.

199) Eve pressed those grapes, and her intention was that by that pressing, the yeast that are swallowed there would come out, and from them Adam and Eve drank from that wine, the cup of poison. The part of the outer ones is called Sitra de Muta [Aramaic: the side of death]. Hence, they were punished by death and brought death upon her. It is also possible that this is the meaning of Rachel's death due to the Teraphim as our sages said.

200) Look and see that in Gematria, grapes are Akev, as mentioned above. Hence, the grapes are stomped on to extract wine out of them only with the Akevim. These grapes are in plural form, which are the above-mentioned two Akevim, each of which is called Elokim, since she is judgments. The two Raglayim are two names Elokim (and with their ten letters they are also grapes in Gematria) and they are Akev in Gematria since Elokim is the root of the judgment in the quality of grapes, and in it, the wine is concealed and swallowed.

201) In truth, since they are two names Elokim, as well as grapes, two is the least plural, (therefore) why are they Akev in Gematria, which is in singular form? The thing is that since the two Akevim are swallowed in the Keter of Rachel, they unite and become one Akev, and this is the Akev of humbleness, and it is not written "Akevim of humbleness."

Simple Light

201) **Since the two Akevim are swallowed in the Keter of Rachel, they unite and become one Akev.** It has already been explained above that during the clothing of Akevim of Leah in the Keter of Rachel, Rachel is in a state of back-to-back, and those Akevim are NH of Leah. For this reason, they are only one phase since NH are regarded as two phases only when they are in the phase of anterior.

202) (It seems to me that I heard from my teacher that this is also the meaning of what is written in the portion *Tezaveh* and in *Sifra de Tzniuta*, the judgments of Nukva are harsh in the beginning and soft in the end, since in the Keter of Rachel are the Akevim of Leah, which are the harshness of the judgments.)

203) Thus we have explained the matter of the sin of Adam HaRishon, how it was with the tree of knowledge, which are in the two bottom thirds of Tifferet of ZA, which are revealed lights of Daat from the phase of Hassadim in it.

204*) Now we must interpret what our sages said in the Midrash and in *The Zohar* in the portion Balak, 208b, that when it writes "Who sees the vision of the Almighty, falling down with uncovered eyes," it speaks of Aza and Azael. Know that Aza and Azael are two angels rooted and created from the same two lights that emerge from the two Akevim of Leah inside the Keter of Rachel. From there, it is the grip of Balak, as was said above, that they are complete judgments and their illumination goes outside. Also, Aza is made of the right Akev and Azael of the illumination of the left Akev.

205) Conversely, Balaam is not from the illumination of the Akevim themselves but from the illumination of the Keter of Rachel which swallows within it the illumination of the two Akevim, as mentioned above. For this reason, he, too, learned all his wisdom from Aza and Azael and suckled from them the way Keter of Rachel suckles from the Akevim of Leah. Since the illuminations of Aza and Azael are revealed in that place, it is called a "vision of the Almighty."

Simple Light

205) **Balaam is not from the illumination of the Akevim themselves but from the illumination of the Keter of Rachel which swallows within it the illumination of the two Akevim.** It was written above that when those Akevim are in the phase of Leah herself, they have sweetening. However, all the judgments in them are revealed when they shine in the Keter of Rachel from the Chazeh and below. This is the meaning of what the ARI tells us here, that Balaam clings to the Akevim of Leah when they shine in the Keter of Rachel, which is why he is discerned as the Sitra Achra.

206) This will explain the matter of the words of our sages in the Midrash and in *The Zohar*, portion *Beresheet*, 35a, that Aza and Azael complained about the creation of Adam HaRishon and the Creator dropped them from their place of Kedusha [holiness], and it was said about them, "The fallen ones were in the land."

207) This is simple, for it is not without reason that they complained about his creation more than the other angels. The reason is that ZON were initially back-to-back, and then Leah and Rachel are one above the other in the above-mentioned manner, since the two Akevim of Leah become concealed inside Rachel's Keter, and then Aza and Azael suckle from there.

208) When He wished to create Adam and Eve, it was so that through his actions, he would correct the Nukva so they would return to face-to-face and make a coupling together, as in "there is no man to till the land."

---
* *Shaar HaPsukim*, Chapter Balak, Mark 24.

209) When ZON are face-to-face, the Akevim of Leah are not inside the Keter of Rachel and all those illuminations that emerged from the Akevim of Leah to the Keter of Rachel, from which Aza and Azael gripped, were now revoked from there and emerged through the anterior side since this is where Rachel stands and there is no place for Aza and Azael to grip there, for their grip is only in the posterior. The illuminations of Aza and Azael were revoked in the creation of Adam, which is why they complained about his creation, due to the harm that comes to them by his creation. Also, know that Aza should be with [the letter] Hey and not with Aleph, and I heard from my teacher that he is ADNI in Gematria with the number twelve letters of the filling.

Simple Light

209) **When ZON are face-to-face, the Akevim of Leah are not inside the Keter of Rachel, etc. The illuminations of Aza and Azael were revoked in the creation of Adam.** All the suckling of Aza and Azael is from the Akevim of Leah in the Keter of Rachel, which is only when she is back-to-back. Since they knew that Adam HaRishon would return ZON to face-to-face, which are the phase of Mochin of Haya, when Rachel takes all of the middle third of Tifferet and corrects also the Akevim of Leah by snatching and stealing, at that time, the illumination of Aza and Azael is completely revoked, "which is why they complained about His creation, due to the harm that comes to them."

210) However, the rest of the lights that emerge to the posterior side are not revoked except for this one, since it emerges only when the Akevim of Leah are inside the Keter of Rachel. Upon her return to the anterior, the rest of the lights of Aza and Azael are revoked.

Chapter 11

211*) Now we will explain to you a different introduction. Know that Adam HaRishon, besides his first sin of eating from the tree of knowledge, continued to sin and engendered demons and ghosts and Lilits.

Simple Light

211) **Adam HaRishon, besides his first sin of eating from the tree of knowledge, continued to sin and engendered demons and ghosts and Lilits.** Through the sin of the tree of knowledge, he ejected a drop of semen in vain because of the serpent, and the stormy wind clothed inside the serpent clung to him. This is regarded as the yeast of the shells, the potion of death, which are shells of Malchut of Nekudim on which the judgments of the first restriction ride. Besides this, he continued to sin during the 130 years when he abstained from his wife and ejected drops of semen in vain. These were from the phase of the scales that rob the souls, meaning from the shells of the second restriction. They are two phases, which are called below "first drops" and "last drops."

There is merit to the first drops of semen that the shells cling only to their Malchut and not at all to the first nine of those drops, since in the phase of the first restriction there is no grip to the shells and judgments in the first nine. However, opposite this there is a great flaw there that is impossible to correct before the end of correction, which is the ten lights placed in the Akev. Opposite this there is merit in the last drops that it is possible to correct them during the six thousand years, as well, through Mochin of Haya. However, a great flaw is discerned in them, that the shells cling to their first nine, too, since they are from the second restriction and from the shells that come from the posterior vessels that operated in Nekudim. Remember well these distinctions between the first drops of semen and the last drops. This is the meaning of "continued to sin and engendered demons," etc., since he caused the shells to grip also to the first nine of these souls, which is an added sin.

212) Initially, he ejected semen in vain. Later, while still doing this bad deed, he came upon his wife, and then Eve was impregnated by him from two drops. From the first drop came Cain, the elder. Then, from the second drop came Abel, his brother.

213) Afterward, he returned to his corruption once again and ejected drops of semen in vain all those 130 years of abstention from his wife until he begot Seth. Thus, there were two drops of semen, one before Cain and one after him, and Cain was in between them.

Simple Light

212-213) **While still doing this bad deed, he came upon his wife, etc., one before Cain and one after him, and Cain was in between them.** This is the meaning the

---

* *Shaar HaPsukim, Yehezkel.*

serpent's coming upon Eve and casting filth in her, since that first drop of semen of the yeast of the shells from the first restriction mixed with Eve when he came upon his wife at that time, and that filth clung to Cain. It is as our sages said that when Israel stood on Mt. Sinai, their filth stopped. But the nations of the world, who did not stand on Mt. Sinai, their filth did not stop. However, besides this, the last drops of the 130 years were also mixed with Cain in a manner that Cain includes both and has the same two faults. This is why he is mostly bad.

214) However, when the drop of Cain emerged from Adam HaRishon and he gave it to Eve, his wife, through connection and copulation, the drop of Cain was still mixed with the drops of semen that preceded him, since the matters were near and followed one another. For this reason, all the drops of semen that emerged from Adam before he engendered the drop of Cain mixed with Cain since they were close together.

215) There is another reason. Since I have already explained to you in Shaar HaGilgulim [Gate of Reincarnations] concerning the Ten Martyrs, that they were from the drops of semen of Joseph. It was explained there that the souls that emerge as drops of semen in vain are greater in merit than the rest of the souls because they are from the phase of Daat itself, since they are from the awakening of the male. The rest of the souls that come by a coupling of male and female are from the awakening of the female and are only from the Hassadim or Gevurot that spread below in VAK of the Guf of ZA. Since they are of great height and merit, the shells have a strong governance over these drops of semen.

Simple Light

215) **The souls that emerge as drops of semen in vain are greater in merit than the rest of the souls because they are from the phase of Daat itself.** The corrected souls that come from the male and female are extended from the VAK of Mochin of Haya as Hesed that is revealed in the Peh of Ima, meaning from the Hassadim that are revealed from the Chazeh of ZA and below. These are VAK of the Guf and not the phase of HGT of ZA, which are GAR of the Guf. However, the souls from the drops of semen come by extensions of GAR of Mochin of Haya because this coupling of GAR does not occur during the six thousand years, since the inner AVI were concealed in RADLA, these souls emerge to the domain of the shells in vain. Thus, the souls of the drops of semen are higher in merit than the corrected souls since they are drawn from the actual Daat, meaning from the GAR of Daat, which bestow upon the Garon and HGT of the Guf, which are the GAR of the Guf.

In VAK of the Guf of ZA, meaning from the Chazeh and below, regarded as VAK of the Guf, since the Garon and HGT are regarded as GAR of the Guf of ZA. The reason for it is that while they are in the Guf, the five phases KHB ZON in the Rosh are called HGT NH, where HGT are KHB of the Guf, or HBD, and NH are ZON of the Guf.

216) Since Cain is the elder, as it is written in *The Book of Tikkunim* about the verse, "If you carry well," these very fine drops of semen mixed with him. Another, third reason, is that since all those drops of semen are Gevurot because the shells called semen can grip them.

Simple Light

216) Cain is the elder, etc., "If you carry well." Even though Cain is the crown of Gevura of Daat of ZA and Adam HaRishon and Abel is the crown of Hassadim in their Daat, and it is known that the crown of Hassadim precedes the crown of Gevura, here, however, due to the sin of the tree of knowledge, a change occurred, that the Gevurot preceded the Hassadim. It is known that the light of Haya that emerges by the Daat is mostly as a female that encircles a man, and the revealing of the light of Haya of Hassadim comes by the Gevurot as reflected light from below upward where the Hassadim receive disclosure of illumination of Hochma from the Gevurot that illuminate for them from below upward. For this reason, Cain is regarded as the elder, meaning illumination of GAR, since any phase of GAR of Abel by an illumination of Cain to him is from below upward. This is the meaning of the words, "And it came to pass that when they were in the field, Cain arose," etc., for he denied him illumination of GAR and thus killed him. This is his complaint, "Am I my brother's keeper?" since in his view, he was not obligated to illuminate to him.

This is the meaning of "And the Lord had regard for Abel and for his offering, but for Cain and for his offering He had no regard," for so is the order of illumination of Daat of ZA, that the Gevurot do not receive for themselves but in order to illuminate from below upward to the Hassadim. It follows that "The Lord had regard for Abel and for his offering," which is the phase of Hassadim of Daat, and not to Cain in his place. This is the meaning of "If you carry well," since it angered Cain that he had to illuminate for Abel his brother from below upward, which is the phase of VAK of the GAR of Haya, for any illumination from below upward is regarded as VAK while he wanted illumination of GAR of Haya that illuminate as direct light instead of HGT of ZA, as it was in the HGT of the seven Melachim. This is why "his countenance fell."

The Creator replied to him about this, "If you carry well," meaning that only in this manner will all your correction come, meaning in a manner of carrying, from below upward, to improve the Hassadim. He warned him about it, "If you do not do well," but want to draw GAR of Mochin of Haya to HGT of ZA, then "Sin crouches at the door," meaning the serpent lies by this door, since this was the sin of the tree of knowledge.

217) Cain is the crown of Gevura. This is why they mixed with him, as they are from his root. For this reason, all the first and final drops of semen were only from the male, since Cain was born from a male and a female, especially that they were from his root. They were all included with him because they are all from the same root and he must correct all of them. This is why Cain was born mostly bad and with little good, since all the above-mentioned drops of semen were included in him and many shells clung to them.

218) Now we will explain the words of our sages about the verse, "And He wiped out every living thing," which is Cain, whom the Creator hung loosely between heaven and earth and the flood came and washed him. The matter concerns what has been explained, that all the first and final drops of semen of Adam HaRishon were included in Cain since they are from the same root, and especially since he was born from a male and a female and had the ability to correct them and was therefore obliged to correct them.

219) Moreover, he continued to sin, as you know that the whole generation of the flood was Cain's sons, Mehujael and Methushael and so forth, and all of them were wasting their sperm on the ground, spoiling even more than initially until they were wiped out by the boiling water of the flood, an eye for an eye.

220) Cain himself was their father. Since the day he had sinned until the flood came, the Creator hung him loosely, meaning that what is made through a male and a female is a strong and persisting drop since they emerge from the male as loose water and enter the female where they congeal as a strong and persisting firmament with a strong and hard Partzuf and organs.

221) But the drop of semen that emerges only from the male has two flaws: 1) It is loose, since it is a drop of water. 2) It hangs in the air since it emerges from the male, who is called heaven, and did not enter the female, who is called earth. This is why it hangs in the air between heaven and earth and has no rest at all until it enters a female.

222) This is what is written about Cain, that he had those two flaws: 1) He was hanging between heaven and earth, and 2) he was loose, and all that was due to those drops of semen that were included in him. When the boiling water of the flood came, an eye for an eye, they found him hanging loosely in the air and wiped him out.

Simple Light

222) **Cain, that he had those two flaws: 1) He was hanging between heaven and earth, and 2) he was loose.** The whole correction of the first drops of semen that were attached to Cain is by congealing into strong organs that are made by the Nukva by the strong boundary in her. But Cain was as a loose drop of water without a strong boundary, which is why he still yearned to draw GAR of Haya as in the act of the sin of the tree of knowledge, as in "And it angered Cain a lot, and his countenance fell." Although in fact, he emerged through the Nukva Eve, he had this through the force of the first drops of semen that had clung to him. Also, he was hung between heaven and earth since his Neshama itself was blemished by the final drops of semen since they are regarded as the shells of the second restriction that blemish all the first nine

of the Neshama. This is why the ARI writes that she has no rest at all, meaning that the Sitra Achra clung to her in that part of Cain's soul which was already sorted in him. This is why he was hung between heaven and earth, meaning in the air, which means complete absence of illumination of GAR, for he could not be depicted in the female and receive GAR from her, as the ARI wrote about demons and ghosts and Lilits. This is why the flood came and wiped him out, as in "And wiped out every living thing," for "every living thing" means GAR. Since he lost the illumination of Haya, the flood controlled him.

223) Had he corrected those souls of drops of semen, the flood would not have wiped them out. But since they had not been corrected, the souls of drops of semen were hanging in the air of the heavens, which are demons and ghosts that are always hanging in the air of the firmament, as mentioned in *The Zohar* in many places, whether in *Idrat Nasso* or in the portion *Aharei Mot* or the portion *Tazria* or the portion *VaYikra*.

224) Since they were not depicted in the female and could not ascend or descend in this world to enter the bodies of children, they were wiped out by the water of the flood, which found them hanging there in the air as demons and ghosts. This is why it is written about Cain that he was hanging between heaven and earth, since heaven is the male and earth is the female, and those drops emerged from heaven, which is the male, and did not reach the earth, which is the female, but remained hanging loosely.

225) This is also the meaning of what our sages said, that the demons and ghosts were created on the eve of Shabbat at twilight, since they are from those drops of semen, which were ghosts without bodies since they were not depicted in a female. You already know that Cain, too, was born on the eve of Shabbat [Sabbath] near the afternoon prayer, at twilight.

226) After those drops of semen were wiped out during the generation of the flood, the shell that clung to them was removed from them. Since then, they have been reentering the upper female where they are corrected and depicted and descend to this world in bodies of the newborn like the rest of the souls. Since then, they have been gradually correcting.

Simple Light

226) **During the generation of the flood, the shell that clung to them was removed from them. Since then, they have been reentering the upper female,** since being completely wiped out from the earth removed from them the shell of the serpent of the first drops, regarded as the yeast of the shells, which cannot be corrected. After this hard shell has been removed from them, they have become fit to receive correction in the female. This is regarded as the first correction, for as long as this hard shell is attached to them, they are completely unfit for any correction.

227) Although all of Adam's drops of semen were included in Cain, they are certainly divided into three divisions: 1) drops of semen before Cain was born, 2) drops of Cain himself, who was from a male and a female, 3) drops of semen after Cain's birth.

228) Know that although we said above that the souls that come from drops of semen are much greater and higher than the souls that come from a coupling of a male and a female, there is still a difference between the drops of semen before Cain was born compared to those after he was born. The first drops of semen, before Cain was born, are much greater and better than the drops of semen after Cain was born.

I have already alerted you that Micah of Moreshet is from the root of Cain and is from those first drops of semen, which are better. Moreshet comes from the word Resheet [beginning/head]. But Nahum the Elkoshite was also from the root of Cain, except he was from the final drops of semen, and this is the meaning of Elkoshite, from the word Malkosh [final rain of the year]. It follows that Micah is Yoreh [first rain of the year], and Nahum is Malkosh, which are the final raindrops. Ezekiel the prophet and Hezekiah King of Judah were both from the root of Cain and are from the first drops of semen, which are better. Since initially, their souls were hanging loose, as mentioned, their souls were mentioned so by the word "strength," to indicate their correction—that they have been completely corrected and were completely strengthened out of their looseness.

Simple Light

228) **The first drops of semen, before Cain was born, are much greater and better than the drops of semen after Cain was born.** It has already been explained above that there is a great merit to the first drops of semen, that the shell grips only to Malchut in them, but the first nine are clean, whereas in the final drops of semen, the shells cling to their first nine, too.

Their souls were hanging loose ... and were completely strengthened out of their looseness. The very possibility to correct the first drops is regarded as congealing of organs with a strong boundary through the Nukva. By this they are certain never to go astray again as with the sin of the tree of knowledge. This is the whole correction that those souls have during the six thousand years. But at the end of correction, they will be completely corrected, as in "legs touching legs."

Chapter 12

229*) The reason that Israel were exiled among the nations has already been explained in the portion Re'eh concerning the commandment to remember the exodus from Egypt. We said that Adam HaRishon contained all the souls and all the worlds. When he sinned, all those souls fell from him into the shells that divide into seventy nations. Israel must be exiled there in each and every nation to collect the lilies of the holy souls that have scattered among those thorns. It is as our sages said in Midrash Rabbah, "Why were Israel exiled among the nations? To add proselytes to them."

230) The matter of the exile in Egypt was also explained there, since at that time, the majority of those souls or all of them were mixed with the shells called "Egypt." Yet, who these specific souls were is explained in the explanation about Passover and the exodus from Egypt.

Simple Light

230) The exile in Egypt... were mixed with the shells called "Egypt." Egypt are the shells corresponding to the Garon of ZA which is a narrow [Tzar] place. This means that they are regarded as shells opposite the GAR of Guf of ZA from the Garon to the Chazeh where the Hassadim are covered, since Hassadim are revealed only from the Chazeh down. This is regarded as the land of Canaan, which is considered VAK of Guf of ZA. As long as the shells of Egypt cling in order to suckle from the GAR of Guf of ZA by making the souls sin by extending illumination of Haya to the place of GAR of Guf of ZA so they, too, can enjoy the abundance, HG of ZA remain concealed in the Rosh and do not spread from the Garon down. This is the meaning of the Garon [throat] becoming a narrow place. This implies blocking of Hassadim due to the grip of the Egyptians in the place of the back of the neck of ZA.

This is the meaning of the exile in Egypt, since the souls of the children of Israel fell under their authority and had to serve them according to their wish, to extend to them revealed Hassadim to the place of GAR of Guf of ZA from the Garon downward. This is why the Mochin of ZA departed and did not illuminate to the children of Israel until they were delivered from under their hands and the Mochin of Haya of ZA were born and expanded in their place from Chazeh of ZA and below. This is the meaning of the exodus from Egypt.

In all those explanations, we must remember that correction can come to the souls of people only through Mochin of Haya of ZA since Nukva of ZA, Rachel, does not have the power to deliver souls before ZA obtains Mochin of Haya, much less souls that are the offspring of the Nukva of ZA. By this you will understand that the exile in Egypt was essentially due to lack of Mochin of Haya in ZA. Egypt's power to enslave Israel was in order to make the souls of Israel sin and draw illumination of Mochin to their

---
* *Shaar HaPsukim, Shemot,* Mark 1

quality, to the place of GAR of Guf of ZA, which is called the "gripping of the back of the neck," which is a continuation of the sin of the tree of knowledge.

However, besides the above-mentioned iniquity, the filth of the serpent that extends from the shells opposite the first restriction, called "death," was also included in them. By this force, they put the children of Israel to death, as in the verse, "If he is a boy, put him to death." This is so because any unsorted phase includes all the phases of the shells. However, the Egyptians' main force of evil was the extension of revealed Hassadim to the forbidden place called the "grip of the back of the neck," regarded as the canceling of the Parsa of the second restriction. This is the meaning of "They made their lives bitter with hard work and mortar and bricks."

231) Now we will explain about them in brief. It was explained above, in the verse, "Go to Joseph; whatever he says to you, you shall do," for he observed in the spirit of holiness that they were sparks of semen of holy souls that Adam HaRishon begot in the first 130 years, called "afflictions of the sons of man," meaning Adam HaRishon. Through the pleasure he felt while emitting them, as in the pleasures of the sons of man, demon and demons, who are Lilit and Naama, etc., they were inverted and became afflictions instead of pleasures. Therefore, he converted them and circumcised them.

Simple Light

231) Therefore, he converted them and circumcised them. Circumcision means removing the foreskin, which is the three evil shells clothed in the impure serpent. Joseph circumcised them in order to remove this hard shell from them, which is the beginning of all the corrections. However, they still remained in their main shell called the "grip of the back of the neck." Those Egyptians that were circumcised by Joseph later reincarnated in the mixed multitude, which Moses toiled to correct them from the grip of the back of the neck, as well.

232) The thing is that concerning what we have clarified about Cain and Abel in the portion Beresheet, the majority of souls come from HG that expand in the Guf of ZA and not from Daat itself, although the drops thrown by the layer of wasted sperm are only from the male's lust, whose Daat awakened to the coupling and he emits those drops above the upper Daat itself and did not find his Nukva ready for it in the world of Atzilut, since she descended due to the flaw. At that time, they went outside and the females of the shells took them, they were depicted in their bodies and they delivered them. These are demons, ghosts and Lilits and they are called "the afflictions of the sons of man."

Simple Light

232) Those drops above the upper Daat itself and did not find the female ready for it. It has been explained above that ZON face-to-face in Mochin of consequence come only from VAK of Haya that shine only to Rachel. One who draws from the phase of Daat, it means from GAR of Haya, since ZA does not have a Nukva that is ready to receive the GAR of Haya because the inner AVI were concealed.

233) It follows that all those demons and ghosts that were created during those 130 years of Adam's abstention from Eve are high and holy souls from the phase of Daat. They were mixed with the shells and require many incarnations in order to cleanse and whiten them until their scum is completely removed from them through many incarnations.

234) For this reason, you find that the Israeli nation was not born before Jacob and onward since the majority of souls were mixed with shells and were being sorted and reincarnated from generation to generation. Their correction did not begin before Jacob, the senior among the patriarchs, who corrected Adam HaRishon. This is also when the correction of his sons began, who are the above-mentioned souls, and they were gradually sorted in the exile in Egypt until Israel departed from Egypt.

235) This is the meaning of the verse, "Has God tried to go to take for Himself a people from within a people?" Our sages said, "It did not say "a nation from within a people," but "a people from within a people." You need to understand this well because they were truly inside the shells and they were gentiles like them, and they were cleansed and whitened and taken from among those actual gentiles.

Simple Light

235) "A people from within a people," etc., they were gentiles like them, and they were cleansed and whitened, etc. In other words, those two forces of impurity of the Egyptian people were truly attached to the children of Israel as to the Egyptians, since this is the meaning of the enslavement under them. For this reason, the children of Israel had to be whitened and sorted until these two forces of impurity are removed from their souls, namely the grip on the back of the neck and the filth of the serpent.

236) The beginning of their incarnation was in the generation of the flood. Since they are from that bitter root that emerged through the wasting of the sperm of the afflictions of the sons of Adam HaRishon, they were rebellious and heretic against the Creator. Their sin was mainly that they wasted their sperm on the ground, as the verse says, "For all flesh had corrupted their way upon the earth."

237) This is the meaning of "And God regretted that He had made man on the earth," said about the generation of the flood, implying that they are as the sons of Adam HaRishon himself, who emerged while he wasted his sperm during those 130 years. This is also the meaning of "And God saw that man's evil was great upon the earth." It is known that one who wastes his sperm is called "bad," as in "And Er, the first born of Judah, was bad in the eyes of the Lord," as mentioned in *The Zohar*, in the portion VaYechi, for this is the meaning of "No harm shall come to

you." It follows that the generation of the flood that emerged by the wasting of the sperm of Adam are called "man's actual evil."

238) It was also said, "And the Lord said, 'I will wipe out the man whom I have created,'" implying that they are souls from the wasting of the sperm of Adam HaRishon himself who was created and who was truly a creation of His hands. This is the meaning of "And all the inclination of the thoughts of his heart is only evil all the day," since all the intensification of their inclination was the wasting of sperm called "bad," since they, too, were extended from there, and then their bodies were wiped out by the flood, for the boiling drop of wasting their sperm on the earth. It is as our sages said, "In boiling they corrupted; in boiling they were sentenced."

239) Afterward, they incarnated a second time during the generation of Babylon, and they, too, acted badly like their fathers, but not by wasting sperm. This is the meaning of the words, "And the Lord descended to see the city and the tower that the sons of man had built." It was explained in *The Zohar* and in the Midrash that they were truly the sons of Adam, Adam HaRishon, implying that they were truly his sons, who emerged when he wasted his sperm.

Afterward, they incarnated a third time in the people of Sodom. This is why it was said about them, "And the people of Sodom were bad and very sinful to the Lord," implying that they were bad in the sense of wasting Adam's sperms, which is called "bad."

Simple Light

239) **They incarnated a second time during the generation of Babylon, and they, too, acted badly like their fathers, but not by wasting sperm.** This means that they did not sin in the male quality, in whom there is the matter of wasting sperm. Rather, they sinned in the quality of the Nukva, to whom this does not apply. However, the matter of the sin was also a continuation from the sin of the tree of knowledge since they wanted to revoke the Parsa of the second restriction called "a firmament dividing between water and water." This is the meaning of what our sages said, "Not all is from Him, He will choose for Himself the upper ones, etc., we will rise to the firmament and fight against Him." That is, they denied the kernel of the world since the Parsa of the second restriction is the kernel of the world, as in the words, "He created them with a Hey," that all the worlds emerged only by the correction of this Parsa, which is the small Hey.

240*) After they incarnated three times in the three above-mentioned generations, and it is written, "God does all these three times with a man," they incarnated a fourth time in Egypt, in the children of Israel who were born then, in that generation of exile, and then they began to be corrected.

---

* *Shaar HaPsukim*, Portion *Shemot*, Mark 1, p 103.

241) This will answer for you one big question that the greatest in the world wondered about, and even in *The Zohar*, in the portion *Shemot*, Rabbi Elazar asked Rashbi [Rabbi Shimon Bar Yochai], his father, about the reason for the exile in Egypt, why was that exile, and why in Egypt over any other land. And there is another question, which is why the exile was in the form of that ugly enslavement, "And they made their lives bitter with hard work with mortar and bricks," etc.

242) The matter is explained with the above-mentioned, that those souls drowned in the shells in the nation of Egypt. Hence, since in the beginning, in the generation of the flood, they sinned by wasting their sperm, which is why they were wiped out then, in the days of the flood, by boiling water. For this reason, now, too, Pharaoh sentenced them that "Every boy who is born, throw him in the Nile." But he sentenced only the males since they sinned by wasting the sperm and not the females.

Simple Light

242) **They were wiped out then, in the days of the flood, etc., now, too, Pharaoh sentenced them that "Every boy who is born, throw him in the Nile."** These souls of the children of Israel are the souls that fell from Adam HaRishon with the sin of the tree of knowledge, as is written above, that there were two kinds of flaws in the sin of the tree of knowledge. The first was the emission of the drop of semen in vain, as yeast of the shells, which is considered as pulling on his foreskin, since he dropped those souls in the three shells of the foreskin called "stormy wind," etc. The second was the matter of revoking the Parsa, since he drew illumination of GAR of Haya from AVI of Nekudim who were concealed in Atzilut. Thus, he revoked the Parsa between Atzilut and BYA, as it happened during the seven Melachim [kings] of Nekudim. This is called "denying the kernel," since he denied the kernel of the world, which is the small Hey of Hibara'am [when they were created], from which all the worlds of ABYA emerged. For this reason, those souls came in two incarnations, one in the generation of the flood, as it is written, "And He wiped out every living thing," when the shell of the foreskin was separated from them. The second was in the generation of Babylon, when the second shell of denying the kernel still remained in those souls, and by which they sinned with the city and the tower with its top in heaven, meaning they wanted to revoke the Parsa and draw lights of Atzilut to BYA. Afterward they came in the people of Sodom, and then in the souls of the people of Israel in the exile in Egypt. For this reason, those two flaws clung to them as to the Egyptians, which are truly these shells.

This is the meaning of **"Since in the beginning, in the generation of the flood, they sinned by wasting their sperm, etc., Pharaoh sentenced them that 'Every boy who is born, throw him in the Nile,'"** since this shell of the foreskin is discerned as death and has correction only in the manner of "and He wiped out every living thing," by which the generation of the flood were sentenced. For this reason, Pharaoh, too, sentenced them, "Every boy who is born, throw him in the Nile," as well as "If it is a boy, you shall put him to death."

This is the meaning of **"Corresponding to what they sinned in the incarnation of the generation of Babylon, etc., to rise and deny the kernel, to fight against Him. This is why now it was said instead, etc., and they made their lives bitter building Pithom and Ramesses opposite those city and tower."** The hard work with mortar and bricks is precisely that same iniquity of denying the kernel of the generation of Babylon, and the Egyptians made the children of Israel sin with it.

We should understand the difference between the two incarnations—the generation of the flood and Babylon, and the generation of the exile in Egypt. In the generation of the flood and Babylon, these two shells were still attached and mixed inside those souls of the drops of semen. Hence, they could not be completely corrected. But after the shells were separated from the souls and clothed in the Egyptians, and the souls themselves in the children of Israel, the correction of the souls of the children of Israel became possible, to bring them out of Egypt, as it is written, "a people from within a people."

243) Corresponding to what they sinned in the incarnation of the generation of Babylon, "Let us make bricks and burn them thoroughly," to build the city and the tower, to rise and deny the essence, to fight against it. This is why now it was said instead, "Let us outwit them, opposite "Let us make bricks," and they made their lives bitter building Pithom and Ramesses opposite those city and tower.

244) Know that there were two phases, since there are souls that were completely corrected and incarnated in those children of Israel in that generation after they descended to Egypt. Among them there are souls that were not corrected and were incarnated in the children of the Egyptians themselves. They are the ones whom Joseph circumcised, as mentioned in the verse (Genesis 41:55), "Go to Joseph; whatever he says to you, you shall do," and as it is written, "He said to his people, 'Behold, the people of the children of Israel.'"

245) First he called them "the people of the children of Israel," and then "They were in dread of the children of Israel," not mentioning "a people." This question was asked in *The Zohar* in the portion Shemot. The thing is that Joseph sentenced circumcision on those Egyptians, and so did Jacob his father. Our sages said that he, too, made conversions in Egypt, and these are the above-mentioned souls.

Chapter 13

246*) Concerning the lights that we say their roots remained in their places and their illumination came out, we will explain this to you about ZA and from it we will conclude about the rest. When Ein Sof emanated Keter, He made it from all five general Partzufim, which are the Keter in it, AVI, and ZON in it. Know that when He emanated the Keter in it, all the Ketarim [pl. of Keter] from there down were included in it one inside the other down to Assiya. How? Keter of Atzilut clothes Keter of Beria, and Keter of Yetzira is over it, and Keter of Assiya is on it, clothing it.

Simple Light

246) Concerning the lights that we say their roots remained in their places and their illumination came out, we will explain this, etc. These words of the ARI from Item 246 through Item 251 are shining keys to the full depth of the wisdom from beginning to end. Without them, we would have no way to understand even one issue to the fullest. Let me present a few questions:

1) Since every Keter of a world or a Partzuf is a branch of its upper Malchut, how can it be understood that Keter in every place is truly the phase of Ein Sof, since if it is only an consequence of Malchut, which is only discerned as a vessel in every place?

2) It is known that there is no degree without twenty-five Partzufim, meaning five Partzufim: AA, AVI, and ZON, clothing one another on an equal level, where each of them has five Partzufim—AA, AVI, and ZON to its length. Accordingly, we should understand the difference between them. For example, what is the difference between the inner AA and AA of Abba that clothes it, and AA of Ima, etc., since they are all AA and discerned as an emanator? Also, what is the difference between AVI of AA in its length, and AVI of AVI in their length., etc.?

3) If the inner AA that clothes the line of Ein Sof also has five Partzufim on the length, meaning AVI and ZON, how then is it possible that AVI, which are the third degree from Ein Sof, will clothe the line of Ein Sof equally with AA, and even more so for ZON, which are the fourth degree from Ein Sof, to clothe the line of Ein Sof, which is four degrees far from them?

4) At one time, it is said that the Partzufim clothe one another on an equal level, and another time, it says that they clothe only one below the other, meaning that the lower one clothes a little bit of the upper one. We should know when they are on an equal level and when they are one below the other, as well as the reason for it.

5) This is the main question around which this text revolves. It is the clarification of what the ARI wrote for us in several places, that even after all the ascents of the worlds that occur during the six thousand years, the ladder of degrees does not change at all, since for example, ZON, in the beginning of their emanation, emerged

---

* *Tree of Life*, Part 2, Gate "The General *ABYA*," Chapter 2.

clothing the NHY of AA. They will never raise themselves above it. Even when they clothe the GAR of AA, they do not change their place, since at that time, AA rises to AB of AK, and his NHY are in the place of the previous GAR. Then ZA is drawn with them to the previous GAR of AA, but it does not change so as to rise above NHY of AA. Thus, the ascents never change the ladder of degrees.

The reason for this is that the main cause of all those ascents of the five Partzufim of Atzilut are the souls of the righteous. They raise MAN to ZON so that ZON would draw Mochin for them. These Mochin that ZON draw are drawn to him from the Partzufim above him through Ein Sof, and it is known that there is no absence in the spiritual and it cannot be said that they move from one place and come to another place. Rather, they stay in all the places they went through, since the root of anything in Kedusha [holiness] remains wherever it is, and only its illumination is extended downward. Moreover, the core and root of their illumination remains in their place, and their illumination exits.

For example, when ZA draws Mochin of Neshama, these Mochin come from Ein Sof to Partzuf Atik, which takes the level of Keter in this Neshama, by which he has an ascent to Partzuf SAG of AK. Afterward, it gives the Mochin to AA and takes the level of Hochma in Neshama, and by this he has an ascent to Partzuf Atik of Atzilut. He gives the rest of the Mochin to AVI, who take for themselves the level of Bina in Neshama, and by this they rise to the previous GAR of AA. They give the rest of the level, meaning VAK in Neshama, to ZA, and he has an ascent from the Tabur of AA to the Chazeh of AA. Thus, Atik took the Keter of Neshama, AA took the Hochma of Neshama, AVI took the Bina of Neshama, and only the VAK from them reached ZA.

It follows that now, too, after obtaining Neshama for ZA, the ladder of degrees has not changed at all, since as ZA grew in VAK, all the ones above him grew to the same extent: AVI in Bina, AA in Hochma, and Atik in Keter. Each one rose to a higher degree so that ZA remained in his initial place, which is Tabur of AA. However, since AA himself grew and ascended to the place of Atik, his Tabur also grew and ascended to the previous place of the Chazeh, and ZA was drawn along with it. It is likewise in the rest of the Mochin that ZA obtains: The upper ones grow first. For example, when ZA acquires Haya, the Chazeh of AA ascends to the place of his Garon and ZA is drawn along with him. In Yechida, the Garon of AA ascends to the place of his Galgalta and ZA is drawn along with him. Thus, the ascents do not change the place of the degrees at all, but there is only an overall growth here.

The ARI further clarifies this matter here, which is why he must clarify here the order of the emanation of the degrees in general and in particular. The ARI regards AA here as Keter and not as Atik, since Atik took Keter of MA and AA only Hochma of MA. The thing is that the ARI wants to detail five Partzufim here—AA, AVI, and ZON—and it is known that there is no existence to Partzuf Nukva before ZA obtains the level of Neshama, since then Nukva has a Partzuf back-to-back from the Chazeh of ZA and below. It is also known that when ZA obtains the level of Neshama, he ascends and clothes the Chazeh of AA, and AVI rise and clothe the GAR of AA where there is Hochma of MA, and AA ascends and clothes the GAR of Atik where there is Keter of MA. Thus, now AA already has the level of Keter, and this is why the ARI regards AA as Keter, AVI as Hochma, YESHSUT as Bina, ZA as Ruach, and Nukva as the Chazeh of ZA and below, which is Nefesh of Atzilut. So is always the conduct of the ARI: When he counts the five Partzufim of Atzilut, he does not count Atik because at that time, Atik has already ascended to SAG of AK and AA ascends to GAR of Atik and becomes Keter of MA, and AVI to Hochma of MA, YESHSUT to Bina of MA, and ZON to VAK of MA. But below, in item 253, when he explains the order of the emanation of the Partzuf, he actually begins with Partzuf Atik.

When Ein Sof emanated Keter, He made it from all five Partzufim, which are the Keter in it, AVI, and ZON in it. Here we should remember the two great distinctions that the ARI presented, and note them in every level of ten Sefirot, both from world to world, and from degree to degree: In the ten Sefirot of direct light, regarded as Keter, and four phases HB TM, there is no division between one world and the next, or between one degree and the next. As they are four phases in Atzilut, so they are at the end of Assiya. The only difference from one world to the next and from one degree to the next is only in the screen.

It is as he explains in the beginning of the chapter, that the ten Sefirot of direct light become coarser in an order of four phases, each coarser than the other. Phase one is Hochma, phase two is Bina, which is coarser than Hochma, phase three is ZA, which is even coarser, etc., and in the vessel of Malchut, a screen was established, which strikes and repels the light back as reflected light. He explained there that initially, the light of Ein Sof expanded by the order of the above-mentioned four phases of direct light until it reached the screen in the vessel of Malchut. Then the screen raised reflected light to the beginning of the level of direct light and clothes them, and then the self dresses in the vessels.

This matter requires a long clarification. I have already explained it in *The Study of Ten Sefirot*, and here I will bring only a brief summary sufficient for the matter before us. The vessel of Malchut is the primary vessel of reception of the Sefirot. All those four phases of coarseness that the ARI presents, in HB TM of direct light, are depicted primarily in the vessel of Malchut itself and in the screen in her. Hence, Malchut and the screen are divided into five phases of coarseness in which there are five levels of coupling by striking in the above manner one below the other.

The rule is that the coarser the screen, the higher the level of reflected light it raises. If the coarseness in the vessel of Malchut is fully complete, meaning in phase four, when the upper light strikes the screen in her, it raises reflected light that clothes up to the level of Keter of direct light. If the coarseness of the vessel Malchut is only of phase three, her reflected light that rises during the coupling by striking reaches only the level of Hochma of direct light, and this level of ten Sefirot lacks Keter. If the coarseness in Malchut is only phase two of coarseness, her reflected light reaches only the level of Bina of direct light, and the level lacks two Sefirot: Keter and Hochma. If there is only coarseness of phase one in Malchut, it clothes only the level of ZA and lacks KHB. If there is no coarseness in her at all, but only as the root phase of coarseness, she elicits only the level of Malchut, lacking the first nine Sefirot.

Through this screen, meaning according to those five phases of coarseness, the worlds were differentiated from one another, since in the world of AK, Malchut from coarseness of phase four operated. For this reason, her reflected light reached the level of Keter. This is why AK is called "the world of Keter." In Atzilut there was coarseness of phase three in Malchut; hence, she elicited there the level of Hochma. In Beria there was coarseness of phase two in her, and thus the screen elicited the level of Bina. In Yetzira there was coarseness of phase one in her, and thus the level of ZA emerged there, and in Assiya there was root coarseness in her, which is why there is only the level of Malchut there.

As the screen distinguishes one world from another, so it distinguishes between the five Partzufim in each world. The Keter of Atzilut emerges through a screen of phase four, and Hochma of Atzilut, called Abba, emerges on a screen of phase three, lacking Keter. Bina of Atzilut, called Ima or YESHSUT, emerges through a screen of phase two and lacks Keter and Hochma, and ZA of Atzilut emerges through a screen of phase one and lacks GAR, which are KHB. Nukva emerges from a screen of the root; hence, she lacks all first nine Sefirot.

All this pertains only to the level of the degree. However the ten Sefirot of direct light KHB ZA and Malchut are equal in all the worlds and all the Partzufim, since even in the world of Assiya, where there is only the level of Malchut, called NHY, lacking the first nine Sefirot, it does not mean that it completely lacks the first nine, since it is inconceivable that any degree would emerge without ten Sefirot of direct light in it: KHB, ZA, and Malchut. Rather, it means that in fact, she does have ten Sefirot, but since the coarseness in her is very faint, her reflected light is faint and reaches only the level of Malchut. As a result, all ten Sefirot in her will be only on the level of Malchut, since Keter will be on the level of Malchut, Hochma on the level of Malchut, Bina on the level of Malchut, ZA in her will be on the level of Malchut, and Malchut herself will be on the level of Malchut, since this distinction of level does not exist at all in the ten Sefirot of direct light.

It is likewise in the world of Yetzira where there is only the level of ZA: All ten Sefirot KHB ZON are on the level of ZA. Likewise, each of the ten Sefirot of Beria is on the level of Bina. Thus, the matter of the ten Sefirot of direct light and the matter of the level in those ten Sefirot are two completely separate distinctions, since there must be ten Sefirot of direct light in each level and in each degree, even in the smallest of the smallest. However, the level of those ten Sefirot is a different matter that depends on the measure of coarseness of the vessel of Malchut that operates in the degree in a coupling by striking, where the coarser it is, the higher the level that its screen raises.

This is the meaning of what the ARI says here, **"When Ein Sof emanated Keter, He made it from all five Partzufim, which are the Keter in it, AVI, and ZON in it,"** since the level of Keter of Atzilut, called Partzuf AA, emerged through a coupling by striking in the screen in the vessel of Malchut of coarseness of phase four. That is, the light of Ein Sof that consists of Keter and the four phases of direct light called HB TM expanded through the screen in the vessel of Malchut of phase four and struck it. By the force of the striking of the descent, it rose again as reflected light and clothed the Keter and the four phases HB TM of direct light. By this, the self clothed in the vessels and the degree was completed. Thus, as soon as these five phases of Keter and HB TM of direct light expand into the abovementioned coupling by striking, they are incorporated in one another and become twenty-five Sefirot, meaning five Sefirot clothing each other to the width, and in each of which there are five Sefirot KHB TM to the length on an even level.

The reason for it is that anything in Kedusha that moves from place to place, it does not mean that it became absent in its first place and came to another place as it is in corporeality. Rather, there is only an addition here, since it remained entirely in the first place even after its arrival at the second place. Since the Sefira of Keter is the root of all four phases of direct light, and they pass through it, they all leave their roots in it. Hence, only the Sefira of Keter contains all five phases KHB TM of direct light.

Also, the three Sefirot Bina and ZON that necessarily pass through the Sefira of Hochma of direct light leave their roots in it, so Hochma contains all four phases HB TM to its length, since all that is coarser from another is regarded as lower than it. For this reason, they seem to be one below the other to the length.

Also, the two Sefirot ZA and Malchut that pass through Bina leave their roots in it. This is why there are three Sefirot in the Sefirot of Bina: Bina, ZA, and Malchut. Similarly, the Sefira of Malchut remains in ZA, which contains two Sefirot, ZA and Malchut, and the Sefira of Malchut has only its own phase of direct light because no Sefira passes through it.

This incorporation is done by the five phases of direct light themselves before the coupling by striking that raises reflected light and clothes them through Keter takes place. At that time, Keter consists of five phases, Hochma of four phases, Bina of three phases, ZA of two, and Malchut of one.

However, after the coupling by striking is done and the reflected light rises and clothes them, the reflected light makes everyone's level even. It follows that now Hochma has gained the Sefira of Keter by the reflected light that clothed it and its level became even with Keter, Bina gained two phases, Keter and Hochma. through the reflected light, and her level, too, became even with Keter, etc., and Malchut gained four Sefirot KHB ZA and her level, too, became even with the Keter. Thus, the level of each of the five phases of direct light KHB TM is even through Keter. They clothe one another in thickness [coarseness], and each of them has five phases KHB TM at their length, for which they become twenty-five Sefirot.

All this is on the degree of the Rosh of the Partzuf. It is known that Malchut of Rosh returns and expands from above downward with the reflected light in her, and like them makes twenty-five Sefirot in the Guf, called the Toch of the Partzuf through the Tabur. Afterward, they expand in the Sof of the Partzuf in twenty-five Sefirot from Tabur down to the Sium Raglayim. Then, after this expansion into Rosh-Toch-Sof, she is called a Partzuf. That is, each Sefira of direct light in her, after expanding into Rosh-Toch-Sof, is called a Partzuf. Thus, those five Sefirot KHB TM that expanded to a coupling by striking in Malchut of the Rosh, and from expanded from there into the Toch-Sof through the Sium Raglayim, are now called five Partzufim AA, AVI, and ZON, which clothe one another on the thickness on an equal level, where each of them has also five Partzufim AA, AVI, and ZON to the length. It follows that the twenty-five Sefirot that emerged through a coupling by striking in Malchut of Rosh have now become twenty-five Partzufim.

This is why the ARI writes, **"When Ein Sof emanated Keter, He made it from all five Partzufim, which are the Keter in it, AVI, and ZON in it,"** as was explained above, that through the five phases of direct light that expanded into a coupling by striking in the screen in the vessel of Malchut, five Partzufim emerge: AA, AVI, and ZON, which clothe one atop the other in thickness on an equal level, and in each of them there are five Partzufim: AA, AVI, and ZON to the length. Together, they are twenty-five Partzufim, as mentioned above. Remember this for the rest of the words of the ARI.

Know that this coupling for Keter of the world of Atzilut was done in Malchut of the world above Atzilut, called "the world of AK." That is, the five phases of direct light that expand from Ein Sof pass through five Partzufim—AA, AVI, and ZON of AK—until they strike the screen in the vessel of Malchut of AK, and the screen raises reflected light that clothes these five phases of direct light. Then the Keter of Atzilut is emanated and becomes the five general Partzufim AA, AVI, and ZON, in thickness, where each of them has five Partzufim AA, AVI, and ZON to the length, and they clothe one another on an equal level. Then they descend from there to their place in Atzilut and clothe the line of Ein Sof that expands in Atzilut.

This thoroughly explains the first question that we asked, how is it possible that Keter will be the actual phase of Ein Sof since it is only a branch emanated by Malchut in the upper world, and Malchut is always a vessel. According to what was explained, it is clear that Keter and the four phases of direct light are extended only from Ein Sof. However, in order to clothe in reflected light, they make a coupling in a coupling by striking with Malchut of the upper one, and from the perspective of this coupling by striking that is done with Malchut of the upper one, this Malchut is regarded as the emanator of the lower world. However, the lights of direct light themselves come only from Ein Sof and pass through the five Partzufim of the upper world, each in its corresponding phase in the five Partzufim of the upper world.

Thus, the installing of Ein Sof—called the Sefira of Keter—on the four phases of direct light, is extended from the actual Ein Sof and passes through Partzuf Keter of AK. From it, the rest of the four phases of direct light expand through the four Partzufim of AK, HB TM, until they come in a coupling by striking in the vessel of Malchut of AK, clothe there in a garment of reflected light, and descend from there to their place in the world of Atzilut.

It follows that Keter is extended only from Ein Sof, it is truly Ein Sof, in itself and all that it receives from Malchut of the upper one is only a clothing in reflected light. Likewise, the other four phases of direct light are only branches of Keter and receive only the clothing of reflected light from Malchut of the upper one. What was said in several places, that Malchut of the upper one becomes Atik for the lower one, is a completely different matter that will be explained in its place. According to what was explained, we can understand the rest of the words of the ARI.

When He emanated the Keter in it, all the Ketarim [pl. of Keter] from there down were included in it one inside the other. Now the ARI explains the order of their clothing one another and the line of Ein Sof in Atzilut after they descended from Malchut of the upper one to their permanent place in Atzilut. Know that the ARI usually calls the five Partzufim to the length of the Partzuf by the names Keter ABYA, where the Rosh of the Partzuf through the Garon is called Keter, from the Garon to the Chazeh, it is called Atzilut, which is Partzuf Abba or AVI, from the Chazeh to the Tabur it is called Beria, and it is Partzuf Ima or YESHSUT, and from the Tabur to the Sium Raglayim of the Partzuf it is called Yetzira and Assiya, or ZON. Thus, there are five Partzufim here on an equal level in thickness—AA, AVI, and ZON—which clothe one another, and each of them has five Partzufim to the length called Keter, Atzilut, Beria, Yetzira, Assiya.

It has already been explained that these five Partzufim to the thickness that clothe one another, which are called AA, AVI, and ZON, are the self of the Sefirot of the five phases of direct light. The five Partzufim that emerged for each of them to the length, which are called Keter ABYA, come only from their incorporation in one another. As they emerge from one another, each leaves its root in the one above it, and for this reason they were incorporated in one another.

We should understand the big difference between the Partzufim of thickness and the Partzufim of length. The Partzufim of thickness are five degrees separate from one another in a manner of cause and consequence at great distances, since Partzuf Keter is the actual phase of Ein Sof and is the phase of emanator and the root of all of them. Partzuf Hochma is very different from it because it is already an emanated light. However, it is considered a second degree to Keter since the vessel in it is very thin and is still regarded as light without a vessel. It is known that as long as the light does not clothe in a vessel, it cannot be discerned as having exited from the state of the Emanator, and it is therefore close to the Keter.

However, Bina has grown far from Partzuf Hochma, which is Abba, since the root of the vessel is already in her, and the light in her is light of Hassadim and not of Hochma. ZA grew even farther because the vessel in him is close to the vessel of Malchut, and Partzuf Malchut is the most separate of all since it is already a complete vessel. This is how the five Partzufim of thickness are so distinguished from one another.

However, the five Partzufim to the length that exist in each of them come only from their incorporation in one another and do not change at all the actual Partzuf in the thickness. For example, Partzuf Keter is regarded as Ein Sof and the root of all four Partzufim. It was said that it comprises all of the other four Partzufim, which expand in it to its length, and are called ABYA. Being the root of Partzuf Hochma, which is Abba, when Abba departed from him, he left his root in him, called Atzilut in him, from the Garon to the Chazeh, and he is called Keter of Atzilut, meaning the root of Abba.

Also, when Keter emanated Partzuf Ima, she left her root in Keter and is called Beria from the Chazeh to the Tabur, and he is called Keter of Beria, meaning the root of Ima. Likewise, when Keter emanated the Partzufim of ZON, they left their root in him. These are called Yetzira and Assiya in Keter from his Tabur to his Sium Raglayim. This is called Keter of Yetzira and Keter of Assiya, meaning the root of ZA and the root of Nukva.

Thus, all those four Partzufim ABYA in Keter are merely roots, meaning they are all discerned as Ein Sof and have nothing of the quality of the four Partzufim, although each of the four Partzufim left its root in Keter because one does not give what one does not have, and also because they went out of him. Thus, it does not change the quality of Ein Sof in him, but rather Keter of Atzilut is regarded as the Keter of Abba, meaning his root. Likewise, Keter of Beria is regarded as the root of Partzuf Ima, and it is Ein Sof, and Yetzira and Assiya in him are regarded as the roots of the Partzufim of ZON, although they are Ein Sof. In this manner, all of those four Partzufim ABYA to the length of AA are all actual Ketarim and do not change in any way because they are roots of the four Partzufim AVI and ZON.

In the same manner, the five Partzufim to the length, Keter and ABYA, that exist in Partzuf Abba in the five Partzufim of thickness do not change the quality of Abba whatsoever. Although it is true that Abba is incorporated in them since he is their root and they passed through him, but the branch cannot change its root in any way. There is nothing of the quality of Ima in Beria of Abba. Rather, she is called Beria because she is the root of Ima, and likewise Yetzira and Assiya in Abba. Thus, all those five Partzufim to the length in Abba are discerned as Abba and are all Hochma. This means that they are the phase of emanated light that has no vessel.

Likewise, the five Partzufim to the length in Bina are all discerned as Ima and are all the phase of light of Hassadim. Although she consists of Keter and Hochma, it does not change her quality since the incorporation does not change the essence of the Partzuf at all. Similarly, the five Partzufim to the length in ZON are all regarded as ZON from their Rosh to their Sof.

This is the meaning of what the ARI says, **"When He emanated the Keter in it, all the Ketarim [pl. of Keter] from there down were included in it one inside the other down to Assiya. How? Keter of Atzilut clothes Keter of Beria, and Keter of Yetzira is over it, and Keter of Assiya is on it, clothing it."** He makes the precision of telling us that all those four Partzufim AVI and ZON included at the length of AA, called ABYA. They do not change his self whatsoever, which is Keter and Ein Sof, and they are all actual Ketarim, meaning they are all actually Ein Sof. However, we should discern in them that Atzilut in it is Keter to the phase of Abba, etc., and Yetzira and Assiya in it are Ketarim to ZON and slightly clothe one another along their length, since from the Garon to the Chazeh it clothes Keter of Atzilut, and from the Chazeh to the Tabur it clothes Keter of Beria, and from the Tabur down are the Ketarim of Yetzira and Assiya. The reason is that any phase that is attributed to the root of a coarser Partzuf is regarded as a lower root. Hence, they are arranged one below the other to their length, since Keter of Beria, which is the root of Ima, is coarser than Partzuf Abba. Therefore, it is considered that the Keter of Beria is below the Keter of Atzilut, which is the root of Abba, etc., likewise.

This reconciles the second question that we asked: Since each of the five Partzufim in the thickness has the same five Partzufim as in the length, what then is the difference between one Partzuf and the other? Now we thoroughly understand the great difference between them. For example, Partzuf Abba in AA, which is called the Atzilut in it, has no similarity at all to all five Partzufim of Abba to the thickness, since Atzilut of AA is truly Ein Sof but it is the phase of Keter of Abba. Conversely, the whole of Partzuf Abba from Rosh to Sof is the phase of emanated light and is not the phase of root and Ein Sof. Even the Keter of Abba of the thickness, which is Ein Sof, is nonetheless not regarded as actual Keter because it is in it only through equalizing the level of the reflected light that evens all the Sefirot to an equal level, and is only an installment of it in it. However, Atzilut of AA is regarded as actual Keter for the light of Ein Sof in the sense that it is the root and the emanator of the phase of Abba. In this way you can discern in each of the twenty-five Partzufim the special quality in it, which is very different from those like it that exist in other Partzufim.

The third question we posed there is also settled. We asked how it was possible that Abba in AA to the thickness could clothe the line of Ein Sof since he is phase two from Ein Sof, and all the more so the rest of the Partzufim Bina and ZON that are included in AA to the length. Now it is very clear, since all those four Partzufim ABYA included in AA to the length are not at all from the four Partzufim, but all of them are actual Ketarim and they are all the phase of Ein Sof. Therefore, all of them clothe the line of Ein Sof.

Similarly, since the five Partzufim to the length of Abba, which are Keter and ABYA of Abba, are all Hochma, which is the second degree of Keter, they clothe the Keter and ABYA of AA on an equal level. Likewise, since the five Partzufim to the length of Ima are all Bina, which are a second degree to Hochma, they clothe Keter and ABYA of Abba, which are Hochma, on an equal level. Similarly, the five Partzufim to the length of ZA, which are all small, clothe Keter and ABYA of Ima on an equal level since they are a second degree to them. In the same way, the five Partzufim to the length—Keter and ABYA of Nukva—are all females, which are a second degree to ZON. Therefore, they clothe Keter and ABYA of ZON on an equal level.

247) In the individual matter, the allegory is in this: Keter of AA and on it Keter Abba, on which there is Keter Ima and on it Keter ZA and on it Keter Nukva, and all this is in Atzilut. It is likewise in Ketarim of Beria and then in Ketarim of Yetzira, and afterward in Assiya.

Simple Light

247) In the individual matter, the allegory is in this: Keter of AA and on it Keter Abba, etc. He tells us here that even if you find that we detail each of the five Partzufim of the length of Keter into five new Partzufim, such as when AA emanates to Nefesh of Nefesh of Nefesh of the lower one, which must emerge from Partzuf Malchut of Assiya of AA, meaning a fifth Partzuf of the quality of Assiya in it, at that time, each of the Partzufim of the length will necessarily divide into five Partzufim again. He tells us that this does not mean that there is something in them from the four Partzufim to the thickness. Rather, even then they are all Ketarim, since the five Partzufim AA, AVI, and ZON that divide in Atzilut of AA are only Ketarim of those five Partzufim, and the five Partzufim AA, AVI, and ZON that divide again in Beria of Partzuf Keter are only Ketarim of five Partzufim and the parts of Yetzira and Assiya of Partzuf AA in a manner that the whole of the new division that was done in the five Partzufim of the length of AA that have now become twenty-five Partzufim to the length does not change the essence of the quality of Partzuf AA in any way, and all twenty-five Partzufim of the length are but twenty-five Ketarim.

Thus far, the ARI spoke only of the inner Partzuf of the five Partzufim of thickness of AA that clothe one another on an equal level, and which is called Partzuf Keter of AA or AA of AA. Initially, he explains the five Partzufim to the length in it, which are called Keter and ABYA of Partzuf Keter of AA. Then he also explains the division of each of these five Partzufim of Keter and ABYA into five new Partzufim to the length which he now calls AA, AVI, and ZON. These are now twenty-five Partzufim which are all only Ketarim.

In Item 248, the ARI explains the other four Partzufim on the thickness of AA, which are called Hochma, Bina, ZA, and Nukva, or AVI, YESHSUT, ZA, and

Nukva. In each of those four Partzufim there are also the same five Partzufim to the length, Keter and ABYA, which were explained here in the Partzuf Keter of AA, and sometimes they are classified into the twenty-five Partzufim of the length, as the ARI wrote about the Partzuf of AA.

Know that the division of the Partzuf at the thickness always precedes the length, for the length becomes itemized only by the incorporation of the parts on the thickness. Thus, once the five Partzufim of the thickness have been detailed into twenty-five Partzufim of the thickness that clothe one another on an equal level, the five Partzufim to the length are also detailed into twenty-five Partzufim one below the other.

248) When he emanated Hochma, all the Hochmot [pl. of Hochma] in the whole world were included in him, as was mentioned. It is likewise in Bina, in which there are all the Binot [pl. of Bina], and in ZA, all the Zeir Anpins in the whole world, and in Nukva, all the Nukvot [pl. of Nukva].

Simple Light

248) When he emanated Hochma, all the Hochmot [pl. of Hochma] in the whole world were included in him, as was mentioned. In other words, when Partzuf Keter of AA that consists of five Partzufim to the length which are all Ketarim emanated Partzuf Hochma of AA that clothes its thickness, it, too, consists of five Partzufim on its length, which are Keter and ABYA, like AA. However, these five Partzufim to the length of Partzuf Abba of the thickness, called Partzuf Hochma, are all Hochmot from its Rosh to its Sof, as written above, that the five Partzufim made in the length of each Partzuf do not change its own quality in any way since these three Partzufim Bina and ZON that were included in Abba as they pass through him do not create in him any coarseness or a vessel, and he remains entirely emanated light without any vessel as with the Sefira Hochma, since these Partzufim Beria, Yetzira, Assiya are only roots of the three Partzufim Bina and ZON to the thickness. Also, the Keter in him is only an induction of AA that is included in him but is not actually Keter like AA. This is the meaning of **"When he emanated Hochma, all the Hochmot [pl. of Hochma] in the whole world were included in him, as was mentioned"** in AA, meaning the Keter in him. Partzuf Atzilut, which is Hochma, dresses over him, and on him Hochma of Beria, and on him Hochma of Yetzira, and on him Hochma of Assiya, as mentioned about Keter and ABYA of AA.

It is likewise in Bina, in which there are all the Binot [pl. of Bina], and in ZA, all the Zeir Anpins in the whole world, and in Nukva, all the Nukvot [pl. of Nukva]. This is as was explained above concerning the two previous Partzufim. Likewise, the five Partzufim to the length of the third Partzuf of AA, which are Keter and ABYA of Bina in him, are all Binot. Also, Keter and ABYA of ZA of AA are all small. Even if those five Partzufim of his were to divide into another five Partzufim and he will have twenty-five Partzufim to the length, they would also be all small and there will not be anything in them that is not from the quality of KHB and not from the quality of Nukva of the thickness, and so forth through the end of the world.

This is so because as was explained above, all the division to the length comes only from the incorporation of the Partzufim in one another. For this reason, they do not change the essence of the Partzuf at all. It is likewise in the five Partzufim to the length—Keter and ABYA of Nukva of AA, for they all have one reason.

Thus, we have explained the twenty-five Partzufim of Partzuf Keter called AA of Atzilut, which are five Partzufim—AA, AVI, and ZON of AA—which clothe one another on an equal level to the thickness. In each of them there are five Partzufim to the length called Keter ABYA. The main difference in degrees is only the Partzufim of thickness, but in the Partzufim to the length there is no difference at all from the actual Partzuf of thickness. Rather, they are arranged one below the other according to the relation of the branches in the thickness, and each root of Hochma on the thickness is placed under Keter, each root of Bina in the thickness is under the Hochma, slightly clothing it, and likewise each root of ZA in the thickness is under Bina, slightly clothing it, and the root of the Nukva is under the root of ZA.

For this reason, Keter ABYA of AA in the thickness clothe the line of Ein Sof, Keter ABYA of Abba in the thickness clothe it on an equal level, Keter ABYA of Ima clothe it on an equal level, Keter ABYA of ZA in the thickness clothe it on an equal level, and Keter ABYA of Nukva in the thickness clothe it on an equal level. But the five Partzufim to the length in each one clothe one another only slightly and not on an equal level. Thus, Atzilut of each one slightly clothes Keter of each one and stands under it; Beria of each one slightly clothes Atzilut of each one and stands under it and so forth likewise.

249) When AA emanated Abba of Atzilut, the Keter in him took AA for himself and placed everything below his degree in Abba. Thus, all the Hochmot are placed in Abba, as was mentioned regarding AA, and likewise in Ima and in ZON, and in all three worlds BYA.

Simple Light

249) When AA emanated Abba of Atzilut, the Keter in him took AA for himself and placed everything below his degree in Abba. Here the ARI begins to explain the four garments of AA called AB, SAG, MA, BON. In each world, there is an inner HaVaYaH from which four Partzufim AB-SAG-MA-BON emerge one below the other. Partzuf AB, called Abba or upper AVI, emerges from the Yod of the inner HaVaYaH. Partzuf SAG that clothe from the Peh of Partzuf AB and below emerges from the Hey of the inner HaVaYaH. Partzuf MA that clothes from the Peh down of Partzuf SAG emerges from Vav of the inner HaVaYaH, and Partzuf BON emerges from the bottom Hey of the inner HaVaYaH.

The inner HaVaYaH of the world of Atzilut are the above-mentioned twenty-five Partzufim of AA, where the inner Keter ABYA of AA in the five Partzufim of the thickness of AA is regarded as the tip of the Yod of this HaVaYaH. The five Partzufim of the length of Abba of AA are Yod of the inner HaVaYaH. The five Partzufim of the length of Ima of AA are the first Hey of the inner HaVaYaH, the first Hey of the length of ZA of AA are the Vav of this HaVaYaH, and the five Partzufim of the length of Nukva of AA are the bottom Hey of this inner HaVaYaH. It has already been explained that all of them are on an equal level.

However, the four Partzufim AB-SAG-MA-BON that emerge from the four letters of the inner HaVaYaH emerge from four special couplings by striking: Partzuf AB emerges from a coupling by striking on a screen of coarseness of phase three, Partzuf SAG emerges through a screen of phase two, and Partzuf MA emerges through a screen of phase one. This is so because just as the five worlds AK and ABYA differ from one another by the coarseness of the screen in the vessel of Malchut, the five inclusive Partzufim in each world differ from one another by the coarseness in the screen.

Thus, Partzuf Keter of Atzilut emerged through a coupling by striking on a screen in a vessel of Malchut whose coarseness is phase four. When Partzuf Keter emanated Partzuf AB of Atzilut that emerges from Yod of his inner HaVaYaH, he extracted it through a coupling by striking on a screen in phase three, whose reflected light does not reach the level of Keter but only the level of Hochma, and that a coupling was done in Peh of Rosh of Partzuf Keter. Hence, it is considered that the level of Keter of Partzuf AB remains in the Peh of Rosh of Partzuf Keter and did not emerge with Partzuf AB that was emanated from it. Thus, all five phases of direct light are lacking on the level of Keter and begin from the light of Hochma.

It is considered that the light of Hochma clothed in Partzuf AB in a vessel of Keter. It follows that Keter has descended below the degree of Hochma. For this reason, Partzuf AB begins from the Peh of Partzuf Keter and below, where there are Hochma of the five Partzufim of the length of Keter. With regard to Keter, it is regarded as having no Rosh. Also, when Partzuf AB emanated Partzuf SAG of Atzilut, called Ima, he emanated it through a coupling by striking on the screen in phase two, whose reflected light reaches only the level of Bina. It follows that Ima, too, has no Hochma and has only from Bina down. When Ima emanated Partzuf ZA, she emanated it through a coupling on a screen of phase one, whose reflected light reaches only the level of VAK, and it has no Bina, too.

Therefore, you find that all the degrees gradually diminish because of the screen. For this reason, each lower one is regarded as having no Rosh compared to its upper one. Thus, AB has no Rosh compared to Keter and begins to clothe it from the Peh of Partzuf Keter downward. Likewise, SAG is regarded as having no Rosh compared to AB, and AB clothes only from the Peh of Rosh of AB and below, and MA, Partzuf ZA, is regarded as having no HGT of SAG, too, and clothes only from the Tabur down.

He says, **"When AA emanated Abba of Atzilut, the Keter in him took AA for himself, and placed everything below his degree in Abba. Thus, all the Hochmot are placed in Abba,"** as it is written, that he emanated Partzuf AB, which is called Abba, through a screen of coarseness of phase three which elicits only the level of Hochma. Thus, Keter of Abba remained in Peh of Rosh AA. This is why he says, **"Keter in him took AA for himself,"** and gave him only what is below his degree, meaning only from the level of Hochma and below. It is known that the essence of the Partzuf is determined by the highest phase in it, at the Rosh of its level. Hence, Abba is regarded as all Hochmot, as he says, **"All the Hochmot are placed in Abba,"** and there is no phase of Keter in him or from the other phases since it is valued entirely according to the uppermost phase in him.

He says, **"as was mentioned regarding AA,"** meaning that Partzuf Abba, too, divides into twenty-five Partzufim that are five Partzufim—AA, AVI, and ZON—that clothe one another on an equal level to the thickness, and in each of which there are five Partzufim Keter and ABYA to its length. The five Partzufim that clothe one another to the thickness and their incorporation in one another that makes in each of them five Partzufim to the length does not depend at all on the level of the degree, since those were made mainly by the five phases of direct light themselves. Rather, the reflected light equals their level to one another, but the level of the reflected light does not add or take away anything concerning the division in length and in thickness.

Thus, in Abba, too, there is an inner Partzuf called AA of Abba in which there is Keter and ABYA to its length, and it clothes from the Peh of the last Partzuf downward in the thickness of Partzuf Keter, meaning a Partzuf Nukva of Keter. On it, Keter and ABYA of Partzuf Abba of Abba clothe on an equal level, and Keter and ABYA of Partzuf Ima of Abba clothe it on an equal level. Keter and ABYA of ZA of Abba clothe it on an equal level, and Keter and ABYA of Nukva of Abba clothe it on an equal level just as has been explained concerning the twenty-five Partzufim of Keter. However, the difference between them is that although we divided between the five Partzufim of Keter that clothe one another to the thickness according to the distinctions of the five phases of direct light, they are all still regarded as Ketarim because their level is that they are all the level of Keter. However, regarding those twenty-five Partzufim of Abba, although for itself, we divide his five Partzufim of thickness according to the distinctions of direct light, they are all only Hochma since the highest phase in them is the level of Hochma.

And likewise in Ima and in ZON, meaning in the three Partzufim SAG, MA, and BON of Atzilut, which are called Ima and ZON that emerge from one another through three special couplings where SAG emerges from a screen of phase two and lacks a Rosh with respect to AB, and Nukva lacks a Rosh with respect to MA, which is ZA. However, in Ima, ZA, and Nukva, there are twenty-five Partzufim in each, as was explained concerning Keter and AB. Yet, all twenty-five Partzufim of Ima are Bina, since the highest phase in them is the level of Bina. Likewise, all twenty-five

Partzufim of ZA are on the level of VAK since the highest phase in them is VAK, and all twenty-five Partzufim of Nukva are Nukva since the highest phase in them is the level of Malchut called "the level of NHY." Nevertheless, we should discern in each of them that his five Partzufim of thickness that clothe one another on an equal level are also discerned according to the distinction in the five phases of direct light, as written above concerning Partzuf AB.

In this manner, there are two discernments to make in each Partzuf: The first is according to the five phases of direct light, where Keter in it is Ein Sof, Hochma in it is light that is emanated in a very thin vessel, Bina is light of Hassadim at the root of the vessel, the vessel of ZA is thicker, and Nukva is already a complete vessel. Likewise, the rest of the discernments that are there are according to the ten Sefirot of direct light. This discernment also applies to the five Partzufim of each degree that clothe the thickness of one another on an equal level.

We should make another discernment: According to values of level, where all twenty-five Partzufim in each degree are arranged according to their level, if the degree is on the level of Keter, all of his twenty-five Partzufim are regarded as Ketarim. If it is the level Hochma, all twenty-five Partzufim are regarded as Hochma. If it is the level of Bina, they are all regarded as Bina, if it is the level of ZA, they are all regarded as ZA, and if it is the level of Malchut, they are all regarded as Malchut. You already know that the level does not depend at all on the five phases of direct light, but only on the measure of coarseness in the screen on which the coupling by striking with the upper light is done.

And in all three worlds BYA, meaning the three worlds BYA below the Parsa of Atzilut. As has been explained concerning the five inclusive Partzufim of Atzilut, in each of which there are twenty-five Partzufim, this also applies to the three worlds BYA that are below the Parsa of the world of Atzilut. Thus, in AA of Beria there are five Partzufim AA and AVI and ZON that clothe one another on an equal level, and in each of them there are five Partzufim Keter and ABYA to the length. Likewise, there are five Partzufim AA, AVI, and ZON in Abba of Beria that clothe one another on an equal level on the thickness where in each of them there are five Partzufim Keter and ABYA on the length. Likewise, Ima of Beria has five Partzufim AA and AVI and ZON that clothe one another at an equal level where in each of them there are five Partzufim Keter and ABYA on the length. These three inclusive Partzufim emerge from one another in three special couplings and clothe one below the other.

We should know that AA of Beria lacks GAR and there is only the light of HGT in his Rosh. Inside the Sof of his Guf there is only light of NHY. And yet, it divides into five Partzufim on the thickness where in each there are five Partzufim on the length, since his Rosh is regarded as his Keter and his Toch through the Chazeh is regarded as Atzilut in him. His Sof from the Chazeh down is regarded as his BYA, and all of his five Partzufim on the thickness divide similarly. The inclusive Abba of Beria also lacks GAR, and light of HGT dresses in his Rosh, and only the light of NHY dresses in his Toch-Sof. Nevertheless, it divides into five Partzufim to the length as was explained regarding AA of Beria. Thus, the inclusive Abba of Beria also contains five Partzufim—Keter, AA, AVI, and ZON—on an equal level that clothe one another on the thickness, where in each of them there are five Partzufim on the length which are called Keter and ABYA.

The inclusive Partzuf Ima of Beria has complete GAR on the level of Bina, and she, too, has five Partzufim that clothe one another on an equal level on the thickness where in each of them there are five Partzufim Keter and ABYA on the length.

It is likewise in the Partzufim in Yetzira and Assiya since the three worlds BYA are regarded as one Partzuf where Beria is the Rosh, the world of Yetzira is regarded as the Toch, and the world of Assiya is regarded as NHY and Sof. Also, it is known that everything that is found in the Rosh is also in the Guf through the Tabur, which is called Toch, and it is also like that from Tabur down, which is called Sof.

250) Let us elaborate for you on the matter of ZA. Initially, ZA was emanated from Keter AA in which all of ZA is included. Then, AA took the part that belongs to the quality AA and the rest emerged in AVI, and then likewise in AVI. You find that the qualities of son and daughter, which are ZON of AA of Keter of Atzilut remain there, and the rest of the phases of ZON emerged (in AVI) in NHY of Tevuna, and then ZON remain there.

Simple Light

250) Let us elaborate for you on the matter of ZA. Initially, ZA was emanated from Keter AA, etc., then AA took the part that belongs to AA. This pertains to the clarification about the five inclusive Partzufim of Atzilut where he says, "When AA emanated Abba of Atzilut, the Keter in him took AA for himself. Thus, all the Hochmot are placed in Abba, and likewise in Ima and in ZON." Now the ARI explains one Partzuf from among them in detail so as to understand from it the four inclusive Partzufim that emerge through special couplings, and whose level gradually decreases because of the screen. This clarification mainly comes to show that with all the ascents that the Partzufim do, the ladder of degrees from the time they were created never changes.

It has been explained above that here the ARI calls Keter of Atzilut by the name AA, and AB of Atzilut by the name AVI, and SAG of Atzilut by the name YESHSUT. He says, **"Initially, ZA was emanated from Keter AA in which all of ZA is included."** This means that when the level of ZA emerged in AA, there was a complete level in him, KHB ZON. **"Then, AA took the part that belongs to the quality AA and the rest emerged in AVI,"** meaning that when he gave the level of ZA to AVI, he did not give them the full level of ZA through the Keter as it emerged in AA. Rather, he gave them from Hochma of ZA and below, and the level of Keter of ZA remains in AA himself. As Abba himself cannot receive from the quality of Keter of AA when he is emanated from him, for the same reason, he cannot receive anything from Keter of ZA. Rather, he receives from Hochma of ZA and below. **"And likewise in AVI,"** meaning that when AVI gave the level of ZA to YESHSUT, they gave only from Bina of ZA and below, while Hochma of ZA remains in AVI since YESHSUT is all Bina and cannot receive anything from the quality of Hochma. Likewise, when YESHSUT elicited the level of ZA from himself to the place of ZA, he gave him only the quality of VAK of VAK since he divides into two Tevunot [pl. of Tevuna] where Bina remains in the first Tevuna, and GAR of VAK are in the second Tevuna. Thus, when the level of ZA emerges, it necessarily emerges from the inner HaVaYaH, which is AA, and traverses the Partzufim AVI and YESHSUT that are above him. You find that the core and root of his illumination, which is Keter Hochma Bina of ZA, remains in those above him: Keter of ZA remains in AA, Hochma of ZA remains in AVI, Bina of ZA remains in YESHSUT, and only the branch comes to him, which is VAK, namely ZA of the level of ZA.

It was said, **"You find that the discernments of son and daughter, which are ZON of AA of Keter of Atzilut remain there."** This means that the quality of Keter ZON in AA is regarded as its ZON. Yetzira and Assiya of AA are Ketarim for ZON, and he remains there. It is written, **"The rest of the phases of ZON emerged (in AVI) in NHY of Tevuna, and then ZON remain there."** This means that after he emerges from AA, he traverses AVI and YESHSUT, and Hochma of ZON and Bina of ZON remain there, and only ZA of ZA reach his place, meaning VAK of ZA lacking his first three, which are Keter Hochma Bina that he left in the ones above him as he passed through them. It is written, **"In a manner that the root of ZON is that part of their Keter that was included in Keter of Atzilut, and the rest of the ZONs of the rest of the worlds and Partzufim are only illuminations."** In other words, the actual root of ZON should be viewed as only that part of ZON that remained in AA, which is the Keter of Atzilut, for "root" means Keter and Ein Sof. All those ZONs that traverse the rest of the Partzufim and worlds besides Keter, meaning in AVI and YESHSUT are regarded as mere illuminations for ZA and not as actual roots, since Hochma of ZA that remains in AVI is already regarded as an illumination of ZA and not as a root, and Bina of ZA that remains in YESHSUT is regarded as an illumination and not as a root. It is likewise in all the details that divide in the Partzufim AVI and YESHSUT, and only what is left in Keter is called root.

As has been explained regarding the beginning of Atzilut of ZON, so it is in all the Mochin and the upper ones of ZON. ZA takes from each degree that comes to him only the VAK, while Keter, Hochma, and Bina of the degree remain in the three inclusive Partzufim preceding him.

251) In a manner that the root of ZON is that part of their Keter that was included in Keter of Atzilut, and the rest of the ZONs of the rest of the worlds

and Partzufim are only illuminations, and so you should conclude about the rest of the Partzufim.

Simple Light

251) So you should also conclude about the rest of the Partzufim. In other words, all the particular and general Partzufim of NRNHY of ZA leave their main illuminations in the three Partzufim above him, for they leave there the Keter, Hochma, and Bina of the Partzuf Mochin, and only their VAK reach ZA. This is what makes the ladder of degrees never to change.

Since this matter is the cornerstone for understanding all the Mochin and ascents of all the Partzufim of ABYA, it is necessary to elaborate on the matters as much as possible. It is known that the ARI regards AA as Keter here, AVI as AB, YESHSUT as SAG, and ZON as MA and BON. It is so because he wants to speak of the five general Partzufim of Atzilut, and this can be depicted only after ZA has achieved GAR of Neshama. At that time, the female Partzufim begin to be built from his Chazeh and below back-to-back. In that state, it is necessary that AA has already risen to GAR of Atik and has become Partzuf Keter of Atzilut. Then AVI, too, rose to GAR of AA and became AB of Atzilut, YESHSUT, too, rose to the place of AVI, meaning from Garon of AA down, and became SAG of Atzilut, and ZA rose to the place of YESHSUT, meaning to Chazeh of AA and became VAK to YESHSUT, meaning VAK of SAG, regarded as Neshama of ZA. ZA always has the same Mochin of YESHSUT because they are regarded as Rosh ZA and ZA as their VAK. Hence, when YESHSUT has Mochin of SAG, ZA has GAR of Neshama. When YESHSUT has Mochin of AB, ZA has GAR of Haya, and when YESHSUT has Mochin of Yechida, ZA has GAR of Yechida, and remember this.

Chapter 14

252*) All four worlds ABYA were sorted by the sorting of the Melachim [kings]: The finest is in Atzilut, the one worse than it in Beria, from which Beria was made, and likewise in Yetzira, and then in Assiya. The worst of all, which could not be sorted and remained as a shell, are very hard judgments that could not be sorted out from the dross. Their sparks of Kedusha [holiness] remained inside the shells, and they are called "eleven marks of incense."

Simple Light

1) Indeed, in order to thoroughly understand the above words of the ARI, we must begin to interpret the five general Partzufim of Atzilut from the beginning of their emanation, from the Mochin that were established in them permanently, and of which they are never deficient. In this regard, the ARI wrote that in all five Partzufim of Atzilut there is only the level of MA, called "the new MA." Atik took Keter of MA, AA took Hochma of MA, AVI and YESHSUT took SAG of MA, and ZON took MA of MA, meaning ZAT of MA. The vessels of GAR and ZAT of Nekudim connected to them, and each one was corrected through its corresponding phase in MA. These vessels are what remained in GAR of Nekudim and are the ones that were sorted out from BYA and were corrected through the five Partzufim of MA of Atzilut. They are called "the five Partzufim of BON of Atzilut."

2) The ARI calls the five inclusive Partzufim of Atzilut by the name ten Sefirot of MA with regard to the five Partzufim of AK. This is so because there is correction to the five Partzufim of Atzilut only by their ascent and clothing the five Partzufim of AK on an equal level, which will happen at the end of correction. However, in the beginning of their correction through the Emanator, they received from the five Partzufim of AK only his level of MA. This means that when each Partzuf of Atzilut was established, it received the level of MA from its corresponding Partzuf in AK. Partzuf Atik received the level of MA from Partzuf Keter of AK, which is below the Tabur of Partzuf Keter of AK since the Rosh of each Partzuf is its Keter, and the Guf of each Partzuf through the Chazeh is Hochma in it or Atzilut or AB. From the Chazeh to the Tabur, it is Bina in it or Beria or SAG, and from Tabur down it is ZON in it, or MA and BON or Yetzira and Assiya.

3) Partzuf AA of Atzilut received from AK, MA of its Partzuf Hochma, meaning from Tabur of AB of AK and below, and it is called Hochma of MA or AB of MA. Partzuf AVI of Atzilut received MA of SAG of AK, called Bina of MA or SAG of MA, and Partzuf ZON received MA of MA of AK, below Tabur of Partzuf MA of AK called VAK of MA or MA of MA. We should know that GAR of Partzuf Nekudim are regarded as MA of AK, and ZAT of Nekudim are regarded as BON of AK. YESHSUT is tags, and MA and ZAT are BON and letters. This refers to MA and

---

* *Tree of Life*, Part 2, Gate "The General *ABYA*," Chapter 3.

BON of AK, which are the internality of GAR and ZAT of Nekudim, from which YESHSUT and ZON of Atzilut receive. YESHSUT receive from MA of AK, which are the internality of GAR of Nekudim, and ZON receive from BON of AK, which are the internality of ZAT of Nekudim.

4) Although Atik does not join the five Partzufim of Atzilut, this pertains only to the BON in him, which is Malchut of AK, the big Hey. But the level of MA is the small Hey of BeHibara'am [when they were created]. For this reason, from the perspective of MA, Atik joins the five Partzufim of Atzilut and is regarded as their Keter. Know that all the ascents of the Partzufim and the worlds are only according to the quality of MA, in which Atik is regarded as Keter and not as AA.

5) You find that each of the five Partzufim of Atzilut is only regarded as VAK, called MA with regard to its corresponding Partzuf in AK, and lacks three degrees— Keter, AB, SAG—with respect to its upper one. These three degrees receive the five Partzufim of Atzilut through the raising of MAN of the lower ones by prayers and Shabbats [pl. of Shabbat (Sabbath)], and special days. At that time, they rise and clothe the five Partzufim of AK. However, it is not permanent since in permanency, each has only the quality of MA of its upper one in AK, which is enough only to sustain the worlds, but not enough for the NRN of the righteous since they will not be able to receive from ZON when he has only VAK of MA. Hence, they raise MAN through good deeds and prayers and draw additions of Mochin to ZON. At that time, the NRN of the righteous will be able to receive their abundance from him. Because these Mochin above VAK of MA come only through good deeds and MAN of the righteous, they are not permanent in ZON since when the lower ones corrupt their actions and are unworthy of receiving abundance from ZON, the added Mochin promptly depart from ZON.

6) When the righteous raise MAN to ZON and draw for them Mochin of SAG, these Mochin must travel from Ein Sof through the Partzufim of AK and through all the Partzufim of Atzilut until they come to ZON from which they receive NRN of the righteous. This causes all the upper worlds to grow by the lower ones' raising of MAN, since the Mochin remains mainly in the upper ones and only a small branch of them reaches the lower ones.

7) When the Mochin come from Ein Sof to the five Partzufim of AK, they take from them everything that belongs to the quality of AK. Then the five Partzufim of AK give the Mochin of SAG to the five Partzufim of Atzilut. First they come to Atik of Atzilut, which is Partzuf Keter, who takes from them the Keter of SAG and gives the rest to AA of Atzilut. AA takes from them the Hochma of SAG and gives the rest to AVI of Atzilut, and AVI take from them the Bina of SAG and give the rest to YESHSUT and ZON of Atzilut, meaning the MA of SAG. YESHSUT take for themselves the Rosh of MA of SAG and give to ZON the VAK of MA of SAG where they become GAR of Neshama, and then the Mochin flow from ZON to the souls

of the righteous. Thus, the lower ones cannot receive anything from ZON before all the upper worlds grow.

8) Likewise, when the lower ones raise MAN in order to draw to ZON Mochin of AB called Mochin of Haya, first, the Mochin are drawn from Ein Sof through the five Partzufim of AK and come to Atik of Atzilut. Then Atik receives the Keter of AB for himself, and AA takes for himself the Hochma of AB and gives the rest to AVI. They take for themselves the Bina of AB, and give MA of Bina of AB to YESHSUT and ZON. YESHSUT receive the Rosh of MA of AB, and ZON the VAK of MA of AB, which become in him GAR of Haya. At that time, ZON take their part and impart the rest to NRN of the righteous. This very order applies also when the lower ones draw the Mochin of Haya: Atik, AA, and AVI take the KHB of Yechida, YESHSUT and ZON the MA of Yechida, where YESHSUT receive the Rosh of MA of Yechida and ZON receive the VAK of MA of Yechida, and the rest is imparted upon the NRN of the righteous.

9) According to the above you will understand the exact order of ascent of the Partzufim and the worlds when the Mochin of Keter AB SAG are bestowed upon the five Partzufim of Atzilut. When the Mochin of SAG of AK are bestowed upon the five Partzufim of Atzilut, Atik takes Keter of SAG. Accordingly, Atik makes one ascent from the place of MA of Partzuf Keter of AK, meaning from the broken place Tabur of Partzuf Keter of AK, and rises and clothes the place of SAG of Partzuf Keter of AK, which is the place of the Chazeh of Partzuf Keter of AK.

Partzuf AA of Atzilut, which takes Hochma of SAG, also makes one ascent from the place of MA of AB of AK, which is from his Tabur and below, to the place of SAG of AB of AK, which is the place of the Chazeh of AB of AK and clothes there.

The Partzufim of AVI of Atzilut also make one ascent from the place of MA of SAG of AK, which is the place below Tabur of SAG of AK to the place of SAG of SAG, meaning the place of Chazeh of SAG of AK.

Likewise, YESHSUT of Atzilut make one ascent from the place of MA of MA of AK, which is from Tabur of MA of AK and below, to the place of SAG of MA of AK, meaning to the place of Chazeh of SAG of MA of AK. Likewise, ZON make one ascent from the place of VAK of MA of MA of AK to the place of VAK of SAG of MA of AK.

Likewise, the souls of the righteous rise along with the world of Beria to the place of Nukva of ZA, meaning to the Chazeh and below of ZA of Atzilut, and Ruach of the righteous rises with the world of Yetzira from their place to the place of Beria. Likewise, Nefesh of the righteous rises with the world of Assiya to the place of Yetzira.

10) When the Mochin of AB of AK are imparted upon the five Partzufim of Atzilut, which are Mochin of Haya, Atik of Atzilut takes from them the Keter of AB and makes a second ascent from the place of Chazeh of Partzuf Keter of AK to the Peh of Partzuf Keter of AK, which is from the place of SAG to the place of AB of Partzuf Keter.

AA takes from them the Hochma of AB and ascends from the place of SAG of AB of AK, which is the place of his Chazeh, to the place of the Peh and below of Partzuf AB of AK which is AB of AB.

Likewise, AVI make a second ascent from the place of SAG of SAG of AK, which is the place of Chazeh of SAG of AK, to the place of the Peh of Partzuf SAG of AK, which is the place of AB of SAG of AK.

Also, YESHSUT rise from the place of SAG of MA of AK, which is the Chazeh, to the place of AB of MA of AK, which is his Peh.

Also, ZON rise from the place of VAK of SAG of MA of AK to the place of VAK of AB of MA of AK which is AB of BON of AK.

In addition, the souls of the righteous ascend with Beria from the place of Nukva of ZA, which is the place from Chazeh of ZA and below, to the place of Peh of ZA, which is from the place of Tabur of AA of Atzilut. Also, Ruach of the righteous ascends with the world of Yetzira to the place of Nukva of Atzilut, which is from Chazeh of ZA and below, and Nefesh of the righteous ascends with the world of Assiya from the place of Yetzira to the place of Beria.

11) When the Mochin of Keter of AK are imparted upon the five Partzufim of Atzilut called Mochin of Yechida of AK, Atik of Atzilut takes from them the Keter of Keter and makes a third ascent from the place of Peh of Partzuf Keter of AK, which is the place of AB, to the place of his Galgalta, and clothes the Rosh of Partzuf Keter of AK which is the place of Yechida of Keter of AK.

Likewise, AA makes a third ascent from the place of Peh of Partzuf AB of AK, which is AB of AB of AK, to the place of Rosh of Partzuf AB of AK, which is the place of Yechida of AB of AK.

Additionally, AVI of Atzilut make a third ascent from the place of Peh of Partzuf SAG of AK to the place of Rosh SAG of AK, where there is Yechida of SAG of AK.

Also, YESHSUT make a third ascent from the place of Peh of Partzuf AB of MA of AK to the place of Rosh MA of AK, where there is Yechida of MA of AK.

And ZA ascends from the place of VAK of AB of MA of AK to the place of VAK of Yechida of MA of AK, which is the Rosh of BON of AK, since in general, VAK of MA are Rosh-Toch-Sof of BON of AK, as mentioned in Item 3.

Also, the souls of the righteous make a third ascent with the world of Beria from the place of Peh of ZA, which is in the place of Tabur of AA, to the place of Rosh ZA of Neshama, which is the place of Chazeh of AA of Atzilut. Also, Ruach of the righteous ascends with the world of Yetzira from the place of Nukva of ZA to the place of Peh of ZA at the place of Tabur of AA, and Nefesh of the righteous ascends with the world of Assiya from the place of Beria to the place of Nukva of Atzilut, which is from Tabur of ZA of Atzilut and below.

You find that now the five Partzufim of Atzilut have ascended and clothed each one its corresponding Partzuf in AK, and the three worlds BYA below Parsa of Atzilut, ascended with the NRN of the righteous and clothed BYA of Atzilut above the Parsa. This is the completion of the ascent of the worlds that unfold during the six thousand years.

12) Indeed, all those ascents that were scrutinized do not mean that each of the five Partzufim of Atzilut entered among the Partzufim of AK to clothe its corresponding Partzuf there. This is impossible since the five Partzufim of AK and the five Partzufim of Atzilut stand and clothe each lower Partzuf from the Peh of the upper one downward. AB dresses Partzuf Keter of AK from his Peh down, SAG dresses AB from the Peh down, MA of AK from Tabur of SAG of AK downward, and BON of AK from the Peh of MA of AK and below. Atik of Atzilut is over MA and BON of AK, which is from Tabur of SAG and below, and AA dresses from Peh of Atik downward. AVI clothe from Peh of AA and below, YESHSUT clothe from Chazeh of AVI and below, and ZON clothe from Tabur of AA and below. This is the order of clothing in the constant state, when there is only the level of the new MA of the five Partzufim of AK in the Partzufim of Atzilut. Accordingly, you will understand that the ascents are actually on the externality of the Partzufim of AK although they aim opposite the Partzuf opposite from it in the internality of AK. It is likewise with the ascents in the five Partzufim of Atzilut themselves, from Partzuf to Partzuf.

To understand this, we must first know the exact meeting points between Keter and ABYA of each lower Partzuf in the place of Keter and ABYA of the Partzuf above it, both in the five Partzufim of AK and in the five Partzufim of Atzilut.

13) You already know that each Partzuf divides into Keter and ABYA where its Rosh is called Keter, its Toch from Peh to Chazeh is called Atzilut or AB, from the Chazeh down to the Tabur it is called Beria or SAG, and from Tabur down to the Sium Raglayim it is called Yetzira and Assiya, or MA and BON, or simply MA. We must always remember that any Rosh is Keter and is Yechida, and its Sium is the Peh. Also, from the Peh to the Chazeh it is Hochma, Atzilut, AB, Haya, and every Chazeh through Tabur is Bina, SAG, Beria, Neshama. Also, anything from Tabur downward is ZON, MA and BON, VAK without a Rosh, Yetzira and Assiya, Ruach Nefesh.

However, this above comparison is completely accurate only in Partzuf Keter which has the level of Keter and Yechida. The NRNHY are divided in it in complete accuracy. In the rest of the Partzufim from Hochma downward, which gradually diminish, the above division is not completely accurate but only relative. That is, it is correct only from its own perspective and not from the general NRNHY.

14) Before we come to arrange the state of the clothing of the Partzufim and their meeting points with one another we should first introduce four truths: The first is that those two Partzufim called MA and BON of AK that we already spoke of have Keter ABYA in each of them. MA begins from Tabur of the inner AK, called Keter, and ends equally with the Raglayim of Atzilut. Clothing ABYA of MA of AK are Keter

and ABYA of BON of AK, which are the internality of GAR and ZAT of Nekudim that clothe them—GAR on MA of AK at an equal level, and ZAT of Nekudim before their breaking clothed BON of AK at an equal level. Now, in the world of correction, when Atik of Atzilut clothes GAR of Nekudim through their Peh, you find that the level of Atik of Atzilut is equal to the level of MA of AK, and it is known that AA of Atzilut clothes from Peh of Atik downward. Thus, it takes the whole place of ZAT of Nekudim whose level was equal with Partzuf BON of AK. You find that the level of AA is equal to Partzuf BON of AK.

The second is that YESHSUT, which are the bottom Partzuf of AVI and are regarded as ZAT of SAG at their source, in order to engender Mochin for ZA, AVI elicited YESHSUT outside of their degree and became Rosh of MA. That is, they became recipients of Mochin for ZA, for the world was unfit to receive the quality of Rosh and GAR were YESHSUT not diminished and emerged from the quality of SAG to the quality of Rosh of MA, since by this they bestow Rosh and GAR to ZA. For this reason, we should make two discernments in YESHSUT: The first YESHSUT is HGT of AVI and ZAT of SAG, and the second YESHSUT is NHY of AVI and GAR of MA.

The third is that all that is imparted upon this second YESHSUT prior to the end of correction is from Partzuf MA of AK as it is regarded as the Rosh of BON of AK, and all that is imparted from AK to ZA is only from BON of AK, regarded as VAK of MA of AK. This depends on what is explained in the second truth.

The fourth is that it is known that AB SAG of AK ended above Tabur of Partzuf Keter of AK. However, when the five Partzufim of AK received the level of the new MA for the purpose of the correction of the five Partzufim of Atzilut, AB SAG of AK grew longer and extended below Tabur of AK through the Tabur of Partzuf MA and BON of AK.

15) Now we will explain the order of the clothing of the five Partzufim of AK and their meeting point with one another. Typically, Partzuf Keter of AK is regarded as the inner HaVaYaH and divides at its length into Keter and ABYA, and the other four Partzufim are its four garments. Keter and ABYA of AB of AK clothes from the Peh down. It is clear that as the uppermost phase of Partzuf AB descended one degree from Partzuf Keter, so does each of the other phases of AB descend one degree. Thus, Keter of AB of AK clothes the Atzilut of Partzuf Keter of AK; therefore, Atzilut of AB also necessarily descends and clothes Beria of Partzuf Keter, Beria of AB clothes Yetzira of Partzuf Keter, and Yetzira and Assiya of AB clothe Assiya of Partzuf Keter.

16) Partzuf SAG of AK also descended one degree from Partzuf AB of AK since it lacked Hochma. Compared to Partzuf Keter, it descended two degrees: Keter as well as Hochma. You find that Keter and ABYA of Partzuf SAG of AK clothe ABYA of Partzuf AB and BYA of Partzuf Keter. Also, Keter SAG of AK clothe Atzilut of AB of AK, meaning from his Peh to his Chazeh, and clothed within him is Beria of Partzuf Keter of AK from his Chazeh to Tabur. Atzilut of Partzuf SAG clothes Beria

of Partzuf AB from the Chazeh to his Tabur, and in him, Yetzira of Partzuf Keter of AK is from his Tabur down. Beria of Partzuf SAG clothes Yetzira of Partzuf AB from his Tabur down, and in him is Assiya of Partzuf Keter of AK, and Yetzira of SAG clothes Assiya of Partzuf AB.

17) Partzuf MA of AK descended one degree from SAG because it lacks Bina, and two degrees HB from Partzuf AB, and three degrees KHB from Partzuf Keter. You find that Keter of Partzuf MA of AK clothes Atzilut of SAG of AK, within which is Beria of AB, within which is Yetzira of Partzuf Keter, meaning below the Tabur. Atzilut of MA clothes Beria of Partzuf SAG, within which is Yetzira of AB, and within it Assiya of Partzuf Keter. Beria of MA clothes Yetzira of SAG within which is Assiya of AB, and Yetzira of MA clothes Assiya of Partzuf SAG.

18) Partzuf BON of AK descends one degree from Partzuf MA of AK, two from SAG, three from AB, and four from Partzuf Keter. Keter of BON clothes Atzilut of MA, within which is Beria of SAG, within which is Yetzira of AB, within which is Assiya of Partzuf Keter of AK. Atzilut of Partzuf BON of AK clothes Beria of MA, within which is Yetzira of SAG, within which is Assiya of AB. Beria of Partzuf BON of AK clothes Yetzira of MA, within which is Assiya of SAG, and Yetzira and Assiya of Partzuf BON of AK clothe Assiya of Partzuf MA of AK.

19) It follows from the above that the Rosh of Partzuf Keter of AK is revealed, and Atzilut of Keter is in the first clothing of Rosh AB, Beria of Partzuf Keter is inside Atzilut of AB inside Rosh of SAG, Yetzira of Partzuf Keter is inside Beria of AB, and inside Atzilut of SAG, inside Keter of MA. Also, Assiya of Partzuf Keter is inside Yetzira of AB, inside Beria of SAG, inside Atzilut of MA, inside the Rosh of BON.

The second part of Assiya of Keter is inside Assiya of AB, inside Yetzira of SAG, inside Beria of MA, inside Atzilut of BON. The third part of Assiya of Keter is inside the second part of Assiya of AB, inside Assiya of SAG, inside Yetzira of MA, inside Beria of BON. Also, Assiya of Partzuf MA is inside Yetzira and Assiya of BON.

20) Now we will thoroughly understand how each of the five Partzufim of Atzilut must extend its Mochin from its corresponding Partzuf in the five Partzufim of AK, and yet does not enter among the Partzufim of AK but only ascends in the externality of all the Partzufim of AK, but aiming opposite the meeting point of its corresponding Partzuf that stands in the internality of AK.

We will begin with the beginning of the emanation of the five Partzufim of Atzilut when they first emerged from the five Partzufim of AK. It has already been explained that initially, they received from AK only its MA. However, this does not pertain to Partzuf MA of AK that clothes from Tabur of Partzuf Keter of AK downward, since this is regarded as the VAK of AK itself. Rather, it pertains to the quality of MA of each and every Partzuf of the five Partzufim of AK, called Yetzira and Assiya of each of the five Partzufim of AK. For this reason, the ARI calls this MA of each of the Partzufim of AK by the name "the new MA," so as not to mistake it for the MA of AK itself.

Atik of Atzilut received Keter of MA and then rose and clothed GAR of Nekudim, which are on the same level as Partzuf MA of AK within which is Atzilut of SAG, within which is Beria of AB of AK, within which are Yetzira and Assiya of Partzuf Keter of AK, which is the MA of Keter of AK. From this MA of Partzuf Keter of AK, Atik receives the Keter of MA since MA of Keter has the same relation as the Keter of MA. Thus, Atik of Atzilut truly clothes the externality of the Partzufim of AK, meaning the Rosh of MA of AK, which is its external Partzuf in this place. However, he does not receive from him because he is attributed to YESHSUT and ZON of Atzilut. Rather, there, in that place in the internality of AK, is the meeting point of MA of Partzuf Keter of AK, which is why he can receive from him the Keter of MA, and it is known that MA of Keter is the same phase as Keter of MA.

21) In this manner, when AA of Atzilut received Hochma of MA, he rose and clothed Atzilut of Atik, which is from Peh of Rosh of Atik and below. There is the meeting point of Yetzira and Assiya and MA of Partzuf AB of AK from which he receives the Hochma of MA, since Atzilut of Atik is on Keter BON of AK, within which is Atzilut of MA of AK, within which is Beria of SAG of AK, within which is MA of Partzuf AB of AK from which AA receives his Hochma of MA, since MA of Hochma of AK has the same relation as Hochma of MA. Thus, the place of Atzilut of Atik, where AA rose when he was emanated, aims for the meeting point with MA of AB that is attributed to AA.

22) Likewise, AVI of Atzilut, who received upon their emanation the level of Bina of MA, need to receive it from Yetzira and Assiya and MA of SAG of AK since they are attributed to Bina. For this reason, they rose to the place of Atzilut of AA from his Peh to his Chazeh, which is the meeting place with MA of SAG of AK, since within Atzilut of AA, Beria of Atik is clothed, and in it Atzilut of BON of AK, within which is Beria of MA of AK, within which are Yetzira and MA of SAG of AK, which are MA of Bina, from which AVI receive Bina of MA since MA of Bina is Bina of MA. Thus, the place of emanation of Atzilut of AA, where AVI rose upon their emanation, aims for the meeting point with Yetzira and Assiya of SAG of AK attributed to AVI.

23) The first YESHSUT are regarded as ZAT of Bina. Hence, they receive the phase of ZAT of the level of Bina of MA together with AVI. The second YESHSUT take GAR of VAK of MA of MA and clothe from the Chazeh of AA and below to Beria of AA which is the meeting place with MA of Partzuf MA of AK.

24) Upon the emanation of ZON that receive only VAK of MA when they are emanated, they must receive from Partzuf BON of AK that is attributed to them. Hence, they rose and clothed Yetzira and Assiya of AA, meaning from his Tabur down, which is the meeting place with Yetzira and Assiya of BON of AK, regarded as VAK of MA, since the level of AA is equal to the level of BON of AK.

Thus we have thoroughly explained the order of the emanation of the five Partzufim of Atzilut from their beginning, meaning in the five levels of MA that took from the five Partzufim of AK, where each clothes its upper one, but aiming opposite the meeting point with the Partzuf of AK attributed to it.

25) You find that Atik of Atzilut, which took GAR of Nekudim, begins from Tabur of AK since GAR of Nekudim began from Tabur of AK. Hence, it clothes MA and BON of AK, meaning on an equal level with Rosh MA of AK and receives through there from Yetzira and Assiya of Partzuf Keter of AK. AA clothes Atzilut of Atik from Peh to the Chazeh, and receives through there Hochma of MA, from Yetzira and Assiya of AB of AK. AVI clothe Atzilut of AA from Peh to [the Chazeh] the Tabur. Through there they receive Bina of MA from Yetzira and Assiya of Partzuf SAG of AK. Also, YESHSUT clothe AVI and receive ZAT of SAG of MA. ZON clothe AA from the Tabur down, and through there, ZAT of VAK of MA receive from Yetzira and Assiya of BON of AK, which is VAK of MA. All these levels of MA that received from the five Partzufim of AK are regarded as the core of their emanation and no diminution or change will ever happen in them because Atik will never diminish more than the level of Keter of MA, or AA from the level of Hochma of MA, or AVI and YESHSUT from the level of Bina of MA, or ZON from ZAT of VAK of MA.

26) The parts of BON that were established with the above-mentioned five levels of MA also stay permanently and no diminution will ever happen in them. It has already been explained above that all the vessels of GAR and ZAT of Nekudim that were revoked and broken are called BON after they were corrected through the five above-mentioned levels of MA.

In Atik, GAR of ZON in Nekudim were corrected, meaning the first five of Keter of Nekudim, and GAR of Abba of Nekudim, and the first four of Ima of Nekudim, and the seven Ketarim. They were connected and merged with the level of Keter MA, which Atik took from MA of Partzuf Keter of AK and they became one Partzuf, Atik and his Nukva. The level of MA is the male of Atik, and the level of BON became his Nukva.

Through Hochma of MA that AA took from MA of AB of AK, the bottom half of Keter of Nekudim was corrected and became Nukva to him. Through Bina of MA that AVI and YESHSUT took from MA of SAG of AK, VAK of Hochma were corrected, Bina of Nekudim. Through ZAT of VAK of MA that ZA took, ZAT of Nekudim were corrected.

27) The reason why the parts of Nekudim were divided specifically among the five Partzufim of Atzilut in the above manner has been thoroughly explained. However, in general, this whole correction that the vessels of Nekudim received through the above-mentioned five levels of MA are nothing more than the VAK of each Partzuf in Nekudim. Even those GAR of Abba and first four of Ima of Nekudim that Atik took are only regarded as VAK of GAR of HB of Nekudim since they are regarded as AVI of Nekudim that emerged in Katnut Nekudim as back-to-back. The reason why nothing more than VAK was corrected in them is simple: Their whole correction came through MA that the five Partzufim of Atzilut received from Yetzira and Assiya

of the five Partzufim of AK, which are regarded as VAK of the five Partzufim of AK, since MA and Yetzira and Assiya, or Nefesh Ruach, are all one and are regarded as VAK without GAR. GAR is called KHB or Keter AB SAG, or Yechida Haya Neshama, and you see that all that was corrected in the constant five Partzufim of Atzilut is only the level of MA, which is VAK from the five Partzufim of AK. Hence, it is enough to come from the judgment in order to be as the accused, and the vessels of Nekudim, too, could be corrected only in the VAK in them.

However, when the five Partzufim of Atzilut permanently receive their missing first three, which are the three phases Keter-AB-SAG, when each Partzuf receives from its corresponding Partzuf in AK, the correction of the vessels of Nekudim will also be completed in their GAR. At that time, all the Parsas will be canceled and this will be the end of correction. Then the five Partzufim of Atzilut will rise and clothe the five Partzufim of AK permanently, on an equal level.

However, even before the correction, the five Partzufim of Atzilut receive GAR of AK through the good deeds and raising MAN of the NRN of the righteous and on special days and Shabbats [Sabbaths], until you find that by the Mincha [afternoon] of Shabbat, each of the five Partzufim of Atzilut has obtained its corresponding GAR in the five Partzufim of AK. At that time, Atik receives the Keter of Partzuf Keter of AK and is with him on the same level, AA receives Keter of Partzuf AB of AK and is with him on the same level, AVI receive the Keter of Partzuf SAG of AK and are with him on the same level, and YESHSUT receive the Keter of Partzuf MA of AK and are with him on the same level. Also, ZA receives the Keter of BON of AK and he is with him on the same level.

However, at that time, Nukva of ZA receives the quality of Atzilut of BON of AK since she will not be able to become corrected even if not permanently before the end of correction. You find that even prior to the end of correction, the five Partzufim of Atzilut will be able to receive their GAR from the five Partzufim of AK. However, there are three flaws here: 1) It is not permanent. 2) The three worlds BYA can receive their lights only through an ascent to Atzilut, above the Parsa, and BYA in their place are devoid of light. 3) The Nukva will not be able to receive her Yechida from Keter BON of AK since her ascent is only through Atzilut of BON. But at the end of correction, Nukva, too, will receive her Keter, the Parsa will be revoked, and the Raglayim of Atzilut will spread to BYA as in Raglayim reaching Raglayim, since the Raglayim of Atzilut will then be equal to the Raglayim of AK that end at the point of this world, and they will remain permanently since all the shells will end. However, afterward there will be many ascents, and we should not prolong.

28) We should also explain the matter of the meeting place of the five Partzufim of Atzilut, each with its corresponding phase in AK when they attain the first three from the five Partzufim of AK. When the lower ones raise MAN and Mochin of SAG are imparted from Ein Sof to the five Partzufim of AK for the purpose of the five

Partzufim of Atzilut, they first reach Atik. Afterward, Atik rises from its permanent place in Keter MA of AK to the place of Rosh of SAG, within which is Atzilut of AB of AK, in which is Beria of Partzuf Keter of AK. From there Atik takes the Mochin of SAG attributed to him, which are Keter of SAG, since SAG of Partzuf Keter has the same relation as Keter SAG.

When AA receives Mochin of SAG, it rises from its permanent place, from the place of Atzilut of Atik, to GAR of Atik in which there is Keter MA of AK, in which is the Atzilut of SAG of AK, within which is Beria of AB of AK. From there he takes Mochin of SAG attributed to him, which are Hochma of SAG, since SAG of AB has the same relation as Hochma of SAG.

When AVI receive Mochin of SAG of AK, they rise from their permanent place, from the place of Atzilut of AA, to the place of GAR of AA, within which is Keter BON of AK, within which is Atzilut of MA of AK, in which is Beria of SAG of AK. From there they take their Mochin of SAG, meaning Bina of SAG, since SAG of SAG of AK has an equal relation to Bina of SAG.

29) When YESHSUT receive Mochin of SAG of AK, they rise from their permanent place, which is in the place of Chazeh of AA and below, where there is Beria of AA, to the place of AVI, the place of Atzilut of AA. In it is Atzilut of BON of AK, within which is Beria of MA of AK, and from there YESHSUT take their Mochin of SAG, which are from Rosh of SAG of MA.

Also, ZON rise from their permanent place of Tabur of AA, to Beria of AA, the place from the Chazeh of AA and below, where Beria of BON of AK is clothed. From there they take their Mochin of SAG, which are the Mochin of VAK of SAG of MA, since BON of AK in general is VAK of MA.

The three worlds BYA below the Parsa are drawn after them. Each of them makes one ascent: Beria to the place of Nukva of Atzilut, the world of Yetzira to the place of the world of Beria, the world of Assiya to the place of the world of Yetzira, and NRN of the righteous rise along with them.

30) When the raising of MAN from the lower ones reaches the extension of Mochin of AB to the five Partzufim of Atzilut and they are imparted from Ein Sof to the five Partzufim AK, they first reach Atik. At that time, Atik ascends from the place of Keter of SAG to the place of Rosh of AB of AK, within which is the Atzilut of Partzuf Keter of AK. From there he takes his Mochin of AB, which are Keter of AB, since AB of Keter is the same phase as Keter of AB.

Also, AA rises from the place of Rosh Atik to the place of Rosh of SAG, within which is Atzilut of AB of AK, and from there he takes his Hochma of AB.

Also, AVI rise from the place of GAR of AA to the Rosh of Atik, in which is Keter of MA of AK, within which is Atzilut of SAG of AK, and from there they take the Bina of AB attributed to them.

Additionally, YESHSUT rise from the place of AVI, which is the place of Atzilut of AA, to the place of GAR of AA, within which is Rosh of BON, within which is Atzilut of MA, and from there they take the Rosh of AB of MA.

Also, ZON rise from Beria of AA to the place of Atzilut of AA, which is the permanent place of AVI, within which Atzilut of AA is clothed, and in it is Atzilut of Partzuf BON of AK. From there they take their Mochin of AB, which are VAK of MA of AB. BYA from below the Parsa of Atzilut are drawn after them, and Beria ascends from the place of Nukva of Atzilut to the place of ZA of Atzilut, Yetzira to the place of Nukva of ZA of Atzilut, and Assiya to the place of Beria of Atzilut, and with them NRN of the righteous ascend, as well.

31) On Shabbat, at Mincha [afternoon prayer], when Mochin of Yechida are drawn to the five Partzufim of Atzilut from the five Partzufim of AK, they reach Atik. At that time, Atik ascends to the Rosh of Partzuf Keter of AK, and from there Keter of Yechida receives what is attributed to him, AA ascends to the Rosh of Partzuf AB of AK and receives from there the Hochma of Yechida attributed to him, AVI ascend to Rosh of SAG of AK and receive from there the Bina of Yechida that is attributed to them, YESHSUT ascend to GAR of Atik within which is Rosh of MA of AK and receive from there GAR of Yechida of MA attributed to them, and ZA ascends to GAR of AA within which is Rosh of BON, regarded as VAK of MA, and from there he receives the VAK of Yechida attributed to him. Following them are the three worlds BYA with the NRN of the righteous, where Beria ascends to the place of YESHSUT of Atzilut in which there is Beria of AA, meaning from the Chazeh of AA and below, Yetzira ascends to the place of ZA of Atzilut from Tabur of AA and below, Assiya ascends to the place of Nukva of Atzilut, leaving the place of the three worlds BYA below the Parsa of Atzilut as an empty space after the three worlds themselves ascended to the place of YESHSUT and ZON of Atzilut, since now they are without the former lights of BYA and there is neither Kedusha nor a shell in their place.

32) We could ask about it that it is known that from the side of BON, AA is regarded as Keter of Atzilut, and from the side of BON, AVI are regarded as Hochma and AB of Atzilut, and YESHSUT from the side of BON are Bina of Atzilut. It therefore follows that AA pertains to Keter of AK, AVI to AB of AK, and YESHSUT to SAG of AK. Thus, why was it said that AA is attributed to AB of AK and AVI to SAG of AK?

The thing is that all the Partzufim of BON cannot receive anything except through MA that bestows upon them. Hence, they can receive from the five Partzufim only through the ascent of the Partzufim of MA. For this reason, all the discernments of ascents of the five Partzufim of Atzilut to receive Mochin from the five Partzufim of AK are only according to the levels of MA, and then they receive from MA. From the perspective of MA, Atik is regarded as Keter of Atzilut, and AA has nothing from Keter of MA and takes only the level of Hochma of MA. Likewise, AVI took only Bina of MA and have nothing from the quality of Hochma. For this reason, in all the values of attainments of the Mochin and ascents to the five Partzufim of AK, Atik relates to Keter of Atzilut who receives from Partzuf Keter of AK, and AA to Hochma of Atzilut who receives from Partzuf AB of AK, and AVI to Bina of Atzilut who receive only from Partzuf SAG of AK.

The whole correction of the Partzufim of BON comes only through ascents of MA. Hence, they truly are devoid of correction since they cannot be completely corrected through the Partzufim of MA because BON of AA must receive from Keter, and AA bestows upon him only from Hochma of AK. Likewise, BON of AVI must receive from Hochma of AK, and AVI bestow upon them only from Bina of AK, and so forth likewise. Thus, the Partzufim of BON have no complete satisfaction from all those Mochin that MA bestows upon them.

This matter will be corrected only at the end of correction after the canceling of the shells, as in the verse, "Death shall be swallowed up forever."

We should know that during the ascent of the Partzufim of Atzilut to AK, the five Partzufim of AK also ascend above them to the same extent. It is a rule in both the Partzufim of Atzilut and in the Partzufim of AK that any upper one raises the lower one along with it. For example, when NHY of AA rise to his HGT, YESHSUT and ZON that clothe NHY of AA are drawn with them and they, too, rise to HGT of AA. Likewise, when HGT of AA rise to his HBD, AVI that clothe HGT of AA are drawn along with them and now they, too, clothe his HGT. Similarly, when HGT of Atik rise and become HBD of Atik, GAR of AA from the garments of HGT of Atik are drawn along with them and they, too, rise to HBD of Atik. It is the same in the Partzufim of AK, since when GAR of MA of AK rise to Rosh SAG of AK, they draw GAR of Atik along with them to Rosh of SAG.

Also, when GAR of MA rose to Rosh of SAG, HGT of SAG of AK necessarily rose first to GAR of SAG, which raised the MA of AK along with them, and HGT of AB necessarily rose first to GAR of AB of AK who raised the Rosh of SAG to Rosh of AB. Also, HGT of Partzuf Keter of AK necessarily rose first and became GAR of Keter of AK, raising with them the Rosh of AB of AK that clothed HGT of AK, and which now clothes the place of GAR of Partzuf Keter.

GAR of Partzuf Keter of AK rose higher still, in a manner that first, the upper Partzufim ascend and draw with them the lower ones that clothe on them. However, they evaluate the level of ascent of the lower one according to the level of permanency of the upper one, for although the upper one ascends, as well, it still leaves its phase below, in his permanent place prior to the ascent. For example, when AVI rise to HBD of AA, they are regarded as clothing GAR of AA although in fact, GAR of AA rose higher up and clothe GAR of Atik. Nevertheless, it was said that AVI are in the place of GAR of AA since there is no absence in spirituality and it cannot be said that as it moves from place to place, it will become absent from the first place. Rather, there is only an addition here and it exists in its first place as in the new place to which it now ascended. This is why it is considered that AVI gained the quality of GAR of AA due to this ascent of theirs although GAR of AA rose from there to GAR of Atik.

It is likewise in all the Partzufim, and always remember this since no ascent in the Partzufim or the worlds can be understood without it. It therefore follows that as any lower one ascends, it reaches the one above its upper one, as well, since through the ascent of AVI to HBD of AA they are included in GAR of AA, too, which rose to HBD of Atik, and this is why AVI have incorporation in GAR of Atik itself, too, since GAR of AA are there now.

Do not be surprised that it is written that GAR of MA of AK rise in one ascent from the place of Tabur of AK to the Rosh of SAG, and you find that it rises two degrees at once—namely HGT of SAG and HBD of SAG of AK—such as which we did not find in all the Partzufim of AK and Atzilut except in MA of AK and Atik of Atzilut that clothes it. The thing is that this MA of AK is indeed from the quality of SAG of AK for it emerged from the Nikvey Einayim of SAG, which is the internality of GAR of Nekudim. Accordingly, it should have clothed from the Peh of Rosh of SAG and below like the rest of the Partzufim of AK, where the lower one clothes HGT of the upper one. However, since there was a new matter here, of the second restriction—where the bottom Hey rose to the Nikvey Einayim and took the AHP from all the degrees outside of the degree—these ten Sefirot could not clothe HGT of SAG, regarded as Akudim of AK, meaning the first restriction, and the screen of the second restriction has no power to rise above its root. Since its root began only in Partzuf Nekudot of SAG below Tabur of AK, it had to descend two degrees from Rosh of SAG and begin to clothe only from Tabur of AK and below.

Thus, you see that the place of MA of AK is indeed with the ten Sefirot of Nekudim in the place of HGT of SAG above Tabur of AK, meaning as YESHSUT clothe from Peh of AVI and below since they are regarded as ZAT of SAG, and only by the connection of the bottom Hey in the Nikvey Einayim did ZAT of SAG descend into being below Tabur and became MA and BON of AK. Therefore, during the imparting of the Mochin of AB SAG of AK, which lower the bottom Hey from the Einayim and breach the Parsas that were made by the second restriction, MA of AK ascends at once to Rosh of SAG of AK, for now, during the coupling, when the power of the second restriction has departed, and HGT of all the Partzufim return to their GAR, GAR of MA are as one with HGT of SAG and rise with them to HBD of SAG. In this manner, just as during the governance of the second restriction, MA of AK, which is YESHSUT, descended two degrees at once, likewise, during the coupling, when all the power of the second restriction has been temporarily canceled, it once again ascends two degrees at once since in relation to the descent, MA and BON are regarded as an ascent, and in relation to an ascent, ZAT of SAG are regarded as they truly are.

By this you can also understand why the third YESHSUT emerged from the phase of SAG and became Rosh of MA. It is so because this third YESHSUT extends from MA of AK, which is also regarded as YESHSUT that has descended and become MA. Remember this, for it is a key to understand all the Mochin of ZON.

There is another thing to scrutinize concerning the matter of the ascent of the worlds and Partzufim: The usual order in the words of the ARI is that AB is Hochma, SAG is Bina, MA is ZA, and BON is Nukva. In regard to this, we find many places in the words of the ARI where AB is Keter, SAG is Hochma, MA is Bina, and BON is ZON. He also says sometimes that AVI are SAG, and YESHSUT are MA. However, after delving in all those places, the matters become very clear and simple. It has already been explained that each of the Partzufim of Atzilut consists of MA and BON. From the perspective of MA, Atik is regarded as Keter, AA as AB and Hochma, AVI as SAG and Bina, the second YESHSUT of AVI are regarded as ZAT of SAG and as ZAT of Bina, the third YESHSUT as GAR of MA, and ZON as VAK of MA or BON. From the perspective of BON, AA is regarded as Keter, AVI as AB and Hochma, YESHSUT as SAG and Bina, ZA as MA, and Nukva as BON.

Therefore, when concerning the matters of BON in the Partzufim, AA is regarded as Keter, AVI as AB, YESHSUT as SAG, and ZON as MA and BON. However, when it concerns only MA, Atik is regarded as Keter, AA as AB, AVI as SAG, YESHSUT and the third Tevuna as MA, and ZON as only VAK of MA. Sometimes, when it concerns a joint relation between MA and BON in the Partzuf, and the main issue revolves around MA, AA is called Keter and AB together, AVI as SAG and Hochma together, YESHSUT as MA and Bina together, and ZON as BON.

This is interpreted in the words of the ARI as he says there: "Yechida is not considered as being in the Partzuf. ...Therefore, now there are four general phases, and it is said that there are AB [72 in Gematria] tastes in Keter, and SAG [63] dots in Hochma, MA [45] tags in Bina, and BON [52] letters in ZAT. We already explained that AB is in Keter, which has Arich and Nukva, SAG is in Hochma AVI, MA YESHSUT, and BON ZON," thus far his words. You therefore clearly see how he mixes the two sides MA and BON in the Partzuf together. He begins with AA, which, from the perspective of BON, he calls Keter. From the perspective of MA, he calls it AB. Likewise, he calls AVI from the perspective of BON Hochma, and from the perspective of MA, SAG. Also, he calls YESHSUT from the perspective of MA by the name MA, and refers to the third YESHSUT, which becomes MA, and he calls ZON BON, since VAK of MA are called BON.

The fourth above-mentioned question has also been thoroughly explained. We asked when were the Partzufim discerned as being on the same level, and when were they discerned as being one below the other. This is explained in the words of the ARI here, that those Partzufim that emerge on a coupling in the same screen, like the twenty-five Partzufim in the inclusive Partzuf AA and in the inclusive Partzuf Abba, etc., these are all on the same level since from the perspective of Keter and the four phases of direct light, there is no difference in the level since they are in the Rosh of AK as they are in the Sof of Assiya. The difference between the worlds and the Partzufim is only because of the changes in the screen in the vessel Malchut on which the coupling by striking was made, as he wrote in *Tree of Life*.

Therefore, only five inclusive Partzufim, meaning that each of them contains twenty-five Partzufim that differ in the screens in them. The inclusive Partzuf Keter emerges on the screen of phase four, and the inclusive Abba, which is AB, emerges on the screen of phase three, the inclusive Ima, which is SAG, on the screen of phase two, and the inclusive ZON on the screen of phase one. For this reason, each one descends by one degree compared to its upper one: Abba that emerges in a screen of phase three has only the level of Hochma and lacks Keter. You find that the light of Hochma dresses in his vessel of Keter, the light of Bina in the vessel of Hochma, and so forth as the ARI explained. This is why you find that Abba, which is AB, dresses from the Peh of Partzuf Keter downward, SAG from the Peh of Partzuf Hochma and below, and so on likewise.

Also, all the worlds divide because of the screen and descend one below the other. The inclusive AK is from the screen of phase four, Atzilut is from phase three, Beria from phase two, Yetzira from phase one, and Assiya from the root phase. However, since all those particular Partzufim in each inclusive Partzuf emerge on one coupling and one screen, their level is completely equal since there is nothing to differentiate their level.

And yet, I saw in the book Rehovot HaNahar by the RASHASH that he had great difficulty explaining the words of the ARI regarding what the ARI wrote, that when he emanated Keter, in whom all the Ketarim were included, etc., that when he emanated Hochma, all the Hochmot [pl. of Hochma] were included in him, etc. He explained that after all five worlds AK and ABYA were emanated and emerged through the end of the bottom world of Assiya, the Emanator inverted their order once again so that all the discernments of length that emerged one below the other in each Partzuf, He corrected them to be thickness, and from all those Partzufim that clothed one another in thickness, He corrected them into being length. Thus, after AK and ABYA emerged, they were included in one another and became twenty-five worlds, since each of the five worlds is included with all of them. Thus, the five worlds of AK and ABYA are to the length in AK, and the five worlds AK and ABYA are to their length in Atzilut, and the five worlds AK and ABYA are to the length of Beria, and likewise in Yetzira and in Assiya. Through this incorporation, they were all made on an equal level to each other where for example, even the bottom world of Assiya ascended and increased his level equally with AK. Hence, now the world of Assiya, too, begins in Ein Sof in the beginning of the line, and ends equally with the Raglayim of AK, and likewise all the worlds.

Afterward, the Emanator swapped the length in them to thickness since He took the five worlds AK that clothed one another on the thickness, which are AK of AK,

AK of Atzilut, AK of Beria, AK of Yetzira, and AK of Assiya, and made them into the length of AK. Thus, AK of Atzilut on the thickness became Atzilut of AK on its length, AK of Beria on the thickness became Beria of AK on its length, AK of Yetzira on the thickness into Yetzira of AK on its length, and AK of Assiya on the thickness into Assiya on the length of AK. He corrected the four worlds ABYA that were previously to the length of AK into being thickness from above, on the four worlds ABYA. He made the world of Atzilut that was on the length of AK into AK of Atzilut, the world of Beria on the length of AK into AK of Beria, the world of Yetzira on the length of AK into AK of Yetzira, and the world of Assiya on the length of AK into AK of Assiya, and likewise the rest of the worlds in general, in particular, and in the particular in the particular. Finally, there is nothing more in the Keter of each world and Partzuf than Ketarim from the beginning of the line through the end of the world of Assiya, and likewise Hochma of each world and Partzuf through the end of Assiya is all only Hochmot, and so forth likewise.

Besides the great difficulty of this interpretation to explain the words of the ARI, since here the ARI says explicitly, **When Ein Sof emanated Keter, He made it from all five Partzufim, etc., and when He emanated the Keter in Him, all the Ketarim [pl. of Keter] were included in it, etc.** Thus, here it speaks of right at the beginning of the emanation of the five Partzufim of the world of Atzilut. Also, he interprets the beginning of Atzilut of the five Partzufim of Beria, and the five Partzufim of Yetzira and Assiya one below the other. How can it be said here that the ARI speaks only of a correction that was done after the emergence of all the worlds? He would not have used the words **"When He emanated"** but the words **"When He corrected."** Also, with such a great innovation that after the emergence of all the worlds, the Emanator reversed their order from length to thickness and from thickness to length, the ARI should have at least presented some hint in all the writings of the ARI. Additionally, besides all the above-said, it is difficult to understand how it is possible that the bottom world of Assiya, which emerged back-to-back in AK and ABYA on the length, and in Partzuf Hochma in it, the ARI says that there is only a dot in it, so how was it later corrected into being equal to the level of AK, and now the world of Assiya begins at the Rosh of the line, attached to Ein Sof like AK?

He wrote there, in Rehovot HaNahar, that these words are presented in the words of the ARI, yet I delved deeply into that above-mentioned Shaar HaTikkun and it is to the contrary. He wrote there explicitly that prior to the end of correction, the Partzufim stand one below the other. Only after the completion of the entire correction, when GAR of ZA emerge, as well as the first nine of Nukva, their level will be equal and they will clothe one another. But during the correction, within the six thousand years, he clarifies there that ZA lacks GAR and Nukva lacks the first nine. To complete this, they need Ibur-Yenika-Mochin each time. Thus, as long as the completion of the whole correction has not been achieved, their level is not the same. Also, in the book Mavo She'arim he [the ARI] does not speak at all about equalizing the level.

He [RASHASH] is probably explaining there the words of the ARI that when it speaks of the completion of the whole correction, it is not quite the end of correction but only the correction of the six thousand years, while the completion of the whole correction that the ARI speaks of pertains to their level being generally equal, and the middle of the correction that the ARI speaks of pertains to the very last item that can be found, in which there is the matter of Ibur-Yenika-Mochin in ZA and they are not on an equal level.

However, according to this, since he explained that first the worlds and Partzufim as a whole were corrected on an equal level and then the particular Partzufim emerged to be made one below the other, you find from this that what the ARI wrote there about the middle of the correction has now become after the completion of the entire correction. You find that the completion of the correction precedes the middle of it? This is very perplexing.

Also, it is not the conduct of the ARI at all to speak in this manner, since the purpose of the whole correction, its meaning is clear: It is the usual end of correction that the ARI always speaks about in all the treatises. Besides, the ARI does not speak there at all of Partzuf AK or of the Partzufim of the three bottom worlds BYA, saying that their level is equal to the world of Atzilut. Rather, he speaks only of the five Partzufim of the world of Atzilut, and there is no intimation here to equalizing the level of the bottom world of Assiya with the Rosh of the line that is attached to Ein Sof.

The RASHASH also says there to delve in Shaarey Kedusha and in the treatises of ABYA where it is explained that after the five worlds AK and ABYA emerged, they clothed each other on the length from above downward from Rosh AK to the end of Assiya, see there in Rehovot HaNahar. I did delve into the treatises of ABYA in *Tree of Life*, and there is no mention there at all of the matter of equalizing the level. Also, in Shaarey Kedusha he explicitly wrote the opposite of his words. He writes there that "All the worlds are included in the name HaVaYaH, etc., and it is likewise in each of the five worlds, etc. All those phases and degrees from the top of Adam Kadmon to the abyss in the bottom world are one above the other and one before the other, since one who is superior to the other dresses inside the one below it like a soul in a body. Yet, the upper one does not dress in the lower one entirely, but only a particular phase in the upper one dresses in the whole of the lower one and so forth likewise until the Sium [end] of the worlds."

Therefore, it is explicitly the opposite of his words, for although they are included in one another, one above the other, and one before the other, the upper one still does not dress in the lower one, but only some of it, only Malchut of the upper one, and their level is not equal. It is very odd that of all the places that he referenced in order to support his words, you find the very opposite there. I scrutinized his holy words a great deal but I did not merit to understand them whatsoever.

There is another oddity I found there in Rehovot HaNahar: He wrote that the level of AA begins at the Tabur of AK and that there is its root. This contradicts the words of the ARI that have been published in several places, that GAR of Atik clothe GAR of Nekudim that remained in their place and were not revoked during the breaking of the vessels, and it begins in Tabur of AK, and this Rosh of Atik is called RADLA, which AA cannot clothe, and AA clothes only the ZAT of Atik which are below GAR of Nekudim, in the place of ZAT of Nekudim. Thus, you find that RADLA stops between Tabur of AK and Rosh of AA. So how does the RASHASH say there that AA begins from Tabur of AK? See in Sha'ar HaTikkun, Chapter 3: "Although the light of Metzah [forehead], which is called MA there, emerged from above the Metzah, it spreads from there downward and begins its existence from the Tabur, etc. The point of Keter extended and spread from her place downward, etc., and this expansion is the full measure called 'the world of Atzilut.' This point is the Nukva of Atik Yomin, and likewise, the male of Atik Yomin that was made of the tastes of MA also spreads in the above measure."

Thus, it is explicitly clarified that both Atik Yomin Nukva and the male of Atik Yomin begin from Tabur of AK and not above it whatsoever. Also, in *Tree of Life*, the ARI wrote as follows: "GAR of Atik cannot clothe inside AA, and it is impossible that he will receive their lights. For this reason, they remain revealed and stand as surrounding of AA. Only the bottom seven of Atik clothe inside AA since KHB of AA clothe HGT of Atik Yomin, and the bottom seven of AA clothe NHY of Atik." Thus, it is explained that Rosh of AA stands in the place of ZAT of Atik, which is the place of ZAT of Nekudim, and does not touch the place of GAR of Nekudim that stand below Tabur of AK even a bit, since it is the place of RADLA.

It is also explained in *Tree of Life* that "The vessels of GAR (of Nekudim) did not descend. One Rosh was made from the vessels of these three Nekudot, and within them three Mochin. This is called RADLA, and it is also called Rosh of Atik Yomin. Thus, the first three of the ten Nekudot are RADLA." Thus, it is explained that Rosh of Atik took the place of GAR of Nekudim that clothe from Tabur of AK downward, and not AA. Also, in *Tree of Life*, he says "The initial place of ZA is in the place that is now AA." Thus, AA stands in the place of ZA of Nekudim.

Moreover, from the above premise that AA begins at Tabur of AK, he got to interpret the order of ascent of the Partzufim of Atzilut to the Partzufim of AK, that when ZA obtains Partzuf Neshama and ascends to the Chazeh of AA, meaning in the first ascent, AA ascends to Rosh SAG of AK. In the second ascent, when ZA ascends to the Garon of AA and obtains Haya, and AA ascends to Rosh AB of AK. In the third ascent, when ZA ascends to Rosh AA and obtains Yechida, AA ascends to the Rosh of Partzuf Galgalta of AK.

According to his words, it follows that on Shabbat, in the Musaf [addition] when the Partzufim are in the second ascent, when ZA rose to the Garon of AA in the place of upper AVI, AA is in Rosh of AB, according to his words. This explicitly contradicts the words of the ARI in the book of intentions in the treatise about the meal on the morning of Shabbat, where he wrote there that at that time, AA ascends to the place of the Heys of Partzuf AB of AK. Also, the ARI instructed to scrutinize this in Shaar Mati veLo Mati [present and not present] where it explains that the place of these Heys is in KHB of the Guf of AB of AK. Thus, on the ascent of the Musaf of Shabbat, AA is in the place of the Guf of AB of AK, meaning in his HGT when he is clothed in Rosh SAG of AK, and not in Rosh of AB of AK. Only in the third ascent, during the Mincha [afternoon] of Shabbat, when ZA ascends to AA, AA rises to Rosh of AB of AK, and Atik rises at that time to Rosh Partzuf Galgalta of AK in a way that in the first ascent, AA rises to Rosh of Atik of Atzilut, and in the second ascent, AA rises to HGT of AB which is the place of Rosh SAG of AK, and in the third ascent, AA rises to Rosh AB of AK.

I found yet another perplexity there in Rehovot HaNahar: He says there that those five mentioned Partzufim of Atzilut that emerge from the new MA refer to MA of AK called ZA of AK, and their five female Partzufim, which are called BON, come from BON of AK Malchut of AK. But these words of his completely contradict what the ARI writes in several places, that the side of BON of the five Partzufim of Atzilut are very high from the side of the male MA, since they are regarded as SAG, who is higher than MA. However, since they are corrected only through MA, their name has been changed into the name BON. Thus, clearly, the Partzufim of BON of Atzilut are not from BON of AK but rather from SAG of AK, who is much higher than even MA of AK himself. It is also odd that according to his words, the new MA is MA of AK. If this is so then why does the ARI call him "the new MA"? Also, how can the male Atik, AA, and AVI receive from GAR of ZA of AK? After all, they are regarded as GAR and must receive from their corresponding phase in the Partzufim of AK, meaning from MA of Partzuf Keter and AB and SAG of AK, and not from ZA of AK, as is written in the words of the ARI above, and this is clear.

He also writes there that the GAR of ZON of BON that Atik took are from the nine Sefirot of BON that emerged anew. This contradicts the words of the ARI, who wrote that they are the old vessels of Nekudim in which there was no breaking.

Also, we have already explained above concerning MA and BON of the five Partzufim of Atzilut, that only the vessels that remained complete from the ten Sefirot of Nekudim, or the vessels that were sorted through the levels of MA that emerge in Atzilut, are called BON. This is due to their descent to receive from the lights of Atzilut which are lower than they are. Although all those lights that emerge in Atzilut emerge only through MAN from the records and the sparks of BON, they are all called MA. It is as the ARI wrote there that only MA emerges through a coupling of AB SAG for the sake of Atzilut, and not BON, who is entirely from Nekudot of SAG of AK, for only the vessels of Nekudim, or those that are sorted from them from BYA, are called BON. The lights in them do not come from the coupling AB SAG of

AK himself but only through their owners, the MA. These words of the ARI are too clear and must not be retracted even as a hairsbreadth.

We should also remember what he says, that the lights of Atzilut are called "the new MA" after the permanent levels of Atzilut in which no diminution will ever occur. These are only what is received from the ZON of each of the five Partzufim of AK, which is called MA, while all the lights that are received from what is above MA of the five Partzufim of AK, which are called Galgalta-AB-SAG of the five Partzufim of AK, which are drawn through MAN from the lower ones by prayers and ascents, are not permanent in Atzilut but rather ascend and descend according to the actions of the lower ones. For this reason, the name Atzilut is not given to them but only to the permanent level of MA in them.

There is another matter that should be mentioned here. I saw in the book Hasdei David [David's Mercies] that AK himself is called Yechida with regard to Atzilut. However, with regard to what is above him, he, too, is called ZON, etc., since the whole of AK stands in the place of half the clothing of the lower one. The complete clothing of the lower one is AB-SAG-MA-BON. When the clothing is divided and the bottom half, called MA and BON, is divided and clothes the upper half, which is AB SAG, that vacant place that was at the place of the bottom half of the clothing is called "primal air," and the ball that is made within it, in which the ten Sefirot of AK stand, is called Tehiro. On top of the Tehiro, between the primal air and the clothing, stand the ten Sefirot of the upper, concealed AK, since AK stands in the place of MA and BON, which is why ZON is called according to what is above it. These words are also found in the words of Rav Menachem Azariah da Fano, in Emek HaMelech, and in Shaarey Gan Eden and in others.

Know that these words came from what the friends received, meaning the other disciples of the ARI and not from Rav Chaim Vital. But not only are they not found in all the writings of Rav Chaim Vital, they also contradict what Rav Chaim Vital received. You can see that *Tree of Life* explains as follows: "This first circle, which is the most attached to Ein Sof, is called Keter of AK." He also writes there: "Know that the first lights," etc., "are regarded as the ten Sefirot whose overall connection is called AK to all the primal ones," see there and in several places. Thus, it explicitly explains that there are no worlds at all above AK, the opposite of those who say that the world of clothing is a special world that precedes AK.

Indeed, all those worlds presented in what the friends received, meaning the first Tehiro and the world of clothing that folded its lower half over its upper half, and the primal air, and the Tehiro inside the primal air, and the blocked AK are all included in the five Partzufim of AK that Rav Chaim Vital explained. It is written in *Tree of Life*: "Let us begin to explain one item that includes and encompasses the whole place of this space, an item from which all the worlds spread, and on which they hang and from which they emerge and become revealed outside. However, that item is called Adam Kadmon [primordial man] before all the primal ones, who precedes all that there is." Thus, it is explained that AK precedes all that exists, and all the worlds are included in it and expand from it.

Know that the world of clothing is included in Partzuf SAG of AK, which prior to the second restriction, expanded through the point of this world. The matter of the folding of the world of clothing was done with the second restriction, for then the world of clothing was also folded due to the ascent of the lights from below Tabur, which are two HaVaYot [pl. of HaVaYaH], MA and BON of AK, to above Tabur, which are two HaVaYot AB SAG of AK. From this you will understand that the worlds "primal air" and the second Tehiro that was made a circle within a square, as presented in what the friends received, emerged in the place of the bottom half of the clothing that had folded. According to the above, you find that they are included in Tabur of AK and below, meaning in the world of Nekudim. Also, the first Tehiro is the first world of restriction. Thus, the world of clothing, and especially the worlds following it, are below the two Partzufim Galgalta and AB of AK.

Besides what is said in the explanation of their words, we are commanded not to mind what the friends received at all, especially where they contradict what Rav Chaim Vital received, as it is written in Shaar HaGilgulim that upon his demise, the ARI gave a will where he forbade all the friends from learning in the writings that they wrote from his words because they did not understand his words. He forbade them from delving into them, with the exception of Rav Chaim Vital. Also, see what the RASHASH wrote in his book Nahar Shalom: "All my engagement and learning is only in the words of the ARI and his disciple Rav Chaim Vital alone. Other than they, I have no dealing with any book from the books of the first and last kabbalists. I did not even learn in the words of the other disciples of the ARI. When I come across a word of their words, I skip it, for by this I am not warning but reminding: For God's sake, let your hands not touch their words."

We should not be surprised about those books that were taken after what the friends received, for they probably did not see the words in Shaar HaGilgulim, and therefore were not careful to distinguish between what Rav Chaim Vital received and what the other friends did. This is what has prompted me to compile the book *Ha'Ilan* [The Tree] and arrange in it the worlds and Partzufim from the Rosh of the line that is attached to Ein Sof through the bottom world of Assiya, established on the purity of the words of Rav Chaim Vital, for all the trees I have seen are mixed with what the friends received. For this reason, they must not be trusted.

253) It is likewise in all of Atzilut itself: The better was sorted in Atik, the worse in AA, and likewise in each and every Sefira in each and every Partzuf in particular. We must not elaborate on this for the pen cannot detail them.

254) Know that once the part of Atik has been completely sorted, he began to sort the part of AA. Once the part of AA alone has been sorted, he sorted

the part of AVI. Once the part of AVI has been sorted, they began to sort the parts of ZON.

255) All this was through couplings and Iburim [conceptions] where the sorted sparks rise from the place of falling and enter the abdomen of Nukva where they stay for the duration of the Ibur and become sweetened there, and there they become discerned as a Partzuf.

256) After all of Atzilut has been sorted, the sorting of Atik of Beria begins to be sorted through Nukva of ZA of Atzilut. Afterward, after sorting Atik of Beria, he sorts the parts of AA of Beria, and so forth likewise in all of Beria. In this manner, it then takes place in Yetzira in all its details, and in this manner in Assiya in every manner and detail. It follows that all four worlds are from the sorting of the seven Melachim [kings], and what was not sorted remained as the eleven marks of incense.

257*) The place of the expansion of all those male and female Partzufim that are made of the connection of MA and BON, as mentioned above, is in the place where initially the Nekudot emerged through the Nikvey Einayim; it is in the Tabur of AK through the Sof of his Raglayim. The light of Metzah is called MA there although it emerged above the Metzah, and spreads from there down and begins its existence from the Tabur through the end of his Sium Raglayim.

258) Yet, what has changed now compared to the beginning, at the time of the emergence of the Nekudot of the Einayim is that then the point of Keter was in its place, alone and on its own, and the point of Hochma was alone and on its own, and likewise all the ten Sefirot. But now a great correction has been added, which is that the point of Keter has been stretched and expanded from its place down to close to the Sium Raglayim of AK, as written in *Tree of Life*. This expansion is the full measure called "the world of Atzilut," and this point is called Nukva of Atik Yomin.

259) Similarly, the male of Atik Yomin that was made of the above-mentioned tastes of MA also expanded in the above measure, and so did all the rest: AA and Nukva, AVI and ZON. They clothed each other through the phase of ZON, so that all the Raglayim of the Partzufim of Atzilut, whether of Atik or of AA or of AVI or ZON are equal at their Sium. They end together, slightly higher than the Sium Raglayim of AK, and there is the Sium of the whole of Atzilut.

260) By this they became Neshama for one another and one clothes the other. Also, by this, the created beings will be able to receive the upper lights which are now covered and clothe one inside the other, and also because they increased their vessels by spreading through the bottom, and in this they have the power to receive their lights, as they are big vessels.

261) This light of new MA that emerges from the Metzah is the eighth Melech [king] mentioned in the portion VaYishlach, and which is called Hadar. No death

---
* *Tree of Life*, Part 1, Gate 10, Chapter 3.

is mentioned in regard to him in the Torah, since he did not die like the others. On the contrary, he corrects and sustains the first seven Melachim who died, which precede him. I have already told you that all those Melachim are kings that are mentioned in the portion *VaYishlach* in the verse, "These are the kings who reigned in the land of Edom."

262) Since when he emerged, he promptly began to sort these phases of Melachim to make them Nukva to him, as they are now called BON of the Heys, it was said about him, "And Hadar reigned after him, and the name of his wife was Mehitab'el. It is written in *The Zohar* that "Until now there was no mention of male and female whatsoever, except for now. And because of it, they all persist," for now there are male and female as we can see and as is mentioned in Idra Rabbah. The thing is that they are regarded as the above-mentioned MA and BON, and now he is called Adam [man] since Adam includes ZON. This is why you find that the name MA in Gematria is Adam.

263) This is not surprising since only the males in Atzilut were made in the name MA, and the Nukva was made from the name BON, so how was he called Adam? The thing is that as it is written, when the name MA emerged, he was sorted from the name BON and connected it to him and was corrected with him. You find that then the light of Nukva was subordinate to him and suckled from it like the son with the daughter, where everything is named after the son and he inherits everything and gives to the daughter only as he wishes. Hence, you find that the daughter is subordinate to the son and is included in him.

264) For this reason, the name BON, which is the daughter, is a Nukva and subordinate to the name MA, who is the male son. She is included in him since he sorts with the name MA, and he is corrected through the MA. Hence, when he sorts, he first takes what he sorts for himself, as is known about the two Ketarim that the son inherited two, (both) Hassadim and Gevura of MA and of BON, and then the son gives to the daughter a Keter of Gevura when he makes a coupling with her, as though he gives her of his own. This is why he alone is called Adam, consisting of both.

265*) However, we should explain the above, since those Nekudot are regarded as SAG, so how are they worse and subordinate to the name, "New MA," and MA is a male and the Nekudot SAG are a female? Also, it is known in several places that the name SAG is greater than the name MA.

266) The answer is that the name "New MA" emerged from the coupling of AB and SAG. Hence, because it extends from AB himself, he is greater than SAG. There is another reason: There were no death or breaking in the name MA as there were in the name SAG himself.

267) A third reason is that these are only the phase of Nekudot of SAG, but the new MA comprises TANTA. Since there are tastes, of course it is superior to the

---

* *Tree of Life*, Part 1, Gate 10, end of Chapter 3.

Nekudot of SAG but not to the tastes of SAG. And there is a fourth reason: Now SAG has a big flaw to him, which is that he was still not fully sorted. Hence, now MA is greater and better than him.

268) But in the future [end of correction], when all the phases of SAG are corrected and all the Melachim live and become completely sorted as in "Death will be swallowed up forever," the name SAG will return to its beginning and to its merit, and the name SAG will govern and shine in the world. At that time, the name MA will be canceled. This is the meaning of the return of the world to Tohu veBohu, as mentioned in the words of our sages about the days of the Messiah. And at that time, MA will be canceled and there will be only two lights, AB and SAG, and that will be enough.

Simple Light

268) **The name SAG will return to its beginning and to its merit, and the name SAG will govern and shine in the world.** This means that SAG of AK was diminished during the second restriction and rose from Sium Raglayim of AK to the place above Tabur of AK and ended on Tabur of AK, below which the Parsa was set up inside the intestines of AK, causing the emergence of the Parsa between Atzilut and Beria. At the end of correction, all those Parsas of the second restriction will be canceled and SAG of AK will return to its initial state and expand through the Sium Raglayim of AK, meaning to the point of this world as he had expanded prior to the second restriction. Also, the name BON—meaning the five Partzufim of BON of the world of Atzilut which come from the ten Sefirot of Nekudim that emerged from SAG of AK from the Nikvey Einayim after he was diminished and rose above Tabur—will return to his root as SAG himself, and he, too, will expand through the point of this world. By this, BYA will return to truly being Atzilut, and you will find that the name SAG from before the second restriction will rule and shine in the world.

At that time, MA will be canceled and there will be only two lights, of AB and SAG, since the new MA, which contains all five male Partzufim of Atzilut emerged from the small Hey of BeHibara'am [when they were created], which is the second restriction that was done in SAG of AK. From this coupling of AB with SAG of the second restriction emerged the new MA. You find that after the second restriction is canceled and SAG spreads once again through the Sium Raglayim of AK as prior to the second restriction, there will no more be a place for the emergence of the new MA, and it, too, will return to his root, to AB of AK, and only AB and SAG will reign. Understand this, for there is nothing more to add.

The Writings of the Last Generation

Editor's Note

The original manuscripts of these writings are stored in the ARI Institute archive.

The publication process was quite complicated due to the condition of the manuscripts, and because of the great density of the texts. First, we located all the writings that belong to the "Writings of the Last Generation" by their content. Subsequently, we meticulously copied the texts without any editing or corrections. Where we could not decipher a word or a part of a word, we marked it with ellipses [...].

We divided the writings into five parts and an introduction, according to their appearance in the manuscripts. It should be noted that the ordering of the parts was done by us. All the titles in the writings were given by Baal HaSulam himself, and where marking a title had to be added we used only letters.

We should pay close attention to the lion share in "The Writings of the Last Generation," Part One. According to the manuscript, the material is in fact divided into two: 1) Essay, 2) Appendices and drafts of the essay.

The Editor

Introduction

There is an allegory about friends who were lost in the desert, hungry and thirsty. One of them had found a settlement filled abundantly with every delight. He remembered his poor brothers, but he had already drawn far off from them and did not know their whereabouts. What did he do? He began to shout out loud and blow the horn, perhaps his poor, hungry friends would hear his voice, approach him, and come to that settlement that is filled with every delight.

So is the matter before us: We have been lost in the terrible desert along with all of humanity, and now we have found a great, abundant treasure, namely the books of Kabbalah in the treasure. They satisfy our yearning souls and fill us abundantly with lushness and contentment; we are satiated and there is more.

Yet, we remember our friends, who were left hopeless in the terrible desert. There is a great distance between us, and words cannot bridge it. For this reason, we have set up this horn to blow out loud so that our brothers might hear and draw near and be as happy as we are.

Know, our brothers, our flesh, that the essence of the wisdom of Kabbalah is the knowledge of how the world descended from its elevated, heavenly place, until it reached our ignoble state. This reality was necessary, as "the end of an act is in the preliminary thought," and His thought acts instantaneously, for He needs no tools to work with as we do. Thus, we emerged in *Ein Sof* [infinity] in utter perfection from the start, and from there we came to this world.

It is therefore very easy to find all the future corrections, which are destined to come, from the perfect worlds that preceded us. Through it we know how to correct our ways henceforth, like man's advantage over the beast, for the spirit of the beast descends, meaning sees only from itself onward, without the intellect or wisdom to look into the past so as to correct the future.

Man's advantage over it is that the spirit of man ascends into the past, and looks into the past as one looks in the mirror and sees one's flaws so as to correct them. Similarly, the mind sees what it went through and corrects its future conducts.

Thus, beasts do not evolve; they are still in the same state in which they were created, for they do not have, as man does, the mirror by which to see how to correct things and gradually evolve. Man develops day by day until his merit is secured and sensed, and he will ride on the high planets.

But all this refers to the natures outside of us, the nature of our surrounding reality, our food and mundane affairs. For this, the natural mind is quite sufficient.

However, internally, within ourselves, although we do evolve a little, we evolve and improve by being pushed from behind through suffering and bloodshed, since we have no tactic by which to obtain a mirror to see inside the people who lived in past generations.

It is even more so regarding the interior of the souls and the worlds, and how they declined to such dreadful ruin as today's, where we have no security in our lives. In the coming years, we will be subject to all sorts of slaughter and death, and all admit that they have no counsel to prevent it.

Imagine, for example, that some historic book were to be found today, depicting the last generations ten thousand years from now. As we feel, the lesson from the suffering and torment will certainly be enough to reform them in good orders.

And these people have before them good orders, sufficient to provide security and complacency, and at the very least, to guarantee their daily lives in peace and quiet.

There is no doubt that if some sage would offer us this book about the wisdom of statesmanship and personal conduct, our leaders would seek out every counsel to arrange life accordingly, and there would be "no outcry in our streets." The slaughters and the terrible suffering would cease, and everything would come peacefully to its place.

Now, distinguished readers, this book lies here before you in a closet. It states explicitly all the wisdom of statesmanship and the conducts of private and public life that will exist at the end of days, meaning the books of Kabbalah [in the manuscript, next to the text beginning here, it was written, "They are the perfection preceding the imperfection"]. In it, the corrected worlds that emerged with the perfection are set, as it says, perfection emerges first from the Creator, then we correct it and come to the perfection that exists in the upper world, emerging from *Ein Sof*, as in "the end of an act is in the preliminary thought." Because the incomplete is not instantly extended from the complete, but rather gradually, and there is no absence in the spiritual, they all remain existing and depicted in their complete perfection, in particular and in general, in the wisdom of Kabbalah.

Open these books and you will find all the good orders that will appear at the end of days, and you will find within them the good lesson by which to arrange mundane matters today as well, for we can learn from the past and by this correct the future.

A Call for the Chosen Ones to Study Kabbalah

I, the writer, know myself and my place, that I am not among the finest in the human race. And if one such as I today has labored and found all this in the books concealed within our cabinets, there is not a shadow of a doubt that if the chosen ones in the generation delve in these books, so much of the happiness and bounty will be available for them and for the entire world.

My Voice that Is in the *Shofar* [Horn], Why Has It Come?

I have seen all that, and I can no longer hold back. I have resolved to disclose of my observations and of what I have found written in those books regarding the conducts of correction of our destined future. And I go out and call upon the people of the world with this horn. I do believe and estimate that it shall suffice to gather all the chosen ones to begin to study and delve in the books, so they may sentence themselves and the entire world to the side of merit.

Part One

The basis of my entire commentary is the will to receive imprinted in every creature, and which is disparity of form to the Creator. Thus, the soul has separated from Him as an organ is separated from the body, since disparity of form in spirituality is like a an axe that separates in corporeality. It is therefore clear that what the Creator wants from us is equivalence of form, at which time we adhere to Him once more, as before we were created.

This is the meaning of the words, "Adhere to His attributes; as He is merciful, etc." It means that we are to change our attribute, which is the will to receive, and adopt the attribute of the Creator, which is only to bestow, so that all our actions will be only to bestow upon our fellow persons and benefit them as best as we can.

By this we come to the goal of adhering to Him, which is equivalence of form. What one is compelled to do for oneself, namely the necessary minimum for one's self and one's family's sustenance, is not considered disparity of form, as "Necessity is neither condemned nor praised." This is the great revelation that will be revealed in full only in the days of the Messiah. When this teaching is accepted, we will be rewarded with complete redemption.

I have already said that there are two ways to discover the completeness: the path of Torah or the path of suffering.

Hence, the Creator has given humanity technology, until they have invented the atom and the hydrogen bombs. If the total ruin that they are destined to bring upon the world is still not evident to the world, they can wait for a third world war, or a fourth one. The bombs will do their thing, and the relics who remain after the ruin will have no other choice but to take upon themselves this work where both individuals and nations will not work for themselves more than is necessary for their sustenance, while everything else they do will be for the good of others. If all the nations of the world agree to it, there will no longer be wars in the world, for no person will be concerned with his own good whatsoever, but only with the good of others.

This law of equivalence of form is the law of the Messiah. It was said about this, "But in the end of days, it shall come to pass, etc., and many nations shall go and say, 'Come, and let us go up, etc., for out of Zion shall go forth the law, etc., and He shall judge between many nations.'" That is, the Messiah will teach them the work of the Creator in equivalence of form, which is the teaching and the law of the Messiah. "And shall prove to mighty nations," meaning He will prove to them that if they do not take upon themselves the work of the Creator, all the nations will be destroyed by wars. But if they do accept His law, it is said about it, "And they shall beat their swords into shovels."

If you take the path of Torah and receive the spice, very well. And if you do not, you will tread the path of suffering, meaning that wars will break out with atom and hydrogen bombs, and all the nations of the world will seek advice how to escape the wars. Then they shall come to the Messiah, to Jerusalem, and He will teach them this law.

*

Before I touch upon this matter, I will present a short introduction concerning human attributes, and say that people are divided into two kinds: egoists and altruists.

"Egoists" means that all that they do is for themselves. If they ever do something for another, they must have a well-paying reward in return for their work, in money, respect, etc.

"Altruists" means that they sacrifice all their days for the well-being of others without any reward. Instead, they always neglect their own needs to help others. Moreover, among them there are those who give their souls and their lives to the benefit of others, such as we find among volunteers who go out to war for their countryfolk.

We have also found more general altruists, who give their hearts and souls to help the stragglers of all the nations of the world, such as communists, who fight for the benefit of oppressed among all the nations of the world. They are willing to pay for this with their very lives.

Egoism is embedded in the nature of every person, as in any animal. Altruism, however, is against human nature. Yet, a chosen few are imparted this nature, and I call them "idealists." Yet, the majority of any society or state is made of simple flesh and blood folk, meaning egoists. Only a few, ten percent at most, are the exceptional altruists.

Now I shall come to the point: For the above reason, that altruists are few in every society, the first communists, before Karl Marx's time, were unsuccessful in spreading communism in the world, as in the saying, "One bird does not make a summer." In addition, some of them even established communal settlements like the kibbutzim in our country, but they failed because they could not endure.

This happened because all the members of the communal society must be altruistic idealists like the founders themselves. Since ninety percent of any society, even the most developed, are egoists, they could not keep up with the conducts of a cooperative society, which is purely altruistic by nature.

This continued until the time of Karl Marx when a very successful plan for the expansion of communism was devised, namely to incorporate the oppressed themselves in the war of communism, so they would fight alongside them against the capitalist bourgeois government. Since the oppressed are interested in this war only for their own good, meaning for egoistic reasons, they immediately accepted the plan, and thus communism spread through all the levels of the stragglers and the oppressed. Since the stragglers are the majority in society, it is no surprise that today communism has succeeded in encircling a third of the world.

However, this coupling of altruist communists with egoistic proletariat, though it was successful in overthrowing the bourgeois government, hated by both, that coupling still fails to keep a cooperative government with just division. The reason is very simple: A person does not make a move unless there is some purpose that necessitates that movement. That purpose serves as the motivating force to make that move like fuel that moves a machine.

For example, one does not move his hand from one place to another unless he thinks that in the other place he will be more comfortable resting his hand. That purpose of seeking a more comfortable place for his hand is the fuel pushing his hand from this place to the other.

Needless to say, a worker who labors all day must have fuel for the laborious movements he makes, and this is the reward he receives for his work. The reward he receives is the fuel that motivates him to his hard work. Thus, if no reward is given for his labor, or if he has no need for that reward, he will not be able to work. He will be like a machine that was not fueled; even the most gullible person in the world will not think that this machine will ever move.

Hence, in a purely communist regime, where the worker knows that he will not be given more if he works more, or receive less if he works less, and all the more so in light of the absolute motto, "Each will work according to his ability and will receive according to his needs," the worker will neither be rewarded for his diligence, nor fear his own negligence.

Thus, he would have no fuel to motivate him to work. The labor productivity of the workers would then drop to zero until they ruin the entire regime. No schooling in the world will help in inverting human nature to be able to work without fuel, meaning without reward.

The exception to this rule is the natural born altruist idealist for whom the best reward is the good of the other. This altruistic fuel is entirely sufficient for him as a motivating force to work, like the egoistic reward for all other people. However, idealists are few; their number is insufficient for society to base itself on them. Thus, you see that communism and altruism are one and the same.

I know there are ways to compel workers to complete their share of the work that the supervisors will give them by the same conducts as in a bourgeois government, where each is rewarded according to his productivity. In addition, harsh punishments can be imposed on the negligent, as in the soviet countries. However, this is not communism whatsoever. Needless to say, it is not the paradise that the communist regime is hoped to bring about, one worthy of giving one's life for.

On the contrary, a government such as this is far worse than the capitalist government for unambiguous reasons that I will present below. Had that compulsive government been a step toward the perfect communism, it would still be possible to accept and tolerate it. However, this is not the case: No training in the world will reverse human nature from egoism to altruism.

Therefore, the oppressive regime applied in the soviet countries is an eternal regime that can never be changed. And when they wish to change it into a truly cooperative regime, the workers will run out of fuel. They will not be able to work and will destroy the government. Thus, egoism and anti-communism are one and the same, identical.

Moreover, a compulsive communist government is completely unsustainable, since a bayonet-dependent government cannot persist, and the majority will ultimately rise against it and abolish it. The idealist ten percent will not be able to rule over the egoistic ninety percent and the anti-communists forever, as we find in soviet and eastern countries.

Moreover, even that handful of communist idealists that lead these countries today are not guaranteed to stay that way for generations, since ideals are not hereditary. Although the progenitors are idealists, there is no guarantee that their progeny will follow suit.

Thus, how can we be certain that the leadership of the second or third generation will be in the hands of communist idealists as it is today? You might say that the majority will always elect them from the public, but this is a grave mistake. The egoistic majority of the public will elect only those who are close to them in spirit, not their opponents.

Moreover, it is common knowledge that today's leaders were not elected by the public at all. Thus, who would see that the elected representatives of the public will always be the idealists in the public? When the egoists are in power, they are sure to revoke that government immediately, or at least turn it into a kind of national communism, "a nation of lords."

All that I have said—when I proved that communism and altruism are the same, and that egoism and anti-communism are the same—is my own view. However, if you ask the communists themselves, they will deny it vehemently. They will claim the opposite: "We are far from any bourgeois morals; we have no sentimentality. It is only justice that we seek, that no man shall exploit another." In other words, it is according to the attribute, "Let mine be mine and let yours be yours," which is, in fact, the attribute of egoists. Hence, I must view the matters from their perspective and review this justice that they seek and to which they devote their lives.

First, according to the development of the communist regimes, I find that the terms "bourgeois" and "proletariat" no longer suffice to explain that economic history, and we need more general terms. It is truer to divide society into a class of diligent and a class of stragglers. In the bourgeois regimes, the diligent are the capitalists and the middle class. The stragglers are the workers who labor for them. In the communist regimes, the diligent are the managers, supervisors, and intellectuals, and the stragglers are the workers who labor for them.

The majority in every society is always the stragglers. The diligent are no more than thirty percent of society. It is a natural law that the class of the diligent will exploit the class of the stragglers as best as they can, like fish at sea, where the strong swallows the weak. It is inconsequential whether the diligent are capitalists and merchants, as in the bourgeois regimes, or whether the diligent are the managers, supervisors, intellectuals, and allotters, as in communist regimes.

Ultimately, the diligent will exploit the laboring stragglers to the best of their ability and will take no pity on them. The diligent will always suck out the butter and the cream, leaving the workers only the meager whey. The only question is what remains for the workers after the ruthless exploitation by the diligent, the measure of enslavement the diligent impose on them, and the measure of freedom and human liberty the diligent allow them. It is only according to the measure of these leftovers, which the diligent leave for the stragglers, that we are to examine every regime, differentiate between the regimes, and choose which one is preferable.

Let us mention once more what we said, that one cannot work without some reward that serves as a fuel for a machine. In a non-altruistic communist regime, the workers must be rewarded for their work and be heavily punished for their negligence.

However, many supervisors are required to watch over them, for without sufficient supervision, the rewards and punishments are certain to be insufficient. However, there is no harder work than standing over people and agonizing them, for no one wants to be a hangman. Hence, even if you place inspectors, appointees over the inspectors, and higher still appointees to watch them, they will all be negligent in their supervision, and will not agonize the workers sufficiently.

There is no cure for this but to provide plenty of fuel to the functionaries, sufficient as reward for such hard labor, meaning the work of the hangman. In other words, they must be given several times more than a simple worker.

Thus, you should not be surprised if functionaries in Russia are paid ten to fifty times more than a simple worker; their work is ten to fifty times harder than that of a simple worker. If they are not sufficiently rewarded, they will be compelled to neglect their office, and the state will be ruined.

Now try to calculate in our country's currency. Let us say that a simple worker earns a hundred Israeli pounds a month. This means that the lowest functionaries will receive a thousand pounds a month, ten times more. Thus, over one year, he will earn twelve thousand pounds, and over ten years, a hundred and twenty thousand pounds.

If we deduct ten percent from this for his sustenance, he will be left with a hundred and eight thousand pounds. It seems that we should consider him a respectable capitalist. It is even more so with higher functionaries.

Thus, within a few decades, the functionaries will become millionaires, at no risk, but strictly through the exploitation of the workers. As I have said, by today's experience, society should no longer be divided into bourgeois and proletariat, but to diligent and stragglers.

You might say that this is but a phase toward pure communism, meaning that through education and public opinion, the public will be tutored until "each will work according to his ability and will receive according to his needs." Then there will be no need for inspectors or supervisors.

This is a big mistake because the motto of each working according to his ability and receiving according to his needs is a strictly altruistic motto. And wherever one can work to the benefit of society without any fuel, it is unnatural unless altruism is the reason and the fuel for the work, as I have shown.

Thus, we must not hope for any change for the better. Quite the contrary, we must fear that that handful of idealist communists who are leading today will not bequeath their leadership to other idealists. The egoistic force of the people will gradually prevail, they will choose a leadership according to their egoistic spirit and will reinstate capitalism. At the very least, they will turn communism into some sort of national communism, a "nation of masters," as did Hitler. They will have no inhibitions about exploiting other nations to benefit themselves, if they only have the power.

You might say that through education and public opinion, the nature of the masses can be inverted into altruism. This is also a grave mistake. Education cannot do more than public opinion, meaning that public opinion will respect the altruists and degrade the egoists.

As long as public opinion sustains altruism by means of respect and ignominy, education will be effective. However, if there comes a time when an experienced and competent speaker gives a daily speech that is the opposite of public opinion, he will undoubtedly be able to change public opinion as he wishes.

We already have such a bitter experience in history with that villain who turned a well-mannered people like the Germans into wild animals through his daily sermons. Several hundred years of education vanished like a bubble of soap, since public opinion had changed, and education had nothing more to rely on, as education cannot exist without the public's support.

Thus, you evidently see that there is no hope to change this compulsive government. There is also no hope that the masses will ever achieve true communism, according to the motto, "Each will work according to his ability and will receive according to his needs."

Rather, the workers must remain eternally under the dreadful rod of managers and supervisors, while the managers and supervisors will always suck the blood of the workers, as bourgeois capitalists do, if not much worse than they. After all, in the compulsory regime of the communists, the workers do not even have the right to strike. Famine and destruction will always hang over their heads, as the Soviet experiment teaches. Moreover, if the compulsory government is ever revoked, society will certainly be ruined instantaneously, for the workers would run out of fuel.

Indeed ... It is said that in a communist regime it is worthwhile for the workers to suffer, since they suffer for themselves, as they are the owners of the productive means, the property, and the surplus, and no one can exploit them. Conversely, in a capitalist regime they only have their daily bread, and all the surplus is given to the capitalists. How lovely these words are on the surface.

Yet, if there is an ounce of truth in these words, then they apply to the diligent, who are the functionaries and the managers, who take all the pleasures of the compulsory regime in any case. But to the proletariat, namely the straggling workers, these are completely empty words.

Let us take our railroads, for example. They are state property, meaning that the ownership of the railroad is in the hands of all the citizens of the state. I ask, do any of us citizens feel our right to ownership of the railroad? Do we have any greater benefit when traveling on a nationalized railway than when traveling on a private, capitalist railway?

We can also take a cooperative owned entirely by the workers, like Solel Boneh (a large construction corporation in Israel), owned solely by the workers. Do the workers who work on their own property have any additional benefit than when working for a foreign, capitalist property?

I fear that one who works for the foreign entrepreneur will feel much more at home than one who works for Solel Boneh, although he is seemingly a co-owner. Only the handful of managers has the entire ownership, and they do with this national property as they see fit. A private citizen is forbidden even to inquire what they are doing, and for what.

Thus, the workers feel no delight in the property of the state and the productive means that is under the hands of the executives and the functionaries, who always oppress and humiliate them as the dust of the earth. What then is the surplus that they have in the compulsory communist regime, more than their daily bread?

I am not at all envious of the workers who are and will be in the compulsory communist regime, under the harsh encumbrance of the functionaries and inspectors, who can torture them with all sorts of atrocities, oblivious to the opinion of the public and the world, as all the advertising mediums is in the hands of the clerks. No one will be able to expose their evil deeds in public.

In addition, everyone will be bound by them, unable to leave the country and escape from them, just as our fathers were locked in Egypt, where no slave could leave there to be free, since every worker leaves all the surplus of his production for the state, so how will they let them go elsewhere when the state loses their surplus? In a word, a non-altruistic communist regime must always consist of two classes: the diligent, who are the managers, the functionaries, and the intellectuals, and the class of the stragglers, who are the productive workers, the majority of society.

For the functioning of the state, the class of the diligent must, willingly or unwillingly, enslave, tantalize, and humiliate the working class mercilessly and shamelessly. They will exploit them ten times more than the bourgeois exploit them, for they will be utterly defenseless, as they will not have the right to strike. They will be unable to disclose the evil deeds of the employers in public, and they will take no pleasure at all in the ownership of the productive means that the functionaries have acquired.

2) One more thing, and this is the most important. Communism must correct more than just the economic order. It must also ensure the minimal existence of the people in the world. In other words, it is to prevent wars so that nations will not destroy one another. I have already screamed like a crane about it back in 1933, in my book *The Peace* pamphlet, warning that wars today have come to such proportions that they endanger the life of the entire world.

The only counsel to prevent this is by all the nations adopting the regime of perfect communism, meaning altruistic. Needless to say, today, after the discovery and use of atom bombs, and the discovery of hydrogen bombs, there is no longer a doubt that after one, two, or three wars, the entire human civilization will be totally ruined, leaving no relics.

Contemporary, modern egoistic communism cannot secure peace in the world, for even if all the nations of the world adopt this communist regime, there will still not be a compelling reason for nations rich in production means, raw materials, and civilization, to share the raw materials and productive means equally with the poor nations.

For example, the nations of America will not want to equalize their standard of living with the Asian or African nations, or even with the European nations. A single nation might have the power to equalize the standard of living of the rich and middle class—the owners of the productive means—with the proletariat, by inciting the poor masses, the majority of society, to destroy the rich and middle class and take their property. However, this counsel will not be of any use in compelling a wealthy nation to share its property and means of production with a poor nation, as the rich nation has already prepared arms and bombs to keep itself from its poor neighbors.

Thus, what good did the communist regime do in the world? It leaves intact the state of envy among the nations just as it is in the capitalist regime, without any relief. A just division within each nation for itself will not assist to a just division among the nations whatsoever.

Hence, while basic sustenance is under such immediate danger, it is a waste of time to improve the economic government. They would be better off using that time to seek counsel to save the very life of all humankind.

You see that the whole problem with today's communist regime is the lack of adequate reward, which is the fuel for the productive force of the workers. Hence, it is impossible to employ them successfully except with the fuel of reward and punishment.

For this reason, we need inspectors, supervisors, and managers to take upon themselves this hard work of supervising the workers and ruthlessly suck their blood and sweat, making their lives endlessly bitter with hardship and enslavement. Also, in return for this hard work, they must be given an adequate reward, which is no less than to make them millionaires, for they will not want to be hangmen of their own free will for any less than that, as we see in the Soviet country.

Also, there is no hope that this reign of terror will ever end, as the optimists promise. Neither bayonets nor education or public opinion can change human nature to work willingly without adequate fuel.

Hence, it is a curse for generations. When the compulsory government is revoked, the workers will no longer yield produce that will suffice for the sustenance of the state. There is no cure for this but to bring faith in spiritual reward and punishment from above into the hearts of the workers, from He who knows the mysteries.

Thus, through the right education and propaganda, that spiritual reward and punishment will be sufficient fuel for the produce of their work. They will no longer need managers or supervisors over their shoulders, but each and every one will work willingly and wholeheartedly for society, to win his or her reward from Heaven.

The Positive

A) Communism is an ideal, meaning moral. The goal "to work according to one's ability and receive according to one's needs" testifies to this.

B) Every moral must have a basis that asserts it, and education and public opinion are a very unsound basis, and the proof is Hitler.

C) Because any concept of the majority is sure to triumph, it is needless to say that the carrying out of the corrected communism is by the majority of the public. Thus, it is necessary to establish the moral level of the majority of the public on a basis that will assert and guarantee that the corrected communism will never be corrupted. The ideal inherent in humans is insufficient, as too few possess it, and they are insignificant compared to the majority of the public.

D) Religion is the only basis sure to raise the level of the collective to the moral level of "working according to the ability and receiving according to the need."

E) Communism must be turned away from the concept, "Let mine be mine and let yours be yours," which is sodomite rule, to the concept, "Let mine be yours and let yours be yours," meaning absolute altruism. When the majority of the public accepts this rule in practice, it will be time to "work according to the ability and receive according to the need." The sign will be that each one will work like a contract worker.

F) It is forbidden to nationalize property before the public reaches this moral level. Before there is a reliable moral factor in the public, the collective will not have fuel for work.

G) The whole world is one family. The framework of communism should eventually encircle the entire world in an equal standard of living for all. However, the actual process is gradual. Each nation whose majority accepts these basic elements practically, and has a guaranteed fuel, may enter the framework of communism right away.

H) The economic and religious form that guarantees communism will be the same for all the nations. Except for religious forms, which do not concern the economy and other conducts, each will have its own form, which must not be changed at all.

I) The world must not be corrected in religious matters before economic correction is guaranteed for the entire world.

J) There should be a detailed program from all the above-mentioned rules and the rest of the rules necessary in this regard. Anyone who comes under the framework of communism must take a solemn oath.

K) First, there must be a small establishment whose majority are altruists to the above-mentioned extent. This means that they will work as diligently as contract workers, ten to twelve hours a day and more. Each and every one will work according to his ability and receive according to his needs.

It will have all the forms of government of a state. In this manner, even if the framework of this institution contains the entire world, and the brute-force government will be revoked completely, nothing will need to change in governance or work.

This institution will be like a global focal point with nations and states surrounding it to the farthest corners of the world. All who enter this framework of communism will have the same program and the same leadership as the center. They will be as one nation in profits, losses, and results.

L) It is absolutely forbidden for anyone from the institution to turn to any of the judicial establishment or any of the forms existing in the brute-force regime. Every conflict is to be resolved among themselves, meaning between the concerned parties. Public opinion, which condemns egoism, will condemn the guilty party for exploiting the righteousness of his friend.

M) It is a fact that the Jews are hated by most nations, and are made fewer by them. It is true for the religious, the secular, and the communists. There is no tactic to fight against it except to bring true altruistic morals into the heart of the nations, to the point of cosmopolitanism.

N) If one is forbidden to exploit one's friends, why should a nation be allowed to exploit its fellow nations? What justifies one nation enjoying the land more than other nations? Therefore, international communism must be instituted.

As there are individuals who have been privileged by diligence, chance, or inheritance from ancestry, to a greater share than the negligent, so it is among the nations. Hence, why should war against individuals be greater than against nations?

O) If you lived on an island of savages that you could not bring to law and order except through religion, would you doubt it and let them destroy one another? Similarly, with regard to altruism, they are all savages, and there is no tactic they will accept unless through religion. Who would hesitate to abandon them to destroy each other with hydrogen bombs?

P) There are three bases to the expansion of faith: 1) Satisfaction of Desires, 2) Proofs, 3) Propaganda.

"Desires" is like the perpetuating of the soul, a reward, as well as a national reward, which is the glorification of the nation.

"Proofs" is that the world cannot exist without it, much less in the days of the atom …

"Propaganda" can be used instead of proof, if it is done with diligence.

Q) Because of the craving for possessions, it is impossible to build altruistic communism unless egoistic communism comes first, as demonstrated by all the societies that wished to establish altruistic communism prior to Marxism. However, now that a third of the world has already laid down their rudiments on an egoistic communist regime, it is possible to begin to establish a sustainable altruistic communism on a religious basis.

R) Altruistic communism will finally completely annul the brute-force regime. Instead, "every man will do that which is right in his own eyes." It should not surprise us, as it was unbelievable that children could be educated by explanation, but only through the cane. But today most people have accepted this and reduce the forceful rule on children.

This regards children who have neither patience nor knowledge. It is even more so with a collective of educated people, knowledgeable people brought up to altruism. They will not need the brute-force regime. Indeed, there is nothing more humiliating and degrading for a person than being under the brute-force government.

Even courthouses will not be necessary, unless some unusual event occurs, where the neighbors do not influence an exceptional individual. In that case, special pedagogues will be needed to turn that person around through argumentation and explanation of the benefit of society until that person is brought back in line.

If a person is stubborn, and it is all to no avail, the public will turn away from that person as though from an outcast until that person rejoins the rules of society.

It turns out that after there is a settlement established on altruistic communism, with a majority of people who have actively taken these rules upon themselves, they will immediately decide not to bring each other to any court, governmental agency, or any other kind of force. Rather, everything will be done by gentle explanation. Hence, no person is to be accepted into the society before he is tested to see if he is so crude that he cannot be tutored into altruism.

S) It is important to make such a correction that no person will demand his needs from society. Instead, there will be selected people who will examine the needs of every person and will provide for every single person. Public opinion will denounce one who claims something for oneself, such as today's thief and scoundrel.

Thus, everyone's thoughts will be devoted to bestowal upon one's fellow person, as is the nature of any edification that calculates it even before one feels one's own needs.

If we want to jump on a table, we must prepare ourselves to jump much higher than the table, and then we will land on the table. However, if we want to jump only as high as the table, we will fall down.

T) Admittedly, the egoistic communism is but a step on the way to justice, a sort of "From *Lo Lishma* [not for Her sake] to *Lishma* [for Her sake]." But I say that the time for the second phase, namely altruistic communism, has come.

First, it must be established in one country, as a model. Afterward, the countries in the first phase will certainly accept it. Time is of the essence, since the shortcomings and brute force used in egoistic communism deter the majority of the cultural world from this method altogether.

Thus, the world must be introduced to the perfect communism, and then most civilized countries in the world will undoubtedly accept it. It is of great concern that imperialism will abolish communism from the world, but if our perfect method is actually publicized, imperialism will certainly be left as a king without armies.

U) Clearly, no stable and proper social life is possible except when controversies among members of society are resolved by the majority. It therefore follows that there cannot be a good regime in a society unless the majority is good. A good society means that the majority in it is good, and a bad society means that the majority in it are bad. As I have said above, Item 3, communism must not be established before the majority of the people in society operate with a desire to bestow.

V) No propaganda can secure a coercive rule over future generations, and neither public opinion nor education will help in this case, for they naturally tend to grow weaker. The exception is religion, whose nature is to grow stronger. We see from experience that nations that accepted religion coercively and compulsively at first, observe them willingly in the following generation. Moreover, they are dedicated and devoted to it.

We must understand that although the fathers took upon themselves altruistic communism because they were idealists, there is no guarantee that their children will follow them in this regime. Needless to say, if the fathers adopted communism by coercion, as is the manner in egoistic communism, it will not endure for generations, but will ultimately be overpowered and revoked. A regime cannot be imposed except through religion.

W) When I say that a communist regime must not be instated before there is an altruistic majority, I do not mean that they will be willingly idealistic. Rather, it means that they will keep it for religious reasons, in addition to public opinion. This coercion is one that will last for generations, for religion is the primary compeller.

X) We must remember all the suffering, poverty, corruption, wars, and the widows and orphans in the world, seeking salvation from the altruistic communism. At that time, it will not be difficult for one to dedicate one's entire life to save them from ruin and the dreadful pains. It is even more so with a young person, whose heart has not been stupefied by one's own shortcomings. That person will certainly support it with one's heart and soul.

The Negative

1) If there is nationalization before the public is ready for it, meaning before each one has a sound basis, and secured cause for fuel to work, it is as though one ruins one's small house before he has the means to build another house.

2) Public equality does not mean equalizing the level of the talented and successful to the level of the negligent and oppressed. This would completely ruin the public. Rather, it means allowing each person in the public a middle class standard of living. Thus, the negligent, too, will enjoy their lives as much the middle class.

3) The freedom of the individual must be kept if it is not harmful to the majority of the public. The detrimental ones must not be pitied and must be made harmless.

4) Current communism endures because of the idealists who lead it. They were idealists before they became communists. However, the second generation, when leaders are elected according to the views of the majority of the public, will gradually be repealed, assuming the form of Nazism or turning back to possessiveness. This is because nothing will stop them from exploiting other, negligent nations.

5) Egoistic communism holds no war preventing element, since the basis of all the wars is living territory, where each wants to build on the ruin of the other, whether justly, or because of envy that the other has more.

Communism based on "Let mine me mine" in a framework of equal division does nothing to remove the envy of the nations with each other, much less the nations' lack of living space. It is also hopeless that the rich nations will give of their share to equalize with the poor because "Let mine be mine and let yours be yours" does not necessitate it. Only communism of "Let mine be yours and let yours be yours" will resolve it.

6) Even today we see that there is a global force that has overpowered and conquered all the communist countries, behaving there as in its own home, just as it was in ancient history in Greece and Rome, etc. There is no doubt that this force will split into pieces in the future, and we already have Tito [Josip Broz Tito]. When they split, they are certain to fight against each other, for how does Russia govern Czechoslovakia, or the others, if not by the sword and the spear?

7) In communism, employers strive to diminish the consumption of the workers and increase their productivity. In imperialism, the employers want, and act, to increase the consumption of the workers, and to equalize their productivity to consumption.

8) The class of rulers and supervisors will eventually create a sort of exile in Egypt over the working class since every worker leaves his or her surplus in the hands of the rulers, who take the greater part of it. Hence, they will not let any worker get away from them to another country. Thus, the workers will be caged, guarded like Israel in Pharaoh's Egypt.

9) The ruling class is destined to finally put to death all the old and handicapped in the working class, arguing that they eat more than they produce and they are parasites on the country. No one will die a natural death.

10) If communism spreads throughout the world, it will put to death every nation that eats more than it produces.

11) If the profiteers and the merchants become allotters, the buyers will become receivers of charity from the allotters, and the allotters will deal with them as they see fit, or as much as they are afraid of the inspectors.

A Regime Cannot Exist on Spears Forever

12) Communism does not exist over an anti-communist society because a regime supported on bayonets and spears is unsustainable. Eventually, the majority in society will prevail and overthrow that government. Hence, an altruistic communist majority must be established first, and the government will be supported on will.

The Habit of Waves of Hatred and Envy Will Later Turn Against the Stragglers

13) Communism that is built on waves of hatred and envy will only succeed in overthrowing the bourgeois, but not in benefiting the stragglers. On the contrary, the same ones that have grown accustomed to hatred and envy will turn the arrows of hatred against the stragglers once the bourgeois are gone.

Egoistic Communism Will Always Be at War with the Public

14) By its very nature, the communist regime will be compelled to always be at war with the anti-communists. This is because each person naturally tends to be possessive. People naturally tend to take the cream and leave the meager whey for others.

Nature does not change by education or public opinion. It is unimaginable that one will ever willingly agree to just division, and army bayonets cannot invert nature, much less education and public opinion.

Naturally-born idealists are few. If you should say that theft and robbery are well guarded in the capitalist regime, I shall tell you that it is because the law permits legal competition. It is comparable to a person who gathers a society where the majority is murderers and robbers, and he wants to rule over them and compel them to keep the law. But regarding the annulment of property, everyone is a robber.

Israel Is Qualified to Set an Example to All the Nations

15) Altruistic communism is seldom found in the human spirit. Hence, the nobler nation must take upon itself to set an example for the entire world.

The Country Is at Risk. Altruistic Communism Will Assist with the Ingathering of the Exiles

16) The nation is at risk since before the economy is stabilized, each will flee to a different place, for not every person can endure the test while there is a way to live comfortably.

In the altruistic communism, the ideal will shine upon all people, giving them satisfaction that will make the suffering worthwhile. Moreover, it will draw the ingathering of the exiles from all the countries because the worries and survival wars everyone experiences overseas will motivate them to return to their land and live in peace and justice.

The Philosophy Is Ready, Meaning Kabbalah Based on Religion

17) Every practical method also requires a renewed idealistic nourishment to contemplate, meaning a philosophy. Concerning our matter, there is already a complete and ready-made philosophy, meaning Kabbalah, though it is intended only for the leaders.

Why Are We the People Chosen for It?

18) We must set a good example to the world because we are better qualified than all other nations. It is not because we are more idealistic than they are, but because we suffered from tyranny more than all other nations. For this reason, we are more prepared to seek counsel that will end tyranny from the land.

19) Ownership and control are not identical. For example, the owners of the railway are the shareholders, and the control is in the hands of the managers, though they have only a single share, or nothing at all. The same applies to the shipping company, whose shareholders have no right to control or advise.

Take warships for example. They are owned by the state, yet no civilian is permitted aboard them. In addition, if the state should be in the hands of the proletariat by way of ownership, the management will ultimately be in the hands of the same managers as now, or others of likewise temper. The workers will have no greater foothold or benefit than they do now, unless the rulers are idealists, caring for the well-being of every single individual.

In a word, with respect to the government, it makes no difference whether the ownership is given to capitalists or to the state. In the end, it is the managers who will control them, not the owners. Hence, the correction of society should relate primarily to the executives. "The Taming of Power," 214 ["The Taming of Power" is a chapter in Bertrand Russell's (British Philosopher, 1872-1970) book, *Power*.]

Likewise, Avniel said in the Knesset (Herut, date ...) [Benjamin Avniel (1906-1993) was an MK (member of Knesset, the Israeli Parliament) from the second elections to the sixth and was part of the Herut party]. In Israel, the gap between the lowest functionary to the highest one is times 1.7. In England, it is times ten, and in the rest of the countries it is more or less the same. But in Russia it is times fifty. Thus, in a proletariat state the functionaries and the managers waste their energy much more than in capitalist countries. This is because the government is oligarchical, and not democratic. In simple words, because the communists control anti-communists, there must be oligarchy. This will never change since a communist means an idealist, which is not the majority.

20) Such a state, where the communists rule over anti-communists is obliged to be in the hands of a group of autocratic executives in absolute dictatorship. All the people in the country will be in their hands as though they are nothing. They must always keep the sword in their hands for killing, incarceration, concealed and revealed punishments, food deprivation, and all sorts of punishments, according to each executive's arbitrary decision. All this is in order to keep the anti-communists in dreadful terror and fear so they work for the state and not ruin it inadvertently or maliciously.

21) In such a state, the executives must make sure the citizens cannot choose a democratic management, since the majority of the country is anti-communist.

22) In such a state, where communists rule over anti-communists, the managers must see that the citizens have no possibility for propaganda, or to disclose the dreadful injustice that is done to the people of the state or to the minorities in the state.

In other words, the printers are not to print, and the administrators of the lecture halls must watch over the speakers so they do not criticize their deeds. They must punish harshly anyone who plans, or even thinks of criticizing their acts. Thus, the government will have full control to deal with them arbitrarily, and there will be no one to detain them (*Power, ...* 21).

23) Ethics cannot rely solely on education and public opinion, because public opinion necessitates only what is in the public's favor. Hence, if one comes and proves that morality is harmful to the public and vulgarity is more beneficial, they will immediately discard morality and choose vulgarity, as Hitler demonstrates.

24) The egoistic communism, based on waves of envy and hate, will never be rid of them. Rather, when there are no bourgeois, they will cast their hate on Israel. We must not be mistaken that egoistic communism will cure the hatred of Israel from the nations. Only altruistic communism can be expected to heal it.

Debate

1) Clearly, the motto, "Each will receive according to his needs and work according to his ability," is absolute altruism. When this is applied, the majority of the public, or all of it, will be armed with the measure, "Let mine be yours." Hence, do tell, which are the elements that can bring the public to this desire? Today's elements, namely the hatred of the capitalists and all sorts of animosities extending from it, will only bring man to the opposite. It will instill the measure of "Let mine be mine and let yours be yours" in people, which is Sodomite Rule, the opposite of love of others.

2) I have nothing to say to those who go with the flow, only with those who have their own opinion and the strength to criticize.

3) Engels' fundamental concept, in the name of Marx, states, "The oppressed and exploited class cannot be liberated from the oppressing and exploiting class without also liberating the entire society from exploitation, oppression and class struggle once and for all."

This contradicts the contemporary communist conduct to slaughter and degenerate all the bourgeois parts of society. This powerful enmity will never be effaced from their children. It contradicts the fact that they are establishing a sovereign, governing class, monitoring the working class. There is no more painful and regrettable class struggle than that. They pump out the fat from the workers' marrow and leave them the leftovers along with constant fear of death, or of being sent to Siberia.

Where is the salvation here? They have replaced the bourgeois class, which was not at all so terrible. In fact, its shadow has been lifted from them since the workers have the power to strike against them. They've substituted it with a sovereign class, governing and ruling over a class of exploited slaves who are perpetually terrorized by punishments far worse than they had in their war against the bourgeois.

4) The country is divided into two classes: the "diligent" and the "stragglers." The diligent are the employers and the leaders; the stragglers are the workers and the led. It is a natural law that the diligent will exploit the stragglers. The only question is how much freedom, equality, and standard of living they leave for the stragglers. Also, how much labor the diligent will demand of them.

The stragglers are always the vast majority in society. The diligent are but ten percent of it, which is the exact measure needed to operate society. If the percentage is increased or decreased, there is a crisis.

These are the crises in the bourgeois society. Crises in the communist society will take a different form, but with the same amount of suffering. The title "diligent" also includes their heirs and those who bribe the diligent. The title "stragglers" relates also to diligent who for some reason have been thrown into the class of the stragglers.

5) Regarding religion: The permanent moral state does not stem from religion, but from science. "Empirio Criticism," 324 [This is a statement made by Lenin in his book, *Materialism and Empirio Criticism*].

6) Morality based on public benefit exists in social animals, too. However, this is not enough since it changes to vulgarity where it is harmful to society, such as the great patriotic murderer, carried on the shoulders of the nationalists. Thus, only religion based morality is durable, valid, and irreplaceable. We find the same among savage nations, whose level of morality is far greater than civilized nations.

7) A society cannot be good unless its majority is good. However, some stun or entice the bad majority with all sorts of contrivances until they are compelled to choose a good leadership. This is what all democracies do. Alas, the majority will finally learn, or others will teach them, and they will choose an evil leadership that matches their ill will.

8) We must understand why Marx and Engels decided that perfection of communism means "Working according to the ability and receiving according to the needs." Who forced it upon them? Why was it not enough to receive according to one's production, and not to equalize one with a negligent, or with a childless? The thing is that communism will not endure by way of egoism, but by the way of altruism, for the above-mentioned reasons.

News

By the very same way they have exterminated the capitalists, they were also forced to exterminate the farmers. In addition, in the sense of the joy of life, they will always be forced to destroy the workers. Although Marx and Engels were the first to place the correction of the world on the workers, it did not occur to them to do it coercively, but rather democratically. For this reason, the workers had to be the majority, and then establish a proletariat government where the leaders of the regime would gradually correct until they come to the abstract altruism: each according to his actions, and each according to his needs.

Lenin added to it the establishment of the communist regime through forcing the minority opinion over the majority, hoping that afterward, altruism would be conducted among them, too. All that was needed for this was an armed camp of workers. Since the property owners are scattered, they could take the government by force, and then come and defeat the weak and unorganized property owners.

In this, he disagreed with Marx and said that it is quite the contrary; in the straggling countries, it is easier to defeat them, as all that is needed was to turn the soldiers into communists and destroyers of the property owners, and to take their property. It is easier to incite soldiers to kill and loot the property owners in a straggling country.

That is why he understood that he will not find a cruder multitude than in his own country, and therefore said that his country will be the first. However, when he saw that in fact it was not enough to destroy the capitalist ten percent, but that millions of farmers must also be destroyed, he grew tired, because it is impossible to destroy half a nation.

Then came Stalin, who said that the end justifies the means, and took upon himself the task of destroying the farmers, too. He was successful.

However, not one of them took into consideration that in the end, they need the good will of the workers, so they would work, and to instill in them the attribute of altruism, which would bring them to this motto. This is utterly impossible. Nature cannot be changed so that not only would one work for one's needs, but for the needs of his friend. This is utterly impossible without coercion and compulsion. Ultimately, the majority will rise and revoke the regime.

Liars are those who say that idealism is either inherent or a result of education. Rather, it is a direct result of religion. As long as religion did not sufficiently expand throughout the world, the entire world was barbaric, without an ounce of conscientiousness.

Only after servants of the Creator expanded did the posterity of the agnostics become idealists. Thus, the idealist is only so because of his ancestry's commandment. However, it is an orphaned commandment, meaning without a commander.

If religion were to be canceled altogether, all governments would then become Hitlers. Nothing would detain them from increasing the country's benefits incessantly. Even today, governments know no sentiments. However, there is still a limit to their acts between the still and the idealists in the country. When religion is revoked, it will not be difficult for rulers to uproot the remaining idealists, just as it was not hard for Hitler and Stalin.

The difference between the idealist and the religious is that the idealist's actions are baseless. He cannot convince anyone of his preference for justice, or who so necessitates it. Perhaps it is but faintness of heart, as Nietzsche said? He will not have a single sensible word to utter, which is why Hitler and Stalin overpowered them. However, the religious will boldly counter that it is so commanded by the Lord, and would give his life for it ...

If my words yield benefit, good. If not, the last generations will know why communism was revoked, that it was not because it could not be sustained, as capitalists say, but because the leaders did not understand how to establish that regime. They erected a regime of egoism where they should have established a regime of altruism.

If anyone should disagree with me and say that education alone will suffice for that, I permit him to establish for himself a society based solely on education, but I will not partake in it. I know all too well that these are idle things. Thus, might he assist me in establishing a religion based society?

Appendices and Drafts

[Fourteen pieces that form appendices or drafts to the essay presented in Part One]

Section One

[This section contains inscriptions that appear to be headlines that the author wrote for his own needs toward writing the essay presented in Part One. It is a kind of first and general draft.]

"Critical communism has never refused, nor refuses now, to fertilize its concepts with the abundance of ideological, ethical, psychological, and educational ideas that may be reached by studying the various forms of communism" (Antonio Labriola (1843-1904), an Italian Marxist theoretician).[*]

2. "Were we to think today as Marx and Engels did, at a time when if they themselves were here today, they would be thinking otherwise ... defending the dead letter of the latter," etc. (from Georgi Plekhanov's (1856-1918) Introductions to the *Communist Manifesto*).[**]

The Positive

1. Evidence for the altruistic communism.

2. For the rules of the altruistic communist society.

3. For the international communism.

4. For a beneficial religion.

5. Promoting the expansion of the religion.

6. Egoistic communism precedes the altruistic communism.

7. For the preservation of Judaism.

The Negative

1. The weakness of the regime of egoistic communism (8).

2. Wars will not become obsolete (9).

3. Proof that egoistic communism cannot last (10).

4. Motives from Zionism (11).

5. Israel must be a role model for the nations (12).

6. Concerning the egoistic regime (13).

7. Ethics (14).

---

[*] Antonio Labriola, *Essays on the Materialist Conception of History*, Part 1: "In Memory of the Communist Manifesto," url: http://www.marxists.org/archive/labriola/works/al00.htm#

[**] Georgi Plekhanov, "The Initial Phases of the Theory of the Class Struggle: An Introduction to the Second Russian Edition of the *Manifesto of the Communist Party*," url: https://www.marxists.org/archive/plekhanov/1898/initial-phases.htm

10/2 14/8 14/4 Communism is egoistic along the way, although eventually it is altruistic.

8/1 3/3 The world should be divided into two kinds: egoists and altruists 0/0.

10/3 10/1 10/2 10/6 The majority of the public is always anti-communist.

8/2 For this reason, the communist regime must rely on bayonets.

13/7 The drawbacks in the egoistic communism governance.

From 8/9 to 9/1 Communism will not save us from wars.

Communism must be international, from 3/2 to 12/1/2.

11/1 Strengthening Zionism, especially the kibbutzim, which are in danger of being canceled.

A communist rule over anti-communists will not survive on bayonets. Those idealists who are in power today will not be elected in the second generation, but rather egoistic managers, like them, and they will turn into Nazism.

I am speaking only to the workers, meaning the stragglers, and to those idealists who dedicate their lives for them. I do not, however, speak to the diligent because they will not be deficient under any regime. Even in the worst regime, they will not be deprived, and it makes no difference whether they are called "industrialists," "merchants," or "managers," "supervisors," or "distributors."

Still, although the coupling of altruists with egoists was so successful in overthrowing the bourgeois government, it is utterly unfit to establish a happy, cooperative society, as the founders wish. Moreover, it is to the contrary, since that coupling of the idealistic communists with the oppressed egoists is bound to break up, leaving social chaos in its wake.

1) How much to leave?

2) What is the measure of enslavement?

3) What is the measure of freedom?

There is no correction to the stragglers unless they choose the committee.

3) The diligent will not let them out of their countries.

3) In the end, they will put to death the elderly and the sick.

1) When traders become distributors, the buyers will become receivers of charity.

2) Ownership and control are not the same.

3) In a compulsory regime, there will not be democratic elections.

2) In such a regime, the citizens are completely inconsequential in the eyes of the government.

2) In such a regime, the managers will enslave even more.

2) In such a regime, the employers will be able to conceal their cruelty.

Explaining Hitlerism

1) Religion is the only sound basis for corrections.

1) Religion is the only sound basis for raising the moral level.

1) Even if it is compulsory at first, in the end it is voluntary.

2) Communism must not be established before altruism has spread through the majority of the public.

1) Religion and ideals complement one another: One is for the few, the other is for the masses.

3) Due to man's craving to work less and receive more, they will be able to assume a communist religion before an egoistic religion has encompassed a third of the world.

4) If you came to an island where savages destroy one another, would you hesitate to offer them a religion by which to save their lives?

5) Man will not be able to settle for dry commandments; he needs a philosophy that will explain to him his good deeds. This is what they have prepared.

Section Two

For the Introduction

1) I have already conveyed the basics of my views in 1933. I also spoke to the leaders of the generation but at the time, my words were not accepted, though I screamed like a crane and warned about the ruin of the world. Alas, it made no impression.

But now, after the atom and hydrogen bombs, I think the world will believe me that the end of the world is nearing rapidly, and Israel will be the first nation to be burned, as was in the previous war. Thus, today it is good to awaken the world to accept its only remedy so they may live and exist.

2) We must understand why Marx and Engels necessitated the ultimate communism, where each works according to his ability and receives according to his needs. Why do we need this strict condition, being the measure of "Let mine be yours and let yours be yours," absolute altruism?

In that regard, I have come to prove in this article that there is no hope for communism to exist, if it is not brought to this end, which is complete altruism. Until then, it is nothing but phases in communism.

Once I have proven the rightness of the motto, "Each according to his ability and each according to his needs," we must see if these phases can yield this outcome.

Today, the terms "bourgeois" and "proletariat" no longer suffice to explain the history of economy. Rather, we need more general terms: the "class of the diligent" and the "class of the stragglers" (above in the section "Debate," Item 4).

After twenty-five years of experience, we are baffled regarding the complete happiness that the communist regime had promised us. Its opponents say it is the absolute evil, and its supporters say that it is heaven on earth.

Indeed, we must not cast off the words of the opponents at a stroke, since when one wants to know another's properties, he must ask both his friends and his foes. It is a rule that the friends know only the virtues and not a single flaw, for "Love will cover all crimes." The foes are the opposite: They know only the faults, for "Hate will cover all virtues."

Thus, one knows the truth when hearing the words of both. I wish to examine communism thoroughly and explain its advantages and disadvantages. Mostly, I wish to explain the corrections, how all its shortcomings can be corrected so that everyone will see and admit that this regime is indeed the regime that brings both justice and happiness.

How happy we were when communism came to practical experimentation in a nation as big as Russia. It was clear to us that after a few years the government of justice and happiness would appear before the entire world, and as a result, the capitalist government would quickly vanish from the world.

Yet, that was not the case. On the contrary, all the civilized nations attribute to the Soviet communist regime every bad flaw. Hence, not only was the bourgeois regime not canceled, it rather grew twice as strong as before the Soviet experiment.

Section Three

Why did communism had to have taken the form of "each according to his ability and each according to his actions"? A communist government cannot endure over an anti-communist society, since a government supported on bayonets is unsustainable.

Communism built on waves of envy can only overthrow and ruin the bourgeois, but not benefit the struggling workers. On the contrary, when the bourgeois are annihilated, the arrows of hatred will aim at the stragglers.

Nothing can guarantee a powerful government over the future generations except religion. Even if the progenitors are idealists, and have taken communism upon themselves, there is no certainty that their progeny will pursue it. Moreover, if the progenitors accepted it by force and coercion, which is the conduct in egoistic communism, they will ultimately rise and demolish it.

A communist regime cannot exist atop an anti-communist society, as it would have to fight the anti-communists throughout its days. This is because every person is naturally possessive, and one cannot work without motivation.

The bayonets of the army will not invert human nature, and the idealists are few. Several thousand years of penalties rest on the heads of the thieves, robbers, and fraudulent, yet they have not changed their nature even though they can obtain everything legally.

It is similar to one who comes upon a society of thieves and murderers and wants to lead them and restrict them to legal ways by force. It must explode.

Double. Double. Double.

Because the majority opinion is guaranteed to win, it is all the more so with the implementation of communism. It will not persist but through the majority of the public. Hence, we must perpetuate the moral level of the majority of the public in such a way that it will never be corrupted.

Religion is the only sound basis that will persist for generations. Communism must be transformed to the mode of "Let mine be yours and let yours be yours," meaning absolute altruism. After the majority of the public achieves it, it will observe, "Each will work according to his ability and receive according to his needs."

Before the majority of the public achieves this level of morality, it is forbidden to nationalize the property for the above-mentioned reasons.

Section Four

Nationalization before the public is ready for it; it is similar to wrecking one's dilapidated house before one has the means to build a strong one.

Just division does not mean equalizing the diligent to the stragglers. This would be ruinous to the public. Rather, it means equalizing the stragglers to the able.

Egoistic communism exists now thanks to a group of idealists that leads it. Yet, in future generations, the public will not elect idealists, but only the most capable, who are not limited by the ideal, and then communism will take on the form of Nazism.

In the egoistic communism, the employers wish to reduce the consumption of the workers and increase their productivity, for there is always a doubt whether it will be sufficient. Imperialism is better than that, since the employers want to increase the consumption of the worker and equalize the productivity to the consumption.

Section Five

The terms "bourgeois" and "proletariat" are no longer sufficient to explain history. Instead, it should be divided into a class of diligent and a class of stragglers.

It is a natural law that the class of the diligent will exploit the class of stragglers like fish at sea, where the strong swallows the weak. It makes no difference if the diligent are bourgeois or functionaries of the communist government. Rather, the question is How much freedom and enjoyment do they leave for the stragglers?

The class of the diligent is ten percent, and the class of stragglers led by them is ninety percent of society. There is no correction for the stragglers unless they themselves choose those diligent who will govern them. If they do not have this power, they will end up being uninhibitedly exploited by the diligent.

Section Six

The class of the diligent, meaning the rulers and the inspectors, are bound to create an exile such as in Egypt over the class of stragglers, who are the workers. This is because the rulers accumulate all the surplus of the workers in their hands and take the lion's share.

In addition, for purposes of the benefit of the public, they will not let any worker escape from them to a different country, and they will guard them like Israel in Egypt. No slave shall leave them and be free. Ultimately, the class of the diligent will put to death all the elderly and handicapped who eat and do not work, or even if they eat more than they can work, as it is detrimental to society, and it is known that they have no sentiments.

When merchants and brokers become allotters, the buyers will become recipients of charity from them. Their fate would be determined by the mercy of the allotters, or as much as they fear the inspectors, should they take interest in that.

Since ownership and control are not the same, for example, a ship that belongs to the state, every citizen has ownership over it, yet no right of entry, but only as the administration that controls it sees fit. Also, even if there is a proletariat government, they will have no preference in government properties than they have now in the bourgeois property, since all the control will be held by the executives alone, which are today's bourgeois, or those like them.

Such a state, where communists govern anti-communists, must be in the hands of an oligarchy, in complete dictatorship, where all the citizens are regarded as nothing, subject to brutal punishments according to the arbitrary heart of each and every executive. Otherwise, they will not secure the sustenance of the needs of the state. In such a regime, the government must ensure that there are no democratic elections since the majority of the public are anti-communists.

Egoistic communism does not liberate the workers whatsoever. On the contrary, instead of bourgeois employers, who are lenient with the workers, they will institute a class of executives and supervisors who will enslave the workers by coercion and harsh and bitter punishments. The oppression and the exploitation will be doubled, and it will not be easier on them in any way if the exploitation is for the good of the country, because in the end, the employers and the oppressors take the cream, and the workers get the meager whey. In return, they are placed under constant fear of death, or punishment harsher than death.

In such a state, where communists rule over anti-communists, the executives must see that the citizens cannot discover the burden and oppression they are under. Thus, after all the works are in their hands, they will forbid the printers from printing, and the speakers from speaking, so they do not criticize their deeds whatsoever. Instead, they will be compelled to lie and cover up for them, and depict a heaven on earth, and their plight will never become known.

It will be even more so with minorities who are not favored by the executives for whatever reason. They will be able to annihilate them without shame or fear that it will become known outside. And what will become of the Jews, whom the majority of the world hates?

Indeed, it is the absolute truth that there cannot be a good and complete society unless its majority is good because the management depicts the quality of society, and the society is elected by the majority. If the majority is bad, the management will necessarily be bad, as well, for the wicked will not place over them rulers of whom they do not approve.

We need not deduce from the modern democracies, as they use various tactics to deceive the constituency. When they grow wiser and understand their cunningness, the majority will certainly elect a management according to their spirit. And their main tactic is that they first sanctify people with good reputations and promote them either as wise or as righteous, and then the masses believe and elect them. But a lie does not persist forever.

This explains Hitlerism. What happened to the Germans is one of nature's wonders. They were considered among the most civilized nations, and all of a sudden, overnight, they became savages, worse than even the most primitive nations in history.

Moreover, Hitler was elected by the majority's vote. In light of the above, it is very simple: Indeed, the majority of the public, which is essentially evil, possesses no opinions, even among the most civilized nations. Rather, they deceive the majority of the public. Hence, even though the majority of the public is evil, there can be a good leadership.

However, should an evil person, capable of uncovering the deceit that the managers employ with the famous people they create, come and present the people that should be elected according to their spirit and desire, as did Hitler (and Lenin and Trotsky [Leon Trotsky, 1879-1940, a Jewish Marxist revolutionary]), it is no wonder that they overthrow the fraudulent and elect evil leaders according to their spirit.

Thus, Hitler was indeed elected democratically, and the majority of the public united behind him. Afterward, he subdued and uprooted all the idealistic people and did with nations as he wished, and as the people wished.

This is the whole novelty. Since the dawn of time, it has never happened that the majority of the public governed a state. Either the autocrats did, who, in the end, do have some measure of morality, or the oligarchy, or the deceitful democrats. But a majority of the simple folk ruled only in the days of Hitler, who, in addition, promoted wickedness toward other nations. He elevated public benefit to the level of devotion since he understood the frame of mind of sadists. When given room to discharge their sadism, they will pay for it with their lives.

Section Seven

Egoistic communism cannot prevent wars, since the diligent nations, or the ones rich in raw materials, will not want to share equally with the poor and straggling nations. Hence, once again we must not hope for peace, except by means of the prevention of wars, meaning by preparing arms to guard against the envy and hatred of the poor and straggling nations, just as today. Moreover, there will be even more wars due to changes in ideals, such as Titoism and Zionism.

I have already spoken and wrote about it in 1933, and I have screamed like a crane that today's wars will destroy the world, but they did not believe. But now, after the atom and hydrogen bombs, I think that everyone will believe me that if we are not saved from wars, it will be the end of the world.

Section Eight

If communism is just toward each nation, it is just toward all the nations. What prerogative and ownership over raw materials in the soil has one nation over others? Who legislated this proprietary law? All the more so when they have acquired it by means of swords and bayonets!

Also, why should one nation exploit another if it is unjust to every individual? In a word: As abolition of property is just for the individual, so it is just for every nation. Only then will there be peace on earth.

Consider this: If proprietary laws and rules of inheritance do not permit possession rights to individuals, why should they permit an entire nation? As just division is applied among individuals within the nation, there should also be internationally just division in raw materials, productive means, and accumulated properties for all the nations equally. There should be no difference between white and black, civilized and primitive, just as among individuals within a single nation. There should be no division whatsoever among individuals, a single nation, or all the nations in the world. While there is any differentiation, wars will not end.

There is no hope of reaching international communism through egoistic communism. Even if America, India, and China should adopt a communist regime, there is still no element that will compel Americans to equalize their standard of living with the savage and primitive Africans and Indians.

All the cures of Marx and Lenin will not help here, inciting the poor class to rob the wealthy class, since the wealthy have already made arms to guard themselves. Thus, if it is to no avail, then the entire egoistic communism was in vain, for it will not prevent wars whatsoever.

Section Nine

It is a fact that Israel is hated by all the nations, whether for religious, racial, capitalist, communist, or for cosmopolitan reasons, etc. It is so because hatred precedes all reasons, but each one resolves the loathing according to one's own psychology. No counsel will help here, except to initiate international, moral, and altruistic communism among all nations.

Israel must be the first among the nations to assume the international, altruistic communism. It must be a model demonstrating the good and beauty of this government because they suffer and will suffer from the tyranny of the nations more than all other nations. They are like the heart that burns before all the other organs. Hence, they are better suited to adopt the proper government first.

Our very existence in the state of Israel is in danger since according to the present economic order, it will take a long time before our economy is stabilized. Very few will be able to endure the experience of the ordeal in our country while they can immigrate to other, wealthy countries. Bit by bit, they will escape the discomfort until too few remain to merit the name State, and they will be swallowed among the Arabs.

But if they accept the international altruistic communist regime, not only will they have the satisfaction of being the avant-garde for the delivery of the world, for which they will know that it is worth the suffering, they will also be able to control their souls and lower the standard of living when needed. They will be able to work hard enough to secure a solid economy for the state.

It is even more so with kibbutzim, whose very existence is built on idealism, which will naturally wane in future generations, as ideals are not hereditary. Undoubtedly, they will be the first to ruin.

Section Ten

Religion is the only sound basis to raise the moral level of society until each person works according to his ability and receives according to his needs.

Unclear ...

If you lived on an island of savages, whose lives you could not save, preventing them from ferociously exterminating themselves, except by means of religion, would you then doubt ordering their lives with a religion that would suffice to save this nation from eradication from the world?

With respect to altruistic communism, everyone is savage. There is no ploy to impose such a regime on the world, except by means of religion, for religious compulsion becomes agreeable in the progeny, as we have seen happen in nations that have accepted religion by force and coercion.

However, in coercion through education and public opinion, which is not hereditary in the progeny, it only diminishes in time. Hence, would you say that it is better that the entire world destroys each other than to impose on them a certain cause to lead them to life and happiness? It is hard to believe that any sane person would hesitate here.

It is impossible to have a stable democratic society except by means of a society whose majority is good and honest, since society is led by the majority, for better or for worse. Hence, the altruistic communist regime must not be established unless the majority of the public is ready to commit to it for generations. That can only be secured through religion because the nature of religion is that even though it begins coercively, it ends voluntarily.

Religion and idealism complement each other. Where the ideal cannot be in the majority, religion forcefully rules the primitive majority, incapable of ideals due to its possessiveness and its desire to work less than his friend and receive more.

It is impossible to erect the altruistic communism before the egoistic communism expands. However, now that a third of the world has assumed the egoistic communism, the power of religion can be used to establish altruistic communism.

Humankind will not suffice with dry decrees without accompanying them with reasonable explanations that support and strengthen these conducts, meaning a philosophic method. In that regard, there is already an entire philosophy concerning the will to bestow, which is the altruistic communism, sufficient to contemplate for one's entire life, and thus strengthen oneself through acts of bestowal.

Section Eleven

Egoistic communism will ultimately adopt the form of complete Nazism, but in the appearance of national communism. However, this difference of names does not inhibit anyone from the satanic acts of Hitler. Thus, the Russians will be the "master nation," and the entire world their submissive servants as in Hitler's way.

In the bourgeois regime, free competition is the primary fuel for success. The industrialists and the merchants play in it, the winners are very happy, and those who do not win suffer a bitter end. In between them are the workers, who have no share in this game. It is seemingly neutral, neither rising nor falling. However, because of its ability to strike, its standard of living is secured.

Ultimately, in both the communist and the bourgeois governments, the stragglers are unfit for leadership, although they are the majority of the public. Rather, they must elect leaders from among the diligent. However, because they are elected by them, they can hope not to be exploited so.

Conversely, in the egoistic communist government, the managers are not elected by the majority of the public, since they are anti-communists, as in Russia and elsewhere, where the elected are only from among the communists. Hence, they face a bitter end indeed, since the workers do not have a single representative in the leadership.

All the above adheres to the rule that the proletariat is anti-communist by nature. The workers are not idealists; they are the straggling majority of society and think that "just division" means that they receive an equal share with the diligent. The diligent will never want that.

My words relate only to the workers, meaning to the stragglers, who are the majority of society. The diligent and the intellectuals will always suck the cream, either in a communist government, or in a bourgeois government. It is reasonable to think that many of them will be better off in a communist regime, since they will not fear criticism, as it is written in Item ...

Only you, the straggling proletariat, will be the worst off in a communist regime. However, the class of the diligent will have a different name: managers and supervisors. They will be better off because they will be rid of the competition, which takes its toll on the bourgeois, and will receive their share persistently and abundantly.

The stragglers have no counsel and contrivance to terminate the fear, unemployment, and ignominy, except for altruistic communism. Hence, my words are not aimed at the diligent and the intellectuals, as they will certainly not accept my words. Only the workers and the stragglers will be able to understand me, and to them I speak, as well as to those who spare the lives of the stragglers and sympathize with their anguish.

It is one of man's freedoms not to be tied to one place, like plants, which cannot leave their habitat. Hence, each country must ensure that it does not inhibit citizens from moving to another country. It must also be ensured that no country closes its gates before strangers and immigrants.

A government of altruistic communism must not be instigated before the majority of the public is prepared for bestowal upon one another.

Ultimately, altruistic communism will encircle the entire world, and the entire world will have the same standard of living. However, the actual process is slow and gradual. Each nation whose majority of the public has been educated to bestowal upon one another will enter the international communist framework first.

All the nations that have already entered the international communist framework will have an equal standard of living. Thus, the surplus of a rich or diligent nation will improve the standard of living of a struggling or poor nation in raw materials and productive means.

The religious form of all the nations should first obligate its members to bestowal upon each other in a manner that (the life of one's friend takes precedence over one's own life), as in "Love your friend as yourself." One will not take pleasure in society more than a struggling friend.

This will be the collective religion of all the nations that will come within the framework of communism. However, besides this, each nation may follow its own religion and tradition, and one must not interfere in the other.

The rules of the equal religion for the entire world are as follows:

1) One should work for the well-being of people as much as one can and even more than one's ability, if needed, until there is no hunger or thirst in the entire world.

2) One may be diligent, but no person shall benefit from the society more than the stragglers. There will be an equal standard of living for all.

3) Although there is religion, tokens of honors should be imparted according to the religion: The greater the benefit one contributes to society, the higher the decoration one shall receive.

4) Refraining from showing one's diligence toward the benefit of society will induce punishment according to the laws of society.

5) Each and every one is committed to the labor of raising ever higher the living standard of the world society, so all the people in the world will enjoy their lives and will feel more and more happiness.

6) The same applies for spirituality, though not everyone is obligated to engage in spirituality, but only special people, depending on the need.

7) There will be a sort of high court. Those who will want to dedicate their labor for spiritual life will have to be permitted to do so by this court.

Also, to elaborate on the other necessary laws:

Anyone, individual, or a group, who comes under the framework of the altruistic communism, must take a solemn oath to keep all this because the Lord has so commanded. At the very least, one must pledge to teach one's children that the Lord has so commanded.

Those who say that the ideal is enough for them should be accepted and tested. If it is so, they may be accepted. However, they must still promise not to pass their heretical ways to their children, but hand them over to be educated by the state. If one accepts neither, he should not be accepted whatsoever. He would corrupt his friends and he would lose more than he would gain.

First, there must be a small establishment, whose majority is willing to work as much as it can and receive as much as it needs for religious reasons. It will work as diligently as contract workers, even more than the eight-hour workday. It will contain all the forms of government of a complete state. In a word, the order of that small society will be sufficient for all the nations in the world, without adding or subtracting.

This institution will be like a global focal point for nations and states surrounding it to the farthest corners of the world. All who enter that framework shall assume the same leadership and the same agenda as the institution. Thus, the entire world will be a single nation, in profits, losses, and results.

Judgments relying on force will be completely revoked in this institution. Rather, all conflicts among the members of society will be resolved among the concerned parties. General public opinion shall condemn anyone who exploits the righteousness of his friend for his own good.

There will still be a courthouse, but it will only serve to sort out doubts that will come between people, but it will not rely on any force. One who rejects the court's decision will be condemned by public opinion, and nothing more.

We should not doubt its sufficiency, as it was unbelievable that children could be educated only by explanation, but only through the cane. However, today, the greater part of civilization has taken upon itself to refrain from beating children, and this upbringing is more successful than the previous method.

If there is one who is exceptional in society, he must not be brought before a court relying on force, but must be reformed through argumentation and explanation and public opinion. If all the counsels do not help him, the public will turn away from that person as though from an outcast. Thus, he will not be able to corrupt others in society.

It is important to establish that no person will demand his needs from society. Instead, there will be appointees who will go from door to door, examining the needs of everyone, and they will provide for him by themselves. Thus, everyone's thoughts will be devoted to bestowal upon one's fellow person, and he will never have to think of his own needs.

It is based on the observation that in consumption we are like any other animal. In addition, every loathsome act in the world stems from consumption. And vice-versa, we see that every joyous act in the world comes from the attribute of bestowal upon one's fellow person. Thus, we should scrimp and reject thoughts of consumption for self, and fill our minds only with thoughts of bestowal upon our fellow person. This is possible in the above manner.

The freedom of the individual must be kept as long as it is not harmful to society. However, one who wishes to leave the society in favor of another must not be detained in any way, even if it is harmful to society, and even then, in a way that the society is not ruined altogether.

Section Twelve

Circulation

There are three rudiments to the expansion of religion: Satisfaction of Desires, Proof, and Circulation.

1) Satisfaction of Desires:

In every person, even in the secular, there is an unknown spark that demands unification with God. When it sometimes awakens, it awakens a passion to know God, or deny God, which is the same. If someone generates the satisfaction of this desire in that person, he will agree to anything. To this we must add the matter of the immortality of the soul, the reward for the next world, glory of the individual, the glory of the nation.

2) Proof:

There is no existence to the world without it, all the more so in the days of the atom and the hydrogen bombs.

3) Circulation:

People must be hired to circulate the above words in the public.

Egoistic communism precedes the altruistic communism, for once it has control so as to abolish property, it is possible to educate that the annulment of property will be due to love of others.

The second phase of communism, being altruistic communism, must be hurried, since the shortcomings and force used in egoistic communism deter the world from this method altogether. Hence, it is time to uncover the final stage of altruistic communism, which possesses all the pleasantness, and has no blemish.

We must also fear, lest the third war breaks out first, and communism will vanish from the world. In a word, there is no harder blow to the capitalist government than this above-mentioned perfect form of communism.

We are already witnessing that the capitalist regime is strong and the workers of the capitalist countries loathe the communist regime. This is happening because of the coercion and the force necessitated in it because of the control of a small group of communists over an anti-communist society.

Hence, we are not to expect that the regime will be canceled by itself. Quite the contrary, time works in their favor. As long as communist governments surround the world, the coercion and subjection entailed in it will be revealed, which every ordinary person utterly loathes, since one will sacrifice everything for one's freedom.

There is another thing: Since communism is not spreading in civilized countries, but in primitive ones, eventually there will be a society of rich countries with a high living standard and a capitalist government, and a society of poor countries with a low standard of living and a communist government. That will be the end of communism. No free person will want to hear of it; it will be abhorred as the concept of slaves sold for life is abhorred today.

For Expansion and Circulation

We must remember that all the agony, poverty, and slaying, etc., can be corrected only through altruistic communism. In that event, it will not be hard for a person to give his life for it.

Judaism must present something new to the nations. This is what they expect from the return of Israel to the land! It is not in other teachings, for in that we never innovated. In them, we have always been their disciples. Rather, it is the wisdom of religion, justice, and peace. In this, most nations are our disciples, and this wisdom is attributed to us alone.

If this return is canceled, Zionism will be canceled altogether. This country is very poor, and its residents are destined to endure much suffering. Undoubtedly, either they or their children will gradually leave the country, and only an insignificant number will remain, which will ultimately be swallowed among the Arabs.

The solution for it is only altruistic communism. Not only does it unite all the nations to be as one, helping one another, it also endows each with tolerance to one another. Most importantly: Communism produces great power to work; hence, productivity will compensate for the disadvantages of poverty.

If they assume this religion, the Temple can be built and the ancient glory restored. This would certainly prove to the nations the rightness of Israel's return to their land, even to the Arabs. Conversely, a secular return such as today's does not impress the nations whatsoever, and we must fear lest they will sell Israel's independence for their needs, and needless to say returning Jerusalem. This would even frighten the Catholics.

Section Thirteen

Thus far, I have shown that communism and altruism are one and the same, and also, that egoism and anti-communism are the same. However, all this is my own doctrine. If you ask the communist leaders themselves, they will deny it unreservedly.

Instead, they would maintain that they are far from any sentimentality and bourgeois morality, and seek only justice by way of "let mine be mine and let yours be yours." (All this has come to them because of their connection with the proletariat.) Thus, let us examine things according to their perception and scrutinize this justice that they seek.

According to the development of today's governments, the terms "bourgeois" and "proletariat" are no longer sufficient to explain history. We need more general definitions. They should be determined by the names "diligent" (which in the second regime are the capitalist, and in the communist regime), and "stragglers."

Any society is divided into diligent and stragglers. Some twenty percent are diligent, and eighty percent are stragglers. It is a natural law that the class of the diligent exploits the class of the stragglers, like fish at sea, where the strong swallow the weak. In that regard, it makes no difference whether the diligent are bourgeois capitalists, or managers, supervisors, or intellectuals. In the end, the same diligent twenty percent will always suck the cream and leave the meager whey to the stragglers. But the question is how much they exploit the stragglers, and which kind exploit the stragglers more—the bourgeois or the managers and supervisors.

Section Fourteen

The basis of this entire explanation is the manifestation of the substance of creation, spiritual and corporeal, being nothing but the will to receive, which is existence from absence. However, what this substance receives extends existence from existence.

Thus, it is clearly known what is good and what the Creator demands of us, namely, equivalence of form. By the nature of its creation, our body is but a desire to receive, and not to bestow at all. This is opposite to the Creator, who is all to bestow, and not to receive at all, because from whom would He receive? It is in this disparity of form that creation has become separated from the Creator.

Hence, we are commanded to deeds in Torah and *Mitzvot* [commandments] that bring contentment to the Maker, and to bestow upon one's fellow person in order to acquire the form of bestowal and adhere once more to the Creator as prior to creation.

The Differences between Me and Schopenhauer
[Arthur Schopenhauer (1788-1860), German philosopher]

1) He perceives it as an essence on its own, while I perceive it as a type and a predicate. Its essence may be unknown, but whatever it may be, it extends existence from existence.

2) He perceives the desire itself as an ambition that no goal can end but is rather a constant ascent and perpetual drive. With me, however, it is limited to receiving certain things, and can be satiated, meaning directed.

However, attaining the goal increases the will to receive, as in, he who has one hundred wants two hundred. Prior to this, the will to receive was limited to obtaining only one hundred; it did not want two hundred. In this manner, the constant desire is expansion of the desire; it is not the will to receive itself.

3) He does not differentiate between the will to bestow and the will to receive. With me, only the will to receive is the essence of the creature, while the will to bestow in it is a Godly light, ascribed to the Creator, not to the creature.

4) He perceives the desire itself as an object, considering it a form and an occurrence in the object. With me, the emphasis is rather on the form of the desire, meaning the will to receive, but the carrier of the form of the will to receive is an unknown essence.

1) ... Since he considers the desire as the subject, he must define some general, formless desire. Thus, he chooses the endless aspiration for materials, and what it wants is the form. Yet, in truth, there is no endless yearning here, but a growing desire that grows according to the direction, and it is a form and a case in the desire.

A) In his method, it is an essence, and in mine, a form.

B) In his method, it is a never-ending desire, and in mine, it is limited in its direction.

C) In his method, there is no difference between bestowing and receiving, and in mine, the will to bestow is a spark of the Creator.

D) In his method, the yearning is a substance, and the quality of the reception, the form, and in mine, the quality of reception is the substance of creation and the carrier of the quality is unknown. Whatever it is, it is existence from existence.

Part Two

Leaders of the Generation

The masses tend to believe that the leader has no personal commitments and interests, but that he has dedicated and abandoned his private life for the common good. Indeed, this is how it should be. If the leader harms a member of the public due to personal interest, he is a traitor and a liar. Once the public knows it, they will immediately trample him to the ground.

There are two kinds of personal interests: 1) material interests, 2) mental interests. There is not a leader in the world who will not fail the public for mental interests. For example, if one is merciful, and hence refrains from uprooting evildoers or warning about them, then he ruins the public in favor of a personal interest. He might also be afraid of vengeance, even the vengeance of the Creator, and thus deters from making necessary corrections.

Thus, if he wishes to annul material interests, he will not wish to annul the idealistic or religious interests in favor of the public, though they may be only his own personal sensations. The general public may have no dealings with them, for they notice only the word "interest," since even the most idealistic thing does not stand in the way of "interest."

Action before Thought

As in desire and love, the exertion over an object creates love toward, and appreciation of the object. In much the same way, good deeds beget love for the Creator, love begets *Dvekut* [adhesion], and *Dvekut* begets intelligence and knowledge.

Three Postulates [Axioms]

Seemingly free, seemingly immortal, seemingly existing [the last word is unclear in the manuscript and is therefore a speculation]. They are relative to practical reason (ethics), to the most sublime good.

Truth and Falsehood

It is known that thought, matter, and desire are two modifications [differences of form] of the same thing. Thus, the psychological replica of physical absence and existence is truth and falsehood. In this manner, truth, like existence, is the thesis, and falsehood, like absence, is the antithesis. The desired synthesis is the progeny of both.

[new page]

[Here and below, the words "new page" mark the beginning of a new page or a new section in the manuscript.]

Personal Opinion and Public Opinion

The opinion of the individual is like a mirror where all the pictures of the beneficial and detrimental acts are gathered. One looks at those experiences, sorts out the good and beneficial ones, and rejects the acts that have harmed him. This is called the "memory brain."

For example, the merchant follows in his mind all kinds of merchandise where he suffered losses, and why. It is likewise with merchandise that yielded profits for him, and the reasons. They are arranged like a mirror of experiences in his mind. Subsequently, he sorts out the good and rejects the bad. Finally, he becomes a good and successful merchant. One deals in much the same way with every experience in life.

Similarly, the public has a collective mind, a memory brain, and collective imagination where all the acts related to the public and the collective are imprinted, from every person, the beneficial ones and the detrimental ones. And they also choose the beneficial acts and doers, and want those who do them to persist. In addition, all the doers of bad deeds that harm the public are imprinted in the imagining and memory brain, and they loathe them and seek tactics to get rid of them.

Hence, they praise and glorify the doers of the beneficial acts in order to increasingly motivate them to these acts. This is where ideals, idealists, and every good attribute come from, as well as the wisdom of ethics.

Conversely, they will strongly condemn the doers of detrimental actions, so as to stop and get rid of them. This is the origin of every evil trait, sin, and ignobility in the human race. Thus, individual opinion operates just like public opinion. Yet, this is true only with regard to benefit and harm.

The Corruption in Public Opinion

The corruption in public opinion is that the public is not arranged according to its majority, but only according to the powerful, meaning the assertive. It is as they say, that twenty people rule all of France. In most cases, they are the rich, which are but ten percent of the public, and they are always the ignorant among the people (even in the eyes of the public).

They harm the public and exploit them. Hence, public opinion is not in control of the world whatsoever. Rather, it is the opinion of the detrimental that controls the public. Thus, even the idealists that were sanctified in the world are but demons and evildoers with regard to the majority of the public. Not only religion, but justice, too, favors only the rich, all the more so ethics and ideals.

The Origin of Democracy and Socialism

This is where the idea of democracy stems from, so the majority of the public will take the judicial system and politics into its own hands. Socialism also calls for the workers to take their destiny into their own hands. In short, the majority wants to determine public opinion, decide between beneficial and detrimental for them, and determine all the laws and ideals accordingly.

The Contradiction between Democracy and Socialism

The contradiction between democracy and socialism, as seen in Russia, is that ten percent control the entire public in absolute dictatorship. The reason is simple: Just division requires idealism. This is not found among the majority of the public. Hence, ultimately, it is bound to fall, and there is no cure for this except through religion, from above, which will turn the entire public into idealists.

[new page]

Contact with Him

People imagine that a person who has contact with Him is a person ... nature, and that they should fear speaking to Him, much less be in His immediate vicinity. It is human nature to fear anything outside the nature of creation. People also fear anything uncommon, such as thunder and loud noises.

However, He is not so. This is because in fact, there is nothing more natural than coming into contact with one's Maker, for He has made nature. In fact, every creature has contact with his Maker, as it is written, "The whole earth is full of His glory," except we do not know or feel it.

Actually, one who is awarded contact with Him attains only the awareness. It is as though one has a treasure in his pocket, and he does not know it. Along comes another and lets him know what is in his pocket. Now he really has become rich.

Yet, there is nothing new here, no cause for excitement. In fact, nothing has been added in the actual reality. The same is true for one who has been granted the gift of knowing that he is the Creator's son: Nothing has changed in his actual reality but the awareness he did not have before.

Consequently, the attaining person becomes very natural, simple, and very humble. It might even be said that before the endowment, that person and all the people were outside of the simple nature. This is because now he is equal, simple, and understands all the people. He is very much involved with them, and no one is closer to the folk than he, and it is only him that they should love, for they have no closer brother than him.

[new page]

Rebuilding the World

See "Personal Opinion and Public Opinion," and "The Contradiction between Democracy and Socialism."

It has been clarified there that until now public opinion evolved and was built according to the powerful ones in society, meaning the assertive. It is only recently that the masses have evolved through religion, through schools, and revolutions, and have perceived the method of democracy and socialism.

However, according to the natural law that "a man is born a wild ass' colt," and man is an upshot of a wild animal and a monkey, according to Darwin's method or that of our sages, after the sin, the human species decline into monkeys, for "All before Eve are as a monkey before the man." However, according to man's merit, who consists in intellectual preparation, he continued to develop through deeds and suffering, and assumed religion, politics, and justice, and finally became civilized. Indeed, this entire development was placed solely on the shoulders of the better part of society, and the masses followed them like a herd.

When the masses opened their eyes to take their fate into their hands, they had to revoke all the corrections and laws of the assertive, being religion, justice, and politics. This is because these were only according to the spirit of the assertive, according to their development and for their own good.

Thus, they had to build the world anew. In other words, they are like prehistoric people, the Darwinian ape, as they are not the ones who experienced these experiences, which brought them their measure of development. Until today, the succession of development was solely on the shoulders of the assertive, not on the masses, who, until now, were virgin soil.

Thus, the world is now in a state of total ruin. It is very primitive in the political sense, as in the age of the cave dwellers. They have not been through the experiences and actions that brought the assertive to take upon themselves religion, manners, and justice.

Hence, if we let the world develop naturally, today's world must undergo all the ruin and torments that the primitive man experienced until they are compelled to assume permanent and beneficial political justice.

The first fruit of the ruin came upon us in the form of Nazism, which is ultimately merely a direct offshoot of democracy and socialism, meaning of the leadership of the majority, once the restraints of religion, manners, and justice have been removed.

Nazism Is Not an Offshoot of Germany

It turns out that the world erroneously considers Nazism a particular offshoot of Germany. In truth, it is the offshoot of a democracy and socialism that were left without religion, manners, and justice. Thus, all the nations are the same in this, and there is no hope at all that Nazism will perish with the victory of the Allies, for tomorrow the Anglo-Saxons will adopt Nazism, since they, too, live in a world of democrats and Nazis.

Remember that democrats, too, must renounce religion, manners, and justice of peace like the Marxists, since all these are loyal servants only of the assertive in the public. They always place obstacles before the democrats, or the better part [majority] of the public.

It is true that thinkers among the democrats keep a watchful eye that religion and manners are not destroyed at once, for they know that the world will be ruined. However, to that extent they also interfere with the government of the majority. Once the majority grows smart and understands them, it will certainly elect other leaders, such as Hitler, since he is a genuine representative of the majority of the public, be it German, Anglo-Saxon, or Polish.

The One Counsel

Unlike the democrats—who wish to cancel religion and manners gradually, and adapt a new politics in a manner that will not ruin the world—the masses will not wait for them at all. Rather, as our sages say, "Do not ruin a synagogue before you can build a new one in its stead." In other words, we are forbidden to let the powerful ones [majority] take the helm of leadership before we build a religion, conducts, and politics suitable for them, for in the meantime the world will be ruined and there will be no one with whom to speak.

[new page]

Nihilism

[a philosophical view that negates all the traditional values and institutions]

Not complete nihilism, but nihilism of values (such as Nietzsche with regards to the values of Christianity), meaning all the values in the religious conducts, ethics, and politics that have been thus far accepted in the perception of humanism.

All these are compromises in the measurements of egoism of the individual, the state, or a servant of the Creator. And I say that any measure of egoism is flawed and detrimental, and there is no other arrangement except altruism, in the individual, the public, and the Creator.

Materialistic Monism

Substance fathers everything, and the thought is the result of actions and sensations, much like a mirror. There is no freedom of will, only freedom of actions. However, not by itself, for evil deeds induce evil deeds, and the freedom of actions is perceived by looking (in the mirror of called upon actions) through another person's mind. Then one has the freedom to obey it. And he will not be able to choose from his own (mirror) mind, since every man's way seems right in his own eyes, and his mind always agrees.

Outside of This World

Outside of this world, we must research and examine only subjectively and pragmatically (practically). This way is the conduct of the research in this world, although it is outside of it, as it contemplates by measurements clothed in the nature of this world, and also according to the practical (pragmatic) benefit.

What Is Outside of This World?

Only the Creator is imperative, since He is the place of the world, and the world is not His place. It is He alone Whom we understand to also be outside of this world, and nothing else, unlike pantheism.

This world is an objective term which can be understood objectively, as well. Its first principles are "time" and "space." Outside of this world, which are the worlds *AK* and *ABYA* [the worlds *Adam Kadmon, Atzilut, Beria, Yetzira,* and *Assiya*], only subjective comprehension is possible, without touching the object whatsoever.

The essence of the objects we define by names in *ABYA* follow the assumption that since everyone perceives so without exception (meaning a chosen few in each generation, which are the tens of thousands and the millions that were, and are destined to be). Thus, we have objective attainment there, though we do not touch the objects whatsoever.

From here come the four worlds above this world, though by nature they are only subjective, clothing the natures of this world in the two ways—expansion and thought—namely psychophysical parallelism. This is so because we know any object by two forms: physical first, and psychic next, and they always go together in a parallel manner.

It is known that in this world, too, many perceive the method of "expressionism," meaning solely by subjective perception. However, I also abide by "impressionism" to explain concepts of this world as objectively as possible, minimizing the interference of subjective reinforcement.

[new page]

The Essence of Religion

The essence of religion is understood only pragmatically, as written by James [William James (1842-1910), American philosopher]. The origin of faith is in the need for the truth in it, inasmuch as it satisfies this need.

There are two kinds of needs: 1) A mental need. Without it, life would become sickeningly detestable. 2) A physical need. This need appears primarily in the social order, such as in ethics and politics, as Kant [Immanuel Kant (1724-1804), German philosopher] had written, "Faith is the basis of morality, and guards it."

Naturally, sages will come solely from among those with the mental need, for they also need it objectively. However, the second part will derive satisfaction, namely truth, also subjectively. However, from *Lo Lishma* [not for Her sake] one comes to *Lishma* [for Her sake]. The need precedes the reason that necessitates faith.

The Leaders of the Public

For oneself, one may choose between expressionism and impressionism. However, the leaders are not permitted to lead the public in any other way but a positive and pragmatic one, meaning according to expressionism. This is because they cannot harm the public for their personal interest.

For example, they cannot instruct a certain faith to the public in order to understand their own impressionism, thus denying moral conduct and ethics from the public. If one cannot control oneself, he had better resign and not harm the public with his ideals.

Perception of the World

The world was created through consequential evolution, according to historic materialism and the dialectics of Hegel [Georg Wilhelm Friedrich Hegel (1770-1831), German philosopher] of thesis, antithesis, and synthesis. Indeed, it corresponds to the sensation of the Creator, from the still, vegetative, animate, and speaking, up to prophecy, or to the knowledge of the Creator. Pleasure is the thesis, affliction is the antithesis, and the sensation outside one's skin is the synthesis.

The Essence of Corruption and Correction Is in the Public Opinion

As private opinion determines one's own gains and losses and brings one to the most successful business, so public opinion determines the policy and chooses the most successful. However, there is quantity and there is quality.

Quantity vs. Quality

Until now, the qualitative [powerful] (who are the assertive) determined and made the views of the entire public, and therefore all the justice and morality. Religion was used to harm the majority, which are 80% of society.

The Majority Is as Primitive as Prehistoric Man

The majority is as primitive as prehistoric man. This is so because they have not tried to utilize justice, religion, and morality, which were used by others until today. However, of course, all these came to the present state only through great pains in the path of causality and dialectics. The majority paid no heed to it, and at any rate, cannot grasp it.

The Quickest Action Is Religion

In order to activate public opinion anew in the majority in an effective manner, there is no quicker way than religion, the loathing of any measure of will to receive, and elevating the beauty of the will to bestow to a great extent. This must be done specifically by actions. Although the psychophysical are parallel, still, the physical precedes the psychic.

[new page]

The Prodigies

The prodigy is a product of the generation; he has a strong tendency to bestow and he does not need anything for himself. As such, he has equivalence of form with the Creator and naturally cleaves to Him. He extends wisdom and pleasure from Him and bestows upon humankind.

They are divided into two kinds: Either they work consciously, meaning to bestow contentment upon their Maker, and hence bestow upon humankind, or they work unconsciously, meaning that they do not feel or know that they are in adhesion with the Creator. They adhere to Him unconsciously and bestow only upon humanity. According to this basis, there is no progress to humanity, except to instill the will to bestow in them and multiply the prodigies in the world.

Teleology

[the science of purpose]

Teleology is necessary in Kabbalah, according to the method of anthropocentricity, that the worlds were created for Israel, and they are the purpose. Moreover, the Creator consulted with the souls of the righteous. Their purpose is also brought in the prophecy: "And the whole earth shall be full of the knowledge of the Lord." There is no more specific purpose than that.

Maimonides takes after the method of dysteleology, and says that the Creator has for creation other purposes besides the human species. It is hard for him to comprehend that the Creator created such a vast creation, with planetary systems, where our planet is like a grain of sand, and all this was only for the purpose of man's completeness.

Purpose is imperative for any mindful being, and one who works purposelessly is mindless. By His actions we know Him. He has created the world in still, vegetative, animate, and speaking. The speaking is the climax of creation since it feels others and bestows upon them. Atop them is the prophet, who feels the Creator and knows Him. This is perceived as pleasing to Him and as His purpose in the entire creation.

Hegel's question is that necessarily, there are purposeless creatures in nature, like many things on our planet, and the countless planets that humankind does not use at all. The answer is according to the law that "The unknown does not conceal the known," and that "The judge has only what his eyes see." Perhaps there is still, vegetative, animate, and speaking on each planet, and on every planet, its purpose is the speaking.

It is likewise with the unknown. And how can that contradict the known and familiar in the way of prophecy? This is simple: It is pleasurable for the Creator to create an object that will be qualified for negotiation with Him and exchange of views, etc. There is also pleasure in having something that is not of the same kind, and we completely trust the prophecy.

Causality and Choice

Causality and choice are a path of pain by which one repays unconsciously by dialectic laws. Within each being, the absence and existence of a being are concealed as long as the absence in it has not been revealed. When the antithesis develops and manifests, it destroys the thesis and brings in its place a more complete being than the first, as it contains the correction of the previous antithesis (since any absence precedes presence.) Hence, the second being is called "synthesis," meaning it includes and is an upshot of both the presence and the absence, which preceded this new being.

Likewise, truth always follows and is perfected by the path of suffering, which is presence and absence, thesis and antithesis, and always yields truer syntheses until the appearance of the perfect syntheses. But what is perfection?

In historical materialism, the above-mentioned path of suffering is clarified only with relation to economic desires, where each thesis means just governance for its time, each antithesis means unjust division in the economy, and each synthesis is governance that settles the antithesis that has been revealed, and nothing more. For this reason, absence is concealed in it, as well. When the absence develops, it destroys that synthesis, too, and so forth until the just division manifests.

The Path of Torah

The path of Torah is placing fate in the hands of the oppressed. This accelerates the end to the extent that the oppressed watch over it. This is called "choice," since now the choice is in the hands of the concerned parties. Thus, the path of pain is an objective act, the path of Torah is a subjective act, and fate is in the hands of the concerned parties.

[new page]

The principle: bestowal upon others. The governance—a regime that mandates a minimum for life, and good deeds toward the standard of living of society. The purpose and the goal: adhesion with Him. In my opinion, this is the final synthesis where absence is no longer concealed.

Good Deeds and *Mitzvot*

Locke [John Locke (1632-1704), English philosopher] said that there is nothing in the mind that does not come in the senses first. In addition, Spinoza [Baruch Spinoza (1632-1677), Jewish Dutch philosopher] said, "I do not want something because it is good, but it is good because I want it." We must add to this that there is nothing in the senses that is not present in actions first.

Thus, the actions engender senses, and senses engender understanding. For example, it is impossible for the senses to take pleasure in bestowal before they actually bestow. Moreover, it is impossible to understand and perceive the great importance of bestowal before it is tasted in the senses.

Likewise, it is impossible to taste pleasure in adhesion before one performs many good deeds that can affect it, meaning by strict observance of this condition to bring Him contentment, meaning to delight in the contentment given to the Creator by performing the commandment. After one feels the great pleasure in the actions, it is possible to understand Him to the extent of that pleasure. And if ... for eternal and perpetual pleasure from bringing contentment to Him, then he will be rewarded with knowing ...

As seen above, there are two modes in religion: 1) *Lo Lishma* [not for Her sake], which is pure utilitarianism, meaning aiming to establish morality for one's own good. One is satisfied when acquiring this tendency. And there is a second tendency to religion, being a mental need to adhere to Him. This is called *Lishma* [for Her sake]. One can be rewarded with the above through actions, and from *Lo Lishma* one comes to *Lishma*.

Life's Direction

There are three views in books and in research: either ideas about how to attain adhesion with Him, or to acquire progress, called utilitarianism, or corporeal pleasure of the flesh, called Hedonism or Cyranism.

I wish the view of Hedonism were true. The trouble is that the pains are greater than the few sensual pleasures that one can delight in. Besides the flaw of the day of death, and the method of utilitarianism to bring progress to the world, there is a big question here: Who enjoys this complete progress ... that I pay so heavily for with pains and torments?

It seems that only ideals whose tendency is man's happiness, thereby improving all the mental forces, impart one with respect in life and a good name after his death. Kant mocked this method of establishing a moral thesis on an egoistic tendency and instructed doing in order not to receive reward.

Modern science has chosen for itself utilitarianism, but only for the common good, meaning to bestow. This is also similar to "in order not to receive reward," and who would want it? There is also the question: What will this progress bring to the generations for which I work with so much pain to give this?

At the very least, I have the right to know what is required of progress, and who will enjoy it. Who would be so gullible as to pay so heavily without knowing its effect? The whole trouble is that the pleasure is brief and the suffering, long.

Life's Purpose

From all the aforementioned, you will find that life's direction is to attain adhesion with Him, strictly to benefit the Creator, or to reward the public with achieving adhesion with Him.

Two Enslavements in the World

There are two enslavements in the world, either enslavement to the Creator, or enslavement to His creatures. One of them is a must. Even a king and a president necessarily serve the people. Indeed, the taste of complete freedom is only to one who is enslaved to the Creator alone, and not to any being in the world. Enslavement is necessary, for reception is obscene; it is beastliness. And bestowal, the question is, "To whom?"

Part Three

Section One

Pragmatic Communism

Accepting the religion of "Love your neighbor as yourself," literally.

Just division of the profits, where each will work according to his ability, and receive according to his needs.

Property is kept, but its owner is forbidden to receive from the profits more than he actually needs. One type of property owners will be kept under public supervisors, another type by self-fiduciary or books.

The unemployed will receive their needs equally with the employed.

Those who live in communes will earn the same wages as workers who are property owners, and the profits made by the communal life will be made into public property belonging to the members of that collective.

There must also be an effort to build communal life for workers in towns.

Advantages

The workers, and even more so those who fear being unemployed, will certainly assume the religion, thus acquiring security in their lives. The idealistic property owners will also assume the religion by indoctrination on a religious basis.

Public opinion must be such that one who takes more than one needs is like a murderer. Because of him, the world will have to continue the slaughter, Hitlerian manners, and terrible wars. Thus, communism will be promoted.

It is possible to make the life of property owners miserable by contracts and strikes, so they assume the religion since they do not touch their properties, only the profits. Since the religion will be international, it will be possible to win the hearts of the Arab Sheiks with money and religious influence — so they assume the religion together with us as one unit, and promote it among the Arab workers and property owners.

That, in turn, will benefit Zionism. Because they will assume the religion that necessitates love and bestowal upon all humankind equally, they will not be envious of the robbing of the land, since they will understand that the land is the Lord's. The standard of living of the Arabs will be equal to the standard of living of the Jews. This will be a great incentive for winning their hearts.

Section Two

Private Opinion and Public Opinion

As there is private opinion, which is one's force of judgment where all the good and bad actions are copied, and as one chooses the good and rejects the bad as though looking in a mirror, so is there a collective mind to the public, where the good actions for society and bad ones are copied. Public opinion sorts out the ones that are good for it, praises their doers, and condemns those who do otherwise. From here emerge idealists, leaders, rules, and reasons.

The Corruption in Public Opinion: the Powerful Ones

Until today, only the assertive had the judgment and the leadership, being the better part, as it is said, that twenty people lead all of France, and they make public opinion. They have arranged justice, morality, and religion to their benefit. Since they exploit the majority of the public, religion, law, and ethics are hence detrimental to the public, meaning to the majority.

Bear in mind that the current government of the assertive was quite sufficient until today since the masses did not have any power to judge. Thus, all the ruins preceding today's political order were only among the assertive. However, they did not come to the present order within one generation, but through terrible ruins until they have conceived the religion, ethics, and law that have brought order to the world.

The New Structure

In recent generations, due to pressure and necessity, and through democracy and socialism, the masses have begun to open their eyes and assume responsibility for the management of society by the majority. Thus, they have concluded that religion, manners, governance, and justice are all to their detriment, as it is true that it serves the assertive ten percent of the public, and harms all the others.

Thus, two images of collective government emerged: either as the Nazis, who have rebelled against religion, manners, and justice, and do as the primitive man, prior to the conducts of life of the assertive, or as the Soviets, where ten percent of the public controls the entire public by dictatorship. This will certainly not last long, in light of the historical dialectic.

If manners are revoked, Israel's enemies will wipe out everyone. In short, we will necessarily and undoubtedly return to being cave dwellers, until (the masses, too) the majority learn the dialectics on their own flesh and bones (as did the powerful ones before them), and finally agree to order.

Thus, Nazism Is Not a German Patent

If we remember that the masses are not idealists, then there is no counsel but religion, from which manners and justice naturally emanate. However, now they only serve the majority. How so? Through the religion of bestowal.

The principle of bestowal upon one's fellow person. The leadership: commitment to a certain minimum, and commanded to a standard of living.

The goal: adhesion with the Creator.

Nazism Is the Fruit of Socialism

Idealists are few, and the true carriers, the workers and the farmers, are egoists. If a preacher such as Hitler were to arise in any nation, saying that National Socialism is more convenient and beneficial to them than internationalism, why would they not listen to him?

[new page]

1) If Nazism and its ruin had been conceived some years earlier, and if some wise men were to devise a plan to save them through devout religion that would suffice for protection, would it have been forbidden in the name of falsehood?

2) If, after the war, the nations come to understand that Israel must be dispersed to the four corners and drive us out of our land, and a certain person would come and reinstate religion (so as to stand devotedly) between us and the nations, thus making them agree to the opposite, that even the Diaspora would come to Israel, would that have been forbidden?

3) If the Nazis, God forbid, prevail and rule the world, and wish to destroy the residue of Jacob, is it permissible to institute religion among all nations in order to save the nation?

Pragmatism

Faith stems from a need; it is true as long as it satisfies that need (James [William James (1842-1910)]). Thus, the need is the reason for faith, and the satisfaction of the need is its trueness.

Two needs: 1) A material need to establish social life; this is its trueness. 2) A mental need, without which life is loathsome; this is *Lishma* [for Her sake].

Of course, the sages of religion come from the mental need, but from *Lo Lishma* [not for Her sake] one comes to *Lishma*, see "Pragmatic Truth."

Life's Direction

1) To bring progress and happiness to society through modern science.

2) By perfecting all of one's mental powers, one will attain dignity in life and a good name after death. Kant mocked it as egoism and indicated that only not in order to receive reward.

We must understand: If it is not worthwhile to live for myself, is it worthwhile to live for a thousand others like me, or a billion? Thus, the direction must be to benefit the Creator, whether for oneself, or for the entire world, to award them adhesion with Him.

Truth and Falsehood

Truth and falsehood are a psychic replica of existence and absence, which are thesis and antithesis, from which stem the "ephemeral truth," which is a synthesis. This is a pragmatic truth, lasting until the "absolute truth" appears, where there will be no falsehood in one's conscience.

Example no. 4 (see above): Would ancient, primitive humanity, which slaughtered and killed each other like wild animals, permit the institution of a religious government?

Example no. 5 (see above): In my childhood, I did not want to read novels so as not to deal with lies. I read only history. When I grew up and understood the value of them, that they develop the imagination, they became truth for me.

[new page]

Necessity

From the perspective of *Lishma* [for Her sake], it is an emotional need. Admittedly, they are few, as it is written, "He saw that the righteous are few... He planted them in every generation," so they would have demand from birth. However, some abhor material life. If they do not accomplish the goal of adhesion, they will commit suicide.

The Religious Principle: From *Lo Lishma* [not for Her sake], one comes to *Lishma* [for Her sake].

Providence has prepared the guidance of people in an egoistic manner, which would necessarily induce the destruction of the world unless they accept the religion of bestowal. Hence, there is a pragmatic need for it, and from that one comes to *Lishma*.

What Is an Emotional Need?

As a blind person cannot perceive color, or a eunuch the joy of sex, it is impossible to depict this need to one who lacks the emotional need. And yet, it is a must.

Performing Mitzvot [commandments]

Performing *Mitzvot* can become for one an emotional need.

Morality Manners

Morality manners means good attributes not in order to receive reward and without external necessity, but based solely on altruism and a sense of responsibility for human society. It is achieved by education. However, education requires public approval to keep and sustain it after one departs from under the authority of the education. But public opinion does not stem from education, but only from the benefit of the public.

The benefit of the public is evaluated only according to the specific state of that public, which necessarily contradicts other states and countries. Hence, how will education help in that? The evidence is that the manner, and even the religion, sufficient for internationality, has not been created, as killing and looting rule everywhere, without any manners whatsoever. Moreover, the greater the murderer one is, the more patriotic and well mannered he is considered. And today, it is international manners that we need.

Public Egoism Can Be Corrected Only by Religion

Public egoism can be corrected only by religion because education that is based on nothing can easily be ruined by any wicked person, and Germany is the evidence. If Hitler occurred in a religious Germany, he would not have done a thing.

Natural Egoism

You will not break natural egoism with artificial means such as public opinion or education. There is no cure for this but a natural religion.

Double Benefit

The religion of bestowal is salutary for both the body and the mind; hence, it is necessitated and agreed upon more than any method in the world (see below at length).

Motive Power

There are two discernments in it: The attracting force, from before, or the impelling force, from behind.

How can education help when one is free, without any motivation for the duties on which he was brought up? After all, there is no attracting force in them, and they are also devoid of the impelling force.

[new page]

The Persistence of the Soul

This is a given, as it is a part of God above. However, it is not included in the wisdom of Kabbalah because no object is attainable. Indeed, the soul appears to the person who carries it only through actions, and its actions are only attainments of Him.

It is therefore clear that the maxim, "Know yourself and you will know everything," is from ... philosophical, since in Kabbalah we should say the opposite, "Know everything and ... attain yourself." An object is not attained at all, only actions, which are attainments of His names, meaning only subjective.

Five Senses

The power in commandments is similar to corporeality, where the actions stimulate the senses. And when the senses remain ... in the memory brain, they become there images of benefit, detriment, and property. And when the mind or the will or the guard ... looks in the image of the memory, one gradually scrutinizes the images and brings the truths closer, meaning the beneficial or the property, and rejects the falsehoods, which are the detrimental.

Man's knowledge grows according to the clarity of the scrutiny. And if in mathematics, he should attach to it images that are beneficial for clarity and validity. They also save time because these help him, as in existing property. The same goes for playing music, healing, and an attribute.

It is similar with the power of spiritual actions, which ... the commandments that stimulate man's spiritual senses. There are two kinds of senses here, or *RASHRAD* [acronym of *Reiyah, Shmia, Reyach, Dibur* (sight, hearing, smell, and speech)], which are ord ... as well as *HGT NH* [*Hesed-Gevura-Tifferet Netzah-Hod*] of the body. It is so because perpetuation of good deeds from ... in one who works the spirit of "love," and when it accumulates into a sizable amount ... in him the sense of "fear" of committing a sin and losing the love. And when he is cer ... of himself that he has the sense of love and fear, a sense of boas ... over his friends who were not rewarded with it is born in him (and this is property).

And following the three senses ... "eternity" is born in him as a mighty one who controls his spirit. According to all the sensations of these four senses, "glory" is born in him as he admits the existence of the Creator.

And with each commandment that he adds, the five above-mentioned lower senses and the flavors of the commandments intensify in him. When they accumulate to the required amount, the five higher senses, sight-hearing-smell-speech, are born in him, to actually see His glory and hear the voice of the Creator, smell the fear of Him, and speak before Him.

And when one is rewarded more, images of the impressions of the five lower senses and the five upper senses remain in him, and he looks as though through the mirror of the brain at these impressions and sorts out the beneficial and the ... and rejects the detrimental. And according to the clarity of the scrutinies, the knowledge of the Creator will increase.

Luxury and Accumulated Property

As in corporeality, so in learning. ... in external teachings there is economics. ... and medicine is regarded as scrutinies that help the standard of living for ... as luxury. This is the first degree of property. The second degree is accumulating property, which is not as usable as wealth. This is the science of ... and an attribute, and playing music.

Likewise, in spirituality, the scrutinies that can be used ... are for a spiritual standard of living, and a non-accumulating property.

There are also higher scrutinies that do not serve for the standard of living, but only as accumulating property and for important possessions such as wealth and the attribute, and philosophy.

However, both come from spiritual images that were once absorbed in the senses. And choosing the beneficial for oneself or for others is called "the knowledge of the Creator." Know that the wisdom of Kabbalah also contains these three kinds of property.

Psychophysical Parallelism

These are two manifestations of the same entity, like thunder and lightning. This is the meaning of "good deeds and Torah." However, a person first feels the psychic explanation, and then the physical one. It is similar to love, where the giver of the present first feels with one's mind that the giver loves him, and then sparks of love flow and spread through him. ...A revealing head is psychic, and inside, it clothes ...

[new page]

The Root Cause of Every Error in the World

The root cause of every error in the world is an idea—when taking an idea or an image that was once clothed in a body, and presenting it as an abstract object that has never been in a body. That is, it is when it is praised or condemned according to that abstract value.

The problem is that once the concept has been stripped of a body, it loses significant parts of its initial meaning while it was clothed in a body. Those who discuss it according to its remaining meaning must necessarily misunderstand.

For example, when truth and falsehood work in the body, we praise the truth according to its benefit to the individual or to the ... and we condemn the lie according to its harm to the collective or to the individual. However, once truth and falsehood have been stripped of the bodies and become abstract concepts, they lose the heart of their meaning ... and acquire sanctity or impurity in their abstract form.

And according to ... it is possible for the evaluator to praise the truth even when it does great harm to the collective or to the individual, and to condemn ... the lie even when it is extremely beneficial to the individual or to the collective. This is a grave mistake that harms the ... and one is not free to ask oneself who sanctified this truth, or ... defiled and forbade this lie.

Benefit, in Fact, Everyone Admits It

Those who dispute it, it is ... that they benefit ... and a moral conduct that at times contradicts the physical benefit. However, essentially, morality and religion are also utilitarian ... everything, except spiritual happiness, and what is the difference?

There is not a fool who will exert without benefit for the body or the mind.

Double Benefit

Accordingly, the law of bestowing upon others is necessary for all the people in the world ... as it is beneficial for both the body and the soul according to the wisdom of Kabbalah.

[new page]

A Vague Complex that Must Be Resolved One at a Time

The main problem is that here there is a ... complicated made of several interweaving doubts:

First: Even when not taking into account the validity, the question remains whether it is actually beneficial.

Second: Even if it is beneficial, is it feasible?

Third: Who are the people to be qualified for training the generation to such a sublime matter?

Fourth: Perhaps this operation will evoke the public's contempt and mockery?

Knowing

Knowing comes in one of three ways: empirical, which is by physical observation (actual experiments), historical, using documents and papers, or mathematical, by joining of sizes and templates (through knowing) ...

And the wisdom of Kabbalah is more confirmed than all three abovementioned ways.

There is also a fourth way to know—through philosophical deductions, either by deductions or by inductions, meaning from the general to the particular, or from the particular to the general. This is strictly forbidden in the wisdom of Kabbalah, since all that we do not attain, we do not know ...

Part Four

Section One

The scrutiny that now, too, we are giving and are not receiving, both because we are not taking the surplus we produce to the grave, and 2) because if a day's exertion awards half a day's pleasure, it is bestowal. And since by and large there is very little pleasure from the exertions people make, we are all only bestowing and not receiving. This is a mathematical calculation.

3) The clarification that we exert today due to the enslavement of society at least 14 hours a day with pain and sorrow, since all our customs come from enslavement to the public.

... The clarification that if we use the "governance of the earth," we can hasten the "last generation" in our generation, too.

4) This matter of competition out of uniqueness in bestowal upon others is not an abstract fantasy, as it is used in practical life, such as those who give away all their possessions to the public, or the most idealistic members of parties, who neglect and lose their lives for the public's benefit, etc.

[new page]

What is this like? It is like a wealthy man who had an old father whom he did not wish to support. He was tried and the verdict was that he would support him at least as respectfully as he supports his own household, or he would face a harsh punishment.

Naturally, he took him into his home and had to support him generously, but his heart was grieving. The old man said to him, "Since you are already giving me every delight that you have on your table, what would you lose if you also had a good intention, which is reasonable in the eyes of every sensible person, to be happy with having the opportunity to honor your father, who spent all his energy on you and made you a respectable man? Why are you so obstinate that you afflict yourself? Can you dismiss yourself even slightly because of it?"

So it is. At the end of the day, we bestow upon society, and only society gains from our lives, since every person, great or small, adds and enriches the treasury of society. But the individual, when weighing the sorrow and pain that he receives, he is in great deficit. Hence, you are giving to your fellow person, but painfully and with great and bitter suffering. So why do you mind the good intention?

Section Two

[This section includes four segments grouped together by context]

Each one of them fills his or her role in service of the public in the best way, albeit without seeing it, since public opinion presses a person even secretly, to the point where one feels that deceiving society by mistake is as grave as mistakenly killing a human being.

Each country is divided into societies where a certain number of people with sufficient means to provide for all their needs connect into a single society.

Each society has a budget and work hours according to the local conditions. Half of that budget is filled by mandatory hours, where each member commits to work a certain number of hours according to one's strength, and the other half by voluntary hours.

A person who fails with self-gain, that person's entire social status vanishes into the thin air of society as clouds in the wind, due to the profound antagonism that such a person receives from the entire nation.

*

For then each person

1) Each person makes him or herself willingly available for the service of the public whenever one is needed.

2) Free competition for every individual, but in bestowal upon others.

3) Disclosing any form of desire to receive for oneself is dishonorable and such a great flaw that such a person is regarded as being among the lowest, most inferior people in society.

4) Each person is medium.

*

1) They have many methodical books of wisdom and morals that prove the glory and sublimity of excellence in bestowing upon others, to a point where the entire nation, from small to great, engage in them wholeheartedly.

2) Each person who is appointed to an important position must first graduate a special training in the above-mentioned teaching.

3) Their courts are busy primarily with awarding accolades marking the level of each person's distinction in bestowal upon others. There is not a person without a medal on the sleeve, and it is a great offense to call a person not by one's title of honor. It is also a great offense for a person to forgive such an insult to one's title.

4) There is such fierce competition in the field of bestowal upon others that most people risk their lives, since public opinion tremendously appreciates and respects the accolades of the highest rank in bestowal upon others.

5) If a person is recognized as having done for oneself a little more than what was decided for him by society, society condemns it so much that it becomes a disgrace to speak with him, and he also gravely blemishes his family's reputation. The only remedy for his plight is to ask for the court's help, which has certain ways by which to

help such miserable people who lost their position in society. But for the most part, they relocate him because of prejudice, since public opinion cannot be changed.

6) There is no such word as "punishment" in the laws of the court, for according to their rules, the guilty ones are always the ones who gain the most. Thus, if one is guilty of not working all his work hours, then his time is either reduced or made easier, or the way he provides it is made easier for him. Sometimes he is given time to spend at school, to teach him the great merit of "bestowal upon others." It all depends on the view of the judges.

*

1) The state is divided into societies. A certain number of people, who can fully provide for themselves, may separate themselves and maintain a special society.

2) That society has a quota of work hours according to the conditions in which they live, meaning according to the local conditions and the preferences of its members.

This quota is filled by mandatory hours and voluntary hours. For the most part, voluntary hours are approximately half of the mandatory hours.

The work hours come from four types and divide into works according to strength: The first type is the weak, the second type is the medium, the third type is the strong, and the fourth type is the quick.

For the work of one hour of type one, type two works two hours, type three four hours, and type four six hours.

Each person is trusted with finding one's appropriate type of work that suits one's strength.

Section Three

1) Humanity's progress is a direct result of religion.

2) The process of religion in circles comes when at the nadir comes the destruction of humanism to the extent of the ruin of religiousness. For this reason, they accept religion against their will, the upward movement begins anew, and a new circle is formed.

3) The size of the circle corresponds to the genuineness of the religion that is regarded as the "basis" at the time of the ascent.

Plan A

Just as we expect actors in the theatre to do their best to make our imagination think that their acting is real, we expect our interpreters of religion to be able to touch our hearts so deeply that we will perceive the faith of religion as the actual reality. The shackles of religion are not at all heavy for those who do not believe, as the demand in commandments between man and man is accepted anyhow, and between man and God, a few commandments observed in public—such as those at one's disposal—are enough.

Plan B

"Nature" in *Gematria* is *Elokim* [God]. Therefore, everything that nature mandates ... the word of the Creator. The benefit of society is the reward, and the damage to society is the punishment.

Accordingly, there is no point turning God into nature, meaning [a cut up word in the manuscript] a blind Creator who does not see or understand the work of His hands. We are better off, and it makes sense to every healthy person that He sees and knows everything, for He punishes and rewards, since everyone sees that nature punishes and rewards, as Hitler proves.

Plan C

All of the anticipated reward from the Creator, and the purpose of the entire creation, are *Dvekut* [adhesion] with the Creator, as in, "A tower filled abundantly, but no guests." This is what they who cling to Him with love receive.

Naturally, first, one emerges from imprisonment, which is emerging from the skin of one's body by bestowal upon others. Subsequently, one comes to the king's palace, which is *Dvekut* with Him through the intention to bestow contentment upon one's maker.

Therefore, the bulk of commandments are between man and man. One who gives preference to the commandments between man and God is as one who climbs to the second step before he has climbed to the first step. Clearly, he will break his legs.

Faith in the Masses

It is written, "The voice of the people is the voice of the Almighty." Indeed, this means that according to reality, they have chosen the least of all evils, and to that extent they always follow the good path. However, of course we must change reality so they can accept the utterly complete path. And it is true that the power of keeping in the masses in general chooses for them a way according to the situation. For this reason, once they have corrupted the interpretation of Torah and *Mitzvot* [commandments], they have become rebellious. However, it is a sacred duty to find a true interpretation in society, and then it will be to the contrary: The power of keeping in the masses will coerce the keeping of Torah and *Mitzvot*.

*

... public of the first degree.

To prepare the way he tried (its reason).

1) Nazism: egoism; the international: altruism.

2) It is possible to destabilize the Nazis only through a religion of altruism.

3) Only the workers are ready for this religion, as it is a revolution in religious perception.

4) This religious perception has three roles:

1) To undermine the Nazis.

2) To qualify the masses to assume collective governance so they do not fail as the Russians have. (This follows the term: The progress of humanity comes only through religion.) It is so because the more the worker needs reward for the work, the regime cannot survive, as Marx said.

3) To take religion from the possessors and turn it into an instrument in the hands of the workers.

4) First, it will be accepted by the workers, and through them by the whole of Israel, and the same goes for the international of all the nations, and through them to all the classes in the nations.

6) Revolution in religious perception means that instead of the hermits being thus far the destructors of the world, when they assume altruism, the hermits will be the builders of the world, since the measure of anxiety can be measured only by the measure of help to society in order to bring contentment to the Maker.

7) This concept is clarified over nearly 2,000 pages that explain all the secrets of Torah that the human eye cannot see. It will make every person believe in its truthfulness, as they will see that they are the words of the Creator, for secrets of a glorious wisdom attributed to prophecy testifies to their truthfulness.

8) The distributor of religion must be capable of Plan A, to bring as much faith as possible to the people.

In addition, he must bring complete sufficiency to the still, vegetative, animate, and speaking. Without it, religion is unsustainable. It is as Maimonides said, that it is like a line of blind people headed by one person who sees. That is, the speaking must stand at the front of the line at every place and in every generation. Hence, any religion that does not guarantee to elicit one man out of a thousand becoming a speaking, that religion is unsustainable.

9) Spreading the religion of love is done by Torah and prayer that can intensify one's quality of bestowal upon others. At that time, the Torah and prayer are as one who sharpens one's knife, so it can cut and finish one's work quickly. Conversely, one who works with a blunt knife believes it is better not to waste time sharpening the knife, and it is wrong because his work becomes much longer.

(It is also clear with the regard to the term that there is no progress for humanity unless through religion.)

10) (Relates to Item 9) The fourth role is in favor of Zionism, for during the truce, when fates of countries are decided, we will not have those enemies from among the conservative, who think we have no religion, as we learn from Weizmann's words [Chaim Weizmann (1874-1952), the first President of the State of Israel], and the mediators are bound to be from among those conservatives.

Part Five

Do Not Destroy

The frivolous have already grasped that it is possible to be built only on the ruin of one's friend. This method is what is frying humanity on a stove to this day, since before one finds a vulnerable place in one's friend, he cannot even conceive building anything. But the minute he finds a weakness in his friend's way, he clasps there with his claws and venom until he destroys him entirely, and there he builds his palace of wisdom.

Thus, all the palaces of science are built in a place of ruin. And for this reason, every researcher is interested only in destroying, and the more one destroys, the more one is famous and praised. Indeed, this is the way that science develops, and it cannot be denied.

However, what is this like? It is similar to the struggle that ruled with its terrible destructions for millions of years before the land had formed over the sea. This, too, was certainly a kind of development. And yet, there is no reason to envy those people who witnessed those upheavals. Rather, we should be more envious of those who came to the world after the making of peace, after the struggling materials made peace, and each found its resting place on Earth as it is today.

Although the struggle persists today, it is nonetheless a minor struggle, and not upheavals where each one destroys its predecessor, who has become entirely exhausted. Rather, they have already understood that it is forbidden to destroy, since "for drowning others, you are drowned, and the end of those who drowned you will be that they, too, will drown" (*Masechet Avot* 2, 6). Rather, the struggle is more about weakening and restricting, while keeping the life of the weak and avoiding destroying it, for he knows full well that the tide will later turn, "And they who drown you will drown." It is similar to the laws of war that the fighters keep while fighting. This, too, is for the same reason.

Now, if we really do learn from practical history, we must not overlook the above-mentioned principle, and we must take reality into consideration, as in a status quo, and punish one who murders a view just as we punish one who murders a person. It is so because a mind without a view is not in the type of emotion of pity, for they are more numerous than all the dunghills and the lakes, and all the air, and because of it they are given to Providence, and we have no tactics by which to assist them.

For this reason, we should presume that the land before us is vast, and there is room for all the views to dwell in it, the good as well as the bad. Indeed, one who kills and destroys a bad view is as one who destroys a corrected view, as there is no such thing as a "bad view" in the world. Rather, an unripe view is bad.

Therefore, we should judge it as one who kills a bad person, where "the voice of the blood of his descendants, and his descendants' descendants," we are redeemed from the evildoer. Likewise, a bad view is a seed that is still unripe for eating, but that will eventually grow and develop.

We should search for a new place for the palace of wisdom that we want to build, a place vacant of others' buildings, meaning without hurting any existing method. The mind is deep and broad, and the words of the wise are heard with pleasure, and the method of abusers and abused is agreed by everyone to be regarded as bad. Hence, this alone should be uprooted as it is obsolete and loathsome, according to everyone.

At the same time, we should keep all the manners of life in a status quo and maintain the freedom of the individual, since they are not required for our new building because in the end it is merely an economic structure. It is similar to a merchant who wants to open his own grocery store but fears the competition, so he burns all the stores in town along with the gold, jewels, gemstones, and clothes. He is too stupid because he will not grow any richer by burning jewelry stores. Rather, grocery stores only would have been enough for his ruin, and let the keepers keep, and they who vacation, let them vacation. At most, one should make a rule that all who keep must add work so as to satiate the examiners.

[new page]

I know what Mark wrote, that once the wounds and troubles of the body have been bandaged, we will begin, and we will have a suitable place for studying ideals. Besides, arguing that this is fundamentally untrue, since we know from experience that a tortured and afflicted body finds knowledge and truth better than a satiated body that knows no lack, even if we let his words be, we should still say, "Do not destroy," at the very least. It is similar to a person cutting down fruit trees because he wants to examine them so they will grow more fruitful. It is foolishness, for if he cut them down they will die and there will be no one picking fruits.

It is likewise in views that have come to us by inheritance from our fathers over hundreds of generations of development. He cuts them down, dries them up, and ruins them, promising us that later, when he is at rest, he will examine them and will improve them, if possible. It is complete folly.

He assumes that religion harms the commune. (But how can he be certain of this assumption? After all, it is a view that is spreading among people of positivity and negativity, and many are the supporters.) He can only dispute the form of understanding that the abusers use to their own benefit. Therefore, we should fight for the understanding, so it does not harm, but sentence it a death sentence.

And yet, his whole theory is built only on religious hatred, similar to structures of scholars of his time concerning hatred of religion, without any motive of economic damage. For this reason, we have permission to demand of the real sages, whose intention is only the economic side, to remove this item from their books. Only then can they hope to win a lasting victory that does not slide on its own vomit.

In a word, there is no joy without calamity, no good without bad. Even the wisest person cannot be saved from a medley of errors, and this is the weaker side in him, which leaves room for those who come to dispute it and completely destroy it. This is the weak side of Marxism, and it is why the occupation is difficult for them, and a hundred fold so the right to exist.

Therefore, if you are true to your method and desire its persistence, hurry up and erase the above-mentioned item from your laws, and then your road will be safely paved.

Has Marx's Prophecy Come True?

On one hand, his prophecy can be regarded as having been fully realized. The powerful people having been sitting for a while on the fear of certain ruin, on wondrous arms that have been accumulated, and of which there is not a shred of hope to be rid or to balance. Also, economists see their ruin in their eyes, and any chance for salvation has been quenched from reality. The hungry multitudes are accumulating in terrible masses each day; the working class has almost completed its ripeness, etc., etc.

Why Were They Cast to the Right?

On the other hand, we find the opposite. Fascism is growing daily, first Italy, now Germany, tomorrow Poland, and America is also on the verge, and so forth. It must be that that prophet had missed a point, which caused his grave error.

The Flaw Is Buried in His Own Theory

The flaw is buried in his own theory, for he has added redundancies in the theory of participation, and these are the hard seeds that history cannot process whatsoever (religiousness and nationalism), and they were rejected to the right.

[new page]

Faulty Policy

The guard does not need to sit and guard the surpluses that do not concern his conservativeness, nor the freedom searcher need pursue freedom for the luxuries of the body, nor the collaborator needs to destroy the views that do not contradict his socialism.

All of these three methods are real and are equally respected by their proponents. If the forces let one sect destroy another for a time, it is an incarnation, and in the end, there must be laws that limit the types of arms, so one will not destroy the other to a greater extent. It is a circle, and one does not know what one's tomorrow will bring.

Therefore, before the day of struggle comes, there is time for the mind to protect from a complete ruin of one of the sides. The current power is not to be relied upon, but rather the certain future.

Considering the truth between the methods, I define this word according to the law of evolution, since each view and each method prepares and makes a way for a better method. As long as it is not made, it must be kept and persisted, since by destroying it you destroy the view and the method whose role is to yield its fruition.

Marx himself had pointed it out … because he says that from the bosom of the great bourgeoisie emerges the working class. Therefore, you will evidently see that if there had been a savior for the working class at the time, to destroy the great bourgeoisie, he would certainly obliterate the foundations of the commune from its root, for this strong law, "do not destroy," is telling you, until the time comes by itself. In that regard, I dispute him because he says that we must force the issue at all cost, and I say, except for the ruin of views, they do not need this end at all.

For everything, there is a time, and the time of socialism has arrived. Woe to the fools who miss the hour and place before them completely redundant obstacles and boundaries, which are as smoke in their eyes. For this reason, before they turn one way or the other, the world will have already overturned and they will find "relief and deliverance from another place," and they and their method will be lost for a long time.

The war over the definition of nationality is completely redundant and is nothing like private property. There is no private property in the spiritual, only in corporeal properties. Who does not desire the development of the wisdom, and who does not know that authors' envy increases wisdom? Therefore, no one disputes it even among the extreme, leftist Marxists. Rather, the war concerns only the corporeal properties, for which envy yields nothing but fright and unnecessary agony. Hence, why should you fight spiritual properties and nationality?

Let us assume that all the nations have reached economic parity and have revoked private property so that the existence of abusers is unthinkable. Instead of the nations competing with one another for corporeal assets, henceforth the competition will be over spiritual assets. That competition is bound to emerge in individuals, just as in the collective. But here, no one speaks of it, even among the most extreme, but would it be so.

Therefore, our debate revolves solely around spiritual assets from the past. You say, "We permit the acquisition of such assets in the future with all the desirable and fitting freedom, but the past you take out of your houses." Is this not sick and twisted? After all, what will be permitted in the future, why should we destroy the great bulk that has been ready from the past? It is like that famous Egyptian king who inherited a library of precious books the size of three streets, and he commanded they be burned because they are not necessary for the existence of religion or for fear of harm.

And besides, no nation will obey your order to destroy all the assets of its past. They will fight over it with devotion (but you are absolutely permitted because you have no need for it at all). Indeed, even if a spirit of madness takes over the land to obey them to do this, they must spare this giant structure of several generations being lost for no reason at all.

Thus, you must leave the "You have chosen us" of each nation intact, to the extent that they want it. Only the corporeal basis of each nation should be abolished, since that basis has now reached its term, and it is in crisis anyhow. For this reason, it might take correction from whichever hand reaches out to it. However, along with it we must give full and complete confidence to each and every nation that their spiritual assets will be kept in full.

We cannot argue about statements that oppose socialism as we do with religion, since both legislators and religious authorities admit that "renunciation of a court is renunciation, and the law of the land is the binding law." For this reason, all those laws that oppose the concept of socialism will remain as obsolete history, for now, too, there is already a large majority concealed and unused.

Before us are three forces in reality, fighting against each other. Although it contradicts the view of Marxists, who take into account only two forces into consideration—abusers and abused—it is an abstract theory that has no more merit than all its preceding theories. However, according to the basis of Marxism itself, we should take into account only what is practical, and not endless theories. Hence, I have chosen to detect three forces as though they were set before our eyes in reality.

New Class Division: Quick and Idle

Let us assume that one nation is idle, and another nation is naturally more nimble. What one does in two hours, the other does in an hour. Naturally, there will be complaints: One will say that all the nations should work the same number of hours, and the other will say that what counts is the amount they produce. And as it is with those who argue, each will insist. What is the basis by which the court will decide? If it is according to the principle, "Give as much as you can and receive as much as you need," it still does not necessitate an equal length of time. And if we judge the nations according to the amount of work, then individuals, too, have a similar argument, and the diligent will work half as much as the weak. Thus, you have prepared for yourself a new class: a class of quick, and a class of idle.

You could say that there is power in the idle majority to force the quick minority in the nation, but there is certainly no such power to one nation over another. Thus, you will create classes among the nations, and abusers and abused among individuals.

The Arrival of the Redeemer

This is not new, for the founders themselves knew it, as he says ... that in the beginning they will see how this is possible through compromise, and will finally come to true ideals, to the highest degree of socialism, where each gives as much as he can and then takes only as much as he needs, meaning the same as the idle. This can be done only by the arrival of the redeemer, when the earth is full of knowledge. Then the giver will understand that he is exerting for his God, giving contentment to his Maker.

[new page]

The idealistic instincts have already struck numerous roots in the human race. They have also come and become antiquated and have gained a foothold in a place where no one can reach, namely the subconscious in the elongated brain, which moves man's nerves by itself, without the person's awareness. This is why they have experimented in Russia, as it is known that they did not do a thing in all their wars. These warriors should know that the human heart will give them anything if they only leave it with its ideals, which have come to it by inheritance from past generations in one's subconscious. If they insist on destroying this legacy, too, they themselves will suffer the consequences, for the heat and the sulfur is accumulating bit by bit until it is filled to the brim and begins to explode.

And besides all that, a new generation is growing, "which did not know Joseph." They do not understand at all the need or necessity to revoke private property from their flesh and blood, but only according to a dry theory. Therefore, the passion for private property that is buried deep in their subconscious from past generations, after all the learning, one fine day they will establish camps of young people from all sides, and they themselves will put the elderly to death with all their property and wisdom. It is so because an ideology does not come to a person from the intellect, but only from life's experiences, out of affection and a combination of good and bad, as with automatic machines. The mind has no control over the body, as it is completely foreign to us. Hence, those young socialists who have acquired knowledge through their own wit cannot be trusted whatsoever, and they will pop like a bubble of soap.

One Last Word of Policy

At that time, three forces will sit on the throne in the councils—right, left, and middle. They will argue and fight with one another: the right opposing the liberty in the left, and the left opposing the reactionism of the right, and the neutral will give room to both, and the majority will solve and determine.

Indeed, in one, they have already come to a solution, namely sharing all necessary and positive needs of life, meaning equal sharing of all the needs of the economy: one land to all who are living on it, and one division in its corporeal pleasures. They will load all the trials and arguments on the suffering of spiritual predicates, along with the three degrees—envy, lust, and honor—they will turn and restrict themselves only to the spiritual boundaries.

This version will indeed be the final word of policy because it will forever remain an inexorable law. It is so because according to the development of the human species, so will views separate and intensify, and each one will be far more obstinate than one is currently so about one's fortune. There is no hope to come out of this strait unless people begin to regress into the form of fools, meaning be emptied from all of their reason.

For this reason, there will be almost as many parties as there are people, and there is no solution to it other than the fixed law, "follow the majority." At that time, people will make among them various compromises until they gather into groups. In the groups, there will be competition with the oppositions until the opposition itself will separate.

Thus, the big groups will split into small ones, and the small ones into tiny ones, and they will trade among themselves, as is customary nowadays. However, this negotiation must acquire a more acrid form each time, precisely according to the measure of development of views without compromise forever, for so it should be forever.

[new page]

However, in one—in private property—they have already arrived at an agreed upon solution: Each will give as much as a successful one can give, and will receive as much as an unsuccessful one, without adding even as much as a hairsbreadth. And the work hours will be equal to all, by order. And besides the mandatory, there will be additional time to the veterans, who will give compared to the weak, to completely exempt them and not afflict them. This is similar to today's charity.

Also, in each city and community, the weak will be distributed equally. And if there are many volunteers in the community, then all the weak will be exempted. If there are few, then only some of them, the weakest, will be exempted.

One who breaks these rules will be punished either by giving his portion or by criminal punishment.

The Anterior of an Idea

The truthfulness of the spirit of pleasure of one who expresses it is evident. I have become a c ... although ... [unclear words in the manuscript] many years prior, while I did not pay attention until I saw them speaking and arguing. Then I recognized the truth as it is. It is a law that one who is completely untroubled will not be satisfied by corporeal possessions. Even when engaged in an ideal, one must feel pleasure during the engagement. The measure of spirit and delight that one feels depends on the truthfulness of the ideal with which he is engaged.

Thus, we have found for truth an anterior face by which to know it, meaning by merely looking at the person who expresses it, whether he is enjoying or not. And the amount of pleasure is the amount of truth. This is what has brought me to believe in this idea, for until then I have never seen anyone expressing an idea with such contentment and delight as they.

The Absolute Truth

If there are no absolute truths, but temporary ones, then I say that each truth in itself is the absolute truth for its time. It is just as it cannot be said about some reality that is about to die that it is regarded as dead, since while it is alive, it is an absolute reality.

[new page]

Everything is operated either voluntarily or by coercion, and the mind does not force. Therefore, we have a question: Who will move the socialist when he acts? What source will spur his desire to move, or by what force will coercion come upon him?

It is so because at that time, movement will become to him a kind of private property, and every person is meticulous about his energy, not to disperse it uselessly even more than about his fortune. And if the socialism is not because he is deficient, due to saving of energy, he will certainly not squander the energy in vain. Thus, from where will justice or compassion come?

Rushing Its Ripening: Through Religion

The socialist idea requires ripening in one's mind for at least three whole generations of peace and general agreement. Hence, many more attempts and cycles will the world endure before it comes to fruition, but there is no easier way to ripen the ideas than through religion.

www.ingramcontent.com/pod-product-compliance
Lightning Source LLC
Chambersburg PA
CBHW080606170426
43209CB00007B/1348